MARKETING AND SOCIETY: CASES AND COMMENTARIES

Roy D. Adler
Assistant Professor of Marketing,
Xavier University

Larry M. Robinson
Vice President, Research
Nationwide Insurance Companies

Jan E. Carlson
Associate Staff Manager,
Southern Bell Telephone Company

239547

Prentice-Hall, Inc., Englewood Cliffs, N.J. 07632

Library of Congress Cataloging in Publication Data

ADLER, ROY D.
  Marketing and society.

  Bibliography: p.
  Includes index.
  1. Marketing—Social aspects—United States—Case
studies. I. Robinson, Larry M., joint author.
II. Carlson, Jan E., joint author. III. Title.
HF5415.1.A533 658.8′02   80-39636
ISBN 0-13-557074-3.

Editorial/production supervision by Anne Bridgman and Marian Hartstein
Text design by Marian Hartstein
Cover design by Carol Zawislak
Manufacturing buyer: Gordon Osborne

Printed in the United States of America

10 9 8 7 6 5 4 3 2 1

Prentice-Hall International, Inc., *London*
Prentice-Hall of Australia Pty. Limited, *Sydney*
Prentice-Hall of Canada, Ltd., *Toronto*
Prentice-Hall of India Private Limited, *New Delhi*
Prentice-Hall of Japan, Inc., *Tokyo*
Prentice-Hall of Southeast Asia Pte. Ltd., *Singapore*
Whitehall Books Limited, *Wellington, New Zealand*

To our wives
Cecilia, Susan, and Carolyn,
and our children
Douglas and Davison;
Vincent, Kristen, Barton, and Nathan

Their sacrifice has been greater than ours.

CONTENTS

Part 3
Promotion: Issues of What to Say and How to Say It   135

Part 4
Pricing: Issues of Satisfaction for Value Received in Voluntary Exchanges   217

Part 5
Place: Issues of Power and Equity
in Channels of Distribution   293

Part 6
Organizing: Social Responsiveness for
Marketers   369

PREFACE

One of the most pleasant tasks in completing a project such as this is recognizing those individuals who contributed so much to the success of this venture. We owe an immense intellectual debt to Frederick Sturdivant at The Ohio State University, whose knowledge and insight convinced us that this book would be a necessary and useful teaching device. Barry Mason and Morris Mayer at the University of Alabama, and Len Berry, McIntire School of Commerce, University of Virginia, then at Georgia State University, were largely responsible for creating exciting environments where this work could flourish. At least two dozen other colleagues contributed more indirectly to the book through positive influences on our careers, and we know they share our sense of accomplishment.

A number of our students conducted research for and wrote preliminary drafts of several of the cases. The dedication and enthusiasm of Lisa Galanti ("McDonalds (A)", "Gulf Oil"), Mike Logan ("Heublein, MACAP 'A' and 'B'"), and Pat Pons ("Life Insurer's Conference") is deeply appreciated. Students at Georgia State and at Xavier provided feedback in the sessions where these materials were class-tested. The comments of Larry Rosenberg, who class-tested the material at New York University, were extremely helpful. The assistance of Carolyn Carlson, who provided editorial help, and Jan Gottemoeller, who unerringly typed the entire manuscript, was invaluable. Finally, the outstanding work of John Connolly, Anne Bridgman, and the other editors and reviewers at Prentice-Hall should be recognized. Their professionalism made the production process extraordinarily smooth.

Much of the credit for what is good about the book belongs to these people. Each author blames the other two for any weaknesses.

Roy D. Adler
Larry M. Robinson
Jan E. Carlson

Part 1 | Introduction: The Social Consequences of Marketing Decisions

INTRODUCTION: THE SOCIAL CONSEQUENCES OF MARKETING DECISIONS

This book is about the social impact of marketing transactions, both on ultimate consumers and on third parties. The position taken throughout this volume is that marketers can, and indeed must, acknowledge, monitor, and begin to *manage* the social consequences of their marketing decisions. The perspective is consistent with the societal marketing concept proposed by Philip Kotler of Northwestern University:

> *The societal marketing concept calls for a* customer orientation *backed by* integrated marketing *aimed at generating* customer satisfaction *and* long-run consumer welfare *as the key to attaining long-run profitable volume.*[1]

As Kotler has noted, "Societally responsible marketing calls for including four considerations in marketing decision making: consumer wants, consumer interests, company requirements, and societal welfare."[2]

The cases and commentaries are not intended to proselytize or to present a pro- or an anti-marketing posture. The book was written to provide a basis for thoughtful dialogue and analysis concerning the role of marketing in a free-enterprise economy. Although much of the material considers public policy issues, the book is not intended as a primer on the legal aspects of marketing.[3] Nor does the book examine all of the critical social concerns that marketers must address, for the issues change, often with dramatic rapidity. The one constant, however, is that social considerations can be expected to continue as important factors in marketing practice.

Although many marketers believed consumerism to be a minority movement of self-appointed consumer representatives, the movement refused to go away during the 1970s. The Sentry Life Insurance Company national study on consumerism concluded in 1978 that "The consumer movement is here to stay, and in fact, is growing stronger. . . . Leadership groups and consumers alike think that many different industries and services are doing a poor job in serving consumers. . . . The business community is sharply out of step with the American public on consumerism issues."[4] These findings, at a time when the American

---

[1] Philip Kotler, "What Consumerism Means for Marketers," *Harvard Business Review,* May–June 1972, pp. 48–57.

[2] Philip Kotler, *Marketing Management: Analysis, Planning, and Control,* 4th edition (Englewood Cliffs, N.J.: Prentice-Hall, Inc., 1980), p. 18.

[3] See, for example, Marshall C. Howard, *Legal Aspects of Marketing* (New York: McGraw-Hill Book Company, 1964), or Earl W. Kintner, *A Primer on the Law of Deceptive Practices* (New York: Macmillan Publishing Co., Inc., 1971), or Martin L. Bell, *Marketing Concepts and Strategy,* 3rd edition (Boston: Houghton Mifflin Company, 1979), pp. 525–552, or G. David Hughes, *Marketing Management* (Reading, Mass.: Addison-Wesley Publishing Co., Inc., 1978), chap. 10.

[4] Sentry Life Insurance Co., *Consumerism at the Crossroads: A National Opinion Research Survey of Public, Activists, Business and Regulator Attitudes toward the Consumer Movement* (Hartford, Conn.: 1978), pp. iii–iv.

marketing system is delivering the highest standard of living in the history of mankind, represent a serious indictment. Clearly, the Sentry study suggests that marketers must make dramatic improvements in the 1980s if they are to continue to merit the support of the American public.

The criticism embodied in the Sentry study echoed the conclusion of Richard N. Farmer of Indiana University from a decade earlier. Farmer, in a widely discussed article, noted that much of marketing practice was perceived by the public as unethical and irrelevant to major world needs.[5] The article concluded, "If that nice young man who has dates with your daughter turns out to be a marketing major, what would you do? I would chase him off the premises fast. Who wants his daughter to marry a huckster?"[6]

Much happened in the 1970s to suggest that some marketers were sensitive to major world needs and to the charge that marketing was unethical in nature. Marketing concepts and techniques became meaningful to many nonprofit organizations involved in the dissemination of social ideas and causes. Also, marketing was much debated and, in many instances, accepted by members of the legal, medical, accounting, and engineering professions.

Many nonprofit organizations turned to marketing for defensive, even survival reasons. However, marketing, with its emphasis on efficient use of scarce resources to create and facilitate voluntary exchanges of values, achieved acceptance in many organizations concerned about major world problems. Although the stigma raised by Farmer remains, he concluded in an update on his earlier view:

> It is becoming difficult to find stereotypes to poke fun at, when the salespersons I meet are bearded males, blacks with afros, and women of all ages, along with more traditional types. It is even tougher to find some stereotypes when I discover the best people can be any of these diverse types. And when serious economic development scholars start talking about market segments for birth control pills, and government people talk about using effective advertising to peddle rapid transit rides, I find it even more difficult to figure out who the villains really are.[7]

This book does not focus on villains, but on real issues faced by marketers in contemporary organizations as they attempt to serve, in a socially responsive way, the needs of customers and the needs of the larger society.

A major aim of this book is to provoke thoughtful discussion and analysis on the social consequences of marketing policies and practices. The cases and commentaries are designed to focus student attention on socially related managerial decisions. For each decision to be made, there is an apparently popular and attractive option in opposition to the status quo. Many consumer issues are very seductive in their simplicity: Who can be opposed to "product safety,"

---

[5] Richard N. Farmer, "Would You Want Your Daughter To Marry a Marketing Man?" *Journal of Marketing*, January 1967, pp. 1–3.

[6] Ibid., p. 3.

[7] Richard N. Farmer, "Would You Want Your Son to Marry a Marketing Lady?" *Journal of Marketing*, January 1977, p. 17.

"higher ethical standards," or "full disclosure?" Yet each of these issues can be carried to an extreme conclusion. For example:

1. *Product safety.* Product safety was included as one of President Kennedy's four consumer rights. The specter of consumers maimed or killed by unsafe products is unpleasant, yet the pursuit of absolute safety is not at all realistic.[8]

Consider automobile safety as an example. Suppose that the first $1,000 in safety equipment on a car saved X lives, the next $1,000 saved $X/2$ lives, the next $1,000 saved $X/4$ lives, and so on until ∞ had saved $2X$ lives. How much safety does a socially responsive automobile manufacturer place on the car to be marketed? If you selected any other figure than ∞, you have opened yourself to the literally true charge that you knowingly traded off lives for dollars. You *would* have saved more lives if you had only spent more on safety.

The same type of cost–benefit rationale can be applied to a host of safety-related products, such as toys, athletic equipment, power tools, or the national speed limit.

2. *Ethical standards.* It is difficult to argue for lowered ethical standards, yet the question of what is right often can only be answered within the context of the situation. Consider two similar disasters in the latter part of the nineteenth century. The passengers and crew of the British liner *Lulworth Hill* were becalmed and had no food. As passengers died one by one, they were solemnly buried at sea by the starving survivors, until only one was left, who also died. In contrast, members of a stranded wagon train at the Donner Pass survived the winter of 1846 by engaging in cannibalism. Which ethical standard was more appropriate in these cases?[9]

Robert Bartels argues persuasively that ethics is a function of the expectations of those affected by business decisions.[10] Thus, if one is expected to live up to a standard higher than the law requires, and does not, the behavior is unethical. It also means that if one is expected to break the law and does *not,* then adherence to the law is unethical conduct. Perhaps the whole concept of ethics is more complicated than it first appears to be.

3. *Full disclosure.* Most thoughtful individuals agree that full disclosure of *all* attributes of a product or advertisement would not be possible, but then suggest that only "important" attributes be disclosed. Who is to decide which are important?

Research conducted at Purdue University has suggested that under high-information conditions, consumers feel better but make worse decisions.[11] If

---

[8] See Walter Guzzardi, Jr., "The Mindless Pursuit of Safety," *Fortune,* April 9, 1979, pp. 54–64, for an excellent discussion of this issue.

[9] These examples were taken from Frederick D. Sturdivant, *Business and Society: A Managerial Approach* (Homewood, Ill.: Richard D. Irwin, Inc., 1977), pp. 102–103.

[10] Robert Bartels, "A Model for Ethics in Marketing," *Journal of Marketing,* 31 (January 1967). p. 21.

[11] See, for example, Jacob Jacoby, Donald Speller, and Carol Kohn, "Brand Choice Behavior as a Function of Information Load," *Journal of Marketing Research,* 11 (February 1974), pp. 63–69; Jacob Jacoby, Donald Speller, and Carol Kohn Berning, "Brand Choice Behavior as a Function of Information Load: Replication and Extension," *Journal of Consumer Research,* 1 (June 1974), pp. 33–42; and J. Edward Russo, "More Information Is Better: A Reevaluation of Jacoby, Speller and Kohn," *Journal of Consumer Research,* 1 (December 1974), pp. 68–72.

these findings were confirmed repeatedly under a variety of conditions, would full disclosure of true information be valuable for its own sake?

The issue of what "truth" is has been debated for centuries, but suppose there is agreement that a message concerning pain pills is literally true. Further, imagine that a person is selected to read this message as a television commercial. Need the individual's name, occupation, and education be prominently disclosed? What if exactly the same message were read by Robert Young wearing a white cotton jacket?[12] When is literal truthfulness not enough?

Clearly, there are difficult managerial decisions to be made even on such seductive "more is better" issues as safety, ethics, and truth. These and other issues will be explored through the cases and commentaries in this book. Throughout the book, text materials summarize and integrate some of the more recent literature concerning various issues, to provide the tools to begin a thoughtful analysis of them.

Mere analysis will not be enough, however. The student will need to commit to specific marketing decisions that strike a balance between social enlightenment and managerial necessity. Such practice will, at minimum, provide an understanding of the difficulties faced by marketers who make socially relevant decisions and, it is hoped, provide an operational framework for making socially responsible marketing decisions in the future.

The first commentary in this introductory section examines the evolution of the marketing discipline. The next two selections consider the need for dialogue on the relationship of business and the larger society. The last reading provides insight into the role of government in regulating marketing practice as viewed by the Chairman of the Federal Trade Commission, perhaps the most activist federal agency.

[12] Robert Young is an actor who is well known for his portrayal, on television, of Dr. Marcus Welby.

Commentaries

MARKETING: AN INTERVIEW WITH PHILIP KOTLER*

- How did you, a graduate of MIT with a PH.D in economics, get involved in the field of marketing?

I was always interested in marketing while I was studying economics because it seemed to be a field with a lot of unanswered questions. We knew that there were a few theories in economics about how to set advertising budgets, how to price, how to use sales resources optimally, and so on. But I didn't feel these theories were either full enough to be correct, nor pragmatic enough to make a difference in business operations. So, my interest was strong in the field of marketing, although I hadn't at that time studied it as marketing. I studied it as economics. And, when I came to Northwestern, I was given an option of teaching either marketing or managerial economics. It seemed to me that marketing would be more challenging because it was less theoretically developed. I saw that challenge as exciting, so I turned to marketing. Ever since, it has just been a very comfortable fit.

- Do you feel that, starting out with your interest predominantly in economics, this background has been a good springboard for entering the marketing field?

Yes. Marketing is really an eclectic area.

One of the strongest contributions to it can be made by good economic theory, but not economics alone. I also did postgraduate work in behavioral science (particularly psychology and sociology)—another mainstay of marketing analysis—and work in mathematics.

- In looking back over the field of marketing for the past 70 years, how has the field been evolving or changing?

I'm glad you said 70 years ago because marketing just about began then. Selling, of course, goes way back to the dawn of history. But marketing is so much more than selling. We have had to go through 200 years of the Industrial Revolution to see

* Condensed from an interview published by Prentice-Hall, Inc., Englewood Cliffs, N.J., in November 1979. Used with permission. Philip Kotler is the Harold T. Martin Professor of Marketing, Northwestern University.

the difference. Yet, in its short history, marketing has gone through important changes about every decade. The central thrust, though, has been toward rigor, away from casual observation on what seems to work.

• Exactly what do you mean when you suggest that the central thrust has been toward rigor?

Rigor in analyzing problems facing managers, so that the problems are carefully understood and then the tools, techniques, and concepts that work are applied to those problems.

Marketing has become technical. It has developed some central concepts in the last two decades which were previously dormant. For instance, the concepts of market segmentation, market targeting, market positioning, marketing mix, marketing planning, and marketing auditing were simply not in the literature then. Today, though, these concepts give us some firm handles on the problems of adapting organizations to rapidly changing environments.

• Can concepts sometimes get out of date and keep us from seeing what really is?

Yes, concepts can get out of date. They must have ecological validity or they won't survive. For example, right now I am playing around with the notion that the marketing mix doesn't quite capture the factors that impinge on the consumer. The marketing mix is a convenient model for what the seller manages, not what the buyer necessarily experiences. We have to define the marketing mix from the buyer's point of view. Maybe we need the concept of a buyer's motivation mix.

In general, there is always the need to reexamine concepts that are unclear . . . or perhaps too clear. Even though the content of marketing may stay the same, we must be ready and willing to apply new concepts. They can alter the context of marketing and shed new light on the content.

• You mentioned strategic planning. How do you view its importance in the field of marketing?

Marketing is one discipline along with several others that make it possible for the firm to survive and grow. Strategic planning helps us realize that the issue for the firm is survival and growth in a rapidly changing environment.

Organizations can no longer expect the future to be like the present. They cannot plan on simply doing more of the same. They can't just extrapolate their sales and market shares and do the older form of long-range planning.

What is happening is that you don't know what the demand for a particular product will be next year. There are so many surprises occurring in the marketplace from month to month, from day to day, that you need to build more adaptable mechanisms for survival. Strategic planning has become the major answer to the problems of the 1970s. Strategic management will probably become the magic term of the 1980s. It all comes down to answering the question of how to make organizations "work" in a rapidly changing environment.

To me, marketing is an essential part of that process of strategic planning. In fact, I can't imagine strategic planners answering their own questions without applying marketing analysis and marketing strategy concepts. So, when I realized that strategic planning is a fundamental process in an organization, I wanted to work out in my own mind where marketing fit in. I am now very comfortable with positioning marketing as the leading component of the strategic planning process.

• The definition of strategic planning seems to imply that it operates more on a corporate level—it provides the directive force to the company rather than to the marketer as an individual. How will the strategic planning process on the corporate level affect the marketing manager in his or her job?

Strategic planning starts at the top and is then repeated throughout the company's divisions, and even at product line levels.

Top management figures out broadly which business divisions should be built, maintained, harvested, and terminated. Then, because each division has some stars, cash cows, question marks, and dogs, strategic planning must be applied here also. Each product line also consists of a portfolio of products that must be separately evaluated for assigning missions and resources. So, basically, I would not confine strategic planning to something that only top management does. Strategic planning thinking works only when it is applied throughout the entire organization and becomes an actual part of the organization's culture.

• How does marketing help determine strategic objectives for different products?

Well, marketing represents a set of skills for analyzing market needs and the company's capacity to profitably deliver values to that market. For instance, the marketer might see no future in certain markets because of their stage in the product life cycle. Or, the marketer might see a great future in an embryonic market. Marketers, then, provide the technical intelligence to assess the quality of the markets.

After the strategic planning process leads to some company decisions and commitments—such as: this business should be expanded, that one should be contracted—marketers have to carry that out. The very interesting thing is that in the past marketers saw themselves as primarily "growth engineers." That is, their job was to build "businesses." Under the regimen of strategic planning, however, marketers are more broadly demand managers. Their assigned task may be demand expansion, maintenance, reduction, or modification. In a sense, marketers have a broader and more exciting job to do because, instead of narrowly being builders of market demand, they now have to be managers of market demand.

One of the other challenges facing marketers of the 1980s will be to find constructive ways to reconcile company profitability, customer satisfaction, and social responsibility.

The job of marketing is to create customer satisfaction as the means by which the organization achieves its goals. The new factor, though, has to do with not only meeting customer wants but also customer interests. This means that companies must now face environmental issues. For example, firms might satisfy customers well with the immediate product, but hurt them in the long run as members of society.

• You mentioned that you use a managerial process framework. What is the benefit of using such an approach?

There are several possible approaches for a marketing management course.

An institutional approach would be highly descriptive—what wholesalers do, what retailers do, what advertising does, what sales forces do—rather than dealing with these same topics from the point of view of what decisions marketers face in using resources effectively. I rejected using an institutional approach—for a marketing management book.

An environmental approach describes the environment to the reader. The question still arises as to what the marketer should do about it to make good decisions.

And, a social approach wouldn't do in itself because marketing is about serving people profitably.

I believe that a managerial approach—that is, analytic management—is the natural approach to use because it has a clear focus on the key decision problems and planning problems of the marketing managers and the company managers.

• Looking beyond any new shifts in thought that occurred recently, what do you foresee in the not-too-near, or distant, future—even beyond the 1980s?

I have been very interested in scenarios of marketing futures. I really believe we are going to have a very different marketing environment. New technologies of transportation, communication, retailing, office management, and so on, will have a tremendous impact on marketing—shaping new opportunities and posing new threats. Just think about home computers and picture telephones. Imagine stores which we don't go to, but order from by seeing pictures on our home computer picture screen. This would change the course of marketing a great deal.

• Do you feel that these technological advances will hamper or restrict the marketing field?

No, I don't. I never think of saving the discipline but of serving the customer. It is a question of what gives customers more value. The developing technologies will give us an opportunity to cut costs, increase convenience, or improve overall satisfaction. So, if it means that stores that depend on you coming to them and handling their merchandise and buying certain things you hadn't thought of buying have a tougher time against stores which are televised to you and from which you order by simply looking up what you need, I am not concerned. Traditional retailers have to be ready to move into new forms or else vanish. I have a kind of Darwinian view about competition and what survives. I don't think the best marketing planning is going to help a poor product or a poor company, one that can't create sufficient value to survive.

The important thing is that new opportunities arise all the time, and for every marketing institution that goes down it is because a new, more vigorous one has arisen. So we should welcome the new when its time has come.

Let's take another development: generic products. It's not clear whether generics will capture 10 or 20, or more, percent of the market. They are a formidable challenge to national brands and will put a real squeeze on the weaker brands. National brands will have to become better or they will have no reason to survive.

I can imagine a textbook of the future dealing more with what constitutes efficient delivery systems for commodities and less with the niceties of brand competition. The marketing problem may be: How do you supply a lot of bread to the marketplace at the lowest possible cost?

HOW SOCIETY CAN HELP BUSINESS*
By Jerry McAfee

Much has been said in recent years about the business corporation's responsibilites to society. This is as it should be. The corporation's obligations to the public today, I suggest, are the result of nothing less than an American renaissance that grew out of the social, political and cultural upheaval that began in the early 1960s. One effect of this revival is that more is now expected of business than ever before.

At the same time, there is another side of this story that one hears much less about: society's responsibilities to the corporation. Admittedly, in a country intent upon reforming its institutions, conspicuously including business, this counterpoint is hardly in vogue, and is often overlooked if not forgotten in our contemporary social debate. But it is no less valid. Because the corporation and the environment in which business functions unavoidably affect one another, their fortunes are linked. Therefore, it is only logical to conclude that the corporation and society have practical responsibilities to each other.

THE BASIC RULES

I think it's time to talk about this other dimension: what society—in its own best interest—owes to the corporation.

From this point of view, and taking into consideration our changing environment, I submit that society's responsibilities to the corporation basically boil down to five:

1. *Set rules that are clear and consistent.* This is one of the fundamental things that society, through government, ought to do. Although it may come as a surprise to some, I believe that industry, and I include the energy industry, actually needs an appropriate measure of regulation. By this I mean that the people of the nation, through their government, should set the bounds within which they want industry to operate.

But the rules have got to be *clear.* Society must spell out clearly what it is it wants the corporations to do. The rules can't be vague and imprecise. Making the rules straight and understandable is really what government is all about. One of my colleagues describes his confusion when he read a section of a regulation that a federal regulatory representative had cited as the

* Jerry McAfee is the chairman of the board and chief executive officer of the Gulf Oil Corp.

reason for a certain decision. He told the official that the regulation did not seem to justify the decision that had been made. "You're right," the official responded, "that's what the regulation says, but that's not what it means."

We in business just can't live with that sort of thing.

2. *Keep the rules technically feasible.* Business cannot be expected to do the impossible. Yet the plain truth is that many of today's regulations are unworkable. Environmental standards have on occasion exceeded those of Mother Nature. For example, the Rio Blanco shale-oil development project in Colorado was delayed by the fact that the air-quality standards, as originally proposed, required a higher quality of air than existed in the natural setting.

3. *Make sure the rules are economically feasible.* Society cannot impose a rule that society is not prepared to pay for because, ultimately, it is the people who must pay, either through higher prices or higher taxes, or both. Furthermore, the costs involved include not only those funds constructively spent to solve problems, but also the increasingly substantial expenditures needed just to comply with the red-tape requirements. Although the total cost of government regulation of business is difficult to compute, it is enormous. To cite an example close to my own company, the Commission on Federal Paperwork last year estimated the energy industry's annual cost of complying with federal energy-reporting requirements at possibly $335 million per year.

4. *Make the rules prospective, not retroactive.* Nowadays, there is an alarming, distressing trend toward retroactivity, toward trying to force retribution for the past. Certain patterns of taxation and some of the regulations and applications of the law are indications of this trend.

A case in point is the "Notices of Proposed Disallowance" issued by the Federal Energy Administration (now the Department of Energy) in 1977 against Gulf, for alleged overcharges on our imported crude oil during the 1973-74 oil embargo. We have denied those charges. The fact is that during those difficult months we were struggling to supply the nation's energy needs, and increasing imports with the government's support. We were doing our level best to follow the existing regulations on pricing imports. The charges against us, as well as many other issues raised by the DOE, were the result of retroactive applications of new regulations or new interpretations of vague, poorly written and confusing regulations.

It is counterproductive to make today's rules apply retroactively to yesterday's ball game.

5. *Make the rules goal-setting, not procedure-prescribing.* The proper way for the people of the nation, through their government, to tell their industries how to operate is to set the goals, set the fences, set the criteria, set the atmosphere, but don't tell us how to do it. Tell us what you want made,

but don't tell us how to make it. Tell us the destination we're seeking, but don't tell us how to get there. Leave it to the ingenuity of American industry to devise the best, the most economical, the most efficient way to get there, for industry's track record in this regard has been pretty good.

TRADE-OFFS

In sum, government must understand more fully that one of its responsibilities is to make sure that the messages it gets from the people are properly sorted out, that the necessary trade-offs are thoroughly evaluated, before the regulations are promulgated. It must not issue confusing and impractical decrees that leave the sorting-out task to the industry. The government's proper job is to balance the trade-offs before it makes the rules.

Fortunately, concerned sectors of society and corporations both appear to be increasingly aware that their responsibilities to each other are a two-way street. If all of us—industrialists and environmentalists, engineers and artists, marketers and consumers—recognize that this is so, we can all play a more constructive role in the new American renaissance.

"OFTEN, WE HAVE BEEN STUPID" SOME NOTEWORTHY COMMENTS FROM AMERICAN BUSINESS LEADERS*

By John Cunniff

New York—Lost amid the cacophony of crisis news, of gasoline shortages that compel attention, for example, are observations worthy of recognition, for their significance if not for their urgency.

Among them are commentaries from the private sector that may be worthy of consideration or even perhaps of reconsideration.

Such as the remarks of Henry Ford II, chairman of Ford Motor Co., at the University of Chicago last April 26, a few days before announcing that he would quit as chief executive officer on October 1.

"In recent decades we businessmen have neglected many genuine problems and turned a blind eye to conditions that should have caught our attention. Often we have simply been stupid.

"We have refused to confront some of the crucial issues of our time, and as a result we have played directly into the hands of our critics and helped to make matters worse.

---

* John Cunniff is a reporter for The Associated Press. *The Atlanta Journal and Constitution,* 1979.

"The whole issue of consumerism is a prime example. . . .

"Maybe we wouldn't have won any prizes if we had answered auto-safety charges more effectively before the consumerists moved into the area, but we would have saved ourselves—and customers—some nightmarish regulations."

Or the comments on big government by Murray Weidenbaum, former assistant secretary of the treasury and now one of the foremost advocates of regulatory reform.

Weidenbaum, director of the Center for the Study of American Business at Washington University, St. Louis, was interviewed by editors of *Exxon USA,* an Exxon Co. magazine for shareholders and others.

"The government cannot be our nanny. I think Americans are sensible enough to know that.

"To my mind there exists a tremendous gap between the view of the formal consumer advocates and the view of the rank and file of consumers.

"Currently, there's a strong movement in the Federal Trade Commission to tell Americans what to eat through regulation of television advertising.

"When a senior FTC official was asked if he thought it was the government's task to tell free Americans what to eat, his response was, 'People eat for the wrong reasons.'

"Talk about Big Brother!"

Walter Hoadley, executive vice president and chief economist of Bank of America, articulated the thoughts of many people in testimony before the Senate Budget Committee.

Almost everyone appearing before the committee had declared his concern about the possibility of recession and with public demands for a restraint on government spending.

"I submit there is another broader force at work which quietly but relentlessly is sapping our fundamental economic strength," Hoadley said.

It is, he said, the "pervasive negative thinking across our country about the future, national and personal." He continued:

"It is crucial that the Congress and the administration try hard to reverse this public attitude through policy changes in the next year or two to cause a sharp increase in private risk-taking investments, innovation, productivity, saving and national confidence.

"The private sector also has major responsibilities to respond positively as government takes the lead.

"If we fail, we must expect chronically slow growth in the economy, which in turn can only mean higher inflation, progressively tougher budget problems, a still weaker dollar and more voter unrest.

"I have absolutely no doubts about our national capability to meet and overcome our problems. However, sometimes I almost despair about our will to do so and when we'll get on with the task."

PERTSCHUK SPEECH ON FTC LITIGATION STRATEGY*

FTC Chairman Michael Pertschuk reviewed the commission's immediate priorities in remarks made to the 1979 Antitrust Section spring program April 6.

Besides emphasizing the importance of FTC litigation in its overall competition efforts, Pertschuk reviewed specific initiatives in the areas of health care, energy, transportation, and food marketing. Pertschuk also gave a glowing preliminary evaluation of the premerger notification program.

Text of his address follows:

Several weeks ago, at the National Press Club, I suggested that the Federal Triangle, within which dwell the nation's regulatory agencies, had become the new red light district of Washington—shunned in the business establishment's preachings; patronized by many of the very same good citizens in the dark of night.

We had a call after that speech from a local history buff who reported that the area now occupied by the Federal Triangle was indeed the red light district of the Nation's capital during the Civil War—so flamboyantly so that President Lincoln instructed the commanding officer of the District to clean it up. The troops performed their task with such zeal that the name of their commanding general has ever since been associated with the activity. He was as you may have guessed by now, none other than General Hooker.

With this history to guide us, I find it very difficult to relinquish the image. And it occurs to me that it also may be an apt metaphor for the relationship between the antitrust and trade regulation bar and the FTC. Once again, we find that we are denounced in broad daylight by our colleagues in the private bar—and solicited in the shadows.

"Your cases are unprecedented, oppressive, untryable, ill-conceived; you pursue trivial and technical violations or obsolete goals devoid of the new learning," I hear you say. Then, *Sotto voce,* "Where are the new cases?"

Again, "Your trade regulation rules are over-broad, indigestible, burdensome, serve no useful purpose; leave the legislating to Congress." Then, again in a whisper, "Why are you proposing so few new TRR's?"

Well, it gives me pleasure to set at least one of the FTC's constituencies at ease. I'm delighted to report to you that the case as an instrument of public policy is alive and well at the FTC; indeed, that more are on the way; not only more but better.

* "Pertschuk Speech on FTC Litigation Strategy," *Legal Times of Washington.* Used with permission.

On the other hand, I'm not about to tell you that we are emerging from the red light district only to enter the numbers racket.

FEWER CASES

The perception that the Commission has brought fewer cases in the last two years than in some earlier years is, as rumors go, a hard one to dispel. That's because it's true.

It is not true, however, that the lower number of new cases reflects a diabolical determination to drive the private defense bar into starvation. The numbers have their root cause in our perception of our mission and the way we have gone about our business since I joined the Commission two years ago this month.

As my tenure as Chairman began, we took a hard look at the agency's priorities and our approach both to case selection and alternative enforcement strategies. These periodic reassessments are necessary, I believe, to take into account changes in the enforcement climate, such as current industry structure, corporate behavior, developments in the law and the degree to which our efforts are complemented by the work of others.

As we began this review, we had to contend with the iron laws of litigative restraint.

PICK CASES CAREFULLY

The first law: *Small may be beautiful, but with fewer than 300 lawyers to police a continent of competitors, you'd better pick your fights carefully.*

A corollary of that first law is that small or minor cases are not proportionately cheaper than major cases.

When the Supreme Court reversed the Commission in the *A&P* case, which involved only a few hundred thousand dollars in alleged discriminations, it brought to a close 110 days in trial, consuming 35,000 work hours over seven and a half years of litigation, for a total cost of the Commission and, of course, the public, of more than a million dollars.

DEFERRAL TO OTHERS

The second law of litigative restraint is this: *If someone else is equally willing and able to bring the case, take two doses of institutional humility and step aside.*

Now that the Justice Department is able to seek stiffened penalties for criminal antitrust violations, we are more pleased than ever to leave to our sister antitrust agency the prosecution of most horizontal collusion cases, especially where there is blatant price fixing and the stuff of felony prosecutions.

We also applaud the emergence of vigorous state antitrust enforcement and the sprouting of state *pareis patriae* suits in the federal courts, fertilized by congressional seed money. We are now in a position to refer a greater number of matters of state or local significance to aggressive antitrust divisions within state governments.

Then there is you: the growth industry of the legal profession. As you well know, private antitrust cases have grown from 659 complaints filed in 1968 to a peak of 1611 filings in 1977. We welcome displacement by private antitrust litigation—the citizen's arrest of competition law enforcement—in those cases where the public interest is likely to be vindicated effectively by a private party.

OTHER APPROACHES

The third law of litigative restraint is this: *Cases are dandy but the paths to competition are many and varied. Or, there may be more than one way to skin a monopoly.*

We are increasingly sought out by congressional committees to explore innovative legislative approaches to persistent competition problems, because they value our independence, and, I believe, our integrity.

More and more we are advocating and intervening before other government agencies, federal and state, where current regulatory schemes needlessly foreclose price competition or the entry of new competitors. We are doing this not simply because the restraints are egregious but because we are being listened to more often and we're achieving results.

We are working with state officials and legislators. We have joined forces with them to devise model state legislation for competition problems best addressed at the same level.

Because we believe that consciousness raising is an appropriate response to nascent problems of competition, we have sponsored public debate through symposia on competition issues on the horizon, most recently the emerging solar energy industry and the growth of media concentration.

We're working directly with corporations to help them take preventive action to avoid antitrust problems. Our staff is now developing a model "antitrust audit" which would enable firms to discover and remedy incipient violations more efficiently.

And rulemaking as a competition law enforcement tool may be about to emerge from its cocoon.

CASE: SILVER BULLET

No doubt the reassessment of priorities begun early in our tenure and the gearing up for new initiatives had the side-effect of slowing the flow of new cases. But it has given us an enhanced ability to generate enforcement responses better suited to the times. All of this you have heard before. What we have perhaps not made so clear is that, while we continue our hunt for the biggest bang for our limited bucks, the case remains the silver bullet of our competition policy.

Let me illustrate: Since April 1977, we have issued 59 complaints alleging the commission of unfair methods of competition. Consent orders have been negotiated in 47 of these. Thirty of these consent orders have been accepted, either initially or finally, since September of last year. Adding the eleven complaints issued since April 1977 that are now in adjudication together with previously issued complaints, we now have 34 ongoing competition cases in litigation.

But where do we go from here, you ask? I expect that in the coming months our enforcement program will concentrate on three broad fronts:

First, actions aimed at vitiating the effects of excessive market power.

Second, cases and other initiatives arising directly from analyses of industries and sectors of the economy of critical importance to consumers.

And third, continued strong presence in traditional law enforcement areas such as mergers, vertical restraints, and compliance.

Let me go over briefly what is likely to happen on these fronts in the coming months.

ABUSE OF MARKET POWER

First, we will continue to focus on firms that have 30, 40 or 50 percent market shares—below traditional monopolization levels—but which possess substantial market power. We are exploring whether some of these dominant firms are engaging in conduct in the marketplace that stifles competition, drives out competitors or intimidates potential competitors, to the detriment of the public.

We are, for example, studying the way the Sherman Act's proscription on attempts to monopolize has been developed in the case law. This is an area where alternative approaches to liability should be explored under Section 5, which I believe can reach beyond the parameters of Sherman Act precedent.

We are also studying and investigating the phenomenon of price signalling and other interdependent activity among oligopolists, short of outright collusion, and considering innovative applications of Section 5. You may have noted our application of Section 5 to interdependent formula pricing in the plywood industry last year in our *Boise Cascade* decision.

And we will continue to pursue traditional monopolization cases under Section 5, while recognizing the need to streamline the discovery and trial processes and focus on effective relief.

SPECIFIC ECONOMIC SECTORS

A second focus of our efforts will continue to be the state of competition in sectors of the economy critical to consumers health, energy, transportation and food. We are exploring market structures and probing entrenched forms of conduct that may straitjacket competition.

A model for this approach is our health care antitrust program which has produced a series of cases and other initiatives. Cases and projects in this area center on:

- alleged professional association restraints on advertising:
- Use of relative value scales to stabilize fees;
- professional associations allegedly condemning acceptance of non-fee-for-service employment by their members;
- preferential payments to physicians by medical laboratories to obtain business;
- alleged boycotts of cost-containment programs set up by insurance plans;
- prospects for competition under national health insurance
- obstacles faced by health maintenance organizations;
- limitations on the scope of practice of allied health practitioners;
- potential cost savings through the use of generic drugs;
- problems in the nursing home field; and
- physician participation in control of open panel medical service plans, like Blue Shield.

Although cases can address many of the possible competitive defects in the health care sector, some cannot be addressed adequately in a case setting. They may require other approaches. For example, doctor control of Blue Shield plans will probably be the subject of the competition staff's first competition trade regulation rule recommendation.

As you know by now, other professions are also getting antitrust checkups from the FTC. And if our diagnosis is that a profession isn't taking care of itself—or is taking too much care of itself—we may prescribe competition as a remedy. And we are prepared to make housecalls where necessary.

In transportation, we will continue to advocate the relaxation of anti-competitive government regulations, especially before the ICC with respect to the railroad and trucking industries. Our presentations to the ICC are good examples of the kind of *competition advocacy* we are doing with increasing frequency before other government agencies.

In the *food* area, our program will probably continue to be heavily litigation-oriented. Significant antitrust problems appear to exist in this sector of the economy as a result of mergers, monopolization and predatory practices. We are especially concerned about the need for competition at the manufacturing-processing level, where the most value is added to food.

In energy, we will proceed with a mix of litigation and advocacy-type interventions, and are exploring the suitability of rulemaking.

Our *third* principal thrust in the coming months will be continuation of our traditional enforcement role, aggressively screening and pursuing anticompetitive mergers, moving against resale price maintenance violations, enforcing the Robinson-Patman Act, ensuring compliance with Commission orders and scrutinizing other alleged unfair and anticompetitive practices as they come to our attention.

HART-SCOTT-RODINO

The Hart-Scott-Rodino premerger notification program and our increased authority to seek preliminary injuctions have greatly improved the speed and efficiency of our merger work. For example, we learned of the proposed merger of Cooper Industries and Gardner-Denver Company in January. By the end of March we had accepted a consent agreement requiring divestiture of assets in two horizontally overlapping markets.

Curiously, Hart-Scott-Rodino may be serving to reduce the size of our adjudicative case load. Since we get information on mergers more quickly, and since the firms involved get a sense of our enforcement intentions faster, a number of proposed mergers have simply evaporated.

According to a preliminary study of premerger notification applications over the past 12 months, we have reason to believe we played a role in the abandonment of at least a dozen planned mergers. For example, the planned merger between the Allendale Mutual Insurance Company and the Arkwright-Boston Manufacturers Mutual Insurance Company was dropped after the Bureau of Competition recommended that the Commission issue a complaint.

Such government impact is not, of course, reflected in our statistics, but should not be overlooked in measuring the Commission's performance.

It works the other way too. Hart-Scott-Rodino saves everyone time and money when information becomes available to us quickly and reveals that a planned merger does not raise significant antitrust problems and, therefore, does not require Commission action.

Of course, some matters do go to litigation. For example, Grand Union's recent acquisition of the Colonial supermarket chain, and Rhinechem's attempt to acquire Chemetron's pigments division.

CONGLOMERATE LEGISLATION

We are continuing to explore the further application of Section 5 and Section 7 to large conglomerate mergers. At the same time, however, we recognize that traditional enforcement analysis may not provide an appropriate basis for challenging many conglomerate mergers. This is an example of how we are supplementing our traditional enforcement role by developing, in cooperation with congressional committees and the Department of Justice, a legislative approach to what we view as a critical problem.

Recently I recommended to Congress that it consider legislation that would limit the growth of large firms through large mergers. The Commission staff's proposal is based on a "spin off" approach, which permits large firms to make large acquisitions, subject to traditional horizontal and vertical concerns, provided they divest or spin off viable business entities of a size comparable to the acquisition.

VERTICAL RESTRAINTS

Vertical restraints have also been a traditional focus of Commission enforcement efforts and this will continue to be the case, even in a "good-bye *Schwinn*," "hello *GTE Sylvania*" world. The *Sylvania* decision has had a major effect at the Commission, for it has sparked a more comprehensive and planned approach to vertical restraints enforcement.

A task force composed of Bureau of Competition, Regional Office and Bureau of Economics staff was formed to consider restraints enforcement and a task force report was prepared. Next, a seminar on vertical restraints was held to upgrade the staff's training in this area—led by senior staff and leaders of the private bar and academic economists. From this process, priorities and ideas for developing the law have been formulated.

To give an example, the Commission may consider a complaint recommendation from our staff that tackles head on that part of the *Col-*

gate doctrine which allows a seller to threaten the cut-off of retailers who refuse to sell at specified price levels.

Although certain offices have the responsibility for coordinating various innovative approaches to vertical restraints, competition has been encouraged: the office that finds the right case gets to pursue it. Competition also seems to work within the FTC.

Although we will be attempting to define new approaches to vertical restraints, resale price maintenance will remain our top priority in this area and will be pursued vigorously by the Commission's staff, especially in the Regional Offices.

Part 2 | Product: Issues of Product Design, Use, and Disposal

PRODUCT: ISSUES OF PRODUCT DESIGN, USE, AND DISPOSAL

In a free enterprise, economy, buyers, and sellers enter the marketplace voluntarily to exchange values. Marketers strive to establish ongoing business relationships with buyers by creating values that satisfy perceived needs. Thus, the product may be viewed conceptually as any offering that has the potential to satisfy functional, psychological, or social needs of prospective buyers.

Products can be considered at four levels of abstraction, as illustrated in Figure 1. At the most elementary level, marketers offer consumers a physical set of attributes, including one or more of the following characteristics: quality level, features, styling, brand name, and packaging. Each of these tangible features may be valued highly by prospective customers. Some marketers follow a management philosophy that presumes that buyers enter markets in search of pro-

FIGURE 1   The Product: Four Levels of Abstraction

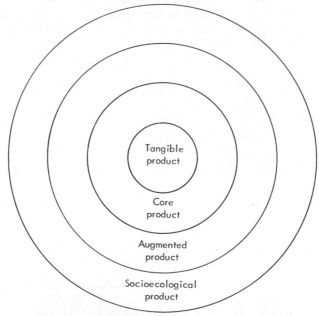

Philip Kotler, *Marketing Management: Analysis, Planning, and Control,* 4th edition (Englewood Cliffs, N.J.: Prentice-Hall, Inc., 1980). For a similar discussion on the application of the concept to *nonprofit* services and social causes see Philip Kotler, *Marketing for Nonprofit Organizations* (Englewood Cliffs, N.J.: Prentice-Hall, Inc., 1975), pp. 164–66; Etienne Cracco and Jacques Rostenne, "The Socioecological Product," *MSU Business Topics,* Summer 1971, pp. 27–34.

ducts that possess certain levels of physical characteristics. By following the so-called "product concept," such marketers develop strategies to make their offerings preferred by consumers. As an example, most hospitals manage relationships with physicians and customers on the basis of this product concept.

At the next level of abstraction, marketers may view customers as problem solvers. This orientation suggests that consumers do not buy products per se; instead, they buy the results of product use. This view, popularized by Theodore Levitt of Harvard, suggests that marketers identify the core product, or essential utility sought by customers.[1] Thus, as Revlon founder Charles Revson noted in his biography, *Fire and Ice,* his competitors sold a tangible product, cosmetics; he sold the core product, "hope." As a second example, many shoe stores sell running shoes as a physical product. Phidippides, a rapidly growing chain of shoe stores, sells "cardiovascular health." Phidippides requires that all managers be experienced marathon runners, salespersons must be active runners, free seminars are offered at each store for runners, and so on. Phidippides has become a successful company by organizing marketing efforts around a concept of the product based on benefits sought by customers.

A third view of the product considers the totality of costs and benefits received or experienced by customers in obtaining the product. The augmented product includes everything that happens to a consumer in the effort to obtain and use the tangible product. Marketers who follow this view seek to minimize the time, energy, and psychic costs involved in product purchase and use. La Quinta, a San Antonio, Texas-based motel chain has followed this product concept with great success. In the late 1970s, La Quinta was the highest occupancy-rate, fastest-growing motel chain in the United States. The La Quinta philosophy was to target marketing efforts toward the repeat business traveler. La Quinta locations were close to places visited by business executives and salespersons, each inn was run by a husband and wife team who could identify and meet individual needs, each room had amenities such as desks and conference tables needed by business travelers, and a 24-hour restaurant was available on the premises. These characteristics of the augmented product combined to make La Quinta the motel of choice for many travelers who sought to minimize non-productive time and effort while maximizing value received from a business trip.

At a fourth level, products can be viewed as more than a bundle of need satisfactions for the buyer. The socioecological product, as defined by Cracco and Rostenne, is "the sum of all positive and negative utilities which must be accepted by society as a whole in order to allow the satisfaction by users of a certain bundle of needs, wants, or desires in a certain way.[2] This perspective requires that marketers consider social, as well as economic, costs of consumption. According to this view, products that prove unsafe in use or contribute to environmental decay should be discontinued or modified. As George Fisk, marketing professor at Syracuse University, has stated in the Theory of Respon-

[1]   Theodore Levitt, "Marketing Myopia," *Harvard Business Review,* July–August 1960, pp. 24–47; see also Theodore Levitt, "Retrospective Commentary on 'Marketing Myopia,'" *Harvard Business Review,* September–October 1975, pp. 177–181.

[2]   Etienne Cracco and Jacques Rostenne, "The Socioecological Product," *MSU Business Topics,* Summer 1971, p. 28.

Table 1   PRODUCT CLASSIFICATION BY IMMEDIATE
SATISFACTION AND LONG–RUN
CONSUMER WELFARE*

| | | Immediate Satisfaction | |
		High	Low
	High	Desirable Products	Salutary Products
Long-Run Consumer Welfare			
	Low	Pleasing Products	Deficient Products

* Philip Kotler, "What Consumerism Means for Marketers," *Harvard Business Review,* May–June 1972, pp. 48–57.

sible Consumption: "Responsible consumption requires that scarce resources be used for their most ecologically valuable purposes."[3]

Products can be classified according to the distinction between immediate satisfaction and long-run consumer welfare, as shown in Table 1. For example, deficient products would include products, such as feminine hygiene sprays, which deliver low immediate satisfaction and may be harmful to the consumer in the longer term. Pleasing products provide immediate satisfaction but offer little, if any, long-term benefits. Cigarettes, soft drinks, and alcoholic beverages are examples of pleasing products. Salutary products produce low levels of immediate satisfaction, but possess long-term benefits. Cod liver oil, spinach, and piano lessons might be classed as salutary products. Desirable products include anything that is both enjoyable and contributory to long-term consumer satisfaction. Nutritious, palatable foods and classics in literature are illustrative of desirable products.

Product-related issues can be found at any of the four levels shown in Figure 1 or with any of the four types of products shown in Table 1. Further, many products satisfy consumer needs but possess social costs for nonusers. The cases and commentaries included in this section focus on several of the more visible, and difficult, product issues that confronted marketers in the early 1980s.

1. *Social desirability of products.* Some group or groups in society may be opposed to a product, often on emotional bases without objective data. The Heublein, Inc., case explores this issue, as some observers charged the Malcolm Hereford Cows line of milk-flavored packaged cocktails with contributing to teenage alcoholism. The product had been the most successful new product introduction in the history of the distilled spirits industry. The emotion-laden charges could undermine the continued viability of the product. What should Heublein, Inc., do, particularly since objective data indicated that the charges were without merit?

2. *Product safety.* Everyone is in favor of safe products. The difficult issue

[3] George Fisk, *Marketing and the Ecological Crisis* (New York: Harper & Row, Publishers, Inc., 1974), p. 23.

involves the trade-off in costs and benefits from increased levels of safety. As suggested in a commentary in *Fortune*, "The Mindless Pursuit of Safety," the social costs to ensure 100 percent safety may be far more than society is willing to pay. The Firestone Tire and Rubber Company case examines this difficult issue. In addition, the discussion on products liability legislation illustrates that considerable disagreement existed with respect to the legal liability of marketers for injuries suffered by consumers in product use.

3. *Socially responsive packaging.* Product packages must identify and protect contents but must also be sensitive to environmental imperatives. For instance, aluminum cans and nonreturnable bottles received much attention in the late 1970s and early 1980s because many observers considered the packaging materials to be environmentally harmful. The Foam-Pak, Inc., case examines the issue of whether foam plastic trays should be made illegal since the possibility existed of deceptive packaging for cuts of meat. The company had to develop a strategy that would forestall unfavorable legislation. Foam-Pak, Inc., was also concerned about the disposal problem for its product.

4. *Product legality.* Products whose sole purpose is to circumvent the law raise a serious moral question. Should one violate laws that are considered wrong? The Electrolert, Inc., case concerns a company whose sole product is the "Fuzzbuster" radar detector. Although the immediate question considers the appropriate marketing strategy for an advanced radar detector, the larger issue concerns the marketing of civil disobedience.

5. *Product proliferation.* The number of new products introduced each year continued to grow dramatically in the 1970s. Is it possible to have too much consumer choice? What are the benefits and costs associated with trivial product differences?

6. *Product labeling.* Marketing critics allege that labels often provide inadequate information for consumer decision-making purposes. How much information is enough?

7. *Trademark protection.* Brand names help customers to make product choices by promising an expected quality level. Can a brand, such as Formica™ be too successful, so that consumers insist on it, even when other brands offer similar quality at substantial price savings? What role should government play in protecting (or prosecuting) brand names?

8. *Imitation products.* Inflation and technology have combined to produce frozen cheese pizzas without cheese, chocolate bars without chocolate, and lemon meringue pies without lemon or meringue as ingredients. Aside from the question of safety, are there limits on the types of substitute ingredients permitted in food products? What disclosure requirements should there be for products that do not contain expected ingredients?

9. *Environmentally sound products.* Many man-made materials are not found in nature and thus are not fully recyclable according to natural processes. Nonbiodegradable materials include aluminum, mercury, DDT, glass, and automobile tires. The issue of the impact of fluorocarbons in the ozone structure illustrates the negative environmental impact of products.

Table 2 provides a summary of product-oriented legislation, designed to help the student recognize the legal constraints relating to any of these issues.

Table 2 A SUMMARY OF IMPORTANT FEDERAL LAWS AFFECTING PRODUCT DEFINITION AND USE

Act	Year Passed	Major Provisions
Sherman Act	1890	Prohibits contracts, combinations, and conspiracies in restraint of trade as well as monopolizing or attempts to monopolize.
Pure Food and Drug Act	1906	Forbids adulterations and misbranding of foods and drugs sold in interstate commerce; amended in 1938 and 1962.
Meat Inspection Act	1907	Provides for inspection of slaughtering, packing, and canning plants that ship products in interstate commerce; amended in 1967 to require states to match federal meat inspection standards.
Federal Food, Drugs, and Cosmetic Act	1938	Extends the FTC's authority over packaging, misbranding, and labeling to include food, drugs, cosmetics, and therapeutic devices.
Wool Products Labeling Act	1939	Requires that the labels on wool products indicate the percentages of wool, reprocessed wool, and reused wool.
Lanham Trademark Act	1946	Provides for the registry of trademarks, collective marks, and certification marks.
Fur Products Labeling Act	1951	Prohibits false advertising and misleading labeling of fur products.
Flammable Fabrics Act	1953	Prohibits manufacture and sale of apparel that is dangerously flammable; extended by amendment in 1968 to cover household furnishings, fabrics, and materials.
Poultry Products Inspection Act	1957	Empowers the Department of Agriculture to inspect poultry sold in interstate commerce; amended in 1968 to encourage states to upgrade their poultry inspection practices.

Table 2 (*continued*)

Act	Year Passed	Major Provisions
Automobile Information Disclosure Act	1958	Designed to prevent deceptive pricing practices in the sale of automobiles; requires that dealers affix to new automobiles the manufacturer's suggested retail price of the automobile and factory-installed accessories.
Textile Fiber Products Identification Act	1958	Regulates the labeling of textile products by requiring identification of various textile fibers by percentage content, the name of the manufacturer or distributor, and the country of origin (if imported); also, synthetic fibers must be identified by generic names assigned by the FTC.
Hazardous Substances Labeling Act	1960	Requires that the proper labels be attached to toxic, corrosive, irritating, or flammable goods that tend to enter into ordinary household use; labels must be specific as to the nature and extent of the danger involved.
Fair Packaging and Labeling Act	1966	Through mandatory and discretionary provisions assures accurate labeling and informative packaging of most household products.
National Traffic and Motor Vehicle Safety Act	1966	Directs the Secretary of Transportation to issue safety standards for new and used motor vehicles.
Consumer Product Safety Act	1972	Created the Consumer Product Safety Commission with power to set safety standards or otherwise to regulate the marketing of unsafe products.
Warranty–FTC Improvement Act	1975	Establishes minimum disclosure standards for written consumer product warranties, identifies minimum content standards, and allows FTC to prescribe rules governing the use of product warranties.

Cases

HEUBLEIN, INC.: A SOCIALLY QUESTIONABLE PRODUCT*

Stuart D. Watson, chairman of the board at Heublein, Inc., sat in his office to review a speech he was to give that evening. The occasion was the annual meeting of the Wine Institute, a trade association of wine producers and distributors. Watson had selected as his topic, "The Corporate Responsibilities Function at Heublein." He would focus in the speech on the importance of monitoring the social and political environment for contingency planning purposes.

In particular, Watson intended to discuss the role at Heublein, Inc., of public affairs and the Corporate Responsibility Committee. Watson was proud of the research sponsored by Heublein on the causes and treatment of alcoholism. He was also pleased that the Corporate Responsibility Committee had provided strong guidance to senior executives on advertising, product, and distribution policies. As an example of the Committee's efforts, he intended to show some recent advertisements that were sensitive to the social consequences of alcohol consumption. The ads depicted people with and without cocktails, all having fun. The intention was not to glamorize drinking as the socially desirable thing to do. The text of the ads stressed moderation. Figure 1 shows an example of the ads Watson intended to show the group.

Just as Watson completed his review, he received a call from John J. Moran, vice president of public affairs. Moran began by saying, "Stuart, did you see the Today Show this morning? Well, I did. I could not believe my eyes. Betty Furness got some fifth graders drunk on Cows and then told

* This case is not intended to provide a precise account of the thinking of the parties involved.

FIGURE 1   Advertisement for Malcolm Hereford's Cows

Malcolm Hereford's Cows are up-to-their-flanks in ice and snow to make a very refreshing point:

When the Sun is high, nothing refreshes better than Malcolm's "herd" on ice.

Enjoy them chilled.
On-the-rocks.
Or in one of the more elaborate manners of Malcolm, himself:

1. How to make COW-SLUSH.
Pour a Cow into your blender, add lots of ice and blend for 30 seconds.
Serve and sip.
Light, Icy, delicious.
2. COWPUNCH serves a "herd".
Just mate two flavors in a large pitcher filled with cracked ice.
(Strawberry and Banana were made for each other.)
And have a party.

At the beach. By the pool.
Whenever you thirst for something cool, spirited, light and delicious, there's only one thing to do:
Adopt a Cow.
An original Hereford Cow.
One of Hereford's 30 Proof "herd," the spirited new breed of drinks that promise one thing for sure:

Ice cold Cows get no beefs.

HEREFORD'S
STRAWBERRY COW
A blend of natural flavors and grain neutral spirits

HEREFORD'S
MOCHA COW
A blend of natural flavors and grain neutral spirits
Thirty Proof
Bottled by Malcolm Hereford Ltd. Hartford, Conn.

Hereford's
BANANA COW
A blend of natural flavors and grain neutral spirits
Thirty Proof

HEREFORD'S
CHOCOLATE MINT COW
A blend of natural flavors and grain neutral spirits
Thirty Proof
Bottled by Malcolm Hereford Ltd. Hartford, Conn.

AN ICE COLD COW IS NOT A BUM STEER.

Malcolm Hereford's 30 Proof Cows. The Spirited New Breed of Drink.

America, 'this proves that Heublein is trying to appeal to kids.' Stuart, we cannot let this one lie like we did in November with the MacNeil–Lehrer Report.'' Watson agreed and asked Moran to prepare his recommendations for an appropriate response. He further requested Moran to add the issue to the agenda of the Corporate Responsibility Committee meeting scheduled for the following day.

COMPANY BACKGROUND

Heublein, Inc., was, in 1977, the largest producer and distributor of distilled spirits and wines in the United States. Corporate-wide revenue was over $799 million for the first half of fiscal 1977. Table 1 shows a steady growth pattern in both revenues and profits for the period 1972–1976. Prior to 1976, the company was organized in three major profit centers: beverage, food, and international. In January 1976, the company reorganized into five groups: spirits, wines, food service and franchising, grocery products, and international. Of these, spirits was the largest, in both sales and profits, with 1976 sales over $300 million and profits of approximately $35 million.

The Heublein product line featured over 200 well-known consumer product brand names, including Smirnoff Vodka, Black and White Scotch, A-1 Steak Sauce, Ortega Chiles and Sauces, Italian Swiss Colony, Lancers, Inglenook, Annie Green Springs, T. J. Swann, Jose Cuervo Tequilla, Black Velvet Canadian Whiskey, Irish Mist, Harvey's Bristol Cream, and Snap-E-Tom Cocktails. In addition, the company had acquired, in 1971, Kentucky Fried Chicken.

Heublein had been plagued by several serious problems in recent years which had the net effect of plummeting Heublein stock from 40½ down to the 20s, even though sales and profits continued to be strong. The Christmas quarter of 1976, normally the strongest sales period, was disappointing, with sales down by 13 percent from the previous year. Preliminary estimates showed that company profits for the first half of the fiscal year 1977 would be up only 1 percent over the previous year.

Several reasons were cited by management for the declining performance of company products. First, in 1975, the Federal Trade Commission challenged Heublein's acquisition of United Vintners, a prestigious and profitable wine group, second only to the E & J Gallo Winery in market share. In negotiations with the FTC, Heublein offered to divest itself of the Petri, Italian Swiss Colony, and Lejon product lines while retaining the

Table 1 HEUBLEIN, INC. CONSOLIDATED SUMMARY OF OPERATIONS (DOLLARS IN THOUSANDS)

	1976	1975	1974	1973	1972
REVENUES					
Beverage	$ 858,706	$ 772,576	$ 697,018	$ 586,423	$ 507,125
Food	489,302	446,792	387,272	315,095	273,154
International	235,125	135,047	155,852	64,620	33,721
	1,583,133	1,414,415	1,240,142	966,139	814,000
Cost of sales	1,099,416	988,474	855,134	660,173	546,674
Selling, advertising, administrative, and general expenses	338,454	290,151	265,660	211,523	181,185
Operating income	$ 145,263	$ 135,790	$ 119,348	$ 94,443	$ 86,141
OPERATING INCOME					
Beverage	$ 72,732	$ 63,226	$ 52,044	$ 42,005	$ 39,080
Food	52,211	55,985	51,458	45,170	43,456
International	20,320	15,579	15,846	7,268	3,605
	145,263	135,790	119,348	94,443	86,141
Interest expense	18,494	16,910	9,830	6,357	7,381
Interest income	2,810	2,147	1,384	1,683	646
Miscellaneous income (expense)—net	763	632	122	(225)	367
Income taxes	64,433	61,661	58,683	46,877	41,474
Income from continuing operations	65,909	55,998	52,341	42,667	38,299
Income (loss) from discontinued operations, less tax effect	7,184	1,498	2,069	1,544	(607)
Income before extraordinary items	73,093	61,496	54,410	44,211	37,692
Extraordinary items, less tax effect	—	—	—	(13,800)	(15,250)
NET INCOME	73,093	61,496	54,410	30,411	22,442
Preferred dividends	—	—	—	—	293
Earnings applicable to common stock	73,093	61,496	54,410	30,411	22,149
Common and common equivalent shares	$21,516,526	$21,216,540	$21,166,002	$20,932,055	$19,607,538
Earnings per common and common equivalent share					
Continuing operations	$3.06	$2.83	$2.47	$2.04	$1.94
Discontinued operations	0.33	0.07	0.10	0.07	(0.03)
Before extraordinary items	3.39	2.90	2.57	2.11	1.91
Extraordinary items	—	—	—	(0.66)	(0.78)
NET EARNINGS	$3.39	$2.90	$2.57	$1.45	$1.13

Source: Heublein Annual Report (May, 1978), pp. 17–18.

Inglenook, T. J. Swann, and Annie Green Springs brands. The FTC rejected this proposal and the case was expected to go to court in late 1977.

Another problem area had been the declining performance of Kentucky Fried Chicken (KFC). As of June 1976, the KFC chain included 4,340 company-owned or franchised outlets, which spent over $30 million on advertising. KFC ranked second in fast-food-industry sales, behind McDonald's, and the company had planned to retain this position by relying on its superior marketing capabilities in spite of a trend of continuous and substantial price increases. Problems occurred when, as one industry analyst put it, "the oil shortage and the nation's economic problem resulted, the economics of a burger meal for the family began to look a lot more attractive than a $9 bucket of chicken . . . they priced themselves into a bind."[1] KFC planned to reduce prices and return to emphasizing a smaller sales package to recapture its declining market share.

The spirits groups also suffered problems during this period. The Black Velvet Whiskey campaign was given the "Keep Her in Her Place" Advertising Award in 1974 by the National Organization for Women for a campaign described as a demeaning "sex-sell." This was followed by an attack from the Oregon State Liquor Commission for "sexually suggestive" advertising.[2] Black and White Scotch, the leading brand of scotch in the 1950s, acquired by Heublein in 1974, experienced a decreasing market share. The company found itself unable to stop the decline. The trend, averaging a decrease of 110,000 cases per year since 1974, represented a drain on corporate profitability.

On the positive side, Heublein had Smirnoff Vodka, which was acquired in 1939 for a mere $14,000 and a small royalty by John G. Martin, grandson of Heublein's founder. Smirnoff was the largest-selling vodka in the country, with sales of 5.5 million cases in 1976. Smirnoff accounted for nearly $15 million in profits in 1976. Smirnoff was the most heavily advertised distilled spirits product in the industry, as suggested by Table 2.

Beyond its more traditional liquor lines, Heublein was the industry leader in the prepared cocktail market, with a market share of over 75 percent. Although experts tended to see the company's expertise primarily in marketing, Heublein's research and development division was the largest and most active in the liquor industry. Researchers worked on developing and testing new products ranging from bottled martinis, manhattans, and canned whiskey sours through plum and peach wines to the "softer" coffee and chocolate liqueurs.

Over 1,000 ideas were generated by the marketing department and

---

[1]   "Top 100 Advertisers," *Advertising Age,* August 18, 1976, pp. 145–146.
[2]   Ibid.

Table 2   ADVERTISING EXPENDITURES
FOR DISTILLED SPIRITS
1976 LEADING 10 BRANDS,
MAGAZINES*

1.	Smirnoff	$4,067,353
2.	Johnnie Walker	3,678,147
3.	Canadian Club	3,614,095
4.	J & B	3,423,641
5.	Chivas Regal	2,817,170
6.	Seagram's V.O.	2,390,809
7.	Dewar's	2,298,070
8.	Hereford's Cows	2,195,269
9.	Beefeater	2,146,536
10.	Heublein Cocktails	2,102,771

* *1977 Liquor Handbook* (New York: Gavin-Jobson Associates, 1977): 320.

other sources throughout the year, and of that number, perhaps 100 were considered practical from a marketing or production viewpoint. The time span from conception to full distribution often took several years. A new product had to be salable and also retain quality and flavor over the months it might sit on a store shelf. Thirteen new drinks were introduced in 1974, the success of which contributed to the spirits division market increase from 9.9 percent to over 13 percent of the total market for distilled spirits.

Heublein noted a sharp trend toward lighter and sweeter drinks, with lower alcohol content. As shown in Table 3, the prepared cocktail market

Table 3   DISTILLED SPIRITS PRODUCTS
PERCENTAGE SALES INCREASES
1961–1980*

	1961–66	*1966–71*	*1971–76*	*1976–80*	*1961–76*
Wine	25.4	29.9	11.5	—	+ 81.68
Vodka	58.6	51.6	55.4	55.4	+ 273.6
Gin	37.7	18.9	4.4	4.4	+ 70.9
Canadian whiskey	66.9	70.6	31.4	31.4	+ 274.0
Scotch	55.1	54.5	8.2	8.2	+ 159.1
Brandy/cognac	46.5	41.3	15.2	15.2	+ 138.5
Prepared cocktails	109.7	30.3	113.5	113.5	+ 483.7
Rum	57.8	77.1	43.1	43.1	+ 300.1

* *1977 Liquor Handbook* (New York: Gavin-Jobson Associates, 1977): 280–319.

was growing at over 20 percent per year. The forecast for 1976–1980 showed a continued trend for this category of distilled spirits. As a result, Heublein had its R&D division working on new prepared cocktail drinks. One result was the introduction in 1975 of Malcolm Hereford's Cows—a sweet 30-proof, milk-type drink—first conceived 6 years earlier.

Hereford's Cows was test marketed in Chicago in the spring of 1975.[3] The product was available in five flavors—banana, strawberry, coconut, chocolate mint, and mocha. The successful results of the Chicago test market led to a decision to distribute nationally in March 1976. The product had originally been targeted for women in the age group 18 to 35. It was subsequently found to have strong appeal for other groups as well, including blacks, young males, and women over 35. Hereford Cows was budgeted for over $3 million in advertising for 1976.

The product achieved market acceptance far in excess of forecasted levels. In fact, with first-year sales at over a million cases, it was the most successful distilled spirits new product introduction in the history of the industry. William V. Elliott, vice president—marketing, stated:

> There's a huge market here because Cows even appeal to non-drinkers. . . . We could spend triple our promotional budget and it still won't be enough. . . . The repeat business on this product has been phenomenal.[4]

Having seen the success of Cows' appearance on the market, Heublein introduced Kickers, a product almost identical to Cows except for packaging. Kickers was designed to increase demand for milk-type "fun" drinks by appealing to those individuals who considered themselves energetic, activity-minded, and "young at heart."

THE CONTROVERSY

Robert MacNeil, in the introduction to a November 5, 1976, airing of the MacNeil–Lehrer Report on the subject of teenage alcoholism, said:

> The appearance of Cows and similar drinks from other manufacturers has alarmed doctors and others concerned with alcoholism. In particular, they are

---

[3] The details that follow were drawn from John J. O'Connor, "Heublein's Hereford's Cows Success Tips Marketers to Hot New Liquor Area," *Advertising Age,* December 1, 1976, pp. 1, 75.

[4] Ibid.

worried that these pop drinks will exacerbate an already serious social prob-
lem, teenage drinking.[5]

The show, which focused on Heublein's 30-proof Hereford's Cows, represented a summation of the social objections which surfaced shortly after the product was successfully test marketed and introduced nationally.

Susan Papas, a spokesperson for Odyssey House, a New York center for the rehabilitation of teenage alcoholics, said the sweet-tasting Cows "can cause the start or beginning of teenage problems." She explained:

Kids that don't like Scotch or Vodka or other types of hard liquors might be
more inclined to drink something that is like a milkshake. And milk is a very
acceptable form of something to drink. And with a bottle like this, that's
equal to two and a half cans of beer, I think they probably get a little surprised
very quickly.[6]

Although Papas admitted that she had no statistics on Cows specifically, she said her experiences at Odyssey House taught her that teenage alcoholics begin by drinking sweet-tasting products. "It's the pop, the lightness; it's the way it's presented."[7]

In addition to objecting to the ready accessibility of these drinks to potential young alcoholics, Papas and others cited advertising the promoted alcohol as the answer to numerous adult situations, "which happen to be the very ones that teenagers find particularly frightening and painful."[8]

Referring to one of Heublein's ads for Kickers, a companion product to the Cows, Nicholas Pace, assistant professor of medicine at New York University–Bellevue Medical Center, president of the New York City Affiliate of the National Council on Alcoholism, and chairman of the New York State Advisory Commission on Alcoholism, told Robert MacNeil:

It seems as if an awful lot of Madison Avenue . . . is sort of geared towards
showing the use of the drug alcohol in a romantic way that would allow people
an escape or a method to dull their senses or to increase their sexual activity
and so on.[9]

Other individuals active in fighting alcoholism objected to Heublein's attitude. Morris Chafetz, a medical psychiatrist who was a former head of the National Institute on Alcohol Abuse and Alcoholism, stated:

[5] "Teenage Alcoholism," *The MacNeil–Lehrer Report,* Library No. 290, Show No. 245, November 4, 1976.
[6] Ibid.
[7] Ibid.
[8] Ibid.
[9] Ibid.

I must say that I am concerned about the Cow drinks. Not because I think they are designed to hook people to alcoholic problems, but because it reflects a lack of sensitivity on the part of the liquor industry.[10]

He further stated:

The liquor industry could be moving ahead faster. . . . It's taking them a little longer to learn that there is no advantage to their product in people suffering from alcohol abuse and alcoholism.[11]

Pace, Chafetz, and Papas all agreed that they didn't believe government regulation of business practices and advertising was the answer to the types of problems they saw represented in Heublein's Cow. Chafetz, in summary, stated that he believed that the people in the liquor industry "are socially responsible and I would like them to downplay their product or remove it."[12]

Heublein did not respond publicly to the allegations and comments made on the MacNeil–Lehrer Report.

Heublein, the manufacturer of Hereford's Cows, declined to send a representative to join us tonight. A company spokesman objected that this program "was making a direct reference to certain products and had already made a decision that we (that's Heublein) were part and parcel of the problem." The Heublein man added, "It's like we're being placed on trial. Besides we had late notice." In fact, our reporter first contacted Heublein a week ago. We should note that Heublein also refused to send a representative to a Senate hearing on this subject last March. The industry's main lobbying organization in Washington, the Distilled Spirits Council of the United States, also declined to join us. So did the advertising agency that handles the Cows account, and the American Association of Advertising Agencies. The U.S. Brewers Association and the Association of National Advertisers did not respond to our phone calls.[13]

In response to objections raised that advertisements for Kickers seemed to be primarily directed at teenagers, Heublein dropped its advertising campaign even though it disputed the complaint. A spokesman for the Institute of Alcohol Abuse later stated that "Heublein acted very responsibly in acknowledging our concern about the problem of teen drinking, which appears on the rise."[14]

The current crisis occurred against this background. Betty Furness, former Special Assistant for Consumer Affairs to President Johnson and currently consumer affairs reporter for NBC-TV, handed out Dixie cups

[10]   Ibid.
[11]   Ibid.
[12]   Ibid.
[13]   Ibid.
[14]   The account of the incident was drawn from Mitchell C. Lynch, "The Day All the Kids Got Booze in Class from Betty Furness," *The Wall Street Journal,* February 12, 1978, pp. 1, 30.

filled with a beverage which later was found to be Strawberry Hereford's Cows to a classroom of 12- to 14-year-olds.[15] The students were unaware that the cups contained an alcoholic beverage. This action was taped for a segment on NBC's Today show to back up earlier statements made by Furness in criticism of Heublein products.

In an effort to prove that kids were attracted by advertising for sweet milk-type drinks, and without disclosing her intentions to either school officials or the students' parents, Furness gave the teenagers a cup of the beverage. She then recorded their enthusiastic responses to her question of whether they preferred the sweet-cream Cows "rather than a shot of scotch." Furness closed the Today show segment with the statement: "This is proof that Heublein is trying to appeal to young people." Furness did not question the students about whether they had seen any of the advertisements being challenged or if they had heard of the product.

THE ALTERNATIVES

Moran hung up the phone after his brief conversation with Watson. He began to consider the options available to Heublein in response to the latest incident involving the Hereford Cows.

Before laying out the alternatives, Moran reviewed the data provided by research and development and by marketing on the Hereford Cows. First, it was clear that most people could not drink more than two or three Cows at one sitting. The product was quite sweet and had a milk base. In fact, research in the R&D Laboratory showed a high probability that a drinker would get physically sick before he or she would become drunk. Also, marketing research showed that the primary adopters of the product were 25- to 39-year-old women.[16] Further, an awareness study showed that only 8 percent of teenagers polled were aware of the product. Perhaps of most importance, the retail price of Cows, $4.50 to $6.00 per fifth, was well above the cost of the alcohol products typically consumed by teenage alcoholics. These data suggested to Moran that the charges were without factual basis.

He looked at his watch. It was nearly noon. The Corporate Responsibility Committee meeting was scheduled for 8:00 A.M. the following day. That left little time to prepare his recommendations for response to the latest incident which threatened the continued success of the Malcolm Hereford's Cows line of packaged cocktails.

[15] Ibid.
[16] "The Furness Fiasco," *Advertising Age,* February 6, 1978, p. 16.

FIRESTONE TIRE AND RUBBER COMPANY:
A VOLUNTARY RECALL OF DEFECTIVE TIRES*

Joseph Wiley caught himself staring plaintively at the blank sheet of paper in his typewriter. He realized that he had been preoccupied unproductively with thoughts that had nothing to do with the task at hand. Since the hour was late and he wasn't getting anywhere with the piece he was working on, Wiley decided that 8 hours of sleep might restore his perspective. If nothing else, it would improve his ability to concentrate.

Wiley was a professor of business administration at a leading north-eastern university. Among his many interests, Wiley was particularly noted for his expertise and knowledge in the field of government regulation of business practices, which was the subject of several textbooks and articles that he had written. In his writings and lectures, Wiley generally leaned toward the view that government regulations were progressively escalating in terms of both the degree and the scope of activities covered. As a result, regulations were becoming so burdensome that any benefits derived were being canceled out by the ensuing passage of costs to the public. He was also quick to point out, however, that there were many areas of business activities that needed to be regulated. A compromise had to be found, he taught, somewhere between *caveat emptor* and *caveat venditor.*

In his business policy course, Wiley used many actual examples of companies that were exposed to undue regulation, as well as situations in which government intervention proved beneficial to the public welfare. In the latter cases, he frequently stressed the role and policy that management had taken in the face of such a situation and questioned his students as to whether they felt that the business had lived up to its responsibilities to both its stockholders and to the public.

Wiley was currently writing an article for the university's quarterly business review publication on the role of corporate strategy in facing regulatory agencies. In the course of his discussion he drew upon several examples of strategies that specific companies had taken in the past. He had spent the better part of a day reading research on a recent business–government confrontation that had been the focus of widespread publicity. Feeling much more alert than the night before, Wiley decided to review his research notes again before writing his analysis on the appropriateness of this particular company's handling of the controversy that it had experienced.

* This case is not intended to provide a precise account of the thinking or behavior of the parties involved.

THE COMPANY

The Firestone Tire & Rubber Company began in 1900 under the direction of Harvey Firestone. Over 78 years later, the Akron, Ohio-based corporation had grown to become the second largest U.S. tire producer and the sixty-third largest U.S. corporation as measured in revenues, which exceeded $4.8 billion in the 1978 fiscal year.

The company describes its principal business as "the development, production, distribution and sales of tires for all types of vehicles both in the United States and in countries around the world."[1] Tire and related products sales account for 80.4 percent of total company revenues. From 1972 to 1977, the steel-belted Radial 500 was the flagship of Firestone's tire line. In 1977, it had been replaced by the Radial 721 Fuel Fighter.

Owing to the technological nature of tire production, Firestone naturally began to diversify into rubber and synthetic rubber-related products. Diversification expanded to include a product line of over 40,000 items, including rims and wheels for trucks, tractors and off-the-road equipment, natural and synthetic rubber, polyurethane foam, metal and industrial rubber products, and textiles and chemicals, among others. Firestone's holdings in rubber plantations make it the largest natural rubber producer in the tire industry.[2]

In 1979, the company operated 15 tire and 41 nontire plants in the United States, and owned manufacturing subsidiaries in 25 foreign countries. Firestone had approximately 1,400 retail outlets within the United States that sold tires, automotive products and services, home appliances, and other consumer products. The company also operated approximately 600 retail stores in 135 foreign countries. The company employed over 112,000 people.

THE INDUSTRY

In 1978, in the midst of the Radial 500 controversy, Firestone watched its market share drop to a little over 18 percent from 23 percent in 1974. Both the original-equipment (tires sold to auto manufacturers for new cars) and the replacement-tire markets were fiercely competitive. Five major producers dominated the industry, and pricing dominated marketing strategies. Firestone was second behind industry giant Goodyear, followed by

---

[1] Firestone Tire & Rubber Company, *1978 Annual Report.*
[2] Ibid.

Uniroyal, B.F. Goodrich, and General Tire & Rubber Company, in the order of their market shares. (See Table 1 for a comparison of key financial statistics of these companies.)

In 1970, the U.S. tire industry was radically affected by the introduction of a new production tire from Europe—the radial tire. First mass-produced by Michelin, the radial tire, which consists of a number of steel or polyester meshed belts that circle the tire between the outer tread layer and the inner body ply or carcass, was a dramatic improvement over earlier bias-ply tires. Radials not only lasted twice as long, with warranties frequently covering a 4-year period or 40,000 miles, but also contributed dramatically to fuel-consumption economy.

When Michelin began selling, and later producing, their tires in the United States, tremendous pressure was put on U.S. manufacturers to develop their own radial tires. Michelin had mastered the production techniques years ahead of domestic manufacturers, and many industry analysts cited the rush to meet new competition and the relative inexperience with the new technology as reasons for the introduction of products that had not yet been completely debugged. However, because of the longer endurance of radial tires, the problems with these earlier production tires began to show up en masse only after the passage of several years. Ironically, by the time defect problems became generally known, the industry production expertise had grown to the point where experts believed that the newer-generation American-built radials were comparable in quality to any built abroad.

By 1978, radial tires accounted for more than 50 percent of all U.S. passenger-car tires, compared to 2.4 percent in 1970. Demand for all tires included original-equipment tires on 9 million new passenger cars and approximately 142 million replacement tires. Radials made up over 70 percent of the original-equipment market and, of these, about 95 percent were steel-belted. In the replacement-tire market, radials comprised between 40 and 45 percent of the demand, of which 75 percent were steel-belted tires.

In recent years the entire tire industry has suffered general financial problems. Most manufacturers were forced to cut back on production of bias-ply tires as demand for radials grew. This often required the closing and subsequent write-off of older production facilities that could not be converted.

In 1978, for example, Firestone was forced to phase out approximately $110 million in such facilities. Foreign-currency-exchange losses also affected most of the domestic manufacturers, as did the growing competition from foreign producers. General demand for replacement tires had been depressed primarily because of the longer life expectancy of the newer radials.

Because of the intensive competitive nature of the industry, price wars

Table 1 FINANCIAL STATISTICS FOR TOP FIVE MANUFACTURERS, FISCAL YEAR 1978*

Company	Assets ($000)	Rank[a]	Sales ($000)	Rank[a]	Net Profits ($000)	Rank[a]	EPS[b]	Number of Employees
Goodyear	$5,231,103	90	$7,489,102	31	$226,127	77	3.12	155,600
Firestone	3,486,000	155	4,878,100	63	(148,300)	—	(2.53)	112,000
Uniroyal	1,870,960	350	2,735,856	146	5,883	—	0.04	49,200
B.F. Goodrich	1,930,551	338	2,593,533	154	70,110	336	4.39	40,600
General Tire & Rubber	1,701,685	385	2,199,220	196	115,519	221	4.97	42,100

[a]Rank among top 500 U.S. corporations.

[b]Earnings per share before extraordinary items.

* "The Forbes 500," Forbes, May 14, 1979, 233–314.

affected the profitability of most companies, as indicated by the relative low return on assets that was characteristic in the industry. Firestone had a reputation for particularly aggressive pricing which some experts felt would intensify as the company tried to recapture part of its lost market share. This heightened competition, as well as lack of funds to build new mechanized plants and to keep abreast of new technologies, was expected to force many of the smaller tire manufacturers to fold. Even some of the larger manufacturers were expected to feel the squeeze. It had been rumored that B.F. Goodrich, for example, was allowing its share of the market to decline as it reinvested capital into more profitable areas, such as chemical and plastic production.

THE CONTROVERSY

Firestone was experienced with all kinds of public controversy. The company had been suffering from various consumer and government complaints long before the Radial 500 controversy began. Following a 1976 National Highway Traffic Safety Administration (NHTSA) investigation of safety problems involving 500s built from late 1973 through early 1974 at the company's Decatur, Illinois, plant, Firestone complied with the agency's suggestion that 400,000 of these tires be voluntarily recalled. The company argued that the recall was due to a temporary production problem at that one plant only, resulting in defects that included improper vulcanizing and rubber compounding "and possible vibrations at high speeds when the tires were overloaded or underinflated."[3] This was the largest tire recall in history at that date.

Other problems plagued the company during this period. Firestone received some bad publicity surrounding its methods of handling the United Rubber Workers 1976 strike. The company had long been accused of aggravating already bad relations with the union prior to the strike. As part of its strategy, the union was successful in drawing attention to its grievances when it called for a nationwide boycott of Firestone products during its 140-day strike.

Firestone also became involved in a political scandal in 1977 when it was revealed that the company's chief financial officer, Robert P. Beasley, had been indicted for stealing company funds. The money turned out to be part of a $1 million illegal political slush fund that Beasley had managed from 1970 to 1973. Beasley was sentenced to 4 years' imprisonment and

---

[3] "Compound Troubles for a Firestone Radial," *Business Week,* May 22, 1978, p. 37.

subsequently has accused Firestone chairman Richard Kiley and general counsel John Flogerg of full knowledge of the secret fund and other illegal company activities.

If 1977 appeared problematic for Firestone, 1978 proved to be much more costly. Despite the gravity of earlier problems, Firestone had managed to escape severe bad publicity. However, government and consumer watchdog agencies continued to monitor the company's activities. In 1978, Firestone took the full brunt of a massive investigation involving two federal agencies, a House subcommittee and a consumer organization, which eventually led to the largest product recall in history. Although the full cost has not yet been fully assessed (by the end of 1979), it was estimated that the recall eventually would cost Firestone well over $200 million.

CHRONOLOGY OF EVENTS

Following the February 1977 recall by Firestone of over 400,000 Radial 500 series tires, the Center for Auto Safety, a Washington, D.C.-based consumer organization formerly associated with Ralph Nader, began their own in-depth investigation of safety-related problems of the 500 tire. Discovering that over half the tire complaints they had on file were in regard to Firestone products, the center fired off a letter to Firestone president Mario Di Federico, revealing their findings and strongly suggesting higher quality-control standards, as well as recall of certain tire lines. The center also sent their findings to the U.S. Department of Transportation's National Highway Traffic Safety Administration (NHTSA), which, it turned out later, began their own informal investigation.

Firestone officials, in various interviews, suggested a "Naderite" conspiracy.[4] They cited certain officials as holding a grudge against the company, including Joan Claybrook, head of the NHTSA; Lowell Dodge, special counsel to Representative John E. Moss's House subcommittee on investigations and oversite; and Clarence Ditlow, head of the Center for Auto Safety. All were former Ralph Nader associates.[5] John Floberg, Firestone's vice president and general counsel, in a later interview commented that "[t] hey scratch each other's backs. They get together and decide to play Ping-Pong or badminton with somebody."[6]

---

[4] Arthur M. Louis, "Lessons from the Firestone Fracas," *Fortune,* April 28, 1978, p. 46.

[5] Ibid., p. 47.

[6] Ibid.

March 1978

As a part of its ongoing investigation into steel-belted radial tires, the NHTSA was continuously amassing evidence and conducting research. Part of this research, begun in late 1977, included an informal survey in the form of a mailed questionnaire to over 87,000 buyers of new cars that were factory equipped with radial tires. The survey began with a question regarding the specific brand of tire on the respondent's car and continued with questions as to whether or not problems such as blowouts or tread separation had been encountered with that brand.

On March 8, Firestone obtained from a federal court a temporary injunction stopping the NHTSA from publishing the results of the survey. The company argued in court that the survey was sloppily designed and highly biased against Firestone. Almost half of the car owners surveyed had purchased Firestone 500-tire-equipped automobiles, while the other half bought cars equipped with steel-belted radials from the other original-equipment suppliers. According to a company spokesman, "the manner in which the survey was designed . . . will provide a distorted and biased view of the quality of Firestone's steel-belted Radial 500 tires."[7]

Experts agreed with Firestone's argument that the survey was poorly designed. David Taylor, senior study director of the National Opinion Research Center at the University of Chicago, stated in an affidavit presented at the court hearing that the survey was conducted "without regard to the most basic and fundamental principles of survey methodology and thus is useless from a statistical standpoint."[8] Judge John Manos agreed with the company's arguments and later extended the injunction on March 31.

Until Firestone decided to raise these issues in a public forum, the company's problems went largely unnoticed by the public. Following the March 8 hearing, the media began speculating on what Firestone had to hide. Most notably, Firestone's action brought the entire situation to the attention of Congressman John E. Moss, chairman of the subcommittee on oversight and investigations of the House Committee on Interstate and Foreign Commerce, who immediately decided to begin collecting evidence for his own investigation into the safety of the Radial 500.

Of more immediate consequence to Firestone, however, was the announcement by the NHTSA on March 9, the day after Firestone obtained its injunction, that it had begun a formal investigation into possible safety-related defects of certain Firestone tires. A spokesman for the agency stated that the investigation was "spurred mainly by more than 500 com-

---

[7] "Firestone Acts to Stop Survey," *The Wall Street Journal,* March 8, 1978, p. 6.

[8] Ibid.

plaint letters from consumers who own cars with the Firestone radial tires."[9] The letters included reports of blowouts at high speeds, as well as contentions of tread separations, resulting in ten accidents and two injuries.

In response, a Firestone spokesman stated that the company felt the agency's action was "totally inappropriate."[10] He stated that studies have shown that tires are responsible for less than 1 percent of vehicle accidents and that most of these are due to abused or improperly inflated tires. The agency's "premature" announcement, he stated, "raises the disturbing question of whether the [NHTSA] has prejudged the issue or is proceeding on the basis of unreliable evidence."[11]

On March 31, Firestone succeeded in obtaining an extension of its injunction against the NHTSA in a court hearing that was widely covered by the media. Unfortunately, on the same day, another event occurred that turned all of Firestone's efforts into a public fiasco while at the same time putting the NHTSA into a very embarrassing position. Following the agency's announcement of a formal investigation, the Center for Auto Safety had filed a request with the agency under the Freedom of Information Act for certain documents pertaining to the case, including a copy of the survey results. The agency later explained that a staff lawyer had released the material, including the survey report, "inadvertently."[12] The agency's negligence appeared to give credence to Firestone's claim that the NHTSA was out to get them.

Any sympathy the company may have received was quickly canceled out, however, when the Center for Auto Safety issued a news release which publicly disclosed for the first time the results of the highly contested survey. The report indicated that only 5,414 car owners responded to the questionnaire out of the 87,000 mailing list.[13] Of these respondents, 1,971 persons indicated that they had experienced blowouts, tread separations, and tire distortions. Out of the 5,414 survey returns, 2,200 indicated that they owned Firestone tires, and out of these over 46 percent complained of some type of defect. The next closest group were Goodyear tire owners, of whom over 32 percent had complaints.[14]

9   "Safety Agency Says Some Firestone Tires Are Subject of Probe," *The Wall Street Journal,* March 9, 1978, p. 16.

10   Ibid.

11   Ibid.

12   Reginald Stuart, "Battle Rages over Recall of Firestone 500's," *The New York Times,* August 6, 1978, p. 7.

13   These figures represent a response rate of a little over 6 percent, indicating the probability of a high sampling error, which would render any conclusions statistically unsound.

14   Stuart, "Battle Rages," p. 7.

Firestone responded to the news leak by repeating its claims that the survey was prejudicial and highly unscientific, and by continuing to question the agency's motives in its investigation. Federal Judge John Manos was sharply critical of the NHTSA's disobedience of the court's injunction and permitted Firestone to subpoena Transportation Secretary Brock Adams and NHTSA director Joan Claybrook in a civil contempt of court action. Firestone continued to argue that the 500 series tire was a very sound product, and any problems were due to abuse and neglect. Many industry observers began expressing their feelings that Firestone's actions were adding fuel to the fire by continuing to bring public attention to itself.

April 1978

Clarence Ditlow, executive director of the Center for Auto Safety, publicly accused Firestone of trying to suppress information about the 500 series tire's high failure rate while at the same time trying to dump its remaining inventories of the tires, which the company claimed it stopped producing in late 1976. The center's director sent a letter to Firestone's president, Mario Di Federico, which stated that they had on file reports of 186 Radial 500 blowouts that resulted in 19 accidents, six serious injuries, and five deaths. Their studies also showed that the 500 was experiencing an "adjustment rate" problem (i.e., the percentage of tires returned to dealers with complaints by customers) that was two to three times the industry average.

The center also publicly accused Firestone of shipping its remaining inventories of the 500 tires to Florida and other southern states, where dealers were selling the radials at half price as a plot to foist a bad product on the market.[15] Firestone responded by explaining that it was phasing the tire out, and that when stocks get down to certain levels it is routine procedure to have clearance sales. Firestone contended again that the 500 was a good-quality product that was safe and would continue to give good mileage with proper care.[16]

In mid-April, Congressman Moss announced that his subcommittee would begin holding public hearings regarding the safety of Radial 500 tires. Moss requested over 16,000 documents from Firestone that pertained to charges that the 500 had an unusually high failure rate. Moss, upon hearing Firestone's response to the Center for Auto Safety's charges, angrily stated that "Firestone owes the public more than a statement in effect blaming reported accidents, injuries, and fatalities on the users of Firestone tires."[17]

[15] "House Panel Probes Firestone," *Advertising Age,* April 17, 1978, p. 8.
[16] Ibid.
[17] Ibid.

Firestone suffered further from the disclosure by Moss's subcommittee that the company was only now discontinuing production of the 500 series. The company had been stating all along, including in court testimony, that they had ceased production of the tire in late 1976, while they had in fact continued to produce one size of the tire. Also in April, Firestone announced losses exceeding $37 million in the first half of its current fiscal year, which ended in October.

July 1978

Following 7 months of investigation, the NHTSA announced on July 7 that it had reached an "initial determination" that there existed a safety-related defect in the Firestone Radial 500 series as well as in tires made by the company for sale by Montgomery Ward & Co. and Shell Oil Co. under their private labels. The agency urged Firestone to voluntarily recall the estimated 13 million 500 radial tires still on the road.[18] They also stated that a formal recall order would not be considered until after a public hearing scheduled for August 7, 1978, at which time Firestone could present its case.

In reaching its determination, the agency, as established in legal precedent, did not have to pinpoint the exact nature of a product defect that was safety-related to order a recall. Justification was legally provided if the government could produce evidence that a pattern of excessive failures exists. The definition of "excessive" was a discretionary decision left up to the agency. In the Firestone case, the NHTSA felt that it established such a pattern based on two types of evidence.

First, the agency had amassed during the course of its investigation over 6,000 reports from consumers that dealt with over 14,000 separate instances of 500 series tire failure, more than 50 injuries, 29 fatalities, and hundreds of incidents of property damage.

Second, the agency felt that Firestone's unusually high adjustment rate on the Radial 500 indicated a pattern of excessive failure of the product. The adjustment rate was calculated by dividing the number of tires returned by the number of tires sold. Firestone's own testimony indicated that the adjustment rate on the 500 was 7.4 percent, compared to the industry average of between 3 and 4 percent. Of course, it was the policy of tire dealers to make adjustments, which included partial as well as full

---

[18] The NHTSA was under pressure by Ralph Nader and other consumer activists to make a formal recall order. Under regulations, the government could require only that a tire manufacturer recall defective tires sold during the 3 years prior to a recall order. It was felt that Firestone could significantly reduce the impact of a recall through legal stalling tactics in the courts in the hope that over time the number of 500s still on the road would be significantly less.

refunds under a variety of circumstances, many of which were not safety-related defects. Further, a high adjustment rate, within reason, could be indicative of a more lenient return policy or a more generous warranty.

The NHTSA reported that in many cases the steel belts, which lie between the outside tread and the inner body ply, had a tendency to develop adhesion problems resulting from heat buildup that could alter the chemical composition of the bonding agent or from improper placement of the steel belt on the body carcass.[19] This situation could lead to tire blowouts, tread separation, distorted tire shape, blistering and cracking of tire sidewalls, or chunks of rubber pulling off.

Firestone responded to the agency's findings by stating that "there's no safety-related reason for the public to be concerned. . . . We contend that the 500 hasn't been proven to our knowledge and satisfaction to be the cause of fatalities in any accident in which it has been involved. . . . We don't think it's fair to recall a tire that doesn't have a safety defect and we believe this position will eventually prevail."[20] They added that most of the problems with the tire could be attributed to the American consumer's relative inexperience with radial tires and that owners too often run their tires underinflated.[21] Vice president John Floberg stated that he attributed the high number of complaints that the agency had on file to the significant amount of bad publicity the company received.[22]

Firestone also came under pressure from within. On July 10, 1978, the company's national dealer advisory council, made up of Firestone dealers, made public a committee memo addressed to Firestone's management that stated: "We know that Firestone is aware of the enormous problems we are having and feel that you must come up with a program so that both Firestone and the dealers can have some credibility with the public."[23]

On July 22, Firestone was exposed to another publicity nightmare that would further deepen its growing credibility gap with the public. Firestone had produced for General Motors a tire called the TPC (which stands for "tire performance criteria"), a steel-belted radial tire of the same basic construction as the 500 but adjusted for specifications set by GM for all of its original-equipment tires. On the above date, a Firestone corporate headquarters employee gave newsmen copies of computer printouts of company tests conducted on the TPC tires back in 1975 which indicated that the tires could not meet industry safety standards after a year or two of storage. The test results were never sent to either the NHTSA or to General Motors.

[19] Stuart, "Battle Rages," p. 7.
[20] "Firestone Could Lessen Financial Impact of Any U.S. Order to Recall '500' Radials," *The Wall Street Journal*, July 10, 1978, p. 10.
[21] Ernest Holsendolph, "Firestone Defends '500' Radial Tires," *The New York Times*, July 11, 1978, p. 12.
[22] Ibid.
[23] Ibid.

Firestone issued a statement saying that these test results, through an oversight, were never sent by the research and development department to company management.[24] Firestone also stated that these particular tests were "among thousands" performed each year, "and general conclusions about the performance of the [Firestone steel-belted radial] tires cannot be drawn from any one test or from limited number of tests."[25]

August 1978

On August 8, Firestone was given its "day in court" when the NHTSA held its final public hearings and the company was asked to show evidence as to why the Radial 500 and related products should not be recalled. On August 7, the company had announced that it had retained the renowned Washington attorney and former Secretary of Defense Clark Clifford as its chief counsel at the hearing.[26]

Firestone continued to argue that there was not clear evidence that there existed a safety-related defect in its tires and that what few accidents had occurred could be attributed to customer misuse. On the second day of the hearings, however, Firestone attorneys began to make the first public gestures that they were interested in facilitating an end to the dispute. Before presenting final defense arguments, an attorney representing Firestone told Joan Claybrook that "I want to advise the administrator of the interest of Firestone's management in taking whatever reasonable and appropriate action may be necessary to allay the obvious public concern over the safety of the steel-belted Radial 500. . . . While Firestone has the utmost confidence in the safety and reliability of this line of tires, our management is itself extremely concerned that, as a result of the extensive media attention to this controversy, many members of the motoring public now perceive the Radial 500 as an unsafe tire."[27] Clark Clifford also confirmed that the company was vigorously pursuing a negotiated settlement with the government. It was Firestone's feeling that a long court fight could cost the company as much as some form of recall in losses from further consumer law suits, extensive legal costs, and loss of goodwill from bad publicity.[28]

---

[24] Ralph E. Winter, "Tire Blowout," *The Wall Street Journal,* July 25, 1978, p. 1.

[25] Ibid.

[26] Prior to taking Firestone on as a client, Clark Clifford's most famous recent position was counsel to former Office of Management and Budget director Bert Lance when the latter was being investigated by Congress for abusive banking practices.

[27] Reginald Stuart, "Firestone, at Hearing, Asserts Its Radials Are Safe," *The New York Times,* August 9, 1978, p. 9.

[28] Ibid.

During the NHTSA hearings, the contents of correspondence between Firestone and its largest private brand customer, the Montgomery Ward Co., were made public. The letters indicated that Firestone had paid Montgomery Ward in 1977 $500,000 for what Montgomery Ward called "excessive tire adjustments" experienced on the "Grappler Radial" 8000 series tire, the private brand name given to the 500 sold by them.[29]

One of the letters to Firestone, dated December 22, 1976, that precipitated the large refund, expressed the following thoughts of Montgomery Ward's management:

> *We think you have failed to give consideration to this being of epidemic proportions, and also that more recent information indicates that adjustments on 1975 production is considerably greater than the 1973 and 1974 production after a year of exposure. This performance does not support your comment regarding ongoing improvement; rather, it amplifies the fact that we were given a bad product. . . . This falls in the area of moral responsibility and if we had any realization that our losses on adjustments would have reached the proportions they have and continue to increase, this tire would never have been introduced.[30]*

During the summer months and ending in August, Firestone had been called on several occasions to give testimony at Representative Moss's subcommittee hearings. John Floberg almost singlehandedly represented the company at these hearings. Floberg had been identified as Firestone's chief tactician acting on chairman Richard Riley's general approval throughout the controversy.[31] One magazine article at the time gave the following account of Floberg's handling of the situation:

> *When John Floberg appeared before the House subcommittee, he found himself in hostile surroundings. Chairman Moss and most of the other subcommittee members were antagonistic toward the company. What's more, Floberg had been preceded to the stand by seven witnesses—two police officers, two consumers, a Firestone dealer, a writer, and Clarence Ditlow—all of whom had testified against the 500 radial. Still, the hearings offered Firestone a broad forum, and a chance to redeem itself in the public eye.*
>
> *The company muffed the chance. Floberg's prepared statement was eloquent at times. But his adversaries on the subcommittee had done their homework, and they managed to trip him up. He lapsed into obfuscations and tortured explanations. The situation called for a heavy dose of candor, but Floberg came across strictly as a lawyer fighting a tough case. . . .*
>
> *An adversary, Representative Albert Gore, Jr., Democrat of Tennessee, wondered about the seemingly high adjustment rate on 500-brand radials.*

[29]   Ibid.
[30]   Ibid.
[31]   Arthur M. Louis, "Lessons from the Firestone Fracas," *Fortune,* August 28, 1978, p. 47.

Floberg tried to show the rate—7.4 percent—might not be out of line. He mentioned that the tire had been Firestone's most expensive and that buyers might therefore be "more likely to seek adjustment when they are unhappy with it." He added that the industry guards its adjustment rates "very jealously" and suggested that the 500 might compare favorably with other top-priced tires. But the subcommittee had demanded adjustment data from the other major tire makers, and none of them indicated a rate even half that of the 500s on competitive steel-belted lines for the years 1975–1977. At Goodyear, Firestone's chief competitor, the highest adjustment rate was 2.9 percent.[32]

August proved to be a difficult period for Firestone in its court battles. Since the beginning of its investigation, the NHTSA had been trying to get Firestone to surrender company records relevant to the 500 controversy, including 1975 consumer complaint letters, warranty-adjustment reports, and other documents. When Firestone failed to comply with the agency's request, the agency obtained a special order from a federal court for Firestone to present the papers in question. Firestone failed to comply and appealed the ruling, arguing that the special order was "unreasonably burdensome" to Firestone and that it exceeded the agency's investigatory authority. On August 16, the U.S. District Court in Washington, D.C., upheld the agency's authority as having a "broad information-gathering power," and ordered Firestone to surrender the requested information within 21 days.[33]

Since production of the 500 series began, Firestone had been faced with over 250 law suits seeking millions of dollars in damages because of alleged defects in the tires. Of these, nine were won by the plaintiffs, 22 cases were won by Firestone, and 64 were settled out of court. The biggest case involved a $1.4 million settlement.[34]

During the month of August, five class-action suits were filed against the company. Four of these suits alleged that Firestone sold the 500 tires knowing that they were defective, as evidenced by the company's own testing and by company knowledge of an unusually high adjustment rate. The fifth suit was filed by a Firestone shareholder on behalf of all persons who purchased Firestone stock between December 1, 1975, and July 24, 1978, on charges that Firestone failed to disclose negative information about their product line. This suit also alleged that Firestone officials had prior knowledge of the defects.

[32]   Ibid., p. 48.
[33]   "Firestone Is Ordered to Give Information on Radials to U.S.," *The Wall Street Journal,* August 16, 1978, p. 17.
[34]   Louis, "Lessons from the Firestone Fracas," p. 46.

September 1978

On September 1, Representative Moss's subcommittee issued a report on their findings, which concluded that the Radial 500 tire poses an unreasonable risk of death and injury and joined the NHTSA in recommending that Firestone voluntarily recall over 13 million of the tires still on the road. Its study contended that the tires "frequently fail on the road even with the most careful tire maintenance."[35] The report also called for a mandatory recall if Firestone did not comply on its own.

Firestone spokesman, Robert Troyer, did not make a detailed rebuttal to the report but reiterated the company position that "to the best of our knowledge, there have not been any proven cases where accidents, injuries or deaths have been caused by a defect in the tire itself."[36]

The subcommittee report also stated that Firestone had actually had a 17 percent adjustment rate on the Radial 500 from the date of its introduction in 1972 to the time it was phased out in 1978. This figure is much higher than the 7.4 percent the company had earlier testified to, which actually represents the adjustment rate for 1975 to 1977. The report also stated that Firestone had had a 7.6 percent adjustment rate on its TPC tire built for General Motors. The members urged that this tire be recalled as well.

During the month of September, the NHTSA continued its efforts to reach a negotiated settlement with Firestone on the details of a voluntary recall. Consumer advocate Ralph Nader continued to try to increase pressure on the agency to make a quick decision, arguing that government delay was saving Firestone $1.25 million weekly because of the declining number of roadworthy 500 series radials with the passage of time.

October 1978

On October 20, Firestone reached an agreement with the NHTSA on the terms of a voluntary recall. The negotiated settlement went into effect without a formal signed agreement which the NHTSA expected to obtain within the next several weeks. In its announcement, the NHTSA revealed its latest findings, that at least 41 deaths and 65 injuries could be attributed to Radial 500 tire defects.

The agreement called for Firestone to begin immediately sending out recall notices covering approximately 10 million 500 series radials estimated to be on the road. Firestone estimated that about half of these tires would actually be returned at an after-tax cost to the company in excess of $135

[35] *The New York Times,* September, 2, 1978, p. 58.
[36] Ibid.

million. The recall would cover all Firestone Steel Belted Radial 500s, private brands of the same construction, and General Motors TPCs. Firestone would replace those 500s that were sold on or after September 1, 1975 free of charge for new 721 series radials. The September 1975 date reflects the NHTSA 3-year statute of limitation on tire recall orders. The NHTSA also agreed to recall, much to the displeasure of consumer advocacy groups, only those radials produced before May 1, 1976. Firestone successfully argued that tires produced since that date reflected improved quality standards and the NHTSA had evidence that these tires had an adjustment rate that was within industry norms. Firestone agreed to replace those 500s sold before September 1975 at half the retail price, although it was not required to by regulation. The company estimated that this would include another 4 million tires. Firestone was required by law to allow those consumers covered by the recall at least 60 days to take advantage of the recall, although the NHTSA hoped to get the company to extend the deadline. Since many of the tires that qualified for recall were not registered, NHTSA insisted that Firestone use extensive advertising to notify consumers of the details of the recall.

On October 23, the Firestone company issued a statement about the recall at a news conference. Firestone's chairman, Richard Riley, said the company had agreed to the recall because resistance in the courts would likely have been extremely lengthy and expensive and the outcome uncertain and that government pressure for a quick settlement had been strong.[37] He also stated that the company was anxious to end the public controversy in order to reassure Firestone customers that their products were sound.[38] Riley continued to insist that there was no safety-related defect in the Radial 500, although the notification of recall sent to eligible customers contained a statement that the NHTSA had determined that such defects do exist.

November 1978

Early in November, the Firestone company's advertising agency successfully negotiated a 3-year, $750,000 plus contract with the venerable actor Jimmy Stewart for television spot commercials praising the company's founder Harvey Firestone, and his devotion to product quality and innovation which was reflected in "today's steel-belted radial 721 tires." Stewart said in the advertisement, "It's a product Harvey Firestone would have been proud of, because you know he always said he wanted Firestone to be

[37] "Firestone Recall on Its '500' Tires Will Begin Soon," *The Wall Street Journal,* October 23, 1978, p. 4.
[38] Ibid.

best today and still better tomorrow."[39] No mention is made of the 500 tire in the commercials. Outwardly, this would appear a strange choice for the 78-year-old, well-respected actor to make for his first-ever television commercial endorsement. It was later disclosed that Jimmy Stewart was a classmate of one of the Firestones at Princeton University, as well as a close friend of the family. He had worked also on several charity projects with the Firestone family.[40]

During the month of November, Firestone and the NHTSA continued negotiations on the still-unsigned recall agreement. The major source of contention at this point was on the scope and the nature of the advertising campaign Firestone was to use to announce the recall details, in addition to the mailed notifications to registered owners of Radial 500s. Another sore point in the talks was the restrictive policy that many dealers were using in replacing the recalled tires. Some dealers were refusing to replace tires if tread-wear indications were too low in those cases where the customer had no proof of purchase. The NHTSA issued a statement saying that there was "nothing in the terms of the agreement that addresses the condition of the tire."[41] The agency also wanted the company to extend the 60-day grace period following notification of eligibility.

On November 29, the Firestone company signed a revised agreement for the recall of 500s. In addition to those conditions previously agreed upon in the October settlement announcement, Firestone agreed to adhere to the following major points:

- The company would pay for advertising in 242 major daily newspapers and send news releases to 3,800 daily and weekly newspapers.[42]
- Firestone would replace all eligible 500 series tires regardless of their condition as long as the tires were still on the owner's car.
- Firestone would refund to customers any balances due to eligible recall tires that had been previously brought back to the dealer for adjustment.
- The company would broadcast 30-second spot commercials on television at times of the day when the company advertised its products.
- The company would recall the same eligible tires that had been sold in the Canadian market, estimated to involve over 1 million tires.
- Firestone agreed to extend the replacement period to April 1, 1980, for those eligible consumers who did not receive a written notification of the recall.

[39] "A New Image," *Forbes,* October 30, 1978, p. 178.
[40] "Why Jimmy Stewart Chose Firestone," *The New York Times,* November 21, 1978, sec. IV, p. 20.
[41] "U.S. Agency Complains to Firestone Tire about Conduct of Company's '500' Recall," *The Wall Street Journal,* November 6, 1978, p. 4.
[42] See Appendix B for a reprint of one of these ad notices.

Richard Riley stated that the company would have to manufacture 400,000 tires a month just to replace those that are recalled. Industry analysts felt that the company would be able to handle the enormous economic burden of the recall. At the time of the recall, Firestone was sitting on cash and marketable securities of over $214 million as well as an untapped bank credit line of $200 million. Also, General Motors and the Ford Motor Co. both announced that they had no plans on cutting back on Firestone orders for original-equipment tires.

The actual financial losses were not too far off from these estimates, although the actual damage would not be known for several years. In fiscal 1978, Firestone listed on its balance sheet an accrued liability estimate for the tire recall of over $227 million, or $147.4 million after taxes. The company had a net income loss that year of $148.3 million. (See Appendix A for Firestone's balance sheet and income statement.)

What proved to be the most damaging factor to Firestone was the considerable loss of goodwill and customer loyalty in the marketplace. One highly respected industry analyst stated that he felt the company may have lost as much as two or three percentage points off its market share, a considerable amount in the multibillion-dollar, highly competitive replacement-tire market.[43] Each point of market share was estimated in 1979 to be worth over $50 million at the wholesale level.

---

[43] "The Case for Firestone," *Forbes,* November 13, 1978, p. 106.

Appendix A Financial Statements

For The Years Ended October 31 *(Dollars in millions, except per share amounts)*	*1978*	*1977*
Net sales	$4,878.1	$4,426.9
Cost of goods sold	3,958.7	3,535.0
Selling, administrative, and general expenses	669.5	610.3
Interest and debt expense (Notes 6, 7, and 8)	100.6	88.5
Other income, net	(23.0)	(22.7)
	4,705.8	4,211.1
Income before provisions for loss on phase-out of facilities and tire recall, income taxes, and minority interests	172.3	215.8
Provision for loss on—phase-out of facilities (Note 14)	110.0	—
—tire recall (Note 15)	234.0	—
Income (loss) before income taxes and minority interests	(171.7)	215.8
Domestic and foreign income taxes, including credits in 1978 applicable to provisions for loss on phase-out of facilities ($37.0) and tire recall ($86.6) (Notes 1, 3, and 6)	(27.2)	102.9
Minority interests in income of subsidiary companies (Note 10)	3.8	2.7
Net income (loss)	$ (148.3)	$ 110.2
Net income (loss) per share of common stock*	$ (2.58)	$ 1.92

*Based on average number of shares outstanding during the year.

Appendix A (*continued*)

THE FIRESTONE TIRE & RUBBER COMPANY
AND CONSOLIDATED SUBSIDIARIES
BALANCE SHEETS

	October 31	
Assets	*1978*	*1977*
(dollars in millions, except per share amounts)		
Current assets		
Cash	$ 26.7	$ 43.3
Time deposits and certificates of deposit (Note 4)	103.4	123.0
Short-term investments (Note 1)	27.1	49.5
	157.2	215.8
Accounts and notes receivable, less allowance for		
doubtful accounts: 1978—$9.8; 1977—$9.8	959.8	793.0
Inventories (Notes 1 and 5)		
Raw materials and supplies	213.3	233.2
Work in process	73.2	70.6
Finished goods	531.6	563.4
	818.1	867.2
Prepaid expenses	13.0	14.2
Total current assets	1,948.1	1,890.2
Properties, plants, and equipment, at cost (Note 9)		
Land and improvements	122.5	113.4
Buildings and building fixtures	637.3	625.1
Machinery and equipment	2,077.7	1,991.8
	2,837.5	2,730.3
Less accumulated depreciation (Note 1)	1,392.6	1,307.8
	1,444.9	1,422.5
Other assets		
Investments, at cost or equity	55.2	44.7
Miscellaneous assets	25.6	22.8
Deferred charges (Note 1)	12.6	15.5
	93.4	83.0
Total assets	$3,486.4	$3,395.7

Liabilities and Stockholders' Equity	October 31 1978	October 31 1977
Current liabilities		
Short-term loans (Note 7)	$ 215.5	$ 215.6
Accounts payable, principally trade (Note 9)	300.8	283.8
Accrued compensation	141.3	131.5
Domestic and foreign taxes (Note 3)	128.0	179.0
Accrued liability for tire recall (Note 15)	227.2	—
Long-term debt due within one year	14.2	23.6
Other accrued liabilities	128.6	102.0
Total current liabilities	1,155.6	935.5
Accrued liability for phase-out of facilities— noncurrent (Note 14)	53.4	—
Long-term debt (Note 8)	616.1	616.1
Long-term capital lease obligations (Note 9)	68.0	74.2
Deferred income taxes (Notes 1 and 3)	94.8	106.7
Minority interests in subsidiary companies (Note 10)	90.7	45.1
Commitments and contingent liabilities (Notes 9 and 16)		
Stockholders' equity		
Serial preferred stock (cumulative), $1 par value, voting, authorized 10,000,000 shares, none issued		
Common stock, without par value, authorized 120,000,000 shares, shares issued: 1978— 60,090,127; 1977—60,082,377 (Notes 8 and 13)	62.6	62.6
Additional paid-in capital	194.7	195.1
Reinvested earnings	1,210.5	1,422.2
	1,467.8	1,679.9
Less common stock in treasury	60.0	61.8
Total stockholders' equity	1,407.8	1,618.1
Total liabilities and stockholders' equity	$3,486.4	$3,395.7

Appendix B A Tire Recall Reminder
From Firestone

WE NEED YOUR HELP—In October, 1978, Firestone and the national Highway Traffic Safety Administration (NHTSA) announced a voluntary recall of certain Firestone Steel Belted Radial "500" and similar passenger tires.

That recall has been going on for the past ten months. We are doing everything possible to complete the recall and to get back all eligible tires.

But we cannot do it alone. The only tires we can replace are the ones you bring in.

This advertisement is being published again to remind motorists who may still have tires eligible for replacement that they should bring them in so that the recall can be completed.

We need your help and cooperation and we strongly urge you to bring in any eligible tires for replacement now. Check your spare tire too—it might also be covered by the recall.

In October, 1978, The Firestone Tire & Rubber Company initiated a voluntary recall of certain Steel Belted Radial 500 and Firestone manufactured Steel Belted Radial TPC passenger car tires. Some private brand steel belted radials manufactured by Firestone were also recalled (see note on page 65).

In July, 1978, The National Highway Traffic Safety Administration (NHTSA) made an initial determination that a defect which relates to motor vehicle safety exists in Steel Belted Radial 500 tires.

In order to resolve this matter, Firestone agreed to replace certain steel belted radials.

A defect of the type referred to in the NHTSA's initial determination may, according to the NHTSA, be first evidenced by the appearance of a bulge or of a noticeable difference in ride characteristics, such as a thumping sound or a roughness in ride, or both. According to the NHTSA, the tires covered by its initial determination may also fail without warning. The NHTSA believes that failure of the tires can result in a loss of air with a possible loss of control of the vehicle which may result in vehicle crash.

If you are a registered owner of eligible tires bought from a Firestone Store or Dealer, or if the tires came to you as original equipment on a new car, you should have received a mailed notice of the recall.

But if you did not, that doesn't mean you're not eligible. That's why we ask you to read carefully all the recall details and procedures spelled out here.

What Tires Are Being Recalled?

Firestone will replace, free of charge—including mounting and balancing—any of the following tires.

1. Firestone Steel Belted Radial 500 tires, with a five-rib tread pattern, that were sold on or after September 1, 1975 and manufactured in the United States or Canada prior to January 1, 1977.

2. Firestone Steel Belted Radial 500 tires and Firestone TPC Radials, with a seven-rib tread pattern, that were sold on or after September 1, 1975 and manufactured in the United States, Sweden, or Canada prior to May 1, 1976.

The Firestone Steel Belted Radial 500 tires and private brand tires of the same or similar internal construction which were purchased as replacement tires and which have serial numbers, as explained below, showing they were manufactured between March 1, 1975 and September 1, 1975 are eligible for replacement if they were not purchased on a 1975 vehicle. Otherwise, to be eligible for replacement, tires manufactured prior to September 1, 1975, must be accompanied by evidence that the tires were first sold new on or after September 1, 1975, either as replacement tires or as original equipment on a new vehicle.

Tires that have been retreaded, previously adjusted or scrapped are not covered by this offer. Tires that have been worn out (2/32nds of an inch or less of the original tread depth remaining as measured at three points on the tire) are not eligible for free replacement unless you are still using them on your car.

In order to obtain a replacement tire, you must present the tire. Proof that you once purchased or owned an eligible tire is not sufficient.

How Can I Identify A Recalled Tire?

Obviously, if you received a mailed notice from Firestone, your tires probably fit into one of the recall groups. But if you did not get a letter, they may be included. Here is how you tell:

First, compare your tire tread pattern with the pictures shown here. Are they five-rib tires or seven-rib tires?

Next, if you have the invoice or other evidence showing the date you bought your tires, compare it with the "sold" date mentioned above. That's your proof of purchase. (In the case of original equipment tires, your car invoice, title, or other evidence of the vehicle purchase date will do just as well.)

Finally, to determine when the tire was made, check the DOT number on the tire sidewall (on the inside wall of a whitewall tire). The picture we have included in this announcement will help you identify the DOT numbers on your tires. The last three digits of the DOT number identify the week and year of manufacture. For example, 355 translates as the thirty-fifth week of 1975.

Still not sure? Ask the man at your nearby Firestone Dealer or Store. He's got the answers, and he really does want to help.

Can Anyone Bring in Tires for Replacement?

Firestone's voluntary recall covers both "owners" and "purchasers" of Firestone tires.

So if you were the first purchaser of eligible tires and are still using them or have them in your possession, you may present them for replacement.

Even if you acquired your eligible tires on a used car, you may as the current "owner" of those tires bring them in for replacement.

Is anyone excluded from the recall? Yes. Manufacturers or retreaders of tires, tire dealers, and persons who sell used or scrapped tires are not eligible.

What Tires Will I Receive As Replacements?

In exchange for an eligible tire, you'll receive a new Firestone Steel Belted Radial 721, TPC or comparable Firestone tire.

You may take your choice of any of these tires that are available in the size of the tire replaced. Or you can wait until the tire you want becomes available. You may also select a lower priced radial tire or even a non-radial tire so long as radials and non-radials are not unsafely matched.

Where and When Will My Tires Be Replaced?

All replacements of Firestone brand tires will be made at Firestone Dealers and Stores. So even if your tires came to you on a new car, bring them in to Firestone. The private brands tires listed below that are also being recalled should be taken back to the local outlet of the private brand.

If your tires came on a new car or your tires were registered when purchased as replacement tires, you should have received a mailed recall notification. Otherwise, we suggest that you visit your Firestone Store or Dealer to have your Firestone "500" or Firestone TPC tires inspected and to make arrangements to have eligible tires replaced. You may find it convenient to make an appointment.

Your Firestone Retailer will inspect your tires, check to see if they're included in the recall, and arrange with you to replace eligible tires as quickly as possible.

It will take approximately 15 to 20 minutes per tire to make the exchange.

If a tire is not available you will receive a "rain check" and will be notified by your Dealer or Store when your tire is available.

How Soon Must I Bring My Tires in for Free Replacement?

The provisions of the recall program require that eligible tires be submitted for replacement within 60 days after you have received notification by mail of the recall.

In the case of those who may not receive a notification letter but where tires are eligible request for replacement must be made by April 1, 1980. After you have been notified that your replacement tires are available you will have 60 days in which to come in to actually have your tires exchanged.

If you do not submit eligible tires for recall within the time required, or fail to have your tires exchanged within 60 days after notification that your replacement tires are available, any exchange of your tires will involve a pro rata charge to you based on the amount of remaining tread and a charge will be made for mounting and balancing.

What If My Tires Were Purchased New Prior to September 1, 1975?

Tires purchased prior to September 1, 1975 are also covered by the initial determination of a safety-related defect by the NHTSA. Although those tires are not required by law to be replaced, to make certain all our Firestone customers are fully satisfied, we are extending a special offer to owners of older tires:

If you own any eligible Steel Belted Radial 500, TPC Radial tires purchased *before* September 1, 1975 we will, if you wish, replace them with equivalent new Firestone tires of your choice, charging you only a pro rata portion of the regular selling price and applicable Federal Excise Tax for the tires based on the amount of remaining tread depth. A charge will be made for mounting and balancing.

A Closing Comment

As you might imagine, this recall has been an enormous undertaking. It has required—and it has received—extraordinary action on our part. We have given it priority in producing tires at our factories and in replacing tires at our stores and dealers.

It has also taken the cooperation of many outside of Firestone—the NHTSA, consumer agencies across the country, our loyal dealers and their employees, our private brand accounts and, of course, all our customers.

Now, with your help, we can go on to finish the task. That's our pledge to you, our valued customer.

Note: The following private brand tires will fall into the free replacement category based on the same production dates and purchase dates as are applicable to the corresponding type Steel Belted Radial 500 tire. **Tires similar to "500" seven rib tires: Atlas Goldenaire II Steel Belted Radial** (Only Atlas Goldenaire II tires having a serial number beginning with VD and ending with 055 thru 176 are involved in this recall. Tires having a serial number beginning with A3, AC, UT and VC are not involved. For replacement, if possible, return these Atlas tires to the oil company service station from which they were purchased.); **JTW Ferrari Steel Radial; National Steel Belted Radial** (78 series only); **Union Radial Steel** * * * * * (five star); **Montgomery Ward Steel-Track, Belted, Grappler Radial II** (Only tires beginning with VD or VK are included). **Tires similar to "500" five rib tires: Montgomery Ward Steel-Track, Belted, Grappler Radial; Super Shell® Steel Radial. In the following lines the BR78-13 and ER78-14 sizes are "500" seven rib type tires, the remaining sizes are "500" five rib type tires: Caravelle Supreme Steel Power Radial; Caravelle Double Steel Radial; Holiday Supreme Steel Power Radial; JTW Ferrari Supreme Steel Power Radial; Lemans Supreme Steel Power Radial; Seiberling RT 78 Steel Belted Radial; and Zenith Supreme Steel Power Radial.**

FOAM-PAK, INC.:
SOCIALLY RESPONSIVE PACKAGING*

On his return flight to Chicago, Clayton Burnett reviewed the meeting of the Association of Plastics Manufacturers (APM) which he had attended earlier in the day. As vice president of marketing for Foam-Pak, Burnett attended all trade association meetings together with Frank Braswell, the

* This case was prepared by Thomas Ingram at Georgia State University, and modified by the authors as the basis for class discussion rather than to illustrate either effective or ineffective handling of an administrative situation. All rights are reserved to Mr. Ingram.

corporate attorney. One point from the meeting had given Burnett cause for extreme concern. If pursued, it would mean that Foam-Pak could literally be legislated out of business.

Braswell shared Burnett's concern that Foam-Pak's sales could be diminished or eliminated by the latest developments. Braswell spoke first:

> *Clayton, we have been working closely together for over 5 years. You can probably look at me and tell that I am more than a little concerned. Frankly, I am scared to death that the company is in real trouble. When we got into the styrofoam meat tray business 10 years ago, I had no idea that we would be in such a vulnerable position at any point in the future.*

Burnett agreed with Braswell and said:

> *I really wasn't too concerned when we first began to run into resistance to our meat trays. After all, we had conducted a lot of research and knew that our trays offered the consumer a better form of packaging than either pulp or clear plastic trays. It didn't really upset me too much when we were banned in the Miami area. But when I found out about the ban against us in the entire state of Connecticut, I began to realize that a nightmare might be unfolding. We could be out of business in another year if we don't do something fast!*

The next morning, Burnett received a call from Frank Decker, sales manager of the southern region. Decker gave Burnett further reason to be concerned as he related the latest developments in South Carolina: "As you know, Clayton, we were able to defeat the bill in the subcommittee last year—by one vote. I just got the word from one of our customers that the bill will be introduced into the subcommittee again when the legislature convenes in two weeks."

Burnett made a quick mental review of the past problems in South Carolina. Two years ago, a then unknown representative from the Charleston area named Caroline Henley introduced a bill requiring clear or grid-bottom pulp meat trays for all meat packaged at the retail level. Henley claimed that it was common knowledge that supermarkets who used foam trays packaged meat with the "bad side down" and that a change to clear or grid-bottom trays would eliminate this practice. Representative Henley had been ridiculed by her own subcommittee for lack of evidence and lost her bid to have the bill introduced on the floor of the House by a margin of 8 to 1.

Immediately after the defeat, Henley called a press conference to denounce "consumer deception in the supermarket industry." The results of the news conference made headlines and established Henley as a pro-consumer state official.

Last year, the vote was 5 to 4 after a bitter debate. Henley still had not produced sufficient evidence to persuade all of the members of the subcommittee, but she did have 25 women testify that they had definitely bought meat in the past which appeared to have been packaged "bad side down." These women were members of the Consumer Rights League of South Carolina.

Burnett was afraid that if the bill made it out of the subcommittee, that other "headline grabbers" would join Henley in pushing for new meat tray packaging requirements.

Decker continued:

We are trying to line up the retailers to testify at the subcommittee hearing, but they seem to be the only ones on our side. When the ban on foam meat packaging passed in Connecticut last week, it made the front page in all the local newspapers. I don't think we will be able to stop it in the subcommittee this year.

After assuring Decker that he could personally handle the testimony for Foam-Pak at the hearing, Burnett asked his secretary to hold all his calls. Burnett needed time to think.

COMPANY BACKGROUND

Foam-Pak was a national manufacturer of styrofoam products, including foam meat trays. Other products include beverage coolers and coffee cups. The foam meat trays accounted for approximately 85 percent of Foam-Pak's annual revenue, which was about $50 million. When Foam-Pak entered the styrofoam meat packaging industry, the styrofoam meat tray was a new product being supplied by small regional manufacturers. Within 5 years, Foam-Pak had proven to be the only national supplier of the product. Their manufacturing facilities had expanded from Chicago to California and Georgia as well.

The manufacturing segment of the meat packaging industry was composed of eight companies manufacturing three different types of meat trays. Three companies manufactured a molded grid bottom pulp tray, and one manufacturer recently began to make a clear, hard plastic tray.

Foam-Pak sold their meat trays for use at the retail store level where the packaging of the meat is actually done. Large chains typically bought directly from Foam-Pak, while the smaller stores bought trays from co-op grocers who had earlier purchased from Foam-Pak. Retailers packaged about 85 percent of their meat, poultry, and seafood in foam trays. The grid bottom pulp tray had 12 percent of the market. With a much higher cost per tray, the clear plastic tray had only about 3 percent of the market.

Foam-Pak was the top supplier of the foam tray in the country, with

50 percent of all foam sales. This position of leadership had not been severely tested by other foam tray manufacturers, but the threat from the other types of trays has become serious in the past year.

THE ISSUE OF VISIBILITY

Citing apparent consumer concern over possible deception in meat packaging, the manufacturers of grid bottom pulp trays and clear plastic trays combined forces to work against the suppliers of opaque foam trays. These manufacturers pointed out that consumers were unable to see the bottom of the cut of meat when it was packaged in a foam tray. They charged that some retailers packaged the meat "bad side down" and that the consumer would not be able to detect this until after the purchase was made.

In Miami and Connecticut, manufacturers organized and supported consumer groups to push for legislation that would ban the usage of foam trays by a retail outlet. Their efforts had paid off. Similar efforts had been mounted in 15 other states, with signs pointing to battles in all states.

CURRENT SITUATION

Clayton Burnett had not sat idly by as his competitors mounted their grassroots campaign against foam meat trays. He had persuaded the other members of the APM to join Foam-Pak in sponsoring an independent research study to investigate the following areas:

1. How important consumers feel the type of meat tray is, relative to other factors, in selecting fresh meats.
2. Whether consumers believe they have ever been misled about the quality or quantity of fresh meat, how often they feel this occurs, and the nature of any deceptive practices they feel they have experienced.
3. What recourse they follow if they feel they have been deceived by a supermarket.
4. How they rate the three main types of meat trays on certain specific attributes.

In addition, APM wanted a technical analysis of over 150 cuts of steaks and roasts to determine if there was any discrepancy by type of trays as to top and bottom quality in the cut of meat. One of the oldest and most reputed consulting firms in the country was commissioned to do both studies.

When the report was complete, Clayton Burnett found the summary to his liking.

1. There was no difference in actual or perceived incidence of the top side of the meat being better than the bottom, among the three types of trays tested.

2. The type of tray did not materially influence the purchase decision. Ninety percent of the purchasers cited factors other than packaging (i.e., price and quality) as the reason for their purchase decision.

3. When given a choice to select meat in the three trays, the consumer showed no significant preference toward any particular tray.

4. Because of the juice that had typically drained and the bunching of heat-sealed protective film, the clear or grid pulp tray did not help the consumer to determine the top-to-bottom quality differential.

5. Ninety-three percent of purchasers report that when deception is perceived, they either return the meat or change to a different store—actions that are an obvious deterrent to deceptive practices by the retailer.

Burnett had also asked two of his staff members to prepare their recommendations with regard to the legislative environment. Although he had asked for these reports only last week, both reports were already on his desk (see Figures 1 and 2).

Burnett reflected back over the 10 years that Foam-Pak had been in the meat tray business. The first major problem Foam-Pak had encountered was high operating costs and the resulting noncompetitive price for their trays in the market. That problem had been solved through increased manufacturing efficiency to the point where Foam-Pak was able to offer trays at a substantially lower price than grid-bottom pulp trays or clear trays. The environmental issue had been a major concern in the early 1970s but had never threatened sales volume.

Clayton Burnett was a persuasive person, having excelled in various sales jobs on his way to becoming vice president of Foam-Pak. He felt that he had the necessary information to "sell" interested parties on foam meat trays in a one-on-one situation. What made him feel uneasy was the realization that the "sale" in this case would apparently have to be made to millions of ultimate consumers.

Another factor which worried Burnett was that his competition had been successful in Miami and Connecticut without ever producing research results documenting the deceptive practices they claimed were widespread. Their emotional appeal had been very effective.

Wishing mightily that Foam-Pak had a public relations department, Clayton Burnett buzzed Frank Braswell on the intercom and said, "Frank, we've got a hot one in South Carolina and it looks like it is spreading. Can you come down to my office to hear what I propose to do?"

FIGURE 1   Interoffice Correspondence

MEMO TO: Clayton Burnett
FROM: R. L. Winslow
           Product Manager—Foam Trays

     This memo contains my recommendations for appropriate action to be taken with regard to the visibility issue and the resulting threat to our business. As you know, our meat tray is demonstrably superior to the pulp and the clear plastic meat tray in terms of cost, handling, product protection, equal in terms of long-term environmental protection, and it is preferred by the supermarkets.

     Prohibitive legislation, however, is aimed at the supermarket, not the suppliers of foam plastic meat trays. The enemy is not the various consumer protection advocates and groups pressing for prohibitive legislation. The enemy is a misconception based on misinformation or a lack of information about meat trays which results in overprotection for the consumer, and discriminatory packaging legislation harmful to foam plastic meat tray manufacturers.

     Conventional advertising and sales promotion methods are not applicable to this situation because *nonplayers* are attempting to determine who can and who can't play in our game based on the rules of an entirely different game called "consumer protection."

     Consumer protection is a "public relations" game—not a "manufacturing–marketing–distribution" game. Therefore, an effective and remedial response should involve:

1. Responding as an *industry* rather than as an individual manufacturer of foam plastic meat trays.
2. Creating and supporting a more effective consumer protection organization so that we can play in their game.
3. A program designed to allow Foam-Pak to exploit the newly created consumer protection program with a hard-hitting industry advertising and promotion campaign of its own.

Proposed Solution

     We propose that Foam-Pak create and operate a FOAM PACKAGING ASSOCIATION (FPA) for the purpose of gathering and disseminating information relative to the problems and practices of packaging and selling fresh meat, poultry, and seafood in food stores, with special emphasis on the consumer protection aspects of such practices as they relate to display merchandising.

     More specifically, FPA's objectives would be:

1. To make the trade and public aware of the fallacies and negative effects of overprotecting the consumer via discriminatory legislation relating to supermarket meat departments in general, and to the visibility issue in particular.

2. To promote the advantages of foam plastic meat trays to appropriate segments of the retail industry and to the meat-buying public.
3. To accomplish the above in such a way that the costs of operating the FPA are distributed equitably among the various suppliers of foam plastic meat trays.

Organization

FPA would be established as an independent entity with its own staff, quarters, budget, and board of directors. Foam-Pak would provide office space and facilities on its premises in Chicago, and manage FPA operations. FPA would consist of one delegate Director from each participating foam plastic meat tray manufacturer. The Board would meet periodically, perhaps in conjunction with appropriate industry conventions to review the activities of the Council.

FPA Acitivities

1. Gather and analyze all available information on
   a. All products used in the manufacture of meat trays,
   b. Meat tray usage, and
   c. Industry and consumer reaction to this form of meat packaging.
2. Instigate, guide, and fund additional product usage and consumer preference surveys—especially on the effects of prohibitive legislation in certain markets.
3. Establish, maintain, and promote a Meat Merchandising Library to facilitate the use of the above information by all interested industry, press, legislative, and consumer groups.
4. Identify individual and group advocates of the visibility legislation.
5. Identify all influential publics interested or potentially interested in the question of consumer protection as it relates to meat trays, and organize the means to reach each of these publics via key spokesmen in industry, the media, and legislative bodies.
6. Prepare and place news stories and feature articles and advertisements favorable to our cause.
7. Prepare background dossiers on FPA projects for industry sales and marketing executives.
8. Coordinate and disseminate information from and for industry spokesmen working with legislative bodies.
9. Prepare semiannual reports on FPA activities for the Board of Directors.

Use of Funds

Administrative

Staff salaries	$ 30,000
Office facilities/phone	8,000
Management fee	26,000
	$ 64,000

Trade/Consumer Communications

Advertising	40,000
Production and printing	24,000
Mailing and postage	15,000
Research	10,000
Travel and entertainment	15,000
	$104,000

Total	$168,000

This budget is tentative. I realize that we did not meet our profit objectives for the last quarter, and our concern must be with controlling costs. Nevertheless, we must view participation in the Association as an investment that will allow us to operate in the future. If you are interested, I will develop more detailed information for your analysis. Let me know what you think at your earliest convenience.

Regards,

R. L. Winslow

FIGURE 2   Interoffice Correspondence

MEMO TO: Clayton Burnett
FROM: T. F. Gorman
                   Sales Promotion Manager

I have conferred with Bob Winslow as you suggested on the meat tray situation. Although I feel that Bob's plan has some good points, we disagree on a basic point. Bob favors industry approach to the problem, while I think Foam-Pak should launch a meaningful two-part trade and consumer communications program under its own banner. One part deals with protecting our market, the other with promoting our product—generally and specifically. These two approaches are interrelated and reinforce each other.

Protecting Our Market

A limited amount of well-timed ads in selected markets could be effective; but ads are obviously self-serving, and so would be discounted by many. I believe that a carefully targeted and sophisticated public relations effort would be more effective and more cost-efficient.

Such a campaign would seek to create articles on "the silly meat tray controversy" (ridiculing the visibility concept), or "how consumer protection is backfiring at the meat counter," or "how some companies are using consumerism against the consumer," or "the negative aspects of overprotection," or "how politicians use phony issues to create a consumer protection image," etc.

The variations on these themes are endless. And so is the market for such stories, e.g., newspaper food editors and syndicated columnists (such as Sylvia Porter), grocery trade journals, news and general business magazines, women's magazines, weekly newspapers, etc.

More indirect, but no less effective, is to supply freelance writers with detailed story ideas and lots of background material so they can write and sell articles that make our point to their regular outlets. The objective here is to get others to tell our story for us. This is not product publicity. This is influencing the public—especially those factions of the general public who can influence consumer legislation in any way.

Promoting Our Product

Simultaneously, Foam-Pak should aggressively promote its foam plastic trays to the trade (distributors and supermarket buyers) via ads, in-store merchandising, and strong field sales tools.

Advertising ($30,000)

Trade ads (in supermarket publications) pointing out

1. The economies, merchandising, and operating advantages of using Foam-Pak trays.
2. Consumer preference for foam plastic trays.

Consumer ads (in *Woman's Day* and/or *Family Circle,* plus newspapers in critical situations) pointing out the fallacies and inflationary of tects of overprotecting the consumer at the meat counter via "see-thru bottoms" (that you can't really see through, because the juice drains to the bottom, and the shrink-wrap bunches at the bottom) and the advantages of the foam plastic tray as a packaging material for meat, poultry, and seafood.

Merchandising Materials ($15,000)

Ad reprints to legislators and supermarket executives.

Meat Department posters/wall banners describing advantages of foam plastic meat trays.

Pamphlets to be given away on meat department counters describing 10 other uses for foam plastic meat trays after you get them home.

Sales Materials ($5,000)

Product sales sheets.

Flip Chart Presentation telling complete foam plastic story for sales presentations.

Although I am still in the development stage, I feel very strongly that we should run our own promotional program and leave our foam tray competitors out of it.

Regards,

T. F. Gorman

ELECTROLERT, INC.: MARKETING CIVIL DISOBEDIENCE*

The blacktop sizzled with the heat from the midday sun and all traces of the brief morning thunderstorm had disappeared, with the exception of the oppressive humidity. Tony Lawrence, vice president of sales for Electrolert, Inc., wondered whether the dampness in the air might affect the performance of the radar unit that had been set up in one of the company cars, located about 4 miles ahead of him on the side of the road.

Lawrence was observing a test of a prototype radar detector that Electrolert had been developing. This new unit consisted of two pieces; a receiver antenna unit designed to fit behind the car's grill, and a control unit designed to fit in or under the car's dash. The field test was being conducted to see how well the device operated on various types of terrain and under different types of traffic conditions. The car Lawrence was riding in was being driven by Alex Gordon, the company engineer who had designed the new detector. Up ahead of them another technician, Sam Goldstein, was sitting behind the wheel of the parked Plymouth they had set up as a mock state trooper cruiser equipped with one of the most advanced police radar units on the market—the Kustom Signals KR-11 K-band moving radar.

Lawrence laughed when he thought about the way Electrolert had purchased the unit. Dale Smith, founder and past chairman of Electrolert, had been unsuccessful in purchasing a KR-11 directly from Kustom Signals. Smith then asked Sam Goldstein to try and get one, because Goldstein was the only employee with an FCC license to operate radar devices and because he had built up a reputation for scrounging hard-to-find parts for various R & D projects. Two days later, Goldstein had showed up with a brand new KR-11 unit still in its shipping carton, complete with a warranty and a bill of sale from Kustom Signals for over $2,900. It had been a matter of joking speculation around the office for a month as to how he had gotten it, since Goldstein refused to tell.

Alex Gordon began calling out mileage readings as their car quickly approached Goldstein's radar setup. There were two, fairly steep hills ahead and Goldstein was parked on the down side of the farthest one. As their car topped the slope of the first hill, the prototype detector gave off an intermittent high-pitched sound and its warning light came on. They were about 1.9 miles away from Goldstein's position. The noise stopped and the warning light extinguished as they continued to drive down the far

---

* This case is not intended to provide a precise account of the thinking or behavior of the parties involved.

side of the first hill. The light and the warning tone came on again, and stayed on this time, as their vehicle was about halfway up the second hill. Gordon said they were three-fourths of a mile away from Goldstein who was hidden on the other side of the rise. Moments later they cruised by his position at a steady 40 mph. They turned into a roadside rest area where Lawrence had parked his own car earlier. Goldstein soon pulled up behind them and the two engineers compared notes. The radar unit still displayed the 40-mph speed reading of their car. Goldstein said the unit had locked in when their car was about a quarter of a mile away from him. That left a comfortable half-mile advance warning distance, plenty of time for any driver to decelerate to the speed limit if necessary. Not bad at all, thought Lawrence. A pretty good margin considering the terrain. The three men talked for a while, discussing the test results and their plans for other types of testing conditions they would set up for the remainder of the afternoon. As Gordon and Goldstein readied their equipment, Lawrence bade the two men goodbye and climbed into his own car. It was about a 20-minute ride back to the office. He had driven out to the test site that morning on a pretext. Actually, he just wanted to get away from the office for a while and he always enjoyed working with the engineers on such tests.

Lawrence had been plagued all week with a strategy problem. Electrolert's executive committee was to meet the next day and the top item on the agenda would be a discussion of a new marketing strategy for the company's top product—the Fuzzbuster II Multi-Band Radar Detector. It was felt that recent political events and judicial trends suggested that the time was right for a new and much more aggressive marketing plan. Lawrence had been given the responsibility for presenting a detailed plan of the new strategy.

Feeling refreshed from his brief escape, Lawrence pulled up to his parking space at the company headquarters. His first task would be to call his wife and try to explain why he would miss dinner for the fourth night in a row. Oh well, he thought, she must be used to it by now and was probably expecting his call.

RADAR HISTORY

Before 1973, radar detectors, shunned by the majority of the "legitimate" electronics industry, appealed principally to gadget buffs and perennial highway speeders. Introduced in the early 1960s, the first detector units were generally poorly constructed "black boxes" being marketed through mail-order advertising at prices ranging from $20 to $30. With the average speed limit of 70 mph on the interstate highway system, the majority of

Americans cruised comfortably without the gnawing fear of encountering a police radar trap. Another factor limiting demand for radar detectors was the consideration that police radar technology at the time was new and fairly primitive. Also, although state troopers used radar, they more often employed VASCAR patrols or simple sight-and-chase techniques to catch errant drivers.

Political and economic events in 1973 and 1974, however, proved to have lasting consequences on American life-styles, not the least of which was on driving habits. Arab oil-producing nations imposed a ban on oil exports to the United States because of its support of Israel in the October 1973 Yom Kippur War. In December 1973, the federal government announced that it would begin enforcing allocations for fuel oil and gasoline, giving priorities to essential services. Also in December, Arab nations announced a doubling of world-market oil prices. For the first time since World War II, Americans experienced a gas shortage. Long lines began forming at gas stations across the country and the government began drawing up plans for a gas-rationing system. Although the Arabs resumed oil exports to the United States beginning in March 1974, the shock of the temporary shortages combined with the permanent escalation of crude oil import prices had begun to change the way Americans viewed their fuel-consumption habits. The government put into effect various plans aimed at reducing fuel oil and gas consumption with the goal of eventually reducing the heavy demand for imported crude oil. On December 20, 1974, Congress voted to make permanent regulations strongly encouraging states to strictly enforce a nationwide 55-mph speed limit on the interstate highway system. States were also required to lower the speed limit on intrastate highways to 55 mph if they expected to receive federal funding. Experts had decided that at 55 mph the average car was performing at optimal fuel-consumption patterns. It was also felt that the lower speed limit should significantly reduce highway fatalities, which had been rising at alarming rates.

With many states being pressured to enforce the new speed limit and many Americans finding it difficult to adjust to this new restriction, it was not hard to predict the ensuing increase in the number of speeding citations, even though most states allowed a grace period when only warnings were issued. Federal funding for enforcement of the law was increased. Manufacturers of police radar units were able to sink more money into research due to increased sales and the state of the art for compact radar unit technology improved dramatically.

Radar was used in the majority of speeding arrests, with some reports ranging as high as 85 to 90 percent of the cases. Radar was popular among police and troopers for two principal reasons: it was easy and simple to operate, and it had been accepted as *prima facie* evidence in courts since

1955. Convictions occurred in over 99 percent of the cases where radar was used as evidence. Drivers who considered stepping over the "double-nickel" (CBer's jargon for 55 mph) line may have considered another formidable fact—it had been estimated that there was at least one radar-equipped patrol car for every 40 miles of interstate highway.[1]

HOW RADAR WORKS

Radar traps were even more frightening because most people did not understand the technology behind them. Actually, police radar units were based on a very simple principle—the Doppler effect. Radar (an acronym for "radio detection and ranging") is actually a very high frequency radio wave. For police radar units, the Federal Communications Commission set aside the frequency range of 9.445 to 24.445 gigahertz, which is classified as being within the microwave spectrum.[2] (A hertz is a frequency level equal to one cycle per second. A gigahertz is equal to 1 billion hertz. The FM radio dial is measured in megahertz or 1 million cycles per second.)

A radar unit both transmits and receives microwaves (very short wavelength radio or electromagnetic beams). The radar used by police transmits at about 1/10-watt power per FCC regulation. A radar unit transmits on only one particular frequency. Over 95 percent of police radar units operate on the X-band frequency (10.525 gigahertz), while the remainder operate on the K-band frequency (24.150 gigahertz).[3]

The radar unit transmits at one of these known frequencies. This is when the Doppler principle comes into effect.

[*When this transmitted*] *beam strikes a stationary object, a part of it is reflected back at the same frequency. If it strikes an object moving away, the reflected wave is returned at a lower frequency. If the object is moving toward the transmitter, the reflected frequency is shifted up. The radar device picks up this reflected frequency, compares it against the original, and uses the difference to compute the speed of the reflecting object.*[4]

The use of a radar unit in a moving patrol car is a bit more complicated. In this case, the radar unit picks up two signals from the same beam. A lower-frequency beam is reflected back from the road surface,

---

[1] Rich Taylor, "Getting on Top of Old Smokey," *Car and Driver,* September 1977, p. 41.

[2] Ibid.

[3] Ibid., p. 42.

[4] Patrick Bedard, "Smoking Out Old Smokey," *Car and Driver,* February 1979, p. 72.

while a higher-frequency beam is reflected off the moving target. This more sophisticated type of radar unit regards itself as being stationary and looks at the road surface as an object moving toward it. The unit then calculates the closing speed between the two objects—the road surface and the target car. By subtracting the reflected frequency differences between the two objects, the unit derives the speed at which the oncoming target is traveling.[5] This type of radar only works if the target is closing the gap between itself and the radar (i.e., moving toward it). If the unit is stationary, however, it can clock the speed of cars moving in either direction.[6]

There were several factors inherent in the technology of police radar that allowed its detection. First, radar beams are microwaves and, like television signals, are capable of traveling only in a straight line.

The microwave beam is often compared to that of a flashlight on a foggy night. The person holding the flashlight can't see around a corner, but someone standing around the corner can see the approaching beam scattering off the fog. A good radar detector finds this scatter and warns you before you drive around a corner or over a hill into the full microwave pattern. . . . [7]

Another factor limiting the effectiveness of radar was the relative difference between a radar unit's transmitting strength and reception sensitivity. At only ¼-watt transmitting strength, a radar unit was capable of hitting an object over 1 mile away. However, even the best radar receiver was not sensitive enough to lock onto and distinguish a speeding passenger car much beyond half a mile. Of course, the larger the object being tracked, the greater its chance of being trapped, because it reflected back a larger microwave pattern that the radar was more likely to distinguish early. The smaller the car, therefore, the less time the police had to accurately track its speed. The typical radar detector, on the other hand, was sensitive enough to pick up microwave signals, within the designated frequency range they were set for, at strengths as low as one one-hundredth of one-millionth of 1 watt. This was about the strength of police radar at 3 miles if unimpaired by intermediate objects.

There was another factor which impeded radar's effectiveness. Radar units had built-in circuitry that requires automatic verification of a target's speed before a reading would be given. This system worked by the radar rejecting erratic signals caused by a target decelerating more than 3.15 mph per second or the target having any stable speed lasting less than one-fourth of a second.

This factor was important when police were using hand-held radar

---

[5]   Taylor, "Getting on Top of Old Smokey," p. 41.
[6]   Ibid., pp. 41–42.
[7]   Bedard, "Smoking Out Old Smokey," p. 71.

guns, where all they needed to do was point the radar at a target within close range to cut the possibility for early detection. The verification circuitry, however, required a full second for the radar to lock in, plus another second or two for the unit to "warm up." If the driver immediately decelerated when his detector went off, say from 70 to 55 mph, he would create an erratic signal that will be rejected.[8]

Although there have been many manufacturers of police radar units, it has been widely held that Kustom Signals, Inc., operating out of Chante, Kansas, was the leading producer. Their KR-11 unit was notorious and considered far ahead technologically of their nearest competitor, as had been its predecessor—the MR-7. The MR-7 had been the first in the industry to reliably track targets while mounted in a moving patrol vehicle according to the principle described earlier. While stationary, the MR-7 could be set to track vehicles moving in either direction, although it could not monitor both lanes of the highway simultaneously. Kustom Signals were also innovators with their HR-8 Hand-Held Radar, which worked like a hand gun with the operator merely pointing the unit at a suspect vehicle and pulling the trigger to get a fix. The MR-7 operated within the X-band frequency, while the HR-8 operated within the K-band (Figures 1 and 2 contain illustrations of these products).

Kustom Signals continuously upgraded and improved their products in order to stay ahead of the growing number of radar detector units that sprouted up with claims of being able to thwart the latest radar technological advances. For this reason, Kustom developed the KR-11, which the company claims was "the first effective countermeasure to all radar detection devices."[9] The KR-11 was one of the first radar units to operate at the higher K-band frequency, thereby destroying the effectiveness of almost all radar detectors on the market at the time, since they all detected X-band radar only. The more devastating characteristic of the KR-11, however, was its ability, through the use of its built-in microprocessor, to track and register speeders by transmitting microwaves in its "pulse mode." Here the unit sent out short bursts of K-band waves which were only erradically picked up by detectors.[10] The KR-11's list price was $2,895, a record high price within the industry. Despite this fact, demand was so high for the product that profits from its sales enabled the company to come out of operating in the red and recapture its leadership position in the industry with a 33 percent market share.[11]

[8]   Taylor, "Getting on Top of Old Smokey," p. 44.

[9]   "Kustom Electronics: Can Its Radar Outwit Electrolert?" *Business Week,* July 3, 1978, p. 105.

[10]   "Electrolert: Aiming to Broaden Sales of Its Police Radar Detector," *Business Week,* July 3, 1978, p. 105.

[11]   Ibid.

FIGURE 1

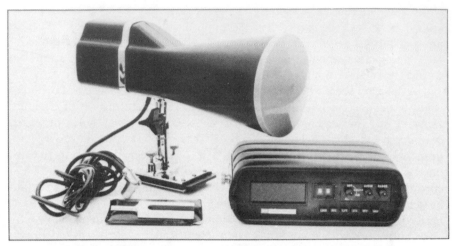

MR-7 MOVING RADAR Kustom Signals, Inc., Chante, Kansas 66720; **Price:** $2385.00; **Dimensions:** 10.5″ L x 6″ W x 3.5″ H (readout unit), 16.5″ L x 6″ W x 6″ H (antenna); **Weight:** 78 ounces (readout unit), 80 ounces (antenna); **Frequency:** 10.525 GHz (X-band); **Overall rating:** Speeder's Enemy Number One.

Rich Taylor, ''Getting on Top of Old Smokey,'' *Car and Driver* (September 1977), p. 42.

FIGURE 2

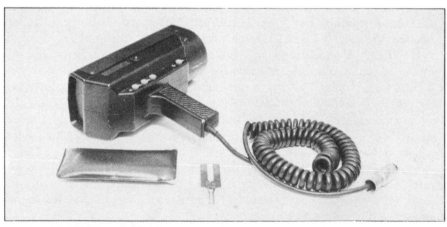

HR-8 HAND-HELD RADAR Kustom Signals, Inc., Chante, Kansas 66720; **Price:** $1385.00; **Dimensions:** 10″ L x 4″ W x 8″ H; **Weight:** 69 ounces; **Frequency:** 24.150 GHz (K-band); **Overall rating:** Deadly in quick-draw speed traps.

Rich Taylor, ''Getting on Top of Old Smokey,'' *Car and Driver* (September 1977), p. 42.

It was obvious that radar manufacturers and detector producers were technologically intertwined industries. A technological breakthrough in one of the industries can make the products in the other partially or wholly obsolete. However, an increase in the demand for either product circuitously creates a demand for its counterpart. For example, as more detector units are sold, the number of speeders able to avoid radar traps increases. As police frustration increases, their demands for more innovative and tricky radar devices that can foil detection increases. According to John L. Aker, Kustom Signals' vice president of research: "The more effective radar detection becomes, the more incentive there is to come up with alternative speed-measuring devices."[12]

ELECTROLERT'S HISTORY

Electrolert, Inc., of Troy, Ohio, had always held the leadership position in the detector market through both their technologically superior product line, the Fuzzbuster series, and their aggressive marketing skills. Electrolert's chairman and founder, Dale T. Smith, developed the Fuzzbuster, a simple X-band detector, back in 1968 after he claimed he was erroneously caught in a radar trap. Like similar products at the time, demand for such units was minimal until the 55-mph law was passed in 1974. Smith formed Electrolert, Inc., that year. Demand was so great that sales of the product reached over $8 million in 1977 and the Fuzzbuster's market share was over 50 percent.[13]

Smith graduated from Harvard University in 1968 with a degree in electrical engineering. Following college, Smith served in the Air Force. Assigned as a research scientist, he helped develop an electronic countermeasure system used by the strategic air command today. After leaving the Air Force, Smith bought a small electronics firm to manufacture police radar units, called Traffic Electronics. Smith sold the company, which had become very successful, in 1972, because of claims that he had become disenchanted with industry business practices and the way such products were being used.

The profit incentive was not the sole motivation that spurred Dale Smith through his hectic business days. In many ways he treated it as a personal crusade against potential injustice. Almost 10 years after Smith received that unjustified speeding ticket, he served as chief technical adviser for the defense in a Dade County, Florida, court hearing on the accuracy of police radar units. After the judge dismissed 80 speeding cases, ruling that

---

[12] "Kustom Electronics," p. 105.
[13] "Electrolert," p. 104.

radar measurement of traffic speed was not reliable enough for court evidence, Smith said he didn't care if the blow to radar cut his company's sales. "I don't think we'll sell many Fuzzbusters in Dade County," Smith told an Associated Press reporter. "I don't think this is going to affect our business in the rest of the country, but I don't care if it does." Smith explained that he "just got teed off" by the inaccuracy of police radar units.[14]

Smith paid for most of the trial expenses himself, amounting to over $40,000, flying in defense witnesses, setting up equipment demonstrations, and managing press relations.[15]

Before the trial, Smith retired as Electrolert's Chairman and now denies any formal connection with the company, although he has been on the company's payroll listed as a consultant. He also owns the patent of the Fuzzbuster and receives the royalties.[16]

In its first few years of operation, Electrolert's marketing strategy was limited. Mass retailing was not possible since large retailers felt that the product was tainted and an obvious ploy to circumvent the law. It was not considered by them to be a legitimate motorist aid, such as a citizens-band radio, which was enjoying great market demand at the time. C.B. radios were at first used mainly by truckers to avoid radar traps and inspection stations. As a communication tool, however, it was quickly legitimized by both manufacturers and retailers by emphasizing its ability to greatly assist in emergency situations. Radar detectors, on the other hand, sadly lacked any obvious redeeming quality. At the time, the issue of whether detectors could be legally sold was not clear as well. Several states made it illegal to sell such devices. In some states, Virginia notably, it was illegal to be in possession of such a device in a vehicle, with violators subject to both fines and confiscation of the detector itself.

Unable to utilize customary retailing channels, Electrolert resorted to using direct mail-order marketing small electronics distributors who sold detectors and C.B. radios primarily to such outlets as truck-stop concessions on a consignment basis. The primary market was considered to be high-mileage highway travelers such as truckers and traveling salesmen.[17] The original suggested retail price for the Fuzzbuster was $109.95. The wholesale price at the time was $75.00. The price to distributors if they bought in minimal one gross (144 units) shipments was $59.00 per unit. Electrolert also gave a co-op advertising allowance of $3.00 per unit.

The original Fuzzbuster was a simple parametric radar receiver

---

[14]   Associated Press wire story, May 8, 1979.
[15]   John Blackmore, "The Man behind the Fuzzbuster," *Police Magazine,* September 1979, p. 28.
[16]   Ibid.
[17]   Ibid.

capable of sensing X-band radar microwaves. Until Kustom Signals introduced their K-band KR-11 police radar, the Fuzzbuster was considered to be the best of the detectors on the market. Like almost all similar products, the Fuzzbuster consisted of a small box that sat on the dashboard and simply plugged into the car's cigarette lighter for a power source. To operate the device, the driver simply had to play with a small knob, called the squelch control on the unit's faceplate that adjusted the device's sensitivity to pick up transient radar signals. If set properly, the detector would give out a high-pitched tone and a bright white warning light would go on as long as the detector was receiving signals within the factory-set frequency range (See Figure 3 for a comparison of several detectors on the market).

DETECTOR PROBLEMS

There were several technological problems inherent in detectors that render them less than the perfect radar escape device. The squelch control was extremely sensitive to adjustment and all too often the detector would sound off from erratic and sometimes nonexistent signals. It would frequently detect signals bouncing off obstacles, such as bridge abutments or nearby buildings, that had originated from radar units far ahead. Such false warnings created an atmosphere of crying wolf one time too many, whereby drivers frequently failed to slow down when a "real" radar signal was detected. To make matters worse, the FCC had set aside the same frequency range that police radars operate within (9.445 to 24.445 gigahertz) for the use of such burglarproof devices as microwave motion detectors and intrusion alarms, thereby compounding the possibility of false readings.[18] If set high, the squelch adjustment could cut down on the number of false readings at the cost of cutting down on the margin of time before a real but weak radar signal would be detected. It took time, as with all the other detectors on the market, to learn how to properly adjust the Fuzzbuster and to correctly interpret its warnings.

The original Fuzzbuster became partially obsolete when Kustom Signals introduced the KR-11. The Fuzzbuster could only detect X-band radar beams. This could hardly be considered devasting, however, when 97 percent of all radar units in use operated in the X-band. Despite this fact, the thought of being caught by a K-band radar unit that could not be detected by a $100 plus warning device was enough to force Electrolert to develop the Fuzzbuster II multiband radar detector. With a suggested retail

[18]   Bedard, "Smoking Out Old Smokey," p. 78.

FIGURE 3

Getting on Top of Old Smokey: The Hardware

The speeder's guide to early warning systems.

FUZZBUSTER II MULTI-BAND
Electrolert, Inc.
4949 South 25 A
Troy, Ohio 45373
Price: $129.95
Dimensions: 5" L x 4" W x 3" H
Weight: 30 ounces
Frequency: all bands
Overall rating: Next best thing to diplomatic immunity.

SUPER ELIMINATOR
Creative Marketing Corp.
2880 LBJ, Suite 307,
Dallas, Texas 75234
Price: $149.95
Dimensions: 3" L x 5.5" W x 7" H
Weight: 19 ounces
Frequency: X-band/K-band
Overall rating: First in line for second fiddle.

SUPER SNOOPER
Autotronics, Inc.
1399 Executive Drive West
Richardson, Texas 75081
Price: $149.95
Dimensions: 4" L x 7" W x 4.5" H
Weight: 25 ounces
Frequency: X-band/K-band
Overall rating: First-class for X-band, but nearsighted on K-band.

FUZZBUSTER
Electrolert, Inc.
4949 South 25 A
Troy, Ohio 45373
Price: $109.95
Dimensions: 5" L x 4" W x 3" H
Weight: 28 ounces
Frequency: X-band
Overall rating: First-class for X-band, but more false alarms than Chicken Little.

FOX II
ComRadar Corporation
4518 Taylorsville Road
Dayton, Ohio 45424
Price: $129.00
Dimensions: 1" L x 8" W x 2" H
Weight: 6.5 ounces
Frequency: X-band
Overall rating: Last on the list of those to which you'd trust your license.

WHISTLER RADAR EYE
Whistler, Inc.
Box 37
Littleton, Massachusetts 01460
Price: $99.95
Dimensions: 4" L x 4" W x 4" H
Weight: 18 ounces
Frequency: X-band
Overall rating: Mostly, it whistles *Dixie*.

SENTURION
Radatron Corporation
2424 Niagara Falls Blvd. North
Tonawanda, N.Y. 14120
Price: $109.95
Dimensions: 6" L x 5.5" W x 6" H
Weight: 35 ounces
Frequency: X-band
Overall rating: Finds radar, but won't tell you.

SNOOPER
Autotronics, Inc.
1399 Executive Drive West
Richardson, Texas 75081
Price: $89.95
Dimensions: 3.5" L x 5.5" W x 5.5" H
Weight: 11.5 ounces
Frequency: X-band
Overall rating: Strictly a placebo.

FOX II REMOTE
ComRadar Corporation
4518 Taylorsville Road
Dayton, Ohio 45424
Price: $169.00
Dimensions: 1" L x 7.5" W x 2" H
Weight: 8 ounces
Frequency: X-band/K-band
Overall rating: Smokey's little helper.

Rich Taylor, "Getting on Top of Old Smokey," *Car and Driver* (September 1977), p. 43.

price of $129.95, the Fuzzbuster II differed from other hastily introduced dual-band receivers in that it used a microprocessor to actually scan the full alloted frequency range of 9 to 25 gigahertz every 2 milliseconds. Competitive units detected either X-band or K-band or both exclusively. The Fuzzbuster II, therefore, was capable of detecting any type of possible radar frequency that could be developed, barring a future change in FCC regulations.

Tony Lawrence had been accumulating a mass of data over the past year to assist him in deciding what the appropriate tactic should be for Electrolert's new and hopefully aggressive marketing strategy. This pile of researched information, consisting mostly of newspaper articles, copies of existing or pending legislation, court transcripts, various editorials, and research reports had already grown to the point that it filled an entire filing cabinet in his office. Lawrence had begun to prepare a report based on the principal facts found in the data. His outline was divided into two main categories: radar and enforcement practices, and legislation and legal precedence pertaining to radar detectors.

Law Enforcement Practices

Until very recently, the courts accepted radar evidence as indisputable. After all, radar was a very technical device based upon fundamental laws of physics. It didn't lie and it didn't discriminate. Unfortunately, radar also was blind and required human intervention to properly operate and to interpret the results. Human intervention meant occasional, if not frequent, human error. Conviction rates were running as high as 99 percent when radar evidence was used, yet some studies indicated that as many as 30 percent of these cases were based on either false or erroneous evidence.[19]

Although this rather high error rate was debatable, there remained several uncontested facts that offered proof of radar's occasional fallability. Although the better devices have some type of circuitry to control radio-frequency interference, it has been demonstrated that radar could be influenced by such diverse electrical radiation sources as neon signs, electric fans, and two-way radios.[20] According to one article in Lawrence's file:

> [A] *Denver news team was able to produce readings as high as 84 mph simply by aiming the radar out the window of a car equipped with a police radio and then keying the mike. Even low-powered CBs have been known to affect radar readings.*[21]

[19]   "The Dubious Witness," *Car and Driver,* February 1979, p. 72.
[20]   Ibid.
[21]   Ibid.

Even the better radar units, such as the Kustom Signal's HR-8, had been demonstrated to be affected by interference stemming from the vibrations put out by transmission housings, defroster fans, and air-conditioning units. Radar responds to sound vibrations of different types. In fact, police radar units were adjusted and calibrated with the use of a tuning fork. This tool, set to a certain frequency level, was struck and held in front of the radar unit's antenna. This would set off an exact reading on the receiver's display. If the reading was incorrect, it was a simple matter to adjust the unit on the spot. Most states required that troopers calibrate their radar before and after each shift to ensure the integrity of their evidence.[22]

Most radar critics argued that unseen interference sources, such as those outlined above, only accounted for a small percentage of radar error. They also were quick to discount the possibility of deliberate falsification of readings by overzealous or quota-deficient officers as a major error factor. The most common error, the critics said, was that the officer simply and unknowingly would arrest the wrong driver. Radar units read and register the strongest signal that is reflected back to the antenna. All other weaker signals are rejected by the unit. The strength of a reflected signal is proportional to the size of the object that the signal is bouncing back from and the distance that the signal had to travel. (It should also be noted that the construction material of the target object also affects the signal. Radar beams will pass through glass, for example. A radar beam might pass through a fiberglass body but be reflected back off the engine.) A small car might be stopped for speeding when, if fact, the radar unit picked up the speed of a large-body car traveling nearby. Typically, the police would stop the car that was in front. Either car could have been stopped because the radar unit picked up the reflection of a speeding tractor-trailer one-fourth of a mile behind them.[23] Clearly, then, there appeared to be more than a reasonable doubt in many speeding arrests.

Legislation and Legal Precedence

The Federal Communications Commission was created by Congress through the Communications Act of 1934. The Act exclusively reserved to the federal government the right to regulate all electromagnetic communications. In later court decisions, the Act was interpreted as the intent of Congress that the federal government have full regulatory powers over all electronic transmissions—including both interstate and intrastate communications. However, Section 605 of the Act (U.S.C. Title 47) explicitly

[22]   Ibid.
[23]   Ibid.

states that the people have the right to receive radio transmissions of any type as long as "no person not authorized by the sender shall intercept the communication and divulge or publish the existence, contents, substance, purport, effect, or meaning of such intercepted communication to any person."[24] The courts have since held that Congress intended that anyone has the right to receive any radio communications, whether interstate or intrastate in origin, as long as the communication is not "divulged or published" to another person without prior consent of the sender.[25] Since radar detectors are simply radio receivers of a specific type, manufacturers of such devices contend that their use is guaranteed by law to be free from state regulation.

Until mid-1978, several states disagreed with this interpretation of U.S.C. Title 47, Section 605. Between 1975 and 1977 the legislatures of Georgia, Minnesota, Louisiana, Oklahoma, Mississippi, Maine, North Carolina, Iowa, and West Virginia, bowing to pressures from police agencies, unsuccessfully attempted to pass laws making it illegal to sell radar detectors as well as the use of such devices. Violators would have been fined or jailed and the devices subject to confiscation. In Georgia, for example, the law died in committee hearings in three consecutive legislature sessions after disclosure that such a law might be in violation of federal statutes. (A copy of the proposed Georgia legislation for the 1979 session appears as Appendix A.)

Four states—New York, Connecticut, Michigan, and Virginia—have had statutes at one time that forbid the use or sale of radar detectors. The laws of New York, Connecticut, and Michigan consistently have been struck down in their courts for lack of proper authority or jurisdiction.[26] Virginia proved stalwart, however. Twice the state legislature tried to repeal the law only to be vetoed by the governor. Finally, in June 1978, the Virginia Supreme Court overturned the only remaining state law that prohibited the use of radar detectors.

This was a landmark day for the executives at Electrolert. Since 1976 it had been Electrolert's policy to fight such legislation. Several tactics were taken in this regard. The company, over the years, had spent over half a million dollars lobbying in 32 states against detector legislation. In those states that had existing legislation, Electrolert offered to assist any of their customers who were arrested for using the Fuzzbuster. In those cases where the detector was confiscated, Electrolert upon request would telex a lengthy legal defense, which, among other arguments, invoked the Communica-

---

[24] Rich Taylor, "Your Right to Bear Radar Detectors," *Car and Driver,* September 1977, p. 59.

[25] Ibid.

[26] Ibid., p. 60.

tions Act of 1934 prohibition of state's restriction of radio reception.[27] In those cases of legal import or of a precedential nature, Electrolert has provided legal counsel in over 250 cases.

A new trend began to take place in courts in recent years in regard to radar evidence. Previously, radar evidence went unquestioned since 1955 in *The State of New Jersey v. Dontonio,* where a federal court held that Doppler-type radar was *prima facie* evidence of speeding violations.[28] Some state courts, however, have begun to question this assumption of unerring accuracy. In Georgia, for example, a state court recently threw out a speeding case when it was proven that the patrol officer had failed to calibrate his radar unit with a tuning fork before he began his patrol. In another case, the arresting officer attested to the fact that a large truck was in the area of the suspect vehicle at the time of the arrest. The judge dismissed the case because there existed a possibility that the passing truck could have been the actual violator since its reflected signal was more likely to be picked up by the radar under the circumstances.

Judges across the country have cited the Dade County ruling of May 7, 1979, as a precedent in rejecting speeding cases based solely upon radar detection. Judge Alfred Nessitt held a hearing on the accuracy of police radar units after he viewed a television report which appeared to show radar units clocking a tree at 85 mph and a house at 28 mph. During the lengthy hearing, experts testified that errors in clocking can be caused by telephone paging devices, two-way radios, or people whistling into citizens-band radio microphones. Nessitt's ruling dismissed cases against 80 accused speeders (Judge Nessitt's decision appears in Appendix B). Shortly after the Dade County case, an Atlanta, Georgia, television station ran a three-part series on police radar problems. The television station offered to send interested viewers a list of questions to ask the arresting police officer in a radar-related speeding case. The answers to these questions could serve as a defense in a traffic court case by establishing circumstances that present reasonable doubt of guilt. (This list of questions appears in Appendix C.)

It occurred to Lawrence that Electrolert in the past had been marketing, in a broad sense, a form of civil disobedience by selling a product that primarily appealed to people who clearly had every intention of using the device to circumvent the law. The mass of data he had been scanning pointed out that Americans were definitely unhappy with the 55-mph speed limit. Failing to have the law repealed, Americans cast their votes instead by simply ignoring the law when they could get away with it, just as they had violated the Volstead Act's prohibition of alcohol back in the twenties. Recognizing this growing trend toward violation of an unpopular

27   Ibid.
28   Taylor, "Getting on Top of Old Smokey," p. 42.

law, the state of California went so far as to forbid the use of any type of radar by its state patrol officers.

Although the magnitude of violators across the country was increasing, the vast majority of Americans were still law-abiding citizens. Lawrence wondered how he could tap into this much larger market to create a demand for the Fuzzbuster. He drew up a list of issues that he wanted the executive committee of Electrolert to address at their afternoon meeting, which he hoped would assist in developing a more aggressive marketing strategy. The main issues were as follows:

- Considering the recent court trends and legislation repeals, how could Electrolert convince mass retailers that there was a real and legitimate demand and need for their product?
- What type of message should the company use in its advertising in order to reach a broader market and stimulate demand for the Fuzzbuster? Should the bulk of advertising be aimed at stimulating primary demand by legitimizing the need for radar detectors in general? How could the company stay clear from any suggestion of disobeying or disrespect for the law or law agencies in its advertising?

Appendix A

SENATE BILL 158

By: Senator Sutton of the 9th

A BILL TO BE ENTITLED AN ACT

To prohibit the use of devices on motor vehicles used to detect the presence of radar upon highways; to prohibit the operation of motor vehicles so equipped; to prohibit the sale of such devices; to provide for penalties; to provide an effective date; to repeal conflicting laws; and for other purposes.

BE IT ENACTED BY THE GENERAL ASSEMBLY OF GEORGIA:

Section 1. Prohibiting use of devices on motor vehicles to detect presence of radar upon highways or operation of motor vehicles so equipped or sale of such devices. It shall be unlawful for any person to operate a motor vehicle upon the highways of this State when such vehicle is equipped with any device or mechanism to detect the emission of radio microwaves in the electromagnetic spectrum, which microwaves are employed by police to measure the speed of motor vehicles upon the highways of this State for law enforcement purposes; it shall be unlawful to use any such device or mechanism upon any such motor vehicle upon the highways; it shall be unlawful to sell any such device or mechanism in this State. Provided, however, that the provisions of this Section shall not apply to any receiver of radio waves of any frequency lawfully licensed by any State or federal agency.

Section 2.   Any person, firm or corporation violating the provision of this Act shall be guilty of a misdemeanor and, upon conviction thereof, shall be punished as for a misdemeanor, and any such prohibited device or mechanism be forfeited to the court trying the case.

Section 3.   The presence of any such prohibited device or mechanism in or upon a motor vehicle upon the highways of this State shall constitute prima facie evidence of the violation of this Section. The State need not prove that the device in question was in an operative condition or being operated.

Section 4.   This Act shall not apply to motor vehicles owned by the State or any political subdivision thereof and which are used by the police of any such government nor to law enforcement officers in their official duties, nor to the sale of any such device or mechanism to law enforcement agencies for use in their official duties.

Section 5.   This Act shall become effective upon its approval by the Governor or upon its becoming a law without his approval.

Section 6.   All laws and parts of laws in conflict with this Act are hereby repealed.

Note: The bill was voted down in Georgia State Senate on February 16, 1979.

Appendix B: The State of Florida vs. Ana Aquilera

IN THE COUNTY COURT
IN AND FOR DADE COUNTY FLORIDA

CASE NOS: 711-101S, 309-104S, 711-307S
496-904R, 644-372P, 332-088Y
725-391S, 622-863S, 829-297X
132-781Y, 956-402Y, 383-145T
634-395S, 123-746S, 233-748S
360-809S, 892-382S, 340-269S
239-297Y, 433-4 5Y, 267-431S
696-977S, 357-500S, 640-416S
115-325S, 250-708S, 429-646Y
647-109X, 163-947Y, 430-798Y
628-352T, 656-725X, 868-898R
160-543Y, 924-944S, 339-214S
649-601X, 713-798S, 381-575T
721-546S, 628-238T, 327-753S
027-343Y, 922-484S, 214-466P
715-593S, 724-088S, 159-266Y
630-823S, 922-147X, 164-103Y
924-561S, 274-986S, 337-364Y
888-320S, 296-236T, 894-270S
742-143S, 427-996Y, 740-304S
897-418S, 240-683S, 894-357S
240-974Y, 730-604S, 206-143T
889-204S, 285-304T 737-886S
910-199S, 302-805Y 420-204T
631-951T, 242-194S, 356-938S
361-942S, 238-100Y, 790-215R
743-461S, 239-062Y

THE STATE OF FLORIDA,   )

      Plaintiff,   )

vs   )

ANA AQUILERA, (AND CONSOLIDATED)
       CASES)
)

      Defendant.
_____)

ORDER GRANTING MOTIONS TO SUPPRESS AND/OR
EXCLUDE

THIS CAUSE came on to be heard on the Defendants' Motions to Suppress and/or Exclude the results of radar speed measuring devices with both the Defendants and the State presenting expert testimony and introducing exhibits to support their respective positions.

At the outset, Messrs Michael Daderberg and Paul Tunis for the Public Defender's office and Mr. Ken Drucker for the State Attorney's office are to be commended for affording the Court an opportunity to truly be informed of the issues in this complex case of first impression, without the necessity of hurdling technical obstacles since all parties have agreed to waive most legal niceties in the search for reasonable answers to the questions involved. Although there have been a few challenges to radar readings in other courts, I say case of first impression because, as far as has been determined, this is the first time that any court has been presented so much testimony and so many exhibits from so many highly qualified experts summoned from all parts of the country. This is undoubtedly due to the fact that no single defendant can afford the tremendous cost in money and time to produce such a defense to a speeding charge.

The Court has heard over two thousand pages of testimony and arguments, and has also examined thirty-three exhibits presented by highly trained and experienced specialists in the fields of mathematics, electrical engineering, and the design, construction and testing of radar devices. Of course, the various and many times diverse opinions of these renowned experts must be tempered by their respective interests in the results of this hearing.

At this point, let us understand that this hearing has dealt only with radar used by police as speed measuring devices in its present mode. There has been no argument with the Doppler system itself, but only as to its use by the current units. Although not having any real bearing on the questions before the court except, perhaps, to emphasize the arguments herein, there has been an apparent belief throughout this hearing that these devices can and should be improved to the extent that they are accurate and identification of the target vehicles can be readily made, under any conditions. Undoubtedly, the manufacturers with their scientific and financial resources can accomplish this in the very near future. The prime inhibition against such success is their quoted awareness that the Purchasing Agents at all levels of the government seem to place economy ahead of quality. If this is true, then it is a disservice to the motoring public, and can place the courts in an untenable position. As the court said in <u>Wisconsin v. Hanson</u> case #76-061, 1978, "For the average law abiding American citizen, minor traffic offenses constitute the only contact such a person will have with the law enforcement and judicial systems. Public confidence rests upon the fairness of such proceedings...fairness dictates that contested prosecutions are conducted according to meaningful standards, which insure the instrument's accuracy. Although the Court there referred to certain guidelines, I feel it is equally applicable to the use of inadequate specifications for the evidentiary speed measuring unit.

With respect to the desire for economy, we should refer to the testimony of Mr. Sargent, a manufacturer's official, who disclosed that in large quantity purchases, they were able to reduce the single purchase price of $2,500 per unit to $375 per unit. Without questioning what may seem to be a strange profit structure, it would behoove us to establish a central purchasing office on the state level for radar units so that advantage can be taken of such substantial reductions. The total number of units required could be determined by the requisition from the various lower governmental entities who would then pay for their share at the discount price. Thus the savings would, at least in part, offset the increased cost of the improved product. In line with this procedure, I would then urge such agency to retain the services of independant, highly skilled radar engineers to establish sufficiently high standards of specifications so that accuracy of speed readings and exact identification of the target vehicle will be assured under any conditions.

I recognize that many millions of dollars in revenue are involved in "speeding" fines but let it be understood once and for all, the function of the traffic court is to convict the guilty, acquit the innocent, and improve traffic safety but not to be merely an arm of any revenue collection office. At the same time, if the errors alleged by the opponents of radar do exist, then one must wonder – What percentage of these millions of dollars has been collected from erroneously convicted defendants? – How many of these defendants have suffered the additional penalties of extremely higher insurance rates, and the unnecessary compiling of points with the consequent loss of drivers' licenses and perhaps jobs?

While not pertaining to the reliability of radar, it is incumbent upon the Court to refer to the part of the testimony which raises the spectre of radiation within the police vehicles. It is conceded that the amounts involved are within government safety limits, however, we must take notice that such limits have been wrong in other areas and unfortunately the effects are sometimes not observed until the next generation. My concern is further enhanced by the statement of the expert witness, Dr. Nichols, that there is an ongoing investigation of the problem.

Without repeating any of the voluminous testimony, suffice it to say that it contained in-depth studies of practically all of the errors alleged to be inherent in varying degree in the vast majority of radar units in present usage. Described therein were the Cosine error; Batching error; Panning and Scanning errors; Shadowing error; errors due to outside interferences such as billboards, overpasses, passing C.B. radios and many other similar causes; errors due to inside interferences such as heater and airconditioning fans, and police radios etc.; errors due to improper mounting of the radar unit; errors due to heat build up; errors due to power surge by shutting off and turning on the radar at the last minute to avoid radar detecting devices; errors due to the auto lock system; errors due to reliance on the auto alarm system; errors due to mirror switch aiming; and errors in the identification of target vehicles due to modern day traffic patterns and the mixture of sizes of vehicles and varied materials in their construction. Admittedly more of these errors pertain to radar in the moving mode than in the stationary mode. Certainly, some of these problems are minimal in degree but their potential has been attested to not only in scientific theory but many have been perceived in actual tests by the witnesses. The State's witnesses have denied these problems but in doing so have expressed a reliance on adequately trained officers recognizing same and not issuing tickets. However, the defense witness, Dr. Nichols, whose expertise and objectivity have been conceded by Mr. Drucker, has prescribed an intensive course of training in both classroom and in the field with written examinations for proof of qualification, conducted by an independent, highly skilled radar operator and not by a manufacturer's agent or his students. Such a program has not apparently been pursued. Even with this type of curriculum, Dr. Nichols seems to imply that there would only be a lessening of the problems.

All of this resolves itself into one main issue, to wit: the reliability of radar speed measuring devices as used today.

Based upon all of the testimony, exhibits, and argument of counsel, I find that the reliability of the radar speed measuring devices as used in their present modes and particularly in these cases, has not been established beyond and to the exclusion of every reasonable doubt and it is therefore,

ORDERED AND ADJUDGED that the Motions to Suppress and/or Exclude herein be and they are hereby granted.

DONE AND ORDERED in Miami, Florida, this 7th day of May, 1979.

_____
JUDGE ALFRED (FRED) NESSITT
COUNTY COURT JUDGE

WAGA-TV 1551 Briarcliff Rd.. NE. Box 4207. Atlanta. Ga. 30302 (404) 875-5551

Dear Viewer:

As requested, I am sending you the following list of questions regarding radar.

1. Did you calibrate your unit with a tuning fork?

2. May I see your tuning fork?

3. What was my speed?

4. Was there a truck or another large vehicle driving near me?

5. May I see the reading on the radar?

6. Was there a truck or another large vehicle driving in front of you?

7. Where was your radar antenna placed?

8. Were there any wires or signs or fence posts between my car and your radar antenna?

9. How do you know I was the speeder?

Thank you very much for your interest and if you have any further questions, please do not hesitate to call me at 875-5551.

Sincerely,

Barbara Nevins
5 News Scene

STORER
STORER BROADCASTING COMPANY

Commentaries

NUMBERS GAME:
MARKET-SHELF PROLIFERATION—PUBLIC PAYS*

By A. Kent MacDougall

In the beginning, there was just Campbell's chicken rice soup.

Today, besides chicken rice soup, Campbell Soup Co. makes chicken gumbo, chicken noodle, chicken noodle O's, curly noodle with chicken, cream of chicken, creamy chicken mushroom, chicken vegetable, chicken alphabet, chicken and stars, chicken'n'dumplings and chicken broth.

These dozen chicken soups and the 40 other varieties in Campbell's familiar line of canned condensed soup exemplify the colorful cornucopia of consumer goods that gives American shoppers a range of choice unsurpassed in history.

But to competitors such as H.J. Heinz Co., which just this month settled a $105 million antitrust suit against Campbell Soup out of court, Campbell's proliferation to three lines of canned soup with a total of 80 varieties is part of a calculated strategy to hog supermarket shelf space, keep out rival brands and protect Campbell's near-monopoly in canned soup.

Whatever the merits of such charges, proliferation on the soup shelves of the nation's supermarkets is mild compared with what is going on elsewhere. Along breakfast cereal row, in the frozen foods display case, on the dog and cat food shelves and up and down most other aisles, a fierce struggle for shelf space and market share is being waged among the two to four big manufacturers that typically dominate each category.

* A. Kent MacDougall is a staff writer for *The Los Angeles Times.*
Copyright, 1979, *Los Angeles Times,* Reprinted by permission.

Rather than undercutting one another on price, the manufacturers are locked in a big-bucks battle to see which can spew out the most new products, advertise and promote them most heavily and tie up the most shelf space.

And far from being new, most of the new brands, sizes, shapes, colors, flavors and scents being showered on the public are only minor variations on existing products, differing mainly in form, packaging and advertised image.

Many new grocery products seem little more than novelties, such as the new line of Buitoni macaroni for children that comes in four varieties, depending on the macaroni's shape: spacemen, spaceships, space robots and moon buggies. Other new products carry specialization to the edge of absurdity; witness Cycle dog food's four versions, one for each stage of a dog's life: puppy, middle years and senior citizen, plus overweight.

It would all be just amusing if consumers who did not want the new products could avoid paying for them. But they cannot. This is because the steep costs of developing, promoting and distributing the four out of five new items that fail to catch on with the public are inevitably loaded onto the prices of existing brands.

What's more, because each new brand threatens the market share of all existing brands in the same category, the existing brands must be defended with stepped-up advertising that inflates their prices as well. Manufacturers end up fighting harder for smaller pieces of the market, and consumers end up paying higher prices.

Many manufacturers are starting to see that brand proliferation is growing counterproductive. Paul F. Enright, a sales manager for Coca-Cola Co.'s foods division, recently took note in a food industry newsletter of "a growing concern within our industry about the rapid proliferation of brands, products, sizes and flavors, many of which bring nothing new to their respective categories, endlessly confuse the consumer and dilute the high-volume sales of a few products to the modest volume of many. In our opinion, it is not in the industry's best interests to continue endless (and sometimes mindless) product proliferation."

Be that as it may, the Coca-Cola foods division seems more caught up in proliferation than ever. Since last June, it has introduced and heavily advertised two new lines of drip coffee, two new varieties of fruit juice and two new lines of powdered drink mixes. The drink mixes come in nine flavors and two sizes. The company also has added a 10th and 11th flavor (peach and tangerine) to its existing Hi-C line of canned fruit drinks.

In the absence of a nonproliferation treaty, which many in marketing might welcome, no company seems willing to be the first to cut back on new product development. The risks are too great, as the fate of Liggett &

Myers Tobacco Co. demonstrates. Once a formidable force in the cigarette industry, with a 20% market share 30 years ago, L & M was too late with too few new brands in recent years. Its market share has shrunk to 3%, and it is in the process of being sold off by its parent, Liggett Group, Inc.

Liggett & Myers' slide to obscurity can be traced to its poor adjustment to the revolution in marketing that got started about 1950. Until then, nearly every consumer goods category was dominated by a few standardized national brands. People smoked Camels, Luckies or (Liggett & Myers') Chesterfields, all uniformly 2¾ inches long, unfiltered and soft-packaged, they washed with Ivory, Lux or Palmolive. Children ate the same breakfast cereals as adults, adding their own sugar. And the entire family drank Coke from 6½-ounce bottles.

From about 1950 on, while continuing to mass-produce standardized brands, manufacturers found even greater profit opportunities in segmenting mass markets and supplying specialized goods for each segment. This increased the cost of doing business, of course, but consumers went along because they had more discretionary income to spend on new products promising convenience, novelty or prestige. Television provided a powerful medium to create rapid consumer acceptance for new brands. And grocery stores expanded to handle the outpouring of new products.

While brand proliferation seemed to suit the affluent and expansive 1950s and 1960s, declining disposable incomes in the economically troubled 1970s have put the marketing ploy increasingly out of joint with the times. Consumers pinched by inflation are more and more looking for bargains in basics rather than new faces on old products.

Shoppers are economizing by buying fewer national brands, according to a recent study for the Food Marketing Institute, and more private-label, or store, brands, which are priced lower. And in the 25% of supermarkets that, within the last two years, have started to stock "generic" grocery products, shoppers are also turning to these even cheaper no-frills, plainly wrapped items.

Supermarkets are as effective a brake as shoppers on the proliferation of high-priced national brands. The typical supermarket has quadrupled its stock, from 2,500 items in 1950 to nearly 10,000 today, but not even the largest can accommodate the deluge of new products.

Since 1971 when A.C. Nielsen Co., the market researcher, began tracking the introduction of new products into supermarkets, it has counted 53,000 new brands, sizes, flavors and other variants that have to be stocked separately if they are to be handled at all. And the Nielsen count excludes thousands of locally produced bakery and dairy products, carbonated beverages and snacks.

Little wonder that Progressive Grocer magazine recently reported "signs of increasing retailer resistance to new items." The Alpha Beta chain of 300 supermarkets in California and Arizona accepts fewer than 10% of the new items offered it, says buyer Pat Bobzin, and "normally, we have to throw out something in the same section to make room."

The biggest manufacturers and advertisers, such as Procter & Gamble Co., General Foods Corp. and Bristol-Myers Co., stand the best chance of winning supermarket acceptance for their brands. This is because of the tens of millions of dollars in advertising, cents-off coupons, free samples and introductory price discounts to retailers they can put behind each new brand. Such pre-selling is hard to resist, for no supermarket wants to disappoint a customer who asks for a new brand, forcing her or him down the street to a competitor.

The generally higher prices and markups that new products command help retailers defray the costs of warehousing, inventorying, shelving and reordering the many slow sellers among the new items. Even so, as the total number of items handled has mounted toward 10,000, supermarket sales per square foot of floor space and employee man-hour—adjusted for inflation—have fallen, pinching supermarket profits and putting even more upward pressure on prices.

The inefficiencies caused by brand proliferation at the retail level are strikingly illustrated by cigarettes. Thirty years ago, the typical retailer could accommodate 88% of his customers by stocking just five brands—Camel, Lucky Strike, Chesterfield, Philip Morris and Pall Mall, each in a single version. To supply the same percentage of smokers today, the retailer must carry no fewer than 58 different items, including variations in length, filter, package, flavor and tar and nicotine content within some brands.

Whereas checkout counter clerks used to dispense both packs and cartons of cigarettes, cartons now are shelved in self-service aisles, increasing pilferage. But at least they take up much less room—an average of 33 feet of shelf space—than most other products.

According to A.C. Nielsen, the average supermaket devotes 176 feet of shelf space to candy and chewing gum, 193 feet to soft drinks (up 75% in six years), 210 feet to cat and dog dinners (up 80% in seven years), 229 feet to refrigerated foods and 290 feet to frozen foods.

Many shoppers revel in the enormous variety available, but an increasing number seem to be losing patience with sorting through the bewildering array of brands, sizes, flavors and forms clamoring for attention.

"The expansion of product variety in supermarkets has served only to confuse the food shopper, make shopping more difficult and time-consuming, and force the shopper to make decisions she would rather not make," says William Nigut, a Chicago supermarket consultant. "The conventional wisdom has been that the longer you keep the shopper in the store, the more she will buy. But many shoppers get so frustrated and aggravated that they have begun to leave the store before finishing their shopping.''

Gordon F. Bloom, a Waltham, Mass., supermarket owner who also is a senior lecturer at Massachusetts Institute of Technology's Sloan School of Management, agrees. ''Merely walking around large supermarkets is a time-consuming undertaking,'' he notes. Customers in a hurry ''have taken their purchases to convenience stores,'' making them the fastest-growing segment of food retailing.

The back-to-work movement among housewives is also bad news for heavily advertised national brands. According to a survey by Cadwell Davis Savage, a New York advertising agency, when other family members do the shopping, they pick a different brand than Mom would have 54% of the time. Even more ''shocking'' to the ad agency: 36% of the husbands ''told us all brands are the same, so they just picked one.''

Husbands who see little difference among brands apparently have good eyesight. Lee Adler, a former New York ad agency executive who now is a professor of marketing at Fairleigh Dickinson University, says that differences among brands ''tend to occur not so much in basic product benefits as in packaging, brand name and imagery, advertising strategy, distribution and sales promotion.'' As a result, advertising copywriters face ''a desperate struggle to find a competitive edge'' for their brand over essentially similar products.

Unfortunately for the copywriters, few new brands offer meaningful improvements to crow about. William D. Tyler, a columnist for Advertising Age, recently lamented a ''growing trend'' in new product introductions of ''warmed-over variations'' on old products. ''New products have become, slowly but surely, *less* new. The greater growth has come about in line extenders: new colors, new flavors, new scents, etc.''

Pat Bobzin of the Alpha Beta supermarket chain notes the same thing: ''Probably less than 5% of the new items presented to us are really new ideas; the rest are variations on what already exists.''

One reason for the proliferation of me-two, me-three and me-four brands is the difficulty, even in this age of rapid technological advances, of coming up with genuinely new products. ''Most of the major product innovations—dried milk, instant coffee, disposable diapers—came before 1963,'' says Martin Friedman, editor of New Product News, a newsletter published by the Dancer-Fitzgerald-Sample ad agency.

Products that differ from what is already available usually must be promoted more heavily, at least initially. Quaker Oats Co. says the $28 million it spent to introduce Ken-L Ration Tender Chunks went largely to convince pet owners of the need for a new kind of dog food. "We started a new category, and we had to explain why our product was different" from existing dry and semimoist dog foods, a Quaker Oats spokeswoman explains.

Many manufacturers prefer to wait for someone else to establish a category and then capitalize on the competitor's mistakes and successes. When R.J. Reynolds Tobacco Co. introduced the first 120 mm. cigarette, More, competitors rushed 13 imitative brands to market within three months. Most have since disappeared, and More still leads the extra-long, thin-cigarette category.

Although More won out over its imitators, it is often the other way around. An A.C. Nielsen study of 20 highly successful new products found that only four had been first on the market. This led Vice President Kenneth O. Carlson to advise manufacturers, "Your chances appear better being second or third with a first-class product than first with a second-class product."

No one denies that product proliferation has given consumers more choice—perhaps more choice than most want or would vote for. And manipulated or not, many people lay great store by even cosmetic features that have no effect on product performance.

One reason there are so many new scents and other minor product pluses is that manufacturers make higher profits from such "value-added" products than from no-frills standardized items. For this reason food manufacturers eschew minimally processed staples that command relatively low profit margins to concentrate their new product development on convenience, gourmet, "natural" and "light" foods that can be promoted as adding value.

Predictably, convenience comes high. Every penny's worth of sugar sprayed onto presweetened corn flakes at the factory adds about two cents to the price the consumer pays for the convenience of not having to spoon on his own sugar at the breakfast table. The additional vitamins and minerals that General Mills, Inc., adds to Wheaties to turn it into Total cost an estimated two cents, yet add about 30 cents to the retail price of a 12-ounce box.

"Consumers could save money if they simply bought a box of Wheaties and a bottle of vitamin pills instead of Total," says Michael Jacobson, executive director of the Center for Science in the Public Interest, which has formally complained to the Federal Trade Commission that Total constitutes "a total rip-off to the consumer."

General Mills won't say what Total's additional fortification costs it, but contends that consumers would have to pay more than the difference in price between Wheaties and Total to get the same additional fortification in the form of nationally branded vitamin pills.

WHAT LABELS DON'T SAY*

By Henry Gilgoff

Food labeling appears to be headed for an overhaul and critics say it is long overdue. The problem, they say, is basic: Labeling tells consumers too little about the food they're buying, even when they need to know more to maintain their health.

Donald Kennedy, commissioner of the U.S. Food and Drug Administration, recently suggested why such significance is attached to the label, and to efforts to stop it from being such an underachiever. "Food labeling is important," Kennedy told the U.S. Senate subcommittee on nutrition, "because consumers have a basic right to know the contents, amounts and nutritive values of food they purchase for themselves and their families.

"Even more important," Kennedy said, "is the direct relation between food labeling and health maintenance. Millions of Americans with special health problems would benefit from more specific labeling, and *all* consumers, whether or not they have specific health problems, stand to gain from more informative and understandable nutrition labeling."

Consumer sentiment that current food labeling is inadequate came through in the thousands of oral or written comments presented in response to a drive by the FDA and two other federal agencies to revise labeling requirements. The other agencies, the Agriculture Department and the Federal Trade Commission, share jurisdiction in food labeling and advertising, but the FDA has the broadest authority in the field. Five public hearings were held on labeling in different parts of the country, and a call for comment was issued. One FDA official now analyzing all the data gave his reading of many of the consumer comments: "People do not feel that the food label is adequate." he said.

That inadequacy is embodied in many flaws, consumer advocates say. Here is a taste of what they find so distasteful:

• Manufacturers list their ingredients in order of predominance by weight, but nothing requires them to explain that it is on this basis that one ingredient is listed before another. So, says Michael Jacobson, executive director of the nonprofit Center for Science in the Public Interest, many consumers are unaware of how to use a basic tool in product selection.

• The *amount* of each ingredient, such as salt or sugar, is not generally listed, so the consumer cannot figure out the quantity of any one ingredient from the label. Recently, Consumer Reports sought to unravel that mystery through a laboratory analysis of salt content in a sampling of products. The results, reported in the March issue of the publication, held several surprises. "One bite tells you that bacon is salty. But how about a sweet pudding? One-half cup of Jell-O Chocolate Flavor Instant Pudding contained 404 milligrams of sodium, 102 milligrams more than our three-slice serving of Oscar Mayer Bacon."

Such information could have significance for a person suffering from high blood pressure or hypertension who is, as a result, attempting to restrict sodium consumption. Salt, or sodium chloride, is the main source of sodium in the American diet, according to Consumer Reports.

• Labeling is sometimes ambiguous, telling consumers only what *may* be in a product. A Hostess cup cake, for example, lists "partially hydrogenated animal and vegetable shortening (may contain beef fat and/or lard and soybean and/or cottonseed and/or palm oil)." So, a consumer reading this label would know that one fat and/or another is used, maybe. Paul Khan, an executive with ITT Continental Baking Co., manufacturer of the Hostess products, said that such flexibility in labeling is necessary so that manufacturers can select shortening sources based on their cost and availability at a particular time.

Robert Kroll of East Meadow, though, sees imprecision from a consumer's viewpoint. He has had open heart surgery and on doctor's advice seeks to limit consumption of saturated fats. Kroll said that the task is made difficult by labeling that does not tell how much saturated fat, if any, is in a particular product.

• Artificial coloring used in a product does not have to be named, even though some consumers have allergic reactions to certain colorings. As one of many examples, Wish-Bone low-calorie Italian dressing discloses on its label that it has artificial coloring but not which one. John Young, senior counsel of Thomas J. Lipton Inc., maker of the Wish-Bone products, said he could not readily determine what coloring is used in that dressing. But, he said, it might be a coloring derived from food, rather than a synthetic dye. As long as a coloring agent is not part of the food it colors—such as beet juice to color lemonade pink—it is legally considered artificial.

Young implied that the FDA's enforcement policy, until recently, made it risky for his firm to do anything but list an artificial coloring without specifying the agent used. To the contrary, said Taylor Quinn, FDA associate director of compliance, the FDA has not done anything to stop specific listings. In fact, he said the agency prefers that companies specify the colorings used even though the law permits the general "artificial coloring" label.

• Labels on some products do not list any or all ingredients, without violating any law or regulation. This happens with products such as ice cream that adhere to "standard" recipes. Ice cream ingredient labeling is now voluntary on many brands, but it will be mandated by a regulation that takes effect in July. That change will not affect other "standard" products, however.

Despite the criticism heard at the government hearings across the country, one industry representative insisted that food labeling is adequate and added that change will not come free of charge. In fact, said Robert Harkins, vice president of scientific affairs for the Grocery Manufacturers of America, "Food labels already offer consumers a wealth of information." It is true, of course, that labels do contain useful information and should be read. But debate over whether labeling is adequate seems much a question of semantics and degree. Harkins said he believes some change is necessary to keep labeling in pace with the times, even though he insists on characterizing labeling as adequate.

Clearly, though, labeling is in for some change. Government officials say they will use the consumer comments as guidance when they seek to change regulations or propose legislation. As the data from the hearings, written comments and surveys of consumer use of labeling are being analyzed, the plan for action calls for publication of a general blueprint for label improvements by early this summer. The first specific proposals may accompany the outline or follow in the months ahead. Consumers and industry will have an opportunity to comment.

Two specific proposals expected to be in the earliest batch would require total sugar and salt content to be disclosed on a product's label, according to Sanford Miller, director of the FDA's Bureau of Foods. A closer look at one of these—the notion of disclosing the amount of salt—shows how a seemingly simple idea can become complex in its execution, particularly when the proposed change reflects an ongoing scientific dispute.

The Center for Science in the Public Interest petitioned the FDA to change salt content labeling last July. In his testimony before the Senate subcommittee on nutrition, FDA Commissioner Kennedy said, "Such labeling is [an] issue we have been considering for some time, because of the importance of sodium intake in regulating hypertension." Miller said the FDA's current thinking is that the level of salt content *should* be on the label. But his agency has yet to decide how the information will be presented on labels and which products will be required to have it. George Brubaker of the FDA's Office of Policy Coordination said that one option being considered is to mandate salt content labeling only on those foods that are now required to have nutritional labeling—that is, only when manufacturers make a claim about the nutritional value of their products—or when the food is enriched with essential nutrients.

While insisting that his organization has no official position on the matter, Harkins of the Grocery Manufacturers of America nonetheless said, "I'm not at all convinced that mandatory disclosure of sodium content would make the life of the hypertensive patient any easier." The person with high blood pressure would probably have to "say goodbye to processed foods," Harkins said, if salt consumption is to be cut sufficiently to make an impact on hypertension.

One problem in making salt labeling meaningful is relating it to consumer awareness of how much is too much, particulary when that is a debatable point (and considering that reaction to salt can vary). The petition from the Center for Science in the Public Interest designates various levels of salt and suggests that products which reach what it terms a highly salted level be labeled as such—and that products with even more salt be required to carry a warning label.

Graham Ward, chief of the health education branch of the National Heart, Lung and Blood Institute, said that hypertensive patients *could* benefit from salt content labeling even if it does not tell consumers everything there is to know. Hypertensive patients may receive some guidance from physicians in cutting salt consumption, Ward said, and persons who do not have high blood pressure can be made more conscious of their salt consumption. Excessive sodium consumption has been implicated in hypertension, but Ward said that the connection is not clear. "We do know," he said, "that the American public consumes far more salt than they need physiologically."

General Mills recently announced that it is moving toward voluntary disclosure of its products' salt content. Ivy Celender, director of nutrition and a vice president of General Mills, said that the first packages with this new labeling are expected to show up on the shelves by late spring. Celender said that her company had opted for the new disclosure because of the consumer's "right to know," rising interest in salt consumption and indications that the FDA is going to mandate the labeling. The labels were to be revised anyway Celender said, and the addition of the salt content data alone would cost a "minuscule" amount per package.

So it is that in labeling battles consumer pressure sometimes couples with signals of approaching regulation in prodding an industry to act on its own. Cereal companies, for example, list the amount of sucrose and other sugars in their products even though they are not required to.

How helpful is that? The required listings on three Kellogg's products, for example, show that sugar ranks first in weight among the ingredients in Apple Jacks and second in both Sugar Frosted Flakes and Rice Krispies.

But they don't say how much sugar separates the cereals. The voluntary labeling, though it has been criticized by consumer advocates as deficient, at least helps parents to know more about the food they feed their children: Apple Jacks has more than five times as much sucrose and other sugars than Rice Krispies, the labeling says. Apple Jacks have 16 grams per ounce; the Frosted Flakes touted by Tony the Tiger have 11, and the Rice Krispies that go Snap, Crackle and Pop have three.

SUIT CHIPS AWAY AT FORMICA™*

By Neil Pickett and
George Fox Rishel

Washington, D.C.—The Federal Trade Commission thinks Formica is like aspirin, cellophane and shredded wheat.

The Formica Corp. says it's closer to Xerox, Kleenex and Vaseline.

What's at issue here is the use of the name. In a novel lawsuit, the FTC has challenged the company's right to exclusive use of the trademark the company gave years ago to the decorative plastic laminate it produces.

The agency claims the public thinks Formica is a generic, not a brand name, and the company gets an unfair competitive advantage when an unwitting consumer asks a salesman for Formica.

While the suit is a year old, it is emerging as a test case that could open up trademarks of other big businesses to scrutiny, say some trademark lawyers and businessmen.

"The FTC must undoubtedly have some kind of trademark hit list of other key brand names it could challenge if successful here," said John Lanahan, immediate past president of the U.S. Trademark Association.

CLASSIC STRUGGLE

The case also could add trademark litigation to the FTC's expanding arsenal of weapons to attack anticompetitive practices. But the success of such litigation depends largely on the results of sophisticated public opinion polls that lawyers say are easily open to challenge.

The Formica suit is a classic struggle between business and government. It is a prototype of legal maneuverings that go on when a regulatory agency tries to expand its power. *FTC v. Formica Corp.*, Trademark Trial and Appeal Board No. 11955.

Formica, a Wayne, N.J., subsidiary of American Cyanamid Co., has worldwide sales of $396 million and is bringing its full economic weight to bear on the case. Its regular outside counsel, Donovan, Leisure, Newton & Irvine of New York, has been joined by New York's Pennie & Edmonds.

Company lawyers estimate that defending the use of the name—which was coined by the company's founders and isn't a shorthand description of anything—will cost several million dollars, which the company is prepared to pay.

* Neil Pickett and George Fox Rishel are staff reporters for *The National Law Journal*. "Suit Chips Away at Formica,™" Neil Pickett, George Fox Rishel, *The National Law Journal;* June 18, 1979, pp. 1, 19, used with permission.

And the case went to the U.S. Supreme Court before discovery even began. *Formica Corp. v. FTC,* 78–1477. The company had raised the now-standard business argument that the FTC had overstepped its authority in bringing the suit and, therefore, had no standing to sue. The court rejected the company's appeal June 4.

But the company isn't limiting its fight to the courts. Already, lobbyists for Formica and other companies have had some success pushing a bill that would effectively kill this litigation and other challenges to existing trademarks by the FTC.

OLD LAW

The FTC brought the case under a long-neglected statute, the 1946 Lanham Trademark Act, which authorizes the commission to challenge trademarks that have fallen into generic use.

Daniel Schwartz, deputy director of the FTC's bureau of competition, said the suit is part of a general policy of maintaining competition. Trademarks, he contends, hurt consumers by causing artificially high prices.

"If we are successful [in the Formica case], we certainly will consider investigating other trademarks, but we'll do it sparingly," said Paul Daw, director of the FTC's Denver office, which is conducting the case against Formica.

Formica claims its brand name isn't hurting consumers and that its trademark still identifies only one brand of plastic laminate. But results of litigation are generally uncertain, and Formica is having better luck getting what it wants in Congress.

The House Commerce Committee recently voted by a wide margin to approve an amendment to the commission's three-year fiscal authorization barring the use of any federal funds to challenge existing trademarks.

The measure was sponsored by Rep. Thomas Luken, D-Ohio, whose district includes the site of Formica's main manufacturing plant. Mr. Luken himself referred to the proposal as the "Formica Amendment," indicating its passage would scuttle the FTC suit.

CASE COULD DIE

If the Formica amendment passes, FTC staffers said their case would be dropped. The growing laissez-faire attitude in Congress has shown businessmen another way to settle lawsuits—win through legislation, not litigation. Last month, for example, the Senate Judiciary Committee added an amendment to an antitrust bill to prevent foreign governments from suing for antitrust damages in U.S. courts unless their countries have similar antitrust laws.

The amendment quickly became known as the "Pfizer Amendment" because it effectively halted a multimillion dollar lawsuit brought against the Pfizer Drug Co. and other leading drug manufacturers by several foreign governments.

If Congress passes the "Formica Amendment," the FTC's only challenge to trademarks might never reach the merits.

"This is a very unusual case. The question of whether a trademark has become generic is normally settled through private litigation," said Robert Silver, head of the trade identity committee of the American Bar Association's Patent, Trademark and Copyright Section.

In fact, Formica's trademark was challenged in a private suit in 1966 brought by the small Newman Corp. At the time, the Trademark Board ruled the mark wasn't generic. But one FTC lawyer blamed the defeat on poor evidence and bad presentation.

This time, the commission—and Formica—will use sophisticated public opinion polls to prove their points. Although language experts and newspaper clippings also will be brought in, the polls will be the centerpiece of both arguments. The attacks are expected to be on the validity and methodology of each other's samplings.

The FTC claims its polls will show that most consumers now think of Formica as a word describing any brand of plastic laminate. Formica will respond with its own studies indicating that buyers still recognize the word as a brand name.

"I fail to see the public's interest in this litigation," Mr. Silver said. "The public is not threatened or endangered by Formica's use of the mark. A trademark has no intrinsic effect on preventing entry into a market by competitors. The FTC is involved in this case because of its monopolization phobia.

"A victory for the FTC would give it selective power of abuse," he said. "The staff could pick out a corporation they don't like and bring costly trademark litigation."

Critics of the FTC's trademark policy say that's exactly what happened to Formica Corp. Commission lawyers deny any prearranged plan to attack the company.

Staffers say that shortly after the FTC's new Denver office opened in 1976, attorneys there looked for ways to advance the commission's policy in new areas. An official at FTC headquarters here led them to the Lanham Act.

The next step was to find a test case. By the end of 1976, the staff lawyers found that Formica fit all their case selection criteria.

"We tested the mark with consumers and found that it had high recognition as a generic word, but was only infrequently recognized as a brand name—the classic characteristics of a trademark that has become generic," an FTC attorney explained.

Staffers also found that Formica carries a price premium, which means that its product sells at higher prices than other laminates sell for because of its name recognition.

"That's another reason we picked this case," the staffer said. "It demonstrates the costs of generic marks. People don't really know they can buy a similar product for less."

Formica claims people pay more for their product because of its quality. The company argues that most Formica is bought by wholesalers who know that other plastic laminates are available.

"But we're concerned about the consumers who tell wholesalers and contractors that they want Formica," the FTC attorney said. "The contractor has to use it."

Formica also has adopted the stance of many large businesses faced with government efforts to stop market concentration. The company says no harm has resulted from Formica's trademark usage and that any objections to the mark should be brought by other companies in the industry.

"Why did the FTC bring this case without first making any test for anticompetitive activities?" asked Formica counsel Lawrence of Pennie & Edmonds. The Lanham Act doesn't require the commission to establish anticompetitive behavior before challenging a trademark, but Mr. Lawrence argues that there is no reason to oppose the mark unless such conditions exist.

An aide to Mr. Luken, explaining the congressman's decision to sponsor the "Formica Amendment," said neither the FTC nor the company's competitors has found any injury stemming from the continued use of the trademark.

"FUNDAMENTAL PURPOSE"

"The basis for the FTC case seems exceedingly weak," Mr. Lanahan said. "This litigation represents a tremendous waste of time, energy and funds.

"The FTC has overlooked the fundamental purpose of trademarks—to protect the public, to make sure they know they're getting exactly what they want and not a cheap copy," he said. "This is another sign of FTC over-reading."

Like many in the trademark bar, David Goldberg of New York's Kaye, Scholer, Fierman, Hays & Handler accused the FTC of "using this particular provision of the Lanham act to attack through the back door what they consider to be market concentration, instead of going through the front door and proving violations of the antitrust laws.

"The FTC thinks they've hit upon a shortcut," he said. "I don't think the FTC cares one way or the other whether the trademark is generic or not. They perceive themselves as going after certain kinds of market concentration."

Mr. Luken's aide pointed out that Formica's market share is now 40 percent and decreasing. But the FTC contends that the company's market share is on the increase again and that the industry has seen an unusually high number of business exits in recent years. The FTC claims four firms control more than 80 percent of the market in an industry that only has moderate barriers to entry.

In light of the Formica suit, trademark lawyers are watching advertising campaigns to make sure companies don't let their marks become generic. The FTC says advertising is one of the best ways to protect a trademark. "Xerox, for example, has gone out of its way in advertisements to emphasize that Xerox is not a verb, but a copier," one staffer said.

Formica, he contends, wasn't careful. "Formica is now emphasizing its brand name, but if the company had done so before, it's doubtful the trademark would have become generic," he said.

IMITATION CHOCOLATE:
IS THE REAL THING AN ENDANGERED SPECIES?[*]

By A. Kent MacDougall

Americans have taken in stride the non-dairy creamer, the reconstituted potato chip, "bacon" made from soybeans and other synthetic foods. So why not the ersatz chocolate bar?

Stung by sharply rising prices for cocoa beans, from which real chocolate is made, manufacturers of chocolate candy, ice cream, beverages, cake mixes and other foods are increasingly turning to substitute ingredients—some natural, most synthetic, all cheaper.

Though less discriminating chocolate lovers don't seem to be noticing the substitutions, manufacturers are proceeding cautiously lest connoisseurs of fine chocolate lose confidence in brands now known for quality.

Hershey Foods Corp. has no present plans to use substitutes in its famous milk chocolate candy bar. But it has been marketing an imitation

[*] A. Kent MacDougall is a staff writer for the *Los Angeles Times*. *The Atlanta Journal and Constitution,* December 18, 1977.

chocolate chip for baking cookies for nearly three years. And it hopes a substitute for cocoa butter that Procter and Gamble Co. has just developed will prove good enough for use in many Hershey products.

The nation's largest candy maker, Mars, Inc., which coats its Snickers, 3 Musketeers, Milky Way and other bars with real chocolate, has just introduced its first candy bar with an imitation "chocolaty" coating.

Manufacturers stand to gain a great deal by using substitutes for the increasingly costly ingredients in real chocolate. Americans spent more than $3 billion on chocolate candy last year, and billions more on chocolate-flavored milk, ice cream, cookies, and other foods. Yet sales of chocolate candy are down this year because of consumer resistance to the higher prices necessitated by increased ingredient costs. Profits are also down—by more than $10 million at Hershey alone.

To make matters worse, chocolate manufacturers find themselves forced to defend products they consider nutritious against charges that they contribute to tooth decay, obesity, and sugar addiction. The federal government is threatening to ban the sale of chocolate candy and other sugared snacks in school lunch rooms. And it is considering restrictions on television commercials that allegedly brainwash impressionable children into becoming junk food junkies.

Urging the government on to even sterner measures is a small but vocal group of nutritionists, consumer advocates and other critics of the food industry. Among other things, they question the safety of many of the synthetic flavors, preservatives, emulsifiers, and other additives that are finding their way into chocolate products and other foods. Though their impact on federal regulators may be minimal, the critics seem to be making the buying public more conscious of the ingredient labels on the highly processed convenience foods that dominate supermarket shelves.

As any vacationer who has stopped for a guided tour of a chocolate factory knows, chocolate itself requires extensive processing. This starts with the cocoa beans that grow in large pods on the tropical cacao tree. At the factory the cocoa beans are cleaned, roasted, crushed, and ground. This produces chocolate liquor, a bitter liquid. Cooled and molded into blocks, chocolate liquor is sold as unsweetened baking chocolate, the nearest-to-natural form of chocolate available to consumers.

Further processing of chocolate liquor squeezes out some of its major constituent, cocoa butter, the fat that gives chocolate its melt-in-the-mouth consistency. This leaves cocoa powder, which is used to flavor cakes, puddings and other foods and, when added with sugar to milk or water, makes hot cocoa, the breakfast beverage.

The Food and Drug Administration, which sets standards of identity for chocolate and cocoa products, allows some products—puddings and ice cream, for example—to be labeled "chocolate" even though they contain no chocolate liquor but only the less flavor-intense cocoa powder.

In contrast, a candy bar must contain chocolate liquor, usually enriched with an extra shot of cocoa butter, to qualify as "chocolate." Other ingredients permitted in chocolate candy include milk solids; sugar, which typically comprises 40 percent to 50 percent of a chocolate bar's weight; emulsifiers to aid mixing and improve consistency; and vanillin, an artificial flavor derived from a by-product of wood pulp that acts to enhance the chocolate flavor.

So-called real chocolate, then, is far from a naturally occurring food. Some natural food devotees avoid it for this reason. Indeed, the extensive processing that chocolate undergoes renders it chemically complex. Chemists have identified 310 compounds in cocoa powder, including 34 hydrocarbons, 28 alcohols, 53 carbonyls, 38 acids, 46 esters, and 33 bases. Many more compounds in cocoa remain unidentified, and chocolate is even more complex.

Undaunted by the formidable task of matching the flavor and aroma of real cocoa and chocolate, manufacturers of imitation flavors have accelerated their efforts to come up with acceptable substitutes. Like medieval alchemists seeking to transmute base metals into gold, flavor chemists across America have been toiling in their laboratories to find the right mix of cheap chemicals and other ingredients.

The chemists labor under some handicaps. They must stick to substances that are regarded as safe by the Food and Drug Administration or the Flavor Extract Manufacturers Association. They cannot use caffeine or theobromine, though both stimulants are present in real chocolate. And they must get along without the most effective coloring agent, Red Dye No. 2, which was banned last year as a suspected cancer-causing agent.

At least 20 companies have artificial cocoa and chocolate flavors on the market. They bear such names as Nocoa, Mate 'n Match and Counterfeit Chocolate. Most are priced substantially below the $2.15 to $2.50 per pound cost of cocoa powder. National Food Ingredient Co., a subsidiary of National Can Corp., charges 62 cents to 93 cents a pound for its dozen artificial cocoa and chocolate flavors.

But do the imitations come close to the real thing? Not really, chocolate manufacturers agree. Wilbur Chocolate Co., a subsidiary of MacAndrews and Forbes Co., reports it has tested 50 imitation flavors and "not a single one was close to the true chocolate flavor." Hershey says it has found none good enough to use in candy.

Be that as it may, makers of the imitation flavors say they are supplying ersatz cocoa flavors to producers of such non-candy products as cake and pudding mixes, ice cream, and beverages. But which brands? Who knows? The flavor makers won't identify their customers. And food processors generally need not specify on ingredient labels which artificial flavors they are using. Ice cream makers need not list any ingredients at all.

If flavor chemists are still a ways from matching chocolate and cocoa flavors, vegetable-fat chemists are close to duplicating cocoa butter. This is because cocoa butter is less complex and the chemists have had 50 years to develop substitutes.

Cocoa butter is unique among vegetable fats because it is a solid at normal room temperatures, melting at 90 to 92 degrees, just below body temperature. Under proper storage conditions, a chocolate bar can be kept for years without deteriorating. If the bar melts and then resolidifies, cocoa butter will infiltrate to the surface, turning it gray or white as the cocoa butter recrystallizes. This condition, called bloom, renders a chocolate bar unsightly and unpalatable, though still safe to eat.

Bloom isn't much of a problem nowadays because most stores selling candy are air-conditioned. But especially in the South in summer, it used to be the scourge of the chocolate trade, seriously depressing sales. "Many chocolate plants closed down for three months a year," recalls L. Russell Cook, a retired chocolate executive and author of the definitive book on the industry. One chocolate manufacturer that decided to do something about the chocolate-melting problem was Curtiss Candy Co. Curtiss developed a coating for its popular Butterfinger and Baby Ruth bars that replaced cocoa butter with hydrogenated vegetable oils that had higher melting points. Such substitute "compound coatings," as they are known in the candy industry, have been used on Butterfinger since the early 1920s and on Baby Ruth since the early 1940s.

Two other popular chocolate-coated bars, Clark and Oh Henry!, went over to compound coatings in the 1950s when cocoa bean prices shot up and spurred substitutions.

How well candy lovers took to the early imitation chocolate is lost in history and the traditional secretiveness that pervades the highly competitive candy industry. Baby Ruth, which Curtiss touted in 1942 as "the nation's best-liked candy," ranked 22nd in sales last year, according to one independent survey of candy wholesalers. Butterfinger ranked 20th, Clark 24th and Oh Henry! 58th. However, the survey didn't measure sales through other channels of distribution, such as vending machines.

The caution with which major chocolate manufacturers are moving toward imitation chocolate is understandable in light of the near-disaster that befell Peter Paul, Inc., when it went ersatz four years ago. Peter Paul switched coatings on its Mounds, Almond Joy, and Caravelle bars and York Peppermint Patties from chocolate to imitation. Some wholesalers refused to handle the reformulated bars, claiming they had been cheapened. Some consumers noticed a difference in taste and stopped buying them. Sales and profits fell, and after two years the company switched back to real chocolate.

Peter Paul officials admit that the imitation coatings were inferior. Sales vice president Walter E. Cohan says they didn't melt in the mouth as fast as real chocolate and were somewhat brittle, even waxy. The chocolate flavor was less intense, just as instant coffee lacks the full-bodied flavor of brewed ground coffee. President Lloyd W. Elston remembers that the imitation chocolate-coated bars "tasted as good when you were chewing them, but they didn't have the same pleasant after-taste."

Chocolate men say it is safer to introduce a new compound-coated bar that has a fresh flavor than to switch coatings on a familiar-tasting bar. Predictably, then, new imitation chocolate bars are proliferating.

A sure tipoff that a candy bar isn't chocolate is the lack of a "chocolate" or "milk chocolate" blurb on the wrapper. That and the presence of hydrogenated vegetable oil and cocoa on the ingredient label.

At present there is no way for a consumer to know specifically which hydrogenated vegetable oil—soybean, cottonseed or whatever—is present in his favorite candy bar. This will change next July when a regulation the FDA announced two and a half years earlier finally takes effect. The regulation will require food processors to label specific oils and fats used. This additional information will permit consumers to follow doctor's orders, religious conviction or personal preference in restricting certain oils and fats.

About the only thing the chocolate industry has reason to be cheery about is that cocoa bean spot prices have eased from their all-time high of $2.60 a pound three months ago, and may fall further as production recovers from the eight-year low set in the crop year ended last September. Assuming, of course, that the weather remains favorable in the hot, humid areas of West Africa and South America where cacao trees thrive.

THE PRODUCT LIABILITY ISSUE:
WOULD CONSUMERS BE RIPPED OFF?[*]

BOTH SIDES OF THE ISSUE
PLEAD FOR THE CONSUMER

The product liability issue may not, at first, seem important. However, it directly concerns everyone of us—as consumers.

Product liability laws allow you to sue for damages when you have been injured or your property has been damaged because a product was de-

[*] *The Atlanta Journal and Constitution,* February 11, 1978.

fective. Of course, the key to any product liability case is whether *a court* decides the product was defective or in some way caused the injury.

That's the rub. On one side, the insurance industry, whose members provide protection for manufacturers against the risk of defective products, argues that liability laws are changing and becoming more liberal in favor of the complaining party. This, insurance advocates say, means bigger awards by the courts which are generally making manufacturers "strictly" liable for anything they produce which has caused injury.

Obviously, such large (and more numerous, they say) awards mean product liability insurance rates must be raised. Therefore, the consumer must suffer higher prices for products.

To keep this from happening, the insurance industry is lobbying the Georgia Assembly on several bills which would change the state's product liability laws, and essentially make it harder not only to win a lawsuit, but also to start one.

One word can describe the position of the folks on the other side of the product liability issue: outrage.

Georgia Trial Lawyers Association spokesmen cut directly to what they believe is at stake here:

An attempt by the insurance industry to take away consumer rights for its own gain. And, the trial lawyers association, whose members are the ones who usually handle product liability lawsuits, says the insurance industry is telling a lot of lies to get its message across.

They says awards have not been so numerous, they really have not been so large and that few lawyers are getting rich from what the insurance industry calls unfair awards by sympathetic juries interpreting loosely constructed statutes.

It's just an artificial "crisis" created by the insurance industry in order to get the laws changed and to justify previously jacked-up rates, the trial lawyers say.

Among the several bills now before the state legislature are four that would:

• Exempt from liability any manufacturer of a faulty product that injured someone if the product was made or designed according to the "state of the art" at the time it was made.

• Forbid the use in evidence of governmental safety regulations issued before or after the manufacture of the product.

• Permit the maker of a defective product to deduct from any damage award the amount of Workman's Compensation payments the injured person had received.

• Repeal "strict" liability and substitute "comparative negligence" (that is, contributing factors such as misuse) in product liability cases.

• Set a new time limit on when a suit can be filed. Instead of the present limit of two years after the injury occurs, no matter how old the product is, the bill would change this to eight to 10 years after it was made, or during the normal useful life of the product, though the suit was filed within two years of the injury.

Certainly Not*

By Robert Knowles

Product liability is the legal responsibility that a manufacturer or seller bears to compensate persons who are injured as a result of using his product. It is a growing problem in Georgia that already is making itself felt in the form of increased prices for many manufactured goods.

Product liability concerns also are causing companies to curtail the development of new products and services. And Georgia's product liability statutes are being carefully scanned by corporations that want to relocate their plants.

PRODUCTS: AN OPEN-ENDED RISK

Twenty years ago, product liability coverage was a small but profitable part of the General Liability insurance line sold to manufacturers by property-liability insurers. Today, product liability is an open-ended risk that is hard for insurers to price and therefore difficult and expensive for manufacturers and distributors to purchase. The reason is that today, courts in Georgia and elsewhere are holding manufacturers and distributors strictly liable for product-related injuries, even in cases where the victim ignored safety instructions, and though the product may have been built 20 years ago.

TEXAS CASE ILLUSTRATES

Manufacturers and distributors even have been found liable in cases where the product was altered by the purchaser to make it unsafe after the sale. Take the Oliver Machinery Company's 1971 saw bench case, for example.

* Robert Knowles is regional manager of the Insurance Information Institute in Atlanta.

The case was described to a U.S. Senate hearing before the Small Business Committee Sept. 8–10, 1976. The testimony was given by Ralph B. Baldwin, the company president.

"In 1942, the Oliver Machinery Company sold to the U.S. Navy in Pearl Harbor, an 88-D Saw Bench which met government specifications. This machine was equipped with the latest safety equipment," Baldwin told the senators, "including guards which differ only slightly from those now being manufactured."

"On Oct. 11, 1971, a man lost part of a hand on this machine. He worked in a plant in El Paso, Texas, which had acquired the machine years later after its rebuilding by a dealer. He testified that he knew the machine was dangerous and that it had no guard."

"The accident occurred," the Oliver Company president continued, "when he [the worker] attempted to cut a large piece of wood and the work lifted on the saw blade and he pushed it down to the table, thereby pushing his hand through the saw blade and cutting off some fingers. Had the guard been on the machine, this accident could not have happened because he would have been pushing down on the guard, not the wood. Still the jury found the Oliver Machinery Company at fault and awarded the amount of $50,000 out of $100,000 asked."

CLAIM CREATES CALIFORNIA MILLIONAIRE

Though charges have been made that some product liability cases have even been fabricated to prove misuse of the tort liability system, the newspapers daily carry accounts of large, if not preposterous, product liability judgments for cases involving almost every kind of product. The most recent such award occurred this week in California. A Santa Ana, Calif., court awarded $127.8 million to a young man who was injured when the gas tank of an automobile exploded. Basic arithmetic shows that an award of that magnitude will produce an annual income from simple 7 percent interest on the $128 million principle of about $8 million a year, for the rest of the plaintiff's life. If the award isn't overturned on appeal, or at least reduced in final settlement, that single case could produce an increase in car cost for 220 million Americans.

INSURERS, MANUFACTURES SAFETY PARTNERS

Responsible manufacturers, insurers and consumers are concerned that Georgians be provided the safest possible products and services. To that end, insurers and manufacturers have worked as partners for many years to foresee and minimize product hazards. The insurance industry also has taken the lead in establishing product safety standards and safety review procedures. It is a prime supporter of the National Safety Council and other volunteer safety movements. Underwriters Laboratories, a private research and testing facility for development of safe products, has been established by the insurance industry.

But how safe can a product be? And how much are Georgians willing to pay to acquire a product that has achieved the almost unattainable ideal of having no foreseeable hazardous aspect for its use or abuse? Clearly, these are important questions that must be answered, soon, if the product liability issue is to be prevented from injuring the Georgia economy.

YOU CAN BET ON IT[*]

By G. Gerald Kunes

The insurance industry is using fraudulent claim information, and false advertising to manufacture a new "product liability crisis" to pass legislation denying consumer protection to Georgians. The legislation will build a new profit base for insurance companies at the expense of the public.

This is nothing new in Georgia. "Crises" have been used before to gain support for changes in the law which benefited the insurers with higher profits and hurt the consumer by taking their rights.

A "crisis" was used in automobile insurance. We were told the only way rates could be reduced was by "no fault." "No fault" was enacted. Auto rates went higher than ever.

MEDICAL MALPRACTICE CRISIS

"Crisis" number one worked, so they tried "crisis" number two: medical malpractice. A picture was painted of hospitals and doctors going out of business because lawyers were collecting huge verdicts. Doctors threatened to strike!

Not becauseof huge jury verdicts, but because insurance companies raised rates. These companies had taken a bath in the stock market. Who

---

[*] Gerald Kunes of Tifton is president of the Georgia Trial Lawyers Association.

could best replace lost profits: doctors who earned great sums of money. The "malpractice crisis" again took the rights of the public. Legislation was passed making it harder to sue negligent doctors. The companies are now making millions in profits.

BIG LIE ADVERTISING

Not satisfied with this bonanza, "big lie" advertising was used to create "crisis" No. 3, the product liability "crisis," now being pushed in our legislature.

Insurance ads claimed one million product liability cases were filed in 1976, but a U.S. Department of Commerce survey showed only 70,000 product cases were filed in 1976.

These insurance ads were big lies to gain public sympathy. One insurer alone spent $5.5 million on these ads in the past 18 months. Another ad proclaimed two men got rich, when they sued, after they were injured using a lawn mower to trim a hedge. This big lie was investigated and it was found no lawn mower existed, no persons were injured, and not one thin dime was paid out.

IMPOSSIBLE TO GET A VERDICT

Pending legislation seeks to further deny consumer rights.

House Bill 681 and Senate Bill 511 will make it impossible for consumers suing for defective products to get a verdict. The legislation makes all products legally free of defects, unless overcome by admissable evidence. The bill also keeps out of evidence: (1) Subsequent improvements in the product. (2) Changes to remedy the defect. And (3) National Safety Standards.

H.B. 682 would decrease product liability payments by amounts paid out in Workmen's Compensation benefits. Workmen's Compensation and product liability have no legal relationship, nor are the insurance premiums for either dependent on the other.

H.B. 683 is the most dangerous, because it will repeal the judicial doctrine of "strict liability." California first announced the doctrine in 1963. In 10 years the highest court in 38 sister states adopted the doctrine.

Georgia just adopted it two years ago. H.B. 683 will now take this right away from the consumer. S.B. 512 and H.B. 684 are bad because they seek to place unreasonable time limits during which an injured consumer can sue. All the above bills are anti-consumer, and should be opposed by all who are interested in the welfare of average citizens of Georgia.

Three bills are pending which protect the consumer. S.B. 504 allows recovery for wrongful death in product liability cases. Georgia law does not allow "strict liability" when a defective product causes death. S.B. 513 and 514 are designed to make sure Georgia manufacturers are not overcharged for product insurance.

LAWYERS DON'T GET RICH

The villain in every insurance "crisis" has been characterized as the lawyer who gets rich off the insurance company. This is another big lie. Lawyers are only hired when legitimate claims are not paid by insurance companies to injured parties. Georgia products cases average about 100 per year. The average paid is about $9,000 per claim.

When special rights are granted special interests under the law, these rights have to be taken away from someone, and that someone is the public. This tilts the scales of justice. Once you lose your right, it's hard to get it back.

THE MINDLESS PURSUIT OF SAFETY[*]

By Walter Guzzardi, Jr.

Out of this nettle, danger, we pluck this flower, safety.

—Henry IV, Part I

Now ascending among the many blessings that the citizenry expects of government in our society is that flower, safety. Popular demand for this latest entitlement has become practically a national frenzy, and the rush is on to give us full protection from those former-friends-turned-enemies, the myriad products and conveniences and adornments of the industrial age. The presumption is that safety can be wrung in ever-larger increments from manufacturers, who are thought to be exposing us all to needless hazards in return for the equally needless addition of a few pennies of profit. Only make them forgo this petty gain, only force them to build more safety into new products and to fix what they have already put out there on the market, and there you have it—behold the bargain-rate splendors of the riskless world.

[*] By Walter Guzzardi, Jr. Reprinted from the April 9, 1979 issue of *Fortune* Magazine by special permission; © 1979, Time, Inc.

Right now, we are pursuing this chimera in two different but related ways, both of which can safely be called dangerous. Carrying out with religious zealotry the sweeping mandates of Congress, regulatory agencies engaged in social governance are forcing the recall of millions of products in the name of consumer protection. And instead of supplying sanity, the courts are regularly interpreting the law to hold manufacturers liable for huge sums when their products can in some way be blamed for injuries. Both agencies and courts frequently ignore or misrepresent true cost and evade the question of who is going to pay it; both accept the appearance of social benefit in place of its reality; and both bring about an uneconomic allocation of risk, shifting too much away from the consumer and back upon the manufacturer. Cost/benefit ratios are admittedly complicated in this field, especially when they concern, as they sometimes must, suffering or death. But it remains inexcusable for our society to be so deceived by the desire for yet another gift by government that we refuse to consider how to-day's policies will run up tomorrow's bills. Relatively speaking, Faust was a long-range planner.

The primary enforcement tool being used to bring us more safety is the product recall, and the most convincing display of its power can be seen in the confrontation between the government and the auto industry. The protagonist there is Joan Claybrook, the intelligent, formidable, Nader-trained, bred-in-the-bones adversary of the industry who is now head of the National Highway Traffic Safety Administration. Cars were being recalled long before Claybrook came to her present eminence. But NHTSA's policy then gave greater weight to working out standards beforehand with man-ufacturers, and ordering recalls when the standards were not met; although the manufacturers groaned about the standards, at least they knew what they had to do. But today, while NHTSA is still writing standards, the agency seems to have lost its interest in them as a means of effecting recalls. "NHTSA's standards have to be so minimal that they would be self-defeating," says Lynn Bradford, director of the office of defects investiga-tion. Besides, NHTSA took one of its few beatings in court after trying to impose complicated standards for air brakes on trucks.

So NHTSA has been moving its legal base to higher ground. It is now making extensive use of its power to order recalls whenever *substantial numbers* of a *safety-related defect* show up, and present an *unreasonable risk* of accident or injury. From those wide-branching concepts, which derive from the Congress, the bodies of the auto companies as we know them today may presently swing. For by its rulings and the generous inter-pretations of the courts, NHTSA has made those italicized words mean almost anything it has wanted them to mean. Any number can be sub-stantial; any failure of any part even after years of good performance can be a defect; any defect may be safety-related; and any defect related to safety can present an unreasonable risk—not literally, but very nearly, that is the legal case today. As one embittered official at Ford Motor says, "There are no standards. Whatever we do, NHTSA and the courts just say we should have done it better."

For a while, Ford and General Motors fought to keep from ensnarement in that particular web. But the courts, which like Congress have felt the heat of the consumer movement, have found NHTSA to be very, very right. For instance:

• A stop at the Pitman Arms. "Pitman arms," part of the steering mechanisms, were failing in some 1959–60 Cadillacs when NHTSA began its investigation in 1974. The failure was coming only with very sharp turns made at very slow speeds—most often when a car was being parked. Since no one could prove injuries as a result of the failures, and since the 43,400 cars of that model still left on the road had gone through 96 percent of their lives, G.M. could not see the "unreasonable risk." But the court held that whenever steering or other vital components fail without warning, that's an unreasonable risk. In the end, G.M. had to notify the owners of the remaining cars (by then eighteen years old) that they had a defect. G.M. made the repairs without charge.

• Breaking point. Seat pins were breaking off one side of the driver's seat in some 1968–69 Mustangs and Cougars. NHTSA cited a failure in fifty-seven out of some 500,000 cars. Ford pointed out that the defect had never led to serious injury. The company lost, and recalled the cars.

• Reinventing the wheel. A number of wheels on some 1960–65 G.M. trucks were collapsing when the load limits of the trucks were exceeded by overweight campers. G.M. argued that the overloading, against which it warned in its instruction manuals, constituted owner abuse. The court held that there was abuse, all right, but it was "reasonably foreseeable"; everybody knows trucks are going to be overloaded. Only "unforeseeable abuse" might have excused G.M.

Supporting a G.M. petition to the Supreme Court, Volkswagenwerk AG made the point that "nearly every accident situation involving an automobile, no matter how bizarre, is foreseeable, if only because in the last fifty years drivers have discovered just about every conceivable way of wrecking an automobile." But the Supreme Court declined to hear the case. Since then, the auto industry has been reluctant to fight NHTSA in the federal courts.

Recalls also dump truckloads of unfavorable publicity on the car companies because of the tone of the letters that the companies have to send out to begin the recall. Millions of copies of the letter may go to owners of the cars being recalled, even when only a small percentage of the cars have that particular defect. The letters, which are practically dictated by NHTSA, recount the horrors that *might* happen: a typical one might say that the owner's car may have this defect, that if it does the part might fail, and if that happens the driver may lose control of the car and there may be an accident. All that is true. But it is also a doomsday scenario.

Just what would happen if the angry Claybrook became angrier still nobody knows, but the scene might do for a movie by Irwin Allen, the master of disaster. In 1975, about 1.5 million vehicles were recalled. In 1976, still pre-Claybrook, the number went to three million. In 1977, however, a record number of 10.7 million vehicles were recalled; that number included about as many cars as were manufactured that year. Last year recalls came down to 7.9 million. But if that made the year a numerical disappointment for NHTSA, there were compensations: victories were won over Firestone (14.5 million tires recalled) and over Ford with the Pinto recall.

As for 1979, it could be a wonderful year for NHTSA. The agency has issued two "consumer advisories," and has got out other kinds of publicity as well, warning that transmissions in some Ford vehicles have been jumping from park into reverse; included in the advisories are allegations that twenty-three deaths occurred as a result. (NHTSA's advice to drivers includes the suggestion that they turn off their engines when they get out of their cars, which would certainly be a cheap fix.) Ford has done enormous amounts of testing, but says it has found no evidence of any defect; it thinks that the information coming in about the number of accidents has been skewed by NHTSA's publicity. But the shadow of a recall, amounting to nine million cars and trucks made from 1970 to 1978, still hangs over Dearborn. Whether NHTSA would ever recognize any limits to recalling is anybody's guess: Frank Berndt, associate administrator for enforcement, muses that "if we were faced with a massive recall, say 15 million cars, we might try something else, rather than destroy the industry."

The crucial questions about all those recalls, of course, are how much they cost, and how much safety they are buying. None of the car companies breaks out figures about recall costs, which consist of payment at retail labor rates to the dealers who do the work, and the cost of the replacement parts plus some profit to the dealers for handling them. Neither will any of them estimate the value of the executive time spent on recalls—Henry Ford II himself worked hard on the Pinto case—or the public-relations damage. Still, there's not much doubt that the auto companies have had to lay out hundreds of millions of dollars for recalls, and that amount is being repaid by new-car buyers. When it passed the law obliging manufacturers to pay for recalls, the Senate Commerce Committee thought it was ensuring that "the consumer never again will be forced to pay for the repair of safety related defects," but its rhetoric was better than its economics. Chester V. Barion, general manager of the parts and service division at Ford, remarks, "These recall costs are substantial, and they will be reflected in future pricing." To whatever the total cost is to the industry must be added, of course, the social cost of operating NHTSA: it has spent $1 billion in its twelve-year life.

As for safety, a very strong inference can be drawn that society could be getting much more of it by spending the money in a different way. Lots of research goes to show that unsafe vehicles cause a very small proportion of highway accidents and deaths. The definitive study on accident causation by a special research group at Indiana University found that some 75 percent of auto accidents are caused by "human factors," generally meaning speeding, inattention on the part of the driver, and bad decision-making in a crisis—all worsened by drinking. "Environmental factors," such as icy roads, obstructed view, and poor highway design are the next most frequent cause. "Vehicle factors" cause only about 5 percent of accidents. Brake failures and bald or underinflated tires take a big chunk of that percentage.

So instead of pressing on with recalls, it would be more rewarding to urge better driver education, regular vehicle inspection, and tougher laws about drinking. But those are unpopular causes to promote. NHTSA has found it politically much more rewarding to wheel up the cannons and open fire on those centers of power around Detroit.

The terrain there is also pocked with shells fired by another body, the Environmental Protection Agency, which has the power to order recalls of cars that do not meet emission standards. Since the advent of the Carter Administration, the EPA, like NHTSA, has been shooting from the high ground. The shift in emphasis has come with the methods of testing for emissions, which have moved from inspection and certification of new cars in the plants to what is called "end-use enforcement"—testing cars chosen at random from models suspected of being in violation after they have been driven for a while by their owners. EPA says this is the way to find out what is happening in the real world. But a Ford executive points out, "In new-car testing, the average is what governs. Now EPA is looking not at averages but at individual cars. We're petrified."

What worries Detroit most is that this shift may oblige the companies to pay for fixes on cars whose antipollution devices have been abused or tampered with by their owners. There's some reason for this fear, because while pollution controls can upgrade the quality of the air, they can also downgrade the performance of the car. Lots of owners make adjustments to get smoother rides and better mileage—and don't worry much if they increase emissions.

Consequently, there's a big battle coming between the industry and EPA over what constitutes proper maintenance, with Chrysler as the point company. EPA wants Chrysler to recall 208,000 of its 1975 cars that the agency insists are exceeding emission standards. Chrysler says the owners have tampered with the carburetion. EPA replies that the fault lies with

Chrysler's carburetor designs and adjustment procedures. Millions of dollars in fixing costs for all the auto companies hang on the case, now before the courts.

Although EPA's new policies toward emissions may greatly increase the costs to the industry and the number of recalled cars, the agency is far from satisfied. Ben Jackson, a deputy assistant administrator at EPA, says, "We could go on ordering recalls and logging numbers and looking good. But it's fool's play to make a numbers game out of this. We want the standards met." Jackson claims that after the manufacturers have been advised that some of their cars aren't qualifying, they present plans for the cheapest possible fixes—"a tweak of the carburetion mixture when a carburetor replacement might be best." Negotiations over what constitutes a proper fix can go on for months, Jackson says, while the companies benefit from the delay: the more time that goes by, the fewer the cars they have to adjust. To end this Ping-Pong game, Jackson wants the EPA to be given more punitive powers, so that the costs of the dilatory tactics to the companies would become too high. Ford denies using such tactics, and shudders at the prospect of still higher costs for emissions control.

By way of its authority over marketing practices, including advertising and warranties, the Federal Trade Commission is also prancing around on the recall stage. Its most interesting role so far began in 1976, when Ford discovered that some of its small cars had pistons that were scuffing cylinder walls. Although the warranties on some of the cars had expired, Ford was making what it calls "goodwill adjustments"—repairs free to those customers who complained. The FTC took the view that the repairs should be offered to all customers, not just complaining ones: what Ford called "goodwill adjustments" the agency looked on as "secret warranties." Ford notified about two million customers that it would make a free fix.

The FTC, though, had got the wind up, and it has gone on to develop a very expansive case against Ford, going far beyond piston scuffing. The commission is charging that Ford is offering "seriously defective cars" for sale, and is misrepresenting them in its advertising as "durable and reliable." In a proposal lunatic even in the religion of regulation, the FTC is suggesting that to protect itself from charges of false advertising, Ford must conspicuously display in every showroom a poster enumerating the twenty principal flaws, both potential and known, to be found in its cars, and must also plaster a defect notice to the windshields of new cars that are "subject to a substantial defect."

Swallowing hard, Ford has responded by saying that its cars are indeed reliable and durable, that it can't find out about defects (which the FTC can't define anyway) until they show up, and besides, in effect, the FTC should drop dead—the case is way beyond its purview. Ford has not got around to suggesting that the FTC should post in its corridors a list of the agency's twenty greatest failings, including its recent questionnaire about practices in the legal profession that the American Bar Association calls "unreasonable, of questionable legality and doubtful usefulness." Still, if the FTC has its way, the auto industry may end up with yet another overseer with de facto power to effect recalls—assuming, that is, that when NHTSA and the EPA get through, there are still some cars left out there.

The FTC has also just worked out with Fedders a consent agreement for the repair of some 40,000 heat pumps. There, the commission contended that selling a product is an implicit assertion that the product is free of defects. That broad theory could serve as the basis for many other FTC-influenced recalls in lots of other industries. Formerly, the FTC confined its recall actions to making manufacturers eat their words. The most famous example involved Warner-Lambert, which was forced to include in its next $10 million of advertising an assertion that "Listerine will not help prevent colds or sore throats."

For all of the deficiencies of those belligerent agencies, they do have generally understandable recall policies, if costly ones, and they never have to wonder what to do. But the Consumer Product Safety Commission, which has played a role in over 1,200 recalls of millions of products during its six-year life, lacks both surety and a proper occupation. The fault lies not with the people but with the purpose. The Consumer Product Safety Act, and the four other acts that Congress has charged the commission with carrying out, add up to the loosest and most indistinct mandate ever conferred on a regulatory body. Without too much exaggeration, the mandate might be summed up as a collective command to make almost everything safer.

Despite the commission's Herculean efforts, there is no way to accomplish that task by regulatory authority. Here and there, the commission may keep or get a perniciously shoddy product off the market. But basically, the CPSC, like NHTSA, has a fatal defect. Its primary thrust has to be directed against product defects and design. But the overwhelming number of product-connected injuries probably come not from faulty products, but from errors or recklessness of the consumer. As E. Patrick McGuire of the Conference Board puts it, "The most dangerous component is the consumer, and there's no way to recall him." By government standards, the CPSC may be a modest spender, but it will cost about $40 million this year, and it requires lots of paperwork from many different companies. On balance, the CPSC just doesn't pass the cost/benefit test.

The troubles and issues go deeper and are far more important at the Food and Drug Administration, but they do not for the most part center on arguments over recall power. The FDA technically has such power only in its oversight over medical devices, such as pacemakers, and over products that emit radiation, such as TV sets and microwave ovens. It has had some disputes over standards with companies like General Electric, Zenith Radio, and RCA in those fields. Besides, while medical devices are usually simple to track down, they can be hard to fix: it's not easy to put a screwdriver to an implanted pacemaker. TV sets, on the other hand, can be fixed readily enough, but they are hard to track after they have been sold to the customer. Generally, though, industry and agency manage to coexist without too much acerbity and waste in this field.

With food, the FDA has the authority to ban or seize what it regards as a menace to health. It cannot order recalls, but the threat of those other measures is usually enough to motivate a company to run its own recall. Although the FDA sometimes leans too hard on publicity as a weapon against food producers, it manages pretty well in the traditional fields, getting adulterated tuna, lye-sprinkled pretzels, poisonous mushrooms, and botulin-infested soup off the shelves about as well as possible, given the long chain of distribution. The more profound difficulties come with the waves of scientific and technological change that have brought food additives, such as nitrites, and products like saccharin. That area is now swirling with conflict and confusion.

The danger is that the FDA, always being carped at for inaction by some pressure group, will end by opting for safety over all other considerations. It may be moving that way with cosmetics, where it wants authority to certify ingredients as safe before they get to market. The FDA for many years has had that kind of authority over ethical drugs, keeping them off the market until they are certified "safe and efficacious"; the results range from dubious to bad. In a study that stands as a landmark in the field, Sam Peltzman of the University of Chicago has shown that the proof-of-efficacy requirement has kept some useless drugs from going on sale. But it has also deprived us of lots of beneficial new drugs, and has kept the prices of existing drugs higher by shielding them from competition. On balance, Peltzman computed a huge net loss.

The growth of the recall phenomenon in the past decade has roughly coincided with an explosion in the number of lawsuits brought against companies, large and small, for injuries associated with the use of their products. The two developments have the same provenance: the sense of rising entitlements, and the efforts of the courts and the Congress to institutionalize it.

In the field of product liability, the change comes close to a doctrinal revolution. Until a few years ago, anyone claiming damages for a product-related injury usually had to prove that the product was defective, in the sense that it failed to meet the manufacturer's own standards. One important case held the Coca Cola Bottling Co. of Fresno liable when a waitress was injured by a bottle of Coke that exploded when she was putting it into a refrigerator. She did not have to prove that there had been negligence somewhere in the long skein of Coke production. Obviously, the company didn't intend its bottles to explode; it was liable when they did.

Now that sensible doctrine is being taken to extremes, and strict liability, like Calvinism, holds the maker responsible for everything. We may be coming to the point where all the fault lies with the product, none with the conduct of its owner. Lawsuits have been entertained claiming that cars are defective (that is, not "crashworthy") when they are demolished by railroad trains, and that a car is unsafe when it hits a pedestrian. If football players sustain head injuries, the maker of helmets didn't design in enough shock resistance. The manufacturer has not yet been held liable when some swinger mashes his thumb with a hammer, but that day may come. And the link of causation has been weakened, too: courts have expanded liability to include defects that enhance or aggravate the injury, rather than directly cause it. And some awards have surpassed even the hopes of the plaintiffs, running up beyond all reason.

Recalls have fed this liability monster in several ways. "The number of recalls has surely disabused the public of the notion that we make perfect cars," dryly remarks one company lawyer. "Twenty years ago, people thought Detroit made a pretty good automobile. Now people— and jurors—are saying, 'Can't you do anything right?' " Corporate lawyers also say that after a big recall, the number of private lawsuits increases. And one of them adds, "We often notice that the legal complaints paraphrase the recall letter"—the doomsday scenario.

Government actions and private litigation also have a way of feeding on each other. When the government starts an investigation, the target company has to produce piles of documents, which later can provide the basis for private suits. The reverse is also true: government agencies monitor civil litigation looking for clues. Warnings issued by regulatory bodies also stir up suits: "Say the FDA starts to talk about side effects from a drug that has been on the market for twenty years," says Michael Hoenig, a lawyer with Herzfeld & Rubin in New York and an authority on products liability. "Shortly thereafter, you might see 200 women claiming to suffer from that complaint." Violations of FDA or CPSC or NHTSA standards can lead to private charges of negligence against a company, but the knife doesn't cut the other way: compliance doesn't immunize a company from strict liability.

In a broad sense, the process at work here is serving a moral imperative. Judges and juries are setting out not to right wrongs, but to compensate the injured. As Reynold M. Sachs, a professor of economics at American University, has explained, the emphasis is not on who is responsible but on who is best able to pay—on who, in other words, has the "deep pocket." So the laws of liability may be turning into a subterranean means for redistributing wealth.

As the trends toward more recalls and more liability go on, manufacturers will indeed make safer products. They will do more testing in their plants and, since absolute safety will remain unattainable, they will take out plenty of liability insurance. But intramural procedures can never be as efficient as the tests of actual use that the consumer carries out, and the premiums for liability insurance have gone up rapidly with the size of the awards being made for damages. So the total costs for putting so much of the incentive for safety on the manufacturer will be very high.

All this will have social effects that Congress, the agencies, and the courts would do well to ponder. To begin with, prices of products will go up to cover these new, forever-escalating components of cost—the added charges for safety. Every consumer, whether he wants or needs the new layer of protection, is going to have to pay the charge: as Reynold Sachs says, "It's a tie-in sale." What is made safe for the village idiot will cost the man of common sense more. Many people would choose to be careful, or to buy their insurance in some other form. Nonsmokers don't want to pay extra for fireproof bedsheets; people who fasten seat belts don't need the costly air bag. But everybody will have to buy such refinements anyway.

Like so many other losses of freedom, this loss will hurt more people than it helps. The beneficiaries will be those who are reckless, for we shall all be guaranteeing them compensation for the injuries they sustain, the cost of which they ought to bear themselves. Further, their ranks may increase as the penalty for recklessness diminishes. To the well off, the cost of subsidizing the reckless won't matter very much; the rich are liable to buy the most expensive products anyway. Most disadvantaged will be the poor, who will find less on the market that they can afford. The low-income man who knows how to handle a chain saw or maintain a truck or take his own fire precautions in a cheap house may find those items beyond his means when they are inseparable from fancy and costly safety devices.

In order to be both free and efficient, it seems better to strive for policies that distribute incentives to avoid accidents more sensibly between consumer and manufacturer. Sometimes manufacturers make sleazy and dangerous products, and the consumer feels powerless to change that. But the corrective action transferring more incentive to the manufacturer to make products safe is now going too far.

Buyers and sellers should share more equitably the total cost of accidents—the costs to the consumer of property damage, medical expenses, and forgone income, and the costs to the manufacturer of making a safer product. One way of doing this, which follows a rule by Learned Hand, starts with the assumption that the cost of an accident is $100,000 and the chance that it will happen is one in a hundred. The expected accident cost is thus $1,000. If the manufacturer could have avoided that accident by an expenditure of, say, $300, he ought to have done so, and should be held liable. If it would have cost him $2,000, it would be uneconomic for him to bear the whole burden; the consumer must share it by taking some risk. Such equations can get complicated and tenuous, but they can help point the way to efficiency.

That kind of analysis is often attacked on the ground that, if pushed far enough, it requires that we assign a value to human life, which is too heartless for a humanitarian society. On one level, that is true: life is price-less, death is final. But all that is beyond the reach of law and government. On a different level, we have to affix a value to life, and we do, all the time: for an additional given number of millions of dollars we could build every bridge, or mine every ton of coal, without losing a life, and we could make every railroad crossing accident-proof. But, in a difficult balance, we have decided that we cannot afford those things. Some of that same contour of thought should enter now as the government strives, from our present net-tle of danger, to bring us that flower, safety.

THE OZONE ISSUE:

Fluorocarbon Battle Expected to Heat Up as the Regulators Move beyond Aerosols[*]

By Jeffrey A. Tannenbaum

Phase Two of the battle over fluorocarbons will touch off a lot more con-troversy than Phase One did.

In Phase One, the government has proposed an almost total phase-out of fluorocarbon aerosols. The reason: Fluorocarbons, used mainly as propellants in many aerosol deodorants and hair sprays, are suspected of damaging the earth's ozone shield. Any such damage will cause an increase in human skin cancer and could do other harm.

The public, which has raised an outcry over proposed saccharin re-strictions, has hardly whimpered over the aerosol ban. That's because aero-sols are widely regarded as inessential to society and because they have readily available, and less expensive, substitutes. Indeed, manufacturers have halved their use of fluorocarbon aerosols over the past three years, and Phase One is winding down quietly. Next month federal regulators are expected to make the phaseout official.

Now, however, the battle is moving beyond aerosols. As Phase Two begins, the regulators are starting to consider how many other types of products, if any, should be banned or otherwise restricted because they contain fluorocarbons. The chemicals are widely used in refrigeration and air conditioning, and as blowing agents to make plastic foam. One product that may come under attack is the automobile air conditioner.

THE SUBSTITUTION PROBLEM

The reason the hue and cry will grow is that in most of their nonaerosol applications, fluorocarbons are generally deemed to have no fully satisfactory substitute. (The use of fluorocarbon refrigerants, which account for perhaps one-third of overall fluorocarbon use, is almost universal because the formerly used alternatives—ammonia, methyl chloride, and sulfur dioxide—are highly toxic or flammable. And new refrigerants, if they are developed, are likely to be more expensive than fluorocarbons.)

Thus, both manufacturers and consumers are likely to be upset by any curbs on nonaerosol fluorocarbons, especially in light of a continuing debate as to whether the ozone is actually being damaged. "What's happening is disturbing and alarming," says Richard B. Ward, a chemist and spokesman for Du Pont Co., the biggest maker and defender of fluorocarbons. "We're going a very long way into the regulatory process before the scientists know what's really going on."

Similarly, the American Chemical Society, a professional group, complains that any fluorocarbon restriction, including an aerosol ban, would be "the first regulation to be based entirely on an unverified scientific prediction" and hence would be "a very dangerous precedent."

At the same time, some scientists and environmental groups are calling for further sharp restrictions on fluorocarbons. "This is a very important issue that concerns a major human health hazard," says Suedeen Gibbons, an attorney for the private Natural Resources Defense Council.

THEORY PRESENTED IN 1974

The theory that the ozone is being damaged by fluorocarbons was first advanced in 1974 by two University of California chemists, F. Sherwood Rowland and Mario J. Molina. The ozone layer, part of the upper atmosphere, prevents much of the sun's dangerous ultraviolet radiation, which causes skin cancer, from reaching the earth's surface.

The complex theory involves the most commonly used fluorocarbons, those that contain chlorine (and are known to chemists as fully halogenated chlorofluoromethanes). When molecules of the chemicals are released into the lower atmosphere, according to the theory, they are eventually wafted up to the ozone layer. There the molecules are broken apart by ultraviolet light, and the chlorine is released.

This chlorine, in theory, then has a profound effect on the ozone, upsetting the natural balance in which ozone is constantly being destroyed and replenished. Then, the theory goes on, each chlorine molecule, becoming involved in what is known as a catalytic chain reaction, manages to destroy thousands of molecules of ozone. According to the original prediction by Messrs. Rowland and Molina, a continuation of fluorocarbon use at recent levels (over 1.6 billion pounds annually world-wide) would eventually cause a 7% to 13% ozone depletion.

In 1975, a federal task force concluded that fluorocarbon restrictions would be necessary "unless new scientific evidence is found to remove the cause for concern." And in 1976, a blue-ribbon scientific panel, having reviewed the evidence for the National Research Council, cited many uncertainties but deemed an eventual ozone depletion of 6% to 7.5% to be probable.

DEPLETION ESTIMATE RAISED

Since then, scientists have increased the estimate of expected ozone depletion. The main reason is that researchers determined that nitric acid, a trace element in the stratosphere, yields the chemical units known as hydroxyl radicals up to 60 times faster than previously thought. The presence of hydroxyl radicals increases the efficiency with which chlorine attacks ozone.

The current estimates of eventual ozone depletion, as outlined in a recent report for the National Aeronautics and Space Administration, range from 10.8% to 16.5%. Even scientists at Du Pont are currently predicting a 12.2% ozone loss. (A scientific panel appointed by the National Research Council says that a 7% ozone loss would be sufficient to cause "a few hundred deaths per year" from the severe form of skin cancer known as melanoma, as well as increases in nonfatal skin cancers.)

However, Du Pont and its supporters continue to insist that the ozone-depletion theory is still unproved, and that further new chemistry may be discovered that undermines the theory. Du Pont and others argue that, in any case, no product should be banned on the basis of a scientific prediction of an adverse effect, but only on the basis of solid evidence that the damage is occurring. But Du Pont's adversaries argue that by the time ozone damage was extensive enough to detect by direct measurement of ozone, the damage would already be too great.

So far, the federal regulators (from the Environmental Protection Agency, the Food and Drug Administration and the Consumer Product Safety Commission) have tended to side with Du Pont's adversaries. The regulators' expected phase-out of fluorocarbon aerosols (not all aerosols contain fluorocarbons) will be fully in effect by April 15, 1979.

TOUGH QUESTIONS REMAIN

But the remaining questions are tougher. Regulators still haven't faced, among other things, the question of how much chlorine, if any, to allow to reach the stratosphere in fluorocarbons. World-wide bans on fluorocarbon aerosols (the U.S. accounts for half of fluorocarbon use) would still leave a predicted ozone loss of 4% to 5% from the other uses of fluorocarbons, the University of California's Mr. Rowland says.

In theory, each 1% ozone loss leads to a 2% increase in skin cancer. "I think any regulator who chooses any number other than zero for the ozone loss will have a difficult time explaining to people why he wants to allow so much damage," Mr. Rowland says. The Natural Resources Defense Council is urging that the ozone loss be held down to 1%, which implies sharp reductions of fluorocarbon use in all applications.

But regulators must also weigh the possible consequences of switching away from fluorocarbons as refrigerants, and such evaluation is difficult because it isn't clear what could replace them, other than the flammable or toxic chemicals formerly used. "Developing new alternatives to fluorocarbons is proving much more difficult than we initially surmised," Du Pont's Mr. Ward says.

An alternative is at least five to 10 years away, Du Pont insists. The company is considering two possible alternatives. One is fluorocarbons that contain hydrogen as well as chlorine (and thus would degrade before reaching the ozone layer), but these are too toxic. The other is fluorocarbons without any chlorine, but Du Pont insists these are too expensive, at least three times as expensive as the fluorocarbons most widely used today.

According to the York Automotive division of Borg-Warner Corp., one drawback of automobile air conditioners using refrigerants other than fluorocarbons would be increased gasoline consumption. Other refrigerants must be contained under higher pressure, requiring slightly heavier equipment that adds to the weight of the auto, thus reducing mileage.

INFORMATIONAL HEARINGS

The regulators hope to decide what to do about all this by next June. They began informational hearings in October.

Beyond the fluorocarbon decision, the regulators may eventually have to consider controlling some other chemicals that are likewise suspected of damaging ozone, though on a smaller scale. For example, there is methylchloroform, a widely used cleaning solvent, which contains chlorine and may reach the upper atmosphere.

In a scientific report published earlier this month, researchers at York University in Canada said it is reasonable to assume that methylchloroform poses a threat to ozone about 20% as large as the threat from fluorocarbons. The use of the chemical has been growing, in part because of restrictions on another chemical, trichloroethylene.

Trichloroethylene, used largely for metal degreasing, has been linked to cancer in test animals and is a contributor to urban air pollution because it readily oxidizes in the lower atmosphere.

Part 3 | Promotion: Issues of What to Say and How to Say It

PROMOTION: ISSUES OF WHAT TO SAY
AND HOW TO SAY IT

Promotion may be viewed as any attempt to communicate with a prospective customer. While much promotional effort is intended to create awareness or to create a shift in attitudes toward a product or marketer, the essence of promotion is persuasive communication. When such communications are face to face, the process is called "personal selling." When delivered via paid space in mass media, it is called "advertising." When the space is not paid for, it is "public relations." In-store persuasion is called "sales promotion." At a somewhat more subtle level, the design of the surroundings in which a marketer and consumer meet to exchange values is also an opportunity to influence consumption choice. Thus, atmospherics can be an important component of a promotional strategy. The common thread is that each seeks to persuade people to change their purchasing behavior.[1]

There are two intended effects of persuasive communication. The demand curve for the product, service, or other offering is shifted to the right, meaning that at any price more is demanded. A second effect of promotional activity is to make demand for the offering inelastic. That is, some consumers may develop or reinforce brand preferences which make them less sensitive to price. More specifically, promotion has one or more of the following purposes:

1. Fulfills one of the classic economic assumptions of perfect competition, that of complete knowledge of the marketplace.[2]
2. Provides a method of quality control, in that products which require repurchase to be economically successful must meet consumer expectations. If they did not, consumers would not repurchase and the promotional investment would be lost.
3. Encourages new products, because existing promotional channels provide a means by which to introduce them to the public.
4. Lowers the cost of goods sold, through economies of scale resulting from the potential of wider immediate customer acceptance.

Promotion, as practiced in the United States, also has a number of social effects which result indirectly from the economic effects. The merits of each of these are largely dependent on the personal values of the individuals making the assessments, but most marketers consider the net social effects of promotion to be positive. The social effects of promotion include:

---

[1]   It is easy to forget that persuasive communication is common to a wide variety of interpersonal and social relationships. Sophisticated examples of behavior are found within religious, legal, interpersonal, and political settings, among others.

[2]   The extent to which promotion provides "complete" information can be debated, but there is little doubt that marketplace information without promotion would be slight.

1. Promotion creates aspirations, by showing how products and services can be easily obtained or productively used by potential consumers.
2. Promotion creates a wide choice of products in the marketplace, because different segments within a total market can be reached with the unique benefits, for them, of purchasing a particular brand.
3. Promotion becomes a time-budgeting mechanism. In the Soviet Union, housewives spend several hours *each day* in shopping activity, because few effective promotional channels exist. The result is a significant physical drain on the citizens and a colossal productivity drain on the economy.
4. Some promotion is considered offensive by some people. Even if promotions were 99-44/100 percent free from objection, the dozens of salespersons and hundreds of advertisements that one comes in contact with each week would leave a few promotions objectionable to someone, but not everyone. Research has shown a wide variance in individual reactions to given promotions.
5. The discussion of the social effects of promotion is often stalled by the differences in definitions between defenders and critics of promotion. Bauer and Greyser's classic work points out the disagreement of the definitions of such basic terms as "product," "need," "competition," "rational," "information," "power," "deception," and "truth."[3]

While the marketer looks at the positive social impact of these elements, the critic focuses on the negative. Promotion *does* encourage people to want things they could live without. A wider consumer choice of brands *does* sometimes lead to confusion. Even one ad offensive to someone is too many. Salespeople are subject to special criticism, because their function is to be persuasive.

> Just take a look, the critics say, at manuals and training courses for salesmen. They are taught how to greet the customer in a positive way, how to find out what she is thinking about, how to ask her for advice, how to induce her to say something that the salesman can later use to his advantage, how to anticipate her objections, and how to ask for the order without seeming to ask for it. Anyone who knows how to get along with people, of course, behaves in this way almost instinctively. In the last analysis, politeness, charm, and good looks themselves can be deceptive.[4]

These areas of potential improvement for promotion have become political concerns institutionalized through federal regulatory agencies. The Federal Communications Commission (FCC) has licensing authority over broadcast media, and can control program content. The ban on liquor and cigarette advertising was accomplished through the FCC. The Food and Drug Administration (FDA) has been involved in food and drug labeling, and is now very active regarding the standardization of package sizes, weights, volumes, and labels. The regulatory activity of the Federal Trade Commission (FTC), however, dwarfed the others in

---

[3] Raymond A. Bauer and Stephen A. Greyser, *Advertising in America: The Consumer View* (Boston: Harvard University, 1968), pp. 385–86.

[4] Charles G. Burck, "High Pressure Consumerism at the Salesman's Door," *Fortune*, July 1972, p. 70.

the 1970s. The FTC enthusiastically pursued a perceived mandate to protect consumers from potential harm resulting from intentional or unintentional business actions, particularly in the areas of fair competition and promotion. Some basic

FIGURE 1   Some Basic FTC Ground Rules for Advertisements[*]

Over the years, there have emerged some basic ground rules for applying the FTC law to advertising. Based largely on the rulings of the Federal Trade Commission and on court decisions, these rules include the following important points.

Total Impression. The courts have held that the overall impression an advertisement gives is the key to whether it is false or misleading. Thus, in one case, although the term "relief" was used in an advertisement, the net impression from the entire context was that the product promised a "cure" for the ailment. Similarly, words like "stops," "ends," and "defeats" may improperly imply permanent rather than temporary relief. If an advertisement has even a "tendency to deceive," the FTC may find it illegal.

Clarity. The statement must be so clear that even a person of low intelligence would not be confused by it. The tendency of the law is to protect the credulous and the gullible. If an advertisement can have two meanings, it is illegal if one of them is false or misleading.

Fact versus Puffery. The courts have held that an advertiser's opinion of the product is tolerated as the legitimate expression of a biased opinion, not as a material statement of fact. However, a statement that might be viewed by a sophisticated person as trade puffery can be misleading to a person of lower intelligence. Much controversy over misleading advertising hovers around the question: "When is a statement trade puffery and when is it a false claim?" All factual claims must be supportable. If you say, "This is an outstanding leather case," and the case is made of vinyl, that is misrepresentation. If you say, "This is an outstanding case," that is a subjective matter of opinion and is considered puffery, which is not a legal matter.

The Question of Taste. The courts have held, "If the advertisement is not false, defendants have a constitutional right to use it even though its content and blatancy may annoy both the Federal Trade Commission and the general public. The issue is falsity. . . . " Hence bad taste is not a matter involving the FTC.

Demonstrations. Demonstrations of product or product performance on television must not mislead viewers. The FTC requires literal accuracy in nutritional ads, both audio and video.

---

* Otto Kleppner, *Advertising Procedure,* 7th edition (Englewood Cliffs, N.J.: Prentice-Hall, Inc., 1979), pp. 550–552.

Exaggerations in the impression conveyed may also be found misleading. Mars, Inc., makers of Milky Way candy bars, had a TV spot showing a glass of milk magically changing into a Milky Way bar. The commercial was held misleading because it gave the impression that a whole glass of milk went into a Milky Way bar.

Warranties. A report on the subject by the FTC says:

"The final disclosure rule . . . applies to written warranties on consumer products . . . costing the consumer more than $15 . . . The warrantor must disclose "in simple and readily understood language" the following items of information, among others:

- What is covered by and, where necessary for clarification, what is excluded from the warranty.

- What the warrantor will do in the event of a defect, malfunction, or failure to conform with the written warranty, including a statement of what items or services will be paid for or provided by the warrantor, and, where necessary for clarification, those that will not be.

- A step-by-step explanation of what the purchaser should do to get the warranty honored.

"Free." Along with related words, "free" is a popular word in advertising: "Buy one—Get one free," "2-for-1 sale," "Gift," "Bonus," and "Without charge." If there are any terms or conditions for getting something free, they must be stated clearly and conspicuously with the word "free." If a purchaser must buy something to get something else free, the purchased product must be at its lowest price (same quality, same size) in 30 days. A "free" offer for a single size may not be advertised for more than 6 months in a market in any 12 month period.

Lotteries. Lotteries are schemes for the distribution of prizes won by chance. If a person has to pay to enter a lottery conducted by a an advertiser (except government lotteries), the U.S. Postal Service calls it illegal and bans the use of the mail for it. If a lottery is advertised in interstate commerce, the FTC also holds it illegal and will proceed to stop it. Prizes in many sweepstakes (which are a form of lottery) are allowable if money need not be paid to enter the sweepstakes.

Federal Trade Commission Guidelines. The FTC, after consulting with members of over 175 industries, has compiled and published trade-practice rules calling attention to illegal practices in each industry. These rules are offered as guidelines for legal operation. All advertisements containing claims that may come under FTC scrutiny should be submitted to an attorney before the ad is produced. For foods, drugs, and cosmetics, particularly, proof of performance must have been available before the advertisement was run.

Corrective Advertising. In the past, when the commission found advertising false and misleading, it would require the advertiser merely to sign a decree consenting to discontinue such advertising. This "consent decree" permits an offending company to avoid pleading guilty if it agrees not to indulge in such practice again. Any violation thereafter is subject to a $10,000 fine for each offense. Meanwhile, however, damage to the public has been done; and formerly, during the long time required for hearings and the advertiser's appeal, the advertising could continue. It was the intent of the FTC, however, by offering the advertiser the option of signing a consent decree, to put an immediate stop to the false advertising. Now, a new philosophy has been introduced: to counteract the residual effects of the deceptive advertising, the FTC may require the advertiser to run advertising at its own expense "to dissipate the effects of that deception." The commission appears to require corrective advertising chiefly when major advertising themes are the bases for consumers' choices. The first corrective advertising case to face court review was that of Listerine.

Some of the major social issues resulting from the use of promotional methods follow.

1. *What is the best response to erroneous information?* Several industries have been beset by widespread and persistent rumors. What is the proper response to counter these rumors? The McDonald's Company case addresses this contemporary problem.

2. *What is deception?* If a statement is literally true but gives a false impression, can it be deception? What guidelines are available for using such terms as "natural," "fresh," and "wholesome"? How does a firm defend itself regarding the charge of deceptive advertising? This issue is examined in the Litton Industries, Inc., case as the leading manufacturer of microwave ovens responded to a charge of deceptive advertising.

3. *Sales ethics.* If one is given the choice of keeping one's standards or keeping one's job, what choice should be made? What guidelines are available to help make this decision? The Jimmy Don Davis case provides an opportunity to evaluate ethical pressures experienced by salespersons.

4. *Who is responsible for an ad's content?* The widespread use of testimonials and comparative advertising raises a number of issues regarding the legal responsibility for the statements made.

5. *Advertising to vulnerable markets.* Should marketers direct promotional efforts for toys and presweetened cereals toward children? Should marketers promote infant formula and soft drinks in underdeveloped countries? Should insurance marketers target sales efforts toward poor, undereducated consumers? Should alcoholic beverages and smoking be marketed in ways appealing to teenagers? The role of industry self-regulation and of government in such markets remains the subject of intense debate.

These and other social issues with respect to marketing communications are discussed in the cases and commentaries included in this section.

To help answer these questions, a listing of major cases regarding persuasive communication is given as Figure 2.

FIGURE 2   A Summary of Recent Cases Regarding Persuasive Communication*

Federal Trade Commission Act (1914)

Section 5:   As amended by the Wheeler-Lea Act (1938), "unfair methods of competition in commerce, and unfair or deceptive acts or practices in commerce, are hereby unlawful." This section, among other things, *prohibits deceptive advertising* and pricing arrangements that treat transportation cost in ways that result in unfair competition.

Recent Cases in Deceptive Advertising:

1. The *Great Atlantic and Pacific Tea Co., Inc. (A&P)* was found by the Federal Trade Commission (1975) to be advertising deceptively, because an FTC survey of newspaper advertisements and store checks revealed that 9.3 percent of the items were not available in the stores and 3.7 percent were priced higher than advertised. The administrative law judge found nothing intentional or willful. The cease-and-desist order provided for the future defenses of sufficient quantities ordered and received, but sold out; ordered but not delivered for reasons beyond the control of A&P (but A&P must immediately revise the advertisement); and offer "rain checks." (*JM* July 1975, p. 90)

2. The television advertising for *Chevron F-310 gasoline* was found to be deceptive by the FTC (1974) because it used illustrations that conveyed the message that its gasoline emissions did not pollute the air. A before-and-after demonstration used a balloon on the exhaust pipe. The deception occurred because the "before" exhaust came from specially formulated dirty gasoline. Furthermore, most pollutants are invisible. Standard Oil of California and its advertising agency—Batten, Barton, Durstine & Osborn—were ordered to cease and desist. (*JM,* July 1975, pp. 88–89)

3. The FTC (1976) ordered the *Fedders Corp.* to cease and desist from advertising that its air conditioners had a unique "reserve cooling power"; in fact, there was no technical advantage over competitors. (*JM,* July 1976, pp. 102–103)

4. The J. B. Williams Co. paid $302,000 in fines, penalties, and interest when the U.S. Court of Appeals (1976) found the *Fem-Iron* advertisements deceptive because they failed to disclose that most people do not feel tired and run down because of an iron deficiency. (*JM,* July 1976, p. 103)

---

* G. David Hughes, *Marketing Management* (Reading, Mass.: Addison-Wesley Publishing Co., Inc., 1978).

5. The FTC (1973) dismissed the complaint against Coca-Cola that its *Hi-C drink* advertisements were false, misleading, and deceptive. This case was unique in that it examined "implied," as distinct from "expressed," product claims. The majority of the commission concluded that there was not persuasive evidence that Hi-C had been claimed to be equivalent to citrus juices in general or to orange juice in particular. (*JM,* April 1974, pp. 81–82)

Recent Cases Requiring Corrective Advertising:

1. ITT Continental Baking Co. was required to devote 25 percent of its media budget for 1 year to correct the claim that *Profile bread* is effective for weight reduction. (The bread is sliced thinner.) (*JM,* October 1971, p. 76)
2. Two *sugar-trade associations* were required to advertise to correct the misconception in previous advertisements that eating sugar before a meal will help in weight reduction. (*JM,* January 1973, p. 80; *JM,* April 1973, p. 85)

Cases

McDONALD'S CORPORATION:
RESPONSE TO RUMORS ABOUT "WORMBURGERS"

As quickly as Marci Phelps,* manager of an Atlanta area McDonald's, could complete a phone conversation with one anxious McDonald's patron, she would see an employee signaling that yet another caller "wanted to speak with the manager." Although the callers had different names and voices, the conversations were nearly identical. Phelps' "Good morning" was invariably met with "Is the rumor true?" or "How many earthworms do you put in each burger?" As if by rote, Phelps responded, "No, our hamburgers contain only beef, without additives, preservatives, or red earthworms."

By mid afternoon, Phelps had received cancellations for three birthday parties scheduled for November and December. The third cancellation prompted Phelps to place a call of her own. She contacted McDonald's regional office, also in Atlanta. She pleaded with the regional manager, Tim Hodges, to do something about the rumor.

Marci Phelps was not the first McDonald's manager to speak with Hodges. In fact, he had been fielding calls from McDonald's managers and customers all day. After his conversation with Phelps, however, Hodges decided to call McDonald's headquarters again. The rumor had lost the humorous aspects that it had previously had. It was clearly hurting business. The regional office requested that headquarters take some dramatic action against the rumor.[1]

*The names of the principal actors in the case have been disguised.
[1]This scenario was reconstructed from "Rumors of Worms in Hamburgers Hurt McDonald's Business," *The Wall Street Journal*, November 16, 1978, p. 21.

INDUSTRY BACKGROUND

Competition in the $21 billion a year fast-food industry was intense at the end of 1978, but despite the competition, McDonald's continued to wrest a greater portion of the increasingly large market. For the previous year, McDonald's had approximately 20 percent of the U.S. fast-food market, up from about 13 percent 5 years earlier.[2] According to *Dun's Review,* McDonald's market was more than double that of Kentucky Fried Chicken, the second-largest chain and nearly four times greater than that of Burger King, the number two hamburger chain.[3] A list of the top 10 chains, ranked by sales, is given in Table 1.

Within the largest subdivision within the fast-food industry, McDonald's, Burger King, and Wendy's were escalating their hamburger war.[4] The three leaders were perceived by most observers to be hurting the smaller fast-food chains more than they were hurting each other. Several smaller fast-food chains were closing stores, abandoning expansion plans, and looking for new ways to boost sales in existing restaurants. Steak 'n Shake, a regional chain based in Indianapolis, closed all 17 of its stores in Chicago and Houston, ending a 2-year effort to crack those markets. Long John Silver's, a fast-fish chain, pulled out of Boston and discarded plans to expand into new markets. In an effort to reverse its recent earning slump, the Jack-in-the-Box chain expanded its menu and instituted new marketing and remodeling programs.[5]

The top three hamburger chains, though, were not unscathed in the fighting. All three had—at best—nearly flat unit sales, if price increases and new store openings were excluded.[6] Indeed, to the distress of large and small restaurant chains alike, rising prices were keeping would-be customers at home.[7]

---

[2]   Jeanette M. Reddish, "People of the Financial World," *Financial World,* August 15, 1977, p. 26.

[3]   "McDonald's Grinds Out Growth," *Dun's Review,* December 1977, p. 50.

[4]   Paul Ingrasia, "Burger King Begins Big Hamburger Fight against McDonald's," *The Wall Street Journal,* April 5, 1978, p. 1.

[5]   Paul Ingrasia and Laurie Cohen, "Smaller Fast-Food Chains Feel the Brunt of Big-Three Companies' Burger War," *The Wall Street Journal,* February 20, 1979, p. 42.

[6]   *Ibid.*

[7]   Gene Marcial, "Sales Slippage in December for McDonald's Leads Analysts to Lower Profit Estimates," *The Wall Street Journal,* January 17, 1979, p. 47.

Table 1 THE LARGEST FAST-FOOD CHAINS RANKED BY SALES, 1976*

Rank	Chain	U.S. Food Sales [a]	Percent Increase over 1975	Market Share in 1976
1.	McDonald's	$2,730.0	21.0	19.6
2.	Kentucky Fried Chicken	1,165.0	16.6	8.4
3.	Burger King	741.6	20.7	5.3
4.	International Dairy Queen	684.0	10.4	4.9
5.	Pizza Hut	374.2	38.2	2.7
6.	Howard Johnson's	358.0	0.8	2.6
7.	Sambo's	348.4	32.4	2.5
8.	Hardee's	324.3	8.9	2.3
9.	Jack-in-the-Box	323.4	17.8	2.3
10.	Burger Chef	305.0	7.0	2.2
18.	Wendy's[b]	187.0	151.1	1.3

* "The Fast-Food Stars: Three Strategies for Fast Growth," *Business Week*, July 11, 1977, p. 56.

[a] Sales are reported in millions of dollars, and include sales franchises and company-owned stores.

[b] Wendy's is included in this list because of its exceptional growth within the industry.

COMPANY BACKGROUND

In 1978, or the end of the first quarter-century of operation, McDonald's had served 25 billion hamburgers with sales of more than $16.5 billion. A total of 4,085 McDonald's outlets were in operation in the United States with 586 in 23 other countries. For the fiscal year 1977, sales by all licensed, affiliated, and company-owned restaurants totaled a record $3.7 billion, up by 22 percent from the 1976 total. This rapid growth in volume had matched a string of enviable earnings gains.[8] Fuller financial data are given in Table 2.

Indeed, McDonald's represented one of the classics of American corporate growth stories. The story of McDonald's began in 1954 with Ray Kroc, a 52-year-old milkshake machine salesman, who approached his customers—Richard and Maurice McDonald—with a proposal to sell franchises for the McDonald brothers' "fast-food" concept. The brothers agreed, and Kroc franchised about 200 stores, each of which paid about $950 as a down payment.[9] The opportunities for his company's expansion

[8] McDonald's Corporation, 1977 Annual Report.
[9] *Dun's Review*, December 1977, p. 51.

Table 2 MCDONALD'S CORPORATION AND SUBSIDIARIES
TEN-YEAR FINANCIAL SUMMARY FOR YEAR DECEMBER 31, 1977.

(Figures in Thousands Except Per Share Amounts and Number of Restaurants)

		1977	1976	1975	1974	1973	1972	1971	1970	1969	1968
Systemwide sales	United States	$3,241,000	$2,730,000	$2,256,000	$1,792,000	$1,420,000	$ 667,000	$761,000	$575,000	$445,000	$333,000
	International	497,000	333,000	222,000	151,000	87,000	46,000	23,000	12,000	6,000	2,000
	Total sales	$3,739,000	$3,063,000	$2,476,000	$1,943,000	$1,507,000	$1,033,000	784,000	$587,000	$451,000	$335,000
Revenues	Company-owned restaurants	$1,097,434	$ 928,197	$ 771,552	$ 630,178	$ 510,730	$ 387,253	$269,158	$190,842	$138,833	$ 88,155
	Licensed restaurants	286,773	233,224	185,183	140,850	104,574	68,700	n/a	39,093	30,094	23,047
	Total revenues	$1,406,148	$1,176,436	$ 972,641	$ 785,432	$ 624,254	$ 442,408	$326,041	$233,453	$172,953	$114,511
Before tax Income		$ 266,796	$ 215,534	$ 171,817	$ 132,203	$ 98,628	$ 69,657	$ 51,450	$ 35,358	$ 28,431	$ 19,944
Net income		136,696	109,180	86,802	64,936	49,505	35,714	26,488	18,516	14,512	9,896

Net income per share	3.37	2.69	2.15	1.61	1.23	.90	.69	.51	.43	.30
Stockholder's equity	643,113	516,690	409,376	318,168	253,484	201,334	133,689	106,095	48,482	36,848
Total assets	$1,645,155	$1,372,174	$1,169,340	$ 952,051	$ 723,579	$ 530,028	$586,172	$296,604	$180,380	$184,061
Number of restaurants at year's end										
Operated by licensees	3,184	2,841	2,495	2,157	1,776	1,465	1,253	1,052	929	830
Operated by company	1,338	1,217	1,123	1,009	896	785	644	540	369	257
Operated by affiliate	149	120	88	66	45	22	7	-	-	-
Total restaurants	4,671	4,178	3,706	3,232	2,717	2,272	1,904	1,592	1,298	1,087

From McDonald's Corporation, Annual Report, 1977.

The data, except for stockholder's equity and total assets, have been restated to include the accounts of pooled businesses for the year of acquisition and the four preceding years.

into a major corporation were limited initially by the franchise fee of 1.9 percent (with 0.5 percent to the McDonald brothers). Kroc soon devised a plan whereby company-owned stores would complement his franchise operations. Franchise stores would now obtain a package which included real estate along with the use of service marks and trademarks.[10]

In the early 1960s, the middle-class population was migrating to the suburbs. The average suburban family had more children, owned more automobiles, and led a more casual life-style than the family of the 1950s. The average suburban family of the 1960s also enjoyed a massive increase in discretionary income.

Kroc examined these factors and derived the concept of QSC—Quality, Service, and Cleanliness—as just what the fast-food market needed.[11] Twenty years later Gerald S. Office, Jr., Ponderosa's chairman, commented that:

> *What impresses* [me] *most* [*about McDonald's*] *is the quality of food and service and the cleanliness . . . in the fast food business there's a tendency to lose control with size. But McDonald's has improved with it.*[12]

As a result of this concept and the expansion attributed to it, in 1978 over 90 percent of McDonald's customers lived within 2 miles of the units they patronized.[13]

In 1965, McDonald's became a publicly held company, and at the beginning of 1977, Fred L. Turner succeeded Kroc as chairman and chief executive of McDonald's. Turner had been with McDonald's since 1956, when he applied for a license to run one of Kroc's "limited menu establishments." The business interested Turner tremendously, and he decided that he would rather work for the company than run a McDonald's restaurant. So Turner went to work as the one-man operations department for the young chain. In 1968, Turner—a one-time Fuller brush man—was made president of McDonald's.[14]

A decade later Chairman Turner noted that McDonald's disliked being classified as a "fast-food company." Turner believed the "fast-food" concept connoted a negative relationship, specifically that quality would be

[10]   Roger D. Blackwell, James F. Engel, and W. Wayne Talarzyk, *Contemporary Cases in Consumer Behavior,* "McDonald's Corporation," (New York: Holt, Rinehart, and Winston, 1969), p. 60.

[11]   *Ibid.*

[12]   "The Fast-Food Stars: Three Strategies for Fast Growth," *Business Week,* July 11, 1977, p. 59.

[13]   Tim Metz, "Earnings of Fast-Food Chains Are Seen Rising in '79, Although Stock Prices May Ebb Briefly," *The Wall Street Journal,* December 22, 1978, p. 22.

[14]   *Financial World,* August 15, 1977, p. 26.

compromised for speed. He preferred to regard McDonald's as a "self-service food operation" that sells "a limited number of products a special way."[15]

THE PRODUCT

McDonald's first menu spotlighted the hamburger. Although product expansion altered the limited menu of the restaurant's early days, 25 years later upgraded hamburgers continued to be McDonald's feature. The Big Mac arrived in 1968, and at the end of 1977 was the company's largest selling item.[16] In 1972, the Quarter Pounder was introduced. In an attempt to stay abreast of widened consumer wants, McDonald's introduced hot apple pies, fish sandwiches, Egg McMuffins, and McDonald Land cookies. Indeed, Kroc attributed McDonald's success to "finding something the public wants, something basic and simple, something that can be sold in volume and sold fast."[17]

McDonald's has never manufactured any of the products sold in its restaurants. McDonald's has relied instead on outside suppliers, none of whom get a contract. Suppliers typically sold their products to local distributors, generally at a price negotiated by McDonald's purchasing department. The distributors sold to the individual restaurants.[18] Over 70 percent of the U.S. McDonald's were serviced by central distribution centers, which operated on a "one-stop-shopping" theme. That is, the center handled all food, packaging, and operating supplies. The exceptions were dairy products and buns, which were purchased locally.[19]

Independent processors provided most of the meat, potatoes, and fish used in McDonald's restaurants. To ensure that the ground beef in McDonald's hamburgers met company standards and specifications, the firm has agricultural and technical experts continually inspect the meat through all stages of processing, packaging, and distribution.[20] McDonald's, like Burger King, shipped patties to the individual restaurants in frozen form.[21]

McDonald's 1977 Annual Report stated that a "McDonald's hamburger should—and does—taste the same in London, Tokyo, New York, or Boise, Idaho. Each aspect of our system—equipment engineering, prod-

---

[15] *Dun's Review,* December 1977, p. 51.
[16] *Ibid.*
[17] Blackwell, Engel, and Talarzyk, "McDonald's Corporation," p. 61.
[18] Peter J. Schylen, "How Keystone's Handshake Turned Golden," *Fortune,* March 13, 1978, p. 79.
[19] McDonald's Corporation, 1977 Annual Report.
[20] *Ibid.*
[21] *The Wall Street Journal,* April 5, 1978, p. 1.

uct development, purchasing, training, operations, and so on—is geared to this end.''

THE RUMOR

In 1977, a rumor maintained that Bubble Yum—a product of Life Savers, Inc.—was loaded with spider eggs.[22] The ''foreign-substance-in-the-food rumor'' for 1978 was that McDonald's supplemented the beef in its hamburgers with protein from ground-up red earthworms.[23] According to one source:

> But . . . the tale did have a squirmy logic: hundreds of worm breeders, hooked into buying worm-ranch franchises from promoters who vastly exaggerated the anglers' market, were still trying to unload their live stock.[24]

Commenting on the rumor's impact, McDonald's spokeswoman Joy McCuen said, ''At first, it was something that we laughed at and said 'You've got to be kidding.' But you don't laugh when you can prove sales resistance.''[25] For example, Jim Taylor, owner of four McDonald's restaurants in suburban Atlanta, reported a sales decline of 30 percent and a staff layoff affecting about a third of his employees.[26] Although one McDonald's spokesman stressed that ''systemwide you can't see the effect on sales,''[27] McCuen maintained that sales had been hurt at 40 to 50 McDonald's restaurants in the Atlanta area.[28]

The rumors seemed to be centered in certain regions of Georgia, Kentucky, Ohio, and Indiana, which is why systemwide performance was not affected.[29] The damage was not being done solely to McDonald's, as the negative impact was spreading to other hamburger outlets as well. This effect on competition prompted McDonald's to reject the notion of a competition-inspired smear campaign.[30]

[22] ''Tall Tales: McDevil Burgers?'' *Newsweek,* October 2, 1978.

[23] *The Wall Street Journal,* November 16, 1978, p. 21.

[24] ''A Wormburger Scare,'' *Newsweek,* November 27, 1978, p. 90.

[25] Joe Brown, ''McDonald's Will Attack Rumors of Worm Meat,'' *The Atlanta Journal and Constitution,* November 14, 1978, p. 8-D.

[26] *Newsweek,* November 27, 1978, p. 90

[27] *The Wall Street Journal,* November 16, 1978, p. 21.

[28] *The Atlanta Journal and Constitution,* November 14, 1978, p. 8-D.

[29] *The Wall Street Journal,* November 16, 1978, p. 21.

[30] *Ibid.*

The origins of the rumor, however, were a mystery. The rumor was believed to have started in May 1978 in Chattanooga, although McDonald's received the majority of customer inquiries in early-to-mid November. Initial reports indicated that people had seen a report on "60 Minutes" or "20/20" indicating that McDonald's added worm to the burgers to increase the protein content. The firm investigated this possibility by speaking several times with representatives of CBS and ABC. Corporate investigator Steve Sammons also talked to representatives of the syndicated Phil Donahue Show. Sammons obtained statements from all three claiming to have "had never run anything" suggesting that McDonald's added earthworms to its hamburgers.[31]

McDonald's also asked a Tulane University social psychologist, Fred Koenig, for help in determining the origin of the rumor. Koenig offered several ideas about the type of person who would circulate the story, but doubted whether the origin of the story would ever be unearthed.[32]

Koenig suggested that the originator was "probably somewhat insecure, of lower status and is spreading it to someone of higher status." Similarly, it could have spread from within a specific neighborhood, originating with one lower-status person who wanted to impress a neighbor of high status. Koenig further believed the rumor has been spread "by people with less education, since anybody who knows anything about food processing is not going to believe that red worms are used in hamburgers because, for one thing, they cost too much." He stated that "it's also possible that the rumor started with a nutritionally-minded person upset with the intrusion of a restaurant into their community or someone concerned with McDonald's replacing 'home virtues' with an impersonal fast-food meal."[33]

Red worms were apparently used in the rumor because their appearance is similar to that of raw red meat. Koenig added that tales about worms in the hamburger business are nothing new. He referred specifically to a worm rumor at McDonald's in Nova Scotia several years ago. But, said Koenig, "it didn't affect the sales because they eat anything in Nova Scotia."[34]

Restaurants in Georgia, Kentucky, Ohio, and Indiana were not as fortunate.

---

[31] *The Atlanta Journal and Constitution,* November 14, 1978, p. 8-D.

[32] John Reetz, "Who's Out to Get Ronald? McDonald's May Never Know," *The Atlanta Journal and Constitution,* November 19, 1978, p. 22-A.

[33] *Ibid.*

[34] *Ibid.*

BACK AT HEADQUARTERS

Doug Timberlake, McDonald's vice president, agreed with Tim Hodges that the situation had lost its humorous aspects. But just what combination of tactics would combat the negative impact without spreading the content of the rumor to other parts of the country? Timberlake had jotted down a few possible plans of attack. He also noted some possible directives, potential consequences, and general concerns associated with each approach. Of course, the list was not exhaustive, and one approach would not necessarily preclude the use of others.

The alternatives were:

1. Do nothing. Let the rumor ride itself out.

Managers would be encouraged to continue to deal—individually and honestly—with the customer calls. But was this realistic or fair? Would this be an efficient use of managers' time? Would restaurant operations and control suffer because managers were too busy fighting the rumors?

2. Try the press-conference approach. Combat damaging rumors by turning them into news.

Would mass media be able to discount the personal influence of a rumor passed from person to person? Would the people who are unaware of the rumor become alarmed and skeptical of the restaurant, even if they don't believe the tale?

3. Institute advertising that attacks the rumor directly.

Essentially a modified press-conference approach, going directly to consumers would eliminate any potential misquotations and would allow total control over the context of the message.

4. Devise advertising messages that stress 100 percent pure beef as the only ingredient in McDonald's patties.

Would the public feel that we have something to hide because we are not confronting the issue directly? Would the increased advertising fuel the American public's distrust in anything "big?" Americans were apparently skeptical of large institutions—government, the CIA, ITT, Lockheed. Would McDonald's be any less susceptible to the public's critical eye?

Note: In November 1978, McDonald's began a series of advertisements featuring former network newscaster Frank Blair. Mr. Blair's message was that, as a newsman, it was his responsibility to get the facts behind every story, and that he knew for sure that McDonald's hamburgers were 100 percent beef. The rumor was not specifically mentioned.

At about the same time, a number of Wendy's ads appeared featuring actor Danny Thomas, whose St. Jude Charity project Wendy's had helped promote at Christmas. Mr. Thomas stressed the wholesome purity of the Wendy's product, and avoided mentioning the rumor.

Neither of these campaigns had been as successful as had been anticipated.

LITTON INDUSTRIES, INC.*

INTRODUCTION

Fridays were always the worst day of the week for Marc Stillwell. As an Administrative Law Judge for the Federal Trade Commission, he frequently considered his workload burdensome, but Fridays always seemed the worst. While many civil servants spent the afternoon clearing off their desks preparing to start off fresh the following Monday, Stillwell was cramming his briefcase with case files and court briefs that would require his attention over the weekend. He felt he would be lucky if he could spare the time to watch a little football on Sunday, judging by the bulge in his briefcase.

The Litton Industries case decision had to be made soon, and as the presiding Administrative Law Judge he would have to prepare a detailed decision, including his reasoning for the conclusions reached. The FTC staff attorneys and the Litton attorneys had both filed their final statements containing their arguments and findings of fact, and he would have to sort out from these conflicting documents what was actually correct.

Although it was not surrounded by the heavy publicity that characterized some of the more dramatic cases on which he had worked in the past, the Litton case was important because it contained some important issues concerning the use of surveys in advertising, and the increasing use of comparisons between competitors in advertising with actual names of competitors being used. He knew it was FTC policy to encourage advertising that uses factual data, such as that obtained from surveys, and that the agency also wanted to encourage comparative advertising. At the same time, he had to decide, in this case, if these goals conflicted with another FTC policy—that no advertising should be unfair or deceptive.

* This case was co-authored by Dr. Kenneth L. Bernhardt, Associate Professor of Marketing, Georgia State University.

In addition to deciding if Litton had engaged in unfair or deceptive advertising and if they had adequate substantiation for the claims made, he also had to determine an appropriate remedy if the company was found guilty. A proposed order had been recommended by the FTC staff attorneys, and he would have to decide if that was reasonable or whether some other order would be better.

THE COMPANY

Litton Industries, Inc., was founded in November 1953 as a small electronics firm in San Carlos, California. Revenues that year were less than $3 million. By the end of fiscal 1978, Litton was the ninety-ninth largest U.S. corporation, with revenues exceeding $3.65 billion.[1] But Litton's management still held to a strategy laid out in the company's first annual report:

> *The company's management [has] planned to first establish a base of profitable operations in advanced electronic development and manufacturing. Utilizing this base, the plan contemplates building a major electronics company by developing new and advanced products and programs and by acquiring others having potential in complementing fields. . . . This plan is designed to establish strong proprietary product values and a "broad base" on which to grow—a profitable balance between commercial and military customers and an integrated but diversified line of electronic products.[2]*

By 1980, Litton had grown to become a widely diversified, international industrial conglomerate with 175 manufacturing and research facilities in the United States and around the world, employing over 90,400 people. The corporation produced such products as business computer systems, business furniture, calculators, copiers, Royal typewriters, Sweda cash registers and POS/retail information systems, machine and hand tools, material-handling systems, specialty metal products, electronic components, biomedical equipment, paper and printed products, medical professional publications (including the *Physicians Desk Reference),* textbook publications, airborne navigation systems, electronic signal surveillance equipment and so on. Litton's Ingalls Shipbuilding subsidiary built U.S. Navy destroyers and nuclear submarines. Table 1 on page 156 contains Litton's sales breakdown by product line.

As can be seen, Litton Industries produced primarily commercial, industrial, and defense-related products. However, the company's Electronic and Electrical Products division successfully produced and marketed at least one major consumer good—microwave ovens.

[1] "The Forbes 500s," *Forbes* (May 14, 1979), p. 234.
[2] Litton Industries, Inc., *Annual Report, Fiscal 1978,* p. 4.

MICROWAVE OVENS

Microwave cooking was first developed shortly after World War II as an offshoot of advancements in radar technology. Although microwave ovens were introduced as early as 1954, principally for institutional and commercial use, consumer models were not mass marketed until early 1970. Improvements in production technology corresponded in time with tremendous demand for convenience goods and fast-food services. In 1970 the industry sold about 40,000 microwave ovens. The Association of Home Appliance Manufacturers estimated that by the end of 1978, market penetration for microwave ovens in American Households would reach 10 percent. Over 2.8 million ovens were sold in 1979, representing sales of over $1.25 billion.

The working principle of microwave cooking is actually quite simple. Microwaves are electromagnetic or radio waves in the gigahertz (in excess of one billion hertz or cycles per second) frequency range with wavelengths between one and one hundred centimeters. The Federal Communication Commission, which regulates all forms of electromagnetic transmissions, has set aside a frequency range equal to 2.45 gigahertz for the use of microwave ovens.

The device inside of these ovens that emits the microwave energy is known as a "magnetron microwave generator." Microwaves, if applied with sufficient energy, will cause the water molecules within food substances to become agitated and start to vibrate. This vibrating action generally begins, unlike conventional cooking, deep within the middle of whatever is being cooked. The vibrating molecules create friction which heats the food, generally in one-fourth the time it would take conventionally.

All microwave ovens work on this simple principle, although most manufacturers have added features to facilitate the process further or to overcome some of the problems inherent in microwave cooking. Generally, foods cooked in a microwave oven are more nutritional and have a better, more natural flavor than conventionally prepared foods, due to less water and natural vitamin content loss. Of course, the most desired feature remains the faster cooking speed.

Microwave cooking is not suitable for all types of food, a factor that ensures conventional ovens will not become obsolete in the near future. Meats and bread products are notable "problem" foods: Meat because it cooks from the inside out in a microwave oven and tends not to brown on the outside, and bread products because their water content quickly evaporates, causing it to harden or to not rise properly. Manufacturers are trying to overcome these problems. Older model ovens were generally

Table 1 LITTON'S SALES BREAKDOWN

Sales and Service Revenues by Product Line—Continuing Operations (Unaudited)

(thousands of dollars) Year Ended July 31,	1978	1977	1976	1975	1974
Business Systems and Equipment					
Business machines and retail information systems	$ 448,109	$ 373,489	$ 389,970	$ 431,941	$ 450,805
Typewriters and office copiers	321,970	302,078	284,903	284,385	302,344
Office products, furniture, and fixtures	177,510	157,899	147,408	143,396	151,638
Intrasegment eliminations	(855)	(1,134)	(1,394)	(9,821)	(2,881)
	946,734	832,332	820,887	849,901	901,906
Industrial Systems and Services					
Machine tools	282,475	252,238	223,678	242,909	219,453
Resource exploration	235,494	161,206	159,632	177,436	135,705
Material handling	95,559	79,705	81,513	91,423	96,677
	613,528	493,149	464,823	511,768	451,835
Electronic and Electrical Products					
Microwave cooking products	**179,640**	**160,104**	**129,400**	**69,431**	**50,585**
Medical and electronic products	160,964	187,762	220,776	217,163	192,527
Electronic and electrical components	398,241	336,742	305,389	313,395	306,880
Intrasegment eliminations	(6,759)	(8,492)	(7,527)	(4,800)	(3,346)
	732,086	676,116	648,038	595,189	546,646

Paper, Printing, and Publishing					
Specialty paper, printing and forms	215,561	194,108	199,630	190,517	165,126
Educational and professional publishing	74,924	64,676	57,388	61,593	64,488
	290,485	258,784	257,518	252,110	229,614
Advanced Electronic Systems					
Navigation and control systems	315,045	276,719	286,278	248,034	212,935
Communications and electronic data systems	222,427	203,809	187,236	205,154	185,761
Intrasegment eliminations	(7,520)	(5,502)	(4,797)	(4,725)	(5,241)
	529,952	475,026	468,717	448,463	393,455
Marine Engineering and Production	616,069	792,213	794,142	906,851	642,618
	3,728,854	3,527,620	3,454,125	3,564,282	3,166,074
Intersegment eliminations	(89,935)	(96,852)	(120,429)	(153,433)	(164,191)
Miscellaneous	14,290	12,156	20,856	1,340	898
Sales and service revenues—continuing operations	$3,653,209	$3,442,924	$3,354,552	$3,412,189	$3,002,781

The above table sets forth the sales and service revenues of continuing operations by classes of similar products or services within the business segments.

Source: Litton Industries, Inc., *1978 Annual Report*

powered at a fixed energy level. Newer models, with a variable temperature feature, can emit microwaves intermittently or at different power settings up to the FCC maximum of 625 watts, which assists in more uniform cooking.

In the 1970s, advancements in another type of technology took place, which vastly affected the nature of microwave cooking. The development of silicon chips and microcircuitry was quickly adopted by the appliance industry to simplify and automate many procedures. Many of today's microwave ovens incorporate such "mini-computers" to facilitate cooking processes. For example, Litton's newest microwave oven, the Model 560 Meal-In-One Oven, uses a microprocessor with four levels of memory. This oven "knows" how to cook, reheat, or defrost 47 types of frequently prepared foods with just a touch of a button on a keyboard-like control panel.

Litton's history in electronic technology allowed the company to be one of the first manufacturers of consumer model microwave ovens. By 1979, the company was the largest manufacturer with a 25 percent market share. Amana, a division of the Raytheon Corp., and another early pioneer in the microwave cooking field, was the second largest producer with 20 percent of the market, followed by Sharp, General Electric, and Tappan with 15, 10, and 10 percent shares respectively. Litton's microwave sales contributed almost $180 million in revenues to the company in 1978.

PRIMARY DEMAND

Until 1978, microwave oven sales for the industry had been increasing at an annual rate exceeding 45 percent and it was estimated that by 1985 almost 50 percent of American households would be using the product. Microwave ovens were capable of handling over 80 percent of a household's normal cooking.

Demand for microwaves began to fall off sharply in mid-1978, surprising analysts who expected sales to begin to decline only after market penetration of America's 80 million households exceeded the 20 percent level. In the first six months of 1978, unit sales were only 14 percent ahead of the same period in the previous year. Comparatively, the growth rate for the first six months of 1977 was 43 percent. This represented a shakeout period in the industry with two manufacturers, Farberware and Admiral, dropping out of the American microwave market.

Industry experts generally concurred on several reasons for the unexpected slump. By 1978 there were 35 different manufacturers with microwave models on the U.S. market. The proliferation of brands, each with its own array of special features, was believed to have injected a great deal of confusion into consumer purchasing decisions. The complicated controls on many of the models also was believed to have scared off potential buyers.

Because it was a new and fairly expensive product, the proper marketing strategy called for knowledgable salespeople to explain and demonstrate the microwave oven's many uses. Industry analysts pointed out that by 1978 most dealers were not putting enough effort into actual cooking demonstrations and other "push-type" marketing stategies. This became especially true as mass merchandise retail chains began selling the product. Such stores had neither the time nor the trained salespeople to devote to the kind of personal selling required for such a product.

Another speculation as to the cause for the sudden slump in sales was related to market segmentation. As the manufacturers struggled to differentiate their products from those of their competitors, they began to upgrade their products by adding such items as probes that could automatically cook meat to the correct temperature, rotating carousels to ensure uniform cooking, browning units, defrosting cycles, variable temperature controls, memory storage, delayed timing controls and so forth. Most manufacturers continued to market the basic, no-frills oven models, but emphasis was placed on the deluxe-type models with all the added features. There was a good reason for this, since the fastest growing market segment, representing 32 percent of dollar volume sold, was for the expensive model ovens with retail prices of $450 and up. Litton's Model 560, for example, retailed for $629 and had been very popular.

To date, therefore, there had been very little incentive for manufacturers and retailers to lower prices to encourage demand. Members of the market segment for the more expensive models tended to have higher incomes and better educations, and were more likely to be familiar with the microwave principle, and to have seen it in actual use by friends or relatives. Such consumers were less likely to misunderstand the safety-related factors that had caused much apprehension in the early, introductory stages.

Industry experts had begun to wonder whether sales to this particular market segment had reached the saturation level. Many felt that it was time that microwave manufacturers began to concentrate on selling to the larger, more price-conscious market segment that had remained mostly untapped. Research studies over a period of several years showed that there was a large segment of the market (86 percent) who consistently had stated that they had no plans to purchase a microwave oven. Trade analysts felt that many of these people could be encouraged to buy if prices were lower.

Although it remained slightly ahead of the industry with a 20 percent growth rate in 1978, Litton felt the effects of the general sales slump. The company reacted aggressively. The 1978 advertising budget already had been increased by 13.5 percent to over $21.5 million. To counter declining demand, the 1979 ad budget was increased to about $50 million. The company decided to stress product education as the key to market growth, and a large portion of the budget was earmarked for sales training, dealer promotions, and in-store demonstrations. Over 2,000 home economists were hired across the country to demonstrate the product in appliance and department stores, shopping malls and grocery chains.

The Federal Trade Commission Complaint

On January 31, 1979, the Federal Trade Commission formally issued a complaint against Litton stating that some of their earlier advertisements constituted "unfair and deceptive acts or practices in or affecting commerce and unfair methods of competition in or affecting commerce in violations of Section 5 of the Federal Trade Commission Act."[3] The complaint concerned a series of 1976 and 1977 ads in such publications as *Newsweek* and *The Wall Street Journal* that featured the results of an "independent" survey. The FTC charged that the ads claimed that:

1. The majority of independent microwave oven service technicians would recommend Litton to their customers.
2. The majority of independent microwave oven service technicians are of the opinion that Litton microwave ovens are superior in quality to all other brands.
3. The majority of independent microwave oven service technicians are of the opinion that Litton microwave ovens require the fewest repairs of all microwave brands.
4. The majority of independent microwave oven service technicians have Litton microwave ovens in their home.[4]

The FTC stated that such claims were deceptive and unfair and that there was "no reasonable basis of support for the representations in those advertisements, at the time those representations were made."[5]

The FTC formally alleged that the survey in no way could be described as "independent." They claimed that Litton hired Custom Research, Inc. to conduct the survey but that Litton designed the survey instrument and analyzed the results themselves and that Custom Research had only engaged in telephoning the respondents who were selected from a list of names supplied by Litton.

---

[3] Federal Trade Commission Complaint, Docket No. 9123 (January 31, **1979**), p. 5.
[4] *Ibid.*, p. 2.
[5] *Ibid.*, p. 4.

The FTC also claimed that the list of respondents were drawn exclusively from a list of Litton-authorized microwave service agencies. The surveys also failed to show that the respondents knew enough about competing brands of microwave ovens to make a comparison to Litton's ovens. The Commission also stated that the base number of respondents was too small to have any statistical significance.

In summary, "the sample surveyed was not representative of the population of independent microwave oven service technicians and the survey was biased,"[6] (Refer to Figure 1 for a copy of the Federal Trade Commission complaint, as well as Figure 2 for a sample copy of the Litton advertisement in question.)

The filing of the FTC complaint was accompanied with the usual notice stating the time and place of an administrative hearing at which Litton would have to show cause why it should not be subject to a cease-and-desist order. Litton did not choose to enter into a consent agreement, whereby the company would have not have admitted any of the charges and would have negotiated an order outlining an agreed upon remedy.

At the time the complaint was originally issued, a Litton spokesperson made the following public response to the charges:

> *We employed an independent research firm to survey our authorized independent microwave service agencies numbering over 500 throughout the U.S. Litton surveyed only those servicemen who repaired at least two brands of ovens, and tabulated their response only as to the brands they serviced. Litton feels the claims made in the ads, that up to 80 percent of the servicemen would recommend purchase of Litton microwave ovens, were accurately represented, and that the FTC's concerns are unfounded.[7]*

THE FEDERAL TRADE COMMISSION

The Federal Trade Commission is an independent law enforcement agency charged by the Congress with protecting the public—consumers and businesspeople alike—against anticompetitive behavior and unfair and deceptive business practices.

The Commission has authority to stop business practices that restrict competition or that deceive or otherwise injure consumers, as long as these practices fall within the legal scope of the Commission's statutes, affect interstate commerce and involve a significant public interest. Such practices may be terminated by cease-and-desist orders issued after an administrative

---

[6] *Ibid.*

[7] "Litton Industries, Inc.'s Microwave Oven Ads Deceptive, FTC Says," *The Wall Street Journal* (February 2, 1979), p. 4.

FIGURE 1 Litton Complaint and Proposed Order

Litton Complaint and Proposed Order

UNITED STATES OF AMERICA
BEFORE FEDERAL TRADE COMMISSION

In the Matter of	)	
	)	
LITTON INDUSTRIES, INC.	)	DOCKET NO. 9123
	)	
a corporation.	)	

COMPLAINT

Pursuant to the provisions of the Federal Trade Commission Act, and by virtue of the authority vested in it by said Act, the Federal Trade Commission, having reason to believe that Litton Industries, Inc., a corporation (hereafter "Respondent" or "Litton"), has violated the provisions of said Act, and it appearing to the Commission that a proceeding by it in respect thereof would be in the public interest, hereby issues its complaint stating its charges in that respect as follows:

PARAGRAPH ONE: Litton Industries, Inc. is a corporation, organized, existing and doing business under and by virtue of the laws of the State of Delaware, with its executive office and principal place of business located at 360 North Crescent Drive, Beverly Hills, California 90210. Litton's Microware Cooking Products Division is located a 1405 Xenium Lane North, Minneapolis, Minnesota 55441.

PARAGRAPH TWO: Litton is now, and for some time in the past has been, engaged in the manufacture, distribution, advertising, and sale of various products including microwave ovens.

PARAGRAPH THREE: Respondent Litton causes the said products, when sold, to be transported from its place of business in various states of the United States to purchasers located in various other states of the United States and in the District of Columbia. Respondent Litton maintains, and at all times mentioned herein has maintained, a course of trade in said products in and affecting commerce. The volume of business in such commerce has been and is substantial.

PARAGRAPH FOUR: In the course and conduct of said business, Litton has disseminated and caused the dissemination of advertisements for microwave ovens manufactured by Litton, by various means in or affecting commerce, including magazines and newspapers distributed by the mail and across state lines, for the purpose of inducing and which were likely to induce, directly or indirectly, the purchase of said microwave ovens.

PARAGRAPH FIVE: Typical and illustrative of the advertisements so disseminated or caused to be disseminated by Litton are the advertisements attached as Exhibits A, B, C and D* designated as the "initial consumer microwave independent technician survey advertisement," the "revised consumer microwave independent technician survey advertisement," the "initial commercial microwave independent technician survey advertisement," and the "revised commercial microwave independent technician survey advertisement," respectively.

PARAGRAPH SIX: In Exhibit A, the "initial consumer microwave independent technician survey advertisement," printed in The Wall Street Journal, October 25 and December 13, 1976, and elsewhere, and in Exhibit B, the "revised consumer microwave independent technician survey advertisement," printed in HFD Retailing Home Furnishings, August 22, 1977, and in other advertisements substantially similar thereto, Litton has represented, directly or by implication, that:

1. The majority of independent microwave oven service technicians would recommend Litton to a friend.
2. The majority of independent microwave oven service technicians are of the opinion that Litton microwave ovens are the easiest to repair of all microwave oven brands.
3. The majority of independent microwave oven service technicians are of the opinion that Litton microwave ovens are superior in quality to all other microwave oven brands.
4. The majority of independent microwave oven service technicians are of the opinion that Litton microwave ovens require the fewest repairs of all microwave oven brands.
5. The majority of independent microwave oven service technicians have Litton microwave ovens in their homes.
6. Representations 1-5 were proved by a survey independently conducted by Custom Research Inc., in June 1976.

PARAGRAPH SEVEN: In Exhibit C, the "initial commercial microwave independent technician survey advertisement," printed in Hospitality (Restaurant), November 1976, and elsewhere, and in Exhibit D, the "revised commercial microwave independent technician survey advertisement," printed in Restaurant Business, September 1977, and elsewhere, and in other advertisements substantially similar thereto, Litton has represented, directly or by implication, that:

1. The majority of independent microwave oven service technicians would recommend Litton to their customers.
2. The majority of independent microwave oven service technicians are of the opinion that Litton commercial microwave ovens are superior in quality to all other microwave oven brands.
3. The majority of independent microwave oven service technicians are of the opinion that Litton commercial microwave ovens are the easiest to repair on location of all microwave oven brands.
4. The majority of independent microwave oven service technicians are of the opinion that Litton commercial microwave ovens require the fewest repairs of all microwave oven brands.

---

*For Exhibit A of this complaint, see Exhibit 2-A. Exhibits B, C, and D of this complaint are not included here.

(continued)

FIGURE 1 *(continued)*

5. The majority of independent microwave oven service technicians are of the opinion that Litton commercial microwave ovens are the least costly to maintain in operation over time of all microwave oven brands.

6. Representations 1-5 were proved by an April 1976 survey independently conducted by Custom Research, Inc.

In addition, in Exhibit C, Litton has represented, directly or by implication, that Litton is the best commercial microwave oven buy and that this representation was proved by the above-referenced survey.

PARAGRAPH EIGHT: In Exhibits A and B, and in other advertisements substantially similar thereto, Litton has represented, directly or by implication, that:

1. Litton microwave ovens are superior in quality to all other microwave oven brands.

2. Litton microwave ovens are the easiest to repair of all microwave oven brands.

3. Litton microwave ovens require the fewest repairs of all microwave oven brands.

PARAGRAPH NINE: In Exhibits C and D, and in other advertisements substantially similar thereto, Litton has represented directly or by implication, that:

1. Litton commercial microwave ovens are superior in quality to all other microwave oven brands.

2. Litton commercial microwave ovens are the easiest to repair on location of all microwave oven brands.

3. Litton commercial microwave ovens require the fewest repairs of all microwave oven brands.

4. Litton commercial microwave ovens are the least costly to maintain in operation over time of all microwave oven brands.

PARAGRAPH TEN: In truth and in fact, the April and June 1976 technician surveys conducted for Litton by Custom Research, Inc., do not prove the representations listed in PARAGRAPHS SIX and SEVEN, for reasons including but not limited to the following:

(a) The survey respondents were drawn exclusively from the list of Litton authorized microwave oven service agents. As such the sample surveyed was not representative of the population of independent microwave oven service technicians and the surveys were biased.

(b) The surveys failed to establish that the survey respondents possessed sufficient expertise with either (1) microwave ovens or (2) competitive brands of microwave ovens to qualify as respondents for a microwave oven comparative brand survey.

(c) In some paired comparisons, the results lacked statistical significance because the base number was too small.

(d) The surveys conducted for Litton by Custom Research, Inc., were not in fact independent surveys. The surveys were designed and analyzed by Litton employees. The role of Custom Research was limited to placing the telephone calls, from a list of names supplied by Litton and conducting the inverviews, from a questionnaire supplied by Litton.

For the above reasons, representation 6 in PARAGRAPHS SIX and SEVEN is false. Therefore, representation 6, contained in Exhibits A, B, C and D, was, and is deceptive and unfair.

PARAGRAPH ELEVEN: In Exhibits A, B, C and D, and other advertisements substantially similar thereto, Litton has represented, directly or by implication, that it had a reasonable basis of support for the representations contained in those advertisements, at the time those representations were made. In truth and in fact, for the reasons enumerated in PARAGRAPH TEN, Litton had no reasonable basis of support for the representations listed in PARAGRAPHS SIX, SEVEN, EIGHT and NINE, at the time those representations were made. Therefore, the representations listed in PARAGRAPHS SIX, SEVEN, EIGHT and NINE were, and are, deceptive and unfair.

PARAGRAPH TWELVE: In the course and conduct of the aforesaid business, and at all times mentioned herein, Litton has been and is now in substantial competition in commerce with corporations, firms, and individuals engaged in the sale and distribution of microwave ovens of the same general kind and nature as those sold by Litton.

PARAGRAPH THIRTEEN: The use by Litton of the aforesaid unfair and deceptive statements, representations and practices has had, and now has, the capacity and tendency to mislead members of the consuming public into the purchase of substantial quantities of microwave ovens manufactured by Litton.

PARAGRAPH FOURTEEN: The aforesaid acts and practices of Litton, as herein alleged, were, and are, all to the prejudice and injury of the public and of respondent's competitors and constituted, and now constitute, unfair and deceptive acts or practices in or affecting commerce and unfair methods of competition in or affecting commerce in violation of Section 5 of the Federal Trade Commission Act.

WHEREFORE, THE PREMISES CONSIDERED, the Federal Trade Commission on this 31st day of January 1979, issues its complaint against said respondent.

NOTICE

Notice is hereby given to the respondent hereinbefore named that the 19th day of March 1979, at 10:00 o'clock A.M. is hereby fixed as the time and Federal Trade Commission Offices, Gelman Building, 2120 "L" Street, Northwest, Washington, D.C. 20580, as the place when and where a hearing will be had before an administrative law judge of the Federal Trade Commission, on the charges set forth in this complaint, at which time you will have the right under said Act to appear and show cause why an order should not be entered requiring you to cease and desist from the violations of law charged in this complaint.

You are notified that the opportunity is afforded you to file with the Commission an answer to this complaint on or before the thirtieth (30) day after service of it upon you. An answer in which the allegations of the complaint are contested shall contain a concise statement of the facts constituting each ground of defense, and specific admission, denial, or explanation of each fact alleged in the complaint or, if you are without knowledge thereof, a statement to that effect. Allegations of the complaint not thus answered shall be deemed to have been admitted.

If you elect not to contest the allegations of fact set forth in the complaint, the answer shall consist of a statement that you admit all of the material allegations to be true. Such an answer shall constitute a waiver of hearings as to the facts alleged in the complaint, and together with the complaint will provide a record basis on which the administrative law judge shall file an initial decision containing appropriate findings and conclusions and an appropriate order disposing of the proceeding. In such answer you may, however, reserve the right to submit proposed

(continued)

FIGURE 1 *(continued)*

findings and conclusions and the right to appeal the initial decision to the Commission under Section 3.52 of the Commission's Rules of Practice for Adjudicative Proceedings.

Failure to answer within the time above provided shall be deemed to constitute a waiver of your right to appear and contest the allegations of the complaint and shall authorize the administrative law judge, without further notice to you, to find the facts to be as alleged in the complaint and to enter an initial decision containing such findings, appropriate conclusions and order.

The following is the form of order which the Commission has reason to believe should issue if the facts are found to be as alleged in the complaint. If, however, the Commission should conclude from the record facts developed in any adjudicative proceedings in this matter, that the proposed order provisions as to Litton Industries, Inc., a corporation, might be inadequate to fully protect the consuming public, the Commission may order such other relief as it finds necessary or appropriate.

<u>ORDER</u>

IT IS ORDERED, that respondent Litton Industries, Inc., a corporation, (hereinafter "Litton") and its successors, assigns, officers, agents, representatives and employees, directly or through any corporation, subsidiary, division or other device, in connection with the advertising, offering for sale, sale or distribution of any commercial microwave oven, any consumer microwave oven, or any other consumer product, in or affecting commerce, as "commerce" is defined in the Federal Trade Commission Act, do cease and desist from:

1. Representing, directly or by implication, that any commercial microwave oven or consumer microwave oven or any other consumer product:

> (a) is able to perform in any respect, or has any characteristic, feature, attribute, or benefit; or
> (b) is superior in any respect to any or all competing products; or
> (c) is recommended, used, chosen, or otherwise preferred in any respect more often than any or all competing products,

unless and only to the extent that respondent possesses and relies upon a reasonable basis for such representation at the time of its initial and each subsequent dissemination. Such reasonable basis shall consist of competent and reliable scientific surveys or tests, and/or other competent and reliable evidence.

2. Advertising the results of a survey unless the respondents in such survey are a representative sample of the population referred to in the advertisement, directly or by implication.

3. Representing, directly or by implication, by reference to a survey or test, that experts recommend, use or otherwise prefer any commercial microwave oven, any consumer microwave oven, or any other consumer product unless:

> (a) such individuals or experts in fact possess the expertise to evaluate such product(s) with respect to such representation;
> (b) such experts actually exercised their expertise by comparatively evaluating or testing the product(s) and based their stated preferences, findings, or opinions on such exercise of their expertise;
> (c) such representation, to the extent it expresses or implies that such product(s) is superior to competing products, is supported by an actual comparison by such experts and a conclusion therefrom that such product(s) is superior in fact to the competing products with respect to the feature(s) compared.

For purposes of this order, an "expert" is an individual, group or institution held out as possessing, as a result of experience, study or training, knowledge of a particular subject, which knowledge is superior to that generally acquired by ordinary individuals.

4. Making representations, directly or by implication, by reference to a survey and/or test, or to any portions or results thereof, concerning the performance or any characteristic, feature, attribute, benefit, recommendation, usage, choice of, or preference for any commercial microwave oven, any consumer microwave oven, or any other consumer product unless:

(a) such survey and/or test is designed, executed and analyzed in a competent and reliable manner so as to prove the claims represented;
(b) in regard to any claims of superiority based thereon, such survey and/or test establishes that such product is superior to each compared product in respect to which the specific representation is made to a degree that will be discernible to or of benefit to the persons to whom the representation is directed; and
(c) such survey and/or test is represented as fully as necessary to assure that all results which are material to the consumer with respect to the specific representations made are disclosed.

For purposes of this order, a survey or test conducted in a "competent and reliable manner" is one in which one or more persons, qualified by professional training and/or education and/or experience, formulate and conduct the survey or test and evaluate its results in an objective manner, using procedures which are generally accepted in the profession, to attain valid and reliable results. The survey or test may be conducted or approved by (i) a reputable and reliable organization which conducts such surveys or tests as one of its principal functions, (ii) an agency or department of the government of the United States, or (iii) persons employed or retained by Litton Industries, Inc. Provided, however, such organization, agency, or persons must be qualified (as defined above in this paragraph) and conduct and evaluate the survey or test in an objective manner.

5. Misrepresenting in any manner, directly or by implication, the purpose, content, validity, reliability, results or conclusions of any survey and/or test.

6. Failing to maintain accurate records, which may be inspected by Commission staff members upon reasonable notice,

(a) which contain documentation in support or contradiction of any claim included in advertising or sales promotional material disseminated or caused to be disseminated by respondent insofar as the text is prepared, authorized or approved by any person who is an officer or employee of respondent, or of any division, subdivision or subsidiary of respondent, or by any advertising agency engaged for such purpose by respondent, or by any of its divisions or subsidiaries;
(b) which provided or contradicted the basis upon which respondent relied at the time of the initial and each subsequent dissemination of the claim; and
(c) which shall be maintained by respondent for a period of three years from the date such advertising or sales promotional material was last disseminated by respondent or any division or subsidiary of respondent.

(continued)

FIGURE 1 *(continued)*

IT IS FURTHER ORDERED, that the respondent shall, within sixty (60) days after service upon it of this order, file with the Commission a report in writing, setting forth in detail the manner and form in which it has complied with this order.

IT IS FURTHER ORDERED, that the respondent shall forthwith distribute a copy of this order to each of its operating divisions.

IT IS FURTHER ORDERED, that respondent notify the Commission at least thirty (30) days prior to any proposed change in the corporate respondent such as dissolution of subsidiaries, or any other change in the corporation which may affect compliance obligations arising out of this order.

By the Commission

Carol Thomas
Secretary

ISSUED: January 31, 1979

FIGURE 2

Quality is No. 1 at Litton!

76% of the independent microwave oven service technicians surveyed recommend Litton.

Litton Model 419 microwave oven.

Litton leads all brands.

PREFERENCE FOR SPECIFIC BRANDS AMONG TECHNICIANS SERVICING THOSE BRANDS				AVERAGE PREFERENCE FOR LITTON VS. ALL COMPETITION –
Brand To Brand	Litton vs. G.E.	Litton vs. Amana	Litton vs. Magic Chef	(weighted average)
Which Microwave Oven Brand would you recommend to a friend?	59% vs 23%	66% vs. 18%	81% vs. 1%	76% vs. 8%
Which Microwave Oven Brand is easiest to repair?	68% vs. 5%	65% vs. 8%	71% vs. 0%	72% vs. 4%
Which Microwave Oven Brand is the best quality?	48% vs. 16%	50% vs. 26%	69% vs. 1%	63% vs. 9%
Which Microwave Oven Brand requires fewest repairs?	38% vs. 22%	42% vs. 24%	59% vs. 3%	53% vs. 12%
Which Microwave Oven Brand do you have in your home?	48% vs 19%	59% vs. 18%.	70% vs. 5%	67% vs 10%

Among independent technicians servicing Litton and competitive microwave ovens, an average of 76% of those surveyed said they would recommend Litton to a friend. And an average of 63% identified Litton brand ovens as having the best quality.

You'll find it in our full line of advanced countertop microwave ovens, double-oven and combination microwave ranges.

Respondents represent independent microwave oven service agencies, who service at least two brands of microwave ovens, (one of them Litton) and do not represent a factory owned service agency. Percentages add to less than 100% due to other responses (other brands and no preference).
© 1976 Litton Systems, Inc.
*Survey conducted by Custom Research, Inc. Complete survey results available on request.

And in such Litton features as Vari-Cook® oven control, Vari-Temp® automatic temperature control and new Memorymatic™ microwave program cooking. Innovative ways to microwave more foods better.

Need any more reasons to buy Litton? Ask your Litton dealer for a microwave cooking demonstration. For his name and number, call us right now, toll free 800-328-7777.

⊞ **LITTON**
Microwave Cooking
1405 Xenium Lane No. Minneapolis Minnesota 55442

Litton... changing the way America Cooks.

hearing, or by injunctions issued by the Federal courts upon application by the Commission.

In addition, the FTC defines practices that violate the law so that businesspeople may know their legal obligations and consumers may recognize those business practices against which legal recourse is available. The Commission does this through the *Trade Regulation Rules and In-*

dustry Guide issued periodically as "do's and don'ts" to business and industry, and through business advice—called Advisory Opinions—given to individuals and corporations requesting it.

When law violations are isolated rather than industrywide, the FTC exercises its corrective responsibility also by issuing complaints and entering orders to halt false advertising or fraudulent selling or to prevent a businessperson or corporation from using unfair tactics against competition. The Commission itself has no authority to imprison or fine. However, if one of its final cease-and-desist orders or Trade Regulation Rules is violated, it can seek civil penalities in Federal court of up to $10,000 a day for each violation. It can also seek redress for those who have been harmed by unfair or deceptive acts or practices. Redress may include cancellation or reformation of contracts, refunds of money, return of property, and payment of damage.

The Commission defines its role, in its literature, as:

> . . . *protecting the free enterprise system from being stifled or fettered by monopoly or anti-competitive practices and protecting consumers from unfair or deceptive practices.*[8]

The remedies available to the FTC are described in Figure 3.

DECEPTIVE PRACTICES

Deceptive or fraudulent trade practices affecting consumers have centered around the misuse of advertising. The trend in the agency has been to identify and counter the more subtle forms of false advertising. Businesses, in arguing against the FTC's jurisdiction, have relied heavily on the First Amendment's protection, specifically freedom of speech. In 1976, the U.S. Supreme Court held in *Virginia State Board v. Virginia Citizens Consumer Council* that:

> *Although an advertiser's interest is purely economic, that hardly disqualifies him from protection under the First Amendment. . . . It is a matter of public interest that [private economic] decisions, in the aggregate, be intelligent and well informed. To this end, the free flow of commerical information is indispensable.*[9]

[8]   This section is based on *Your FTC: What It Is and What It Does,* pamphlet published by the Federal Trade Commission, Washington DC.

[9]   William Sklar, "Ads Are Finally Getting Bleeped at the FTC," *Business and Society Review* (September 1978), p. 41.

FIGURE 3   FTC Remedies*

I. Assurance of Voluntary Compliance (Non-Adjudicative)

If the Commission believes the public interest will be fully safeguarded, it may dispose of a matter under investigation by accepting a promise that the questioned practice will be discontinued. A number of factors are considered by the Commission in the rare cases in which it accepts such a promise, including (1) the nature and gravity of the practice in question, and (2) the prior record and good faith of the party.

II. Consent Order

Instead of litigating a complaint a respondent may execute an appropriate agreement containing an order for consideration by the Commission. If the agreement is accepted by the Commission, the order is placed on the public record for sixty (60) days during which time comments or views concerning the order may be filed by any interested persons. Upon receipt of such comments or views, the Commission may withdraw its acceptance and set the matter down for a formal proceeding, issue the complaint and order in accordance with the agreement, or take such action as it may consider appropriate. Respondents in consent orders do not admit violations of the law, but such orders have the same force and effect as adjudicative orders.

III. Adjudicative Order

An adjudicative order is based on evidence of record obtained during an adjudicative proceeding that starts when a complaint is issued. The proceeding is conducted before an Administrative Law Judge who serves as the initial trier of facts. After the hearings the judge within 90 days issues his initial decision, which is subject to review by the Commission on the motion of either party or on the Commission's own motion. Appeals from a final Commission decision and order may be made to any proper Court of Appeals and ultimately to the Supreme Court.

IV. Preliminary Injunctions

The Federal Trade Commission has statutory authority to seek preliminary injunctive relief in Federal district court against anyone who is violating or about to violate any provision of law enforced by the FTC.

* *Your FTC: What It Is and What It Does,* Federal Trade Commission, p. 26.

The Court was reaffirming the First Amendment rights of business enterprises through the right of the public to know facts relevant to decision making in the marketplace.

The Supreme Court, however, held in *Bates v. State of Arizona* in 1977 that this First Amendment protection of advertising was entirely dependent upon its truthfulness. "The public and private benefits from commercial speech derive from confidence in its accuracy and reliability."[10] In other cases, the courts have gone on to say that truthfulness in advertising includes completeness of information, as well as the absence of misleading or incorrect information.

The key legal requirement of advertising is that the advertiser have a "reasonable basis" to substantiate the claims made before an ad has been run. Not having a reasonable basis beforehand has been found by the courts to be a violation of Section 5 of the FTC Act as an unfair marketing practice, even if the ad is not deceptive.

It has long been argued that the FTC's simple enforcement power to issue cease-and-desist orders in regard to false advertising was largely ineffectual, since it occurred after the fact and offered no remedial sanctions. Unscrupulous advertisers could get by with a simple admonition to "go and sin no more." Recently, however, the FTC has been increasing the use of such remedial actions as corrective advertising, the most severe of possible penalities facing legitimate marketers.

In 1975, for example, the FTC ordered the Warner-Lambert Co. to include a corrective message in their next $10 million of advertising. The message would have to say that Listerine was not effective against colds and sore throats, a statement which contradicted the company's earlier advertising. The Commission argued that if, under Section 5(b) of the FTC Act, it had:

> . . . the authority to impose the severe and drastic remedy of divestiture in antitrust cases in order to restore competition to a market, surely it had the authority to order corrective advertising to restore truth to the marketplace.[11]

On April 3, 1978, the Supreme Court upheld the FTC order by denying a request to review a lower court's decision.

The FTC, as a rule, has required corrective advertising only when it found that such ads are necessary to present to the public "the honest and complete information" about an advertised product to dispel "the lingering effects of years of false advertising."[12] Without such measures, advertisers would:

[10]　*Ibid.*, p. 42.
[11]　"Corrective Ad Order Not Anti-Free Speech: FTC," *Advertising Age* (September 13, 1976), p. 2.
[12]　*Ibid.*

. . . remain free to misrepresent their products to the public, knowing full well that even if the FTC chooses to prosecute, they will be required only to cease an advertising campaign which by that point will, in all likelihood, have served its purpose.[13]

SUMMARY OF THE FTC'S ARGUMENTS AGAINST LITTON

In a national advertising campaign that stretched over a year and a half in at least 26 states, Litton Microwave Cooking Products promoted the results of a survey of microwave oven service technicians. (See the sample ad at the end of Exhibit 2.) The advertisements represented the majority of service technicians as recommending Litton microwave ovens on the basis of quality, fewest repairs, and ease of repairs. These advertisements are held by the Federal Trade Commission to be unfair and deceptive in that the survey as conducted does not substantiate the advertisements' claims.

The survey is represented as an independent survey conducted by Custom Research, Inc. In fact, Litton designed the survey, developed the questionnaire, provided the sampling frame, and analyzed the results. Custom Research personnel made the actual phone interviews.

Errors existed in the survey design, which biased the results of the study, thus precluding the results being projected to the population of service technicians as represented in the ads. Litton was aware of these biases prior to the implementation of the ad campaign, but ran the advertisements anyway. A memorandum, sent to executives by Litton's manager of marketing analysis, noted that the surveys were likely to be biased and recommended that the source of the sample be kept confidential. The sample used for survey was limited to those service technicians on a list of 500 Litton-authorized service agencies. No attempt was made to draw a sample from technicians authorized to service other brands of microwave ovens.

Only one technician from each agency and the technician selected by the person answering the phone was interviewed. Even with this limited, easily accessible sample, response rates were between 42 and 47 percent. Little was done to improve the response rate, and what was done is uncertain since no written instructions were provided for interviewers.

With the majority of respondents authorized only by Litton, their familiarity with Litton products would tend to bias their responses. In addition, no screening was conducted to detemine if the respondent had recently or ever serviced Litton or the brand compared, thereby failing to establish a level of expertise necessary for answering the questionnaire.

---

[13] *Ibid.*

With the survey biased to the point that it cannot be held to substantiate the advertisements' claims, the FTC has proposed an order for Litton Industries, the parent corporation, and all divisions, to cease and desist advertisements and representations based on faulty survey techniques or testing. This "strong order," which refers to all of Litton's consumer products and representations, is necessary to "protect the public interest and to deter respondents from future unfair and deceptive acts."

Details of the specific FTC arguments are included in Figure 4.

FIGURE 4   FTC Case Against Litton*

> The findings as developed by the FTC are summarized by the following outline:
>
> **A.** The FTC has *jurisdiction* over the alleged misleading advertisements since substantiation provided by Litton does not constitute a reasonable basis for the advertisement claims.
> **B.** The advertisements are misleading in representing the results of the survey as *projectable to the total population*.
> Problems exist relative to:
> 1. Survey design and statistical significance of the results
> 2. Deficiencies in sampling
> 3. Low response rate
> 4. Representing survey as "independent" survey
> 5. Respondents' possesion of "necessary expertise"
> 6. Respondents' familiarity with Litton as basis for answers
> 7. Definition of "independent technician"
> **C.** The FTC has the right to issue a "strong order."
>
> The national advertisements distributed by Litton has represented, directly or by implication that the majority of independent microwave service technicians:
>
> - would recommend Litton to a friend.
> - are of the opinion that Litton microwaves are the easiest to repair.
> - are of the opinion that Litton microwaves are superior in quality to other brands.
> - are of the opinion that Litton microwaves are the easiest to repair.
> - have Litton microwaves in their homes.
>
> ### A. Jurisdiction
>
> Litton is "engaged in the manufacture, distribution, advertising, and sale of various products including microwave ovens."
> Litton causes their products "to be transported from their place of business . . . to purchasers located in various other states."

* *Your FTC: What It Is and What It Does,* Federal Trade Commission, p. 26.

Litton has been and is now "in substantial competition in commerce with corporations, firms, and individuals engaged in the sale" of microwave ovens similar to those sold by Litton.

National advertisements based on the service technician surveys were disseminated in four magazines, 28 newspapers, and six trade publications.

114 ads ran during a year-and-a-half period.

Litton Industries is a proper respondent to this proceeding since it owns and controls Litton Systems of which Litton Microwave Cooking Products is a division.

B. Survey Results As Advertised Are Misleading.

The advertisements represent the results of the surveys as projectable to the entire population of independent microwave oven service technicians.

The disclaimer attempts (the use of "technicians surveyed" or "of those surveyed") in no way limit the representations of the ads as projectable to all technicians.

"The ad does not state that those service technicians actually interviewed. . . are in any way different from or might hold differing views than the general population of service technicians."

The many defects in the surveys preclude their results from being capable of supporting *"any* conclusions about the attitudes of . . . microwave oven service technicians."

The surveys do not substantiate the advertised claims.

1. Deficiencies in survey design limit the use of the survey.

There were no written interviewer instructions.

The screening questions on Litton's survey were ambiguous in whether the questions applied to "your company" or "you yourself."

Litton failed to test whether the survey results were statistically significant.

2. Deficiencies in *sampling* procedure preclude projecting results to the population.

The surveys "do not provide accurate and reliable results because the surveys suffer from basic deficiencies in sample design."

All sampling was from lists of Litton approved service agencies (Litton had in its possession but did not use lists of Magic Chef and Sharp technicians. Lists were also available for other technicians. Technicians not on Litton's authorized list had no chance of being interviewed.)

Litton asserted that samples obtained from their lists of authorized technicians were representative of all independent service technicians.

Litton vastly underestimated the universe of independent microwave oven service agencies. Litton's National Field Service Manager estimated their list of 500 Litton authorized technicians represented 85–90% of all microwave service technicians and that there were not more than 100 independent agencies servicing microwave ovens that were not on the Litton list. But, in addition to the list of 500 used as a sampling frame, Litton had a list of 1700 servicing dealers who repaired Litton microwave ovens under warranty. Other dealers' service networks included numerous additional service agencies: Sharp, 1,480; General Electric, 5,000; Amana, 2,500; Magic Chef, 1,323. These numbers do not include service networks for additional suppliers such as Tappan, Panasonic, Frymaster, and Hobart.

From the results of a survey by an independent research company for the FTC, it is estimated that Litton excluded from its consumer survey between 414 and 715 (low and high projections) agencies which serviced Litton plus at least one other brand. At most, 421 service agencies were included in Litton's study. Therefore, Litton excluded at least as many service agencies that service Litton and another brand as it included.

Less than half the technicians surveyed were authorized to service the brand they compared to Litton. Many were therefore comparing a brand for which they were authorized with one for which they were not authorized, a source of substantial bias.

Litton's survey methodology of interviewing only one technician per agency, and that technician selected by the person answering the phone, further limited the possibility of a technician in the population being interviewed and led to biases:

a. small firms may have been over-represented
b. technicians who work in the field would have been excluded (Litton's policy was to do warranty work in the home).

3. The *response rates* in the Litton surveys were low (47% for the consumer survey, 42% for the commercial survey) leading to nonresponse biases.

4. "The Litton consumer and commercial surveys were not independent surveys," as the ads suggested. Custom Research merely placed telephone calls to agencies on a list provided by Litton and asked questions from a questionnaire designed by Litton.

5. "Litton failed to establish that the respondents to the . . . surveys possessed the necessary expertise or relied upon that expertise to compare various brands of microwave ovens."

6. The Litton survey respondents, as Litton-authorized technicians, were likely to have expressed preferences for Litton microwave ovens because they were most familiar with that brand.

7. The term "independent microwave oven service technicians" in the ad headlines conveys the meaning of technicians working for independent agencies not owned by a manufacturer. The footnote stating only technicians who serviced Litton microwaves were interviewed, does not qualify the representation of the headline. In fact, a Litton executive was unable to read the fine print of the footnote when asked to do so in court.

C. "The Proposed Order is Required
   to Protect the Public From Further
   Deceptive and Unfair Practices."

The respondents' conduct justifies a broad order to protect the public, since:

1. Litton disseminated a large scale deceptive advertising campaign.
2. The survey claims are a prominent and material component of the advertisements.
3. Litton knowingly disseminated results of a biased study.
4. Litton is a leader in the advertising and marketing of microwave ovens.
5. Litton sells a number of consumer products to the public.

SUMMARY OF LITTON'S DEFENSE

The original complaint in this action challenged certain advertisements run by Litton Industries as being in violation of Section 5 of the Federal Trade Commission Act. The complaint was preceded by a two-year investigation of a limited number of magazine and newspaper ads run October through December of 1976 and August and September of 1977.

Complaint counsel has not met the burden of proving that the advertisements were "deceptive" within the meaning of Section 5. Complaint counsel and their witnesses did nothing more than identify "potential" deviations from *ideal* survey procedures that "might" have influenced the survey results. The procedures used were perfectly reasonable, were in accord with generally accepted survey practice, and yielded reliable results.

Even if one were to assume that a technical violation of Section 5 has occurred, the unintentional, minor nature of any such violation, and the public policy implications of the proposed order dictate that no order should be issued. The proposed order covers all products of Litton Industries. As such, it is punitive in nature, sweeping far beyond the violations, if any, that occurred.

In essence, the complaint charges that the ads contained three categories of representations: (1) alleged representations concerning the actual superiority of Litton microwave ovens over competitor brands, (2) alleged representations concerning the opinions of the "majority" of independent microwave oven service technicians relative to the superiority of Litton microwave ovens over competitive brands, and (3) alleged representations that the Litton surveys "proved" the first two representations. Only the third category is alleged to be false and misleading. Complaint counsel did not seek to prove that Litton was *not* superior to competitive brands on the attributes listed or even that independent service technicians were *not* of that opinion. The main issue was not the specific allegations in the ads but, rather, the sufficiency of the surveys upon which the ads were based.

The key issues, then, are (1) whether the ads were interpreted by the readers of those ads in the manner alleged in the complaint, and if so, (2) if the survey provided a "reasonable basis" for any representations that were made. On both issues, complaint counsel bears the burden of proof. A careful examination of the record reveals that complaint counsel misconceived the nature of their burden of proof and fell far short of meeting it. What the record does reveal is that Litton Industries attempted in good faith to conduct reliable surveys aimed at guiding its future marketing and engineering decisions. The surveys were designed and conducted in a manner that would lead to results upon which a "reasonably prudent businessman" could rely.

The surveys were designed and conducted as part of the business planning function at Litton. Specifically, the surveys were in response to advertising and point-of-sale literature by Amana, which directly and implicitly raised questions concerning the quality of Litton microwave ovens. These Amana ads emphasized the fact that Amana had received an exemption from a warning label requirement and caused certain Litton dealers to question the quality of Litton microwave ovens. As a result of the Amana ads, Litton dealers began encountering problems on the sales floors. Their concerns were communicated to Litton management.

The problems caused by Amana's attacks on the quality of Litton microwave ovens persisted. As a result, product quality became a frequent subject of discussion. The Litton Marketing Division President and Litton Microwave Consumer Products President became very concerned that perhaps the quality of Litton microwave ovens was in fact deteriorating and that they were not being adequately informed. Thus, in the early spring of 1976, Litton decided to investigate the quality of Litton microwave ovens through market research studies.

It was only after Litton conducted its studies for internal management purposes and analyzed the results that the idea of incorporating the results into advertising germinated. That possibility was not even seriously considered until September 1976. In fact, the ads were not included in the advertising budget for 1976–1977. As a result, special approval had to be obtained from the President of Litton Microwave Consumer Products in order to prepare the ads.

The advertising copy that ultimately emerged from the surveys presented the results fairly, at a level of detail so complete that it threatened their effectiveness as an advertising tool. The decision to present the data fully was made so that the ads would withstand any subsequent scrutiny.

This case was chosen by Federal Trade Commission staff as a "test" case for establishing industrywide standards for the advertising of survey results and for the procedures which must be followed in such surveys. Indeed, the Commission press release announcing the issuance of the complaint identified it as a test case that would set standards for advertising surveys and tests. Thus, the key issue is whether Litton had a "reasonable basis" upon which to make the claims included in the ads.

The arguments made by Litton as their defense are summarized in Figure 5.

FIGURE 5   Summary of Litton's Defense

A. Litton Acted in Good Faith in Designing and Conducting the Surveys.

Litton confined the surveys to independent microwave oven service agencies servicing multiple brands, including Litton.

Litton followed the definition of independent microwave service agency commonly used in the industry: one which services but does not sell microwave ovens (this definition excluded over 1,700 Litton dealers who serviced Litton microwave ovens).

Independent service technicians eliminated a potential source of bias since they have no special tie to one manufacturer and are experienced in servicing many makes of microwave ovens.

Litton used a list of independent service agencies identified by a nationally known expert as the most reliable source. The list was nearly exhaustive and thus was representative of the universe of independent service agencies.

Interviewers were specifically instructed to ask for an experienced service technician. The respondent had to have worked for the agency for at least one year. The agency had to have serviced microwave ovens for at least one year. Only technicians who serviced at least two brands, including Litton, were interviewed.

To ensure unbiased representation of all brands serviced by the technicians surveyed, those comparisons were made between Litton and other brands only if the respondents serviced both brands.

A reputable outside organization, Custom Research, Inc., conducted the surveys.

Litton's identity as the research sponsor was never disclosed to the respondents. Also, the interviewers were not aware of the survey purpose.

In each ad, the headline prominently states that results pertain only to those "independent microwave service technicians surveyed."

The ads carefully delineate the groups surveyed, and that the survey was conducted by Custom Research, Inc.

The ads were targeted to a special audience of businesspeople and microwave oven purchasers who were characterized by complaint counsel witnesses as upscale, sophisticated, and knowledgeable.

The total cost of all the survey ads was $215,384.29, only 2.1 percent of the Litton microwave advertising budget for the 1976–1977 year.

When the FTC challenged the initial ads, Litton modified-the ads in response to the criticisms.

B. The Specialized Audience Interpreted the Representations in a Distinctly Limited Manner.

Complaint counsel, under Section 5 of the FTC Act must prove that the ads were interpreted by the audience in a way which suggests "the capacity or tendency to mislead." Yet complaint counsel developed no empirical data nor called any expert to testify on the issue.

Expert testimony concluded that the small portion of the audience which attached any significance to the ads would merely perceive that a study had been done, that it involved people with major biasing ties to a manufacturer who were qualified to service microwave ovens, and that their opinions were obtained on various characterisitics of microwave ovens.

The most which the ads could have possibly done was to convince a small number of readers who were otherwise uncertain that Litton was one of the brands worthy of further considerations.

The ads did not state, as alleged in the Complaint that a "majority" of *all* independent service technicians preferred Litton.

The combination of *low* public trust in surveys, the *lower* public trust in surveys conducted by private companies, the inherent cautiousness of readers of ads generally, and the even greater caution exercised by "upscale" readers lead to the conclusion the interpretations alleged in the Complaint did not occur.

C. The Surveys Were Conducted in Accordance with Generally Accepted Practices in the Survey Research Community

To prove that the Litton surveys did not provide a "reasonable basis" for representations made in the ads, complaint counsel had to establish that (1) generally accepted standards for survey and market research exist within the industry, (2) the procedures followed by Litton represent substantial, unreasonable deviations from those standards, and (3) such deviations resulted in demonstrable biases favoring Litton and thus in advertising which was "deceptive" within the reasoning of Section 5 of the FTC Act. Complaint counsel met *none* of the three requirements.

Expert witnesses were unable to define generally accepted survey research standards.

The Litton survey was, in the opinion of expert witnesses, "indicative of typical industry practice."

D. The Surveys were Conducted in an Accurate and Unbiased Manner.

The universe was carefully defined to eliminate any significant risk of bias.

The Litton surveys were an attempted census of the ascertainable agencies in the universe.

The procedures to respond to the survey were reasonable and produced reliable results.

The use of Litton's authorized service agency lists was proper and introduced no bias into the survey results.

The questionnaires used adequately qualified respondents and produced accurate results.

Response rates were within normal and accepted ranges and did not create any biases.

Test of statistical significance were neither necessary nor proper.

Litton's role in the surveys was consistent with normal survey procedures and with the advertised claims.

Interviewer instruction and supervision was entirely adequate.

JIMMY DON DAVIS:
SALES ETHICS*

Jimmy Don Davis was employed by a major oil company within the marketing division. Although his work encompassed almost every phase of business (e.g., finance, marketing, and production), his main concern lay in three areas. First, he was responsible for about 50 service stations and the dealers who operated them. Second, he acted as facilitator between the oil company and his 10 wholesalers. Third, he was responsible for real estate development within his area. Geographically, the area of responsibility was generally eastern Alabama and western Georgia. His headquarters was located in a town some 70 miles from the company's district office, so that he had personal contact with the district manager no more than once a month.

During his first 7 years with the company, he progressed even more rapidly than he had anticipated. Jimmy Don had begun with the company as a sales representative and was now a district sales supervisor. He was, by all corporate measurements, a successful salesman and employee.

Each town in his sales area could be characterized as a "farm town," in that each had one or more feed and fertilizer stores, a grain elevator, a tractor supply company, and a Farm Bureau Cooperative organization. Virtually every citizen was to some extent dependent on agriculture for his livelihood. The largest town in the area contained two large retail outlets, which could be characterized as discount stores.

At about the time of Jimmy Don's promotion to district sales supervisor, his firm purchased a controlling interest in a fertilizer company. With the increase in leisure time, the lawn fertilizer industry was becoming one of the country's leading growth industries, and the extrapolated economic potential was good. The oil company already had under its trademark some 40,000 retail outlets across the country, and there was some common production expertise between petrochemicals and chemical fertilizer. Furthermore, the philosophy of the gasoline industry was fast becoming a scrambled one of "whatever can be put into or on the car should be sold by the service station," so that the combination seemed like a natural one.

The oil company began producing a lawn fertilizer called "Green Lawn." There were several meetings held to enthuse the salesmen about the product and to explain to them the new "scrambled merchandising" phil-

* This case was prepared by Assistant Professor Ronald P. Allison, Loyola University of New Orleans, and modified by the editors as the basis for class discussion. All rights reserved to Professor Allison.

osophy. They were told that a survey had revealed that the 40,000 service stations could easily sell 50 bags per month for the 3-month lawn fertilizer use period. Because the district manager had committed himself to the survey team sent out by the home office, this became the salesmen's quota. During the meeting, the district manager reiterated this commitment by expressing his confidence that "all the men on his team would carry the ball." The management team reported this to the home office. This quota coincided with the amount that had been projected by management during its analysis of the data upon which the decision to purchase the fertilizer company was based. Since this was a new product, sales were to be monitored very closely.

In terms of units, Jimmy Don became responsible for selling 2,500 bags of Green Lawn fertilizer. His initial success in selling his dealers this product was marginal, because they realized that the season for using lawn fertilizer was very short, about 60 to 90 days in the spring. In fact, Jimmy Don didn't receive his shipment of Green Lawn until the end of the first 30 days of the use period. Management pressure was designed to grow as the season matured. Thirty days after the start of the season, Jimmy Don had to send in a weekly report to the district manager as to the number of bags sold. After 40 days, a biweekly report was necessary; at 60 days, a triweekly report. At 70 days, a report was sent each day, and after 90 days, he had to phone the district manager at the end of each day to tell him what had been sold that day and what plans were being formulated for selling the remaining bags.

At the end of 90 days, his warehouse still had about 2,100 bags of Green Lawn and the phone reports became routine in content. Jimmy Don believed that he had expended every effort to sell the fertilizer. Every ethical sales technique he could think of had been utilized. He had literally run out of ideas, and the sales of other products in his district were suffering from lack of attention.

During one of the routinely embarrassing telephone reports, Jimmy Don's district manager mentioned that Jimmy Don didn't seem to be "on the team," since the other salesmen had already sold their quota. The suggestion by Jimmy Don that these other salesmen might then be able to sell his quota was not met with enthusiasm. Subsequent conversations contained references to "salesmanship not up to usual standards," "lack of team spirit," "perhaps there is need to reevaluate your work record," and "possible need to replace you with someone more actively involved and committed to corporate expectations."

Jimmy Don was faced with an ethical dilemma not of his own making. During the last conversation, the district manager had stated that if Jimmy Don wanted to retain his job, he had to sell the 2,100 bags left in his warehouse within the next 8 days. Yet it was obviously impossible to sell the fertilizer to the service-station dealers, since the season was over. Given these factors, there were at least four alternatives available.

Jimmy Don could, of course, resign from the company. His work record was excellent and the skills he had learned were readily transferable. He would get a very good job recommendation. His was not the only major oil company in the region, and he anticipated very little trouble in finding a similar job with another firm. Furthermore, although he liked the area of the country in which he lived, he was not married and considered himself to be highly mobile.

A second alternative was to wait and see what steps, if any, management would take. This step would be, in essence, calling management's bluff. Jimmy Don found it hard to believe that an intelligent management would actually let a productive salesman be fired because he failed to do an impossible task. On the other hand, the district manager had stated the threat in no uncertain terms and might need to follow through in order to save face with subordinates and his peers.

As a third alternative, he could try some "wheeling and dealing" as a survival device. One method Jimmy Don could use to implement this option was quite simple. The 10 wholesalers he called on were equally divided between consignees and distributors. The oil company provided consignees with certain farm equipment, which they in turn loaned to farm accounts. This equipment included aboveground gasoline storage tanks for farm equipment fuel. When a consignee informed that he had a farm tank that needed replacing, Jimmy Don could simply charge it off and order a replacement. There was no inspection of or set means of disposing of the old tank. It was only necessary to take the consignee's word regarding its condition.

What Jimmy Don could do would be to go to each of his distributors and ask them to buy the fertilizer from him, for which he would give them an equal value of gasoline storage tanks. He would do this by charging off nonexistent farm gasoline tanks in consignee areas and ordering new ones. When the tanks arrived at the consignee's place of business, Jimmy Don would inform the respective distributors, who would then pick them up. This would satisfy management because the Green Lawn fertilizer would show up on the records as having been sold. This would not be the first time actions of this nature had been undertaken in this industry.

Finally, Jimmy Don could take an active stance within the company regarding the absurd position in which he had found himself. The higher levels of management must certainly contain persons of intelligence and insight, and if he pursued the matter diligently enough, he would certainly find some backing at the higher levels. A good place to start might be the current vice president of sales, whom Jimmy Don had met on three occasions. The sales vice president had warmly praised Jimmy Don's work on one occasion, and assured him that "his door is always open" regarding questions or advice. The downside risk of the activist strategy was the all-or-nothing nature of the outcome. Either Jimmy Don or his boss would have to go. It would be inconceivable to imagine the two working in the same division after the actions he was considering.

As he debated alternative strategies, Jimmy Don ran across an article on "whistle blowing" by employees on shady or unethical practices by their employers (see Appendix A). Mechanisms for whistle-blowing had become institutionalized in some firms, and it was very similar to the activist strategy he was considering.

Appendix A: Why People Inform on Their Bosses[1]

In January 1971, the world champion whistle blower, Ralph Nader, gathered a group of associates and admirers together at the Mayflower Hotel in Washington to talk about the fuzzy lines between corporate loyalty and public duty.

The question of the day was: At what point should an employee's obligations to society take precedence over his employer's well being and move him to publicly blow the whistle on defective products, concealed hazards, pollution, public waste, and corruption?

From those discussions has come a new book, *Whistle Blowing,* by Mr. Nader and two colleagues, Peter J. Petkas and Kate Blackwell (Grossman Publishers, Inc., 398 pages, $6.95). It's dull and dated in places, a bit too shrill in others, but it probably deserves far wider readership at all levels of the corporate ladder than it is likely to get.

The book starts with a yawn and ends with a sermon. The first four chapters explain why whistle blowing is good for the soul, good for the free enterprise system, and essential for the nation's well being, designating Dwight Eisenhower "the modern father of whistle blowing" for his farewell address warning Americans to beware the "military industrial complex." The final four discuss strategies for would be whistle blowers, explain what laws are on their side (practically none), and plead for organizational change from within.

[1]   Richard Martin, *The Wall Street Journal,* October 17, 1972, p. 2.

FASCINATING CASE HISTORIES

It's the middle of the book that makes the whole thing worthwhile, 142 pages of brief, fascinating case histories of 33 whistle blowers, detailing their motives and methods, their gains and suffering. They are mostly conscience-stricken persons with little in common but a strong sense of individual responsibility and a determination not to be ignored.

A sampling of some who spoke out against corrupt, illegal or otherwise harmful activities of their organizations:

• Dr. A. Dale Console, former medical director at E. R. Squibb, who started a public outcry over worthless drugs and misleading pharmaceutical advertising in 1960. "I reached a point where I could no longer live with myself," he says.

• Christopher Pyle and Ralph Stein, ex-Army intelligence men, who brought to light the Army's massive clandestine civilian surveillance operations in 1970. So thoroughly had they thought out and documented their "responsible dissent" that when the Army lied and clamped a tight lid on the affair they blew it right off again.

• Charles Pettis, a crack civil engineer at Brown and Root Overseas, who exposed fraud, waste, and unsafe construction on a Morrison-Knudsen road project in Peru in 1968. He was fired, blackballed from the engineering field, and hounded out of South America. He's still unemployed, in Spain, but he says, "You've got to stand up against pressures on that kind of thing to live with yourself."

• Seven employes of Colt Firearms, who in 1971, disclosed massive tampering with test results on Colt M-16 rifles to conceal poor quality and frequent malfunctions. The seven testers whistled, not because troops were going into combat carrying faulty weapons, but because the testers themselves were being forced to work in unhealthy conditions—on indoor firing ranges choked with lead-filled dust. Soon after the brief public outcry, new ventilation systems were installed.

• Edward Gregory, a senior quality control inspector for General Motors in St. Louis, who forced a 1969 recall of 2.4 million Chevrolets with built-in faults that allowed carbon monoxide to seep into passenger compartments. He started trying to get the fault fixed in 1966, and kept beating management over the head with its own rules while doggedly sticking within the routine GM channels. He was bullied, ridiculed, and downgraded before he finally won. Then, without admitting it should have heeded his early warnings, GM awarded him $10,000 for previously ignored suggestions he made for sealing the cars. He spent $2,700 of it on an 18-foot boat and Polaroid camera which he uses on weekends to patrol the polluted Mississippi near his home. So far, complaints he has filed against a railroad, a steel plant, and a glass company have brought crackdowns and cleanups.

• A. Ernest Fitzgerald, one of the Pentagon's top civilian cost reduction specialists (with a Civil Service rank equivalent to major general), who revealed to congressional investigators in 1969 the $2 billion cost overrun on Lockheed's C5A transport for the Air Force. He became a pariah overnight and was shunted off to study cost problems of bowling alleys in Thailand. Air Force sleuths probed his private life, but found nothing more damning than that he was a "pinch-penny type person" who drove an old Rambler. With cruel irony, they finally abolished his job in an "economy move." He's trying to build a small consulting business now, similar to the one he abandoned for the Pentagon in 1965. His horror story deserves lengthier treatment than a *Whistle Blowing* vignette, fortunately, Mr. Fitzgerald has provided it in a new book of his own, *The High Priests of Waste* (W. W. Norton, 416 pages, $8.95).

It's a lousy title, but a book worth reading. His straightforward prose plods in places and is tinged occasionally with understandable bitterness, but he documents his charges well, recounting enough instances of bungling, chiseling, waste, fraud, collusion, and moral turpitude to make a taxpaying reader dizzy with outrage.

There are Arthur Young & Co. accountants helping to conceal monumental overruns. And McKinsey & Co. consultants inventing a cost estimating system which specifically prohibited Air Force use of industrial engineering techniques that could tip off cost padding by defense contractors. And General Electric engineers subjecting nosy visitors at one plant to "The Ordeal by Alcohol" before ushering them into briefings in an office "which had been set up as a kind of recovery room . . . mercifully dim, lighted only by some subdued desk lamps and a large illuminated aquarium in which tropical fish were swimming about soothingly."

And there are many more: Boeing, General Dynamics, Grumman, Lockheed, Martin Marietta, North American, Rand Corp., TRW, United Aircraft, NASA—he has something on all of them.

Mr. Fitzgerald reveals an unnatural selection process in which the least fit not only survive but prosper more than their competitors. The system punishes those who strive to cut waste and insure quality, and rewards cheats and incompetents for weapons that don't work.

"By producing an airplane inferior to the one they had promised to build originally, General Dynamics had nearly doubled its profits (more than $80 million)," he says. In contrast, Col. Joe Warren led a "tiger team" of cost cutters that got too aggressive and suddenly he was on the way to Addis Ababa as air attache, his career ruined. (At that, he fared better than the tough civilian contract officer who was cast out and reduced to washing dishes for a living or the physicist weapons analyst whose honesty left him jobless, homeless, and penniless.)

LITTLE HOPE OF IMPROVEMENT

The author holds out little hope for improvement. "Fat means high, risk-free sales for the giant corporations, an easy, comfortable, prosperous life for all the feeders at the procurement trough, and immense economic and political power for dispensers of this largesse," he explains.

"Flimsy C5As can be continually patched up to fulfill at least some of their missions. With enough of the taxpayers' hard-earned cash, some of it can be used to adapt substandard F111s to some kind of service. Extra equipment can be bought to replace junky Minuteman missile hardware. . . . All this is undoubtedly good for the business of the giant contractors who make money correcting their own errors."

Public indignation, demonstrations, even congressional restrictions on the way money should be spent "have little effect on the Pentagonists," he contends. Only drastic, across-the-board budget cuts can "provide sufficient incentive for management reform in the military . . . and also reduce the Pentagon's patronage power to manageable proportions."

But for that to happen, he adds, "some of the same hot indignation that has settled upon the hapless welfare mothers" must be directed against military waste. And, "this kind of indignation has been woefully short in congressional and 'new priorities' groups."

Commentaries

WHAT'S NATURAL, ANYHOW?*

Marilyn Stephenson

It's probably fair to say that the more people know about food and nutrition, the more likely they are to develop eating habits that contribute to good health. Therefore, the growing interest of consumers in the safety and nutritional quality of the American diet is a welcome development.

Regrettably, however, much of this interest has been colored by alarmists who state or imply that the American food supply is unsafe or somehow inadequate to meet our nutritional needs.

Advocates of "health," "organic," and "natural" foods—terms for which there is little agreement as to their exact meaning—frequently proclaim (or at least strongly imply) that such products are safer and more nutritious than conventionally grown and marketed foods. Although most of these claims are not supported by scientific evidence, it is difficult for the public to evaluate truth from fancy.

This is particularly true in regard to use of the term "natural" for everything from whole-grain flour or bread to potato chips. Claims or suggestions that certain health foods or diets prevent or cure disease or provide other special health benefits are, for the most part, folklore—and sometimes fabrication.

Almost daily the public is besieged by claims for new "anti-cancer" foods, "no-aging" diets, "no-hunger" breads, "new" (non-essential) vitamins, and endless other varieties of quackery. Many consumers do not know that the 1st Amendment to the U.S. Constitution places some kinds

* *The Miami News,* 1978.

of statements about food and nutrition beyond t

tion through its protection of free speech and

If the label on a food product makes false

Food and Drug Administration can take action

product is mislabeled or misbranded. If false cla

other material directly promoting the product, t

sion may be able to take action.

But the labels on or promotion for fad fo

make any direct claims that can be shown to be

a book, a pamphlet, a speech or a magazine a

product. Thus, these indirect promotions receiv

Amendment.

Scientific rebuttal of food and nutrition m

uated in faddist literature often is futile. As D

recently retired from the Mayo Clinic, has

hogwash.''

We have fables that natural vitamins are

mins, that the soil in this country is ''all worn ou

tilizers results in better crops than those deriv

factured fertilizers. And we have many minor m

ed) eggs are nutritiously superior to infertile eg

than pasteurized, and the like.

The terms ''organic,'' ''natural,'' and ''h

often interchangeably used that they are diffic

that the FDA has taken no position on their u

The FTC in its proposed Food Advertising

the words ''organic'' and ''natural'' in food adv

about the ability of consumers to understand t

and confusing ways they are used. The commi

prohibit the term ''health food'' in advertising

may fool consumers into thinking a particul

health.

One thing all health, organic, and natural

in common is that they cost the consumer more

survey by the U.S. Department of Agriculture i

supermarket can run twice as much for heal

foods. The price for comparable foods, and so

foods, rises steadily from the regular superma r

section of the supermarket to the health-food s

ing health food sections in some major fo

popularity of these items. In 1974 it was projec

sales would reach $3 billion in 1980 up from $

Use of these foods often is tied to the desire for a simpler, pre-technology lifestyle. But users are misled if they think such foods can maintain health or provide better nutritional quality or safety than conventional foods. There is real cause for concern if consumers, particularly those with limited incomes, distrust the regular food supply and buy the more expensive health foods.

The FDA has not tried to arrive at a legal definition of these terms for food labeling because enforcement would be difficult or impossible, as well as costly. Organically grown foods, once they are removed from the field, cannot be told from commercially fertilized plants. Plant roots absorb nutrients in an organic form regardless of the source, and there is no scientific basis for claiming organic foods are more nutritious than conventional foods.

According to Dr. Emil M. Mrak, former chancellor of the University of California at Davis and a world authority on agriculture, scientific experiments conducted for 25 years in Michigan, at Cornell University and in England have established no nutritional or chemical differences between organic or health foods and foods treated with manufactured fertilizers.

Differences in the nutrient content of food from plants of the same species depend on their genetic nature, the climate, the nutrients available for growth, and the stage of maturity at which they are harvested. For example, wide variation in Vitamin A content has been found in different varieties of carrots and in Valencia oranges grown in different parts of the country.

One of the alleged advantages of organically grown foods is that no pesticides are used on them and thus the so-called organic products the consumers buy are supposedly free of traces or residues of pesticides. But the fact is that many of these foods do contain pesticide residues. Even if no pesticides are used on a particular crop, some chemical residues often remain in the soil for years after the last application of a pesticide on a previous crop. In addition, fresh residues may be deposited from drifting sprays and dusts or from rainfall runoff from nearby farms. Traces of pesticides may be found in both organic and conventional foods, but these residues normally are within federal tolerance levels, which are set low enough to protect consumers.

Since chemically and organically grown foods do not differ in looks, taste, or chemical analysis, the only way to assure that a product labeled as "organically grown" is truthfully labeled would be to keep watch over the product from planting to harvest to sale, and to check soil and water reports. Such a program, of course, would be prohibitively expensive.

The possibility for fraud is apparent when the consumer doesn't know if the storekeeper is honest, when the storekeeper can't tell if the distributor is honest and when the distributor doesn't know if his suppliers are living up to their promises. Undoubtedly conventional foods at times have been substituted for organic foods.

If the FDA can identify fraud in the labeling of a natural or organic or health food, it can take action. The agency also can act if claims are made suggesting that a certain food or combination of foods can be used to treat a disease condition, if the statements are untrue.

It would be inaccurate to imply that all elements of the health-food industry engage in shady marketing practices. Some distributors and growers supply affidavits or certificates for foods grown and handled according to "organic and natural" precepts. Many health-food operations truly believe in health foods and are sincere in trying to provide consumers the "real" thing.

Reading the labels and trusting in the health-food store manager appear to be the best protection for the consumer interested in purchasing these foods. Recently it was reported that a natural-food store in California removed all vitamins, which are high-profit items, from its shelves.

The management had learned that most of a product labeled "Rose Hips Vitamin C from Natural Sources" was synthetic. Unable to confirm that similar practices do not occur in other natural vitamin supplements, the store stopped handling vitamins and suggested that people get them from a pharmacy where the pills aren't labeled as natural and they're cheaper.

That's excellent advice from both a scientific and an economic viewpoint. Vitamins from natural sources have no nutritional superiority over synthetic vitamins, and the Food and Drug Administration prohibits such claims in food labeling.

The FDA also prohibits claims of nutritional significance in behalf of para-amino-benzoic acid (PABA), rutin and other bioflavonoids, lecithin, and many other such supplements not essential for human nutrition which are sold in health-food stores. The continuing market for an ever-increasing variety of these and other food supplements feeds on various myths promoted in the fad literature.

One practice is to falsely promote a substance as a vitamin. A recent example is pangamic acid, which has falsely been called Vitamin B-15. Vitamins are organic substances required in minute amounts in the diet of animals for normal growth, maintenance of health, and reproduction. Each vitamin has a unique function in the body, and an inadequate amount or the absence of a vitamin in the diet produces a specific deficiency disease condition. For instance, a deficiency or lack of Vitamin C causes scurvy.

For a substance to be established as a legitimate vitamin it must be tested under controlled conditions to prove that its absence in the diet causes abnormal body functioning. All animals need some vitamins, but not all known vitamins are needed by all animals. Therefore, testing must also establish that a vitamin is essential in the human diet before it can be said to be essential in the diet of animals for the normal functioning of the body.

Many people are lured to health foods in the belief that, since they're natural, they're totally safe—or at least safer than conventional foods. There's not much known here. Hundreds of toxicants are known to occur naturally in foods. For example, aflatoxin, a mold product which grows naturally under some conditions on corn, peanuts, and other grains, is a powerful carcinogen. The FDA monitors food for aflatoxin and has established safe minimum levels in some foods, such as peanut butter and milk. Peanut butter or milk containing aflatoxin above these levels cannot be marketed. But there's no way the FDA or anyone can assure that all foods are entirely free of such naturally occuring toxins.

Herb teas, which are favored by many health food advocates, contain thousands of chemical compounds that have not been tested for safety. Sassafras root was found to contain safrole, which produces liver cancer in rats, and the sale of sassafras tea was banned by the FDA in 1976 for that reason.

Lead, arsenic, cadmium, and other heavy metals occur naturally at very low levels in many foods. In extracts and concentrates made from foods, the level of such substances may be much higher. Some bone meal has been found to contain high levels of lead.

Kelp tablets, a food supplement commonly sold in health-food stores, may contain high levels of arsenic, as may many other products from the sea. Studies of industrial workers exposed to arsenic indicate a greater occurrence of cancer among those so exposed. Researchers have found elevated levels of urinary arsenic in individuals who have consumed kelp tablet supplements.

Many commonly used foods whether sold as health or conventional foods, contain low levels of toxic substances. Oxalic acid is present in several vegetables including spinach. Carrots, lettuce, and celery leaves contain nitrate and nitrate compounds.

Does this mean that we need to be fearful of using these foods? Not at all. The best thing to do is to exercise care and common sense by eating a balanced diet from a wide variety of foods.

SHOULD THE FTC BAN CHILDREN'S COMMERCIALS?*

Pressured from all sides, the agency is trying
to decide how much control is necessary and proper

By Irwin B. Arieff

Do television ads aimed at young children take unfair advantage of their unschooled minds and lack of judgment, or are these ads merely a harmless way to make money to pay for children's programs?

Should children's television advertisers be left alone, regulated by the Government, or should their ads be banned from the airwaves altogether?

These difficult questions figure in a far-reaching effort to place strict Government controls on television advertising directed toward children. The effort is being directed by the Federal Trade Commission (FTC), a five-member commission whose job, under the law, is to police unfair and deceptive advertising. The commission is continuing to pursue restraints despite a hectic year of concerted industry opposition.

The FTC staff, after a study, came to the conclusion that very young children don't understand what televison advertisements are. It recommended that the commission ban all TV ads aimed at them, while restricting certain other ads aimed at their older brothers and sisters.

According to the FTC staff's report, the average American child (aged 2 to 11) sees more than 20,000 TV commericials during a typical year. Though estimates vary, most experts say that TV advertising to children amount to about a half-billion dollars in billings every year.

The broadcasting, candy, soft drink, toy, cereal, and sugar industries, however, disagreed with the staff's recommendations, and took their case to their congressmen and the courts.

Within months, the FTC was to find its chairman barred from participating in the children's television investigation by a Federal judge, and its independence and its very survival threatened by an angry Congress.

For the past decade, efforts have been made to have the Federal government regulate children's television advertising. But the FTC's current regulatory activity stems from two petitions filed with the commission in 1977.

Two organizations, Action for Children's Television and the Center for Science in the Public Interest, asked the FTC for controls on the advertising of heavily sugared foods to young children. What TV told kids to eat, the groups argued, had become more influential than what their parents told them. And the resulting steady diet of heavily sugared foods was harming children's teeth and keeping them from eating more nutritious fare, or so it was claimed.

As a result of the petitions, the staff of the FTC prepared a 400-page report on children's television advertising for the members to study. The staff report recommended that the FTC consider adopting three proposals:

- A total ban on all TV ads directed at children under 8. These children, the staff argued, "are too young to understand the selling purpose of, or otherwise comprehend or evaluate, the advertising."
- A ban on the advertising of heavily sugared products aimed at children aged 8 through 11. Though children by that age probably can understand what commercials are all about, the staff reasoned, these products pose "the most serious dental-health risks."
- A requirement that the advertisers of less heavily sugared products pitch in to pay for the production and broadcasting of "counteradvertising"—commercial spots designed to promote good nutrition and health.

Industry spokesmen bitterly attacked the FTC staff's proposals. The recommendations, stated candy manufacturer Mars, Inc., "would be without any valid scientific, sociological or legal basis." The proposed actions, the National Association of Broadcasters commented, "are founded upon conjecture and supposition. . . . There is no cause-and-effect relationship between (1) sugar content and tooth decay, (2) sugar-product advertisements and tooth decay, or (3) sugar-product advertisements and a belief that 'sugar is good for you.'"

Despite the strong opposition, the FTC voted in February 1978 to move ahead with the investigation. Worried that they may have moved too far, too fast, however, the FTC members decided not to simply offer for comment the staff's recommendations. Instead, they voted to explore a variety of possible regulatory approaches, and set a deadline of two years for a final recommendation to be placed before them.

Before the new inquiry had even begun, however, the industries that advertise on children's television programs had set to work to counter the commission's actions.

First, they turned their attention to the members of the Congressional committees that supervise the FTC's activities and determine the agency's annual budget. The various industry trade associations and their members began urging the committee members to press for an end to the FTC's inquiry.

At the same time, three advertising associations and the Toy Manufacturers of America asked FTC chairman Michael Pertschuk to disqualify himself from participating in the inquiry. They charged that the chairman, in his public statements, had shown that he had made up his mind on the issues before all the evidence was in.

Pertschuk is a former consumer advocate who, while chief counsel to the Senate Commerce Committee, helped draft much of the Nation's consumer legislation. To underline his desire for action on the children's television advertising issue, Pertschuk, in January 1978, had promised to donate his salary to dental research for every month past February that the staff was late in making its recommendations. (The staff came through, completing the recommendations on February 27.)

When Pertschuk refused to disqualify himself voluntarily, the four groups asked a Federal court to do so.

In May, the House subcommittee charged with drawing up the FTC budget recommended that Congress forbid it from spending any money on the inquiry. Its recommendation, a Congressional aide explained, was an attempt "to send a clear message that [the FTC's proposal] to ban perfectly legal products, just because they are addressed to children, is not acceptable." The House Committee on Appropriations later softened the recommendation, voting merely to prevent the FTC from issuing a final decision before September 30, 1979, the end of the current fiscal year. The Senate also expressed concern about the FTC's proposed bans, and when the Congress finally voted funds for FY 1979, it was with the understanding that no ruling would be made this year.

In October, Congress defeated a bill to renew the FTC's charter for 1978-79, because House members wanted a provision added to the charter permitting either the House or the Senate to block any FTC action they disagreed with. The children's television inquiry played a major role in the House's deliberations. (Though, technically, the FTC could not operate without a charter, it has stayed alive because of a loophole in Congress's rules.)

And in November, U.S. District Judge Gerhard Gesell ordered Chairman Pertschuk to disqualify himself from the investigation because he was biased against children's television advertising. Another commissioner previously had disqualified himself (because of an earlier association with a public-interest law group representing one of the original petitioners) and yet another retired in March 1979. All this left the FTC with only two members able to participate in the proceeding.

Despite the opposition, the FTC voted in December to continue its inquiry and to appeal Judge Gesell's ruling. Preliminary hearings began in January and ran through the end of March. The commission has voted to postpone a second set of hearings until a new commissioner is appointed to replace the retiring member. A final vote on what action the FTC will take, if any, is tentatively set for mid 1980—well beyond the time limit established by Congress.

To the TV industry, commercials are a must. Take away the ads, the industry argues, and there won't be any money to put on the shows. To its critics, however, the industry—by advertising sweets to children—is taking unfair advantage.

Children's television ads are profitable. Broadcasters, however, say they don't put on children's programs for money. "The fact is that we do make a profit from children's programming," an NBC spokesman explains. "But if you're looking to make a buck, that isn't where to look. Our children's-shows' contribution to overhead is the lowest of any day-part of all NBC programming."

Nonetheless, in the TV industry, even small profits can be significant. NBC, for example, brought in $23 million in advertising revenues from children's shows in 1976 (the last year for which figures are available), of which $4 to $5 million was profit, according to Dr. Alan Pearce, a telecommunications economist. NBC denies this, but won't disclose its own figures.

Children's programming, Pearce concludes, "is disproportionately profitable for the amount of time and money spent by the networks on it."

In the past, the Government has done little to regulate children's TV advertising. Both the broadcast and advertising industries have set up "self-regulatory" groups to establish guidelines for children's ads and to police them. On the few occasions that an ad practice has attracted attention, the self-regulatory groups have responded by adopting additional rules, and the Government has not acted.

During the period from 1973 to 1976, for example, under pressure from the Federal Communications Commission, the Television Code Review Board of the National Association of Broadcasters reduced the permissible level of Saturday- and Sunday-morning television ad time from 16 minutes an hour (the highest then found in any day-part) to 9½ minutes an hour—the same as for prime time.

In January 1979, ABC went one step further, announcing that it would unilaterally cut back by 20 percent the amount of advertising aimed at children during Saturday- and Sunday-morning programming, beginning in January 1980.

The NAB doesn't seem about to alter its current rules concerning the advertising of cereals and candy, however. Instead, they, along with various advertising associations, are gearing up to fight the FTC proposals, which they deem unfair.

The Television Code, they say, already warns its station subscribers of their "special responsibility" toward children. Further, candy, soft

drink, and snack ads "shall not recommend indiscriminate and/or im-
moderate use of the product," according to the Code's children's TV
advertising guidelines, while cereal spots are to show the product as only
one part of a balanced breakfast.

In practice, of course, these guidelines can be conveniently interpreted. For example, one breakfast-cereal ad fulfills its promise to portray
the product "within the framework of a balanced regimen" by stating that
Fruit Scruples cereal (not its real name) "is a yummy part of any good
breakfast."

Does this say to the average child that he or she should eat Fruit
Scruples along with milk, fruit, and eggs—as the Code intends—or that no
breakfast is complete without Fruit Scruples? (Fruit Scruples, by the way,
are 44.1 percent sugar by weight, about the same as an almond Hershey
bar.)

In opposing the FTC staff's proposals, broadcasters, advertisers, and
other affected groups can be expected to advance a number of arguments.
Among them are that a ban on TV ads—but not affecting radio or comic
books—would discriminate against television. They are likely to argue that
a ban on advertising of any kind would violate the broadcasters' First
Amendment rights and that such a ban wouldn't be effective anyway.
Finally, they believe, if sugar is bad for kids' teeth, it should be banned
from the marketplace altogether, and not just from TV ads. Why should
the Government interfere with the parent–child relationship and try to dictate what a child should or shouldn't eat or drink?

"We in the broadcast community readily acknowledge the vulner-
abilities and, therefore, the special needs of children in advertising and programming," commented Amercian Broadcasting Companies president
Elton H. Rule. "At all three networks, broadcast standards apply stringent
rules to television advertising aimed at children to insure that the ads are
not deceptive or unfair. If the idea behind the FTC's proposal is to get
children to eat less sugar, they are raising a question that goes beyond television advertising. Kids will still have a sweet tooth; the FTC won't change
that. The targeted products will still be on the grocery shelves; that won't
change. The sugar bowl and jelly jar will still be on the breakfast table; that
won't change. Even the presence of advertising for these products won't
change—in any medium but television.

"Still more worrisome, though, is the reasoning behind the proposals," Rule went on. "The FTC staff proposals are saying very bluntly
that most people are incompetent to bring up their own children, and,
therefore, an appointed commission of five people—by tradition, all
lawyers—should step in and act as national nannies."

The ability of the broadcasters and advertisers to mobilize public opinion is not lost on the FTC staff, which will have to recommend action in the deliberations to come. In fact, the staff has been gearing up for its own public-relations battle. It will get help from a coalition of 46 national groups that have decided to back the FTC inquiry. Among the groups are the American Academy of Pediatrics, the NAACP, the United Steel Workers, and the Congressional Wives Task Force.

Despite the controversy so far, the FTC's Tracy Westen, who is deeply involved in the staff's efforts, feels the proceeding is still in good shape. "The public is still strongly in support of our doing something," Westen said. "We've received thousands of letters, and they're running four to one in favor of doing something. We expect congressmen to be swayed, too, as the mass of evidence comes out in our hearings. I think people's mind may be changed on this issue."

Westen disputes claims that the staff's recommendations, if approved, might result in fewer children's programs. "I don't think stations and networks will cut out programs for children," he says. "I don't believe it. It's in their interest to present sustained (unsponsored) programming. It's in a sponsor's interest to continue to present the programs even without ads—much as is already being done on public television."

Westen admits that the FTC has been stung by the criticism that it's trying to butt into family affairs, but calls the issue "a red herring."

"If there's any interfering," he says, "it's in beaming 20,000 ads a year to a child, when it's the parent who does the buying. Why doesn't the Kellogg Co. just aim its ads at parents?"

Westen concludes, "The FTC is trying to free parents, to let them make choices without that massive interference from television in the form of advertisements beamed at their children."

How the FTC commissioners will resolve the conflict remains to be seen. A few reasonably safe predictions can be made, however.

Because of the controversial nature of the issues, the final FTC rules, if any are approved at all, are almost certain to be weaker than the original FTC staff proposals.

No matter how weak the final rules, however, they are almost certain to be appealed to the courts—perhaps by both sides. The appeals—along with FTC reconsideration, if either side succeeds in its challenge—could add another five or even 10 years to the proceeding.

By that time, it is likely that both industry and Government will have undergone changes that will make the original regulatory proposals obsolete or irrelevant. The process could begin all over again. Commented one industry lawyer: "God only knows how long it could drag out."

OH, FOR THE GOOD OLD DAYS
OF BRAND X*

Comparative Ads Upset Industry; F.T.C. Adamant

By Edwin McDowell

There was a time when the average advertising executive would sooner be caught with ring around his buttondown collar than mention a competitive product in a client's ad. If it were absolutely necessary to trumpet the superiority of one's own product, it could always be compared with that ubiquitous scapegoat, Brand X.

But the Federal Trade Commission argued that comparative advertising could increase competition and serve to educate the public, and in 1972, the TV network ban on ads that mention the competition by name was ended at the F.T.C.'s urging. The field exploded, taking over 8 to 10 percent of the advertising market overall, and perhaps twice that proportion of television commercials, and then—like many an ad fad before it—comparative advertising lost its glamour and settled down for a long but no-growth, undramatic run.

Now, suddenly, the field is exploding again—not in terms of revenues but in terms of controversy. There are indications that the advertising community is losing patience. Earlier objections on grounds of taste and ethics have been broadened to include attacks on comparative advertising's value to consumers. Ad men have complained that the F.T.C. has been "pushing" the technique, and in fact Michael Pertschuk, the commission's chairman, has recently warned advertisers against "no-comparative-advertising" agreements and urged the use of the technique for alcoholic beverages. Moreover, two contretemps—both involving the Gillette Company—have set the industry on its ear.

Last month, Gillette and the J. Walter Thompson advertising agency agreed to pay the Alberto-Culver Company $4.25 million to settle a law suit over a television comparative ad that Alberto-Culver claimed "disparaged and destroyed" its Alberto Balsam hair conditioner. On the other hand, Gillette is a complainant as regards comparative ads run by the Bic Pen Corporation, claiming they are based on faulty research.

Such developments are not calculated to increase enthusiasm for the technique. The Alberto-Culver settlement, for example, "will certainly make people think twice about comparative advertising, I won't deny that," said Mitch Paul, a staff attorney in the commission's bureau of consumer protection.

Yet even before the settlement, comparative advertising appeared to have peaked. "It gained rapidly in the beginning, but now it's about where it has been for a couple of years," said Ralph Daniels, vice president of broadcast standards for NBC, to which some 47,000 separate advertisements were submitted last year.

Even some of comparative advertising's longtime champions wonder what went wrong. "It's not growing, there's no bandwagon for it, that's for sure," admitted Stanley I. Tannenbaum, vice chairman of Kenyon & Eckhardt Enterprises, a longtime supporter of the concept.

Why? "I have a lot of theories, but no proof," said Mr. Tannenbaum. "I think some people just don't know how to use it. Other people are afraid of the law. Maybe there isn't a clear-cut product difference. Maybe agencies aren't digging hard enough to find ways to apply it."

Moreover, even the benefits to consumers appear to be fewer than had been expected. Ogilvy & Mather, one of four United States ad agencies that billed over $1 billion last year, conducted three separate investigations into the effects of comparative advertising. Each time it concluded that the method failed to heighten consumer discrimination or lessen confusion.

"If it were effective, there'd be a lot more of it being used, and I think its use is decreasing," said Philip Levine, Ogilvy & Mather's executive director of research.

Most advertising is comparative to some degree. And even when advertisers compared the virtues of their products to that despicable, imperfect or undesirable Brand X, most consumers had little doubt who or what Brand X represented. Even now, according to Mr. Daniels, NBC defines comparative advertising as that where the identity of the competitive product is implicit as well as explicit.

Moreover, even those who regard such advertising as unseemly or unethical admit that—regardless of the legal perils, and regardless of what research studies indicate—it will always have a certain amount of appeal to advertisers who are trying to overtake the leader.

"It's not the kind of advertising that everybody is going to do," said the F.T.C.'s Mr. Paul. "Why should your Procter & Gamble, which spends millions and millions of dollars on advertising its products, give free mention to its competitors? But it's probably the most effective advertising technique for also rans and for the new entrants. It's a good way to tell people, 'Look, I'm the new boy on the block.'"

Mr. Tannenbaum agrees. "One of my principles is that the leader, the person who's No. 1 in the marketplace, shouldn't ever use it." His agency created the ads favorably comparing the Mercury Monarch to the Mercedes-Benz.

While enthusiasts and disparagers often disagree about the effects of comparative advertising, there is general agreement that it has sometimes helped users to increase sales or market share.

The Vivitar Corporation's ads in 1975, with Arthur Godfrey comparing the less expensive Vivitar 600 pocket camera with the Kodak 28, are credited with helping to sharply increase Vivitar's sales and expand its market share. Opel doubled its share of the American imported car market in 1977 with the help of an estimated $4 million ad campaign comparing it with the VW Rabbit, the Toyota Corolla, the Datsun B-210, and the Subaru DL.

Others cite the success of ads for Dynamo liquid detergent (comparing it with Tide); Louis Sherry ice cream (comparing it with Breyer's), and Carefree Sugarless Gum (comparing it with Trident).

In most cases, companies whose product are compared unfavorably tend to shrug off such ads, as though disparagement is a small price to endure for the sake of industry leadership.

But turning the other cheek has its limits, and there are signs that those limits are being reached sooner than ever before. For example, about 20 percent of the advertisements reviewed in 1977 for the National Advertising Review Board involved comparative advertising. Last year's comparable figure was 36 percent.

The review board was established in 1971 by the Council of Better Business Bureaus and three advertising groups. Its five-member panels adjudicate questions of truth and accuracy in specific advertisements, after they have been reviewed and investigated by the Council's National Advertising Division, and only after that division is unable to resolve them.

Although the board has no enforcement powers, it publishes the panel reports, favorable or unfavorable. If an advertiser is found guilty and refuses to cooperate, usually by halting the offending ads, the board's chairman publicly refers the matter to the appropriate regulatory agency. The threat of adverse publicity is usually an inducement for compliance.

In one of the earliest tests of comparative advertising, the review board ruled in 1973 that the campaign for the Schick Flexamatic electric shaver, which was touted as superior to shavers made by Norelco, Remington, and Sunbeam, was "false in some details and misleading in its overall implications." It ordered Schick to stop running the ads.

The company said that although it disagreed with the panel, in the interest of industry self-regulation any future advertising created on the basis of its tests would be "guided by the recommendations of the panel."

But some companies have been so enraged by competitor's comparative ads that they have raced straight to the courts, bypassing the industry review panel. The most notable case: that of Gillette and Alberto-Culver.

The first commercial was broadcast in May 1974. Two months later, after failing to get a preliminary injunction to stop the commercial, Alberto

Balsam sued Gillette and J. Walter Thompson, saying the ad violated Federal antitrust laws and Illinois deceptive trade practices, consumer fraud, and trade libel law. It demanded that Gillette be forced to run ads to correct what it said was an effort to show that Alberto Balsam "left an oily, greasy residue on the hair. . . . "

According to testimony developed during the eight-day trial in United States District Court in Chicago, when the comparative ad campaign began Alberto Balsam commanded almost 12 percent of the market (compared with Tame's 17 percent). By September 1974 that share had fallen to about 6 percent and by 1976—even though the company spent $2 million in advertising in 1975 and 1976—it was below 3 percent. Finally, after sales sank 75 percent below previous levels, the product was taken off the market.

Alberto-Culver originally sought $23.5 million in lost profits, actual and potential, but it settled for $4.25 million. Neither Gillette nor J. Walter Thompson would give details except to say that the settlement is not an admission of guilt, that they expect to recover their share of the settlement from insurance, and that the payment will not affect their financial results.

But one highly placed Gillette source spoke bitterly about comparative advertising and the fact that the F.T.C. had "pushed" companies to use it. Last November, Michael Pertschuk, the commission's chairman, warned advertisers that if they agree "expressly or tacitly" not to resort to comparative advertising they are liable to be talking to the commission.

The F.T.C. has been moving on another front, as well, recently urging the Bureau of Alcohol, Tobacco and Firearms to support comparative advertising for the alcohol beverage industry—something to which the bureau has been strongly opposed.

Gillette has long been ambivalent about the virtues of comparative advertising. Recently it complained to the National Advertising Review Board about Bic commercials asserting that the Bic throwaway shaver is as good as the more expensive Gillette Trac II. Gillette charged that the Bic claim is based on "contrived and artificial research," but the review board has not yet investigated.

Gillette also asked the television networks not to run the 30-second Bic commercials and requested them to demand greater substantiation from Bic. "We are going to require some changes in the Bic advertising," said Richard Gitter, ABC vice president of broadcast standards and practices.

Gillette is comfortably ahead with some 58 percent of the market share of disposable razors, which account for about 15 percent of the $425 million blade market. Bic claims that they will eventually represent about 40 percent, but Gillette views the disposable market as only about half that. Yet it has no intention of surrendering its lead without a fight—particularly since, like Alberto-Culver, it considers itself the victim of unfair advertising.

Similarly, several years ago, after complaining that its Right Guard deodorant was being put at a competitive disadvantage by other antiperspirant deodorants, Gillette asked the networks to declare a moratorium on comparative advertising as "confusing and misleading." But before long its ads were favorably comparing its pump-spray version of Right Guard to Ban Basic, the industry leader.

How, given the industry's system of checks and balances, do misleading or false comparisons ever appear on television or in print?

The big companies have huge testing facilities or access to independent testing labs. The big advertising agencies review the results of those tests before developing the ad campaigns. And the television networks have detailed guidelines to insure that ads adhere to their own stringent policies, as well as the policies and codes of the Federal Communications Commission, the F.T.C., the National Association of Broadcasters, the Civil Aeronautics Board (if they involve airlines), state agencies (insurance ads), and a host of other agencies.

Throughout this entire process, test results, theoretically at least, are analyzed by a battery of vice presidents, product managers, editors, lawyers, and copywriters down to the least detail. When Gillette set out to prove the superiority of its twin blade some years ago, it built a high-speed movie camera that would film 1,400 feet in three seconds.

So how then did that controversial Gillette ad get on the air? Gillette won't say, and those who don't hide behind 'no comment' are not able to provide a terribly satisfactory explanation beyond the catch-phrase "human error."

"We made numerous changes in the advertising before it was submitted, we spent a great deal of time examining the substantiation and in reviewing the challenge," said Richard Gitter, vice president of broadcast standards and practices at ABC. He added that of some 50,000 individual ads submitted to the network last year, 5 percent were rejected outright, some 30 percent were accepted without modification, and the remainder accepted only after modification and substantiation.

An anonymous Gillette official had a different explanation of the expensive contretemps. "The case hinged on the question of disparagement," he said. "Some judges might think that comparative advertising is disparagement per se."

But for the most part, friends and foes of comparative advertising were at a loss to explain how the fail-safe system upon which the advertising industry prides itself could have failed to sound the necessary alarm. "Gillette wasn't found guilty," said a source close to the case. "But from the second day, the judge urged the defendants to settle, so he must have thought Alberto-Culver had a good case, and remember, that represents the first big cash settlement of any kind in those matters.''

"I can't explain that case," said Mr. Tannenbaum. "I really don't know how it happened."

Mr. Tannenbaum is quick to say, however, that one of the principal tenets of comparative advertising is not to disparage a competitor or be condescending. "You're basically challenging the judgment of the person who uses the other guy's product, and he's likely to get his back up if you put down that product too much," he said.

He added: "You need to develop points of superiority that are important to consumers—the ride of a car, the taste or durability of a product—something that people care about. You should say that the other guy has a great box of cereal, but we have 32 raisins and they only have 14. By pointing out these real differences, you can force the other guy to improve his product. That's really what comparative advertising is all about.

ADVENTURES WITH STP*

One Consumer Sets Out to Learn Why So Many Motorists Stick to the Much Maligned Goo

By Jeremy Main

Why do we buy plots of land we've never seen? Why do we buy options on foreign commodities we know nothing about over the phone from salesmen we've never met? Why do we send good money off in the mail and expect in return a genuine miracle weight reducer, or a breast enlarger or the secrets of the lazy man's way to riches? Even the most preposterous offer seems to find a taker. We are gullible. There's something about panaceas and nostrums that gets to us all. We've been told often enough that Listerine and Geritol aren't all they're cracked up to be, but we go on buying them. We gorge indiscriminately on vitamins. Some people who ridicule Laetrile fill up on vitamin C at the first sniffle.

Clever advertising helps, but the successful nostrum, it would seem, has to aim at what really concerns people—looks, health, age, money, cars, houses. For the loving car owner, STP has been the panacea, and I recently got interested in finding out why its appeal is so durable. I don't tinker with

* By Jeremy Main. Reprinted from the October 1978 issue of MONEY magazine by special permission; © 1978, Time Inc. All Rights Reserved.

engines—when I got my first car I was planning to put the antifreeze in the gasoline until someone set me straight—and I've never used the stuff.

As nostrums go, STP is hard to beat. It cost only $1.29 a can, which is nothing if you consider all the good things it is supposed to be capable of doing for your $5,000 car. It gives the racer his "edge," hushes noisy valve lifters, cleans up smoking tailpipes, seals worn piston rings, prolongs bearing life and just generally perks up a tired engine. None of this has been proved, but it is widely believed. "I add some of that goo, and it makes me feel better," says one addict who wants to remain anonymous because he has a respectable job in the auto industry in Detroit. The point is, does the car feel better?

Whatever it does inside your engine, in the marketplace STP is just about indestructible. In 1971, Consumers Union, after testing STP, characterized it as useless and possibly harmful. Detroit derides it as "mouse's milk"—hypocritically, as we'll see in a moment. The Federal Trade Commission put STP under a consent order in 1976 to tone down its advertising. This year, for violating the order, STP had to pay a $500,000 fine and spend another $200,000 to advertise its sins. (As often happens, the biggest penalty was levied by STP's lawyers, whose fees amounted to more than the government fine.) Yet STP keeps on selling.

To understand why STP sells so well you have to remember Andy Granatelli. He was a poor boy from Chicago who started with a gas station and built it into a chain of hot-rod shops. He became the perennial sponsor and occasional driver of Indianapolis 500 cars. Eventually Studebaker put him in charge of a subsidiary called STP (which doesn't stand for anything).

As chairman of STP, Granatelli managed to remain the mechanic who could talk straight, or at least convincingly, to all those do-it-yourself mechanics out there. Half the car owners in the U.S. put an oil treatment in their engines. Granatelli made sure that STP became the best known of the additives.

He made his pitch colorfully on TV, and he gave extra prize money to racing drivers who put the big STP decals on their cars—if they won. Of course, what a racing car needs has nothing to do with what the family car needs, but still it feels good to use the same goo as the big drivers do at Indy.

Granatelli was eased out of STP in 1973 when profits fell to $1 million. At 54, he is an auto engineering consultant in Los Angeles. I called him to see how he feels about STP now. Without any encouragement, he peeled off into his pitch. "That product is out of this world, okay?" he demanded, without waiting for a response. "It really does work. You put in one pint of oil treatment and it will stop oil consumption immediately and forever—you know, for 50,000 to 75,000 miles."

He raced on: "All the time I was at the company, we sold STP with a money-back guarantee. You know how many customers wrote in for their money back out of 100 million cans sold every year? It was less than 50 in any one year." (Just to make a stab at setting the record straight, STP never sold more than 60 million cans a year, according to the company records, and it now sells about 40 million cans.)

"You, personally," Granatelli ordered me, "get a pint of STP and get your engine good and hot and you personally pour the can into the engine while it is running and you will notice before the can is even empty your engine will get smoother and quieter."

So challenged, I had to try a can of STP. I started at the NAPA auto-parts dealer, who carries, as I might have expected, NAPA products and not STP products. He wanted to know why I would ever use junk like STP. He had a NAPA oil treatment that was better. "It's lighter," he said, handing me a can so I could feel how light it was.

DARING CLAIMS

At the Chevron station, Nick said he didn't carry the stuff and told me not to use it unless I had a very old car. "It makes it real hard to start in the winter," said Nick. Big John at the Exxon station gave me an odd look and took me to a back room where he rummaged around for some oil treatment. "We don't get much call for this," he said. He came up with a can of Atlas oil treatment, an Exxon product, at $3 for 15 ounces. The label made claims STP wouldn't dare make today, such as "aids in reducing oil consumption."

The new mechanic at the Mobil station warned me off STP. "It'll really gum up your engine," he said. "I've taken engines apart and I've seen what STP does to them. They're full of gunk." He wanted me to buy instead an 11-ounce can of Wynn's Xtend for about $3. But I have never heard Andy Granatelli, or anyone else, mention Wynn's Xtend.

I finally found a can of STP at the local branch of the Caldor discount chain, which is probably where any knowledgeable do-it-yourselfer would have gone in the first place. At $1.29 for 15 ounces, it cost less than half as much as the other treatments I had been offered. The label made no claims at all. Before committing this liquid to my 1976 Volaré—not the healthiest of cars—I decided to get an opinion from the makers in Detroit. Chrysler gave me a terse, ominous response: "We don't recommend STP. It can be harmful if misused, especially at low temperatures." Well, Chrysler is only the smallest of the Big Three, so I called Ford and General Motors too. Their people chuckled about "mouse's milk" but then said primly they couldn't comment on another company's product. They did, however, send me their owner's manuals.

The 1978 Chevrolet manual says your car probably doesn't need an oil additive, but if you must use one, use "GM Super Engine Oil Supplement." Ford's seems to suggest that for certain unintelligible reasons you may want to add to your oil "Ford Part No. D2AZ–19579–A," which turns out to be an oil treatment. By now I was getting the impression that nearly everyone who derided STP had "mouse's milk" of their own to sell. Their prices are generally higher than STP's but otherwise there is no way of comparing the products because the labels don't tell you what is inside the cans.

In pursuit of ultimate truth, I went to the Society of Automotive Engineers convention in Detroit. I passed by a BG Products Inc. oil treatment display ("7% fuel savings with BG") and looked up Ted Selby, a bearded physical chemist of 49 recommended to me by an authority at the University of Michigan as a leading lubrication expert. Selby changes the oil in his own car every two months, regardless of the mileage (and would do so even if the car sat in the garage for two months) and he doesn't use STP.

Slowly and carefully, Selby explained that on top of a base of mineral oil, STP contains two principal additives: ZDDP and a polymer. ZDDP, derived from zinc, combats wear, rust, and corrosion. The polymer makes the oil thicker, counteracting the inclination of oils to lose their lubricating quality as they heat up.

THE ELUSIVE MOMENT

Both additives, says Selby, are useful and legitimate. In fact, high-quality oils (such as those whose cans display an SE rating) already contain them. "In extreme conditions and over a period of time, every oil now made will lose the benefits of its additives," says Selby. Extreme conditions include short-haul suburban driving as well as hauling trailers or racing at Indy.

The trouble is, Selby continues, neither you nor your mechanic will know when the moment has come to add the treatment. You don't know how much ZDDP or polymer is left in your oil and you don't know how much you're adding because the label doesn't tell you. Too much ZDDP can cause more rather than less wear. Too much viscosity can make the car hard to start in the cold. Without more data, it makes more sense just to change the oil.

It was an attempt to produce plausible data that got STP into its latest round of trouble with the FTC. While operating under a consent order that prohibited it from making unsubstantiated claims, STP ran some ads in 1976 saying that STP could reduce oil consumption by over 20%.

A respectable Texas company, Automotive Research Associates, had made the elaborate tests that produced these results. Unfortunately, as STP and the FTC soon learned, there was an elementary mistake in the tests—in measuring how much oil had been used up in the crankcases of the test cars, ARA forgot to allow for the STP that had been added. Adjusted for this mistake, the tests showed STP made no significant difference in oil consumption.

UNDAUNTED

"Those tests were botched up, no doubt about it," says Craig Nalen, 47, who now has Granatelli's job as chairman. A handsome Princetonian with a blue-chip background at Procter & Gamble and General Mills, Nalen is hardly another blue-collar hero. But he seems to be what STP needs. Sitting in his Fort Lauderdale headquarters, with a racer's stripe in STP colors running diagonally across his carpet, Nalen appeared undaunted by the $700,000 penalty and the humiliating ads STP was forced to run announcing the fine for "certain allegedly inaccurate past advertisements." When he joined the company in 1975, STP stock was selling at $6. By last winter the stock was up to $14, and it hardly gave a tremor when the fine was announced. Then in May, Esmark Inc. took over STP for $22.50 a share. Nalen stood to make almost $2 million on his stock options.

Nalen is spending $300,000 to test STP all over again and he says the results this time are showing savings in oil varying from zero to 35%. But he won't use the results in any ads. Anyway, he says, no one seemed to notice the claims last time except the FTC.

By now, I knew all that any sensible person could want to know about STP, and more. I also had that $1.29 can of STP sitting in the garage. By any rational standard, it wasn't going to do my car any good, and it might even do some harm. STP might stuff up the rings of an old clunker enough to make it run better for awhile, but my Volaré is a younger clunker. Still, I owed it to Granatelli. Just as he had told me, I warmed up the engine, let it idle and then slowly poured in the can of STP. Andy, I have to say that nothing changed.

SHOULD UTILITIES USE CONSUMER MONEY TO ADVERTISE?*

Yes

By George W. Edwards

The issue of utility advertising has come up again, but this time with the new twist of implying that consumers write the checks for utility media expenditures. Let's clear up that misconception first.

When customers receive their bills from Georgia Power, they are paying for a service—in this case, the manufacture and delivery of electricity in their homes. Once customers have mailed checks to cover the bills or have paid the customer service representative in their local office, that money becomes part of the company's resources.

At Georgia Power, an extremely small fraction of those resources, less than one tenth of one percent, is channelled into advertising. Why is even this small amount earmarked for such an expenditure? Because it is one of the most effective and inexpensive ways we've found to encourage customers to use less of our product, to use their kilowatt-hours more efficiently and to save money on an essential service whose cost, in the face of worldwide inflation, has nowhere to go but up.

Would a company, especially a monopoly in the case of utilities, be responsible it if kept information affecting energy use to itself instead of sharing it with the public? We at Georgia Power would certainly answer "no," and a recent statewide public opinion survey shows that our customers agree.

In fact, an overwhelming 80 percent stated that they were in favor of electric company advertising, and 89 percent stated that we should run ads telling people how to conserve or use less electricity.

Our survey results also showed that customers have learned the most effective way to save on their electric bills is to use proper thermostat settings for heating and cooling. Just one year ago our customers thought the best way to save electricity was to turn off lights. While that is a good idea, it isn't nearly as effective as setting the thermostat properly. This encouraging reversal can be primarily attributed to our recent advertising campaigns dealing with thermostat settings.

The cost of advertising is minimal when compared with such impressive results. Georgia Power's 1977 media expenditures break down to ap-

* *The Atlantia Journal and Constitution,* February 12, 1978: 1-C, 13-C.
George W. Edwards is vice president of public affairs for Georgia Power Company. Sidney L. Moore, Jr., is with the Consumers' Utility counsel.

proximately 4 cents per customer per month, an amount that is easily saved by following just one of the company's advertised energy conservation tips. To relate these tips in one letter to each customer would cost the company well over $100,000 in postage alone.

At Georgia Power, advertising is actually just one part of a comprehensive customer communications program that includes bill inserts, brochures available at local offices, and free home energy audits—all provided with one objective: helping customers keep their electric bills as low as possible.

A final point in favor of utility advertising is one that is rarely addressed by critics. It applies irrespective of the advertising content. Corporations, be they retail outlets, newspapers, or regulated businesses such as utilities, are entitled to the same First Amendment guarantee to free speech as are individuals.

To limit the right of a company to communicate freely with the public is to say that it may not participate fully in the public debates on the many issues related to utilities.

No

By Sidney L. Moore, Jr.

About one dime out of every $100 of Georgia Power Company's revenue goes to advertising expenses—one-tenth of one percent.

Why then, does advertising evoke so much public comment and hostility? In almost any discussion of electric rates this subject, along with the company's charitable donations, will arise.

Several arguments have been advanced against advertising. First, many contend that since the power company is a monopoly there is no business justification for advertising, and it is simply a waste of the ratepayers' money.

This may be the weakest argument, since electricity does compete with natural gas for many purposes. One may assume that if there were no "business justifications" for advertising, the power company would not do it. All activities of the company, including both advertising and charitable donations, are designed to increase the company's profits.

But what is good for the power company may not be good for the consumer. There are several very fundamental ways in which advertising by public utility companies interest the public.

Some advertising tends to stimulate growth in the use of energy at a time when it is in short supply. This is called "promotional" advertising. Some of it is direct, as when the company runs advertisements in national business magazines to encourage industry to move to Georgia and plug into the system. Some of it is indirect, as when the company plants an article in the food section of the daily newspaper to encourage the use of electric appliances, or inserts information in the utility bill envelope saying that electric space heaters are "100% efficient."

Other advertisements are simply to improve the public image of the utility. Ads in high school annuals and football programs, like charitable donations, tend to raise public confidence in the power company, which decreases hostilities when the company asks for a rate increase.

The effect of advertising to win friends in the news media also cannot be overlooked. While the editorial staff may oppose higher electric rates, the advertising department is knocking on the utilities' door trying to sell ads. Newpapers, radio, and television are all guilty of this. One large utility, contacted in relation to this article, pleaded that the breakdown of expenditures among television, radio, and newspapers not be printed, lest the one on the short end get angry with the company.

There is some advertising which on the surface seems beneficial to consumers. So called "conservation" ads encouraging higher thermostats in the summer and lower thermostats in the winter seem to run counter to the company's interests. These advertisements have two major benefits for the company.

First, added expenses are incurred when it is necessary to use all available generating facilities during "peak load" situations. Most electricity is used during the summer when all air conditioners are on. Older plants which are ordinarily shut down are put into operation to supply this additional or "peak load" electricity. Often "peak load" electricity costs the company more than it can sell it for.

The other advertising benefit is that the conservation image builds "goodwill" which helps hold down adverse comment.

It is not the dime on a $100 power bill, then, that causes the problem. It is the way advertising affects consumer behavior and the behavior of the Public Service Commission that counts. The regulation of advertising, consequently, should deal more with the type of ad and intent of the ad than with its cost.

SHOULD LAWYERS BE ALLOWED TO ADVERTISE ON RADIO AND TV?*

Yes

By Tom Watson Brown

In June 1977, the U.S. Supreme Court, in Bates v. State Bar of Arizona, rules that the legal profession's self-imposed ban on advertising was unconstitutional, thereby eliminating the bar's historic reforms of previous years in this area. The issue now is what guidelines and rules will govern the efforts of attorneys and legal groups in advertising their services.

The Supreme Court of Georgia, which is vested with the power to set rules to govern the conduct of Georgia attorneys, all of whom must be members of the state bar, is currently considering proposals on attorney advertising submitted by the bar's Board of Governors.

I believe that attorneys should have the right, should they so elect, to advertise on radio and television, as well as in newspapers, magazines, and other printed media. The avowed purpose of allowing attorneys to advertise at all is to educate the public to the availability of legal services and to provide basic information for use in selecting an attorney.

Many of the people who are least likely to know an attorney and who most need this information depend for information (as well as entertainment) on the broadcast media, to the almost total exclusion of printed media. Without lawyer advertisements on radio and television, a large segment of the population would not even be exposed to this information.

The First Amendment to the Constitution has now been extended to protect the rights of lawyers to advertise. When the freedom of press concept was written into the Constitution, radio and television were, of course, unknown media. But no rational distinction in principle exists today between radio and television on the one hand, and the press on the other, in application of the Constitutional protection of freedom of press. To allow lawyers to advertise in newspapers, but not in electronic media, is clearly disciminatory against the broadcasting industry.

The oft-expressed fears of "huckstering" and enticement if broadcast advertising is available to attorneys can easily be quelled by adoption of reasonable rules and regulations as to the form and content of radio and television commercials by lawyers. Both radio and television advertisements can be preserved indefinitely by taping so as to permit disciplinary

* *The Atlanta Journal and Constitution,* March 19, 1978, pp. 1-C, 9-C.

Tom Watson Brown is an Atlanta lawyer who represents the Georgia Association of Broadcasters. Emmet J. Bondurant is an Atlanta attorney.

actions against attorneys who abuse the privilege and flout the bar's regulations.

The state bar has consistently solicited radio and television stations to furnish free time for bar promotions such as recognition of Law Day, free legal services for the indigent, consumer relief and the need for legal advice when undertaking such activities as drafting a will, entering into a contract, buying a home and so forth. The broadcast industry has fully cooperated, furnishing its services for free.

These public service announcements have been of high quality and dignity. There is no indication that the public has been abused or unduly persuaded by exposure to them. And, too, the courts of Georgia have permitted broadcast coverage of courtroom proceedings with extremely satisfactory results. To repudiate these past successful examples of the splendid cooperation between the bar and the broadcast media by prohibiting commercial lawyer advertising under reasonable restrictions would be a harsh and discriminatory decision and a studied insult to the broadcasting industry.

While only newspaper advertising was at issue in the Bates case, the court, by observing that electronic broadcast media advertising warranted "special consideration," indicated its tacit acceptance of the principle of lawyer advertising on radio and television. It is obvious that the very concept of advertising embraces radio and television as well as newsprint. Broadcasting is generally recognized as by far the most effective means to widely disseminate information to the public, as demonstrated by its ever-increasing audiences, in contrast to the dwindling circulations of daily newspapers.

There is no rational objection to broadcast advertising that cannot easily be remedied by reasonable regulation. If attorney advertising is to be permitted at all, then it should be available through both electronic and printed media, if the public is to truly benefit.

No

By Emmet J. Bondurant

June 1977 the Supreme Court ruled that the historic ethical prohibitions on advertising by lawyers violated the First Amendment. At the same time the court recognized that the solicitation of clients by lawyers has great potential for abuse and that the state courts and legislatures retain the power to impose "reasonable restrictions upon the time, place and manner of advertising" by lawyers.

The ruling comes at a time when the legal profession is under heavy criticism for not effectively policing unethical conduct of lawyers, and raises a complex host of new ethical problems in a context with which the bar associations and courts have had little experience.

The Georgia Supreme Court is considering new ethical rules that will permit factual advertising by lawyers in newspapers and periodicals, but will prohibit lawyers from advertising for clients on radio and television.

The Georgia Association of Broadcasters has objected to the proposed rules as unwarranted "discrimination" against its members, that deprives the operators of the radio and television stations of the opportunity to sell commercial advertising to lawyers.

Insofar as these objections are based on the Constitution, they are without merit. For example, Congress has, with the approval of the Supreme Court, prohibited the advertisement of cigarettes on radio and television, but not in newspapers and magazines. In its decision permitting advertising of so called "routine" services by lawyers in newspapers, the Supreme Court pointed out that radio and television advertisements by lawyers presented "special problems" not present in printed advertisements which warrant different treatment.

Radio and television advertising by lawyers would present very difficult enforcement problems for the bar, not presented by printed advertisements. More than any other advertising medium, radio and television utilize what Vance Packard has called "hidden persuaders"—a sophisticated combination of sounds, symbols, images, colors, and buzz-words—not to impart factual information about the merits of the sponsor's product, but to trigger a largely emotional and subconscious demand for one particular brand over another.

The Federal Trade Commission, with its huge staff of experts and multimillion dollar budget, has not been able to adequately cope with deceptive advertising of ordinary consumer goods. Bar associations lack the expertise and resources to adequately police radio and television ads by lawyers.

Radio-TV ads differ from other forms of advertising in another respect. If advertising by lawyers is restricted to newspapers and magazines, no one will be forced to read an ad who does not have some interest in employing a lawyer. Radio and television ads are unavoidable. While no one turns on a radio to listen to commercials, he is compelled to subject himself to the bombardment of commercials as the price of "free" radio and television service.

Advertising by lawyers serves a public interest, as contrasted with the commercial interest of lawyers and media only to the extent that it provides the public with objective information that is relevant to the selection of an individual lawyer. The public interest will be harmed if the right of lawyers to advertise becomes a license for lawyers, who are unable to attract clients based on their reputations, to solicit clients by appeals that, while not demonstrably false, make use of hard-sell Madison Avenue techniques to stimulate a consumer demand for his services.

Since radio or television commercials promoting lawyers will both undermine the dignity of the legal profession, and mislead the public through exaggerated claims, hucksterish promotions, and hidden appeals to pride or avarice, the rules proposed by the state bar prohibiting such advertisements by lawyers are in the public interest.

Part 4 | Pricing: Issues of Satisfaction for Value Received in Voluntary Exchanges

PRICING: ISSUES OF SATISFACTION FOR
VALUE RECEIVED IN VOLUNTARY EXCHANGES

The issue of providing fair value is, at once, as old as the concept of exchange and as new as the idea of institutionalized consumer protection. In the earliest notions of exchange, the parties in negotiation were the sole arbiters of detemining what constituted "fair value." The principle of *caveat emptor* ("let the buyer beware") was well accepted, and success in trade accrued to those who were the most wary and knowledgeable regarding products and market needs.

The discipline of economics grew from an analysis of how the "invisible hand" made up of countless individual transactions guided the marketplace. Economic principles of elasticity, cost-oriented pricing, demand-oriented pricing, and various models of reactions to price changes were developed independently of the concept of fair value. The implicit assumption was that if one of the parties believed that fair value was not offered, no exchange would take place.

During the late nineteenth century, however, the technological complexity of producing and distributing many new products to national markets in the United States brought tremendous economies of scale to producers. The formation of monopolies and trusts allowed producers to lower costs significantly while maintaining high prices. With diminished competition, the option of not buying monopolized goods was effectively eliminated. While government intervention through the passage of antitrust legislation was designed to maintain competition, it also had the effect of assuring a range of choices for consumers.

By the late 1930s, federal legislation had begun to specify pricing situations that were permissible and not permissible, as part of a perceived duty to maintain competition. The Clayton Act (1914) prohibited certain types of price discrimination, and the Robinson-Patman Act (1936) provided the Federal Trade Commission (FTC) with the right to establish limits on quantity discounts, to forbid brokerage allowances except to independent brokers, and to prohibit promotional allowances except where made available to all on proportionately equal terms. The Wheeler-Lea Act (1938) amended the FTC Act (1914) to read that "unfair methods of competition and unfair or deceptive acts or practices in commerce are unlawful." The Wheeler-Lea Act, by including "unfair or deceptive acts or practices" toward consumers as well as business entities, opened the door to governmental arbitration as the way to maintain fairness of various pricing practices toward consumers. At the same time, however, the Miller-Tydings Act (1937) exempted fair-trade agreements (which were essentially retail price-fixing agreements) from antitrust prosecution, in order to allow independent stores to compete against newly formed chain stores that could underprice them in the absence of price fixing.

These acts were clearly designed to protect competition. The specification of prohibited and permissible pricing practices was a tactical step necessary to resolve major issues regarding competition at the time. The impact of some acts declined; the Miller-Tydings Act was widely unenforced and finally repealed in

1976. The impact of the Wheeler-Lea Act became very strong, however, as the federal government was asked to arbitrate cases regarding unfair pricing practices toward consumers.

As the consumer movement of the late 1960s and 1970s grew, consumers were quick to see examples of what they believed were unfairness in pricing. There was moral outrage when durable goods and food products were found to be priced higher in poor neighborhoods than were the same products in suburban neighborhoods. Premium-priced products that shared components with lower-priced products (e.g., Oldsmobiles with Chevrolet engines) were denounced as rip-offs. Many consumers believed that among the many obligations that business owed society was the obligation to provide goods at the lowest possible price. When shortages and inflation raised the cost of items to producers, their attempts to raise the selling prices were met with charges of price "gouging." A major function of the Department of Energy became the determination of whether price increases by petroleum companies were "fair."

In the 1960s and 1970s, the responsibility for assuring the inclusion of fair value in a transaction passed from the participants to representatives of society in many instances. Although adherents of laissez-faire capitalism may pine for a return to *caveat emptor,* such an expectation would be unrealistic. The history of the consumer movement since 1900 has shown no retreat from consumerist-generated programs once they have been institutionalized into the operating principles of American business.

The issues involved in providing fair value are diverse and only a partial list can be furnished. Some of the major ones are:

1. *Price disclosure.* Users of automated grocery checkout systems have prices "hidden" in a computer program. Who should bear the costs of protection against potential abuse? The "Giant Foods, Inc." case explores this issue. More "price disclosure" has been favorably regarded, but some industries may have characteristics where more pricing information may *not* be better. The insurance industry, for example, could disclose so much information that the typical customer would be left utterly confused. Is more information always better?

2. *Pricing to the vulnerable.* Should there be protection of consumers when a unique *potential* for taking advantage of a pricing situation exists but no advantage has been taken? Buyers of funeral services make decisions under severe emotional and time constraints. The Davis Gardiner Funeral Home case illustrates this social concern, by inclusion of the charges made by the FTC concerning funeral-home pricing practices. The Life Insurers Conference case also considers pricing practices of firms whose customers often are unable to evaluate price–value relationships in an analytical manner.

3. *Price competition in the professions.* Supreme Court decisions in the late 1970s made clear that advertising and price competition were legal in the professions. "Pricing in the professions" is an issue with

several facets. Is it unethical for professionals (e.g., doctors, lawyers, dentists, accountants, opticians, etc.) to stimulate selective demand, charging low prices to their customers, and to advertise the availability of those low prices? One of the commentaries examines price as a variable in the dentistry profession.

4. *Price discrimination.* Bribery is clearly illegal, but to what extent are such items as "sales commissions," "promotional allowance," "rebates," "trade gifts," "premiums," and "consultant fees" thinly disguised bribes? Are these legitimate costs to be covered by a final price?

5. *Price signaling.* Price fixing is illegal, but not "price signaling," which is a pattern of price changes over time that signals competitors what a firm's ultimate price will be. Is not price signaling simply a method of obtaining *de facto* price fixing?

6. *Price comparisons.* Are price comparisons, assembled and advertised by a competing firm, fair and honest if not all available items are compared on a price basis? In other words, are consumers misled if only comparisons that favor the advertiser are reported? Is there a net gain in consumer information by this process?

These and other issues are addressed in the cases and commentaries in this section. In analyzing them, it might be useful to keep in mind the historical background concerning the development of the idea of providing fair value, specific pricing objectives and legislation (given in Figures 1 and 2), and the role of pricing in the making of managerial decisions.

FIGURE 1   Potential Pricing Objectives*

1. Maximum long-run profits
2. Maximum short-run profits
3. Growth
4. Stabilize market
5. Desensitize customers to price
6. Maintain price-leadership arrangement
7. Discourage entrants
8. Speed exit of marginal firms
9. Avoid government investigation and control
10. Maintain loyalty of middlemen and get their sales support
11. Avoid demands for "more" from suppliers—labor in particular
12. Enhance image of firm and its offerings
13. Be regarded as "fair" by customers (ultimate)

* Excerpted from Alfred R. Oxenfeldt, "A Decision-Making Structure for Price Decisions," *Journal of Marketing,* January 1973, pp. 48–53, with permission of the publisher, the American Marketing Association.

14. Create interest and excitement about the item
15. Be considered trustworthy and reliable by rivals
16. Help in the sale of weak items in the line
17. Discourage others from cutting prices
18. Make a product "visible"
19. "Spoil market" to obtain high price for sale of business
20. Build traffic

FIGURE 2   Recent Cases Regarding Pricing Legislation*

Sherman Antitrust Act (1890)

Section 1: Price fixing is prohibited. (Vertical price fixing was permitted between 1937 and 1976 under the Miller-Tydings Amendment, 1937, and the McGuire Act, 1952. These "Fair Trade" acts were repealed on March 11, 1976.)

Recent Cases

1. The Court (1975) found that *Adolph Coors Co.* controlled prices of its beer by terminating distributors who did not follow company pricing policy. Exclusive geographic territories prevented dealers from using alternative sources of Coors. Coors argued that exclusive territories were necessary to justify the dealers' investment in refrigerated warehouses to maintain the quality of Coors beer, which is not pasteurized.
2. In 1926 the Supreme Court approved *General Electric*'s consignment system for setting the retail prices of lamp bulbs. In 1966 the Antitrust Division of the Justice Department charged GE with price fixing. In 1973 the district court concluded that the system should be outlawed in the future. (*JM,* January 1974, p. 72)
3. The Supreme Court (1967) found *Arnold, Schwinn & Co.* in violation of Section 1, per se, because of its vertical restrictions on the distributors and retailers of its bicycles. Distributors were limited to dealing with franchised dealers, and dealers were limited to dealing only with consumers. (*JM,* January 1968, p. 73)

Section 2: Monopolization, attempts to monopolize, and conspiracies to monopolize are forbidden. The seminal monopolization case may well be *Standard Oil Co. v. United States* (1911); a collection of firms, which first dominated the beginning oil industry through the device of a common-law trust and later through a New Jersey holding company, was held to be an illegal monopoly and was ordered dissolved.

1. The Justice Department (1976) dropped its antitrust suits against *Goodyear Tire & Rubber Co.* and *Firestone Tire & Rubber Co.* because it could not prove its charge

* G. David Hughes, *Marketing Management* (Reading, Mass.: Addison-Wesley Publishing Co., Inc., 1978), pp. 244–45.

that the companies were using predatory price cutting to drive competitors out of the replacement-tire market. The Justice Department spent $1 million on pretrial work. The suit charged that price cuts were predatory because they were made when material and labor costs increased. The suit failed to consider the fact that new manufacturing operations offset some of these costs. Furthermore, consumers had switched to lower-priced grades. Thus the companies seemed to be taking a short-term profit-maximizing course that reflected changes in costs and demand. *The Wall Street Journal,* March 3, 1976, p. 3)

2. The Supreme Court (1967) found three national *frozen-pie makers* in violation of the Robinson-Patman Act for predatory price cutting in the Salt Lake City market. It rejected the defense that there was no competitive injury to the Utah Pie Company, because it was able to cut prices, increase sales volume, and maintain profits. (*JM,* October 1967, p. 74)

Clayton Act (1914)

Section 2: As amended by the Robinson-Patman Act (1936), this section *prohibits price discrimination that may substantially lessen competition.* This discrimination may take the form of direct price differences, differential discounts, a brokerage allowance to a phantom broker, or advertising allowances that are not given proportionally to all buyers in competition with each other. Furthermore, the section makes it unlawful to knowingly induce or receive a price discrimination.

Recent Case

The Great Atlantic & Pacific Tea Company, Inc. (A&P) was found in violation of Section 2(f) of the Robinson-Patman Act and Section 5 of the FTC Act by an FTC administrative law judge (1975) for knowingly inducing discriminatory prices for dairy products from Borden, Inc. A&P induced from Borden an offer that was much better than the competitive offer. Furthermore, the competitive offer was not operative, because A&P could not meet the required volume and the competitor could not meet the delivery schedule. The Borden offer would be justified only on the grounds of meeting competition, not on a cost saving. (*JM,* April 1976, p. 92)

Cases

GIANT FOODS, INC.:
ISSUES WITH SUPERMARKET PRICE SCANNERS*

The company limousine pulled off the expressway and began threading its way through traffic in downtown Washington, D.C. Joseph B. Danzansky put aside the reports he had been studying since he left the Giant Foods headquarters in Landover, Maryland. He noticed some black children playing in a small park and remembered the burned-out storefront that had occupied the site following the devastating 1968 riots. The neat apartment buildings, the freshly painted storefronts, and the sleek new offices gave Danzansky a proprietary sense of pride. He recalled Giant's community relations triumph that had put his food chain in the forefront of the then-burgeoning consumer movement.

During the 1968 Poor People's March on Washington, he had persuaded other local chains and some large manufacturers to join Giant Foods in feeding the 3,000 demonstrators camping in "Resurrection City" on the capitol mall. As a result of such community efforts, Giant Stores were protected by black employees during the riots that followed the assassination of Dr. Martin Luther King, Jr. Danzansky also had headed a committee of civic leaders which instituted a relief program for the riot-torn areas of the nation's capitol. Later, black civil rights leaders officially exempted Giant Foods from Operation Bread Basket, a movement that boycotted stores in 14 cities, including Washington, regarding minority hiring.

As the limousine pulled out of the reconstructed area and toward the Pennsylvania Avenue intersection, Danzansky recalled his comment during an interview the year before: "I feel we have demonstrated that consumer

* This case is not intended to provide a precise account of the thinking or behavior of the parties involved.

action and community action are good business.''[1] He smiled at this thought, remembering the day in 1970 that he hired Esther Peterson, former White House Special Assistant for Consumer Affairs, as vice president—consumer affairs for Giant Foods. He told the same interviewer that "at the time she was anathema to the food industry and very few of our colleagues would speak to her."[2] The smile broke into a brief grin when he thought about some of the uncomplimentary comments others had made to him over that decision—one of the best business decisions, he felt, that he had ever made.

When the limousine began to pull away from an ensnarled intersection, Danzansky caught a glimpse of the capitol dome between the trees adjoining the avenue, triggering an abrupt ending to his reverie over some of his past successes. The 20-minute trip from company headquarters to Capitol Hill had become quite familiar to him over the past year, as he and Mrs. Peterson had been called to testify before Senator Frank Moss' Senate Subcommittee on Consumers. The subcommittee was investigating the new computerized checkout systems and the Universal Product Code that the food industry had begun to employ. The Senate hearings had been harrowing at times, as had been the meetings with consumer groups, activists, and the Retail Clerks International Union that had occurred over the last two years. When he had first proposed to test the new checkout system, he had never thought that the UPC concept, consumerism, and the issue of item pricing would combine to become such a political hot potato.

Danzansky was on his way to a luncheon meeting and conference with Israel Cohen, senior vice president and chief operating officer of Giant Foods and one of the cofounders of the chain back in 1938. The events of the past two years could well culminate at their meeting, since they were going to decide Giant's future commitment to computerized checkout systems. Because of the vast amounts of capital expenditures involved, and the degree of concern by consumers and organized labor over this issue, Danzansky realized they were about to decide Giant's entire future. Danzansky was not prone to dramatics, but because of the effect of food price changes on inflation, he felt that their decision could have a widespread impact. Giant had been in the forefront of innovations in the industry under his leadership and the company was widely respected and recognized as a leader in the field. Danzansky decided to review highlights of the reports that had been lying idle in his lap for the past 10 minutes.

---

[1]   "Joseph B. Danzansky of Giant Foods: Consumerism as a Competitive Tool," *Nation's Business*, October 1974, p. 53.
[2]   Ibid.

COMPANY BACKGROUND

As of 1978, Giant Foods had 115 outlets operating principally in the Virginia–Baltimore–Washington, D.C., area. Giant also operated nonsupermarket subsidiaries, including seven carpet stores, six optical shops, two auto service centers, 37 pharmacies (as part of the food units), 14 Pants Corrals, and four Giant Department Stores (of approximately 100,000 square feet each). The food units typically were between 25,000 and 40,000 square feet. As of 1978, the average food store had annual revenues of $7.8 million. Sales growth over the past few years had been impressive.

The Washington, D.C., area was considered to be dominated by the "Big 2"—Giant and Safeway. Since 1968 Giant had increased its market share from 25 percent to 30 percent while Safeway had remained at 31 percent, despite the fact that Safeway had more than one and one-half times the number of stores in the area. Industry sources estimated that Safeway Stores grossed about $100,000 in sales a week, compared to Giant's typical store average of $140,000.[3] Safeway had approximately 2,450 stores operating in 28 states. Other major competitors in the area included A&P, with about 10 percent of the market, and Grand Union, with an 8 to 9 percent market share. Although only a regional chain, Giant ranked nationally as the 19th largest chain store in sales volume.

The Washington, D.C., area is a very unique market for retailers, especially for supermarkets. For example, independent stores had only 10 percent of total market sales in D.C. compared to 32 percent nationally. In 1972 about 98 percent of all grocery firms in the country were independents (defined as having four or less stores). As of 1974 the D.C. area had the highest average household income of all SMSA markets, while per capita effective buying income was sixth highest. The district also ranked first in per household retail sales, supermarket sales, and furniture, household, and appliance sales.[4]

Not all of the market peculiarities were favorable to Giant, however. The population turnover in Washington was 35 percent every 5 years and regional chains like Giant had to attract newcomers to a chain they have probably never heard of. Giant also had to contend with the fact that it was located in the nation's capitol, and therefore under constant scrutiny

[3] Marion C. Burke and Leonard L. Berry, "Do Social Actions of a Corporation Influence Store Image and Profits?" *Journal of Retailing,* Winter 1974–1975, p. 63.
[4] Kathryn Hanson, "Giant Foods," *Intercollegiate Case Clearing House,* 1977, p. 4.

from legislators, regulators, and leading consumer activist organizations. Chains in the area, therefore, had to be very aware of changing social, political, and consumer issues. As Giant's President Danzansky put it: "Getting some of the heat is just part of the price of being in the kitchen. . . . Whenever legislators—or worse, regulators—get interested in the grocery industry, they look at us."[5]

Danzansky had been president of Giant since 1964 and sales more than tripled under his leadership. Prior to becoming the chief executive officer, Danzansky served on the board of directors and was a highly successful Washington corporate lawyer, earning over $100,000 a year. Giant was one of his clients as early as 1944. A self-starter from the beginning, Danzansky, whose father was a Rumanian-born funeral director in Washington, was voted class president four years in a row while working his way through George Washington University. In honor of his leadership and management abilities, Danzansky was elected chairman of the board of the National Association of Food Chains.

Danzansky had established an excellent reputation for Giant over the years and the company was often cited as one of the best managed chains in the country.

Realizing early that consumerism was a serious and growing trend, Danzansky convinced the board of directors to fully commit the company to meet consumer issues head on. In 1970 he hired Esther Peterson as vice president for consumer affairs. Peterson had been Consumer Advisor to Presidents Kennedy and Johnson, was influential in developing Kennedy's Consumer Bill of Rights, and was one of the most highly regarded members of the consumerism movement. She headed a committee of key Giant executives, and formalized their objectives for their consumer program in the Giant's Consumer Bill of Rights. The key areas of the program were:

- The Right to Safety
- The Right to Be Informed
- The Right to Be Heard
- The Right to Choose
- The Right to Redress[6]

Giant's program on the right to be informed, for example, led to improved point-of-purchase product information. They were early pioneers in both unit pricing (prices per comparable unit of measure) and open

[5]   "In a Fishbowl," *Forbes,* December 1, 1975, p. 80.
[6]   Burke and Berry, "Social Actions," p. 62.

dating, as well as educational institutional advertising. Extensive nutritional labeling was included on all of Giant's private-label merchandise. Danzansky's policy was to ensure that all of Giant's private-label products were equal to or better in quality than branded goods at competitive or lower prices. Peterson employed advisory committees (including housewives and consumer representatives) that ensured quick and individualized responses to customer complaints. Furthermore, Danzansky instituted an unconditional money-back guarantee on all products.

Unfortunately, such service and consumer extras had reduced Giant's return on equity to 14 percent, which was only fair in the industry. Although the program was proving costly, Danzansky has said that "In general, they (the extras) are part of our image[7]. . . we had decided that consumerism was here to stay, that its premises were valid. We had decided to go the whole way and embrace it. In fact, to make it a competitive tool."[8] Market share increases and record sales and earnings during this period indicated that the pioneering strategy was working.

The results of one study also indicated to management how important these programs were to consumers. The survey showed that 29.7 percent of the respondents felt that consumer programs and service were the most important factors in store choice. Of those surveyed, 47.3 percent mentioned Giant Foods when asked which grocery chain in the D.C. area had the most concern for the consumer, compared to 4.7 percent mentioning Safeway and 3.4 percent mentioning A&P.[9] Educating the consumer regarding the benefits of the computer-assisted checkout system utilizing the Universal Product Code could turn out to be Giant's most ambitious and costly consumer-related program to date. Danzansky, therefore, set out to determine as best as possible all the consequences that the program could have on both the company itself as well as for the consumers. In the summer of 1974, he formed an executive committee to review the costs and benefits of the system. At the same time, he asked Peterson to have her Consumer Advisory Committee study consumer concerns regarding the computer-assisted checkout. Between the two committees, Danzansky hoped to find the answers to questions that had been plaguing him since the idea's conception:

- Would the system be justified purely on a cost-benefit basis?
- How much of a competitive advantage would it afford?
- How could Giant handle the item-pricing issue?
- How could Giant sell the system to consumers?

[7] "In a Fishbowl," p. 80.
[8] "Joseph B. Danzansky of Giant Foods," p. 53.
[9] Burke and Berry, "Social Actions," pp. 65–67.

THE UNIVERSAL PRODUCT CODE AND LASER
SCANNING CHECKOUTS

In April 1973, an ad hoc committee of industry associations recommended the adoption of the UPC, a package coding system which consisted of bar symbols and 10 digits that would be readable by some type of scanning device. Every manufacturer in the United States would be assigned an indentification number (the left side, first five digits) as well as a code for each of their products (the right-hand side, second set of five digits). Actually, the code had 11 digits which were machine-readable. The eleventh digit, which was not printed, was one of the first bar symbols the scanner reads. This digit, which was zero for grocery products, was added to allow integration of other industries' products, such as books, health and beauty aids, stationery, and other convenience items that were sold in grocery stores. The UPC symbol had three principal parts or sections: the Number System Character (the industry code), the Manufacturers Identification Number, and the Product/Part Code Number.[10] The bar symbols were computer-designed in such a manner that the scanner-related hardware would know whether a particular bar character was on the left or right-hand side of the symbol.

The UPC was controlled and marketed by Distribution Codes, Inc., which was owned jointly by the Uniform Grocery Product Code Council and the National Association of Wholesalers/Distributors. DCI assigned manufacturers an identification code once the company applied for membership in the Universal Product Code organization. The manufacturer then selected one of several companies to produce a computer-generated glass master plate (film projection) of the bar code that was precise to 0.0001 of an inch. The manufacturer used that master film, either through its own facilities or through packaging companies, to have the code stamped on its product's package. A consulting firm, commissioned by the Grocery Industry Ad Hoc Committee—Universal Product Code, estimated that it would cost between $50,000 and $1,500,000 for a manufacturer to convert to UPC. As of 1978, the UPC had been widely adopted, as shown in the following table[11]:

[10]   Thomas V. Sobczak, "The UPC: An Introduction to What It Means for Consumers," *Computers and People,* December 1975, p. 8.
[11]   Joseph S. Coyle, "Scanning Lights Up a Dark World for Grocers," *Fortune,* March 27, 1978, p. 76; and "Breaking the Code," *Forbes,* March 6, 1978, p. 50.

Date	Portion of Grocery SKUs [a]
10/74	50 percent
1/76	60–65 percent
3/78	85 percent
7/78	91 percent

[a]SKU = stock-keeping units.

The code would be read by a high-speed laser scanner system attached to a minicomputer at the store which was also linked to the master computer at the company headquarters. There were three types of scanners: fixed-beam, moving-beam, and hand-held or pen readers. For a grocery chain, fast "throughput" at the checkout required stationary high-speed optical scanners (using a laser projecting a figure-eight-shaped beam through a slot) that were set flush with the checkout counter. The UPC coded item was read as the checker pulled the package across the slot from any direction and in the same motion bagged the product. The scanner converted the bar images to binary-coded digits. The in-store computer searched its memory for both price and product information. The product name, size, and price were printed on the sales receipt as well as on a cathode-ray tube located at the checkout for the consumer to see. By storing price information in the computer, stores would no longer have to individually price-ticket every can or package on the shelves.

Although the UPC had found wide acceptance and use by manufacturers, the adoption of scanners in supermarkets was extremely slow. As of July 1978, only 250 out of the country's 37,000 supermarkets had utilized scanners, up from 60 two years before.[12] There were three principal hurdles blocking widespread usage of scanners.

First, scanning equipment was very expensive. For a 10-lane supermarket, costs would range anywhere from $110,000 to $130,000. McKinsey & Company, the consultants originally hired by the UPC Ad Hoc Committee to study the feasibility of the system, estimated that if 5,000 to 10,000 stores utilized scanners, industry savings could amount to over $140 million a year—an astronomical figure for an industry whose before-tax profit in 1977 was only $1 billion, with the typical store having about a ¾ of 1 percent margin on sales. McKinsey & Company also estimated, however, that

[12] "ARF's UPC Study: Golddust Now, Paydirt Later," *Purchasing,* June 3, 1975, p. 73.

a store must have gross sales of at least $100,000 per week to utilize the system profitably, effectively ruling out 80 percent of U.S. supermarkets. Although costs appeared to be prohibitive, there were over 50,000 electronic registers in use that would be capable of being upgraded into UPC scanners at less than half the price of new units.[13]

Second, the UPC concept was not viewed favorably by labor, specifically the Retail Clerks International Union of the AFL–CIO. Publicly raising consumer issues, such as abandonment of item pricing, as their main reasons for opposal, the Union was clearly afraid of layoffs due to the scanner's ability to dramatically reduce the labor-intensive nature of the industry operation, through checkout and inventory efficiency.

Third, and by far the most worrisome and visible aspect, was opposition by consumer activists and organizations. Although these groups raised several issues, the major concern was over item pricing. Fearing that companies could change the price on the computer without upkeeping the shelf markers (where every item or SKU would have the price clearly displayed below it on the shelf lip), they suggested that the consumer would not know what the price really was. Consumer groups also complained that the system would impede price comparison.

There were other factors that inhibited adoption of scanner devices—the most important being bad timing. From 1974 through 1976, wholesale and retail prices were skyrocketing and it was felt that budget-conscious consumers, already upset by rising grocery prices, would be very leery of innovative changes in their shopping routine and would be especially suspicious of shelf rather than item pricing. This period also was a time of overexpansion in the industry accompanied by devastating price wars. Typical chain stores were returning two-thirds of a penny on a dollar sale. Automated computerized warehousing and upgraded electronic registers (nonscanning) had drastically weakened debt-to-equity ratios of most companies through increasing capital intensiveness. Profits on food items were so low that 50 percent of net profits in the industry came from general merchandise items, such as health and beauty aids, magazines, household goods—categories that accounted for only 5 percent of sales.[14]

Danzansky was only too familiar with these problems, but he felt that the benefits and opportunities outweighed the risks of installing the system. Although he felt that he had the labor issue under control for the time being at least, and that the system would pay for itself through "hard" savings benefits within a few years after installation, he knew that the consumer acceptance issue would be the greatest hurdle. That issue had

[13]   Coyle, "Scanning," p. 77.
[14]   Ibid, p. 78.

dominated his time in late 1975 when he testified before the Senate Commerce Subcommittee on Consumers. Subcommittee Chairman Moss was greatly concerned that the $3 billion cost of implementing the UPC would be passed on to the consumer. The majority of the summary reports that Danzansky was reviewing on his way to his luncheon meeting were the latest results from the test stores that were utilizing the system. He had asked an executive committee to prepare the reports on results to date with implications for management and the potential risks and benefits for full-scale implementation.

The system so far had demonstrated substantial "hard" or tangible savings in day-to-day operations. Giant's savings were an average $5,530 per month in a typical store with a monthly sales volume of $560,000. The major parts of this savings were about $2,500 in reduced cashier labor and about $900 in reduced "underrings" errors. If these savings were representative, they could equal the after-tax net profit of the average store, effectively doubling income. Hard savings alone indicated a payback period of 2 to 4 years. Other hard savings could amount to $2,745 a month in reduced labor costs, if Giant were able to eliminate item pricing.[15]

Less tangible benefits had also been demonstrated by the test stores. Some of Giant's top management felt that these benefits, although difficult to measure, could have an even greater impact on corporate profitability. For one thing, merchandise supplied directly from local wholesalers, which was not controlled by Giant's computerized warehouse inventory system, could be carefully tracked by the in-store computer system. The "shrinkage" or error and theft savings alone could amount to as much as 20 weeks of net profit for the average store.[16]

Since 30 percent of the typical store's 1,500 SKUs (stock keeping units) or product types were nonwarehouse items, the computers could monitor sales of specific items on a daily, if not hourly, basis. This feature could permit store managers and headquarters to test the effects of price changes, point-of-sale promotions, coupon redemption, sales displays, and ad campaigns. New product or pricing strategies therefore could be tested, revised, or canceled with very little delay.[17]

Another advantage of the scanner system was its ability to inventory and reorder products. Stores could be able to routinely alter product mixes exactly for maximum inventory turnover and return. Product lines, inventories, pricing, and shelf space could be uniquely tailored to meet each store's needs. This would effectively convert a large chain supermarket,

[15] Ibid, p. 77.
[16] Ibid. p. 78.
[17] Ibid.

whose operations had always been based on standardization for economies of scales, into a neighborhood, supersophisticated Mom-and-Pop-
type store catering to local trends.

Since chains could be able to pretest every marketing decision they
made, they would no longer be dependent on manufacturers' salespeople
and representatives for product information. The store could remove a
bad-selling product despite the amount of promotional support from the
manufacturer. Chains also could be more aggressive in marketing private-
label products, which almost always carry higher gross margins than
branded merchandise. The system, therefore, could be capable of shifting
industry control away from suppliers and back to the grocers—one reason
why wholesalers have been generally opposed to the UPC concept.

The potential benefits were very impressive, but Danzansky was quick
to realize that success hinged on consumer, as well as employee acceptance
of the system. The reports indicated that each of the test stores had experienced a short increase in sales during the testing period—an average of 25
percent—but he felt this might be attributed to the novelty effect of the
system's introduction.[18]

Danzansky had decided that the first step was, if not to gain employee
and union acceptance of the system, to at least stem the tide of their active
opposition. Unfortunately, consumer issues were the party platform for the
Retail Clerks International Union's mounting campaign against the scanner
issue and item pricing. As James T. Housewright, president of the Retail
Clerks Union, stated to the Senate Consumer Subcommittee:

> *Our members are particularly aware of such things as the reliability of shelf
> prices, the attitudes of customers, the intense pressure on individual store
> managers to produce profits, and the clever manipulation and motivation of
> customers by refined advertising and merchandising techniques.*[19]

Danzansky had told others that "eventually labor will have to realize
that featherbedding won't bring better conditions even for their own people."[20] He realized, however, that labor was really worried about its jobs
and that the consumer issues it expressed were a smoke screen. The confusion of issues was reinforced by the fact that Jay Foreman, a top officer
of the Retail Clerks, was the husband of Carol Foreman, then head of the
militant Consumer Federation of America.

If labor's opposition could at least be silenced, Giant could gain a
major step forward toward consumer acceptance. With this objective in

---

[18]   Ibid, p. 76.
[19]   Walter Davis, "Packages without Prices—An Electronic Threat,"
American Federationist, January 1976, p. 23.
[20]   "In a Fishbowl," p. 80.

mind, Danzansky had signed the 1974 union contracts with the RCIU and the Amalgated Meat Cutters Unions with a clause guaranteeing that no one would lose their jobs due to automation for the length of the 3-year contract. It was estimated that the cost of this settlement over the 3-year period would be equivalent to the 1973 earnings before taxes for the company, or roughly $14 million in the first year in added benefits and lost opportunities for economies of operation.[21]

Consumerists had taken the issue of item pricing to the forefront of their continuing campaign against corporate practices. Various consumer organizations had lobbied, with the help of labor unions, in several state legislatures on this issue. By 1976, six states (California, Connecticut, Massachusetts, Michigan, New York, and Rhode Island) had already passed mandatory item-pricing statutes, and similar legislation was pending in 12 others. Fourteen cities, including Chicago, had passed similar laws.[22]

The Maryland Citizens Consumers Council had listed the reasons for the necessity of item pricing:

- Price marking is essential to comparison shopping.
- Price changes can be made with impunity unless there is mandatory price marketing legislation.
- Shelf tags are inaccurate and package pricing is the only way to insure accuracy of the price and the only easily used, readily available element of price information.[23]

The Consumers Federation of America, the NAACP, the National Council of Senior Citizens, the National Consumers Congress, various city and state consumer officials, and organized labor had all used similar reasoning in their lobbying efforts. For example, the National Council of Senior Citizens had argued:

Readable and legible prices marked on each purchase item will ensure that the older adults' shopping trips will not be occasions of stress, isolation and possible despair, but pleasant opportunities to mingle, independently and with dignity, with their fellow members of society.[24]

In Danzansky's various testimony before the Senate Subcommittee he had said that the system's savings could help stabilize prices, while doubling the store's operating income to 1.4 percent of sales. Low margins and intense competition had been forcing the closure of many chains. Con-

---

21   Hanson, "Giant Foods," p. 13.
22   Coyle, "Scanning," p. 77.
23   Davis, "Packages without Prices," p. 23.
24   Ibid.

tinued competition was the only way to ensure reasonable food prices in the long run, and the potential economies of the UPC system might prove to be the only way to assure competition in the industry in the future if current cost trends continue.[25]

The argument that the industry was governed by market pressures had apparently fallen on deaf ears. Senator Vance Hartke (D–Ind.) had countered with a demand for proof that any UPC system savings would be passed on to consumers.[26]

Esther Peterson had argued before the committee that legislation to mandate item pricing at the retail level (Price Disclosure Act, S.997) was premature and should be held up until the problems and benefits of the scanning systems could be more fully explored. "We've concentrated so much energy on the problems (of UPC) that we haven't begun to look at the benefits . . . price marking is miniscule compared with other issues. Let's cool it until we know more."[27]

The food industry was not without its own influence and lobbying power. Arguing that the system should be given a chance to demonstrate potential benefits to grocers and consumers alike, the industry had managed to kill or postpone mandatory item pricing legislation in Maryland, Virginia, Washington, and Illinois, and similar legislation was stuck in committees in at least eight other legislatures.

Some grocers had decided to take the issue right to the consumer. Associated Grocers of Seattle had been using scanners successfully since 1975. When a mandatory price bill was introduced in the Washington state legislature, Associated Grocers handed out to shoppers the names and phone numbers of legislators and asked their customers to help fight the law. Customers were apparently pleased with the faster checkout lanes and convinced that it was helping to keep prices down. Associated had used only shelf pricing since they installed the system, and consumers were apparently satisfied with the system to the degree that the legislation was dropped in committee. Another large chain used similar tactics to stop legislation in Illinois.[28]

Focusing on addressing the item pricing issue head-on, Danzansky had formulated a committee to explore the possibilities of protecting against errors due to discrepancies between prices listed on the computer and those on the shelf. One of the recommendations of the committee was to install a self-operating scanner at some strategic place in the store that would allow the customer to check for himself the price of the merchan-

[25]   "In a Fishbowl," p. 80.

[26]   "UPC Foes Play on Consumer Mistrust to Win Passage of Restrictive Law," *Progressive Grocer*, January 1976, p. 25.

[27]   Ibid.

[28]   Coyle, "Scanning," p. 78.

dise. The small scanner's screen would indicate all the information, including unit pricing, so that the consumer could more easily compare prices among products.[29]

Donald Buchanan, vice president–data processing, had his division come up with a checking procedure which they believed would prevent price discrepancies. Headquarters would send price-change forms to data processing each Tuesday. The latter department would check each item before entering the change onto the computer. On Wednesday the master list would be sent to a printer for shelf and unit price labels. On Thursday the labels would be returned, rechecked against the master list, and sent to the stores by courier, together with a copy of the master list for stores to use to double-check themselves. On Monday the price changes would go into effect, with stores placing the labels on the shelf and data processing entering the price change concurrently.[30] The reports led Danzansky to feel that not only was the system cost-justified, but that it could easily provide an important competitive edge in the Baltimore–Washington area. Although the scanning system could be profitably employed in most of his stores without removing price labels, he was concerned that keeping item pricing would reduce potential savings 20 to 30 percent.

Danzansky had committed 10 years of time, effort, and money into creating a strong image of consumer responsibility for his company. He and Cohen had to decide whether eliminating package prices would dent this image. It also occurred to him that it was possible that this long-lasting perception of Giant could prove to be the only tool to sell consumers on the system. After all, if Giant couldn't gain consumers' confidence, how could Safeway or any other competitor hope to?

The list of reports on his lap and the memory of testifying at Senator Moss' subcommittee reminded Danzansky that it would be an uphill fight to elicit consumers' acceptance of the system and convince them that Giant was certainly aware and genuinely concerned with their reservations.

[29]   Hanson, "Giant Foods," p. 11.
[30]   Ibid, p. 14.

DAVIS-GARDINER FUNERAL HOME: FUNERAL SERVICE PRICING*

In 1974, at the suggestion of his father, Stephen Gardiner completed a study of the public records office and discovered that Davis-Gardiner was Shreveport, Louisiana's third largest funeral home. This news astounded the directors, who since the mid-1960s had presumed their position to be fifth or sixth among the 20-some area homes. As this elating fact sank into the directors' heads, it had an energizing effect, and they began to ponder how they might improve their position still further.

The president's son, Stephen, fresh from his college business curriculum, had a host of ideas and an enthusiasm for the project that the directors hoped would net the firm some real advances. It wasn't easy marketing a commodity as unique as a funeral. The directors knew, that as with all high-fixed-cost industries, volume was the real key to success. Yet industry volume was, of course, limited by one major constraint.

To build sales, Stephen was considering two alternatives:

1. Follow industry tradition and build a new home in a new section of town.
2. Break with tradition and institute an innovative marketing plan, stressing expanded information to potential buyers.

Stephen had designed the second alternative and personally favored it, but many people told him that social norms and professional ethics would not permit its success.

ORIGIN OF AMERICAN FUNERAL INDUSTRY

American funeral practices were adopted from old English traditions. Cabinetmakers and livery men provided the basic services necessary for early ceremonies. During the Civil War, embalming with the use of preserving chemicals was first introduced in America. Although this practice was not completely accepted until after the turn of the century, it did help to reduce the spread of disease during the war. By 1880, there emerged an occu-

---

* This case was prepared by Robert Biringer, Stephen Danner, Kevin Kane, Andrew Modrall, and Cameron Morton under the direction of Associate Professor Jeffrey A. Barach at the Graduate School of Business Administration, Tulane University. It was designed as a basis for classroom discussion and not to illustrate either effective or ineffective handling of an administrative situation, and was modified by the authors for inclusion in this book. Copyright © 1976 by the Graduate School of Business Administration, Tulane University. Reproduced by permission.

pational group serving both humanitarian and sanitation needs. Thus the role of the funeral director became an accepted profession. In 1882, the first convention of the National Funeral Directors Association was held.

Prior to the end of World War I, funeral directors performed their duties in the home of the deceased. Services were simple and usually attended by relatives and close friends. With the growing popularity of smaller homes and apartments in urban America, funeral directors began converting stores and residences into undertaking establishments. It became common practice to perform embalming functions there and also make the funeral home available for visitation.

Following World War I, people came to rely on the funeral director to provide them with motor vehicles for transportation to increasingly distant cemeteries. During the 1930s, the introduction of casket showrooms into funeral homes meant that the funeral director no longer had to take the bereaved to manufacturers' warehouses to select a casket. This provided an added convenience to the family of the deceased. In his role as a provider of services, the funeral director was increasing the conveniences available to his customers. After World War II, funeral homes began expanding geographically as the public migrated from the city to suburban areas.

PROPOSED REGULATION OF THE INDUSTRY

With the arrival of consumerism in the 1960s, the funeral industry became the subject of intense scrutiny. The publication of Jessica Mitford's *The American Way of Death* inspired critics to begin questioning the necessity for funerals and the practices within the industry (see Appendix A).

There were two unique characteristics of the industry which aroused public criticism. First, the funeral director played a dual role in society, that of a businessman and a professional. The consumer relied on him as a professional serving emotional and technical needs. In his position as counselor, the funeral director could help the family through the traumatic period following death. He encouraged a high degree of trust from the consumer, who released personal financial information and depended on the funeral director to help plan the funeral. At the same time, the funeral director was also a businessman. He had to market funerals in a way to maximize consumer satisfaction and at the same time ensure an adequate profit for himself.

The second aspect stemmed from the unique buying position of the consumer. Under stress the person was not as concerned with the cost of the funeral as he would be in certain other transactions. Not having the time to shop around, the consumer was more concerned with "doing what is right'' than with cost. The reputable funeral director had a responsibility to match the cost of the funeral with a price that the buyer could reasonably afford.

In the early 1970s, the Federal Trade Commission undertook an investigation of the funeral industry, which resulted in a set of proposed rules to govern the industry (see Appendix B). In defense of the industry, many funeral directors wrote to the FTC expressing their indignation at the thought of federal control. One complaint was that the proposed rules were based on a survey conducted in the only unregulated area of the United States, the District of Columbia. The hearings contained some sharp exchanges between members of the FTC and members of congressional subcommittees (see Appendix C).

FUNERAL PRICING

Surveys showed that prices varied greatly from one funeral home to another.[1] This lack of information in the marketplace about price differences was believed by some to be a sign of a poor competitive environment. Because of a lack of publicized market prices, the usual approach to pricing had been a cost-plus procedure. This required calculation of the estimated fixed charge per funeral and to this was added the variable casket price plus the funeral home's profit.

A nationwide survey of the National Funeral Directors Association indicated that funeral services selected in 1974 were priced as follows[2]:

- 10.1% under $800
- 15.2% $800 to $1,000
- 41.5% $1,000 to $1,500
- 11.6% $1,500 to $2,000
- 2.5% above $2,000

The remaining 19.1 percent included:

- 3.9% (child funeral services) averaged $246
- 2.6% (welfare adult services) averaged $365
- 12.6% (partial adult services) averaged $424

---

[1] "FTC Survey of Funeral Prices in the District of Columbia," p. 52. (Note: Each home's price included varying combinations of services.)

[2] Published by the National Funeral Directors' Association in "Answers to Questions about Funeral Costs," September 1975.

"Funeral service" here was defined as a complete adult service. It included all charges except the following: (1) interment receptacles or burial vaults, which started at $350; (2) burial space (the cost of an individual grave varied from $350 to $1,000 and the cost of opening and closing a grave averaged $150); (3) additional transportation charges (typically long-distance shipping); (4) $125 crematorium charges; (5) monument or marker, which averaged $500; and (6) a variety of miscellaneous charges.

FUNERAL MARKETING

The funeral industry was a traditional business, usually handed down from father to son. It had a low failure rate but also a low growth rate; deaths in the United States were projected to grow at a rate of 2.5 percent per annum for the next decade.[3] In 1974, there were 22,000 funeral homes in the United States, which serviced the 1.9 million deaths. Nonaggressive marketing techniques best described the approach used almost universally by funeral directors. "One of the musts of the industry, of course, is decorum: no flashy ads and no television jingles . . . [owners] are anxious to keep the name of the funeral home intact."[4] Advertising was, in fact, widely considered to be unethical in this profession, although it was not prohibited. The feelings of many directors were summed up in the experience of one discouraged advertiser: "It's just like selling an engagement ring. You either need one or you don't."[5]

Building a reputation and maintaining a good public image have always been the keys to traditional funeral promotion. Homes encouraged their employees to get involved in prominent community affairs. The clergy was recognized as a valuable source of referral business. They were often the recipients of extra services and perquisites from funeral directors. Quite important, as much as "80 percent of an established home's customers use it [the same funeral home] because of their past association with it."[6] This fact more than any other kept new firms from entering the field.

Traditionally, any marketing effort beyond these means entailed a large fixed investment to build a new home, which typically netted an annual return on investment of 10 percent. Accompanying this outlay was the risk of selecting a poor location. In the 1970s, larger homes which were affiliated with insurance companies began selling preneed burial arrangements. Typically, a single premium insurance policy was sold for $800.

3   "Merchants of Death," *Forbes,* November 15, 1970, p. 59.
4   "Undertaker/Entrepreneur," *Barron's,* August 2, 1971, p. 15.
5   Ibid.
6   "Merchants of Death," p. 58.

This provided $1,000 worth of burial benefits upon the death of the insured. The advantage to the funeral home was that of locking up sales in advance. The insurance company was able to invest the premium at 10 to 12 percent, or to loan some of the funds back to the funeral home if needed to supplement cash flow. Consumers could benefit by sparing their relatives the stress of arranging a funeral at the time of death. The policyholder had the option of choosing the general style of casket he or she desired, or merely purchasing the policy without arrangement.

COMPANY HISTORY

In 1976, Davis-Gardner (D–G) operated three funeral homes and a full-line insurance company. The original home was in the old central neighborhood of Shreveport, the second home was located across the river from Shreveport in Bossier City, and the most successful home was located in a newly growing suburb of Shreveport. In 1975 the firm's volume was 650 units. The three homes had a combined capacity of 12 units per day. It was expected that the new suburban home would reach 340 units in 1976 and thus raise the total volume close to 700 units.

D–G began in 1887, when Stephen's great-grandfather combined his cabinetmaking skills with his livery stable to provide simple funeral services for the community. In 1920, a family marriage allowed a merger with the Davis Burial Company. In 1926, to capitalize on the growing popularity of burial associations, the Gardiners introduced death insurance to Shreveport. This greatly helped the poor to confirm their burial arrangements. The post–World War II population growth prompted the Davis-Gardiner home to expand in order to recover a falling market share. This move in 1947 consisted of buying a new home across the Red River in Bossier City, an area that seemed likely to grow. However, subsequently constructed highways were not located in this area. By 1975, this home was responsible for 7 percent of the company's business. It had proved to be an example of the consequences a funeral director faced when he incorrectly anticipated the area of growth.

By 1968, the city was expanding again and to build their market share the family constructed a new $600,000 home in a new suburban area of Shreveport. In building, the family tried to differentiate this home by breaking local tradition and building a chapel within the funeral home. This move, they felt, would provide more service and convenience for consumers and thus prove to be appreciated. The family's competitors ridiculed this move. Seven years later, however, 80 percent of the city's funeral homes had followed suit. By this time, the new home was doing 300 units per year.

COMPANY MARKETING

Stephen's family had always felt a strong sense of responsibility to the public, and this feeling dominated their pricing policy and sales techniques. To establish an equitable price range, the family utilized "functional pricing" (cost-plus) policies. This involved estimating total "professional and personnel" costs for the year, together with projected "facilities and equipment" costs, increasing the total by 10 percent as an inflation hedge, and dividing each category by the number of estimated annual adult funerals. This gave the professional-personnel charge per funeral ($400 in 1974), and the facilities-equipment charge per funeral ($500 in 1974). To these was added the retail price of the casket with a 50 percent markup to obtain the overall charge for the unique funeral service. This total charge, together with its functional breakdown, was then clearly posted in each casket within the showroom.

In the showroom it was the company's belief that, "if a wide variety of caskets are provided, in a well-lit room, in a manner that facilitated comparison and contrast, with prices clearly visible, then the consumer can easily make the best decision with minimal interference from the funeral director." Typically, Stephen would say:

> There are three basic types of caskets in this room: (1) cloth-covered wood (he points to one of these); (2) the hardwoods, which are finished like a piece of furniture. These are made of a variety of different types of woods (he then points to one of these); and (3) metal, which seals out air and water. The quality of these is determined from the gauge of the metal utilized (he then points to one of these). You will find a complete price within each casket [see Appendix D]; please just look around.

There were complete funeral services employing cloth-covered woods for $890, 20–gauge metal for $1,300, polished cottonwood for $1,400, solid oak for $1,440, redwood for $1,800, solid copper (no rust) for $2,400, and on up in price to a beautiful solid bronze casket with a tufted champagne velvet interior for $4,300. The D–G experience had been that the most popular price range for a complete funeral service was between $1,300 and 1,500. Appendix D shows a copy of the format for the itemized bill used by Davis-Gardiner.

Rationale for Stephen's Marketing Plan

The basis of Stephen's two-stage program was twofold. First, the results of his own survey of Shreveport citizens revealed that 41 percent of those polled desired to know more about funeral arrangements (see Appendix E). Because of this Stephen had designed as a campaign theme the quote, "Davis-Gardiner is concerned enough to let you know."

Second, Stephen personally believed that traditional funerals were of real psychological value to society. He desired to communicate this to the public and so thought that this was the perspective from which he should design the D–G marketing campaign.

Stephen was sharply aware of the people who favored cremation or immediate disposition followed by a memorial service a few weeks later, and also of the people who desired body donation to medical science. A growing problem was the critic who said, "Put me in a pine box and skip the funeral altogether; I certainly will not appreciate it and it will only add to the strain on my family."

Stephen felt that there were sound reasons behind the service portion of the traditional funeral. A traditional funeral was good for people. It included complete body preparation of the deceased, a casket, viewing the body and public visitation, chapel service, professional cars, and a procession to the final committal. It was the time-tested way to honor the deceased and at the same time make adjustment to the fact that death had occurred and life must go on. Stephen had heard several opinions along these lines:

> *I recently returned from England where they have gone from one extreme to another in their funeral services. Many years ago, they allowed the poorly prepared body to be exposed for days. It was horrible. The lingering presence left a bad psychological impression upon the viewers. In recent years in their services, the body is whisked away in a closed casket before the bereaved can actually view the remains. This has caused some severe cases of lingering grief, as survivors refuse to admit that death has occurred. I believe the American funeral is a happy medium, allowing the bereaved to express his grief and reinforce the finality of death.[7]*

> *I was recently again reminded of how valuable and legitimate a funeral service can be. I was accompanied by a friend to his mother's funeral. She had died of a chronic and wasting illness. My friend experienced a deep and profound consolation seeing his mother with the lines of suffering erased from her face and lying at peace.[8]*

Stephen felt that the time-honored role of the casket allowed the comforting thought of some protection for the deceased, and he knew it served the functional purpose of facilitating transportation. He knew that complete body preparation was necessary to ensure sanitary disposal of the deceased, while hastening an acceptable memory picture for the bereaved, especially if the death was violent or the body wasted away. An acceptable

---

[7]   Henry Gardiner, president, Davis-Gardiner Funeral Home.

[8]   Charles W. Wahl, Chief, Psychosomatic Service, UCLA, quoted in Howard D. Raether, "The Place of the Funeral, the Role of the Funeral Director in Contemporary America," *Omega,* 1, no. 2 (1971).

memory picture minimized the probability of future psychological repercussions. Stephen knew that having the body at the wake encouraged a healthy confrontation with the finality of the death.

In addition, he reasoned that public visitation served two other important psychological needs: (1) it allowed for the sharing of grief that was too personal to bear alone, and (2) it allowed the bereaved to receive the community's condolences in unison, instead of over the ensuing months. Thus the public visitation helped to prevent the forced return of painful thoughts. Stephen knew that the chapel service in the funeral home allowed the actual service to proceed without the bereaved having to be troubled by transportation complications. And the final component of the traditional funeral service, the procession to the final committal, provides a "symbolic demonstration . . . that the relationship is at an end."[9] Here the public had an excellent opportunity to act out their respect.

Stephen strongly believed that incorporation of these views into his marketing compaign would not only increase his total profits, which was his prime desire, but would also allow him to promote his professional image, by educating the public.

The Plan

Stage one of the two-stage campaign would be the creation of a tasteful brochure for public distribution. This booklet would first stress the idea that traditional funerals are soundly based social customs. Furthermore, the booklet would give a short history of funerals, some information on costs, the wide range of services available to people at their time of need . . . all the time stressing the quality of Davis-Gardiner, a firm that "cares enough to let you know." This free booklet could either be mailed directly to homes near their three branches, or advertised publicly throughout the city. Stephen favored a 13-week series of 30-second prime-time TV spots to announce the availability of the brochure. These ads would primarily be aired on quiet family shows. Interested persons could then telephone and receive a copy by mail or pick one up in person at the home.

This would spread the Davis-Gardiner name widely throughout the metropolitan area (via TV) while limiting printing and distribution costs to those already interested. Stephen estimated the cost of the brochure to be $30,000 and then a $70,000 outlay for prime-time TV ads ($300 for a 30-second spot), a total that was five times the home's normal budget. He knew that the family would have to tighten its belt to pay for this and also that the employees would have to lengthen their hours while having their fringe benefits reduced.

9 Irion, Paul, *The Funeral Directors and the Mourners* (New York: Abingdon Press, 1954).

The second stage would be a high-quality direct-mail campaign stressing the benefits of preneed arrangements. This could be directed to specific neighborhoods and followed up by calls from Davis-Gardiner Insurance Company salespeople. This stage would continue for 18 to 24 months, rotating by calendar quarter to affluent sections of the city, which were undominated by any other funeral home, yet within range of one of the three Davis-Gardiner locations.

On the horizon was potential FTC regulation of the funeral industry. Regulation would be in the form of increased disclosure, particularly in terms of pricing. It seemed to Stephen that the industry could either (1) pretend that this was not going to happen and continue with traditional practices, or (2) meet these expressed concerns with the kind of marketing plan that would make D–G appear to be an industry leader. Stephen clearly favored the second approach, yet he realized that there were risks in it.

If the concerns raised by the FTC were *not* widely felt by potential buyers, the innovative marketing plan would have little effect, even if the FTC rules would later be enacted. Furthermore, if the FTC rules were *not* enacted, D–G might well be abandoning a traditional approach for one that would neither be attractive to potential users nor later required by law.

He was disconcerted when he explained his plan to an old friend of the family, a local funeral director who had recently retired after 45 successful years managing a cemetary and a separate funeral home. After listening to Stephen's entire plan, the friend quietly replied, "Steve, I see absolutely no hope for the success of your two-stage campaign. People do not like to hear about funerals; we live in a death-denying society. This will thwart your pre-need and advertising campaign. In all probability this would lose you business, not gain business for you. If this were a profitable idea, I would have done it 40 years ago. In general, Steve, the cost of your suggested campaign would provide a larger return if invested in the construction of a traditional funeral home, if you really seek an increase in market share."

Appendix A   Jessica Mitford, *The American Way of Death* *

A new mythology, essential to the twentieth-century American funeral rite, has grown up—or rather has been built up—to justify the peculiar customs surrounding the disposal of our dead. . . . The industry has had to "sell itself" on its articles of faith in the course of passing them on the public.

* Mitford, Jessica, *The American Way of Death* (New York: Simon and Schuster, 1963), pp. 36–37.

The first of these is the tenet that today's funeral procedures are founded in "American tradition." American funerals of past times have stressed simplicity to the point of starkness, the pine box, the laying out of the dead by friends and family, who also bore the coffin to the grave. . . .

Secondly, there is the myth that the American public is only being given what it wants—an opportunity to keep up with the Joneses to the end. "In keeping with our high standard of living, there should be an equally high standard of dying," says the past president of the Funeral Directors of San Francisco. . .

Thirdly, there is an assortment of myths based on half-digested psychiatric theories. The importance of the "memory picture" is stressed—in an open casket, done up with the latest in embalming techniques and finished off with a dusting of make-up. . . .

Lastly, a whole new terminology has been invented by the funeral industry to replace the direct and serviceable vocabulary of former times. Undertakers are "funeral directors" or "morticians," coffins are "caskets," hearses are "professional cars" or "coaches," flowers are "floral tributes," corpses are generally "loved ones," but mortuary etiquette dictates that a specific corpse be referred to by name only—as, Mr. Jones.

Appendix B Selected FTC-Identified Issues

1. Have funeral service industry members sought to prevent price–value comparisons by customers—by displaying merchandise in ways which make such comparisons difficult?
2. Have funeral service industry members displayed less expensive caskets in colors known to be unattractive to many customers for the purpose . . . of encouraging customers to purchase the higher priced caskets?
3. Have funeral service industry members disparaged or otherwise sought to discourage or prevent a customer's consideration of or concern about price?
4. Have funeral service industry members prevented or discouraged customers from purchasing less expensive caskets by not displaying such caskets, defacing or disparaging them, placing them in different rooms or inaccessible locations or displaying them in surroundings which are markedly inferior to the way other caskets are displayed?
5. Have funeral service industry members failed to disclose or make available prior to selection by customers by means of price lists, signs or cards and telephone disclosures information on the price and availability of individual items of service and merchandise commonly selected such as embalming, use of facilities for services, caskets and burial vaults?
6. Have funeral service industry members used sales commissions and other employee compensation plans to encourage sales of higher-priced products and services to customers and to discourage or penalize sales of lower-priced ones?

7. Have funeral industry service members failed to provide customers with a written accounting of the products and services used in the funeral service selected and an itemization of their individual prices?

8. Will mandatory itemization as required above force funeral service industry members to increase the prices of funerals, especially the least expensive funerals? What costs, economic or otherwise, to funeral homes, especially those which are small businesses, would result from implementation of the proposed rule, and how could such costs be minimized?

Appendix C The FTC Priorities in Deciding to Propose Funeral Regulations*

Mr. Russo asked, "Why did you investigate the funeral industry in the first place?" . . . Mr. Angel responded, "We looked into the funeral industry because it occurred to us this was a transaction in which there was a potential for the consumer to be vicitimized due to bereavement and the commonsense notion that a person who is making funeral arrangements operates at some emotional disadvantage." (Hearing transcript, September 15, 1976, p. 117)

The staff indicated that when they first began to look into problems associated with the funeral industry, the FTC had "less than a dozen" consumer complaints and at present they have approximately 700 to 1,000 letters from consumers.

The concern so vigorously voiced by members of the Subcommittee was that with less than a dozen complaints, the FTC would launch into a $500,000 project when there were so many other areas in which complaints existed that demanded attention by the FTC. . . Congresswoman Fenwick, for example, who, as the Director of the Division of Consumer Affairs for the State of New Jersey, was responsible for New Jersey's implementation of funeral regulations, queried:

> MRS. FENWICK: Did you consult the various consumer divisions of the
> states to see what they had in the way of complaints?
> MR. ANGEL: Number of consumer complaints? Only sporadically, only in
> a couple of states did we do that.
> MRS. FENWICK: Well, now, gentlemen, seriously, your own kind hearts
> and six letters—they have consumer divisions in almost

---

* "Federal Trade Commission's Proposed Funeral Industry Trade Regulation Rule: Its Effect on Small Business," Report of the Subcommittee on Activities of Regulatory Agencies of the Committee on Small Business, House of Representatives, October 20, 1976 (Washington, D.C.: U.S. Government Printing Office, 1976), pp. 16–17.

every state of the Union, and all you have to do is write a letter. In many states it is the Division of Law and Public Safety it comes under, and in some the Department of Agriculture . . . which I don't understand.

But nevertheless, there are consumer divisions and they receive complaints. And this surely would be the first obligation, and it really constituted an inexpensive way of finding out what the situation is in the nation. If you had written and had found out they had 15 complaints in 8 years, wouldn't that have told you something?

MR. ANGEL: It would have told us something, but not everything, Congresswoman. The point, I think, that really needs to be emphasized here is that consumer complaints simply do not give you anywhere near the full picture of what kinds of abuses or problems exist.

MRS. FENWICK: What makes you think so, sir?

MR. ANGEL: Three and a half years of research, interviewing people.

MRS. FENWICK: I ran the division of consumer affairs.

MR. ANGEL: I understand that.

MRS. FENWICK: And I promulgated regulations. I just simply do not agree with you, there is no better way of knowing. If I were a Federal Trade Commissioner I would have taken a bit more interest in the Pyramid case now there is real abuse, involving activities in one state very difficult to control on another state level. The Federal Trade Commission has certain things, in my opinion, that only it can do. Package deals that stranded poor schoolchildren in Paris, and I couldn't control it because it was organized in another state. I have dozens of things that I could hand you in the way of problems. To get triggered off by six letters and your kind hearts when you have thousands of consumers begging for help in other areas is to me absolutely an incredible way of operating an agency.

Appendix D Format for Itemized Bill

SPECIAL SERVICES

For your convenience, and at your specific request, we arrange, and pay in advance, for such special services as . . .

Extra Cars—Special Music—Toll Call and Telegrams—Grave Opening and Closing—Railroad or Airline Transportation—Family Flowers—Certified Transcripts—Out of Town Charges—Additional Limousines, etc.

There is a well-chosen assortment of specially tailored dresses and suits from which to make an appropriate selection.

The money paid for these, and similar items over which we have no control, will be itemized as Money Advanced in Your Behalf on our statement, and prompt repayment is requested.

TERMS: Net 30 days, after which a *FINANCE CHARGE* at the rate of 1% per month *(ANNUAL PERCENTAGE RATE OF 12%)* will be added to the debt or any portion thereof unpaid on the last day of each month. If this agreement is placed in the hands of an attorney for collection, purchaser agrees to pay attorney's fees of fifteen percent (15%) of all principal and interest owing or a minimum of twenty dollars ($20).

FOR PROFESSIONAL AND PERSONAL SERVICES

Personal and staff services including transfer from home or hospital, embalming and related preparations, procurement and filing of certificates and permits, arrangements pertaining to funeral service, clergy, cemetery, etc., and assistance with filing for social security, insurance, veterans or other benefits . . . twenty-four hour attention to all details and personnel for conduct of the funeral service. Newspaper notice, and Clergyman's record.

USE OF FUNERAL HOME FACILITIES AND EQUIPMENT

Complete funeral home facilities including operating room, visitation room, and chapel or equipment necessary for a home or church service. Acknowledgment cards, Visitor register, and other customary memorials. Devotional equipment as required. Service car for transfer, Casket Coach and limousines (   ), for service, within the limits of our local zone.

$_____

FOR THE CASKET SELECTED $_____

   *Made of*_____

   *Finish*_____

   *Interior Fabric*_____

   *Made by*_____   _____

TOTAL SERVICES, FACILITIES
   AND CASKET $_____

Appendix E Selections from the Davis-Gardiner Survey of 520 Local Citizens

1. Question: "Which funeral home (A, B, D–G, E, F, don't know) would you call if a death were to occur in your family today?" Their responses follow:

| | Socioeconomic Status | | | |
Home	Low	Middle	High	Total
A	41	71	3	115
B	40	50	8	98
D–G	25	49	5	79
E	3	30	27	60
F	8	24	7	39
Don't Know	6	116	7	129
				520

2. Question: "Would you be interested in receiving information on how funerals are arranged and their costs?" Their replies follow:

| | Socioeconomic Status | | | |
	Low	Middle	High	Total
Yes	24	176	9	209
No	42	29	74	145
Indifferent	55	48	63	166
				520

3. Question (directed at those who desired information on funerals): "Would you be interested in purchasing a burial insurance policy?"

- Strongly interested   58%
- Mildly interested   22%
- Not interested   15%
- Indifferent   5%

LIFE INSURERS' CONFERENCE: PRICING AND SALES PRACTICE FOR DEBIT LIFE INSURANCE

Late on a Friday afternoon in early March 1979, G. Mason Connell, Jr., sat wearily at his desk and surveyed the stacks of materials that covered it. He was president of the Life Insurers Conference, a national trade organization made up of over 90 life insurance companies, headquartered in Richmond, Virginia. The past several months had been extremely demanding. The debit[1] life insurance industry (also known as "home service"[2] life insurance) had increasingly become the focus of attack from several directions. Connell was engrossed in a review of documents which outlined the issues and industry positions on the issues. He was acutely aware that the outcome of his efforts in this difficult time would have a critical impact upon the future of the industry. His immediate challenge was to prepare remarks to be read before the Senate Judiciary Antitrust Subcommittee, which had been holding hearings on abuses in the home service insurance industry. The remarks would be read by C. A. Craig, II, the chairman of the Life Insurers Conference, who was also senior vice president of National Life and Accident Insurance Company. Craig had requested that responses be prepared as well for likely questions which might be asked by Subcommittee members. Connell decided that, before he began to prepare the written statement for Craig, he would review once again the series of recent events that had combined to threaten the continued vitality of his industry.

---

[1]   "Debit" refers to both (1) the total amount of weekly premiums collected by an agent on individual life insurance contracts in force within his assigned territory, and (2) the designated territory itself.

[2]   Home service was a method of marketing insurance providing for an agent to sell and service policies in the policyholder's home within a certain territory and includes collection of premium payments on a regular basis.

HISTORY OF THE DEBIT INSURANCE INDUSTRY

Industrial insurance had its origins in England, where the early nineteenth century witnessed the development of "collecting friendly societies." These societies resulted from the ordinary man's need of assurance of avoiding for his family the disgrace of a pauper's burial.

In the United States during the late nineteenth and early twentieth centuries, mutual benefit societies sprang up among poor and unskilled workers. Their growth was stimulated by the failure of the existing insurance system to provide coverage in small amounts for the working class. Industrial life insurance, it was widely believed, evolved from these societies.

Industrial life insurance was originally designed to meet the needs of families that did not have the economic and educational resources necessary to obtain the benefits associated with ordinary insurance. Since the primary purpose of insurance was burial, face values (and premiums) were low. It was generally assumed that purchasers did not have the education and/or economic discipline necessary to pay annual premiums on a notice basis—consequently, premiums were collected on a weekly basis at the insured's home. This system, although expensive, was quite effective in maintaining small amounts of insurance in force for individuals in its target market.

In 1900, there was $1,449 million of industrial life insurance in force in the United States; this represented approximately 19 percent of the total amount of life insurance in force. Through the end of World War II, the growth of industrial life insurance paralleled that of the industry as a whole. However, since 1950, industrial life had shrunk from 14.3 percent of total in force to 1.8 percent in 1975.

Factors and trends affecting the industry included (1) shifts in income distribution, with steady improvement in average family income and increased discretionary spending power; (2) increase in fringe benefits, including greater availability of employee group insurance; (3) the need for insurance in amounts greater than $1000; (4) increased consumer sophistication; and (5) increasing urbanization and mobility of the population, together with a renewed emphasis upon service industries in general.

It was significant that, in the late 1960s, the "big 3," Prudential Insurance Company of America, Metropolitan Life Insurance Company, and John Hancock Mutual Life Insurance Company, elected to withdraw from the industrial life insurance industry altogether. Those companies cited increased costs of operation and a secular downward trend in sales potential. Other companies adopted aggressive marketing strategies in an attempt to gain an increased percentage of the declining market. A third group attempted a "combination" strategy of retaining industrial business while broadening the product line to include other types of insurance, such as monthly debit ordinary (MDO), premium notice ordinary, and property/liability.

CHARACTERISTICS OF DEBIT INSURANCE

Industrial insurance, also known as "debit" or home service insurance, consisted of small policies sold by agents on a door-to-door basis, largely to low-income people. The weekly or monthly premium payments were collected by the agents at policyholder's homes.

The two basic types of policies were:

1. Weekly "industrial"—usually representing $1,000 or less in death benefits.
2 "Monthly debit ordinary" (MDO)—averaging about $3,000 in face value.

Ownership of multiple industrial and MDO policies was a common practice. Although sales of industrial life insurance were concentrated in the Southeast, the product was available nationwide. Since 1940, there had been a decline in the number of policies in force (the number of industrial policies fell from 85 million in 1940 to 71 million in 1974, whereas the number of ordinary contracts rose from 37 million to 131 million). However, sales of MDO more than offset the decline in industrial sales, so the debit (home service) life insurance industry as a whole was growing. The FTC's Office of Policy Planning estimated that, in 1976, there were more than 100 million active debit policies in the United States, with estimated total premiums of $3 billion per year.[3]

The industry was regulated exclusively at the state level under provisions of the McCarran-Ferguson Act, which made antitrust laws inapplicable to insurance. Regulation was generally less strict in nature than requirements for ordinary insurance. One problem, as reported by *Consumer Reports* in 1978, was that some state regulators felt that stringent regulation of the debit insurance program might result in depriving a certain segment of the economy from access to *any* form of life insurance.[4] In actual practice, most state regulatory insurance agencies had neither the time nor the staff to pursue possible abuses.

---

[3]   Elizabeth D. LaPorte, *Life Insurance Sold to the Poor: Industrial and Other Debit Insurance,* Policy Planning Issues Paper, Office of Policy Planning, Federal Trade Commission, January 1979, p. i.

[4]   "Insurance That Preys on the Poor," *Consumer Reports,* November 1978, pp. 658–661.

THE LIFE INSURERS' CONFERENCE

The LIC was organized in 1910 as a national insurance trade association. In 1979, it represented 93 companies, of which 86 sold insurance through the home service method of marketing. The 93 companies had home offices in 21 states, the District of Columbia, Puerto Rico, the Bahamas, and the Philippines. According to LIC, the total life insurance in force of these companies in 1977 was $272 billion, with over $57 billion of home service life insurance in force. The collective companies had assets of over $34 billion and were supported by over 88,500 field representatives and 38,300 other company employees. In 1977, there were 101 million home service policies in force in U.S. life insurance companies.

RECENT EVENTS

Connell began his review of the criticisms by reading *A Mini-Guide to Industrial Life Insurance*, which had been published by Pennsylvania Insurance Department in 1974 under the direction of Insurance Commissioner Herbert S. Denenberg, who had become a well-known consumer advocate. The *Mini-Guide* recommended that consumers not buy industrial life insurance "unless you absolutely cannot afford straight life,"[5] citing higher premium charges. The *Mini-Guide* had also been critical of built-in benefits in industrial life policies, stating: "Some built-in benefits are similar to the accident policy covering you only if you get run over by a herd of buffalo in Times Square on New Year's Eve. The many different built-in benefits in various industrial policies obscure the cost and often make cost comparisons meaningless."[6] Connell recalled that the *Mini-Guide* had no measurable effect on the industry in 1974, and that LIC had decided to remain silent unless criticism came from other sources as well.

In recent months, legislative, consumerist, and media pressures had been mounting, in the form of keen criticism of industry practices, together with demands for federal regulation. Typical of these was a series of articles appearing in *The Tennessean* in August 1978.[7]

[5] Pennsylvania Insurance Department, *A Mini-Guide to Industrial Life Insurance* (Weekly Premium Policies), Harrisburg, Pa., 1974, p. 2.

[6] Ibid.

[7] Carolyn Shoulders and Linda Solomon, "Industrial Policy Premiums Pay Firms Big Profit," *The Tennessean,* August 20, 1978, pp. 1, 8; "Payoff Risk Slight under Policy Terms," August 21, 1978, pp. 1, 4; "Insurance Test Not Important Ex-agents Say," August 23, 1978, pp. 1, 4; "Commissioner Says Hands Tied on Industrial Insurance," August 24, 1978, pp. 1, 9; "Insurance Firms Say Industrial Policies Needed," August 25, 1978, pp. 1, 8; "Industrial Policy 'Savings' Claims False, Buyers Find," August 26, 1978, pp. 1, 4; "Industrial Life Policies Often 100% Costlier," August 27, 1978, pp. 1, 6.

A team of *Tennessean* reporters spent 6 weeks exploring the impact of industrial insurance on the Nashville market. Their extensive interviews among policyholders who resided in low-income housing (and most of whom lived on welfare) reportedly revealed a strong tradition among the poor to purchase as much insurance as affordable, on the theory that it would pay for funeral expenses for themselves or their family members. In addition, some consumers expressed pride in the *number* of policies they held. The investigative team revealed that other consumers harbored the mistaken impression that buying policies on their children—even infants—would somehow provide protection and security. (see Figure 1).

The *Tennessean* reporters also claimed that the industrial insurance segments of many major insurance carriers provided these companies with more profits than either group insurance programs or ordinary life insurance plan sales (Table 1). Their interviews revealed that many people were unaware of either benefits or limitations (most had not read the policy) and disclosed the following problems:

1. Agents usually collected monthly, although policyholders were actually paying higher rates for weekly collection service.
2. Overlapping or unnecessary coverage was frequently the case, resulting from purchasing several policies from various companies (the agents received a commission every time they sold a new policy).
3. Policies were characterized by low cash value, with no loan provisions.
4. Family policies, allowing for cheaper total coverage, were rarely available.
5. Hard-sell techniques were used by some agents.
6. Payments often exceeded the amount that policyholders could ever realize in return.
7. No effort was made by agents to explain policy language or optional policy provisions.
8. Policyholders often paid for benefits they were unlikely ever to use (such as accident benefits). Age limitations, exclusions, and carefully worded definitions all exempted companies from paying for a variety of possible accidents.
9. Policyholders are not required to answer extensive health questionnaires. As a result, all buyers are considered high risks and are charged accordingly.

In January 1979, pressures upon the industry were intensified by the appearance of a Federal Trade Commission (FTC) staff report, citing the following abuses by the home service insurance industry[8]:

1. *Overloading.* Agents encourage policyholders to buy more insurance (a greater number of policies) than they need or can afford. Even so, the total insurance coverage for many customers remained well below the national average.
2. *Misrepresentation.* Agents advise parents to buy life insurance policies for

[8]   LaPorte, *Life Insurance,* pp. 38–46.

FIGURE 1   Examples of Debit Life Insurance Customers*

Hattie Webster, 47, whose monthly income is $285, has been paying 26% of it—or $74—on 33 life insurance policies to "protect" her seven children, eight grandchildren and her boyfriend.

Nannie Lewis, 52, whose income each month is $995, pays $105 of that on 20 life insurance policies to "protect" the five children and three grandchildren she supports.

Willie N. Green, 83, whose income is $207.80 per month, spends $22 of it on eight insurance policies to "protect" her family. But she has paid more to the insurance companies on all but one of these policies than she or the beneficiaries ever could collect. Still, she must continue to pay the premiums to keep the policies in force.

Joseph Hibbett, 66, and his wife Mary, 76, have a total monthly income of $499 and $32 of it goes regularly to pay for seven policies. Like Willie Green, they have paid the companies insuring them more money than they ever could collect on the policies. But they must keep paying to get anything back on what they have invested.

"We trust our insurance agent," says Joseph Hibbett. "We like him. He is a nice man."

* Carolyn Shoulders and Linda Solomon, "Industrial Policy Premiums Pay Firms Big Profit," *The Tennessean,* August 20, 1978, p. 8.

Table 1   PROFITS OF VARIOUS LIFE INSURANCE PLANS*

	Ordinary and Other	Group	Industrial
Kentucky Central	$ 473,780	$ 209,510	$ 2,098,240
Independent Life	5,786,952	2,074,581	12,605,702
Home Beneficial	6,004,329	28,113	8,483,109
Liberty National	15,871,946	253,251	19,363,067
National Life & Accident	39,079,490	230,348	39,966,933
American National	13,922,187	710,774	8,182,411
Washington National	2,675,965	2,333,767	4,541,307
Life of Virginia	9,786,845	1,832,946	8,144,444

* Carolyn Shoulders and Linda Solomon, "Industrial Policy Premiums Pay Firms Big Profit," *The Tennessean,* August 20, 1978, p. 1.

children's education, failing to inform that policies typically do not pay back as much as is invested and that the *full* face amount is paid only if the child dies.

3. *Misinformation.* Agents convince customers to cash in an old policy and use part of the money to pay the first premium on a new policy, thereby having both cash and a new policy. This is misleading because, if the old policy is less than 5 years old, it cannot surrender *any* cash benefits and customers can lose all or part of the old policy's investment.

Abuses, claimed the FTC, were the result of buyers' ignorance of when they were being cheated, coupled with their not knowing how or when to complain when they realized they had been deceived.

On state regulation of the home service insurance industry, the report stated:

> Extensive reporting requirements govern reporting by companies to states on life insurance operations, broken down by industrial, ordinary and group lines, MDO is a curious exception . . . . This lack of separate reporting on MDO, except for volume of MDO business, shelters from public scrutiny a set of insurance activities of increasing significance.[9]

The FTC's recommendations included four principal options for the development of public policy, each with several alternatives that might be adopted separately or together:

1. Measures designed to improve price and quality.[10]
   a. States could impose on industrial and monthly debit ordinary insurance lines of debit companies a maximum administrative cost ratio.
   b. States could require companies to issue paid-up policies to those policyholders still paying on policies even after they have already paid in equal to or more than they can ever receive in death benefits.
   c. States could require companies to reduce premiums to policyholders who pay premiums directly or pay premiums less often and could require companies to give notice of these options.
   d. States could end sales of certain debit policies such as 20-year endowments which have high lapse rates.
   e. States could protect cash value and nonforfeiture benefts of debit life insurance policyholders in the event of a policy lapse.
   f. States could require companies to give notice, in simple language, prior to allowing policies to lapse.
   g. States could require home offices to improve home office recordkeeping to minimize potential for sales agent abuse.

Connell knew that the last option would increase policy service costs dramatically. In fact, each of the recommendations would increase industry costs, in his view.

[9] Ibid., p. 59.
[10] Ibid., pp. 68–75.

2. Measures designed to reduce inappropriate sales of debit life insurance.[11]
   a. Social Security death benefits could be restructured into a need basis to assure payment of funeral expenses.
   b. Agent commission structures could be revised to eliminate the incentive for agents to sell high commission policies which may not be needed.
   c. The amount of debit insurance per household could be limited and sales of more than one small policy could be prohibited where one larger one would be less costly.
   d. Enforcement of existing laws and regulations designed to protect consumers could have stronger enforcement.

On the issue of agent abuses, Connell knew that Delores Matulis, a former agent for Herald Life, a subsidiary of Independent Life and Accident Company, had described alleged agent abuses in detail to the United States Office of Consumer Affairs in a forthcoming article in *Consumer News:*

> Matulis said the major reason debit agents are cheating consumers is because the insurance companies put pressure on agents to increase their intake every week. The more money agents take in, the more they earn, so they often use whatever means available to increase their collections, including, according to Matulis, "fenceposting," or writing policies and making claims for non-existent people.
>
> Matulis also said some agents cash in a person's paid-up policy without telling the buyer, then forge the check and pocket the money. She claimed one company she worked for even had a "tracing machine" that "could be used by others (in the company) if the agent forgot to forge the signature himself.
>
> She added that agents can get away with these abuses because "policyholders receive benefits through their agents, and in many cases buyers are rural people, poor and uneducated, and don't know they are being taken advantage of by their agents.
>
> The Herald Life spokesman, who asked that his name not be used, told Consumer News *many of Matulis' claims were "false." He said all companies "occasionally hire someone unethical," but that the employers would fire him or her if they found out about those practices.[12]*

3. Measures designed to improve access of low-income people to lower-cost alternatives (regular ordinary life policies, nonconventional group insurance, etc.).[13]
   a. Enforcement of laws against "red-lining" could be strengthened.
   b. States could encourage group insurance plans for nonconventional groups such as the principal buyers of debit life insurance.

---

[11]   Ibid., pp. 76–80.

[12]   "Life Insurance Abuses," *Consumer News,* 9, no. 7 (April 1, 1979),
p. 3.

[13]   LaPorte, *Life Insurance,* pp. 80–81.

4. Measures designed to increase consumer information about insurance, especially to low-income people.[14]
   a. Insurance information could be disseminated through radio and television programs and public service announcements.
   b. Education on insurance could be increased in high school and adult education programs.
   c. States could encourage development of third-party insurance information brokers and financial counsellors for low-income people.

Following the LaPorte report, the National Consumers League went on record to urge the life insurance industry to stop selling industrial insurance, praised the FTC report, and recommended increased regulation of the debit life insurance industry.

In March 1979, the industry was the subject of hearings held by a Senate Antitrust Subcommittee chaired by Senator Metzenbaum. These hearings exerted additional pressure upon the industry to make an internal effort to minimize abuses. Meanwhile, the FTC and the Antitrust Committee were considering legislation to strengthen consumer rights in the debit insurance industry. It was in this hostile setting that Craig would testify on March 16. Connell decided to review the industry response to the series of recent events.

INDUSTRY EFFORTS AT SELF REGULATION

The industry had, for some time, acknowledged the existence of some consumer problems. After the "big 3" left the industry in the 1960s, an industry trade association formed a task force, which proposed voluntary company reforms:

1. Mandatory "participation limits" to prevent overloading of low-income families.
2. Mandatory discounts to weekly premium holders currently paying on a monthly basis.
3. Ending sales of plans exhibiting low persistency on a debit basis, such as 20-year endowments.
4. Ending "socioeconomic underwriting," if it is a disguise for racial underwriting.

The extent of voluntary attempts to apply these recommendations was unknown. However, the very nature of the system prevented implementation. High agent turnover (according to the FTC, only 16 percent of agents stayed more than 4 years with one company) plus the debit field system, whereby most transactions were cash and most accounting was

[14]   Ibid., pp. 81–85.

done in the field, inhibited company efforts to ensure agent compliance. Critics claimed that the recommended voluntary reforms did not, however, address the major issue of high price for relatively small benefits.

INDUSTRY REBUTTAL

In the face of increasing charges of consumer abuse, industrial insurance company spokesmen defended the product by arguing that they were providing a service to the poor by sending agents door-to-door. In the process of selling insurance and collecting payments, these agents declared that a "bond of trust" often developed between clients and salespeople.

The industry saw itself as providing insurance to a low-income target market that would otherwise find itself uninsured. The weekly collection plan was designed to accommodate their customers' needs and even encouraged the discipline of thrift, although it was an additional expense to the company.

Although opponents recommended that industrial insurance should not be sold in any case, many insurers honestly felt there was a positive need for a program of this type (policyholders lack suitable alternatives; industrial was better than no insurance at all). However, they insisted that benefits be spelled out to consumers and that the sales of such policies provide for policyholders the best insurance bargain their money could buy.

Industry leaders pointed up the need to make for the public a clear distinction between industrial insurance as a *product* and the home service method of *marketing*, which was a delivery mechanism.

Other industry representatives contended that federal regulation would put some member companies out of business and deprive a specific segment of the population of insurance coverage. They saw the FTC drive for regulation as intended to eliminate certain types of insurance, and they maintained that state regulation was adequate.

A formal rebuttal to the FTC report ("Life Insurers Conference Response to the Elizabeth LaPorte Report," March 9, 1976) consisted of virtually a line-by-line retort, response, or statement of clarification. On the issue of high profits, it was explained that the majority of policies in force in 1976 were sold during the 1930s, 1940s, and 1950s, when average interest rates on invested assets ranged from 2.5 percent to 4 percent. Meanwhile, mortality rates had decreased, while administrative costs had risen.

After the article in *Consumer Reports,* LIC had prepared *The LIC Position Paper on Industrial Insurance and the Home Service Method of Marketing Insurance* (Figure 2). The position paper asserted the right of every U.S. citizen to purchase life insurance in appropriate amounts and forms, regardless of income or life-style. Also stated was a commitment to provide the consumer with information necessary to purchase insurance intelligently. The LIC developed a consumer education program, with a pamphlet to explain the various aspects of life insurance (Figure 3).

The best solution to industry problems according to LIC was seen to be the industry itself, by support of industry self-regulation in such areas as:

1. An increase in on-the-job training for agents and field management.
2. Development of safeguards in policy application (request list of any other policies).
3. Further improve lines of communication between the insurance industry, regulatory agencies, and consumers.

Connell knew that his task was to prepare approximately 10 minutes of written testimony. In addition, he decided to list issues, together with the position of LIC on each, to provide Craig with a thorough preparation for the upcoming testimony.

FIGURE 2   Life Insurance Conference Position Paper on Industrial Insurance and the Home Service Method of Marketing Insurance

---

Introduction

Each individual in the United States should have the right to purchase life insurance in amounts appropriate for his own economic situation and in a form most suitable for his lifestyle. Even people of very modest income want, need, and can afford life insurance. It is best provided through private, individual policies rather than the very costly federal programs adopted in some other nations.

To insure that everyone who wants insurance coverage can in fact purchase it, life insurance is available in many forms, known by many different names. Some of the most common are whole life, term life, credit, group, permanent, ordinary, limited pay, and industrial, each designed to meet the different needs of individuals of varying income levels in varying circumstances. All are sold in various policy sizes.

Just as there are different types of life insurance, there are many different methods of marketing these products. Some policies are sold by agents calling on consumers in their home or office, some are bought as a result of advertisements in Sunday newspapers, or direct mail solicitation, some are purchased through payroll deduction, and some are bought in the course of making a loan or a major credit purchase.

Some policies are paid for with checks mailed to the company, others with cash payments at a local office, others through bank account deduction or payroll deduction plans, and some are collected by an agent who comes to the home. All methods of payment are right for some customers and serve a purpose in the maintenance of insurance coverage.

To eliminate any one of these forms of insurance, or any of the methods of marketing life insurance would effectively exclude a large body of consumers from their right to own insurance.

It is important to remember that no matter what kind of insurance is purchased or how it is purchased and paid for, insurance is a risk which is shared by all policyholders, with the company simply serving as the medium through which the risks are selected, premiums collected and invested, and benefits paid out.

Some types of insurance serve only as protection against accidents, damage or illness and may never provide the policyholder with any return on his investment. For example, almost all automobile owners have insurance coverage against accidents; however, they will not receive any cash benefits from their policy unless they are involved in an accident. The same is true of health insurance, homeowners insurance, or fire insurance. Life insurance is one of the few forms of insurance which not only provides beneficiaries with cash payment on the death of the policyholder, but, except for term life, also provides for the policyholder to receive the option of various forms of financial return while he or she is alive.

In recent months, industrial life insurance and the home service method of marketing life insurance have been the focus of increasing attention by the insurance industry, regulatory agencies and the news media. There has been some confusion as to the relative value of these segments of the insurance business, and to their importance in assuring everyone's right to insure his life.

The purpose of this paper is to provide a better understanding of the home service method of marketing insurance and its importance to policyowners and the insurance industry, and to clarify, define and explain industrial insurance, and its relationship to the rest of the market.

The Home Service Method of Marketing Insurance

The home service method of marketing insurance is now used by many leading companies in the industry. Approximately 30 percent of the 136,000 agents who are members of the National Association of Life Underwriters are home service agents. The Life Insurers Conference believes that the home service method of marketing will continue to flourish in the future. Though industrial life insurance was the early product marketed in this manner, the effectiveness of such a marketing program was easily adapted to the whole spectrum of life insurance policies and to other types of insurance—even property and casualty insurance and health insurance. Agents generally have assigned territories, known in the business as 'debits,' where they are responsible for selling and collecting premiums from all policyholders in the area. The debit may include a few city blocks, a suburb or an entire rural community.

While policies sold via home service are often of a small face value, there are no limitations on the type or amount of life insurance that can be purchased through a home service agent. As a matter of fact, the most recent data available shows that regular ordinary policies constitute almost 44 percent of the business sold by home service or debit agents, and that home service agents sold 52 percent of all the individual policies sold in the entire life insurance industry. Consumers can buy a $1,000, $100,000 or even a $1,000,000 policy from a home service agent. The same is true of premium payments. If a policyholder with $50,000 worth of coverage chose to have the agent come to his home to collect the premium payments on a monthly basis, the agent could do so. Of course, the policyholder would also have the option of being billed and making the premium payment by mail, on a monthly, quarterly, semi-annual or annual basis.

The Costs and Benefits of Home Service

Many consumers operate on a pay-as-you-go basis, revolving around their weekly or monthly paycheck. They buy most goods and services weekly, at the grocery store or the laundromat and must set aside funds regularly to meet monthly obligations such as rent and utilities. A study made by the Federal Reserve Bank of Atlanta in the Atlanta metropolitan area found that over 54 percent of the labor force were paid weekly, another 40 percent were paid twice a month and only 5.5 percent were paid on a monthly basis. For many of these policyholders, home collection is not only a convenience, but can be of service as a means of self-discipline in budgeting their payments. They know the bill is due at a time when the money is available. If it weren't collected by the agent at that time, the money might otherwise be spent elsewhere and the needed protection lost.

Whether a policy premium is paid weekly or monthly, it stands to reason that a policy with a small face value and frequent collection mode will cost more per unit than a larger policy with less frequent premium payment. The cost of calling on a policyholder once a week or once a month can obviously be greater than mailing out a statement and receiving a check back by the same means at any frequency, although the cost effectiveness of collection versus billing depends upon the amount of the premium.

When low income policyholders are given the choice of paying on a semi-annual or annual basis, many of those who do opt for one of these less frequent alternatives soon change back to the weekly or monthly method. A Louis Harris poll revealed that 22 percent of all Americans 18 years of age and older lack any kind of checking account, and among minority and low income groups this percentage is as much as 50 percent. For many of these families who do not have checking accounts, weekly or monthly collection of life insurance premiums fits best into their lifestyles.

The Role of Home Service Insurance— Now and in the Future

The LIC submits that to eliminate small policies and home marketing service would take away the opportunity for many low and middle income individuals to have insurance protection. Many other kinds of products, such as newspapers, milk, even cosmetics and cleaning supplies, are delivered in the same way. As a matter of fact, in the case of the low or middle income individual, who often does not have a private business office, nor any means of transportation, the home is the best environment for the discussion of life insurance needs, preferably with the spouse present and involved.

Generally, the mode of premium payment should be the least frequent the policyholder can afford. Many policy holders prefer more frequent payments as they require the least outlay of cash per payment. As previously stated, there is still a large segment of the population which is subject to the weekly pay cycle. While many policyholders still on weekly payment plans, do at certain times of the year prepay a few weeks worth of ment plans, do at certain times of the year prepay a few weeks worth of premiums in advance, their pattern of payment through the year is often erratic due to seasonal effects on employment of the head of the household and similar effects on expenses such as utility bills.

The flexibility of home service marketing allows policyholders to work out these changes in their payment schedule with their agent when necessary without allowing their policy to lapse.

The future of home service life insurance should rest in the hands of the public and the insurance companies. As long as policyholders desire the services and products provided through home service, these should be available to them. Should the services and products be no longer desired or needed by the life insurance buying public, then home service insurance will no longer be a necessary service.

Industrial Insurance

In most states, industrial life insurance is defined by law as a policy of $1,000 or less, sold or collected for in the consumer's home, usually on a weekly basis. This form of insurance has been marketed in the United States for over 100 years, primarily to individuals in low and middle income brackets.

Even though there are more than 67 million industrial insurance policies still in force in the United States today, the future of the product has been seriously weakened by inflation. Many consumers find that the small $500 and $1,000 policies they bought in the past are not adequate to meet their needs today and have found it necessary to supplement their coverage with additional policies.

Whether an individual has industrial or ordinary coverage, it is not unusual to have several life insurance policies. Most consumers purchase life insurance at least seven times in their lifetimes. For example, when a young person graduates from school and begins working, he may purchase a small industrial policy. A few years later, he gets married, has additional financial obligations and purchases another policy on his life and possibly one to cover the life of his spouse. In another few years, the newlyweds have their first child, again posing additional obligations, and again, additional coverage may be purchased not only for the heads of the household, but this time, also for the child.

This is basically the pattern most life insurance consumers follow in adding to their coverage, whether they are buying industrial policies, ordinary life or even term life insurance.

Profitability

Critics of home service insurance have charged companies with making disproportionate profits from the sales of industrial insurance as compared to ordinary insurance. When all factors are considered, the industrial insurance sold today is not more profitable than other types of insurance and in many cases the opposite is true.

Any insurance policy is less profitable during the first few years it is in force due to expenses such as underwriting and commissions. Therefore, lines of business which are presently being sold in greater volume will show less profit annually than industrial insurance, which represents a large number of policies in force, but comparatively fewer new policies.

The price of any insurance policy is based on many variables. First, the amount of income to be received from premium payments must be estimated by the company. The amount of interest that will be earned by the reserve funds which the company is required to maintain to pay claims and benefits must also be taken into consideration. These earnings are then offset by the amount of money that will actually be paid out in benefits and the expenses involved in maintaining and servicing the policies.

While the company makes every effort to estimate these figures exactly, in these changing economic times, many outside factors may affect their computations during the time a policy remains in force. The interest rate may drop or increase, expenses may do the same, or mortality rates may change.

This in fact is what has happened. The majority of the industrial policies which are in force today were sold during the 1930's, 40's, and 50's. At that time average interest rates on invested assets ranged from 2.5 percent to 4 percent as compared to today's total portfolio average of 7 percent to 7.5 percent. Since that time, mortality rates have decreased, while administrative costs have risen significantly, all affecting the profitability of the product which was sold years ago, but remains in force.

Risks of Industrial Insurance

It has been stated that some industrial policyholders will never get back in benefits or cash value all the premiums they pay in. It's worth repeating that life insurance, like many other types of insurance, is a risk shared by all policyholders.

In the case of life insurance of any form, some policyholders will die early and their beneficiaries will collect, some will die later and their beneficiaries will also collect. If an individual could predict when he was going to die, he could wait longer to buy life insurance and reduce his outlay just as he could wait to buy health insurance if he knew when he was going to get sick.

It is true for example that a policyholder who has $1,000 worth of coverage may pay over $1,000 dollars in premiums during the 40 or more years it may take for the policy to mature. However, that policyholder has had a guarantee of $1,000 in benefits should his death occur any time during or after the 40-year period. Even if the policyholder dies the day after the policy is issued, his beneficiaries will receive the full $1,000 in benefits. The same applies to a $100,000 or a $1,000,000 policy.

On Behalf of the Consumer

The LIC has worked and will continue to work towards providing the consumer with the information necessary to intelligently purchase insurance while providing insurance protection which meets the needs, economic and otherwise, of the consumer at the lowest possible price for the protection provided.

We are in the process of formalizing a consumer education program to directly assist each purchaser of insurance to more fully understand the product which he is purchasing.

The LIC is developing a simple pamphlet explaining in plain language various aspects of life insurance which will be available to agents to distribute to life insurance policyholders as well as to prospective buyers of small policies. This will also contribute to a better understanding of the different kinds of life insurance, their benefits and their costs.

All LIC member companies are also committed to the elimination from the industry of the relatively few individuals who put any other considerations ahead of meeting the consumer's needs.

We feel the best entity to solve the problems of the insurance industry is the insurance industry itself, working in close cooperation with state regulatory agencies. The means of control already are integrated into the industry and in most cases are working.

Steps have already been taken to increase on-the-job training for agents and field management. These programs include continuing emphasis on the effects of allowing a policy to lapse before maturity.

Other safeguards to protect the consumer are included on the policy application. Many companies ask the prospective insurance purchaser to list any other policies which he owns on his application. Insurance applications are turned down each year because the company finds that the applicants already have adequate coverage to meet their needs. Many companies have also adopted limits on the amount of insurance their agents can sell to an individual receiving welfare payments.

In addition, the LIC is working to further strengthen the lines of communication between the insurance industry, regulatory agencies and consumers and to better inform consumers about the insurance industry in general.

Conclusion

Recent charges made against the home service insurance industry, ranging from accusations of disproportionate profits earned from the sale of industrial insurance to taking advantage of the poor by selling them too many policies at too high a premium, are not true. There continues to be a definite established need for small life insurance policies with home service in the United States today and the companies in the LIC will continue to meet that need.

There is no room within the industry for abuse, however, and the members of LIC do not condone any unscrupulous practices. We stand ready to not only police ourselves, but to cooperate with all state insurance departments trying to improve the life insurance industry's overall service to the small policy market.

The LIC is dedicated to providing insurance to meet the needs of consumers at all income levels at the lowest possible price and committed to continuing its efforts to reduce the cost of insurance within the constraints of present day inflationary pressures and general economic conditions. We are in the business of providing protection for all economic segments of the marketplace, and it is our vow to treat them all equitably.

FIGURE 3 Consumer Education Pamphlet on Debit Life Insurance

The Right Insurance For You

Questions and Answers to Help You Understand

Produced by

Life Insurers Conference
1004 North Thompson Street
Box 6856
Richmond, Virginia 23230

Q: What's Home-Service Insurance?

A. Home service is a method of marketing insurance which is now used by many leading companies in the industry. Agents generally have assigned territories, known in the business as debits, where they are responsible for selling and collecting premiums from all policyholders in the area. The debit may include a few city blocks, a suburb or an entire rural community.

Q: What Is Insurance?

A. Insurance, available in different forms, provides protection against accidents, damage, illness or death. Simply stated, it is a risk which is shared by all policyholders with the insurance company serving as the medium through which the risks are selected, premiums collected and invested and benefits paid out.

Q: What Kind of Policies Are Sold Via Home Service?

A. While policies sold via home service are often of a small face value, there are no limitations on the type or amount of life insurance that can be purchased through a home service agent. As a matter of fact, in 1976, regular ordinary policies constituted almost 44% of the business sold by home service agents.

Q: What Is Industrial Insurance?

A. In most states, industrial life insurance is defined by law as a policy of $1,000 or less, sold and collected for in the consumer's home, usually on a weekly basis. This form of insurance has been marketed in the United States for over 100 years and was the first insurance product marketed by the home service method in this country.

Q: What Is the Future of Industrial Insurance in the United States?

A. Even though there are more than 67 million industrial insurance policies still in force in the United States today, the future of the product has been seriously weakened by inflation. Many consumers find that the small $500 and $1,000 policies they bought in the past are not adequate to meet their needs today and have found it necessary to supplement their coverage with additional policies.

Q: What Is Monthly Debit Ordinary Insurance?

A. Monthly debit ordinary insurance is insurance sold by home service agents with a small face value, usually less than $5,000. Premiums for these policies are collected by the agent on a monthly basis in the policyholder's home. The policyholder does, however, have the option of making payments on a less frequent basis or making payments directly to the company.

Q: What Is The Difference Between Industrial Insurance and Home Service or Debit Insurance?

A. Industrial insurance is a product. Home service or debit insurance is a method of delivery, or a marketing system to get the product to the consumer.

Q: Do The Small Policies Most Often Marketed Through Home Service Cost More Than Insurance Which Is Marketed In Other Ways?

A. Any policy with a small face amount and frequent premium payments will cost more per unit than a larger policy with less frequent payments. Home office administrative and accounting expenses are the same per policy for keeping records of premium due dates, mailing notices, paying postage, followup for reinstatement, handling correspondence with policyholders, etc. This per policy allocation of administrative expenses causes all companies, whether they are home service or not, to have a higher cost per $1,000 of coverage for policies with small face amounts.

Q: What Are Some of the Benefits of Home Service?

A. Many consumers operate on a pay-as-you-go basis, revolving around their weekly or monthly paycheck. They buy most goods and services weekly, whether at the grocery store or the laundromat and must set aside funds regularly to meet monthly obligations such as rent and utilities. For many of these policyholders home collection is not only a convenience but can be of service as a means of self-discipline in budgeting their payments. If the premium wasn't collected by the agent the money might otherwise be spent elsewhere and the needed protection lost.

Q: Is Industrial More Profitable Than Other Types of Insurance?

A. When all factors are considered, the industrial insurance sold today is not more profitable than other types of insurance and in many cases the opposite is true. Any insurance policy is less profitable during the first few years it is in force due to expenses such as underwriting and commissions. Therefore, lines of business which are presently being sold in greater volume will show less profits annually than industrial insurance which represents a large number of policies in force but comparatively fewer new policies.

The majority of industrial policies in force today were sold in the 1930's, 40's and 50's. Since that time, the interest rates on invested assets have risen, mortality rates have improved and administrative costs have risen significantly, all affecting the profitability of the product which was sold years ago, but remains in force. These are variables which affect the profitability of an insurance product, that the companies had no control over and could not have predicted when the policies were first priced 20 to 40 years ago.

Q: What Is The Life Insurers Conference?

A. The Life Insurers Conference is an association of 93 life insurance companies, 86 of which are home service companies. Member companies have home offices in 21 states, the District of Columbia, Puerto Rico, the Bahamas and the Philippines.

Q: What Is Being Done Within the Industry to Discourage Abuses of the Home Service System?

A. There is no room within the industry for abuses and the members of LIC do not condone any unscrupulous practices. Steps have been taken to increase on-the-job training for agents and field management, with continuing emphasis on the effects of allowing a policy to lapse before maturity. Policy applications ask prospective customers to list other policies to determine if the applicant already has adequate coverage. In addition, consumer education programs are being formalized to educate the general public about the industry as well as directly assist each purchaser of insurance to more fully understand the product which he is purchasing.

Commentaries

ROBINSON-PATMAN APPEARS HERE TO STAY*

By Larry Lempert

"Sometimes praised, sometimes abused, much interpreted, little understood, and capable of producing instant arguments of infinite variety." Former Federal Trade Commission Chairman Earl W. Kintner, in his antitrust primer, so described the Robinson-Patman Act.

Despite occasional rumblings among government enforcers and members of the bar, the act is here to stay, Kintner said last week. And discussions with FTC officials support his view. These officials indicate, too, that the agency's enforcement of the anti-price-discrimination law will be neither as relaxed as the abusers, nor as spirited as the enthusiasts, would like.

The act, unchanged since its enactment in 1936, forbids price discriminations unless they can be cost-justified by the seller or are made in good faith to meet competition. Robinson-Patman detractors, who believe the statute inhibits valid competition, were encouraged recently by the Supreme Court's decision in the A&P case (see *Legal Times,* March 12, p. 9).

Donald Baker of Jones, Day, Reavis & Pogue wrote with satisfaction in the *National Law Journal* that the combination of A&P and United States Gypsum, 98 S. Ct. 2364 (1978), "drills a pretty good hole" in the act by promoting market uncertainty among sellers. Baker, as Antitrust Division chief two years ago, led the division out on a limb with a report highly critical of the act.

* *The Legal Times of Washington,* April 23, 1979, p. 8. Reprinted with permission.

NO CHANGE FORESEEN

Nonetheless, officials at the FTC, the agency primarily responsible for enforcement, foresee no change in direction. That means that the act, although it is not a priority, definitely remains on the list of responsibilities to be taken seriously by the agency. Alfred Dougherty, Jr., director of the competition bureau, said that A&P, by making it more difficult to prove violations under the inducement provisions, section 20, might make enforcement more costly. "But we shouldn't be ready to say that we won't enforce Robinson-Patman," Dougherty said.

In A&P, the Court exonerated a buyer on the basis of its seller's "meeting competition" defense. This is "one little wrinkle on one kind of violation" and will not put any big dents in the agency's enforcement effort, another antitrust official said.

In a recent speech pledging to continue the FTC's traditional antitrust responsibilities, Chairman Michael Pertschuk tucked Robinson-Patman securely in the middle of his enforcement list (see *Legal Times,* April 16, pp. 19, 20).

These assurances have to be taken with at least two grains of salt. First grain: Robinson-Patman is dear to the hearts of small business and its defenders in Congress, and the FTC is as Hill-conscious an agency as any in Washington. The act has proven to be resilient, and bad-mouthing it at a time when change is unlikely would serve no useful purpose.

Second grain: over the long haul of a decade, investigations that used to number in the dozens have dropped to a handful. The competition bureau provided these figures on formal investigations initiated and number of complaints issued per year:

- 1965   75, 80
- 1966   81, 6
- 1967   159, 8
- 1968   73, 14
- 1969   53, 4
- 1970   36, 5
- 1971   18, 8
- 1972   9, 1
- 1973   5, 1
- 1974   8, 6
- 1975   3, 1
- 1976   10, 2
- 1977   4, 4
- 1978   0, 5

Robert Reich, director of the Office of Policy Planning, said that investigational time going to vertical restraints, including Robinson-Patman violations, amounted to 7 percent of the competition bureau's total in 1978. In 1977, the figure was 11 percent; in 1976, 13 percent.

EQUILIBRIUM REACHED

Robinson-Patman enforcement appears, then, to have reached a new equilibrium, at a level far below that of the halcyon days of the '60s. The halcyon levels, indeed, had prompted strong criticism. An influential American Bar Association study on the FTC, published in 1969, recommended that the commission focus its efforts, targeting "instances in which injury to competition is clear, taking into account the consumer interest in vigorous price competition."

According to FTC officials, that is precisely what the agency is doing now—careful case selection is the watchword, they say. "We're looking for major, industry-wide practices that really harm competition," said James Sneed, the assistant bureau director who supervises food cases.

Commissioner Robert Pitofsky is considered by sources both inside and outside the agency to be the least likely to vote for issuance of a Robinson-Patman complaint. However, he does not advocate repeal; rather, he said, he is sensitive to the tension he sees between Robinson-Patman and the Sherman Act.

"There is a need for careful review and analysis of the record to see that real rather than hypothetical injury to competition has occurred," Pitofsky said.

The commission also has its outspoken Robinson-Patman supporter, Commissioner Paul Rand Dixon. The other commissioners say they will go forward with a Robinson-Patman case given the right set of facts, Dixon said. But he complained of a lack of enthusiasm on the part of the staff and said that staff recommendations urging Robinson-Patman enforcement are too few and far between.

The need for selectivity, which has been voiced by Pertschuk as well, does not spring out of theoretical principles alone. Pertschuk has noted that the A&P case consumed 35,000 work hours and cost the commission more than 1 million dollars. Similarly, a competition bureau attorney said, the *Gibson* case No. 9016 awaiting commission consideration has taken 26,751 hours—and that's before logging any court time.

Building the factual foundation for a price discrimiation case in an expensive process, this attorney said. He cited, as a good example of careful selection, the *Los Angeles Times Mirror* case now before an administrative law judge (No. 9103). The main issue there—is advertising a "commodity"—is a legal and not a factual one, he said.

Kintner, who is perhaps the bar's most avid Robinson-Patman supporter, said that private enforcement of the act through treble-damage actions should not be overlooked. In fact, he said, the legal frontiers in the field of price discrimination are being plowed by private and not by government enforcement—and privately brought cases are making "some of the best, most useful law."

Another former FTC official, now in private antitrust practice, said that this potential for treble-damage liability creates a difficult counseling problem. Even if the commission officials are skeptical about much of the law developed under Robinson-Patman, the whole body of law remains in effect and businesses still have to comply, he said.

The commission is being "two-faced," this attorney said—bringing enough Robinson-Patman cases to keep congressional defenders of small business "off their backs" but leaving business to deal with a substantial body of restrictive law.

This restriction is good or bad, depending which side of the perennial Robinson-Patman debate you're on. The debate seems to have subsided since the fiery Justice Department report issued in January 1977 failed to ignite sparks anywhere else. The issues—whether the Act encourages the stabilizing of prices, whether it restricts new entry, whether it plays a meaningful role in protecting small business, and whether it is too burdensome to establish a Robinson-Patman defense—still excite advocates on both sides, but FTC officials see no prospects for congressional action.

Extensive hearings were held in 1975 before an ad hoc congressional subcommittee and before a White House Domestic Council Review Group. But the alternatives that Justice put forward, a more narrowly drawn predatory practices act and a Robinson-Patman reform bill, garnered little support.

COZY COMPETITORS:
PRICE-FIXING CHARGES RISE IN PAPER INDUSTRY DESPITE CONVICTIONS*

Trend Dating to '30s Includes 36 Judgments Recently
And 100 Cases Pending

"They Never Seem To Learn"

By Timothy D. Schellhardt

The paper industry is acquiring a reputation as the nation's biggest price-fixer.

The dubious distinction, deserved or not, reflects a rash of suits in the past few years against leading makers of paper and paper products. In three major federal cases in the past three years alone, 36 companies were found guilty of, or pleaded no contest to, charges that they fixed prices on products ranging from bags for coffee and pet foods to labels and folding cartons. They paid fines totaling more than $1 million.

In those same cases, 59 paper-industry executives also were judged guilty of price fixing or entered no-contest pleas to such charges. Of these, 14 have gone to jail, five have been required to tell civic groups what they "learned" from their prosecution, and eight have had to work in service projects in hospitals, prisons and Boy Scout troops. Most of the rest were fined or put on probation.

MORE THAN 100 SUITS

But that is just the tip of the industry's antitrust travails. Still pending are more than 100 suits filed in the past several months by the Justice Department, states and private companies charging dozens of paper concerns with fixing prices of corrugated boxes, folding-cartons, stationery and other paper products. A federal grand jury in Philadelphia is in the midst of the broadest antitrust investigation yet of paper-industry pricing practices, and the inquiry could result in felony indictments.

The industry's anticompetitive conduct has followed a simple pattern, according to testimony and evidence taken in the three most recent price-fixing trials. Repeatedly over the past two decades, executives from some paper companies met at posh resorts, during trade-association conventions, and even at a sick colleague's bedside, to agree on price changes for certain products or to decide not to undercut a competitor's prices.

At such gatherings, industry officials testified, executives of companies that didn't live up to pricing agreements often were berated by their colleagues. For instance, at an April 1974 meeting of consumer-bag producers at the famed Antoine's restaurant in New Orleans, an executive of Chase Bag Co. of Greenwich, Conn., began needling Stanley Schottland, president of American Bag & Paper Corp. of Philadelphia, for dragging his feet on a price increase, testimony given in federal court in Philadelphia shows. "This was a real nasty confrontation," one paper company executive testified. He added, "Stanley invited him outside to have a good fist fight." (In this case, a jury found Chase Bag Co. guilty of price fixing. Mr. Schottland and American Bag pleaded no contest to similar charges. They haven't been sentenced yet.)

NO LESSON FROM HISTORY

Antitrust officials are dismayed that such practices have continued despite a string of successful prosecutions against the industry dating back to before the 1930s, when one paper-industry executive raised a storm about being fingerprinted in a price-fixing case. "It's amazing. They just never seem to learn their lesson," one Justice Department official says.

Particularly unsettling to antitrust enforcers is that otherwise, the multibillion-dollar-a-year paper and paper-products industry is considered highly competitive. The industry consists of hundreds of companies, many of them small. "If price collusion can go on so rampantly in that industry, where there's lots of competition, what must be happening in industries where competition isn't as great?"

Paper-company officials deny that price fixing is rampant in their industry. "I don't think the paper industry is all that incredibly unique," asserts William L. Lurie, executive vice president and general counsel of International Paper Co. in New York, the industry's largest company. "Right now, we just seem to have a little more than our fair share of troubles," says Mr. Lurie, whose company is a defendant in all but one of the major price-fixing suits.

FEW ACQUITTALS

Mr. Lurie stresses that being indicted or sued doesn't mean a company or individual is guilty. "An indictment is a lot different than a conviction," he says, suggesting that many, if not all, the pending antitrust charges against paper concerns are without merit.

Obviously, any pending or future charges will have to be proved, antitrust prosecutors agree. But they note their record in such cases is strong. Of the scores of paper companies and their officials charged in the three recent federal suits, only one company and six individuals were acquitted. And the cases produced solid evidence of price fixing.

During a two-week trial in February 1975 of two label manufacturers—Michigan Lithographing Co. of Grand Rapids, Mich., and the Litton Business Systems subsidiary of Litton Industries Inc., Beverly Hills, Calif.,—government lawyers entered as evidence five years of notes of price-fixing activities kept by an official of H.S. Crocker Co., a San Bruno, Calif., label maker. At the trial, in federal court in San Francisco, other industry executives confirmed the substance of the notes and testified that companies wouldn't undercut the price quotes of competitors' accounts.

Here's one exchange between government prosecutors and Thomas Dosdall, vice president of H.M. Smyth Co., St. Paul.

Q: Did you undercut Fort Dearborn's pricing, sir? (The reference was to Fort Dearborn Lithograph Co. of Chicago.)

A: No.

Q: Would you explain why not?

A: Well, you couldn't very well call up your friend and ask him for the price and then turn around and undercut it, I don't think.

Q: Was this your understanding when obtaining price information from a competitor, that you weren't to undercut the information he gave you?

A: Yes.

Michigan Lithographing and the Litton subsidiary were convicted of price fixing. Another seven companies pleaded no contest.

At a January 1977 trial against a folding-carton producer, Consolidated Packaging Corp. of Chicago, Justice Department prosecutors introduced as evidence notes from one former industry executive reflecting hundreds of conversations about prices with competitors in the folding-carton industry. Testimony during the trial in federal court in Chicago showed that members of the Paper Board Packaging Council would gather during meetings of that trade association to discuss prices they charged on various accounts. Consolidated Packaging was the only one of 23 folding-carton makers charged with price fixing that went to trial instead of pleading no contest. Consolidated was found guilty.

At the trial of three consumer-bag producers in Philadelphia last fall, industry executives testified of meetings attended by officials from several companies at resorts in Pebble Beach, Calif.; Hamilton, Bermuda, and Hilton Head, S.C., among other places. Pricing actions were discussed at all of the meetings, they testified. Another meeting was held at the home of an executive who was ill, because, one official testified, "a price increase was coming up, and people had to talk about it."

The executives who discussed prices realized what they were doing was probably illegal, according to witnesses in the trial. One executive testified that he recalled a meeting where another associate said, "If they send us to jail, we will at least have enough to make a ball team—a baseball team."

THE "OLD DOG" THEORY

Antitrust-law experts and paper-industry watchers offer several explanations for the industry's persistent antitrust troubles. And they say many of the reasons could apply to any industry in which price-fixing violations have occurred.

The simplest explanation: It's difficult to teach old dogs new tricks. "Because industry executives have communicated so freely among themselves for years about prices, it's hard for them to stop," one private antitrust lawyer says.

He notes that industry officials continued to meet and agree on price changes despite a noted 1969 Supreme Court ruling involving such practices by paper companies; the decision set strict rules prohibiting exchanges of current price information among competitors in all but the most unusual circumstances. That case involved Container Corp. of America, a Chicago subsidiary of Marcor Inc., and 17 other producers of cardboard boxes that for years had an informal practice of exchanging price information.

A common ingredient in recent price-fixing actions is that "the same companies come up in all the cases," adds another antitrust lawyer. Most of the cases have involved three of the industry's largest companies—International Paper, Weyerhaeuser Co. of Tacoma, Wash., and Champion International Corp. of Stamford, Conn. Indeed, the only company among the industry's eight biggest producers to escape antitrust problems has been Kimberly-Clark Corp. of Neenah, Wis., which several years ago dropped its membership in industry trade associations.

Mr. Lurie of International Paper says one factor in the industry's troubles is the "very diverse, very fragmented and very competitive" nature of the industry. "Competition in the industry is so intense, maybe sometimes people take risks they wouldn't otherwise take," he says.

In an effort to prevent antitrust problems, International Paper requires 7,000 of its employes to review the company's written antitrust policy annually and to acknowledge in writing that they understand it and intend to comply with it. Mr. Lurie says that, as part of an antitrust education program, he also periodically sends articles on antitrust issues to all of the company's 50,000 employes. But, he adds, "You can't police 50,000 people all the time."

Antitrust enforcers also note that until two years ago price fixing was a misdemeanor, and penalties were relatively limited. The stakes are much higher since Congress passed a federal antitrust statute in 1976 that makes price fixing a felony. The statute also increased the maximum penalty for a corporation to $1 million from $50,000, and it raised the top penalty for an individual to three years in prison and a $100,000 fine from one year in prison and a $50,000 fine.

As a result, "The era of the gentlemanly crime is over," antitrust lawyer Ira Millstein of New York says. "A felony is a felony whether it's burglary or price fixing." Judges, too, are sending more convicted price-fixers to jail. Justice Department statistics show that judges recently have sentenced 60% of convicted antitrust felons to prison terms.

ANOTHER BIG SUIT

The department early this year filed one of its biggest antitrust suits yet against paper companies, charging both criminal and civil violations. The suit, filed in federal court in Houston, accuses 14 companies and 26 of their executives with fixing prices of corrugated boxes.

In recent months, 12 states also have brought separate civil suits charging 21 manufacturers of fine paper, such as stationery, with fixing prices. All of the suits are pending. Class-action suits filed by customers of paper producers are climbing too. About 50 companies have filed actions against cardboard-box makers, and about as many concerns have brought suits against folding-carton producers. These companies generally buy boxes and cartons for their own products.

If the paper companies lose the class-action suits, they stand to pay millions of dollars in damages. Attorneys for paper-industry customers charge that price collusion in the paper industry also has cost consumers millions of dollars because their clients have had to pass along the higher costs.

NO BODY LANGUAGE, PLEASE*

You know you're going to raise your prices to industrial customers in 30 days and it would be decent to let them know what's coming, but you daren't. Why? It's against the law.

Or you're an editor and you tell your ace reporter to find out how much steel is going up. Hope your reporter doesn't find out; he could end up in jail.

1984? Maybe, if the Federal Trade Commission has its way. The FTC has just brought its first case, against four major companies selling gasoline lead additives. The complaint: that by publicly announcing their prices through the press the four have fixed prices. The proposed remedy: no more public or press announcements on prices, no more selling at a transportation-included price, no more promising to give any customer the best price you gave anyone else.

The four— Ethyl Corp., E.I. du Pont de Nemours & Co., PPG Industries, Inc. and Nalco Chemical Co.—will fight the FTC order. And the FTC probably will keep appealing, if it loses, as the case works up from an administrative law judge through the four-member commission itself, and then into the federal courts. The First Amendment to the Constitution—the one about freedom of speech and of the press—is a bit of a problem, admits the FTC, but not necessarily that important compared with the risk of possible anticompetitive pricing.

The government's theory is called "price signaling." The idea is that smart operators who want to fix prices, particularly in concentrated industries, don't need to meet in smoke-filled hotel rooms at midnight. They just tell the world what they are doing and, *voila,* everybody gets the message and falls into line.

This isn't the first time the government has tried to convince the courts that businessmen shouldn't be allowed to talk publicly about prices.

Back in 1972 the Justice Department brought Sherman antitrust charges against General Motors Corp. and the Ford Motor Co. charging price-fixing—actually eliminating price discounts on fleet vehicle sales—by signaling each other about their positions and coming actions through speeches and stories to the press. Eventually the federal judge and jury threw out the auto price-signaling criminal and civil cases, but zealous bureaucrats don't quit.

Last year John H. Shenefield, the Administration's chief trustbuster, told *Forbes* he supported the conspiracy-via-signaling theory. It's enough, he said, for an industry such as steel to tell the *government* what it's doing.

* Reprinted by permission of *Forbes Magazine* from the June 25, 1979 issue.

"As to whether it's a fit subject for general public consideration, I'm not sure," the assistant attorney general said.

In the Detroit case the government couldn't prove any conspiracy, but with the FTC rules the proof of conspiracy isn't even necessary.

The FTC's complaint is that the companies sell their additives only at a transportation-included price; that some promise their buyers as low a price as anyone gets; that all use a 30-day-advance-notice-of-price-change clause, and often tell the press and even potential customers of coming price changes.

Is this just sensible marketing? Not to the FTC gumshoes. "The practices amount, under the circumstances in this industry, to a modern form of price-fixing," says Alfred F. Dougherty Jr., director of FTC's Bureau of Competition; "sophisticated advanced price signaling, usually coupled with other practices, achieves similar results while avoiding traditional agreements."

Couldn't companies in concentrated industries discover their competitors' prices even without "signaling," just by asking their customers? "Yes," says an FTC man, "but the customer has a tendency to lie."

"They drive you out of business, and when you act like you do when you're going out of business they say 'we're filing antitrust suits,'" says Irving S. Shapiro, Du Pont's chairman. His point: The government emission regulations have doomed the lead additive business. So, with sales falling anyway, no one will allow business to be lost because a competitor cuts prices. That being the case, who will cut prices to gain market share, he asks? Also, "it's absolutely necessary for us to advise our customers in advance what they'll have to pay for raw materials," he says.

Dougherty says there were 18 lockstep price increases in 4 years; Du Pont's lawyer says that is untrue: There were 18 price changes, including 6 price cuts, and 9 changes connected to changes in the price of lead.

Prices on consumer items, such as automobiles, are different. "In consumer products the public interest might outweigh the anticompetitive aspects," says the agency. But a few years ago the Justice Department did try to use the signaling theory in a case against carmakers.

As for free speech and freedom of the press, Shapiro of Du Pont says: "That's a prior restraint if I ever heard of one." Dougherty of the FTC says, "The test under the First Amendment, basically, is whether a restraint on speech is reasonably necessary to prevent the unfair competitive practices. We believe that that necessity will be established by the record in this case."

What about the press? If an editor tells his reporter to get the steel industry's prices, and he gets them, wouldn't the FTC want to know where the price information came from, to see if it was signaling? And if the reporter wouldn't talk, and they often don't, couldn't he end up in jail?

The FTC lawyer smiles and says it probably wouldn't come to that. But no guarantees. What about extrasensory perception? The FTC apparently hasn't figured out what to do about that. Yet.

THE KROGER CASE:
REGULATION AMOK*

By Robert J. Samuelson

These are strange times. In a period of rapid inflation, the last thing you would expect the government to do is to rap a company for successfully competing on the basis of low prices. And yet, that is precisely the practical effect of a preliminary decision by the Federal Trade Commission against the Kroger Co., one of the nation's largest supermarket chains.

This is one of those sad regulatory stories in which the process seems primarily to serve the regulators and the parasitic industries—consultants, law firms—that thrive on regulation. It is not a story of evil, but one of subtle subversion. Rules acquire independent meaning and momentum, and regulation's ultimate goal of improving the public welfare gets lost in the shuffle.

It's worth remembering that this is not always the case. In advertising, the government has clearly provided for some information that improves consumer choice and competition: gasoline mileage ratings, for example. Though the ratings may not always reflect actual driving experience, they do provide a common basis for comparison.

But the government cannot protect consumers against every slight imperfection in product performance or every strained advertising claim. The regulatory process' main liability is not that it is inherently power hungry, but that its standards are usually imprecise and absolutist. Once it tiptoes into a new regulatory area, government finds it difficult to impose limits on itself.

The result as in the Kroger case—is often frivolous, wasteful and self-defeating.

Back in 1972, Kroger decided to change its corporate image from a high-priced "quality" chain to an aggressive price leader. It shifted its basic strategy, targeted prices in major markets to the lowest-price competitors and established internal surveys to monitor compliance.

* "The Kroger Case: Regulation AMOK," by Robert J. Samuelson, *The National Journal,* 1979, reprinted in *The Washington Post,* July 10, 1979, D–6, used with permission.

To all outward appearances, the corporate strategy succeeded admirably, profits rose sharply, and Kroger passed A&P as the nation's second-largest food chain, behind Safeway. Part of that success involved a highly promoted advertising campaign called "price-patrol," in which Kroger had local checkers make weekly comparisons of about 150 brand-name articles—such as HI-C fruit drinks or Betty Crocker cake mixes—sold by its major local competitors.

Then, resorting to massive advertising on television and in newspapers, Kroger blasted out the results. "For 74 straight weeks, the price patrol proves Kroger is the low-price leader," said an advertisement in Dallas. Or, "Here's documented proof that Kroger leads with low prices in Nashville."

Reading the ruling by FTC administrative law judge Montgomery K. Hyun, you might conclude the Kroger's advertisements represent massive deception. As Hyun points out, the price comparisons didn't include "private label" goods, meats, fresh fruits and vegetables, which together accounted for about half of Kroger's sales.

And the items weren't randomly selected. Merchandising managers picked the items to go on the "price patrol" lists, but they also knew which items benefited from so-called roller programs. These are programs in which major manufacturers give temporary discounts on their products, which may or may not be "rolled" through to customers. Clearly, an opportunity for bias existed.

To highlight these flaws, though, is to miss a more important reality: as Hyun also indicated, Kroger was highly competitive in its prices and, by and large, its "price patrol represented a good-conscience effort to make comparisons."

Full lists comparisons were posted in stores for public viewing. When Kroger lost, it said so. When the comparison shoppers made obvious pricing mistakes, Kroger eliminated the errors that worked to its advantage and kept those that didn't. "Roller" items may have been somewhat over-represented, but still apparently constituted only about 10 percent of the sample. Manufacturers are required to give the same discounts to all stores: if other stores had passed on the discounts, the distortion would have been minimal.

As for meat, its exclusion may have been somewhat self-serving; the evidence is ambiguous about whether Kroger's meat prices exceeded the average. But including meat would have created huge technical problems, because quality differences obscure genuine price comparisons. The same difficulty applied to fruits, vegetables and private-label products.

Kroger's more elaborate (but less frequent) internal price surveillance system—which included surveys by an outside consulting firm—showed remarkable success in underpricing the competition. About 90 percent of the time, Kroger had more items (including meats) priced lower than competitors. But, if absolute truth in advertising is the standard, Kroger flunked. In about a fourth of the tests between 1973 and 1978, at least one competitor had more lower-priced items.

Hyun flunked Kroger, arguing that it didn't have a "reasonable basis" for making its advertising claim. Unfortunately, finding a "reasonable basis" isn't as simple as it sounds. The FTC staff spent years trying to devise a workable random sample for food price comparisons, but apparently concluded that quality differences made comprehensiveness impractical and expensive. Hyun conceded this, but nevertheless insisted that such a survey was required for any unqualified price comparisons.

Even if Kroger had acted totally irresponsibly, it's questionable whether this complaint should ever have been brought. As Robert Pitofsky—an FTC commissioner who once headed the agency's Bureau of Consumer Protection—wrote last year: "Where advertising fraud will be exposed by consumers sampling low-cost, repeat-purchase items, there is less reason for the government to intervene. . . . Much alleged deceptive pricing is almost certainly innocuous. . . . "

Common sense. But government works differently. In 1972, the FTC adopted its "reasonable basis" theory, and new doctrines often lead quickly to unpredictable and silly results. With the FTC action pending, Kroger dropped its "price patrol" last year.

GENERIC DRUGS ARE A HOT TICKET FOR CHAIN STORES*

By Howie Kurtz

Several drugstore chains in the Washington area, armed with new evidence from the Food and Drug Administration, are stepping up their advertising campaigns to tout the benefits of lower-priced generic drugs.

Drug Fair is the most recent pharmacy chain to jump on the generic bandwagon, with a media compaign featuring cartoons in which an animated generic pill waves a copy of "test results" to prove he is just as good as his brandname counterparts.

Drug Fair's 104 stores in the metropolitan area have now joined People's and Giant Food in aggressive advertising of the benefits of generic

---

* "Generic Drugs Are a Hot Ticket for Chain Stores," by Howie Kurtz, *Washington Star,* April 11, 1979, p. DC-1, DC-2, used with permission.

drugs, a rapidly growing market that is just beginning to emerge from the shadow of the major pharmaceutical companies.

In the last few years, some 40 states have adopted laws allowing pharmacies to substitute a chemical equivalent for a doctor's brand-name prescription. This kind of substitution is freely allowed in the District and Maryland, but requires the doctor's permission in Virginia.

"Generic drugs are just coming into maturity where we can really rely on them," said Paul Forbes, a Drug Fair vice president who handled a similar program when he was with Giant Food. "They must meet the same FDA standards as the brand-name drugs. We've had a significant increase in the number of people who come in and talk to us about generics."

FDA officials are now completing a list of 2,400 generic drugs which they certify are equivalent to the brand-name versions. Another agency is recording the tremendous price savings to be had from buying, say, chlordiazapoxide hydrochloride instead of Librium.

But the Pharmaceutical Manufacturers Association, fighting a rearguard action, has sued to prevent the government from distributing these lists. Many big drug firms, however, have capitulated to the movement and are now making their own generic drugs and selling them under different names.

"The industry would prefer that we don't push generics as hard as we do," said Joseph Pollard, vice president of People's Drug Stores. "But we're selling a lot more generics than we did three years ago. There's a lot less confusion than there used to be because most chain drug stores are trying to educate consumers."

People's took a survey of local doctors a few years ago and found they favored generic drugs by a margin of 3 to 1. Both People's and Drug Fair buy their generics from another company that specializes in the less expensive drugs.

"Our supplier identifies companies with great strength in making different drugs and does the necessary testing." said Drug Fair's Forbes. "They ship them out under their own name and it saves us a lot of headaches. We don't have the resources to do that kind of job."

Giant Food, meanwhile, has set up its own laboratory and technicians to test the generics it sells in its supermarket pharmacies.

Drug Fair's television campaign is aimed at reassuring senior citizens and others who might be uneasy about buying drugs made by small, unknown companies. "Drug Fair will never substitute their judgment for your doctor's," the ads say. "But you'll save up to 50 percent on generics and get precisely what your doctor ordered."

But the industry has fought back with its own advertising blitz, aimed primarily at doctors who write the prescriptions. "The FDA really can't inspect every drug manufacturer," said C. Joseph Stetler of the Pharmaceutical Manufacturers Association. "They leave the consumer vulnerable because smaller firms are not getting the same scrutiny."

Stetler says his group agrees that more price information should be offered to consumers, but is not convinced that all generic products are as good as the brand-name versions. "A manufacturer has to be able to put his credentials behind a product and stand behind it," he insisted.

FDA officials, however, emphasize that they must test and approve random batches of every drug, regardless of the manufacturer. "This administration is firmly behind the increased use of generic drugs," said FDA spokesman Wayne Pines.

"We've provided the states with a draft list of generic drugs that we've approved and can be substituted with confidence. I think the industry has exaggerated its point as to whether generics are equivalent to brand-name products."

Federal officials say the government is now saving $10 million a year by putting price ceilings on many of the drugs it purchases. The price limits have forced the government to practice what it preaches and buy generic drugs for millions of Medicare and Medicaid patients.

WHEN CRITICS POINT TO FEES, DOCTORS CITE THEIR RECORDS*

By Howie Kurtz

Dr. Yussef Akbari, a Northeast Washington physician, charges $325 for a tonsillectomy, more than twice as much as many local doctors ask for the same procedure.

"Am I the only one charging $325?" Akbari asked. "Well, I'm not surprised. The reason is, we don't charge for preoperative or follow-up visits. All we get is one lump sum fee."

The veteran doctor added, "I have a very good record. My patients are usually out of the hospital the next morning, and complications are almost nil. I'm not saying that someone who charges $150 or $200 is doing a worse job than I am, but I have a very good record."

Many doctors in the Washington area consider their surgical fees a highly personal statement, a product of their special talents and experience, a private charge they would not want bandied about like the price of hamburger.

* "When Critics Point to Fees, Doctors Cite Their Record," by Howie Kurtz, *Washington Star,* April 8, 1979, p. A-12, used with permission.

The older surgeons say you can't put a price tag on their years of experience, that their patients don't mind paying hundreds of dollars more, especially for a serious operation.

But many younger doctors are charging even more than their older colleagues these days because they have huge debts to repay from medical school and the cost of starting a practice.

"It's like paying off a mortgage," said Dr. Barry Aron, a Gaithersburg urologist. "Tuition at Georgetown Medical School is now about $12,000 a year, and you're 10 or 12 years behind your classmates who became accountants. You've got to open an office at $10 or $12 a square foot, and you're living off the bank.

"You've been a parasite for 10 years, and that debt has to be taken care of. Forget profit, forget standard of living. You've got to cover your overhead, and inflation hurts the new guy starting out even more."

The great disparity in surgical fees throughout the Washington area is also caused, in part, by geographical differences. Doctors in affluent Montgomery County say they have to charge more because their rent and nurses' salaries are substantially higher than in Anacostia or Seat Pleasant.

The widespread public ignorance of the large variation in medical fees, however, gradually is coming to an end.

While the medical profession has long been insulated from the pressures of comparison shopping—especially since insurance companies pay most of the bills—a growing number of doctors are now being asked to explain why they charge far more for a given operation than a colleague across town charges.

The veil of secrecy was lifted further recently when Ralph Nader's Health Research Group revealed a "huge" variation in the fees that 500 local doctors charge for a dozen typical operations.

Federal officials also are getting into the act. The Federal Trade Commission is upset because many doctors are using a "relative value scale" which rates procedures according to their difficulty but can also be used as a price list if each rating is multiplied by a certain dollar figure.

The commission recently secured consent orders from four physician groups—including organizations of radiologists, gynecologists and orthopedic surgeons—in which they promised to stop using these lists to set prices.

The wide variation in fees, Dr. Aron contends, "speaks to a free-market situation. It belies the argument Nader makes that doctors are in collusion to fix fees."

Aron, who charges $1,065 for a prostate operation—nearly twice the $550 that some local doctors ask—says he has higher overhead costs because he practices in Montgomery.

And, he says, "if I spend a half-hour with a patient, they get a lot of attention. Some people are volume operators. They see a lot of people and can afford to charge low fees. It's analagous to the Medicaid mills."

Some women have questioned why Dr. Robert Greenfield and his partners were charging $500 for an abortion, when the Women's Medical Center of Washington is offering the same procedure for just $125.

The Greenfield group, it turns out, hired a Philadelphia consulting firm a couple of years ago to help set the fees for its doctors. The consultants didn't survey the rates in the metropolitan area, but nevertheless advised the doctors to charge $500 for the procedure.

"We sort of agreed to it, but we later decided that seems a little high," said Dr. John Niles, a partner in the group, which has offices in Southeast Washington and Seat Pleasant. "Now we charge $325 because we talked around and found others aren't charging as much.

"The group believes we offer increased safety because the procedure is performed under general anesthesia in a hospital. We don't do it in a hospital just in order to make more money out of it.

"In a clinic, you walk in, have the procedure, walk out, and that's the end of their responsibility. Medicine is a business—you have to make a profit. But you're making medicine sound like a product. It's not like buying a car at a discount, you know."

Yet, Hannah Ticktin, director of the non-profit Women's Medical Center, insists there are many ways to keep costs down. "Our fees are set according to exactly what it costs us," she explained. "Our salaries may be a little lower, but the people here want to work in this sort of setting. We try to provide service at a low fee without any reduction in quality."

Some state and federal officials admit that the government inadvertently helps push up health costs because Medicaid pays 80 percent of the "usual and customary" fees that local doctors charge. If most Washington area physicians suddenly decided to double their fees for, say, tonsillectomies, the government would have little choice but to pay the increased charges.

"Some doctors set a target income for themselves and adjust their fees to reach that figure," said one federal official. "Very few businesses can create more demand, but doctors can raise their income by ordering more tests and marginal procedures."

Many people also don't bother to compare prices because their private insurance coverage pays most of the bills, says Harold Cohen, a Maryland official who regulates state hospital costs.

"The market doesn't work because the incentives have been taken away," he said. "What do you care if an operation costs your insurance company another couple of hundred bucks?"

Added Cohen: "You don't need 20 years of experience to do a tonsillectomy."

Doctors at the Malin Medical Group in Riverdale, for example, charge $150 for a tonsillectomy, compared to Dr. Akbari's $325. "Our doctors are very conscientious about keeping the prices low," said business manager Dominic Colangelo. "We don't turn anybody away. But our group is really struggling financially to make ends meet."

Dr. Ernest L. Hopkins, whose office is on upper 16th Street NW, charges $910 for a normal delivery of a baby, compared to the $360 that some charge.

"The patients we see have complicated obstetric problems, and the figure may include more than 15 visits per pregnancy," Hopkins said. "My malpractice insurance last year was $18,000 just for me. But I still deliver some people for nothing because they just don't have the money."

Dr. Basdeo Balkissoon charges $400 to $500 for a hernia repair, which is in the high range, but he says "experience is a factor you just can't measure. Your patients come back to you because they know you're skilled. I never hear any squawking about money, and if I do I work out whatever the person can pay."

Many local doctors charge $250 for an appendectomy, but Dr. Felix Paolucci, who has offices in Hyattsville and Northeast Washington, asks $450 for the same procedure. "I don't make up a fee after I look at a guy's financial statement," he said, "That's what I charge in order for me to make a reasonable profit and live the way I'm used to living."

Paoluccci, who is chief of surgery at Providence Hospital, says he specializes in complicated cases and that the $450 covers all necessary treatment. "Some of the fees sounded horrendous in the paper, I grant you," he said, referring to an earlier news story on the Nader report. "But compared to New York City, where they get $1,500 for a gall bladder operation, we're pikers."

While some doctors resent their private fees being publicized, Paolucci says he appreciates it when his patients are frank about money. "I don't make it a mystical thing," he said. "If someone is buying a service from me, he has a right to know what it's going to cost beforehand.

"Anyone who doesn't have money I'll still treat because I make plenty of money, but I'm not going to give my services away for free, either."

The Nader group, which based its figures on 1976 data from Blue Shield, the largest local Medicare carrier, says the large difference in surgical fees "can't be justified."

The group insists there is no evidence that someone paying $2,110 for a hysterectomy here is getting better treatment than a patient who pays $550 for the same procedure.

But several doctors say they resent this growing trend toward competitive advertising.

"How do you measure what it costs a doctor in terms of the stress on his family life?" asked Aron. "When you call at 3 a.m. with a kidney stone, we are there. If a patient is bleeding after an operation, I will babysit with him all night. How do you put an amount on that?"

$50 DENTURES:
ASSEMBLY-LINE DENTAL MACHINE SPITS OUT FALSE TEETH ON DEMAND*

By Ena Naunton

Henry Ford did it with automobiles.

Now a few dentists are doing it for teeth.

"It's an assembly line—you go in one way and come out the other," said a patient, waiting with about 60 others at a North Dade dental clinic.

People with wobbly dentures, bad teeth or no teeth at all are lining up for cut-rate dentistry at the practice of Dr. Harvey Pallen and Dr. Stanley Richardson, 1395 NW 167th St.

Pallen and Richardson charge $50 for one denture, $95 for two; $5 for an extraction, $10 for an X-ray. The average cost of dentures in South Florida is between $400 and $500, according to the East Coast Dental Society.

Although relaxation of advertising restrictions has caused a number of Florida dentists to offer cheaper, faster services for simpler treatments, Pallen and Richardson have the largest and most streamlined operation. They have, in fact, produced a dental machine, modeled on a larger one, the Sexton Dental Clinic in Florence, S.C., and similar to clinics in Jackson, Tenn. and Clarksburg, W. Va.

Cut-rate dentistry is the latest sign of the changing times in professions which previously restricted or banned advertising. Professional organizations for opticians first, then lawyers and now dentists, threatened with legal action by the Federal Trade Commission which claimed they smothered competition, have been forced to lift their advertising bans. Legislative and Supreme Court action made previous state laws enforcing such bans invalid.

---

* "$50 Dentures: Assembly-Line Dental Machine Spits Out False Teeth on Demand," by Ena Naunton, *The Miami Herald,* March 17, 1979, pp. D1, D3, used with permission.

This has put eyeglasses and dentistry into some department stores and allowed the public to compare prices for legal services, such as preparation of wills and divorces.

Pallen and Richardson were ready when the Florida law changed last June 30. They were among the first dentists in the state to advertise their prices. But they had spent 18 months preparing their 14-room office layout and production-line operation before quitting a successful, traditional practice on Miami Beach. There, Richardson said, each man would see an average of about 12 patients a day. Now he and Pallen together see 50 to 70 a day. Their waiting room holds 100 and frequently every seat is taken, with some spillover into the parking lot. But Richardson said the crowd usually includes some relatives who have accompanied patients for treatment.

While patients line up on chairs outside the treatment rooms, with notes pinned to their shoulders to describe the treatment each needs, a staff of 26 works on the production line that promises the patient who is in by 10 a.m. will get his new dentures the same afternoon.

Here an employe fills dozens of little paper cups full of white powder. There, another adds water to mix the glop that a third fixes into molds to take gum impressions for dentures. In another room, a lineup of technicians is molding, setting, trimming and smoothing dentures.

After 20 years of making dentures alone, Felix Jacomino, working alongside three other technicians, with a total of 51 years of experience among them, said he likes the production line: "It's fast and it's still the same quality," he said.

While acknowledging the similarity to Henry Ford's division of labor, which revolutionized the auto industry, Richardson said, "This is more difficult. Every Ford comes out the same, but every patient has a different mouth."

In another cut-rate practice in North Miami Beach, Dr. Seth Rhodes says satisfaction with the $50 dentures depends upon the patient's expectations.

Rhodes, who had practiced traditional dentistry in North Miami Beach for 26 years before concentrating on dentures in the past year, said, "I think I have the same ratio of complainers as when I got much more money for my dentures than I do now. If I was good then, I am good now. I am not saying I can produce a denture as good as a man charging $500 to $1,000, because he gives more time. . . but we think we put out a good product and we try to help our patients as much as we can. However, there are limits."

From a choice of eight to 10 different sizes and colors of false teeth, Rhodes said he and his three partners (Drs. Harold Chambers, Tyrone Cheeping and Gary Rosen) offer a kind of wardrobe of dentures, which are selected to fit the mouth and face of the patient. But if someone wants the teeth set in some "cosmetic" fashion, the cut price doesn't apply, said Rhodes. Every person getting a denture in this practice is given one free return visit, if a fitting adjustment is necessary. Any subsequent fitting costs $10. Patients who have teeth extracted and dentures fitted on the same visit are told that their gums will shrink and, after three or four months, their dentures could need to be tightened or relined, said Rhodes. That costs $25.

"If some have 10 or 12 teeth extracted from the upper jaw, they are told there is a good chance that the denture will be loose and that tightening up will not be sufficient," said Rhodes. In that case, the patient has the choice to pay for a new denture later or get along with a loose one.

Regardless of the cost, said Rhodes, "If a patient expects more than he can get from a denture, he is not going to be happy. There is no perfect fit, in my opinion, whether (the denture) costs $50 or $500."

Other dentists in the practice do extractions, fillings and permanent bridges (the latter not at cut rates). Rhodes concentrates only on dentures. He says he misses the old, friendly relationships he built with patients over years of caring for their teeth.

"For $95, I can't take the time," he said. He wouldn't be specific about how much time he budgets for each patient, but he admitted that it probably is less than 10 minutes (he does the morning impressions; one of his partners fits the completed teeth in the afternoon.)

Traditional dentistry still frowns on the production-line approach.

"The construction and fitting of a denture is not the same as the purchase of eyeglasses," said Dr. Clifford Marks, orthodontist and president of the East Coast Dental Society. "It is not a question of filling a prescription for a certain lens that has definite refractive powers. Each denture has to be fitted to the patient's mouth. It's not a commodity type of thing."

While Pallen and Richardson say that they fit every denture after it is made, giving one free return visit and charging $8 for any subsequent fitting, Marks argues: "The fee for a denture is determined by the dentist, based upon the care and time that he puts into the evaluation, fabrication and fitting of that denture for the patient. That's the reason for the fee range of dentures."

Marks points out that the new regulations concerning dentists advertising specifies that prices may only be quoted for "routine dental services" including "simple" extractions and "basic" full upper and lower dentures.

Richardson agrees that, in streamlining their practice for the production line, he and Pallen decided to stick to basics and abandon some of the more time-consuming treatments each had done for more than 20 years.

"We don't do gold crowns, permanent bridges or fillings," he said. "We can offer our service by concentrating on the limited area of dentures and those things related to dentures (including $5 uncomplicated extractions). It's like any other business, when you just do one or two things, you can do a good job and perhaps do it less expensively than if we did root canals and gum work. This is designed and developed only for denture work."

Asked if such a comparatively cheap service would encourage people to have their teeth extracted when another dentist might have worked to save them, Richardson said, "I will not take out good teeth. One of the biggest problems I have in diagnosis is (that) people want teeth out and I won't take them out because they are salvageable." He said he refers such patients to other dentists.

But a number of the patients who show up for treatment at the Richardson-Pallen practice have neglected their teeth for years. Pallen said young men and women want partial dentures to replace lost front teeth, because their poor appearance has kept them from getting jobs.

One woman, who said she had recently pulled out one of her own teeth with ease because of the gum disease pyorrhea, said, "I have been losing my teeth little by little and I am down to my last ones." Waiting patiently to have them extracted and to be fitted with a denture, she refused to be identified because, "what would my regular dentist say?"

"People who work in Florida don't get paid enough to go to high-priced dentists," said the woman who claimed to make about the minimum wage of $2.90 an hour. (Marks said that the Florida Dental Association has a toll-free referral service for persons needing dentures. More than 100 Miami area dentists are enrolled and willing to do denture work—not "restorative dentistry" such as fillings and crowns—at fees scaled according to the patient's ability to pay. The phone is 1–800–282–9117. Medicare does not pay for dental work, unless it is part of treatment for facial injuries.)

The speed of the production line service appeals to some patients.

"We have a lot of truck drivers who are in and out of town and need one-day service," said Richardson. The woman who had been pulling out her own teeth was one of the early morning patients who expected to have her remaining teeth pulled and a denture fitted the same afternoon and return to work at 6:30 the next morning.

Dental bargain hunters sometimes get up very early. On Thursday, Meredith Welshams, 64, left Fort Myers Beach at 4:45 a.m. and was at Rhodes' North Miami Beach office at 8 a.m. By 3:30 p.m., he was being fitted with his new top and bottom dentures that cost him $95.

Welshams said he paid $700 for his last dentures, which he wore for 10 years. "They were clicking a little and my face was starting to recede."

He was pleased with the new dentures' fit, although he said, "I'll know for sure when I eat dinner."

Although Rhodes and his partners speeded up their denture construction operation and increased the number of technicians from two to four, Rhodes doesn't like the word "streamlining" because, he said, "it sounds like cutting corners." The dentists work in eight treatment rooms. Their waiting room holds about 25 people.

"One of our secrets is consistency," said Richardson. "Everything is done the same way, all the time, from laboratory work and X-rays to handling the patients out front (in the waiting room, where numbers are used instead of names). With the volume of people we see, you can't afford to have too much error."

Part 5 | Place: Issues of Power and Equity in Channels of Distribution

Cases

1. Champions of Breakfast: Formulation of a Public Relations Program for the Cereal Industry
2. Gulf Oil Corporation: Responding to a Lawsuit from a Disgruntled Franchisee
3. Northrop Corporation: Development of a Policy on International Sales Commissions

Commentaries

1. Soft-Drink Lobby Claims Its Due
2. The Franchising Industry Acquires Maturity
3. How the Law Lets You Lose in those Cash Machines
4. Mail Fraud: A Thriving Business
5. A Boycott Over Infant Formula
6. U.S. Enters Debate Over Laws: "Criminals" Take Bite of Dental Business

PLACE: ISSUES OF POWER AND EQUITY
IN CHANNELS OF DISTRIBUTION

In order to gain insight into the development of social issues regarding channels of distribution, an understanding of two important concepts is needed. The first of these is the *behavioral nature of channels of distribution*. A channel is not a structure, but a set of negotiated relationships between marketers. As in any ongoing business relationship, the elements of power, trust, competence, and efficiency are continually evaluated by each party in the relationship, which creates an undercurrent of cooperation and conflict. One of the clearest explanations of how these elements relate to each other has been given by Robicheaux and El-Ansary (Figure 1).

It is usual that the channel member with the most power becomes the leader or "channel captain," and makes major policy decisions affecting the channel and its operating efficiency. The channel captain seeks to establish cooperation between channel members and arbitrate areas of extreme conflict, but the give and take of some mixture of cooperation and conflict is probably essential to the vitality of the channel concept. Increasing tension would spotlight a need for a member to either improve efficiency in the given area or withdraw from the function. A reduction of the necessary dynamic tension *could* result from a perfect match of competency and needs. It has been more common, however, that tension was suppressed by an extremely powerful channel member fully exercising available power. In such a case, the affected channel members were forced out of the channel or sought some type of offsetting power.

The second channels concept is that of *countervailing power,* defined as the exertion of "force against an opposing and often bad or harmful force or influence." Popularized by Harvard economist John D. Galbraith, this concept has been used to examine the evolution of channels and the resolution of channel conflict. The concept dates to the late nineteenth century, when the federal government sought to counterbalance the power of monopolies in oil, sugar, steel, and other concentrated industries. Since that time, legislation and regulatory developments have focused on means to provide an environment supportive of fair competition. A summary of legislation and landmark cases on issues related to channels of distribution are included in Figure 2 on page 297.

As the decade of the 1980s began, businessmen and other citizens expressed increasing concern about the growing degree of government intervention in their lives. By the 1980s, it was evident that the bill for this service was more than anticipated and that many governmental agencies were eager to provide controls—often without being asked. Representative Elliott Levitas of Georgia and others sought the right of congressional veto over government regulators. The Federal Trade Commission found its mandate and budget under threat of revision due to its activist stance on antitrust matters and industry trade regulation. The airline industry had been deregulated by passage of the Airline

FIGURE 1   Channel Member Interaction

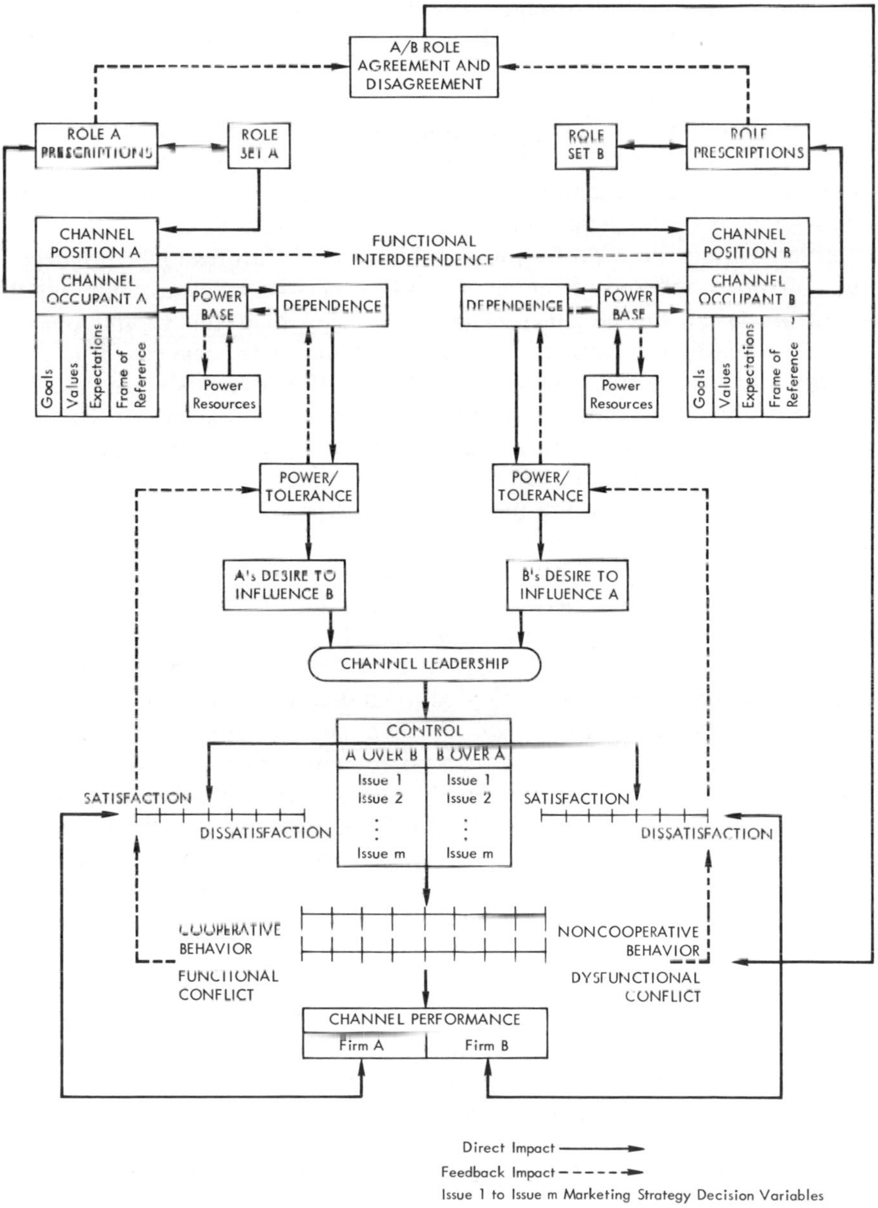

Direct Impact ————→
Feedback Impact ————→
Issue 1 to Issue m Marketing Strategy Decision Variables

Source: Robert A. Robicheaux and Abel I. El-Ansary. "A General Model for Understanding Channel Member Behavior," *Journal of Retailing,* 52 (Winter 1976–1977), p. 16.

Deregulation Act of 1978; trucking and natural gas were under review for deregulation as well. In short, the American society had begun to seriously question the role of government in the provision of countervailing power.

Some of the principal issues involved in channel relationships in the early 1980s included:

1. *Barriers to entry.* Enforcement of the law is perverse regarding barriers to enter markets for goods and services. Physicians and lawyers have professional organizations that control promotional methods and limit the supply of medical and legal services, essentially eliminating competition within those professions. A blanket of "professional privilege" has provided immunity from what would otherwise be clear violations of antitrust laws. At the other extreme, as shown in the Champions of Breakfast case, the ready-to-eat cereal companies were challenged because of *too much* competition within the industry. The government, in charging the top firms in the industry with shared monopoly, argued that vigorous nonprice competition constituted a barrier to entry for new brands entering the market from outside the top four firms in the industry. How active should the FTC be in raising and lowering barriers to entry in individual industries?

2. *The franchisee/franchisor balance of power.* The Gulf Oil case documents the conflict between a franchisee and a major oil company. Issues within the soft drink industry regarding territorial exclusivity have threatened to void the entire concept of franchising on the basis of geographic areas. Will franchising be a valid concept in the future?

3. *International distribution.* When a manufacturer extends distribution internationally, problems can arise with many elements of the marketing mix. Sales "commissions" necessary to secure foreign business may be considered bribes in the United States. Products perfectly acceptable in the domestic market, such as infant formula, have been denounced as lethal when sold in third-world cultures whose sanitation facilities and living standards cannot support the product. What general guidelines exist regarding international distribution channels?

4. *Protectionism.* By its very nature, countervailing power from government is protective of some element in the channel of distribution. Most business managers are scornful of government "interference" and "regulation," except for that which benefits their own firms. What is the proper role of government in providing countervailing power? What general guidelines are available for determining how much is enough? The article on concentration within the beer industry suggests that government regulation can be anticompetitive if it favors large companies in industries where production and distribution economies accrue to larger firms.

5. *Fraud in using channels.* Mail frauds and pyramid schemes proliferated during the 1970s. As laws became more specific, perpetrators

FIGURE 2 A Summary of the Most Significant Legislation Regarding Channels of Distribution

| | | Prevents the below listed actions which have impact on: | | | |
Legislation	Key Phrase	Channels	Product	Price	Promotion
Sherman Act (1890)	'monopoly or conspiracy in restraint of trade"	monopoly or conspiracy to control distribution channels	monopoly or conspiracy to control a product	monopoly or conspiracy to control prices	
Clayton Act (1914)	"substantially lessen competition"	exclusive dealing contracts which limit buyers' sources	tying contracts that force the sale of some products with others	price discrimination in the form of base point systems	
FTC Act (1914)	"unfair methods of competition"	unfair policies		deceptive pricing	deceptive advertising
Robinson-Patman Act (1936)	"tends to injure competition"	allowances to direct buyers in lieu of middlemen		price discrimination on goods of like grade and quality unless cost-justified	discrimination in advertising allowances or other promotional help
Wheeler-Lea Amendment (1938)	"unfair or deceptive practices"		deceptive packaging or branding	deceptive pricing	deceptive advertising or selling claims
Antimerger Act (1950)	"lessen competition"	buying producers or distributors	buying competitors		

became more sophisticated and the chances of punishment declined dramatically. How can enforcement keep pace with potential abuse in distribution practices?

6. *Innovations in channels.* With the advent of distribution innovations, such as automated banking services, there arose new sets of potential conflicts. What is the proper role, if any, of government in protecting the interests of users of such systems?

While it is instructive to consider specific legislation that relates to each of the elements of the marketing mix, the major acts are not *confined* to any one specific area of the marketing mix. Each piece of major legislation, in fact, tends to touch upon at least three of the traditional "4 Ps," as shown in Figure 2.

Of the sections of laws that touch upon channels of distribution, the following are especially important. Each of these is followed by recent court cases that establish precedents in given areas.

Sherman Antitrust Act (1890)[1]

Section 1:   Price fixing is prohibited. (Vertical price fixing was permitted between 1937 and 1976 under the Miller-Tydings Amendment, 1937, and the McGuire Act, 1952. These "Fair Trade" acts were repealed on March 11, 1976.)

Recent Cases:

1. The Court (1975) found that *Adolph Coors Co.* controlled prices of its beer by terminating distributors who did not follow company pricing policy. Exclusive geographic territories prevented dealers from using alternative sources of Coors. Coors argued that exclusive territories were necessary to justify the dealers' investment in refrigerated warehouses to maintain the quality of Coors beer, which is not pasteurized.

2. *Topco* was a cooperative of independently owned local grocery chains which was formed in 1940 to compete with the larger chains. By 1967, Topco had sales of $2.3 billion and was fourth after A&P, Safeway, and Kroger. Members agreed not to sell Topco-brand products outside their assigned territories. The Supreme Court [405 U.S. 596 (1972)] held that this was a per se violation of Section 1 because it was a horizontal territorial limitation.

3. In 1926, the Supreme Court approved *General Electric's* consignment system for setting the retail prices of lamp bulbs. In 1966, the Antitrust Division of the Justice

---

[1]   This section was summarized from G. David Hughes, *Marketing Management* (Reading, Mass.: Addison-Wesley Publishing Co., Inc., 1978), pp. 244–248.

Department charged GE with price fixing. In 1973, the district court concluded that the system should be outlawed in the future. (*JM,* January 1974, p. 72)

4. The Supreme Court (1967) found *Arnold, Schwinn & Co.* in violation of Section 1, per se, because of its vertical restrictions on the distributors and retailers of its bicycles. Distributors were limited to dealing with franchised dealers, and dealers were limited to dealing only with consumers. (*JM,* January 1968, p. 73)

5. An FTC administrative law judge ruled that exclusive territories for *Coca-Cola and Pepsi Cola distributors* did not restrain trade, because the restrictions protected smaller bottlers who would be eliminated without this protection, thereby reducing the number of competitors. He concluded that additional benefits were: that returnable bottles would not be used by large bottlers, thus raising prices and damaging the ecology; that market power would increase, resulting in higher prices to the consumer; and that the territories encourage the development of marketing effort. He concluded further that there was sufficient interbrand competition to offset the lack of intrabrand competition. (*JM,* April 1976, pp. 94, 95)

Clayton Act (1914)

Section 2:   As amended by the Robinson-Patman Act (1936), this section *prohibits price discrimination that may substantially lessen competition.* This discrimination may take the form of direct price differences, differential discounts, a brokerage allowance to a phantom broker, or advertising allowances that are not given proportionally to all buyers in competition with each other. Furthermore, the section makes it unlawful to knowingly induce or receive an illegal price discrimination.

Recent Case:

The *Great Atlantic & Pacific Tea Company, Inc.,* (A&P), was found in violation of Section 2(f) of the Robinson-Patman Act and Section 5 of the FTC Act by an FTC administrative law judge (1975) for knowingly inducing discriminatory prices for dairy products from Borden, Inc. A&P induced from Borden an offer that was much better than the competitive offer. Furthermore, the competitive offer was not operative, because A&P could not meet the required volume and the competitor could not meet the delivery schedule. The Borden offer would be justified only on the grounds of meeting competition, not on a cost savings. (*JM,* April 1976, p. 92)

Section 3:   This section *prevents tying contracts and exclusive dealership arrangements* when they may substantially lessen competition. A *tying* contract may occur when a manufacturer requires a retailer to carry the full line of its products. Oil companies have violated this act when they required a retailer to sell their products exclusively.

Classic Cases in Tying Contracts:

1. In 1949, *American Can Company* was found in violation of Section 3 because it required food-processing lessees of its can-closing machinery to buy all of their cans from American Can on a 5-year contract. To encourage this purchase the machines were leased at low rentals.

2. *International Business Machine* (IBM) was prevented (1936) from tying the leasing of business machines to the purchase of tabulating cards.

Classic Cases in Exclusive Dealerships:

1. *Standard Fashion Co.* was prohibited (1922) from exclusive dealership arrangements in the sale of its dress patterns because it controlled 40 percent of the market.

2. *Carter Carburetor Corporation's* exclusive dealership arrangement violated (1940) Section 3 because it had a 30 percent market share.

Section 7: This section *prohibits mergers* that would reduce the number of producers or distributors of a product, thereby substantially lessening competition.

Classic Cases:

1. In 1967, the Supreme Court ordered Procter & Gamble Co. to divest itself of *Clorox Bleach*. The original FTC complaint was in 1957; the key issues were that P&G was a potential competitor of Clorox, that Clorox had a 40 percent market share, and that P&G could "command one-third more advertising per dollar of expenditure" than competitors because it received large discounts from the mass media as the largest user of advertising. The relevant criteria were the effect that the Clorox acquisition would have on competition by raising the barriers to entry by new competitors and eliminating P&G as a potential competitor.

2. The Supreme Court (1962) held that Brown Shoe Co.'s acquisition of G. R. Kinney Co., Inc., might substantially lessen competition even though Kinney had only a 0.5 percent share and Brown had a 4 percent share. (Each had larger shares in specific markets.) The Court concluded that because this was a fragmented industry, rank, not share, was important. Brown was the fourth largest and Kinney was the twelfth largest producer. (There were vertical aspects of the case, because Brown had retail outlets.)

Cases

CHAMPIONS OF BREAKFAST:
FORMULATION OF A PUBLIC RELATIONS PROGRAM
FOR THE CEREAL INDUSTRY*

Jason Shaw, executive vice president of the Chicago public relations firm of Humble & Small, faced the biggest decision of his career. His firm had been one of three invited by the American Cereal Manufacturer's Association (ACMA), the trade association of the breakfast cereal industry, to make a presentation of their ideas and capabilities. A successful presentation of this nature usually landed the account, and this account could be worth about $500,000 per year in billings to Humble & Small.

Shaw would normally be ecstatic at the potential opportunity thus presented, but in this case he was very cautious. His firm, currently billing about $4 million per year, was fully extended. A major new account would require additional staffing. Although growth had always been an objective at Humble & Small, the firm had always looked for controlled growth with only those accounts that offered virtual certainty of successful long-term relationships. Although he was convinced that his firm could do as well as any other, Shaw was not at all certain that Humble & Small could achieve the ACMA's goals of disarming organized opposition and creating a generally favorable impression with the general public. If the goals were not met, the relationship would be unpleasant, brief, and probably unprofitable for Humble & Small.

Shaw was fond of reminding his people that big problems often disguise bigger opportunities. As he reviewed the track record of the industry over the last decade, however, he reminded himself that sometimes big problems also disguise nothing but larger ones.

* Humble & Small and the American Cereal Manufacturer's Association are fictitious organizations. Any resemblance between them and actual organizations is purely coincidental.

BACKGROUND ON THE INDUSTRY

The major corporations producing ready-to-eat (RTE) cereals were founded around the turn of the century. Their operations were designed primarily to turn low-value bulk grains into higher-value semimanufactured products as close to the point of harvest as practical. In that way, less money would need to be spent on transporting heavy products that would lose weight eventually through manufacture. Table 1 gives a brief background on the major cereal-producing firms in the United States.

For each of the major firms, over half of corporate sales volume was generated by products other than RTE cereals, such as flour products, animal feed and pet foods, snack foods, and frozen foods. RTE cereals became an important revenue producer to most firms relatively recently. During the 1930s, sales of RTE cereals were far behind those of breakfast cereals requiring cooking. By 1940, about 450 million pounds of RTE cereal were produced annually. By 1960, that figure had doubled and, by 1978, it had nearly tripled.[1]

The period of the late 1960s was one of concern for the social welfare of American citizens, especially the poor. Because the purchase of food products required a large percentage of the household budget of the poor, the products of all food manufacturers came under close scrutiny. The basic charge made by several researchers that the poor pay more for food than did more affluent citizens was widely circulated.[2] The 1969 White House Conference on Food and Nutrition focused on the increasing use of refined white sugar in the American diet.[3] Because of the higher sugar content of RTE cereals than had been generally supposed, the increased use of those products (especially by the poor), and the high visibility of them through television advertising, U.S. Senate Subcommittee hearings on the nutritional value of RTE cereals were begun in the summer of 1970.

[1] Figures summarized from the Federal Trade Commission Complaint, Docket No. 8883, 1972.

[2] See, for example, Phyllis Groom, "Prices in Poor Neighborhoods," *Monthly Labor Review,* October 1966, pp. 1085–1090; Charles S. Goodman, "Do the Poor Pay More?" *Journal of Marketing,* January 1968, p. 23; Robert F. Krampf and David L. Kurtz, "Do the Poor Pay More? Some Comments . . . ," *Memphis State Business Review,* September 1969, pp. 6–11; and L. E. Boone and J. A. Bonno, "The Plight of the Poor . . . ," *Business Studies,* Spring 1969, pp. 40–45, for studies of food purchases conducted in the late 1960s.

[3] Some individuals attending the conference labeled purified white sugar "the white death" and "the epitome of what is wrong with American Society" according to industry observer Seymour Banks, address at Georgia State University, January 26, 1979.

Table 1   MAJOR MANUFACTURERS OF READY-TO-EAT CEREALS

Rank	Firm	Home Office	Year Founded	RTE[a] Share	RTE[b] Sales	Percent[c] of Corporate Sales
1	Kellogg Company	Battle Creek	1906	46	$825	49
2	General Mills, Inc.	Minneapolis	1928	25	450	14
3	General Foods Corporation	White Plains	1922	14	250	5
4	Quaker Oats Company	Chicago	1901	9	160	9
5	Nabisco, Inc.	New York	1898	3	60	3
6	Ralston Purina Company	St. Louis	1894	3	55	1

[a]Estimated by the casewriter.

[b]Total sales of ready-to-eat (RTE) cereal firms was estimated by the casewriter in millions of dollars for 1978.

[c]Approximate RTE sales as a percent of total corporate sales.

Source: Data summarized from the FTC Complaint: United States of America, Before Federal Trade Commission, Docket No. 8883, 1970, except as noted.

THE SEDUCTION OF THE INNOCENT

On July 23, 1970, Robert B. Choate testified before the Subcommittee on the Consumer-Committee on Commerce of the U.S. Senate, headed by Senator Frank Moss (D–Utah). A civil engineer by training, Choate headed a consulting firm involved in a number of governmental projects regarding social welfare.[4] The testimony that he presented on the nutritional value of RTE cereals and methods used to market them was covered extensively by mass media and generated a national controversy. Excerpts from his testimony, entitled "Seduction of the Innocent," follow:[5]

> *A study of 60 ready-to-eat cereals reveals that they are primarily calorie sources, the nutrient content of 40 of the 60 being so low as to remind this observer of the term "empty calories," a term thus far applied to alcohol and sugar. In short, they fatten but do little to prevent malnutrition. . . .*
>
> *To compare the nutrient worth of various products is difficult. All told, there may be 30 or more different nutrients, all needed in various amounts and time periods. . . . Recognizing the need for balanced nutrient intake, we have added together the individual nutrient percentages of a typical human's daily needs to ascertain a purely numerical rating for each cereal. . . . In this way we have been able to compare the nutritional merits of sixty dry cereals. . . .*
>
> *We believe it is useful to provide such a graphic display of the comparative value of cereals, especially since the variations are so great. While such a graph oversimplifies the interaction of nutrients, it does portray what the cereal companies are boasting about on their own boxes. In short it uses their standards. . . .*
>
> *A child watching 73 spots in a total of 200 minutes of Saturday television would gather (1) that cereals with sugar are great energy sources, (2) that energy and action are equivalent to happiness, and (3) that ability and health are a product of eating ready-to-eat, preferably sweet, cereals. Is this true? . . .*
>
> *We claim that our children are deliberately being sold the sponsor's less nutritious products; that our children are being programmed to demand sugar and sweetness in every food; and that our children are being counter-educated*

---

[4] Choate, a descendent of the founders of the prestigious Choate School in Wallingford, Connecticut, was a student at Harvard during World War II and graduated with a degree in civil engineering from California in 1949. Married and divorced twice, he has had at least three separate careers: that of engineer (1949 to about 1956), real estate investments officer (1957 to about 1965), and social activist (since 1962). The social causes he has been connected with have included careers for youth; crusade against poverty; children, media, and merchandising; food, nutrition, and health; effective Congress; juvenile delinquency; and representing deaf and blind children.

[5] Chaote's entire testimony, from which these excerpts were taken, appears in Ralph Nader, ed, *The Consumer and Corporate Accountability* (New York: Harcourt Brace Jovanovich, Inc., 1973), pp. 106–124.

away from nutrition knowledge by being sold products on a non-nutritive basis.

These practices dominate the cereal world. In part, they are found in the marketing of every major food group. The consumer is the victim. The industry shows little inclination to stress comparative food values. The industry shows little inclination to correct our nutritional illiteracy. . . .

I ask this Senate Subcommittee to investigate the policies of the cereal industry as it shapes the counter-nutritional message that is beamed to our children approximately 14 hours per week. I request that you analyze the content of the industry's advertising messages. I ask that you examine the reluctance of advertising agencies to stress nutrition; and I ask you to explore how both script and scenario writers and sponsors and networks alike can deliver this country from its nutritional illiteracy. Finally, I ask that you review the strange policies of the Food and Drug Administration, the Federal Trade Commission, and the Department of Agriculture, which perpetuate the misleading of the American consumer by those in the world of food production and marketing.

Fifteen days later, Michael E. Latham, professor of international nutrition at Cornell testified in general support of Choate, and excerpts follow:

My testimony today will not have as its thesis that breakfast cereals are a worthless or even a poor food. They are not. It is a fact however that those breakfast cereals sold in greatest quantity are not nutritionally superior and in many respects are nutritionally inferior to many very common and much cheaper foods such as bread, rice, beans and corn products. The public are unaware of this, for the advertising tactics of the industry have in an indirect and subtle way misled the consumer. A special advertising onslaught has been made on our children. It seems that the less nutritious breakfast cereals and those that are sweet are especially being peddled to the young. In a country where there is a considerable amount of malnutrition among the poor and where the rates of infant mortality are disgracefully high, this advertising may be indirectly contributing to ill health and mortality. . . .

Mr. Robert Choate in his testimony used an unorthodox way to rate or to score the cumulative nutrient content of cereals. He did this because there is no universally accepted way of doing this. It was not a dishonest, or a particularly inaccurate, way of doing it although there are some errors in his data. The method he used is not the one that I or most of my colleagues would have used. Although the rating is unorthodox, I do not think that a different system which somehow used protein, vitamin and mineral content would alter very much the relative positions of the breakfast cereals on the list. . . .

I believe that Robert Choate's research into cereal advertising and his testimony in this respect was most valuable. . . .

I think it bad that the TV networks make an annual profit of about 20 million dollars from Saturday morning children's programs; I am appalled to learn that 50 percent of all the nation's 2 to 11 year olds are in place before their TV sets every Saturday morning instead of in parks, woods or beaches or doing something intellectually stimulating; and I think it terrible that three com-

panies spent over 42 million dollars on TV advertising of dry breakfast cereals in 1969. One is inescapably led to think how the money of these firms and the time of American children could be put to better use. . . .

In conclusion I would ask whether we are going to continue for another generation to mollycoddle the rich and over-protect corporate enterprises while at the same time withholding from our minorities and failing to provide adequately for the poor. If so, then there will be no peace in this great land.

THE INDUSTRY DEFENSE

Summaries of Choate's dramatic testimony were reported on major network news programs and on the front pages of many newspapers. The RTE cereal industry was not fully prepared for the impact of the testimony on the public. Nevertheless, within two weeks a battery of experts had been assembled to provide the comments which follow.[6]

Frederick J. Stare, chairman of the Department of Nutrition of the Harvard University School of Public Health, sharply criticized a ranking of 60 dry cereals presented to the subcommittee July 24 by Robert B. Choate as "grossly misleading" and "absolutely meaningless. In nearly 40 years of studying nutrition I don't recall having seen or heard of an arbitrary scale comparable to Mr. Choate's cumulative nutrient content," he said. "Why then all this rumpus that most breakfast cereals are not very nutritious? . . . Mr. Choate is not a nutritionist or food expert. As far as I know he doesn't pretend to be one, and he certainly was ill-advised on his nutritional comments. . . ."

W. H. Sebrell, Jr., M.D., director of the Institute of Human Nutrition at Columbia University, said the Choate testimony "appears to have created a feeling of apprehension in many people concerning the wholesomeness and nutritional value of breakfast cereals for children." This method of evaluation "leads to erroneous and dangerous conclusions." Sebrell also defended the practice of selling presweetened cereals because it furnishes energy children need and induces them to eat more cereal with milk.

L. M. Henderson, professor and head of the department of biochemistry at the University of Minnesota, said, "With or without the usual accompanying milk it is clear that prepared cereals are substantial sources of many nutrients."

Robert O. Nesheim, vice president—research and development for Quaker Oats, said: "Mr. Choate's testimony before this Committee on July 23 did not perform a constructive service to good nutrition, especially

---

[6] This information is taken from a press release from The Cereal Institute, August 4, 1970.

among the poor. As a nutritional scientist, I am concerned about a 'rating system' which forms a framework for describing 40 of 60 cereals as 'having little nutritional value.' I am concerned about rhetoric and headlines which describe cereals as 'empty calories' or 'junk,' which do nothing but make you fat. . . . These statements are false.''

A. S. Clausi, vice president and director of technical research for General Foods, said, ''if other breakfast foods were rated on the same basis as the Choate ranking of cereals, then a large egg, two slices of bacon or two slices of enriched toast would have to be classified as 'empty calories.'''

To emphasize the unfair nature of the ''cumulative nutrient content'' scale, the staff of one of the leading cereal manufacturers produced the chart given as Table 2.

L. C. Roll, chairman of the Kellogg Company, submitted a written statement for the subcommittee record, which read in part:

> *Contrary to the impression given in the many press reports dealing with his testimony, Mr. Choate is not a nutritionist. . . . He . . . indicates that much of the data underlying his report is based upon a study done by Dr. Morris C. Matt of The Academy of Food Marketing, St. Joseph's College, Philadelphia. We understand that Dr. Matt has written a letter to the subcommittee disassociating himself with Mr. Choate's testimony and the conclusions he reached. . . .*

In spite of the efforts of the industry to publicize their side of the story, Robert Choate continued to command the attention of the press.

Choate issued a statement later in which he contended that from the testimony from industry witnesses one would gather that cereals were identically good, that television advertising had no role in shaping food patterns and that eggs and bacon were the All-American breakfast threat.

Choate declared, ''The witnesses today, I am afraid, represent less of a solution to our nutritional woes; they are part of the problem.''

The subcommittee chairman, Senator Moss, said Choate's claims about TV advertising ''stand unrefuted. In fact, testimony today confirms my own worst fears about the way in which food advertising policies are set. Sugar frosted flakes may be less nutritious than some products, but given present advertising practices you can bet Tony will never be a paper tiger to the millions of children plopped in front of their television sets on Saturday morning.''

Choate added that the industry's response to his findings, he said, ''exemplifies the worry [I] expressed over the independence and forthrightness of the nation's leading nutritionists.[7]

[7] Richard H. Stewart, ''Cereal's Value Defended by Dr. Stare,'' *The Boston Globe,* August 5, 1970.

Product (one standard serving)[a]		Total "Points"[b]
1-4 Kellogg's Product 19 General Mills Kaboom General Mills Total Quaker Oats King Vitamin	all approximately	700
5. Nabisco 100% Bran		440
6. Quaker Oats Life		330
7. General Foods Fortified Oat Flakes		270
8. Kellogg's Special K		240
9. General Foods Special Sugar Crisp		220
10. Kellogg's Sugar Smacks		205
11. Milk, whole (8 oz)		146
12. Quaker Oats Quake		145
13. Ground beef (4 oz)		143
14. Quaker Oats Quisp		140
15. Egg, 1 large		71
16. Bacon, 3 slices		45
17. Apple		39
18. Sweet roll, one commercial		30
19. Doughnut, one cake-type, frosted		29
20. Whole wheat bread, one slice, toasted		24

Note: Twenty products (19 typical breakfast foods plus ground beef) ranked by "points" on the basis of the percentage they contribute toward 60 grams of protein per day and Minimum Daily Adult Requirements for calcium, iron, vitamin A, vitamin C, vitamin D, niacin, thiamine, and riboflavin. This is the ranking system used for 60 cereal products by Robert B. Choate in his testimony before the Senate Commerce Sub-Committee on July 23, 1970.

[a]No milk included for any of the cereals.

[b]Point value for all cereals are as read from Choate's exhibit of 60 cereals, July 23, 1970.

REFORMULATION

During the Senate subcommittee hearings, several witnesses had testified that it was technically feasible to add nutrients to RTE cereals. For example, Harvard professor Jean Mayer, who had chaired the White House Council of Food, Nutrition, and Health, testified that "because of the place of cereals in the national diet, it is obviously important that they be as nutritious as possible. . . . There are wide differences in nutritional value between various types of breakfast cereals. With present technology and using modern knowledge of nutrition, such differences could easily be avoided and many products upgraded. Big food companies have the resources and the expertise necessary to do this.[8]

In response to apparent widespread agreement with this position, the cereal companies reformulated many of their products during the autumn of 1970. The standard achieved was 25 percent of the minimum daily adult requirement for several vitamins and minerals for a normal serving.

Reformulation led directly to severe criticism from the Food and Drug Administration, which had been conducting hearings on regulations that would curtail the addition of vitamins and other nutrients to some foods, including cereals. Publicity surrounding these hearings had mobilized a large group of citizens concerned with artificial additives in foods. These individuals, some of whom had earlier demanded fortification, now demanded that the addition of vitamins and other nutrients be stopped. Members of the industry compromised by bringing out an additional line of "natural" cereals.

In March 1972, Choate returned to the subcommittee to testify that, although 26 of the 40 cereals he had singled out for criticism had been fortified with vitamins and minerals, this did not result in any "real improvement of protein quantity, or protein quality." His associates went on to present testimony highly critical of the current nutritive content of cereals.

In March 1973, in testimony before the Senate Select Committee on Nutrition and Human Needs, nutrition and dental experts urged that television advertisements for sugared cereals that were directed at children be banned. Senator George McGovern, who chaired the hearings, announced in session that eight executives of food producers and their advertising agencies, scheduled to testify, had declined to appear as witnesses.

SHARED MONOPOLY

While Senate subcommittees were still hearing testimony regarding the nutrition controversy, the Federal Trade Commission (FTC) charged the four largest manufacturers of RTE cereals (Kelloggs, General Mills, General Foods, and Quaker Oats) with illegally monopolizing the market.

The charge was somewhat complex, but in essence the extreme competition within the industry was seen as keeping potential market entrants out and assuring supracompetitive profits for the incumbents, cheating consumers, and making otherwise legal actions illegal. The complaint was

---

[8] "Cereal Could Be Better, Panel Told," *Boston Evening Globe,* August 5, 1970.

possible because Section 5 of the FTC Act prohibited "unfair" methods of competition; anything that restrains competition may be challenged as unfair under Section 5. In the past, antitrust laws had sought to preserve competition between major firms in an industry. This case was unique in that extreme competition itself was "unfair."

The focus on competition came about in the following manner. The industry as a whole had higher-than-normal profits. This usually would trigger new entrants into the market, but no such entrants appeared. The classic barriers to entry of the needed economies of scale or lack of access to essential factors of production were not present. Perhaps competition itself was a barrier to entry.

Competition could be a barrier for three reasons. First, the large amount spent of advertising by the industry could dissuade new firms from entering. Second, brand proliferation—the continual introduction of new brands by existing firms—could be a barrier in that new brands from new firms would simply get lost in the shuffle. Finally, monopoly of shelf "facings" by existing firms might keep new brands from being visible to consumers.

The FTC had originally made its charge on January 24, 1972, then officially lodged its complaint on March 26 of that year. Proceedings had continued through 1978, although Quaker Oats had been released as a respondent that year primarily because of its small size relative to the others.

Although the suit continued into its seventh year, government lawyers conceded that "few, if any, of the manufacturers' actions are per se illegal."[9]

THE KIDVID ISSUE

While the shared monopoly case continued, new FTC hearings began concerning television advertising to children. At issue was the proposed "Kidvid" rule, which would:

1. Ban all advertising to children on television at times when children provided a given percentage of the audience.
2. Ban advertising of products containing a set amount of sugar.
3. Require food advertisers directing messages at children to also sponsor health and/or nutritional disclosure messages.

[9] Walter Kiechel, "The Soggy Case against the Cereal Industry," *Fortune,* April 10, 1978, 49–51.

Table 3 CONCERNS RESULTING IN THE "KIDVID" ISSUE*

1. Basic distrust of Big Business.
2. Concern over the increasing amount of sugar in the American diet.
3. Power of television in shaping social behavior.
4. Effect of the following on children's cognitive processing:
   a. Ability to distinguish commercials from programs.
   b. Children's perceptions of commercial messages.
   c. Effect of the source (spokesman) on children.
   d. Effect of premium offers on purchase.
   e. Effect of violence and unsafe acts on behavior.
   f. Volume and repetition of ads.
5. Advertising's impact on the family:
   a. How children learn consumer skills.
   b. Advertising in parent–child relationships.
6. Advertising of special products:
   a. Proprietary medicine advertising.
   b. Food advertising.

* The first three of these concerns were suggested by Seymour Banks, address at Georgia State University, January 26, 1979. The remaining concerns were the results of a survey by Richard Adler, Gerald Lesser, Bernard Friedlader, Thomas Robertson, John Rossiter, and Scott Ward, *Research on the Effects of Television Advertising on Children* (Washington: National Science Foundation, 1977), and reported in Scott Ward, "Compromise in Commercials for Children," *Harvard Business Review,* November–December 1978, pp. 128–136.

The proposed Kidvid rule was a fusion of a number of earlier concerns, listed briefly in Table 3. As Harvard professor Scott Ward, a noted expert in the area, observed:

> *The issues are diverse, but they are similar in their extraordinary complexity. Moreover, the evidence available from research cannot simply supply a solution, partly because the issues are confounded with personal values, rendering empirical information irrelevant, partly because even the research is not conclusive.*[10]

Even such basic underlying questions as the healthfulness of products containing sugar, what constituted an ad "directed at" children, and what was an audience of children were matters of opinion, not research evidence. One advertising industry publication referred to the entire area of children's advertising as a "quagmire."[11]

Hearings began in San Francisco in January 1979. Those favoring the

[10] Scott Ward, "Compromise in Commercials for Children," *Harvard Business Review,* November–December 1978, p. 132.
[11] Richard L. Gordon, "Kids' Ad Hearings Resume and Feeling Total TV Ban Unlikely," *Advertising Age,* March 12, 1979, p. 2.

ban were generally associated with the Boston-based Action for Children's Television (ACT), the Oakland-based Children's Advocacy Center, or Robert Choate's new Washington-based Council on Children, Media, and Merchandising. FTC hearings officer Morton Needelman continually asked witnesses in favor of the ban for "clear evidence of harm,"[12] which they were largely unable to provide.

A second round of hearings began in Washington in March 1979. Since RTE cereal manufacturers were the largest advertisers on Saturday morning television, they had a huge stake not only in the outcome of the hearings but in publicity surrounding the hearings.

THE DECISION

The evidence clearly indicated that the industry had been the uninterrupted focus of both consumerist and government regulatory effort for 10 years. It appeared that as soon as industry spokesmen could mobilize to fight one charge, another would take its place. The American Cereal Manufacturers Association was searching for a public relations agency to anticipate and combat future charges before they become national issues.

Shaw knew that the public often believed that where there was smoke, there was fire. The RTE cereal producers had been on the defensive for so long that he saw virtually no chance of being able to achieve a positive image for cereals with the public.

A presentation would cost several thousand dollars plus the time of valuable personnel to produce. It would be foolish to make a presentation for an account one would not accept. Shaw faced two major decisions:

1. Should he accept the invitation?
2. If so, what key directions would Humble & Small recommend to the ACMA to accomplish their goals of:
   a. Disarming organized opposition.
   b. Creating a generally favorable impression with the general public.

[12]   The term "clear evidence of harm" means: if the ads were removed, what evidence is there that the harm would disappear?

GULF OIL CORPORATION:
RESPONDING TO A LAWSUIT FROM A DISGRUNTLED
FRANCHISEE

Amanda Kent, investigative reporter for the monthly magazine *National Retailer,* was searching for a focus for her August 1979 assignment—a story on the conflict between gasoline producers and retailers in the channels of distribution for their product. Without a focal person, the story would be impersonal and, quite probably, dull. Then she noticed the following lead paragraph in a May 1978 issue of *The Atlanta Journal and Constitution:*

> *A Cobb County service station operator has answered an eviction notice from Gulf Oil Corporation with a $1.25 million damage suit claiming the oil giant is illegally trying to take away his business.*[1]

While the nation wondered whether increasing gasoline prices and lines would ever end, Kent wondered whether the service station operator—Larry McIntyre—and the Gulf Oil Corporation had settled their dispute, and if so, what the result was.

Kent decided to satisfy her need to know by arranging to meet Larry McIntyre and finding out if he was still in business. She prepared herself for meeting the operator by examining the history and distribution strategy of Gulf Oil.

BACKGROUND ON GULF OIL

A diversified petroleum company, Gulf Oil Corporation was, by 1979, in its seventy-seventh year of operation. With 1978 corporation sales totaling more than $18 billion, Gulf Oil ranked ninth by sales on *Fortune's* list of 500 largest industrial corporations, and represented the fifth largest oil corporation, preceded only by Exxon, Mobil, Texaco, and Standard Oil of California, in that order. If the industrial corporations were ranked by income, Gulf, with a 1978 income of $791 million, would fall to the thirteenth position among all corporations and eighth among the oil companies.

The corporation's largest and most profitable division was the Gulf

---

[1] Hyde Post, "Cobb Service Station Operator Sues, Promises Fight after Eviction Notice," *The Atlanta Journal and Constitution,* May 14, 1978, p. 14–B.

Oil Exploration and Production Company. This company was the seventh largest producer of crude oil and the fifth largest producer of natural gas in the United States. Its worldwide assets exceeded $4.5 billion, with this figure excluding the value of Gulf's extensive gas and oil reserves.

Gulf's Refining and Marketing Company had worldwide assets of $3 billion, and was the fifth largest seller of gasoline in the United States. Gulf had captured approximately 8 percent of the market in its 29-state marketing area (East, South, and Southwest). According to the 1978 Annual Report:

> On a total volume basis, Gulf is a leading seller of refined products in an 11-state area along the Atlantic and Gulf Coasts from Maryland to Texas. . . . Abroad, the Company operates in 16 countries and is the most prominent in Western Europe, where it holds 5 percent of the motor fuels market in eight countries.[2]

GULF'S MARKETING STRATEGY

Gulf's primary marketing strategy in 1978 was straightforward: "emphasize the maintenance and improvement of market shares in areas of strength and the selective withdrawal, or conversion to unbranded outlets, in areas of weakness."[3] In other words, Gulf intended to eliminate marginally profitable stations. The 1978 sale of surplus property resulted in cash recoveries by the company of nearly $50 million. At year's-end, Gulf had 17,900 retail outlets, of which 5 percent were company-operated.

As a concurrent geographic strategy, Gulf penetrated further into the South and Southeast, areas in which the nation's greatest growth was occurring, and into the metropolitan areas, where the company capitalized on opportunities to exploit profitable, high-volume, self-serve stations. The company was finding tremendous success with its combination of self-serve pumps with fast-service convenience stores. An internal 1978 Gulf marketing goal was "to simplify its marketing organization by consolidating division offices."[4] For example, Gulf's Georgia–South Carolina district office served an area that was, only 6 years ago, managed by five separate district offices.

In 60 key markets, Gulf utilized a brand-reputation advertising program with a theme centered on "Gulf—The Stop That Keeps America Going." In addition, Gulf introduced a new tire marketing program featuring

---

[2] Gulf Oil Corporation, 1978 Annual Report.
[3] Ibid.
[4] Ibid.

"Every Day Low Prices." For 1978, The Refining and Marketing Company garnered about $265 million in operating profit, which was about one-third of total corporate profits.

THE SEARCH FOR LARRY MCINTYRE

Armed with what she considered to be ample basic background information, Kent sought out Larry McIntyre. She reached for the Atlanta Directory yellow pages, and looked under "Service Stations—Gulf." McIntyre's station was not listed. Undaunted, the reporter looked under McIntyre, in both the yellow and white pages. She did not find a listing for the service station there, either. She tried using the reported I-285/US 41 address as the key item, but that proved ineffective, as well.

Kent thought for a moment and decided to call Gulf's Georgia–South Carolina District Office. She asked to be connected with the public information office. The reporter explained that she was doing a follow-up story on a Gulf-dealer relationship. Kent continued quickly by asking for Larry McIntyre's number. The woman responded immediately with an address and telephone number.

Kent wasted no time in trying the number. Sure enough, Larry McIntyre answered. He was not only willing to talk with the reporter, but also invited her to the station whenever it was convenient for her. Kent went that evening.

LARRY MCINTYRE

Larry McIntyre approached Gulf in 1971 because he "had some extra money"[5] and wanted to invest it in a business of his own. Prior to his venture with Gulf, McIntyre had sold houses for National Homes (a manufacturer of prefabricated housing) and worked for U.S. Industries as a southeastern sales representative. McIntyre received a franchise within 1 month after his application. Figure 1 shows the key stipulations in the franchise agreement.

Upon completing Gulf's training program for station operators, McIntyre began operating the Gulf Station at Interstate 285 and US 41.[6] He had been there ever since, which, compared to the station's previous

---

[5] Personal conversation between McIntyre and the casewriter, July 1979.

[6] Because of an unusual exit-ramp arrangement, Kent earlier overlooked two of the stations in the area, one of them McIntyre's.

FIGURE 1 Service Station Lease

> Concurrently herewith Lessor and Lessee have entered into a Contract of Sale covering petroleum products. Lessee agrees, as a convenant of this lease, that the breach of any of the terms or conditions of said Contract of Sale shall constitute a breach of this lease, and that termination of said Contract of Sale shall, at the option of Lessor, terminate this lease . . .
>
> The leased premises shall be used for the storage and sale of petroleum products and such other articles as are customarily sold at automotive service stations, and Lessee agrees to maintain adequate supplies of petroleum products, tires, batteries, accessories, and specialties for sale to the motoring public . . .
>
> Lessee recognizes that the premises have an intrinsic value as a gasoline service station location and agrees to conduct his business thereon in such manner that its value as such will not depreciate, and in order to accomplish this purpose he will furnish such services and accommodations to retail gasoline customers as are customarily provided by gasoline service stations, including, but not limited to . . . keeping said premises, buildings, equipment, fixtures, rest rooms, sidewalks, approaches, and driveways in good condition, properly lighted, clean, safe, sanitary, and free of trash, rubbish, and other debris, keeping the approaches, driveways, and service areas uncluttered and free of parked vehicles, trailers, and other obstructions at all times . . .
>
> None of the provisions of this lease shall be construed as reserving to Lessor any right to exercise control over the service station business and operations of the Lessee conducted upon the leased premises, or to direct in any manner how Lessee shall conduct his business. It is understood and agreed that the entire control and direction of said activities shall be and remain in Lessee, and neither Lessee nor any other persons employed by him shall be deemed or considered employees or agents of Lessor.

history of 13 dealers in 6 years, was an accomplishment of some note. McIntyre turned the station from a "dismal economic failure"[7] (i.e., pumping 6,000 to 8,000 gallons of gas per month) into a "moderate success"[8] (35,000 to 40,000 gallons per month). Across the street, a competitor with nine pumps, compared to McIntrye's six, sold 125,000 gallons a month.

During his second year with Gulf, McIntyre received the Company's "Presidential Award." McIntyre attributed his success to his practice of "taking risks more than anyone else"[9] and in building his business with the long range in mind, an approach to service station operation that contrasted with most dealers. McIntyre contended that the typical Gulf dealer

[7] Personal conversation between McIntyre and the casewriter, July 1979.
[8] Ibid.
[9] Ibid.

FIGURE 2 The Structure of Larry McIntyre's Organization

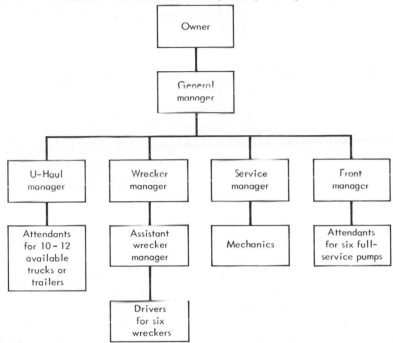

depended on Gulf's formula for station operation, which stressed "pumping gas." McIntyre believed Gulf's prescription for station success dampened rather than stimulated entrepreneurial creative efforts.

McIntyre devised his own formula for success and built an organization consisting of four divisions—the "front" (i.e., gas pumps), repair services, wrecker services, and U-Haul rental[10]—each with its own manager and attendants. McIntyre tacked his organization chart (Figure 2) conspicuously on a wall in the mobile home that served as his office. In addition, McIntyre took advantage of holiday seasons to sell products such as Christmas trees or pumpkins. McIntyre claimed that he would have "an easy job if [he] only pumped gas."[11] He was quick to say, however, that he did not want it easy; he wanted to "build a business."[12]

As Kent was leaving, McIntyre mentioned casually that Cobb County

[10] Gulf severed its contractual relationship with U-Haul in 1973, yet some individual stations remained U-Haul dealers. In 1978, McIntyre's station was second in sales among the 1,973 dealers in the state of Georgia. McIntyre contended that Gulf ended the relationship with U-Haul because the trucks occupied space that could be used for gas pumps.

[11] Ibid.

[12] Ibid.

police had served him with a warrant for illegal operation of a junk yard. He proved that each car on the lot was accompanied by a work order, and thus dodged the warrant. But the official's impression of the place was accurate: the station was a crowded mess and the grass needed to be attacked with a sickle.

McIntyre's station reported a $21,073 net income for the year ending December 31, 1977. The income generated by the trailer rental business was $25,268.20; the service station reported a $4,194.49 loss. For 1976, McIntrye's station reported $21,450.76 as its net income, with $2,937.64 generated by the service station and $18,513.12 generated by the trailer rental business.[13]

THE "NO GAS" SIGN

On Friday, May 12, 1978, McIntyre stood in front of his pumps, to which painted signs proclaiming "No Gas" were affixed. On an 8- by 16-foot portable sign positioned at the roadside, the station operator pleaded his case: "No Gas. Gulf Oil Unfair to Dealer—Forced Out of Gas Business."

Gulf had refused to sell gasoline to McIntyre. The operator contended that Gulf Oil wanted him out of business "not because the company was not making money from the station, but because Gulf felt it was 'not making enough.'"[14] The Department of Energy intervened, though, and ruled that as long as the case remained in litigation, Gulf could neither evict McIntyre nor refuse to sell him gas. Figure 3 shows a summary of dealer rights at lease termination or renewal.

ANTECEDENT EVENTS

The events leading to McIntyre's $1.25 million damage suit against Gulf Oil Corporation began with a rent dispute. According to McIntyre, Gulf offered to buy him out in early 1978 for $18,000. The station operator responded with a $35,000 to $40,000 counteroffer, which Gulf refused. Gulf's next step, contended McIntyre, was more severe. McIntyre's lease expired April 1, 1978, at which time the oil company offered him a new deal, but one that McIntyre could not afford to accept: "pay a monthly rental of $1,500, two and one-half times what [I] had been paying, or be out

---

[13]   Perimeter Gulf Financial Statement, William C. Caye, CPA. The financial statements were not audited by Caye and, accordingly, he did "not express an opinion on them."

[14]   See footnote 5.

FIGURE 3   Summary of Dealer Rights at Termination
or Nonrenewal
Department of Energy
Summary of Title I of the
Petroleum Marketing Practices Act

AGENCY: Department of Energy

ACTION: Notice

SUMMARY: This notice contains a summary of Title I of the Petroleum Marketing Practices Act, a new federal law enacted on June 19, 1978. The law is intended to protect franchised distributors and retailers of gasoline and diesel motor fuel against arbitrary or discriminatory termination or nonrenewal of franchises. The summary describes the reasons for which a franchise may be terminated or not renewed under the new law, the responsibilities of franchisors, and the remedies and relief available to franchisees. Franchisors must give franchisees copies of the summary contained in this notice whenever notification of termination or nonrenewal of a franchise is given.

SUPPLEMENTARY INFORMATION:

Title I of the Petroleum Marketing Practices Act, Pub L 95-297 (the "Act"), enacted on June 19, 1978, provides for the protection of franchised distributors and retailers of motor fuel by establishing minimum Federal standards governing the termination of franchises and the nonrenewal of franchise relationships by the franchisor or distributor of such fuel. Section 104(d)(1) of the Act provides that the Secretary of Energy shall prepare and publish in the *Federal Register,* not later than 30 days after enactment of the Act, a simple and concise summary of the provisions of Title I, including a statement of the respective responsibilities of, and the remedies and relief available to, franchisors and franchisees under that title.

As required by section 104(d)(1) of the Act, the following is a summary statement of the respective responsibilities of, and the remedies and relief available to, franchisors and franchisees. Franchisors must give copies of this summary statement to their franchisees when entering an agreement to terminate the franchise or not to renew the franchise relationship, and when giving notification of termination or nonrenewal. In addition to the summary of the provisions of Title I, a more detailed description of the definitions contained in the Act and of the legal remedies available to franchisees is also included in this notice, following the summary statement.

SUMMARY OF LEGAL RIGHTS OF MOTOR FUEL FRANCHISEES

This is a summary of the franchise protection provisions of the federal Petroleum Marketing Practices Act. This summary must be given to you, as a person holding a franchise for the sale, consignment or distribution of gasoline or diesel motor fuel, in connection with any termination or nonrenewal of your franchise by your franchising company (referred to in this summary as your supplier).

The franchise protection provisions of the Act apply to a variety of franchise arrangements. The term "franchise" is broadly defined as a license to use a motor fuel trademark which is owned or controlled by a refiner, and it includes secondary arrangements such as leases of real property and motor fuel supply agreements which have existed continuously since May 15, 1973 regardless of a subsequent withdrawal of a trademark. Thus, if you have lost the use of a trademark previously granted by your supplier but have continued to receive motor fuel supplies through a continuation of a supply agreement with your supplier, you are protected under the Act.

You should read this summary carefully, and refer to the Act if necessary, to determine whether a proposed termination or nonrenewal of your franchise is lawful, and what legal remedies are available to you if you think the proposed termination or failure to renew is not lawful. In addition, if you think your supplier has failed to comply with the Act, you may wish to consult an attorney in order to enforce your legal rights.

The Act is intended to protect you, whether you are a distributor or a retailer, from arbitrary or discriminatory termination or nonrenewal of your franchise agreement. To accomplish this, the

Act first lists the reasons for which termination or nonrenewal is permitted. Any notice of termination or nonrenewal must state the precise reason, as listed in the Act, for which the particular termination or nonrenewal is being made. These reasons are described below under the headings "Reasons for Termination" and "Reasons for Nonrenewal."

You should note that the Act does not restrict the reasons which may be given for the *termination* of a franchise agreement entered into before the June 19, 1978 effective date of the Act. However, any *nonrenewal* of such a terminated franchise must be based on one of the reasons for nonrenewal summarized below.

The Act also requires your supplier to give you a written notice of termination or intention not to renew the franchise within certain time periods. These requirements are summarized below under the heading "Notice Requirements for Termination or Nonrenewal."

The Act allows trial and interim franchise agreements, which are described below under the heading "Trial Franchises and Interim Franchises."

The Act gives you certain legal rights if your supplier terminates or does not renew your franchise in a way that is not permitted by the Act. These legal rights are described below under the heading "Your Legal Rights."

This summary is intended as a simple and concise description of the general nature of your rights under the Act. For a more detailed description of these rights, you should read the text of the Petroleum Marketing Practices Act itself (Pub L 95–297, 92 Stat 322., 15 U.S.C. 2801).

I. Reasons for Termination

The following is a list of the only reasons for which your franchise is permitted to be terminated by the Act. One or more of these reasons must be specified if your franchise was entered into on or after June 19, 1978 and is being terminated. If your franchise was entered into before June 19, 1978, as discussed above, there is no statutory restriction on the reasons for which it may be terminated. If such a franchise is terminated, however, the Act requires the supplier to renew the franchise relationship unless one of the reasons listed under this heading or one of the additional reasons for nonrenewal described under the heading "Reasons for Nonrenewal" exists.

If your supplier attempts to terminate a franchise which you entered into on or after June 19, 1978 for a reason that is not listed under this heading, you can take the legal action against your supplier that is described below under the heading "Your Legal Rights."

Non-Compliance with Franchise Agreement

Your supplier may terminate your franchise if you do not comply with a reasonable and important requirement of the franchise relationship. In order to use this reason, your supplier must have learned of this non-compliance recently. The Act limits the time period within which your supplier must have learned of your non-compliance to various periods, the longest of which is 120 days, before you receive notification of the termination.

Lack of Good Faith Efforts

Your supplier may terminate your franchise if you have not made good faith efforts to carry out the requirements of the franchise, provided you are first notified in writing that you are not meeting a requirement of the franchise and you are given an opportunity to make a good faith effort to carry out the requirement. This reason can be used by your supplier only if you fail to make good faith efforts to carry out the requirements of the franchise for a period of 180 days before you receive the notice of termination.

Mutual Agreement to Terminate the Franchise

A franchise can be terminated by an agreement in writing between you and your supplier if the agreement is entered into not more than 180 days before the effective date of the termination and you receive a copy of this agreement, together with this summary statement of your rights under the Act. You may cancel the agreement to terminate within 7 days after you receive a copy of the agreement, by mailing (by certified mail) a written statement to this effect to your supplier.

Withdrawal from the Market Area

Under certain conditions the Act permits your supplier to terminate your franchise if your supplier is withdrawing from marketing activities in the entire geographic area in which you operate. You should read the Act for a more detailed description of the conditions under which market withdrawal terminations are permitted.

Other Events Permitting a Termination

If your supplier learns within the time period specified in the Act (which in no case is more than 120 days prior to the termination notice) that one of the following events has occurred, your supplier may terminate your franchise agreement.

1. Fraud or criminal misconduct by you that relates to the operation of your marketing premises.
2. You declare bankruptcy or a court determines that you are insolvent.
3. You have a severe physical or mental disability lasting at least 3 months which makes you unable to provide for the continued proper operation of the marketing premises.
4. Expiration of your supplier's underlying lease to the leased marketing premises, *if* you were given written notice before the beginning of the term of the franchise of the duration of the underlying lease *and* that the underlying lease might expire and not be renewed during the term of the franchise.
5. Condemnation or other taking by the government, in whole or in part, of the marketing premises pursuant to the power of eminent domain. If the termination is based on a condemnation or other taking, your supplier must give you a fair share of any compensation which he receives for any loss of business opportunity or good will.
6. Loss of your supplier's right to grant the use of the trademark that is the subject of the franchise, unless the loss was because of bad faith actions by your supplier relating to trademark abuse, violation of Federal or State law, or other fault or negligence.
7. Destruction (other than by your supplier) of all or a substantial part of your marketing premises. If the termination is based on the destruction of the marketing premises and if the premises are rebuilt or replaced by your supplier and operated under a franchise, your supplier must give you a right of first refusal to this new franchise.
8. Your failure to make payments to your supplier of any sums to which your supplier is legally entitled.
9. Your failure to operate the marketing premises for 7 consecutive days, or any shorter period of time which, taking into account facts and circumstances, amounts to an unreasonable period of time not to operate.
10. Your intentional adulteration, mislabeling or misbranding of motor fuels or other trademark violations.
11. Your failure to comply with Federal, State, or local laws or regulations of which you have knowledge and that relate to the operation of the marketing premises.
12. Your conviction of any felony involving moral turpitude.

13. Any event that affects the franchise relationship and as result of which termination is reasonable.

II. Reasons for Nonrenewal

If your supplier gives notice that he does not intend to renew any franchise agreement, the Act requires that the reason for nonrenewal must be either one of the reasons for termination listed immediately above, or one of the reasons for nonrenewal listed below.

Failure to Agree on Changes or Additions to Franchise

If you and your supplier fail to agree to changes in the franchise that your supplier in good faith has determined are required, and your supplier's insistence on the changes is not for the purpose of preventing renewal of the franchise, your supplier may decline to renew the franchise.

Customer Complaints

If your supplier has received numerous customer complaints relating to the condition of your marketing premises or to the conduct of any of your employees, and you have failed to take prompt corrective action after having been notified of these complaints, your supplier may decline to renew the franchise.

Unsafe or Unhealthful Operations

If you have failed repeatedly to operate your marketing premises in a clean, safe and healthful manner after repeated notices from your supplier, your supplier may decline to renew the franchise.

Operation of Franchise is Uneconomical

Under certain conditions specified in the Act, your supplier may decline to renew your franchise if he has determined that renewal of the franchise is likely to be uneconomical. Your supplier may also decline to renew your franchise if he has decided to convert your marketing premises to a use other than for the sale of motor fuel, to sell the premises, or to materially alter, add to, or replace the premises.

III. Notice Requirements for Termination or Nonrenewal

The following is a description of the requirements for the notice which your supplier must give you before he may terminate your franchise or decline to renew your franchise relationship. These notice requirements apply to all franchise terminations, including franchises entered into before June 19, 1978 and trial and interim franchises, as well as to all nonrenewals of franchise relationships.

How Much Notice is Required

In most cases, your supplier must give you notice of termination or nonrenewal at least 90 days before the termination or nonrenewal takes effect.

In circumstances where it would not be reasonable for your supplier to give you 90 days notice, he must give you notice as soon as he can do so. In addition, if the franchise involves leased marketing premises, your supplier may not establish a new franchise relationship involving the same premises until 30 days after notice was given to you or the date the termination or nonrenewal takes effect, whichever is later. If the franchise agreement permits, your supplier may repossess the premises and, in reasonable circumstances, operate them through his employees or agents.

If the termination or nonrenewal is based upon a determination to withdraw from the marketing of motor fuel in the area, your supplier must give you notice at least 180 days before the termination or nonrenewal takes effect.

Manner and Contents of Notice

To be valid, the notice must be in writing and must be sent by certified mail or personally delivered to you. It must contain:

1. a statement of your supplier's intention to terminate the franchise or not to renew the franchise relationship together with his reasons for this action,
2. the date the termination or nonrenewal takes effect, and
3. a copy of this summary.

IV. Trial Franchises and Interim Franchises

The following is a description of the special requirements that apply to trial and interim franchises.

Trial Franchises

A trial franchise is a franchise entered into on or after June 19, 1978, in which the franchisee has not previously been a party to a franchise with the franchisor and which has an initial term of one year or less. A trial franchise must be in writing and must make certain disclosures, including that it is a trial franchise, and that the franchisor has the right not to renew the franchise relationship at the end of the initial term by giving the franchisee proper notice.

The unexpired portion of a transferred franchise (other than a trial franchise, as described above) does not qualify as a trial franchise.

In exercising his right not to renew a trial franchise at the end of its initial term, your supplier must comply with the notice requirements described above under the heading "Notice Requirements for Termination or Nonrenewal."

Interim Franchises

An interim franchise is a franchise, entered into on or after June 19, 1978, the duration of which, when combined with the terms of all prior interim franchises between the franchisor and the franchisee, does not exceed 3 years, and which begins immediately after the expiration of a prior franchise involving the same marketing premises which was not renewed, based upon a lawful determination by the franchisor to withdraw from marketing activities in the geographic area in which the franchisee operates.

An interim franchise must be in writing and must make certain disclosures, including that it is an interim franchise and that the franchisor has the right not to renew the franchise at the end of the term based upon a lawful determination to withdraw from marketing activities in the geographic area in which the franchisee operates.

In exercising his right not to renew a franchise relationship under an interim franchise at the end of its term, your supplier must comply with the notice requirements described above under the heading "Notice Requirements for Termination or Nonrenewal."

V. Your Legal Rights

Under the enforcement provisions of the Act, you have the right to sue your supplier if he fails to comply with the requirements of the Act. The courts are authorized to grant whatever equitable relief is necessary to remedy the effects of your supplier's failure to comply with the requirements of the Act, including declaratory judgment, mandatory or prohibitive injunction relief, and interim equitable relief. Actual damages, exemplary (punitive) damages under certain circumstances, and reasonable attorney and expert witness fees are also authorized. For a more detailed description of these legal remedies you should read the text of the Act.

FURTHER DISCUSSIONS OF TITLE I— DEFINITIONS AND LEGAL REMEDIES

I. Definitions

Section 101 of the Petroleum Marketing Practices Act sets forth definitions of the key terms used throughout the franchise protection provisions of the Act. The definitions from the Act which are listed below are of those terms which are most essential for purposes of the foregoing summary statement. (You should consult section 101 of the Act for additional definitions not included here).

Franchise

A franchise is any contract between a refiner and a distributor, between a refiner and a retailer, between a distributor and another distributor, or between a distributor and a retailer, under which a refiner or distributor (as the case may be) authorizes or permits a retailer or distributor to use, in connection with the sale, consignment, or distribution of motor fuel, a trademark which is owned or controlled by such refiner or by a refiner which supplies motor fuel to the distributor which authorizes or permits such use.

The term "franchise" includes any contract under which a retailer or distributor (as the case may be) is authorized or permitted to occupy leased marketing premises, which premises are to be employed in connection with the sale, consignment, or distribution of motor fuel under a trademark which is owned or controlled by such refiner or by a refiner which supplies motor fuel to the distributor which authorizes or permits such occupancy. The term also includes any contract pertaining to the supply of motor fuel which is to be sold, consigned or distributed under a trademark owned or controlled by a refiner, or under a contract which has existed continuously since May 15, 1973, and pursuant to which, on May 15, 1973, motor fuel was sold, consigned or distributed under a trademark owned or controlled on such date by a refiner. The unexpired portion of a transferred franchise is also included in the definition of the term.

Franchise Relationship

The term "franchise relationship" refers to the respective motor fuel marketing or distribution obligations and responsibilities of a franchisor and a franchisee which result from the marketing of motor fuel under a franchise.

Franchisee

A franchisee is a retailer or distributor who is authorized or permitted, under a franchise, to use a trademark in connection with the sale, consignment, or distribution of motor fuel.

Franchisor

A franchisor is a refiner or distributor who authorizes or permits, under a franchise, a retailer or distributor to use a trademark in connection with the sale, consignment, or distribution of motor fuel.

Marketing Premises

Marketing premises are the premises which, under a franchise, are to be employed by the franchisee in connection with sale, consignment, or distribution of motor fuel.

Leased Marketing Premises

Leased marketing premises are marketing premises owned, leased, or in any way controlled by a franchisor and which the franchisee is authorized or permitted, under the franchise, to employ in connection with the sale, consignment, or distribution of motor fuel.

Fail to Renew or Nonrenewal

The terms "fail to renew" and "nonrenewal" refer to a failure to reinstate, continue, or extend a franchise relationship (1) at the conclusion of the term, or on the expiration date, stated in the relevant franchise, (2) at any time, in the case of the relevant franchise which does not state a term of duration or an expiration date, or (3) following a termination (on or after June 19, 1978) of the relevant franchise which was entered into prior to June 19, 1978 and has not been renewed after such date.

ii. Legal Remedies Available to Franchisee

The following is a more detailed description of the remedies available to the franchisee if a franchise is terminated or not renewed in a way that fails to comply with the Act.

Franchisee's Right to Sue

A franchisee may bring a civil action in United States District Court against a franchisor who does not comply with the requirements of the Act. The action must be brought within one year after the date of termination or nonrenewal or the date the franchisor fails to comply with the requirements of the law, whichever is later.

Equitable Relief

Courts are authorized to grant whatever equitable relief is necessary to remedy the effects of a violation of the law's requirements. Courts are directed to grant a preliminary injunction if the franchisee shows that there are sufficiently serious questions, going to the merits of the case to make them a fair ground for litigation, and if, on balance, the hardship which the franchisee would suffer if the preliminary injunction is not granted will be greater than the hardship which the franchisor would suffer if such relief is granted.

Courts are not required to order continuation or renewal of the franchise relationship if the action was brought after the expiration of the period during which the franchisee was on notice concerning the franchisor's intention to terminate or not renew the franchise agreement.

Burden of Proof

In an action under the Act, the franchisee has the burden of proving that the franchise was terminated or not renewed. The franchisor has the burden of proving, as an affirmative defense, that the termination or nonrenewal was permitted under the Act, and, if applicable, that the franchisor complied with certain other requirements relating to terminations and nonrenewals based on condemnation or destruction of the marketing premises.

Damages

A franchisee who prevails in an action under the Act is entitled to actual damages and reasonable attorney and expert witness fees. If the action was based upon conduct of the franchisor which was in willful disregard of the law's requirements or the franchisee's rights under the law, exemplary (punitive) damages may be awarded where appropriate. The court, and not the jury, will decide whether to award exemplary damages and, if so, in what amount.

On the other hand, if the court finds that the franchisee's action is frivolous, it may order the franchisee to pay reasonable attorney and expert witness fees.

Franchisor's Defense to Permanent Injunctive Relief

Courts may not order a continuation or renewal of a franchise relationship if the franchisor shows that the basis of the nonrenewal of the franchise relationship was a determination made in good faith and in the normal course of business:

1. to convert the leased marketing premises to a use other than the sale or distribution of motor fuel.

2. to materially alter, add to, or replace such premises.

3. to sell such premises.

4. to withdraw from marketing activities in the geographic area in which such premises are located, or

5. that renewal of the franchise relationship is likely to be uneconomical to the franchisor despite any reasonable changes or additions to the franchise provisions which may be acceptable to the franchisee.

In making the defense, the franchisor also must show that he has complied with the notice requirements of the Act.

This defense to permanent injunctive relief, however, does not affect the franchisee's right to recover actual damages and reasonable attorney and expert witness fees if the nonrenewal is otherwise prohibited under the Act.

Issued in Washington, D.C. on August 23, 1978.

in 30 days."[15] McIntyre believed it was his refusal to agree to the new rental arrangement, or to get out, that prompted Gulf to file the eviction notice. McIntrye responded with the $1.25 million damage suit.

McIntrye admitted surprise at Gulf's "hard and fast handling" of the situation, because in prior years Gulf had allowed the lease to "run unrenewed for months without calling him to renegotiate."[16] Al Johnson, McIntyre's attorney, believed his client had fallen victim to "a trend among the oil companies. They don't have to cater to the public anymore."[17] Jack Houston, executive director of the Georgia Petroleum Retailers Association, told the *Atlanta Journal-Constitution* that in recent years his office had received a "mass of complaints from service station operators claiming that an oil company was trying to jack up the rent unreasonably." Houston added that "Gulf had been the focus of more than its share of complaints."[18]

McIntyre admitted that several of Gulf's services were valuable to him, such as the Gulf image and reputation, the Gulf credit card (the dealer does not pay interest on gasoline and Gulf-related items), national advertising campaigns, and Gulf's initial arrangement with U-Haul. McIntyre summarized his position by contending that he only wanted the fair business ar-

---

[15]   Ibid.
[16]   Ibid.
[17]   *The Atlanta Journal and Constitution,* May 14, 1978, p. 14-B.
[18]   Ibid.

rangement that had prevailed over the past 6 years. He would pay a (reasonably) higher rent to Gulf and pay higher prices for Gulf products; in return he would sell their products to ultimate consumers and assume the entrepreneurial risk of making a profit.

Indeed, Larry McIntyre was a reporter's dream. No question perturbed him, and no subject was off-limits for discussion. He offered Kent financial records, suggested that she talk with Gulf's district sales manager, and insisted that the reporter call if she had further questions. Buoyed by McIntyre's responsiveness, Kent found it easy to sympathize with the operator's plight. In an attempt to balance the story, however, she forced herself to call representatives of the oil giant to get their version of the story.

THE MEETING WITH GULF

Kent's attempt to arrange an appointment with the district sales manager, whose name was—incredibly—Mr. Sales, was thwarted. According to Sales' secretary, he was going to be tied up in court for several weeks on a case involving a "dealer relationship." Kent agreed to see the assistant sales manager, R. B. Manton. The very cordial meeting lasted a little over an hour.

Manton talked freely about Gulf's philosophy, exploration and production, the gasoline crunch, and just about any topic mentioned by Kent. But Manton could not comment specifically on Larry McIntyre. Manton pointed out that Gulf—with marketing headquarters in Houston—had 112 items in its product line. The oil company did not, however, force its dealers to purchase Gulf tires, batteries, and accessories (TBAs) for resale to station customers, but "hoped that Gulf dealers would want to sell Gulf products."[19] Gulf supported sales of its branded TBAs with corporate promotional efforts, but the giveaway promotions and games that used to be so common at gas stations were almost a thing of the past, according to Manton.[20]

---

[19] Conversation between Manton and the casewriter, July 1979. Regarding related products, McIntyre claimed to be proud of his good parts inventory. The products, though, were acquired from local salesmen from whom McIntyre could get the same types of products as those offered by Gulf, but at lower prices. McIntyre said that he passed this cost savings onto his customers. McIntyre did, however, purchase Gulf tires.

[20] McIntyre had commented that he had signed up for one of the promotions, but that Gulf "didn't like him" and thus refused to allow him to participate.

Station operators were free to determine their own operating hours.[21] Gulf did, however, provide each station operator with an estimate of his location's potential volume of gasoline sales. This estimate was based on traffic patterns and site characteristics. Manton could not reveal the estimate attached to McIntyre's station.

Manton explained that Gulf employed local real estate appraisers once every 3 years to determine the fair market value of each piece of Gulf property. The Company used this information to derive the monthly rental fee charged to each station. Essentially, stated Manton, Gulf divided the fair market value of the property by 12 months, and assessed that monthly figure to the station operator. When asked, then, if McIntyre's station was valued at $18,000, Manton said simply that he couldn't discuss it. Manton stressed that Gulf did not want to be in the real estate business, and sold property only when a site was not profitable. He explained that the corporation expected a fair return on its investments.

Kent was left with the problem of structuring the issues that contributed to conflict between producers and retailers in the channels of distribution for petroleum products. McIntyre clearly felt that he represented 115,444 independent service station operators nationwide. He had had two friends who were eased out of their Gulf franchises with a suggestion that they would be relocated, but they had not been. McIntyre was making a stand against the ability of an international giant to destroy an independent businessperson.

On a broader basis, McIntyre also believed that he represented the interests of the American public. The convenient locations and wide variety of one-stop automotive services that the motoring public enjoyed were the direct results of having a large number of retail outlets run by independent business managers like himself. If they were swept from the scene and replaced by a fewer number of "gas-only" stations owned by the major oil companies, the American public would be the loser.

---

[21] McIntyre's station hours were 7 A.M. to midnight, Sunday through Thursday, and until 2 A.M. on Friday and Saturday nights.

NORTHROP CORPORATION:
DEVELOPMENT OF A POLICY ON INTERNATIONAL
SALES COMMISSIONS*

The small parachute exploded from the tail of the Air Force fighter jet landing on the huge runway at Mathis Air Force Base near Sacramento, California. The harsh vibrations that accompanied this braking technique ended the most thrilling experience Bob Merriam had had in over 20 years. As he climbed out of the cockpit with wobbly knees, he could swear that his stomach was still up there, doing tight banking turns and barrel rolls at 600 mph, 20,000 feet over the California countryside.

Merriam was aware that the test pilot had barely touched on the amazing capabilities of the relatively small jet. Despite his physical discomfort, Merriam was very grateful for the opportunity that O. Meredith Wilson had afforded him to fly in such a jet. Wilson, a long-time friend of Merriam's, had recently been appointed to the board of directors at the Northrop Corporation. He had come to Merriam the week before to ask his professional advice on a problem that Northrop's executive committee was encountering. Merriam grinned as he recalled the look of shock on Wilson's face when Merriam stated that one of the conditions for his assistance would be a flight on one of Northrop's new fighter aircraft. Merriam later explained that he had always had an intense interest in flying, stemming from his experience as a fighter pilot during the Korean war. Although he had never flown in any combat missions during that war, Merriam had built up a lot of flight time on a variety of aircraft, including one of Northrop's earliest jet models, the F-89J Scorpion.

The Scorpion had flown like a buzzard compared to the T-38 Talon he had just climbed down from. The Scorpion had been a comparatively large jet with straight wings, two engines, and two seats for a pilot and radar operator. It was used for domestic air defense against the threat of bombers, because the Scorpion's relatively low top speed of 550 mph had made it too clumsy to use in the dogfight air battles in Korea, where the swift F-86 Sabre jet and the Russian MiG-15s were used. The T-38, on the other hand, was a nimble, two-seat, advanced trainer version of Northrop's widely marketed F-5 aircraft. The Air Force had adopted the plane in 1962 as a logical 1,100-mph bridge between the 500-mph T-33 used for training and the 1,500-mph F-4 Phantom used in combat missions.

The Northrop fighter was first flown on July 30, 1959, as the N-156, an aircraft specifically designed to enter the competition to become the standard NATO fighter. Sleek and easy to fly, the plane was an immediate

* This case is not intended to provide a precise account of the thinking or behavior of the parties involved.

hit with pilots. The thrust of 10,000 pounds and superior capability allowed the pilot to "power out" of virtually any dangerous situation. In addition, the plane had no adverse yaw (sideways slippage) characteristics at all, so it could be flown routinely without the necessity of using the rudder pedals. A comparison of the N-156 with other popular fighters of the time is given in Table 1. A photograph of the aircraft appears as Figure 1.

The one drawback to the aircraft was its extremely limited range, which was as low as 75 miles when fully loaded. This consideration was of higher priority with policy makers than with pilots, and resulted in the aircraft being rejected as the NATO fighter. In the early 1960s, Northrop scrambled to find a market for the plane. Engineers successfully adapted the jet for the Air Force to use as a trainer.

In the early 1970s the Air Force Thunderbirds precision aerobatic unit began using the T-38 because of its superb flight characteristics. Perhaps the most dramatic of the Thunderbirds' show maneuvers is a flight down the runway with five planes in a very tight X-shaped formation. The planes travel at 600 mph, 20 feet above the runway, 2 feet apart, with the center plane in the formation flying upside down.

Northrop also developed a fighter version of the T-38 called the F-5 Freedom Fighter, and convinced the U.S. State Department to allow sales to Third World allies. From the State Department's viewpoint, the range limitation became a virtue: Governments of small, developing countries would be geographically limited in their ability to cause trouble with their neighbors. The plane became the standard fighter for the Military Assistance Program through the remainder of the 1960s and 1970s.

As Merriam was changing out of the borrowed flight suit, he reflected upon the request from O. Meredith Wilson to unofficially advise and

FIGURE 1   The Northrop Fighter

Table 1 COMPARISON OF THE NORTHROP T-38/F-5 WITH OTHER COMPETITIVE FIGHTERS

	Folland Gnat	*MiG-21*	*Northrop N-156/T-38/F-5*	*McDonnell Douglas F-4 (Phantom)*
Country of origin	U.K.	U.S.S.R.	U.S.A.	U.S.A.
First flight	1955	1955	1959	1958
Engines/thrust (each)	1/4,400 lbs.	1/12,500 lbs.	2/5,000 lbs.	2/9,500 lbs.
Wing span	24 ft.	24 ft.	27 ft.	38 ft.
Length	38 ft.	44 ft.	48 ft.	53 ft.
Weight	8,100 lbs.	11,900 lbs.	11,800 lbs.	50,000 lbs.
Armament	2 × 30 mm	1 × 30 mm	2 × 20 mm	missiles
Top speed (in Mach[a])	1.15	2.25	1.60	2.00

[a] A speed of "Mach 1" equals approximately 736 mph at sea level.

counsel the new executive committee at Northrop both as a lawyer and as an acknowledged expert in Middle East business dealings. Wilson, a former chairman of the Federal Reserve Bank of San Francisco and former president of the University of Oregon, was one of the four new outside board directors to be appointed at Northrop as part of the settlement of an unusual law suit filed by one of Northrop's stockholders, which concerned misleading proxy statements that voided the results of a corporate election. This case was expected to serve as a precedent for directors of all large multinational corporations. As a lawyer, Merriam had followed the case closely and had been quick to realize the ramifications of such a decision.

As Merriam was passing through the main gate on his way out from Mathis Air Force Base, he heard and felt a deep thrusting rumble and looked out the side window of his car in time to see two Talon trainers zoom low overhead on their final approach for landing. It sure had been one hell of an experience, he thought. Since Wilson had lived up to his part of their bargain, Merriam felt he had better start working on his end. The drive back to San Francisco would take several hours and he decided to spend the time reviewing the events leading up to Northrop's present dilemma.

COMPANY BACKGROUND

The Northrop Corporation was not the largest U.S. corporation in the world arms trade market, where U.S. exports hit a record $13 billion in 1978. Under the leadership of chairman and chief executive officer Thomas Jones, however, Northrop became one of the most aggressive and profitable aerospace companies in competition for foreign markets. Although its sales volume was only half the size of Lockheed's and General Dynamics', Northrop's return on sales was among the highest in the industry and annual productivity growth was 20 percent above the industry's average.[1] Table 2 shows Northrop's standing relative to the industry giants.

Unlike its competitors, over half of Northrop's income came from its dealings with foreign nations. The heart of the company's product line was the F-5 Tiger Freedom Fighter aircraft—the most widely deployed U.S. supersonic fighter in the world. As of 1978, Northrop sold over 2,200 F-5s to twenty-five nations. The F-5 was a lightweight, economy-model fighter that evoked little controversy over the years due to its limited combat range (300 miles) and firepower. It sold for about $3 million—about one-fifth the price of a top-of-the-line American tactical fighter, such as Grumman's

[1]   Louis Kraar, "Everyone at Northrop Is in Marketing," *Fortune,* April 10, 1978, p. 52.

Table 2   SALES OF U.S. AEROSPACE FIRMS 1978

	1978 Sales (Millions)	% Change Over 1977	Rank[a]	1978 Profit (Thousands)	% Change Over 1977	Rank[a]
Boeing	$5,463	35.9	54	$322.9	79.1	45
McDonnell Douglas	$4,130	16.5	84	$161.1	31.0	123
Lockheed	$3,485	3.3	109	$ 64.9	17.1	364
General Dynamics	$3,205	10.5	124	$(48.1)	—	—
Northrop	$1,830	14.3	244	$ 88.4	33.6	271
Grumman	$1,455	16.3	306	$ 19.9	—	—

[a] Rank among top 500 U.S. companies.

Source: "The Forbes 500s," *Forbes* May 14, 1979, pp. 233–250.

F-14 ($12 million) or McDonnell-Douglas' F-15 ($12.5 million). The F-5's only real competition on the world market was the Soviet MiG-21 jet fighter.

INTERNATIONAL SALES STRATEGY

Thomas Jones was chiefly responsible for Northrop's success since he became the chief executive officer in 1960. One of his first strategic steps was to ensure diversification within the defense industry. Aside from military aircraft, such as the F-5 and the new F-18 program for the U.S. Navy and the U.S. Marine Corps, Northrop produced the main fuselage sections for Boeing 747s, and the MQM-74C remotely piloted target aircraft for the U.S. Navy. The electronics and communications division built such items as the electronic countermeasures systems (ECM) for F-15s and B-1 bombers, the inertial guidance and computer systems for ICBMs, guidance system assemblies for the Navy's Harpoon missile, and the laser-augmented target acquisition and recognition (LATAR) system used for missile guidance on F-5 aircraft.

Northrop also provided important services to its foreign customers. For example, under a series of agreements between the governments of the U.S. and Saudi Arabia, Northrop provided F-5 aircraft and related maintenance and support services to the Royal Saudi Arabian Air Force since 1972 in a program known as Peace Hawk. A recent phase of this program, called Peace Hawk V, did not include further aircraft deliveries, yet it earned Northrop about $1.4 billion in revenues through mid-1979. The company built three Saudi air bases—from taxiways to snack bars—and trained local workers to repair and maintain their fighters. "What we're selling," Northrop President Dr. Thomas Paine said, "is bringing more and more of their people into the Twentieth Century."[2] Northrop was negotiating a follow-up contract expected to be worth over $1 billion. Paine explained, "You never finish building a modern air force."[3]

Northrop's success had been mainly attributed to Jones' longstanding marketing strategy of not just selling an aircraft but delivering a total package tailored to each of its customer countries' unique economic, political, and military needs. Northrop's research reports allegedly contained more extensive analysis of political developments and foreign policy than were available to many diplomats. According to Jones, "Everyone at Northrop is in marketing."[4] Instead of salespeople, aircraft designers were the first company representatives to meet with potential customers. Engineers and other specialists worked from the beginning at meeting cost targets rather than building maximum possible performance. By reducing technical risks and cost overruns from the start, Northrop always delivered on time and at the promised price.

Many of Northrop's contracts were geared to meet economic, non-military needs of its customers. For example, a contract with Spain offered that country the opportunity to assemble the aircraft it contracted for when it expressed concern for employment opportunities and production knowledge.

An even more unique contractual arrangement concerned the sale of 72 F-5s to Switzerland in 1977. The Swiss needed help in marketing and exporting a variety of products manufactured by relatively small companies that lacked international experience and facilities outside of Europe.

In response, Northrop developed the "Swiss Offset Program," so named because it was designed to find new business for Swiss manufacturers amounting to at least one-third of the F-5's purchase price of $450 million over an 8-year period. Northrop required that every division of the corporation purchase a yearly dollar target of Swiss-built equipment and supplies. Although the Swiss products were not competitively priced for U.S. markets, due to the steady rise of the Swiss franc, their high-quality products could compete in many of the countries where Northrop had developed good connections and marketing expertise. Northrop tied the Swiss arrangement into the Saudi Arabian Peace Hawk program, for example, where construction work had provided markets for Swiss-built steel shelving, power generators, and other products.

Northrop lined up another unique contract in a joint effort with the McDonnell Douglas Corporation regarding the sale of 800 models of the new version F-18 Hornet fighter aircraft to the U.S. Navy. McDonnell

[2] Ibid., p. 53.
[3] Ibid., p. 54.
[4] Ibid., p. 52.

Douglas was the prime contractor for the Navy version operating from aircraft carriers, and Northrop was the primary producer of the land-based export model.[5] McDonnell Douglas received 60 percent of the work and Northrop got 40 percent, with the shares reversed for the F-18L export model. The F-18 Hornet was a midpriced fighter by aircraft standards, selling at the fixed price of about $9 million. Unfortunately, Northrop faced stiff competition for this type of aircraft, not only from McDonnell Douglas' efforts to sell NATO countries the carrier-based model, but also such foreign-built fighters as the French Mirage, the Swedish Viggen, and Russian MiG-21s. In spite of such opposition, Jones felt confident that the company eventually could sell as many as 1,500 F-18Ls overseas.

Jones' strategy had paid off in the past. In 1977, the company experienced its 27th straight year of profits, with earnings of $66 million on sales of $1.6 billion jumping 82 percent over the 1976 level. Table 3 shows the Northrop financial data for 1973-1977.

Unfortunately, the Northrop Corporation had more than its share of bad publicity. If Jones could be credited for Northrop's success, he also could be held responsible for the series of disastrous events in the mid-1970s that embroiled the corporation in controversy and scandal.

DOMESTIC LEGAL DIFFICULTIES

During the course of the Watergate hearings and trials, it was discovered that many large corporations had made illegal contributions to President Richard Nixon's 1972 re-election campaign. Specifically, Special Watergate prosecutor Leon Jaworski brought charges against Northrop, Jones, and other top executives for making payments in violation of a 1940 law prohibiting companies that get large government contracts from making campaign donations. About 46 percent of Northrop's 1973 sales had been to the federal government.[6]

At the trial it was discovered that since 1961, Jones had maintained a secret political slush fund that involved large sums of money. In regard to Watergate, Jones and his assistant, James Allen, were accused of contributing $150,000 in corporate funds to the Nixon campaign. The contributions—$100,000 in checks and $50,000 in cash—were channeled through William A. Savy, a Northrop consultant based in Paris. The money was listed on Northrop's ledgers as "consultant fees." Part of this contribution was made with $5,000 checks to 20 Nixon campaign committees and were

[5] "Trials and Tribulations," *Forbes,* November 1, 1977, pp. 35-36.
[6] "Northrop Corp., Two Officers Fined for Nixon Gifts," *The Wall Street Journal,* May 2, 1974, p. 14.

Table 3 NORTHROP FINANCIAL DATA 1973–1977

SUMMARY OF OPERATIONS (IN THOUSANDS, EXCEPT PER SHARE)

Year ended December 31	1977	1976	1975	1974	1973
Net sales	$1,601,374	1,265,009	988,123	853,293	698,967
Cost of sales	1,485,210	1,173,569	937,453	820,207	678,120
Operating margin	116,164	91,440	50,670	33,086	20,847
Interest income	16,536	4,498	4,226	5,082	3,944
Other income, net	4,432	1,879	999	237	3,640
Interest expense	(5,413)	(4,535)	(6,069)	(4,990)	(8,348)
Unusual items, net		(23,537)			
Income before income taxes	131,719	69,745	49,826	33,415	20,083
Income taxes	65,559	33,493	25,094	15,279	8,475
Net income	$ 66,160	36,252	24,732	18,136	11,608
Net income less preferred dividends	$ 66,160	36,152	24,446	17,724	11,167
Average common shares outstanding					
Primary	13,776	12,554	11,324	10,948	11,418
Full diluted	13,776	13,118	13,256	13,134	13,976
Earnings per common share					
Primary	$ 4.80	2.88	2.16	1.62	0.98
Fully diluted	4.80	2.79	1.90	1.42	0.89
Dividends per share					
Common	1.15	0.68	0.55	0.46	0.34
Preferred		0.37	0.73	0.73	0.73

Source: Northrop 1977 Annual Report, pp. 28–29, 35–37.

Other Information (Dollars in Thousands, Except Per Share)

Year ended December 31	1977	1976	1975	1974	1973
Net working capital	$ 164,826	115,536	113,850	97,503	97,977
Current ratio	1.43 to 1	1.48 to 1	1.56 to 1	1.52 to 1	1.61 to 1
Long-term debt	$ 25,945	48,719	63,902	59,056	60,619
Other long-term obligations	34,151	18,156			
Shareholders' equity	285,247	225,770	185,297	164,174	155,578
Per common share	20.33	16.93	15.25	14.09	12.77
Long-term debt as a percentage of equity	9.10%	21.58%	34.49%	35.97%	38.96%
Net income as a percentage of					
Sales	4.13	2.87	2.50	2.13	1.66
Average assets	10.19	7.14	5.57	4.51	3.19
Average shareholders' equity	25.89	17.64	14.15	11.34	7.55
Order backlog	$1,858,300	2,351,200	1,166,200	1,122,900	1,165,500
Independent research and development	31,459	25,754	22,108	20,413	17,703
Payroll and employee benefits	613,169	529,578	468,258	426,809	347,532
Number of employees	26,200	24,000	23,300	26,200	24,900
Number of shareholders	15,174	14,213	15,647	16,086	16,662
Floor area (thousands of square feet)					
Owned	5,592	5,477	5,045	4,747	4,752
Leased	3,348	3,477	3,363	4,141	3,289
Government owned	416	416	352	293	226

CONSOLIDATED STATEMENTS OF INCOME

Year ended December 31	1977	1976
Net sales—	$1,601,374,000	$1,265,009,000
Cost of sales, including administrative and general expenses—	1,485,210,000	1,173,569,000
Operating margin	116,164,000	91,440,000
Other income (deductions)		
Interest income	16,536,000	4,498,000
Other income, net	4,432,000	1,879,000
Interest expense	(5,413,000)	(4,535,000)
Claim settlement—		9,234,000
Write-off of interest in affiliated company—		(32,771,000)
Income before income taxes	131,719,000	69,745,000
Federal and foreign income taxes—	65,559,000	33,493,000
Net income	$ 66,160,000	$ 36,252,000
Earnings per common share—		
Primary	$4.80	$2.88
Fully diluted	4.80	2.79

CONSOLIDATED STATEMENTS OF FINANCIAL POSITION

Assets	December 31 1977	(Restated) 1976
Current assets		
Cash—	$ 5,920,000	$ 13,738,000
Certificates of deposit and other short-term investments	266,198,000	84,555,000
Accounts receivable—	121,619,000	128,962,000
Refundable federal income taxes	5,115,000	
Inventoried costs related to long-term contracts—	415,922,000	395,127,000
Less progress payments received	291,409,000	292,221,000
	124,513,000	102,906,000
Product inventories—at the lower of average cost or market	13,475,000	18,331,000
Prepaid expenses	9,673,000	8,487,000
Total current assets	546,513,000	356,979,000
Property, plant, and equipment at cost—		
Land and land improvements	20,586,000	21,206,000
Buildings	95,197,000	90,257,000
Machinery and other equipment	172,357,000	154,889,000
Leasehold improvements	4,793,000	4,540,000
	292,933,000	270,892,000
Less accumulated depreciation and amortization	147,812,000	132,958,000
	145,121,000	137,934,000
Other assets		
Notes and accounts receivable and sundry assets—	25,217,000	24,488,000
Net investment in leases, less current portion	24,358,000	25,846,000
Investments in and advances to affiliates	6,224,000	5,688,000
	55,799,000	56,022,000
	$747,433,000	$550,935,000

Liabilities and Shareholders' Equity December 31	1977	(Restated) 1976
Current liabilities		
Trade accounts payable	$ 61,081,000	$ 50,619,000
Advances on contracts	99,999,000	57,635,000
Accrued employees' compensation	57,697,000	44,105,000
Other current liabilities	54,418,000	54,454,000
Income taxes payable—including deferred taxes of $97,587,000 in 1977 and $12,511,000 in 1976—	103,073,000	27,373,000
Current maturities of long-term debt and capital lease obligations	5,419,000	7,257,000
Total current liabilities	381,687,000	241,443,000
Long-term debt—	25,945,000	48,719,000
Other long-term obligations—	34,151,000	18,156,000
Deferred taxes and credit—	20,403,000	16,847,000
Uncertainties—		
Shareholders' equity—		
Preferred stock—$1.45 cumulative, par value $1 a share Shares authorized—1,000,000; none issued		
Common stock—par value $1 a share Shares authorized—20,000,000; 14,029,432 issued in 1977 and 7,966,755, including 1,297,810 in treasury, issued in 1976	14,029,000	7,967,000
Additional capital paid in	64,704,000	55,887,000
Retained earnings	206,514,000	161,916,000
	285,247,000	225,770,000
	$747,433,000	$550,935,000

drawn by Savy from his account in a Luxembourg bank.[7] The money was returned to Northrop and handled outside the company's normal accounting procedures by Allen. Jones converted the $100,000 in corporate funds into a personal contribution by pledging $45,000 of it himself and obtaining personal committments from Allen and two other vice presidents for the remaining $55,000. Jones and Allen prepared backdated documents to show that the contributions had consisted of personal funds given by Northrop executives.

On May 2, 1974, Northrop, Jones, and Allen pleaded guilty to the charges. The Northrop Corporation and Jones were each fined the maximum $5,000 for "nonwillful violation" of the 1940 law, a misdemeanor. Allen was fined $1,000.[8] Leon Jaworski later made the statement that his office could find no evidence to indicate that the political contributions were in any way linked to, or intended to influence, government contracts.[9]

In November 1974, this wound was reopened during the Watergate trial in Judge John Sirica's court. Herbert Kalmbach, President Nixon's personal attorney and top fund raiser, testified that he had received $75,000 in $100 bills from Thomas Jones in a meeting at Jones' office in August 1972. Kalmbach testified that he collected the money in response to a directive from John Ehrlichman, Nixon's top domestic adviser, to raise "hush money" for the Watergate defendants. Ehrlichman had told Kalmbach that absolute secrecy must be maintained about the payments to the burglars. Kalmbach broke into tears when he testified that Jones never knew what the money was for and that he felt that he had betrayed their friendship.[10]

One crisis seemed to follow on the heels of another during this period. During the House defense appropriations hearings regarding the Navy's possible purchase of F-18s from Northrop and McDonnell Douglas, it was revealed that key military officers, congressional aides, and even some members of Congress were taking advantage of Northrop's offer to use the private hunting lodge that Northrop maintained near Easton, Maryland. Some of the officials cited as accepting such "gifts" included Vice Admiral W. D. Houser, deputy chief of naval operations for air warfare, and politicians such as Robert Sikes of Florida, then ranking Democrat on the House Defense Appropriations Subcommittee, and Senator Howard Cannon

---

[7]   "Political Gifts Spur Northrop Shakeup," *Aviation Week and Space Technology,* November 25, 1974, p. 26.

[8]   James Allen resigned as a director shortly after pleading guilty, and resigned/retired from his position as vice president in November 1974. Also in late May 1974, Jones resigned as a director from the boards of U.S. Steel Corp., Times Mirror Co., and Wells Fargo & Co.

[9]   "Northrop Corp., Two Officers Fined for Nixon Gifts," p. 14.

[10]   "Kalmbach Is in Tears at Watergate Trial," *The Wall Street Journal,* November 13, 1974, p. 8.

(D-Nev.), chairman of the Senate Subcommittee on Tactical Air Power. Pentagon cost accountants, investigating Northrop's contractual agreements with the government, claimed that the company had also tried to pass the cost of running the lodge by improperly billing the taxpayers for some entertainment expenses. They pointed out that the guest list at the lodge was disproportionately weighted toward Navy procurement people at the precise time that Northrop was negotiating for the F-18 contract. Further, Northrop was accused of handing out tickets for hard-to-get Washington Redskins football games to top Pentagon and Congressional figures, as well as ferrying many of them around the country on the company's Gulfstream jet. All of these acts were in violation of the Defense Department's standard-of-conduct regulations, issued in August 1967, which specifically prohibit any officers of civilian officials from taking any gift, gratuity, entertainment, or favor from any company doing business with the government.[11]

The Restructuring of the Board

In May 1974, an event occurred that would have far-reaching effects on Northrop as well as set a precedent for all corporations' board of directors activities. On May 29, 1974, a class-action suit was filed in federal district court in Los Angeles against Northrop and four of its top officials, including Thomas Jones. The suit was filed by the Center for Law in the Public Interest, a nonprofit concern funded mainly by foundation grants, on behalf of Jay Springer, a Belle Harbor New York attorney and holder of two shares of Northrop stock. The civil suit enumerated many of the same charges leveled by Leon Jaworksi and then alleged that Northrop issued false and misleading proxy soliciation material in both 1973 and 1974. The suit charged that the current board of directors were not legally elected because of the misleading information, and asked that Jones and two other officials be removed from the board of directors. The suit also asked that Jones make full restitution to Northrop of any corporate expenditures made in connection with the illegal contributions, such as fines and attorney's fees. Attorneys also sued for punitive and compensatory damages for alleged injuries to Northrop, including damage to goodwill and "loss of reputation as a law-abiding corporation."[12]

The class-action suit was tentatively settled in November 1974. Federal district court judge William J. Fergusen, in whose court the case

---

[11]   "Pentagon, Northrop Team Up to Protect High-Ranking Aides Who Took Favors," *The Wall Street Journal,* September 30, 1975, p. 80.

[12]   "Northrop Holder Files Lawsuit Against Firm Over Campaign Gift," *The Wall Street Journal,* May 29, 1974, p. 4.

was tried, noted that "[T]his is going to have a serious impact not only on Northrop but as a precedent for all large corporations. There's no question it's a landmark."[13] The tentative settlement called for Thomas Jones, who had been serving as chairman, president, and chief executive officer, to relinquish his post as president within 18 months.[14] The settlement proved costly to Jones, as he was required to pay his fine, reimburse the company for some of his expenses and for $95,000 of the Nixon contribution—for a total of $155,000. Jones, of course, had also to pay his personal legal expenditures amounting to over $250,000.[15]

More important to Northrop's future, the settlement called for the selection, subject to the approval of Springer and the Center for Law in the Public Interest, of four new outside directors for Northrop's board, and specified that 60 percent of the company's directors would henceforth have to be outsiders. Further, Northrop's executive committee would be revised so that five of its six directors would be outsiders. A new nominating committee composed solely of outside directors was essential. These new bodies, not just management, would control the use of corporate funds for proxy fights and have access to financial data generated by outside auditors.[16]

An outside audit firm that would be hired (or fired) by stockholders at their annual meeting was another requirement of the settlement. Most companies must get stockholder approval to hire auditors. "But I don't know a single case where management must get stockholder permission to dismiss them," said Melvin A. Eisenberg, law professor at the University of California at Berkeley and a corporate reform expert who helped Springer's attorneys draw up the Northrop settlement.[17] "The power to fire is what's really important—it makes the auditors beholden to management."[18]

Before the Springer suit, Northrop's old board of directors had commissioned two independent auditing firms, Ernst & Ernst Company and Price Waterhouse and Company, to separately conduct a special audit and investigation into any unusual financial activities or practices in Northrop's past. It was their investigation that uncovered the fact that Jones and Allen

---

[13] "Northrop's Punishment for Campaign Giving," *Business Week,* February 24, 1975, p. 60.

[14] In mid-1976, Jones was replaced as Northrop's president and chief operating officer by Thomas Paine, a former vice president of General Electric and former head of the National Aeronautic and Space Administration.

[15] "Silver Cloud, Dark Lining," *Forbes,* December 15, 1974, p. 40.

[16] "Northrop Tentatively Settles Class Action Suit," *The Wall Street Journal,* November 21, 1974, p. 26.

[17] "Northrop's Punishment for Campaign Giving," p. 60.

[18] Ibid.

had supervised the secret political slush fund that had been used in every federal political campaign since 1961, and that had amounted to over $1.2 million over the years. The auditing report indicated that corporate funds were not used by any officer or director for personal gain or for influencing government contracts.

The Springer settlement required that the first tasks of the newly-formed executive committee would include having the auditing firms continue their investigation into the slush fund, investigate any bribes the company may have paid to win Middle East fighter-plane orders, and investigate any alleged kickbacks Jones or other executives may have received from Northrop's foreign consultants. Northrop had paid these consultants $1.2 million from 1961 to 1974, getting back $550,000 for the slush fund. The remaining $600,000 was "unaccounted for," according to Springer's attorneys.

Aside from the executive committee's responsibility to continue the inquiry into Northrop's relationship with its foreign consultants, it was charged with recommending reforms in Northrop's dealings with its foreign agents, possibly including changes in personnel, accounting and administrative procedures.[19] According to one report, the company asked the Defense Department, as well as industry associations, to re-examine rules applicable to the use of foreign agents to make sure Northrop's practices and policies in the future would be consistent with the law.

In accordance with the ruling handed down by the federal district court, the newly-formed executive committee of Northrop commissioned its independent auditing firm, Ernst & Ernst Company, to investigate the company's relationship with its foreign consultants and to identify any bribes Northrop might have paid in its efforts to secure contracts with its foreign customers. Although bribes paid to agents were not illegal per se, a company violated Security and Exchange Commission rules if it failed to report such payments. By concealing such payments, a corporation might also expose itself to the threat of a civil suit. The Springer suit against Northrop for distributing false proxy information to the stockholders (such as failing to list the Nixon campaign contributions in the annual report) was a prime example of the dangers involved in questionable corporate business practices.

Wilson's Need for Merriam's Help

O. Meredith Wilson was one of the four new outside board directors appointed at Northrop following the Springer settlement. His appointment, as well as those of the others, was by the mutual agreement and approval of

---

[19]   "Northrop Tentatively Settles Class Action," p. 26.

Springer's attorneys, the Center for Law in the Public Interest, and the district court judge. Wilson was asked to chair the nominating committee as well as serve on the company's executive broad. This latter committee was to meet shortly to discuss the preliminary findings of the auditing firm, which had been actively investigating Northrop's past dealings with foreign agents. The committee was also charged with the duty of recommending to the board the policy course that Northrop should follow in future foreign business dealings.

Wilson already had received an advance copy of the auditors' report. Their findings had been disconcerting to Wilson. Wilson sought out Merriam not only because he was a lawyer but also because of his longstanding reputation as a person with sound business sense and acumen. Merriam was uniquely qualified for this task in other respects as well. As a specialist in international law, he had served as counsel to several large corporations having foreign operations, and he had helped shape their policies for dealing with foreign agents. He had been asked several years earlier, by World Bank president Robert S. McNamara, to serve as counsel to the World Bank regarding a special project investigating financial dealings of large corporations in developing nations. The project had required Merriam to make several trips to the Middle East, and he had developed firsthand knowledge of the peculiarities of business dealings in such countries.

Wilson had sent a copy of the auditors' preliminary report to Merriam for his review and thoughts. The 200-page report represented nearly six months of intensive research. After reading the principal findings, Merriam understood Wilson's concern but also understood that Northrop's situation represented a typical method of conducting business abroad.

Back at the Office

Merriam's work on another case was interrupted when his secretary informed him that Wilson was on the phone. Wilson apologized for his abruptness, and explained that he had just been apprised by Northrop's chairman of a new development requiring the immediate attention of Northrop's executive committee. Wilson explained that for the last several weeks there were rumors about a possible Senate subcommitte investigation into the foreign business practices of U.S. multinational corporations. Northrop was rumored to be one of the main companies on which the investigation would focus. The executive committee had asked that the corporation's legal department prepare for such a possibility, and it had passed on to that department the Ernst & Ernst Company preliminary audit and investigative report.

Wilson told Merriam that he had been informed a few hours earlier by Thomas Jones that Senator Frank Church's Subcommittee on Multinational Corporations was preparing to hold public hearings the following week. Not only had Jones been asked to testify, but the subcommittee had subpoenaed the Ernst & Ernst Company report and would make it public by reading the findings into the record at that time. Jones had asked that the executive committee hold an emergency meeting over the weekend to consider this situation. He wanted the company to release its own report to the press on Monday, in response to the principal findings of the investigation, to avoid the appearance of the company "being caught with its pants down." Jones also had informed Wilson that part of the findings had already been leaked to the press—specifically that Northrop was alleged to have spent over $30 million since 1971 in soliciting business overseas, and that a substantial portion of this sum represented bribes and kickbacks.

Wilson and Merriam knew from their readings of the report that such an allegation was largely unfounded and that evidence of company malfeasance was limited to a few small but highly controversial and embarrasssing incidents. Wilson told Merriam that he felt that the preparation of a public statement to "beat the committee to the punch" was highly appropriate, and the executive committee would hold a meeting to draft it the following day. He told Merriam that the company's legal department would provide any technical advice that they might need. He wanted Merriam to attend the meeting and to assist the committee in preparing the statement. Specifically, he wanted Merriam to advise the committee on the traditional peculiarities of business practices in the Middle East, to assist in preparing a rebuttal as to the appropriateness of Northrop's past dealings with such countries as outlined in the Ernst & Ernst Company report, and to help the committee in addressing the ethical considerations in doing business abroad.

Wilson apologized to Merriam for the short notice of his request but expressed his hope that Merriam could immediately set the necessary time aside to re-examine the report and prepare his recommendations for the meeting the next day. As Merriam hung up the phone, he noted that the urgency in Wilson's voice had not diminished in the least during the course of their conversation. He immediately turned his attention back to the report.

The Company Report

Northrop's executive committee released a 44-page report to the press, after their weekend meeting, which was prefaced as an effort to quell "often erroneous characterizations" about the contents of the Ernst & Ernst Company document, which raised questions about $30 million that Northrop had spent on foreign consultants since 1971. "The company possessed no legal right to control the ultimate disposition of the funds disbursed to these independent representatives. Thus, contrary to certain press reports, there was no $30 million 'slush fund.' "[20] The executive committee admitted, however, that a little over $500,000 had been used for possibly improper purposes, "In the mistaken belief that to do so was in the best interests of the company—obviously a serious error in judgment in each case that cannot be condoned by the board of directors."[21]

The executive committee report gave an account of events. In 1971, Northrop was employing the services of Adnan Khashoggi, a Saudi Arabian businessman who provided consulting and marketing services for several large U.S. corporations, including Northrop, Lockheed Aircraft Corporation, Chrysler Corporation, and Raytheon Company in the Middle East. Khashoggi enjoyed a widespread reputation of being the wealthiest and most influential consultant and representative in the Middle East.

Khashoggi's empire was controlled by his Triad Holding Corporation, which was incorporated in Luxembourg but based in Beirut. Triad had several operating subsidiaries, but nearly one-third of its revenues were derived through arms sales negotiations. One article gave the following description of some of Khashoggi's activities:

> *Mr. Khashoggi attracts press attention partly because of his flair for luxury. He logs 40,000 miles a year in his own DC-9, jetting to and from a half-dozen residences in Europe and the Middle East as well as his worldwide business interests. As he wheels and deals to build a conglomerate empire, a high powered staff of lawyers and business analysts in California devises strategy while a Washington, D.C., public relations concern watches over his U.S. image . . . [H]is holdings [in the United States], mostly acquired over the past six to eight years, are estimated at $100 million and comprise a quarter of his total worldwide investments.[22]*

Khashoggi was Northrop's representative in an arms contract with the Saudi Arabian Air Force for the sale of F-5 aircraft. Khashoggi's commission was to be in excess of over $68 million, which would be tacked on to the price of the contract by Northrop without informing the Saudi government of the nature of the expense. This type of arrangement, although larger than most, was the typical practice in most arms dealings with Third World countries and was not considered illegal in the United States. Following the publicity surrounding the Senate hearings, however, the U.S. Defense Department began notifying Third World governments that agent's commissions were included in the cost of arms deals. The Saudi government reacted to this by declining to pay Khashoggi the $68 million

[20]   "Northrop Committee Admits Firm Paid $45,000 Intended to Bribe Two Saudis," *The Wall Street Journal,* June 6, 1975, p. 5.

[21]   Ibid.

[22]   "Saudi Who Tried to Buy California Bank Returns to Controversy in Northrop Affair," *The Wall Street Journal,* June 9, 1975, p. 5.

commission for putting together the contract. Khashoggi proceeded to file suit against Northrop for the full amount.[23]

In 1971, Khashoggi asked Northrop for $250,000, in addition to his fee, which he said was needed to pay a Saudi general who could make the arms negotiation severely difficult if he was not paid. Because Northrop's sales to Saudi Arabia had already exceeded $200 million at that time, company officers decided not to take any risks, and paid the Triad Company the $250,000. In 1972, Khashoggi again came to Northrop saying that another general was demanding $150,000. When Northrop tried to resist, the Saudi general, according to Khashoggi, was angered and bumped his demand to $200,000, which Northrop subsequently paid. Company officials claimed they had only Khashoggi's word that the money was actually paid to the generals, although the arms deal eventually went through, and did result in revenues to Northrop in excess of $1 billion.

The executive committee report also disclosed other incidents of questionable conduct. Besides the Saudi bribes, Khashoggi assigned part of his fee to Prince Khalid bin Abdullah when the prince approached Northrop for a commission. Northrop stated that, "The prince wasn't a government official but a registered commercial agent, and he was paid unspecified amounts for unspecified services to the company."[24]

In another example, the report indicated that Northrop paid a lawyer, Frank DeFrancis, $100,000 a year for his "ability to understand the German government."[25] DeFrancis, who admitted that he "did not know a damn thing about an airplane" used his contacts among politicians and officials to obtain research funds from the German government for Northrop.[26] It was also reported that Northrop had set up a huge fund in Switzerland for paying successful agents on a no-questions-asked basis.

Surprisingly, one of the most publicized and controversial incidents was one of the smallest in terms of dollar amount and involved one of the most legitimate of Northrop's retainers. Northrop was paying General Stehlin, former chief of staff of the French air force, approximately $7,500 a year as a retainer for his services as advisor on French and NATO affairs. In late 1974, General Stehlin was forced to resign as vice president of the French National Assembly, after publicly claiming that the Northrop YF-17 and the General Dynamics YF-16 were both technically superior to the French-manufactured Mirage. Such a statement became disastrous when it was made one day before the Belgian government announced its decision to buy the YF-16 in preference to the Mirage.

[23] "All in the Normal Course of Selling Aeroplanes," *The Economist,* January 24, 1976, pp. 87–88.
[24] Ibid.
[25] "The Northrop Rap," *The Economist,* June 14, 1975, p. 73.
[26] Ibid.

The report argued that most of the $30 million paid to agents was not only essential to conducting business abroad but was in almost all of the cases extremely profitable. For example, Northrop employed Kermit Roosevelt, a former CIA official and a close friend of the Shah of Iran. Northrop had been dealing with Roosevelt for nearly 10 years and was paying him about $75,000 annually. Roosevelt's use of his contracts enabled Northrop to beat Lockheed on an arms deal that eventually landed sales exceeding $1 billion.

The committee's interim report concluded that "Northrop's foreign representatives provided legitimate technical, financial and marketing services . . . and the company paid or committed less in fees than other U.S. companies doing business where Northrop makes its sales."[27] The report also stated that all of the above findings "must be regarded in the context of reports over the past few months which have created the impression that Northrop had engaged in widespread or direct payments to foreign government officials—a false impression which can be dispelled by the results of the [auditors'] investigation."[28]

The Senate Hearings

Shortly after the company issued its version of events, the Senate subcommittee made public the 200-page Ernst & Ernst Company version, and began calling witnesses to testify at their public hearings. One of the first to be called was Thomas Jones, who testified for over 2½ hours. Apparently still suffering from the ordeal of the Nixon campaign contribution scandal, Jones was reticent in his testimony and hardly made an effort to defend U.S. business practices abroad or his own company's policy of employing foreign agents. In a later interview, Jones explained:

> *It's difficult to speak about a complex matter in public when everything is being simplified. Suddenly labels are being attached, and an agent's fee becomes a bribe, consultants are influence peddlers, and respect for privacy means secrecy and evil.[29]*

Jones added that, unlike a "true" multinational, Northrop had no factories or marketing staff abroad.

> *[Northrop] is therefore dependent upon well-informed local agents. The use of agents is acceptable all over the U.S.—in buying and selling houses—and*

---

[27] "Northrop Hired Many High-Level Agents to Help Foreign Sales, Documents Show," *The Wall Street Journal,* June 9, 1975, p. 6.

[28] "Northrop Committee Admits Firm Paid $450,000," p. 5.

[29] "The Northrop Rap," p. 73.

Northrop regularly buys supplies from manufacturers' representatives who are agents.[30]

In another interview Jones stated that "agents open doors and keep you apprised. They are a stethoscope of the workings of a government. . . . Personal relationships aren't any less important than product or price in registering foreign sales."[31]

Developing a Foreign Business Practice Policy

By late February 1976, Robert Merriam could think back on his brief involvement with the Northrop Corporation the previous summer. In the hiatus following those hectic days of hammering out press releases in rebuttal to allegations and rumors, Merriam had reflected that he had really participated only minimally in the decisions made at the time. Although Wilson had been earnest in asking Merriam's advice for developing corporate policies, the executive committee members had been more concerned in quelling possible public and stockholders misconception of events surrounding the Senate hearings than in addressing abstract ethical issues that might have affected future foreign operations.

Merriam was surprised when Wilson paid a rare visit to his office one afternoon, because he had seen Wilson only on a few social occasions since the previous summer. Wilson appeared much more relaxed than at their last business meeting. They had a long and casual conversation before Wilson brought up the reason for his visit. He informed Merriam that Northrop was preparing to enter into negotiations with Saudi Arabia regarding the next phase of the Peace Hawk program, which had the potential of over $1 billion dollars in revenue over the next several years. The executive committee, he told Merriam, was unsure of how to proceed, since they obviously could not use their usual agent in such negotiations—Adnan Khashoggi. Agents' and consultants' fees had become a sore point, yet the necessity of using local representation in Middle East business transactions was beyond question. Wilson asked if Merriam would attend a committee meeting the following week to help resolve these issues. When Merriam appeared reluctant, Wilson assured him that the other directors were prepared to address themselves to the long-range policy issues this time and they would be depending on his input.

Although he had agreed, Merriam had second thoughts about his ability to provide meaningful input to the committee's deliberations. Ethical considerations in business practices were much more than mere abstractions, as post-Watergate morality and disclosure had taken hold in the

[30]   Ibid.
[31]   "Northrop Hired Many High-Level Agents," p. 6.

business community. Still, he thought, ethical issues tended to become obscured by the more immediate and practical considerations when huge sums were involved in negotiations. In the absence of governing laws, he wondered, should a company such as Northrop be obligated to give first consideration to the wealth of its stockholders or to the welfare of society? The shared values, rules, and ethics governing social welfare were as different among divergent societies as their respective politics and cultures. The committee, he felt, must address itself to this consideration of conflicting standards of ethics between nations as they prepared their foreign business practice policy.

Commentaries

SOFT-DRINK LOBBY CLAIMS ITS DUE*

By Ed Zuckerman

WASHINGTON—After years of throwing fancy parties for members of Congress and giving big money to their political campaigns, the $11.5 billion soft drink industry wants something in return.

What it wants from Congress is a quick political fix.

Specifically, it wants a law allowing the soft drink industry to ignore a provision of the federal antitrust laws.

Last year, the Federal Trade Commission (FTC) ruled that the industry violated antitrust laws by granting exclusive territories to distributors. There may be hundreds of distributors of a particular brand of soft drink but, to a retailer buying that brand, the only one who counts is the distributor with the exclusive territory who has a monopoly, the FTC determined.

To get around the ruling, the industry is engaged in a massive lobbying campaign in behalf of proposed legislation it calls "The Soft Drink Interbrand Competition Act."

Its name aside, the legislation would do nothing to promote interbrand competition—the kind that now exists among rival brands. Instead, it would excuse the industry from a requirement that it engage in "intrabrand" competition—that is, competition between producers of the same brand of soft drink.

The campaign by the National Soft Drink Association (NSDA) to attain that end is, by all accounts the most serious and best-financed lobbying effort ever waged by the industry. But the industry does not want to talk about it.

"It is in too delicate a condition" said NSDA spokesman Jay Smith in explaining why the trade group would answer no questions about its legislative proposal or its lobbying campaign.

Delicate or not, the campaign has been most effective.

So far, a majority in both the Senate and the House is co-sponsoring the industry's legislation. In the 100-member Senate, 77 senators have their names on the bill that was introduced in early March by Sen. Birch Bayh (D., Ind.). In the 435-member House, 259 members of Congress have co-sponsored the bill that was introduced April 10 by Rep. Sam Hall (D., Tex.).

Conspicuously absent from the list of co-signers, however, are the committee chairmen who have jurisdiction over antitrust legislation. That absence may forecast failure for the legislation; the chairmen involved are, in fact, said to look with disfavor on the bill.

To round up support on Capitol Hill, the industry has dispatched seasoned Washington lobbyists and a veritable army of bottling company executives.

The professional lobbyists have approached their assignments with their usual sophistication. But the less-patient bottlers have left some Capitol Hill aides with vivid recollections.

"He was huge, he had a big scar on his nose and a big diamond ring on his finger," said one aide about the beefy, menacing bottler who paid a recent visit.

"He kept leaning over my desk and, sounding like Marlon Brando kept asking over and over: 'Don't you like jobs and people, don't you like jobs and people?'"

Soft drink bottlers from all over the country have been confronting members of Congress wherever they could be found to demand support for their bill.

Bayh, for example, did not agree to support the industry's legislation "until he was corralled in his Indianapolis office by 20 or 30 angry Hoosier bottlers," one source said. Bayh usually is a supporter of strict enforcement of antitrust laws.

The industry has been threatened with antitrust action by the FTC since 1971, when the FTC filed complaints against eight manufacturers of soft drink syrup. But more than the manufacturers, the issue affects the franchise distributors who use the syrup to produce the finished soft drink.

Last year, in the first two decisions stemming from the FTC complaints, the industry's undisputed giants—Coca-Cola Co. of Atlanta and

Pepsi Co. of Purchase, N.Y.—were ordered by the FTC to remove any of their barriers that confined distributors within specific marketing territories.

Coke and Pepsi have appealed that decision in the federal courts.

Action in the six other cases is awaiting final resolution in the courts before the FTC proceeds with them. They involve Crush International Ltd. of Evanston, Ill.; Dr. Pepper Co. of Dallas; Seven-Up Co. of St. Louis, Royal Crown Cola Co. of Atlanta; National Industries of Louisville, Ky. (parent of the Cott Beverage Corp.); and Norton Simon Inc. of New York City (parent of the Canada Dry Corp.).

While the syrup companies support a political solution to their problem, it is their franchise distributors who fear they have the most to lose from unbridled competition and who are pushing hardest through NSDA, their trade group, for the legislation.

NSDA has been collecting money since 1972 for its "Special Franchise Fund" that was established to finance lobbying for the legislation.

By the end of last year, a total of $1,042,103 had been collected but only $145,361 spent, according to reports filed by the NSDA. From those reports, it would appear that the NSDA began 1979 with a fund of $896,742 to help persuade Congress that their bill should become law.

In the past, the fund has been used for such things as giving receptions for members of Congress and paying a $10,395 fee to a University of Chicago law professor who testified in favor of the industry's bill before a House committee.

During last year's election season, NSDA established a political action committee (PAC) to make contributions to candidates. Although $13,098 was collected for it, not a single donation was made.

Nevertheless, many of the lawmakers who are co-sponsoring the industry's legislation received donations last year from three syrup companies that sponsor PACs—Coke, Pepsi, and Dr. Pepper.

Last year, Coke's Non-Partisan Committee for Good Government dispensed $56,950 to 37 Senate and 98 House candidates. The Pepsi Co. Concerned Citizens Fund split $32,135 among 30 Senate and 64 House candidates, and the Dr. Pepper PAC gave $13,100 to 12 Senate and 17 House candidates.

Coke and Pepsi made donations without apparent regard to political ideology. Dr. Pepper's donations went only to conservative Republicans.

Actually, there are two versions of the bill the industry is touting.

The first version, plainly labeled "The Soft Drink Bottlers Protection Act," was introduced in January by Sen. John Durkin (D., N.H.) and was co-sponsored by 15 other senators.

A 16th senator apparently could not make up his mind. Sen. Larry Pressler (R., N.D.) a self-proclaimed champion of strict antitrust enforcement, was a co-sponsor on March 1, withdrew on March 5, became a co-sponsor for a second time on March 7, and withdrew for a second time on March 8.

On March 8, Pressler was listed as a co-sponsor of the second version of the industry's bill, "The Soft Drink Interbrand Competition Act," that Bayh introduced that day.

"It was all a mistake," Pressler said of his "on again, off again" support for the original version.

"In February, I told some South Dakota bottlers I would support their bill and one member of my staff erroneously put me on the Durkin bill when it was the Bayh bill I intended to support. The mistake was in Durkin's office the second time . . . the whole thing was a snafu."

Of 29 senators who received soft drink donations for their campaigns last year, only one—Sen. Bill Bradley (D., N.J.)—is not listed as a co-sponsor on the industry's bill.

Sen. Joseph Biden (D., Del.) who received a $1,000 gift from the Coke fund last February, long after the election, waited for more than a month before agreeing to co-sponsor the legislation.

Biden is a member of the Senate Judiciary Committee, which has jurisdiction over antitrust matters. With the addition of Biden, all but four of the committee's 17 members are backing the legislation.

One Judiciary Committee member who is absent from the list is Sen. Robert J. Dole (R., Kan.). Dole's wife, former FTC member Elizabeth Hanford Dole—who recently resigned her post to help her husband seek the 1980 GOP presidential nomination—wrote the FTC's Coke and Pepsi decisions seeking to end monopoly distributorships.

Dole is frequently confronted by bottlers during his presidential campaign appearances, according to an aide.

"Why can't you control your wife?" the candidate was asked recently by some angry bottlers in New Hampshire.

In response, Dole lectured them on the "separation of powers" theory—first on its application to the American system of government and then on its application to the Dole household.

Even with all those co-sponsors, the measure's adoption by Congress is not a foregone conclusion.

"My guess is that much of the support is soft," said a House aide who is close to Rep. Peter Rodino (D., N.J.), chairman of both the House Judiciary Committee and its antitrust subcommittee.

THE FRANCHISING INDUSTRY ACQUIRES MATURITY*

By Thomas Watterson

It started with gas stations. Individual entrepreneurs got to be self-employed businessmen by selling the products and services of one of the major oil companies.

Then, hotels and motels got into the act as names like Holiday Inn and Howard Johnson's began offering overnight accommodations.

Today, it includes barber shops, disco music, real estate, brake repair, cheese shops, and the ubiquitous hamburger. Soon, a brand-new set of federal regulations will govern it.

"It" is franchising, and in recent years a new boom has been burgeoning from what was a deeply troubled industry in the late 1960s—the end of an earlier boom that was marked by numerous failures of franchise firms, poor management, and more than a few less-than-ethical business practices.

In recent years franchising has grown to the point where the US Department of Commerce calls it "a dynamic and mature business activity. . . ." Sales by all franchise outlets are expected to reach nearly $300 billion in 1979, an 18 percent increase over 1977.

INTEREST RENEWS

"There is a renewed expansion in franchising," says Collin Weschke, spokesman for the International Franchise Association. "It's part of the old entrepreneurial dream. I just bought a franchise myself." He will be leaving the IFA soon to open a printing shop, he said.

"There's probably nothing that can't be franchised if you have a relatively simple system that can be taught," Mr. Weschke added. He feels this is a major reason for the rapid expansion of recent years.

And the growth has not been limited to the United States. According to the Commerce Department, 244 US franchise firms had 14,217 outlets in other countries in 1977. Although over 5,600 of these were in Canada, more and more companies are reaching into Europe and Japan. Japan, in fact, is the second largest market for US franchisers, with 1,950 franchises, mostly American-style fast food restaurants and doughnut shops.

But even this recent growth has not been without its hazards—of people investing thousands of dollars to become a franchisee only to discover the overall company (or franchiser) has been headed by someone who failed with another franchise attempt, recurring costs that were not spelled out beforehand, or that there was inadequate statistical information on the company.

Regulations imposed by many states and closer policing of franchisers within the industry itself have made these increasingly infrequent occurrences, but the US Government still feels, apparently, that a nationwide set of standards governing the franchise industry are in order.

These standards, in the form of Federal Trade Commission (FTC) regulations, are aimed at providing potential franchisees with all the information they may need about the franchiser before making an investment—one that is often at least $10,000.

The regulations take effect this July 21 and require disclosure of information covering some 20 areas, including:

- Business experience of the franchiser and key executives.
- Litigation and bankruptcy history of the franchiser.
- Financial information on the franchiser.
- Initial and recurring costs to be paid by the franchisee.
- Information on the number of franchises and company-owned outlets.
- Termination, cancellation, and renewal provisions of the franchise contract.
- Number of franchises closed during the past year and the reasons for termination.
- Any restrictions on how the franchisee operates his business, including types of goods to be sold, suppliers, and geographic areas where the franchisee may operate.

"These are the first federal regulations governing franchising," said John M. Tifford, an attorney with the FTC. The FTC proposed similar regulations in 1971, but these will be the first to take effect.

"We find no problem with them [the regulations] at all," said Allen Vermiere, director of franchising for Dunkin' Donuts of America, Inc. "Many states already have similar disclosure statements, and in some they're much tougher."

"They're going to be terrible," said David B. Slater, chairman of Mutual Enterprises, Inc., which operates ABC Mobile Brake Systems, a brake repair service with vans that travel between service stations and auto repair shops, regrinding brakes and replacing brake pads. The regulations, Mr. Slater pointed out, have to be updated every 90 days. "Between the time a franchisee first approaches us and the time he signs the contract the information in the disclosure statement is old."

These days, say franchise operators, it takes more than disclosure statements to make a successful franchise.

DISCIPLINE REQUIRED

"Discipline," said Sam M. Ross, owner of Fantastic Sam's, a chain of haircutting establishments appealing to youngsters and their parents. "You've got to have discipline. Without it you haven't got a franchise. You've got to have an idea that can be taught easily."

"You have to make it idiot-proof," Mr. Slater said of his success with the brake franchise. Not only the service itself has to be simple, but the steps needed to manage the business, keep books, and buy supplies have to be simple enough to make it possible to require a high level of quality control.

Mr. Ross's franchise is an example of the new directions the industry has been moving in in recent years. After leaving a successful business in Milwaukee, Mr. Ross moved to Memphis, obtained a barber's license, and went to work for an established barber. After a disagreement with his boss in 1974, Mr. Ross bought the shop and changed it to appeal to a younger clientele.

The shop was so successful that he began franchising the operation in 1976. Since then, some 130 "Fantastic Sam's" have opened in 21 states, mostly in the South.

For the future of franchising, Mr. Ross sees possibilities in bakeries, shoe repair, butcher shops where customers can selected each cut of meat, lawn and garden service, house cleaning, and a wide variety of specialty foods like cheese. This last has already begun. Mr. Ross encouraged a friend of his to start a specialty cheese franchise a little while ago "and he's doing very well."

HOW THE LAW LETS YOU LOSE IN THOSE CASH MACHINES*

By Albert A. Foer

It's Saturday night, you've got big plans which require the use of cash—and an empty wallet. What to do? The solution may be simple if you own a plastic "debit card" and have a tolerance for abbreviations, com-

* Mr. Foer, assistant director of the Federal Trade Commission's Bureau of Competition, served on the National Commission on Electronic Fund Transfers. The views expressed here are his own, not the FTC's. Reprinted by permission from *The Christian Science Monitor* © 1979. The Christian Science Publishing Society. All Rights Reserved.

puters, and the newest methods of moving money. You go to a 24-hour cash machine which provides instant access to a depository account you've set up with your bank; slip in your card; punch in your secret personal identification number (PIN) and specific instructions; and, in a moment, your cash flow problem is fixed.

Let's look at some of the things that could go wrong when you use that debit card. (The word "debit" implies that the card removes your own funds from the bank; a credit card, in contradistinction, triggers a loan.)

- You are mailed a debit card by your bank, but someone intercepts both the card and your PIN—and uses them to empty your account.
- You receive your card and PIN, but can't remember your PIN.
- You write the PIN on the card to remember it, but you can't find your card; someone else uses it to empty your account. Not only that, but your line of overdraft credit, which was accessible by your debit card, has also been used up.
- The machine malfunctions and you don't receive all the cash your account is charged for.
- The machine works well, but a month later you receive an erroneous bank statement.
- The machine is broken, and you can't get the last-minute cash you are depending on.

These are a few of the possible problems that worried the National Commission on Electronic Fund Transfers, a 26-member study group which reported to Congress in October, 1977. They also worried Senator Riegle, Congressman Annunzio, and others, who engineered passage of the Electronic Fund Transfer (EFT) Act, one of the newest consumer protection laws.

The new law has generally been praised, though with reservations, by both consumer and banking interests. It represents an unusually quick and workable response by Congress to technological change. Yet the law will need to be reconsidered and strengthened after more experience is gained. It certainly won't solve all problems created by EFT.

What will the new law do?

First, it requires that a variety of essential disclosures be made to the consumer when a contract for EFT services is entered. These disclosures should assist consumers in deciding whether to use EFT and facilitate their comparison shopping. Without more information than is provided by the disclosures, however, many consumers may not really understand what they are getting into. The same can be said, of course, about checking accounts and credit cards, but this only emphasizes the need for more effective consumer education by schools, the various agencies of government, and local consumer groups.

Second, the law sets out rules and limits for liability. The key point to remember is that you, the consumer, share the risk of an unauthorized transfer with the bank. If there is an unauthorized transfer from your account, notify the bank within two days after you learn of it. Your liability will then be limited to a maximum of $50, as with a credit card, although you can incur this loss even if you were in no way negligent.

If you report between the second and 60th day, protection may be diminished to losses over $500. And if you wait until 60 days have passed, your entire savings account could be wiped out, without effective recourse.

Your best bet would be to keep only a limited amount of funds in any account reachable by EFT, and to watch your account with the hawkishness that the legislation seeks to promote. One question for Congress to review in a couple of years will be how many consumers get hurt for being sloths rather than hawks.

The rest of the law deals with issues such as the right to receive documentation of transfers; procedures for the correction of errors; restrictions on the issuance of unsolicited cards; and standards for civil and criminal liability. State laws—and there are already many—will be pre-empted if they are inconsistent and fail to provide greater protection than the federal law. Finally, don't expect even this much federal protection until the law becomes fully effective in May, 1980. Only those provisions of the law relating to liability and the distribution of unsolicited debit cards become effective in February, 1979.

I'm not advising against the use of cash machines or other EFT mechanisms which I have not discussed, such as telephone transfers and point-of-sale systems.

With relatively little evidence of how many or how severe the injuries are likely to be, Congress should not be seriously faulted for going no further this time. In effect, it has challenged the marketplace to demonstrate that EFT can work satisfactorily for consumers without more stringent regulation. This is a test that opponents of regulation should welcome.

MAIL FRAUD: A THRIVING BUSINESS*

By Sylvia Porter

Fraud by mail is big, big, business, growing rapidly year after year, showing no sign of diminishing despite all the efforts of the giant legitimate mail-order industry and of policing authorities to curb it. And in fact, this

* From YOUR MONEY'S WORTH by Sylvia Porter © 1979, Field Enterprises, Inc. Courtesy of Field Newspaper Syndicate.

type of fraud is sure to grow even faster when the U.S. economy stalls and joblessness begins to swell again.

Although only an estimated 1 percent of the $60 billion-plus a year mail-order industry is condemned as part of the swindling fringe, this comes to a minimum of $600 million annually—no meager take. And experts chart the rise in frauds steadily upward from $515 million in 1977 and under $400 million in 1976.

What's more, the published figures on mail fraud don't even begin to measure the degree to which consumers are being vicitimized. Less than 5 percent of all victims report it when they've been fleeced through the mails, a Postal Service spokesman observes. Meaning: estimates of gyps via mail-order get-rich-quick schemes may be indicating only the tiniest slice of the problem.

Most significant, as the economy's slowdown forces up the unemployment totals, countless numbers of you will be lured into "investing" your savings in subtle get-rich schemes that are nothing more than ripoffs: the real estate scam, the easy-to-make-money-at-home promise, the free-offer swindle, some franchise hoaxes.

Whoever you are, wherever you are, you are a potential target. But particularly vulnerable are the elderly, the handicapped and the over-45 jobless. You may be naive or greedy, rich or poor—no matter. The words that will tempt you will be "no risk," "money back," "guaranteed," "you can't lose."

Not surprisingly, the centers of the major mail frauds are also centers for advertising and communications—New York, Chicago, Los Angeles. New York City rates the dubious title of the capital of mail-fraud schemes; accounting for as much as one-third of mail-fraud complaints, the U.S. Postal Service notes—possible because it is the heart of the advertising industry.

New York also has the record for cracking down hardest on mail swindlers with a higher incidence of arrests, convictions and jail sentences than anywhere else in the nation. Getting started on a mail-fraud scam may be easiest in New York, but the risks are the highest as well.

While prosecutors push vigorously for stiffer jail penalties for the convicted mail swindler, the fact is that the potential profits in these shady ventures are so great that the gypsters are willing to accept the risks. And it is so easy to set up a mail-order operation that a swindler—as well as a legitimate business owner—can establish a base virtually anywhere.

What it comes down to is your own awareness that you are a possible victim, and your own knowledge of ways to avoid becoming the victim of a ripoff. Here's how to minimize your risks:

- Ask the company to substantiate its claims. You may never again hear from the promoter of what you suspect is a questionable offer (such as a miracle hairgrower) simply by this one move.

- Be highly skeptical of ads that provide "easy money" or dangle a similar lure.

- Do not buy into any venture on impulse. First, shop your local stores, compare the item offered to you via mail with other comparable items in the stores. Check prices.

- When buying through the mail from a source that is new to you, request a catalog. Test the source by purchasing an inexpensive item from the catalog. This will give you a reliable clue to the quality of the merchandise.

- Before you sign any contract, study it carefully against the ad that appealed to you for contradictions (if not outright lies). Do the same with any promotional literature.

If you feel you have been misled, write the company about your complaint. If you get no reply after two or three weeks, write the local Better Business Bureau, the Federal Trade Commission, your local postal inspector, and the Direct Mail-Marketing Assn., headquarters in New York City. State where you first saw the ad.

Summarize your experience. Provide the company name, address, ad claims, where the ad appeared and how much you may have lost. It may be too late for you to recover—but you'll help safeguard others against similar exploitation.

In sum: beware the mail-order swindlers now swarming across the land; and be on guard against even tougher gyps.

A BOYCOTT OVER INFANT FORMULA*

From a corporate perspective, it appeared to be wise and even humane to market powdered infant formula in less developed countries (LDCs), where a large percentage of babies die from malnutrition and disease before they reach the age of five. Yet for the companies involved, that decision has turned into a public relations nightmare.

Church groups advocating breast-feeding have charged that bottle-feeding is contributing to—not alleviating—infant mortality in LDCs, mainly because the formula is often mixed with contaminated water. Using shareholder proposals and a boycott as their major weapons, the church groups have kept pressure on the corporations to change their marketing practices. And this perseverance may be paying off.

The target of the American boycott, Switzerland-based Nestlé Co., has 15 people in the U.S. working on boycott matters, five of them full time. Nestlé also has engaged the New York public relations firm of Hill & Knowlton Inc. to publicize its story. In recent months, Nestlé has explained its viewpoint in a letter mailed to virtually every U.S. clergyman—numbering about 300,000. The company has stopped sending public relations officials to meetings with the boycotters and now dispatches line and marketing executives.

Nestlé officials deny that the boycott has injured sales, but the adverse publicity has undoubtedly damaged the multinational's corporate image. "My interpretation is that they are feeling the heat of this boycott," says the Reverend J. Bryan Hehir, an associate secretary of the U.S. Catholic Conference.

Proposals. Behind the boycott is the Infant Formula Action Coalition (INFACT), based in Minneapolis and operating on a yearly budget of $29,000 that is provided by contributions from churches and individuals. Douglas B. Clement, boycott coordinator, says that Nestlé was singled out because it has the largest share (reportedly nearly 50%) of the infant formula market worldwide.

Nestlé does not sell infant formula in the U.S., but its other products, such as chocolate and instant coffee and tea, are easily recognized by the American consumer. Also, Clement says, the boycott was a response to the difficulty of using legal and shareholder action against a foreign-based company.

At least three of the U.S. corporations that sell infant formula abroad—Bristol Myers, American Home Products, and Abbott Laboratories—will face shareholder proposals relating to the product this month at their annual meetings. Among other requests, the proposals ask that the companies set up committees to study their marketing of infant formula. In the past, these proposals have been voted down, and Edward C. Baer, a consultant for the Interfaith Center on Corporate Responsibility, a group related to the National Council of Churches, believes that it is unlikely the shareholder proposals will ever pass. "But there is pressure being generated," Baer says. "Companies do not like shareholder resolutions. They go a long way toward trying to convince us to withdraw them."

INFACT and other groups want the companies operating in LDCs to stop promoting the infant formula, to halt the distribution of free samples to mothers, and to end the promotion of the products to health professionals. INFACT maintains that these practices serve to place the infant formula in the hands of the consumers least able to afford them or to use them correctly: illiterate women in rural areas living in housing without running water or electricity. Nursing Sister Margaret Gitau, who works in Kenya, says that the young mothers like the prestige attached to using a bottle from Europe or the U.S. But these women are unable to read the instructions and fail to observe even the most basic standards of hygiene, she says. "Water is the major problem," says Gitau. "It must be carried back to the home in cans, so that the bottles are very likely to be contaminated.

'Economic suicide.'   Dr. Roy E. Brown, a nutritionist and pediatrician at New York's Mount Sinai School of Medicine, who spent 10 years working in LDCs, says that an infant's system is unable to fight off bacteria from polluted water. The infant may develop gastroenteritis, with vomiting and diarrhea causing severe dehydration and often death, he says.

The companies claim that their promotions are not aimed at poor people in LDCs. "It would be economic suicide to concentrate any sales effort in rural areas, where people can't afford our product," says Henry G. Ciocca, Nestlé's assistant secretary. Ciocca claims that most of Nestlé's powdered milk products are sold in urban areas, where women can afford them and use them properly.

But under pressure from the church groups, Nestlé, Bristol-Myers, AHP, and Abbott have agreed to stop mass-media advertising of their infant formulas in LDCs. Ciocca notes that in the 1950s Nestlé was one of three companies selling infant formula in the LDCs. "Fierce competition developed when the number of companies grew to 17," he says, adding: "I think there were some inappropriate marketing techniques used."

The companies, church groups, and the World Health Organization agree on the desirability of breast-feeding. "Mother's milk is still superior to any infant food product," says Manuel Carballo, a scientist in WHO's unit of maternal and child health. The companies now state prominently in their literature and on packages that breast-feeding is the preferred method of feeding a baby. But the companies believe that their products are valuable as supplemental and weaning foods, while INFACT and WHO officials state that local foods should be developed instead.

Women's choice.   However, the companies say that there is a real need for their products in Third World countries. "Government and medical personnel in these countries tell us that if we [stopped selling infant foods] we would be killing a lot of babies," says Ernest Saunders, Nestlé's vice-president for infant nutrition products. And in many of these countries, women are choosing not to breast-feed. "In this society, where the rich don't want to bother with breast-feeding because they have nursemaids and the poor want the status symbol of the fatter baby that formula produces, Nestlé doesn't even have to advertise," says an American nurse in São Paulo, Brazil.

A conference on infant feeding will be held in Geneva in October by WHO and the U.N. Children's Fund. Officials hope that the groups will set guidelines for marketing infant formula that can be followed by all companies operating in LDCs. "To commercially push infant foods as just another product is too dangerous," maintains WHO's Carballo.

THE CHEMICAL THREAT IN MOTHER'S MILK

While mothers in undeveloped countries consider powdered milk and bottles a measure of progress, mothers in the U.S. and Europe are returning with increased enthusiasm to breast-feeding. But the federal government and environmental groups are worried that products of the industrialized world—pesticides and chemicals—contaminate mother's milk and may harm infants.

"It's a very significant problem," says Joseph H. Highland, chief scientist for the Environmental Defense Fund (EDF). Of particular concern is the presence of a highly toxic group of chemicals, polychlorinated biphenyls (PCBs), that do not rapidly break down in the environment. These chemicals, as well as pesticides such as DDT, become part of the food chain and accumulate in the body's fat content, especially the tissue in the breast. The chemicals are then easily passed along to a nursing infant.

Low levels. The Environmental Protection Agency collected samples from more than 1,000 nursing women in 1975 and found that about one-third of the milk contained measurable amounts of PCBs. Although the agency did not try to discourage women from breast-feeding, it had enough concern to order three follow-up studies now under way at the National Institute of Environmental Health Sciences (NIEHS).

The levels of the chemicals are low—less than one part per million. But scientists are unsure about the long-term effects of the substances. "PCBs have been found to be toxic at low levels," says Dr. Walter J. Rogan on NIEHS. But he thinks that the amounts currently being detected do not warrant alarm.

The La Leche League, a worldwide organization that promotes breast-feeding, also does not think the problem is severe. However, it has helped line up volunteers to participate in a three-year NIEHS study that will trace the connections between the diet and the milk of nursing mothers.

Some environmentalists are convinced that no more data are needed. And an EDF booklet warns: "Because PCBs cause cancer, they present a risk to the baby, regardless of how small the residue in the milk may seem."

U.S. ENTERS DEBATE OVER LAWS:
"CRIMINALS" TAKE BITE OF DENTAL BUSINESS*

By Ward Sinclair

WASHINGTON—Quick profile of a criminal:

He works in a laboratory in his suburban home, mixing exotic substances, guarding his name from strangers, keeping one wary eye open for the law and the other on his workbench.

He is not a dope peddler, not a counterfeiter, not a spy. He learned his craft from his father; he is respected in his community and his services are sought.

He is making false teeth, fitting them and selling them to the people who will use them. And his work is illegal.

The scene is in the Virginia suburbs of Washington, but it could be in any of the other 48 states that make the denturist's craft illegal, punishable by fine or jailing.

Oregon last November became the first state to break from the pack. Voters overwhelmingly approved a ballot issue removing the dentists' monopoly over the fitting and selling of false teeth.

Oregon's denturism law, as it is called, will take effect in mid-1980, after standards have been written for dental laboratory technicians who wish to sell the teeth they make directly to patients.

The consumer and senior-citizen groups that pushed for the change think other states will follow suit. The American Dental Assn. apparently agrees. It sent more than $300,000 to Oregon to combat the denturism law.

The battle in Oregon was only another round in a debate that has gone on for years. Mostly behind closed doors and in their trade journals, dentists and the technicians who make dentures long have argued about the restrictive state laws.

Now it has become a federal case. With a great deal of money and a lot of false teeth hanging in the balance, the debate has become more intense.

The Federal Trade Commission's western regional staff in San Francisco is considering a proposal that would override state laws and allow technicians to provide denture care.

The San Francisco office expects to make its recommendations to the FTC in Washington soon. If the FTC likes the idea, more months or years could go by before hearings and final federal action.

Ann Grover, a staff attorney who headed a two-year nationwide

* Ward Sinclair, "'Criminals' Take Bite of Dental Business," *The Washington Post,* April 22, 1979. Reprinted with permission.

study of the denture situation, said her office's request for comment drew a heavy response—both for and against the idea.

According to FTC calculations, 23.4 million Americans have no teeth of their own. About 80% of them have dentures. Another 10 million need either an upper or a lower denture. But many—no one knows how many—cannot pay the price.

The FTC staff's study found that about 40% of toothless Americans either have no dentures, have ill-fitting dentures, or fail to receive regular dental care.

So, Grover said, a basic point of the inquiry was related to consumer protection: if nondentists could fit and sell the dentures they make, would prices fall and competition increase? Would the people who need them be able to obtain them more readily?

The American Dental Assn., the dentists' professional organization, responded to the FTC request for comment with a lengthy attack on the proposal. It dealt more with health than cost.

ADA's major contentions: that untrained technicians have no business in medicine; that denturists cannot recognize bone and oral tissue diseases; that only a dentist can properly prescribe and fit dentures; that regulation should be left in the hands of the states.

The ADA also objected to a proposal that would require dentists to tell patients what portion of their denture service fee was paid to the laboratory that manufactured the teeth.

The ADA's response included a lengthy compilation of affidavits alleging mistreatment and unhappy results among people who turned to illegal denturists for their false teeth.

Whatever unhappy results may come from the work of denturists, there apparently is another, more felicitous side to the story—many thousands of denture wearers are pleased and healthy with their illicit, lower-cost choppers.

"Denturism has been going on for 50 years. There is no question that it is widespread," said Markus Ring, a former president of the National Assn. of Dental Laboratories.

"There always have been technicians around who would provide teeth for their relatives and friends. By and large, they have caused no catastrophic problems dentally. There is a lot of dentistry being practiced in this country that a denturist could do," he said.

Ring, however, happens to be one of the dental technicians who has no desire to go into denturism. He and many other laboratory association members say they believe their best work can be done in the lab, not a patient's mouth.

"Oregon is definitely a foot in the door for denturism, and I think it will have drastic reverberations around the country. This situation is a real sleeping giant—there are too many technicians teed off at dentists these days,'' Ring said.

There are various reasons for that, but a central reason is related to money. Some denture makers, not convinced of the magic of dentistry, say they think dentists are overpaid for inadequate service.

That, in combination with patients' displeasure with their dentists, helps keep the illegal practice of the Virginia denturist flourishing.

"This began as a referral service, with my friends and friends of theirs," he said. "These are people who are afraid of dentists or who feel they have been ripped off by dentists.

"Yes, I can provide them with dentures at lower cost, but my concern is the quality of dentures. The whole delivery system is wrong—the dentists don't give us information on the shape of the face, the type of color of a tooth and skin. We have no idea what the patient looks like. These dentists are just not doing their job, and that's why my success rate is so high—the personal attention I can give to each client."

The situation has arisen because very few dentists now produce the teeth they prescribe for patients.

Part 6 | Organizing: Social Responsiveness for Marketers

ORGANIZING: SOCIAL RESPONSIVENESS FOR MARKETERS

Business historian Alfred D. Chandler has noted that "structure follows strategy" in the organizational structure of businesses.[1] In his study of the evolution of such corporate giants as General Motors, Dupont, and Standard Oil, he found that after a new function was performed for several years, an organizational change occurred to institutionalize the function. The phenomenon noted by Chandler also occurred in the 1970s as marketers sought to respond effectively to a myriad of social issues. As consumer discontent increased in the late 1960s and early 1970s, many companies developed consumer affairs departments. As noted by E. Patrick McGuire, the duties and authority of consumer affairs departments varied widely.[2] However, as the consumer affairs function became institutionalized, tools and techniques were developed for effective corporate responses to consumer issues.[3]

COMMON STAGES IN EVOLUTION OF SOCIAL ISSUES

The cases and commentaries in this book consider examples of social consequences of marketer decisions. Some of the issues were of recent origin, triggered by technology, inflation, or changes in public policy. Others were of longer standing, being indigenous to the give and take of dialogue in a democratic society. At the risk of oversimplification, it is suggested that the life of any given social issue can be subdivided into discrete phases, as shown in Figure 1. First, awareness of the issue typically follows a dramatic event. For instance, automobile safety was focused as an issue when the president of General Motors admitted before a Senate subcommittee that his company had harassed Ralph Nader, a little-known lawyer. James Roche in his apology stated:

> I deplore the kind of harassment to which Mr. Nader has apparently been subjected. I am just as shocked and outraged . . . as the members of the subcommittee. I am not here to excuse, condone, or justify in any way our investigating Mr. Nader. To the extent that General Motors has responsibility, I want to apologize here and now.[4]

Much of the subsequent concern and action about automobile safety can be traced directly to public reaction to this sensational development. Similarly, in an

---

[1] Alfred D. Chandler, Jr., *Strategy and Structure: Chapters in the History of the Industrial Enterprise* (Cambridge, Mass.: The MIT Press, 1962), p. 395.

[2] E. Patrick McGuire, *The Consumer Affairs Department: Organization and Function* (New York: The Conference Board, Inc., 1973).

[3] The development in the early 1970s of Society of Consumer Affairs Professionals (SOCAP) was an important step. By 1980, SOCAP had over 1,000 companies represented in its membership.

[4] Reported in Jac Acton and Alan LeMond, *Ralph Nader: A Man and A Movement* (New York: Warner Paperback Library, 1972), pp. 59–60.

earlier era, Upton Sinclair's book, *The Jungle,* which depicted graphically the unsanitary conditions in the meat-packing industry, focused attention on food safety. For most issues discussed in this book, a dramatic event can be isolated which signaled the beginning of societal concern.

In order for an issue to have staying power, a champion must emerge who can capture the imagination of the public. The leader may be an individual, such as a legislator or a consumer advocate; an organization, such as Action for Children's Television; or even a competitor, whose self-interest may dictate public airing of a position on the issue. As an example of the last situation, Gerald C. Wojta, President of Philips Roxane Laboratories, Inc., a manufacturer of generic drugs, became an active spokesperson for the movement to allow pharmacists to substitute lower-cost generic drugs for brand-name medications prescribed by doctors.[5] The ultimate success of his efforts had measurable economic benefits to his company.

The third predictable event is business antipathy, or even open hostility, to the issue. As outlined in the commentary entitled "Business Responds to Consumerism," business has often followed a sequence of: deny everything, blame small companies, discredit the critics, hire a public relations expert, defang the legislation, launch a fact-finding committee, actually do something. Several of the cases included in this volume follow this classic outline of events. The big losers in such a myopic procedure, as noted by Jeremy Main in a review of truth in packaging legislation, are the companies involved.[6]

The next stage shown in Figure 1 is public policy debate and action, often extending over a period of several years. In such a debate, experts argue in hearings, and legislation is introduced. Often, industries involved make attempts at self-regulatory changes sufficient to appease critics while minimizing costs to affected businesses.

FIGURE 1   Predictable Stages in Evolution of a Social Issue in Business

- Theatrical Event, Widely Disseminated
- Emergence of Leaders to Champion the Cause
- Business Antipathy or Hostility
- Public Policy Debate and Action
- Institutionalization of Response to the Issue

Finally, the policy debates conclude, perhaps with passage of laws which only partially accomplish the goals of critics. As Ralph Nader noted after passage of the Truth-in-Packaging Law, which featured voluntary compliance and no funds for enforcement: "The Truth-in-Packaging Law is the most deceptive package of all." Still, within a brief time standardized and misleading terms such as "Giant" and "Jumbo" disappeared from the supermarket shelves.

[5]   For details, see "Philips Roxane Laboratories, Inc.," in Frederick D. Sturdivant and Larry M. Robinson, *The Corporate Social Challenge: Cases and Commentaries* (Homewood, Ill.: Richard D. Irwin, Inc., 1977), pp. 140–151.

[6]   Jeremy Main, "Industry Still Has Something to Learn about Congress," *Fortune,* February 1967, pp. 128–129, 191–192, 194.

Not all issues follow the sequence shown in Figure 1. There are abundant examples of companies and issues for which a different series of steps was followed. For instance, Johnson & Johnson eliminated fluorocarbon propellants from their products before most of the public were aware fully of the danger posed by fluorocarbons to the ozone structure. Whirlpool and American Motors Company simplified warranty statements and extended coverage long before warranty legislation passed Congress; Giant Foods had unit pricing, open dating, and expanded labeling disclosure well before public attention centered on these issues. Still, there are significant barriers to the development of effective responses to social issues faced by marketers.

BARRIERS TO MANAGING SOCIAL RESPONSIVENESS

As Frederick D. Sturdivant of Ohio State University has noted, there are at least five impediments to the management of social responsiveness by businesses.[7] The first barrier is the widespread practice of *ad hoc, crisis-oriented, firefighting* approach to social issues. Many companies are accustomed to waiting until a crisis occurs before energy is focused on an issue. Under this management approach, a formal complaint by a government agency or appearance of a negative story in a major publication occurs before management reacts.

The second barrier is the *public relations approach* to social issues. Many companies do not bother to assess the rightness or wrongness of a critic's position. Although public relations is an important and valued function in a modern business, its purpose is to emphasize the positive about a company. As several of the cases in this volume attest, the public relations response to social issues may do little more than keep the issue alive.

Third, many companies and industries fail to address substantively social issues due to what might be called a *secret state mentality*. In such an approach, information is not provided on an issue because of concern that competitors might benefit. As a result, the public may conclude that there is more substance to the issue than really exists.

Fourth, *organization structures and reward systems may inhibit effective response* to a social issue. There are often economic costs to eliminating secret warranties or acknowledging a product defect or in improving the level of product information on a label. In such instances, there is little incentive to respond promptly and fully to social costs.

Perhaps the most significant barrier is the *problem of measuring social performance.* Objective measures of performance are lacking on most issues examined in this book. The best available data may be mere surrogates for performance. For instance, the number of product liability lawsuits or recalls compared with earlier periods or with key competitors can be considered only as a weak approximation of the safety levels of a company's products.

---

[7] Frederick D. Sturdivant, *Business and Society: A Managerial Approach* (Homewood, Ill.: Richard D. Irwin, Inc., 1977), pp. 114–117.

MANAGING RESPONSIVENESS TO SOCIAL ISSUES IN MARKETING

Many companies respond effectively, and often proactively, to issues that concern their relationships with customers or society. The common denominators to such efforts include measurement of customer satisfaction, continuous monitoring of developments that affect or might affect relationships with customers or society, consumer involvement in decisions that affect their welfare, and performance measurement incorporated into a planning and evaluation system.

Measurement of Customer Satisfaction

The marketing concept calls for identification and satisfaction of customer needs at a profit. Yet many companies fail to measure explicitly their performance as perceived by customers. General Electric, the company that popularized the marketing concept in the mid-1950s, measures customer satisfaction by monthly in-home interviews with 1,000 families selected to be representative of all owners of General Electric products. The results serve not only as trend information but also as an early warning system for emergent problems.

Many companies have followed the lead of Whirlpool in establishing toll-free phone numbers for communication of problems and to handle requests for information. Perhaps a greater number, particularly in service industries such as restaurants, lodging, and airlines, have developed customer feedback forms to capture satisfaction with services. Still others have utilized the concept of "mystery shoppers" to determine the effectiveness of customer contact personnel in such industries as banking and supermarkets.

It should be noted that mere solicitation of customer feedback is an inadequate approach to the measurement of customer satisfaction. An effective system for measuring customer satisfaction should.

- Identify overall level of customer satisfaction.
- Develop trend data on customer satisfaction.
- Identify most frequent complaints and compliments.
- Identify exceptional properties, products, regions, and so forth.
- Follow up on complaints and compliments.
- Evaluate and reward managers for high levels of customer satisfaction.

The measurement system outlined in the Days Inns of America, Inc., case accomplished these objectives by holding employees *accountable* for high levels of customer satisfaction. As highlighted in the case, the measurement system became the baseline for further development intended to improve further the responsiveness of the company to problems and needs of customers.

Continuous Monitoring of Environment

Marketers can take a proactive stance in responding to social issues that affect or might affect their customers. Such a posture requires monitoring of media for stories of potential interest to customers. It includes, as well, the notion of gathering and evaluating recent scientific evidence related to products, materials and processes involved in the manufacture and distribution of products and services offered to the public. Competitive and legislative developments should also be routinely assessed for impact on customers and society. The commentary on the social screening process used by Anheuser-Busch is illustrative of an approach to environmental monitoring.

Consumer Involvement in Marketing Decisions

Consumers should be included at each stage in the development of new products, revision of existing products, and in the development of promotional, pricing, and distribution decisions. Giant Foods has found, along with many other companies, that customer panels can provide cost-effective input into strategic decisions which affect their welfare.[8] Focus group sessions, in-depth interviews, periodic surveys, and in-store intercepts can provide useful feedback on what concerns customers have about company operations. An even more important source of consumer input can come from disaffected former customers, as bankers and airlines can attest.

Performance Measurement Incorporated Into Planning and Evaluation Systems

Once management becomes aware of a social concern related to its marketing activities, it becomes imperative that progress on the issue be measured and necessary corrective actions taken. For instance, warranty problems should feed directly into quality control efforts and into product planning efforts for future products.

Robert W. Ackerman of Harvard University has noted that even in companies which successfully respond to social demands in areas such as consumerism, there is typically a 6- to 8-year cycle before performance evaluation includes social as well as economic performance.[9] Such a finding suggests that development of corporate commitment to meaningful response to social concerns is a slow process. Many companies stop far short of implementing the societal marketing concept. The conclusion reached by Frederick E. Webster, Jr., of Dartmouth College would seem to be a logical conclusion for this book as well:

[8]   Esther Peterson, "Consumerism as a Retailer's Asset," *Harvard Business Review,* May–June 1974, pp. 91–101.

[9]   Robert W. Ackerman, "How Companies Respond to Social Demands," *Harvard Business Review,* July–August 1973, p. 95.

It is a different world from the world of the 1950s that spawned the marketing concept. A more socially responsible consumer will be calling more and more loudly for a more socially responsible marketer. How to add social criteria into our view of marketing is a piece of unfinished business currently facing the marketing profession.

There is an alternative—to maintain the old concept of marketing and let the consumer find remedies for its shortcomings in the political system, thus preserving the integrity of the marketplace as the arbiter of solely economic questions. To argue for this view is to come down on the side of the fence that favors more legislation, regulation, and government intervention and preserves the adversary relationships between business and government.

Most professional managers would prefer to accept the greater challenge of implementing a revised marketing concept, one which places public welfare ahead of individual consumer welfare as the ultimate criterion for socially responsible decision making in marketing.[10]

---

[10]   Frederick E. Webster, Jr., *The Social Aspects of Marketing* (Englewood Cliffs, N.J.: Prentice-Hall, Inc., 1974), p. 110.

Cases

GENERAL MILLS (A): THE THING
THE PROFESSOR FORGOT*

In October 1975, John Roberts, General Mills child cereal product manager, sat in his Minneapolis office reviewing nutrition education materials for an upcoming promotion. The promotion was to be conducted in cooperation with the United States Department of Agriculture (USDA) and had involved more than twelve months of negotiations and preparation. Now, final details were falling into place and prospects looked good for a successful undertaking.

COMPANY BACKGROUND

General Mills, Inc., located in Minneapolis, Minnesota is a diversified manufacturer of consumer food and non-food products. According to the company's annual report, sales for the 1976 fiscal year totaled $2,645,000,000 and net earnings were $100,538,000. Food products constitute approximately seventy percent of General Mills' sales and operating profits. The company manufactures such branded lines as *Big G*® ready-to-eat breakfast cereals, *Betty Crocker*® dessert, casserole and potato products, *Bisquick*® baking mix, and *Gold Medal*® and other flour products. Other food lines include *Tom's*® snacks, *Gorton's*® seafood products and *Saluto*® frozen pizzas. General Mills manufactures products for the food service industry and owns and operates more than 200 family restaurants

---

* Copyright © 1977 by the President and Fellows of Harvard College. Reproduced by permission. This case was prepared by Craig Shulstad under the supervision of James E. Austin. This case is intended to serve as a basis of classroom discussion rather than to illustrate either effective or ineffective handling of an administrative situation.

under the *Red Lobster Inn* and *York Steakhouse* names. The company also produces games, toys and craft items, and manufactures men's and women's apparel, costume jewelry, and hobby and recreational items.

THE BREAKFAST CEREAL INDUSTRY

General Mills is one of six major manufacturers of ready-to-eat breakfast cereals in the United States. The company produces more than a dozen breakfast cereal products that it distributes and advertises on a national basis. The breakfast cereal industry has experienced substantial sales growth on both a dollar and tonnage basis during the 1970s, and retail sales of ready-to-eat breakfast cereals are now estimated to exceed $2,000,000,000 annually. General Mills' share of the total breakfast cereal market is estimated to be approximately 20 percent.

General Mills manufactures primarily three types of breakfast cereals. Unsweetened and highly fortified cereals, such as *Total* and *Buc Wheats,* are marketed principally for and consumed primarily by adults. Other unsweetened cereals, such as *Wheaties* and *Cheerios,* are consumed by both adults and children. A third category, presweetened cereal, includes brands marketed primarily to children, such as *Trix* and *Cocoa Puffs.* Child cereals constitute approximately 25 percent of total industry cereal sales.

An integral part of the marketing strategy of General Mills and other cereal manufacturers' child brands are commercial package promotions designed to stimulate the purchase of the particular brand featuring them or to reinforce the image of the brand. One type of promotion, in-pack premiums features inexpensive plastic or paper toys packed inside the box of cereal. A typical in-pack premium promotion is featured on between three to twenty million child cereal packages depending upon the size of the brand and has national supermarket shelf visability of between six weeks and two months. Because of the high volume of packages involved, in-pack premium promotions are relatively expensive to employ; per unit costs usually range between one half cent and four cents per premium. However, good in-pack premiums are regarded as strong promotional and competitive tools capable of generating incremental volume for the brand offering them.

A second type of package promotion consists of a toy or game offered through the mail and costing the customer ordinarily between fifty cents and two dollars. Most of these kinds of promotional items are priced on a break-even, i.e., self-liquidating promotions require cash purchases from customers. They are regarded more as vehicles to reinforce brand image or to promote customer goodwill than to increase cereal sales. A self-liquidating promotion typically generates a response rate of approximately 1/4 of one percent of packages printed.

A third type of package promotion employed for child cereals, free-in-the-mail promotions, are regarded as somewhere in between free in-pack premiums and self-liquidating items in terms of effect on sales. Free-in-the-mail promotions are similar to self-liquidating promotions with respect to the items offered, but cereal customers receive the items at no direct cost, usually in exchange for multiple proofs of cereal purchase. Because they do not require customers to send in money, free-in-the-mail promotions draw significantly greater responses than self-liquidating promotions, usually between 1 and 2 percent of the total packages printed.

PRESWEETENED CEREALS: THE NUTRITION CONTROVERSY

Because most breakfast cereals are consumed with milk and with added sugar, beginning in the 1950s General Mills and other major cereal manufacturers began marketing a number of cereal brands to which sugar was already added. While reputable nutritionists and other health professionals generally regard unsweetened cereals as being high in nutritive value, presweetened cereals are sometimes criticized by nutritionists as well as by consumer activists for their allegedly high sugar content. To many of these critics, presweetened cereals symbolize what they regard as a dangerous deterioration of the American diet. They argue that presweetened cereals (1) contain excessive amounts of sugar which leads to tooth decay; (2) constitute "empty calories" which kill the appetite; and (3) preclude consumption of more healthful foods.

General Mills officials regard such criticism as undeserved. They maintain that presweetened cereals contribute positively to the diets of children by providing them with needed nutrients at breakfast time in a food form which children will eat. General Mills and other major cereal manufacturers fortify all of their presweetened child cereal brands with vitamins and minerals so that one bowl—generally a one ounce serving—provides 25 percent of a child's recommended daily allowance of essential vitamins and iron as established by the United States Government.

In response to criticism that presweetened cereals contain excessive amounts of sugar, General Mills officials cite data on food consumption patterns compiled by the Economic Research Service of the U.S. Department of Agriculture which indicate that less than 3 percent of an average child's total sugar consumption comes from presweetened cereals. They also observe that children add as much—and sometimes more—sugar to unsweetened cereals such as *Cheerios* as they consume via presweetened brands. Finally, though presweetened child cereals are sometimes blamed for causing dental cavities, General Mills officials point out that all scientifically conducted dental studies involving presweetened cereals which have been conducted to date indicate that no significant differences in incidence of dental cavities has been detected between children who consume presweetened cereal and those who do not.[1,2,3]

GENERAL MILLS PUBLIC SERVICE ACTIVITIES

General Mills commits a significant amount of its resources to corporate citizenship and maintains a philosophy that corporations as well as individuals must contribute to the well-being of society. As part of its commitment to corporate citizenship, and sensitive to criticism of its presweetened cereal products, General Mills in the early 1970s initiated a series of cooperative public service promotions involving its *Big G* child cereal line and various agencies of the United States Government. For the company this series involved providing space on its cereal packages to Federal agencies for public service messages and to publicize the availability of educational materials produced and distributed by the Government. For example, during 1973, General Mills' child cereal brands carried information about a free coloring book on drugs entitled "Katy's Coloring Book" produced by and available from the United States Department of Justice Division of Narcotics and Dangerous Drugs. "Katy's Coloring Book" was featured on 66 million packages of General Mills' child cereals and resulted in requests for 450,000 copies. In 1974, a second cooperative promotion was executed with the Environmental Protection Agency. That promotion consisted of the offer of a free children's fact and games booklet on ecology which was featured on 65 million packages of General Mills' child cereals during the year. As a result, 730,000 booklets were requested and distributed. In both of these instances, General Mills' role was to provide advertising space on its packages and did not involve developing, editing or distributing any of the government materials.

Another area of public service in which General Mills has been active

---

[1] Glass, R. L. and Fleisch, S.: Diet and dental caries: Dental caries incidence and the consumption of ready-to-eat cereals. J. Amer. Dent. Assoc. 88:807–813 (1974).

[2] Rowe, N. H., Anderson, R. H., and Wanninger, L. A.: Effects of ready-to-eat breakfast cereals on dental caries experience in adolescent children. J. Dent. Res. 53:33–36 (1975).

[3] Finn, S. B. and Homer Jamison. 1969. The Relative Effect on Dental Caries of Three Food Supplements to the Diet. Presented at International Association for Dental Research, 47th General Meeting.

has been nutrition education. The company has long believed that as a major food company it has a special responsibility to promote good nutrition among its consumers. The company's 1976 annual report observed that during that year:

> *New nutrition education information was featured on 450,000,000 food packages. . . . Supplementary nutrition booklets were offered on 166,000,000 packages; nutrition articles were prepared and published by newspapers with circulation of 5,000,000; more than 25,000 health professionals were reached via nutrition exhibits at conventions; more than 37,000 were addressed directly in speeches, and 260,000 pieces of nutrition literature were distributed.*

NUTRITION EDUCATION AND PRESWEETENED CEREALS

As a product manager of child cereals at General Mills in 1974, John Roberts was assigned the responsibility by his marketing director for developing a third cooperative promotion with the United States Government. While upper management was committed to a third promotion, Roberts was not certain that continuing public service activity was readily accepted by his fellow child cereal product managers in the company. General Mills product managers are responsible for maximizing the sales and profits of the brands assigned to them and public service activity is difficult to evaluate in those terms, whereas commercial promotions lend themselves more easily to quantitative evaluation and profit contribution analysis.

In thinking about how to proceed, Roberts knew that the U.S. Department of Justice had been pleased with the results of the 1973 "Katy's Coloring Book" drug project and had expressed interest in exploring possibilities for another promotion. Mr. Roberts reasoned, however, that in the interest of variety, other government agencies as well as other subject matters should be considered first. He wondered whether nutrition education might be an appropriate subject for a public service promotion on cereals. Nutrition seemed a logical subject choice in view of General Mills' historic role in nutrition education activity and because of the company's position as a major national food manufacturer.

From his work as a product manager on consumer foods, Roberts was aware that many children are not familiar with the basic concepts of nutrition. During the summer of 1974, he attended a convention of the Society of Nutrition Education, a national organization composed of professional nutritionists, dieticians, home economists and other nutrition educators. The convention included a workshop on new nutrition education materials for children, and Roberts expressed surprise at the inferior quality of the materials being promoted. He reported to General Mills:

> *It is clear that one of the reasons children know so little about nutrition is that there exists very little nutrition material written in language that kids can understand. What I saw at the Society for Nutrition Education convention workshop was a mish-mash of adult copy with kindergarten visuals. I can't tell you what the materials were supposed to be teaching, and I doubt that many of the kids upon whom such stuff is imposed can either. We at General Mills would never tolerate that standard of quality in our food advertising. . . .*
>
> *The point is that the resources for nutrition information—both financial and creative—are not available to most traditional nutrition educators. Where are these resources? They exist within our company and within our advertising agencies. We're the ones who know how to communicate with consumers about food.*

Roberts determined that the United States Department of Agriculture was an appropriate Government agency to approach regarding a cooperative promotion in nutrition education because of the vast quantities of educational materials which the USDA annually produces and distributes. Therefore, in August of 1974 he contacted Ted Crane, Chief, Special Reports Division, Office of Communications, in the USDA's headquarters in Washington, D.C. This telephone conversation was followed by a trip to Washington where Roberts reviewed with Crane General Mills' past activities involving the Department of Justice and the Environmental Protection Agency, and proposed that General Mills and the USDA cooperate in organizing an educational promotion on nutrition. The company proposed utilizing existing USDA materials, or, if suitable materials were not available, enlisting General Mills' in house advertising agency personnel to work with USDA officials in developing appropriate child-oriented materials.

In addition to offering creative assistance, General Mills presented the USDA with an option to disseminate the materials by means of advertising on 40,000,000 of the company's child cereal packages. Consumer market data indicate that in a typical three-month period, more than 60,000,000 U.S. households, representing 85 percent of total households in the country, consume cereal for breakfast. An average package of cereal provides approximately ten servings. Because advertising or publicity would be key to the promotion's success, General Mills' offer to promote the materials did not preclude the USDA from using other dissemination vehicles such as television or magazines. The estimated cost of commercial media for reaching children was approximately $1.25–$1.50 per thousand impressions for weekend network child television and approximately $2.00 per thousand impressions for child print media such as comic books.

Summarizing, General Mills proposed the following cooperative agreement with the USDA:

1. General Mills would agree, if requested by Department of Agriculture, to provide the creative and artistic services of its in-house advertising agency to help create nutrition education material for children;

2. General Mills would agree to provide space on 40 million of its child cereal packages to enable the Department of Agriculture to promote nutrition and to advertise the availability of its nutrition education materials;

3. The Department of Agriculture would agree to furnish whatever materials would be promoted. In doing so, they would maintain all editorial and production rights, e.g., the right to specify inclusion or exclusion of editorial content, the right to make production decisions regarding quality of paper to be used in the materials, etc.

4. The Department of Agriculture would also agree to bear the costs of distributing the materials via the Government's national Consumer Information Center in Pueblo, Colorado.

In agreeing to assume the above responsibilities, the Department of Agriculture and General Mills would observe the following ground rules:

1. Per Department of Agriculture policy, none of the material promoted would identify General Mills or otherwise promote the company;

2. None of the material promoted would contain any commercial food messages or branded product endorsements;

3. All material would be subject to Department of Agriculture final approval.

Department of Agriculture Response

Crane expressed immediate interest in General Mills' proposal. The Department Office of Communications shared the company's desire to do something about the scarcity of good nutrition education material for children. In addition to the opportunity for expanded distribution of materials afforded by the advertising donated by General Mills, Crane reasoned that the company's cereal packages themselves offered a good vehicle for communicating nutrition messages. In addition, Crane was aware that the Department of Agriculture's most popular consumer publication to date, a booklet entitled "Food is More than Something to Eat," was also the result of a cooperative effort with private industry. That booklet involved the Advertising Council, the Grocery Manufacturers of America Trade Association, and the National Academy of Sciences.

Shortly before contact with General Mills, the USDA's Office of Communications had initiated development of four children's posters illustrating the Basic Four Food Groups—meat products, dairy products, bread and cereal products, and fruits and vegetables. Crane showed one of the posters to Roberts and inquired whether, when all four were completed, they might be appropriate materials to promote on cereal packages. He also wondered if, in light of General Mills' offer to provide creative and artistic assistance, the company might be willing to provide constructive criticism regarding the posters.

General Mills Response

When Roberts returned to General Mills' head offices in Minneapolis, he showed the USDA posters to the company's in-house advertising agency creative director, Joe Weaver, and to one of his copywriters, Dick Gerberding. Both Weaver and Gerberding reacted negatively to the posters. They observed that the visual concept of associating each food group with an animal character was geared to very young children, whereas the copy and games, e.g., crossword puzzles, were oriented to much older children. "The Department of Agriculture has not sufficiently defined its audience," said Gerberding, "which is the first thing it must do. These posters try to reach children of all ages and by doing so risk reaching no one. I really don't see what we can do to improve them without starting over from scratch."

Roberts agreed that Gerberding had a point. However, he was not sure that the posters would be unsuitable for use in a cooperative promotion. He had shown the posters to his marketing director and the other child cereal product managers, and they had tentatively approved using them. Moreover, he knew that it would be much easier to implement a promotion using materials already developed by the USDA than to have to create new ones. He envisioned long delays in getting the Department of Agriculture to approve material developed by General Mills, even though in discussions to date Crane had been extremely cooperative and encouraging.

Gerberding and Weaver continued, however, to emphasize that *most nutrition materials, including the Department of Agriculture posters, try to teach too much and therefore end up teaching nothing.* Both men pointed out that this was particularly important to keep in mind in writing for children, where the ideal strategy should be one of concentration on a single and simple message put forth in an entertaining manner. The two men stated that they would like to see whether they could transform what the USDA posters were trying to accomplish into a story book format. Roberts became persuaded and encouraged them to see what they could do.

In December of 1974, General Mills' in-house advertising agency presented a first draft of a twenty-page storybook entitled "The Thing the Professor Forgot." It was designed to be read to children and also to function as a coloring book. The message was simple: there are four groups of food, and everyone should eat foods from each group every day. This theme was developed along with the storyline, and was executed in rhyme for added interest. Roberts, pleased by what had been created and convinced that the effort was a significant improvement over the USDA poster concept, quickly obtained review and approval from his marketing director and other child cereal product managers. The storybook draft was also reviewed by General Mills' Law Department and approved for factual accuracy by the Company's Nutrition Department. When all internal approvals had been obtained, "The Thing the Professor Forgot" was researched among groups of kindergarten children and teachers in a suburban Minneapolis elementary school in order to determine whether the objectives of the material were being met.

In January of 1975, "The Thing the Professor Forgot" was presented to Crane in a meeting in Minneapolis. Shortly after returning to Washington, Crane called Roberts to advise that, once the Department of Agriculture's nutrition staff had had the opportunity to review the storybook closely and to approve and/or revise its contents, a formal letter of agreement for a cooperative promotion would be executed. Roberts commented to one of his assistant managers, "It has taken us six months, but I think we're 90 percent there!"

GENERAL MILLS (B): THE THING
THE PROFESSOR FORGOT*

MATERIALS DEVELOPMENT

"The Thing the Professor Forgot" was presented to officials of the Department of Agriculture in January, 1975, and was enthusiastically received. Both General Mills and Department of Agriculture personnel involved in the project seemed to agree that the material represented a classic example of what can be accomplished when government and business work together for the public good. During the next several months Roberts and Gerberding conferred by telephone with Crane in editing the draft as Department of Agriculture nutritionists reviewed the storybook's contents and requested that changes be incorporated. None of the changes was substantial or posed unsurmountable problems, although at one point

Gerberding remarked that "Government bureaucrats, even more than marketing men, think they know how to write copy." An example was a Department of Agriculture request to include peanut butter and beans in the Meat Group of foods, since peanut butter and beans contribute significant amounts of protein to the diet. While this presented no problem graphically, Gerberding did not find it easy to insert the words peanut butter and beans into the storybook's verse.

As final editorial changes were incorporated, plans were completed with General Mills child cereal product managers for the booklet to be advertised on eight brands of the company's cereals beginning November 1975, and extending into the spring of 1976. Plans were made for each brand to feature the promotion on one half of its back panel for approximately two months. Roberts told Crane that he estimated that "The Thing the Professor Forgot" would generate requests equal to approximately two percent of total packages printed. This estimate was based on the responses generated from previous General Mills–U.S. Government promotions. The Department of Agriculture proceeded to print 1,000,000 copies in October, 1975, in order to satisfy the anticipated needs of the promotion.

PLANNED PUBLICITY

No special publicity was planned by either the Department of Agriculture or General Mills in launching "The Thing the Professor Forgot" beyond that expected to be generated by the cereal package backs themselves. Crane explained that the Department of Agriculture routinely announced new materials available from the Department. Therefore, as the cereal packages began to appear on supermarket shelves around the country, the Department of Agriculture issued a brief press release announcing the promotion. Crane submitted the press release to General Mills for review prior to its release (Figure 1), and Roberts determined that its content was appropriate. Other than to go along with the Government press announcement, General Mills sought to draw no special recognition to its involvement in the promotion.

UNPLANNED PUBLICITY

The week following the Department of Agriculture's announcement, Roberts received a telephone call from General Mills' Public Relations Department. The USDA informed him that a United Press International (UPI) wire services reporter assigned to the Department of Agriculture had

FIGURE 1   Press Release

NEWS
U.S. DEPARTMENT OF AGRICULTURE

USDA Announces Storybook on Food for Children:

Washington, Oct. 1—The U.S. Department of Agriculture today announced the availability of a new storybook on nutrition for children. "The Thing the Professor Forgot" tells the story of good eating habits in pictures and rhyme.

The 20-page booklet is designed to be read to pre-schoolers and to be used by children in the first years of school as a picture book and learning aid.

"The Thing the Professor Forgot" was developed by the General Mills Corporation with the cooperation of the Department. The booklet, along with a message on good nutrition, will be promoted on about 40 million General Mills cereal boxes. The boxes will be distributed during the next several months.

Distribution of the booklet is being handled by the Consumer Information Center in Pueblo, Colo.

The booklet is part of a continuing effort by the Department of Agriculture to provide the public, and especially young people, with more information about food and nutrition. Projects have been developed in cooperation with private industry, with other government agencies, and with volunteer organizations in order to reach the widest possible audience with available resources.

For a single free copy, write to: Consumer Information; Dept. Q; Pueblo, Colo. 81009. Copies are not available from the Department of Agriculture.

---

written a story critical of "The Thing the Professor Forgot" promotion. Roberts subsequently learned that the Associated Press (AP) had issued a similar story (Figures 2 and 3). Both wire services characterized the project as big business exploitation which used taxpayer's money to finance a General Mills promotion. The stories also accused the material of endorsing breakfast cereals, thereby implying that the storybook was self-serving. Roberts asked the Public Relations Department to determine how many newspapers across the country carried the UPI and AP stories; however it was impossible to estimate accurately.

Approximately one month later, General Mills learned that U.S. Congressman Benjamin Rosenthal of New York had written an internal U.S.

FIGURE 2   UPI Press Release

UP—095

  (NUTRITION BOOK)
  (BY BERNARD BRENNER)

WASHINGTON (UPI)—A NEW CHILDREN'S STORYBOOK PLUG-GING NUTRITION IS BEING DISTRIBUTED BY THE GOVERNMENT WITH LABELING INDICATING IT IS PREPARED BY THE AGRICULTURE DEPARTMENT.

ACTUALLY, OFFICIALS SAID, ALL THE TEXT AND PICTURES WERE FURNISHED BY GENERAL MILLS CORPORATION WHICH WILL BE PRINTING NOTICES ON ABOUT 40 MILLION CEREAL BOXES DURING THE NEXT FEW MONTHS TO PROMOTE DISTRIBUTION OF THE BOOK.

THE BOOK ITSELF GIVES NO INDICATION IT WAS NOT WRITTEN BY GOVERNMENT SPECIALISTS. ITS COVER BEARS ON THE TITLE, "THE THING THE PROFESSOR FORGOT," AND THE WORDS, "OFFICE OF COMMUNICATIONS, U.S. DEPARTMENT OF AGRICULTURE."

IN A PRESS RELEASE ANNOUNCING THE PUBLICATION, HOWEVER, AGRICULTURE OFFICIALS SAID IT WAS "DEVELOPED BY THE GENERAL MILLS CORPORATION WITH THE COOPERATION OF THE DEPARTMENT."

AN OFFICE OF COMMUNICATIONS OFFICIAL, THEODORE CRANE, SAID THE COOPERATION INCLUDED RIGID EDITING BY DEPARTMENT NUTRITION EXPERTS OF ONE PAGE AT THE BACK OF THE BOOK. THE PAGE IS ADDRESSED TO PARENTS TO SUM UP RECOM-MENDATIONS ON BUILDING A BALANCED DIET FROM FOUR BASIC FOOD GROUPS—MEAT, MILK, FRUITS AND VEGETABLES, AND CEREALS AND BREADS, PLUS OTHER FOODS TO ROUND OUT MEALS AND SATISFY APPETITES."

ALSO, CRANE SAID, THE DEPARTMENT IS PUTTING UP $71,000 TO PAY FOR PRINTING 1.25 MILLION COPIES OF THE 20-PAGE BOOK WHICH WILL BE DISTRIBUTED FREE ON REQUEST FROM THE GOVERN-MENT'S CONSUMER INFORMATION CENTER, DEPT. Q, PUEBLO, COL. 51009.

THE BOOK, DESIGNED TO BE READ TO PRE-SCHOOLERS AND USED BY CHILDREN IN EARLY GRADES, IS A RHYMING TALE OF A BOY, A GIRL, AND PROFESSOR OONOOSE Q. ECKWOOSE WHO HAS "MY DEGREE IN FOODOLOGY." WITH CHILDREN'S-STYLE ILLUSTRATIONS, THE TEXT EXPLAINS THE FOUR FOOD GROUPS AND WHY THEY'RE ALL NEEDED FOR GOOD HEALTH.

  UPI 10-03 02:33 PED

UP—096

FIGURE 3   A.P. Press Release

U.S. AID FOR CEREAL FIRM

Associated Press

The Agriculture Department has spent $71,000 to help General Mills Corp. tell children what they should eat as they munch on the company's cereal products.

Officials said the promotion, announced yesterday, will be printed on 40 million boxes of cereal as "part of a continuing effort by the department to provide the public, and especially young people, with more information about food and nutrition."

The project involves a 20-page storybook designed to teach children about the four major food groups of meat, vegetables and fruit, cereals and bread, and milk.

Theodore R. Crane, head of special reports in USDA's Office of Communication, said the booklet and a "nutrition message" will be promoted on 15.8 million boxes of General Mills' presweetened cereals, including Monsters, Cocoa Puffs, Trix and Lucky Charms. Information about the booklet will be printed on 25 million boxes of Cheerios.

Crane said the company spent about $25,000 designing the booklet. The $71,000 spent by the USDA is for the government printing of 1,250,000 copies, he said.

The department said free single copies of the storybook, designed to be read to preschoolers and for use by those in early school years, can be ordered from the Consumer Information Center, Pueblo, Colo. Officials said USDA had none for distribution.

Washington Star, October 2, 1975. Reprinted by permission of the Associated Press.

House of Representatives memorandum based on the wire services stories. Representative Rosenthal's memorandum went further charging the U.S. Government Printing Office as well as the USDA with promoting General Mills at the expense of the American taxpayer.

In late December 1975, "The Thing the Professor Forgot" received still more unfavorable attention. An article about the promotion appeared in the nationally syndicated column of Washington political commentator Jack Anderson. Anderson reported the contents of Congressman Rosenthal's House memorandum as saying that the USDA had paid $71,000 for printing the booklet and would pay perhaps as much as $100,000 for mailing it to General Mills' customers. He further quoted the House memorandum as saying: "There appears to be a conscious effort to conceal General Mills' role in this project. Plus a not-too-subtle attempt by the cereal manufacturer to convey an image on nutrition consciousness by virtue of advertising free government booklets on its projects." Anderson paraphrased the memo as stating the booklet failed to say what children should not eat, such as some of General Mills' cereals, which were alleged to be of "questionable nutritional value." Anderson, however, refrained from making any personal observations as to whether or not he regarded Representative Rosenthal's charges as accurate.

The only favorable publicity which "The Thing the Professor Forgot" received in the popular press appeared in the September, 1976 issue of *Good Housekeeping* magazine (Figure 4). Otherwise, positive critical response appeared only in the professional media, and it, too, was limited. For example, the Society for Nutrition Education included a review of "The Thing the Professor Forgot" in the January–March, 1976 issue of its *Journal of Nutrition Education* (Figure 5).

All of the publicity in the popular press resulted in a half dozen letters to General Mills concerning the company's cooperation with the USDA. The number of letters was significantly smaller than might have been anticipated, since the company's Consumer Center, Nutrition Department and other departments annually receive more than seven million "inputs" from consumers in the form of letters and telephone calls.

A few of the letters to the company were from stockholders, however, and one of the letters was mailed directly to the president of General Mills. On the day this letter arrived, Roberts received a telephone call from the president's secretary asking for an explanation. Roberts hurriedly drafted a letter of reply for General Mills' president to sign and which could be used in responding to any other letters the president might receive.

All the unfavorable publicity both surprised and concerned General Mills officials. Neither the Justice Department nor the Environmental Protection Agency promotions had generated any kind of significant criticism; to the contrary, both preceding cooperative promotions had earned public as well as private sector praise. Roberts was somewhat disconcerted by the

FIGURE 4 Review of Booklet

BOOKLETS WORTH WRITING FOR

The Thing the Professor Forgot. This 19-page illustrated, rhyming nutrition lesson is a terrific way to teach young children how to develop good eating habits. Children under grade-school age will love having it read to them! Free from Consumer Information Center, Dept. 254D, Pueblo, Colo., 81009.

Good Housekeeping, September 1976. Reprinted by permission.

FIGURE 5   Nutrition Education Material Review

Preschool/Elementary

The Thing the Professor Forgot, Office of Communications, USDA, 1975. From Consumer Information, Dept. Q, Pueblo, CO 81009, 18 pp., free.

It's Professor Eckwoose's turn this time, to tell of Four Food Groups in picture and rhyme. (The rhyme is contagious!) This charming booklet is designed to be read to preschoolers and to be used independently by early elementary school children as a picture book and learning aid. Professor Eckwoose tells what the groups are, why they are needed, and foods that are in them. This is a good example of a joint project developed by government and private industry (General Mills). The booklet is currently promoted on General Mills cereal package backs.

The Journal of Nutrition Education, January-March 1976. Reprinted by permission.

Department of Agriculture's seemingly matter-of-fact attitude about the problem. "Don't worry," Crane told him. "This kind of thing happens to us all the time. After a while you get so that it doesn't bother you. 'The Thing the Professor Forgot' is a good promotion. We all know that, and the public will think so, too."

Roberts was not concerned that the negative publicity would have an impact on General Mills cereal sales. He was, however, concerned about the effects of the publicity on the results of the promotion, despite Crane's assurances.

PROMOTION RESULTS: AN APPRAISAL

The Department of Agriculture agreed to provide General Mills with progress reports on the number of copies of "The Thing the Professor Forgot" which were distributed to consumers as a result of the promotion. The following data were received by General Mills during the ensuing twelve months:

Number of Months	Total Number of Copies Distributed
6	630,000
9	898,000
12	1,250,000

In reporting the above information, the Department of Agriculture observed that approximately 82% of requests received were single copy (and small order) requests indicating that consumer response to the promotion was widespread. The Department of Agriculture informed General Mills that in terms of number of copies requested and distributed, "The Thing the Professor Forgot" was the most popular consumer publication ever offered by an agency of the Federal Government. General Mills learned that at least one county school system in Alabama involving forty-nine schools had incorporated "The Thing the Professor Forgot" into its curriculum, and feedback received by the USDA was uniformly complimentary (Figure 6).

FIGURE 6   The Thing the Professor Forgot (B)
Excerpts from Letters to the Department of Agriculture

"After receiving a copy of 'The Thing the Professor Forgot' from General Mills, I feel this publication would greatly benefit our Expanded Nutrition Education Program."

—Janet F. Renner, Extension Nutrition Assistant, West Chester, Pennsylvania

"We recently saw a copy of the book 'The Thing the Professor Forgot.' We were very impressed with the content of this material and would like to have some copies for our students and teachers to use as a unit in the classroom."

—Tom Dalser, Principal, Pioneer, Ohio

"As a teacher I feel that your pamphlet entitled 'The Thing the Professor Forgot' would be of great value. Several classes at Skycrest Christian would like to use it. . . "

—Dawn Gaimezy, Clearwater, Fla.

"I have seen your storybook entitled 'The Thing the Professor Forgot' and found it to be very beneficial in helping children study good nutrition. I have 32 children in my class (second graders) and would. . . ."

—Mrs. H. Vinegar, Queens Village, New York

"Recently I took advantage of an offer on a cereal box to receive a free copy of your publication called 'The Thing the Professor Forgot.' I was very impressed by this book. The children at our local elementary school could learn a lot from this very informative booklet. It would really impress upon them the importance of good nutrition. Would it be possible to send us about three hundred copies. . . ."

—Esther L. Lassard, Treasurer, Westfield, Mass. PTA Council

> "These ["The Thing the Professor Forgot"] are to be given to the children at Washington Elementary School by the P.T.A. of the School to be incorporated by the teacher into her lesson plans. We think they would be very helpful to the children and would very much appreciate 450 more copies. . . ."
>
> —**Mrs. Betty Rickinbach, Camden, New Jersey**

> "As part of the Expanded Food and Nutrition Educational Program in Fond du Lac County, we are sponsoring a youth nutrition program. Through my research I have come across your publication of 'The Thing the Professor Forgot.' I have found it to be extremely informative and much to the children's delight."
>
> —**Donna L. Macke, Extension Home Economist-Nutrition, Fond du Lac County, Wis.**

> "I have received a copy of the coloring book for children called 'The Thing the Professor Forgot.' I find this a very interesting and informative book and I want to incorporate it into my Community Services program. I have written a small article on it in my union's National Publication, the Postal Record."
>
> —**Harold A. Wright, National Association of Letter Carriers, AFL-CIO, Office of Comm. Services, Belleville, Illinois**

EXTERNAL REPERCUSSIONS

During the early stages of development of the joint General Mills-Department of Agriculture promotion, officials of the U.S. Food and Drug Administration (FDA) of the U.S. Department of Health, Education and Welfare, had met with Mr. Roberts and with Dr. Ivy Celender, Vice President and Director of Nutrition at General Mills. The purpose of the meeting had been to discuss the possibility of organizing a promotion similar to "The Thing the Professor Forgot" to publicize one of the FDA's consumer programs, nutrition labeling. Officials of the FDA appeared enthusiastic about the prospect of working with General Mills. A year later, however, in August 1976 officials of the FDA informed General Mills that plans for the cooperative promotion were being abandoned. Subsequently, the company learned that FDA officials had encountered pressures from the Center for Science in the Public Interest and other consumer activist organizations, and that FDA feared publicity which might result from participating in a joint effort with industry. In the September 1976 issue of *Nutrition Action,* a consumer activist publication, FDA Deputy Chief Counsel Alvin Gottlieb was quoted as saying: "I don't like this playing footsie with industry and all that crap. We're too goddam friendly with the people we should be regulating."

EVALUATION

The past fourteen months had been rather tumultuous ones for officials of General Mills involved in "The Thing the Professor Forgot" project. The promotion had been conceived as a meaningful public service activity in an area where the company felt it had a special social responsibility. Significant corporate effort and resources had been employed in planning and implementing the project. The backlash of negative publicity was unexpected and disturbing. Mr. Roberts felt that it was incumbent upon him to review "The Thing the Professor Forgot" experience and present recommendations to top management regarding whether and how General Mills should continue its nutrition education activities, especially in regard to cooperative efforts with the Government.

MAJOR APPLIANCE CONSUMER ACTION PANEL (A): AN EVALUATION OF THE CONSUMER ACTION PANEL CONCEPT*

James F. Nolan, administrator for the Major Appliance Consumer Action Panel (MACAP), had just accepted an invitation to appear as a guest speaker. The occasion was the annual information exchange meeting of the Society for Consumer Affairs Professionals (SOCAP), whose conference theme was to be "Consumer Affairs in the 80s: Challenges and Opportunities." One session was scheduled for complaint-handling approaches, including mediation and arbitration programs. Many of the 1,000 SOCAP members were interested in mediation, so he was asked to speak on "Consumer Action Panels: Progress and Prospects." He had been asked to speak to the assembled members because MACAP was viewed as the pioneer in the role of mediator for consumer complaints for an entire industry, and to date, was also the most successful. He was now considering what remarks he could make that would be of value to the group. Nolan was aware that of the five industry-wide consumer action panels that had been established, two had failed.

Nolan decided he would review the histories of various consumer

* This case is not intended to provide a precise account of the thinking of the parties involved.

panels, highlighting reasons for their success or failure, and then he would suggest several industries which appeared to have the most potential for positive application of this mediation technique.

BACKGROUND ON CONSUMER ACTION PANELS

In early 1969, Virginia Knauer, director of the White House Office of Consumer Affairs, challenged the major appliance industry to respond effectively to problems cited in the *Final Report of the Presidential Task Force on Appliance Warranties.* The report described major appliances as the second most frequently complained-about product purchased by American consumers. The report detailed warranty, repair, and product-quality problems for which many consumers were unable to achieve appropriate remedy. The report concluded with recommendation of warranty legislation unless the industry established a system that would assure consumers of prompt, fair handling of their complaints, and provide for mediation or arbitration of consumer disputes where appropriate.

The Consumer Affairs Committee of the Association of Home Appliance Manufacturers (AHAM) responded to the challenge by proposing the formation of a panel of consumer-oriented people, entirely independent of the industry or any part of its distribution structure. The Gas Appliance Manufacturers Association (GAMA) and the National Retail Merchants Association (NRMA) joined AHAM in creating, in March 1970, the then-unique Major Appliance Consumer Action Panel (MACAP). MACAP was established "to assure that consumers do, in fact, have a clear course to fair and honest handling of each case, that they are informed of this and how to avail themselves of it. . . . "[1]

After MACAP was created, other industries developed consumer action panels, including AUTOCAP (1973, automobiles), FICAP (1973, furniture), CRICAP (1973, carpets and rugs), and ICAP (1976, insurance). Of these, AUTOCAP was the most successful. By 1979, there were 45 AUTOCAPs in operation, mostly in major cities around the United States.[2] FICAP, sponsored by the Southern Furniture Manufacturers Association, was also a success, processing over 700 complaints per year. FICAP claimed over 46 percent customer satisfaction with results of

---

[1]   Major Appliance Consumer Action Panel, "Prospectus," March 6, 1970, p. 1.

[2]   *The Auto Dealer and the Consumer,* prepared jointly by Automotive Trade Association Managers and National Automobile Dealers Association (Washington, D.C.: 1979).

mediation.[3] CRICAP discontinued operations in August 1975, after processing fewer than 1,000 complaints.[4] ICAP, in a 1-year trial, processed fewer than 300 complaints, and was discontinued.[5]

Virginia Knauer was perhaps the most ardent advocate of industry-sponsored consumer action panels. She described consumer action panels as "a breakthrough in consumer complaint handling: an innovation of the decade."[6] Knauer suggested that the two key elements in consumer action panel success are consumer involvement and industry-wide involvement.

The success of consumer action panels depended upon consumer confidence that the panel existed to provide "fair and speedy resolution of any complaint that cannot be resolved directly with the company." One of the continuing challenges for the panels was the creation of consumer awareness of their services. Another challenge lay in the design of each panel to recognize the differences in industry structure, marketing practices, and technology of products.

A standardized model did not exist for a consumer action panel. As stated by Robert F. Longenecker, consumer affairs executive at Coca-Cola, and a leader in the development of the Society of Consumer Affairs Professionals (SOCAP):

A complaint system for the automobile industry, for the food industry, for the small appliance manufacturing industry would necessarily differ in procedures, format, and other unanticipated ways from either MACAP or CRICAP.[7]

Thus the AUTOCAPs were regional in coverage, staffed in part with dealers and trade association executives, whereas MACAP was national in scope and staffed mostly with consumer representatives. Yet, consumer action panels in both industries were quite successful in mediating consumer complaints.

---

[3] *1977 Audit of FICAP Operations,* Management Analysis Center Incorporated, p. 2.

[4] Maurice E. McDonald, *CRICAP Resolved Consumer Complaint Audit and Study,* A report to the Carpet and Rug Industry Consumer Action Professional Insurance Agents, Panel, December 20, 1974.

[5] *Insurance Consumer Action Panel Final Report* (Washington, D.C.: 1978).

[6] Virginia H. Knauer, "Consumer Redress: Some Encouraging Signs," in Sal Divita and Frank McLaughlin, eds., *Consumer Complaints: Public Policy Alternatives* (Washington, D.C.: Acropolis Books Ltd., 1975), p. 24.

[7] Robert F. Longenecker, "Complaint Handling by the Consumer Action Panels: MACAP and CRICAP," in Divita and McLaughlin, *Consumer Complaints,* p. 59.

MACAP ORGANIZATION

MACAP was cosponsored by the three industry-wide trade associations, representing manufacturers and distributors of major appliances and providers of appliance repair services. Individual appliance manufacturers and retailers comprised the membership of AHAM, GAMA, and NRMA. These three sponsoring associations shared the cost of MACAP in "proportion to the number of complaints directed to each association's member companies."[8] By 1978, the operating budget, in excess of $360,000, covered expenses for panel meetings, travel, MACAP publicity, and the MACAP chairman's per diem. In addition to funding, the sponsors provided executive and clerical staffs to handle correspondence and maintain individual complaint files.

The 10 MACAP panelists were academic and consumer organization people, who served without personal compensation except for travel expenses. The value of their time was estimated at $150,000 annually. The criteria governing selection as a panelist were (1) total independence of the appliance industry, and (2) a "special and varied" professional background. The panel met for 1½ to 3 days every 6 or 7 weeks and sought not only to resolve consumer appliance problems, but also to prevent them. Panelists advised and counseled industry in ways to improve its service to consumers and educated consumers on proper appliance purchase, use, and care.

Public Awareness

MACAP communicated appliance information and promoted MACAP services through public appearances, news releases, appliance labels, use and care manuals, newsletters, and encouragement of referrals. Panelists made public appearances as keynote speakers, lecturers, and panel participants at conferences and workshops throughout the country. Panelists made collectively over 90 television and 60 radio appearances from 1975 through 1977.

In addition to personal appearances, MACAP distributed news releases after each meeting and annually to review the progress of the panel's efforts. Periodically, MACAP also distributed national news releases with the purpose of keeping consumers up to date on appliance trends and innovations. Some of the releases dealt with new refrigerator-freezer operating noise, automatic oven cleaning expectations, and budgeting for appliance repairs.

[8] Material on MACAP organization and operation abstracted from *MACAP in Action: A Progress Report 1975–1977* (Chicago: MACAP, 1978), pp. 1–22.

In 1976, MACAP issued its first quarterly newsletter. *News and Notes* was distributed to about 3,500 consumer organizations, government representatives, key educators, home extension specialists, MACAP volunteers, appliance trade press, and selected consumer press. *News and Notes* provided a summary of cases handled by MACAP and provided advice that might aid in resolving complaints at the local level.

In addition, MACAP was publicized through labels affixed to appliances and by prominent reference in use and care manuals. By 1978, the majority of major appliances sold in the United States contained information about MACAP as an industry-sponsored mediation service available at no cost to all consumers.

MACAP also encouraged consumer agencies to forward appliance complaints to the panel for mediation. State consumer councils and local Better Business Bureaus, as well as federal agencies (such as the FTC and the President's Office of Consumer Affairs), referred consumer appliance problems to MACAP.

In its public awareness campaigns, MACAP recommended that consumers follow three steps prior to contacting MACAP. First, MACAP advised consumers to check fuses, plugs, use and cleaning procedures, and proper operation of controls. Consumers were then requested to work with the local dealer or a recommended service agency. If these steps were ineffective, MACAP suggested that the consumer contact the warrantor of the brand involved, either retailer or manufacturer; should the customer remain dissatisfied, the problem should be forwarded to MACAP. Experience showed that the majority of problems were resolved within the first three steps.

MACAP Complaint-Handling Procedure

MACAP required the following information to process a consumer complaint:

1. Consumer name, address, and telephone number.
2. Appliance type, brand name, model, and serial numbers.
3. Date of purchase.
4. Name and address of local dealer or service agency.
5. Clear description of the problem, and service required.
6. Copies of receipts and previous correspondence with service agency, dealer, and manufacturer or retailer.

MACAP's complaint-handling procedure consisted of two phases—communications and study—as shown in Figure 1. Every complaint was processed by MACAP through the communications phase, providing the

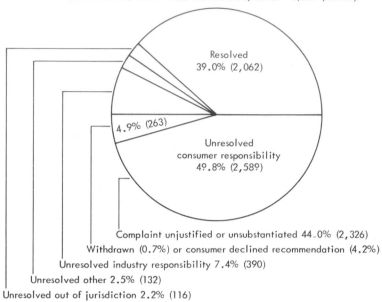

FIGURE 1   Analysis of Complaints Reviewed in Panel Meetings (Study Phase)
Complaints Processed and Closed from January 1968 through
December 31, 1977. Total closed complaints—5,289 (100%).

Resolved
39.0% (2,062)

4.9% (263)

Unresolved
consumer responsibility
49.8% (2,589)

Complaint unjustified or unsubstantiated 44.0% (2,326)
Withdrawn (0.7%) or consumer declined recommendation (4.2%)
Unresolved industry responsibility 7.4% (390)
Unresolved other 2.5% (132)
Unresolved out of jurisdiction 2.2% (116)

manufacturer or brand owner another chance to act on a complaint before
involving the panel. The complaint entered the study phase only if the company and consumer were unable to resolve the situation. Table 1 shows that
most MACAP complaints were resolved before the study phase.

Case Resolution

As shown in Table 1, individual cases were closed as resolved or
unresolved. Over the first 7 years of operation, 84.3 percent of complaints
were considered resolved. Any one of three situations prompted a file to be
"closed—resolved."

1. Both MACAP and the consumer were satisfied with the final resolution.
2. Consumer was satisfied, but the panel was not.
3. The panel was satisfied with company action taken since the complaint was referred to MACAP, but the consumer wanted further concessions.

Any one of four situations resulted in a "closed—unresolved" file:

1. Consumer withdrew complaint.
2. Consumer or company refused to accept a panel recommendation.

Table 1 DISPOSITION OF MACAP COMPLAINTS—CUMULATIVE
(PROCESSED FROM JANUARY 1968 TO DECEMBER 31, 1977)

	Total		Communications Phase		Study Phase	
Resolved						
Resolved	21,002	80.5%	18,940	72.6%	2,062	7.9%
Presumed resolved	591	3.8%	991	3.8%	—	—
Subtotal	21,593	84.3%	19,931	76.4%	2,062	7.9%
Unresolved						
Consumer's responsibility						
Complaint unjustified or unsubstantiated	2,326	8.9%	—		2,326	8.9%
Complaint withdrawn or consumer declined panel recommendation	565	2.2%	302	1.2%	263	1.0%
Subtotal	2,891	11.1%	302	1.2%	2,589	9.9%
Industry's responsibility						
Manufacturer or brand owner declined MACAP recommendation	390	1.5%	—	—	390	1.5%
Subtotal	390	1.5%	—	—	390	1.5%
Other						
Closed for other reasons	132	0.5%	—		132	0.5%
Closed out of jurisdiction	137	0.5%	21	0.1%	116	0.4%
Subtotal	269	1.0%	21	0.1%	248	0.9%
Complaints pending 12/31/77	543	2.1%	483	1.9%	60	0.2%
Subtotal	543	2.1%	483	1.9%	60	0.2%
Total	26,086	100.0%	20,737	79.6%	5,349	20.4%

Source: *MACAP 1977 Annual Audit*, Chicago.

3. Panel considered the complaint unjustified.
4. Complaint was out of MACAP's jurisdiction.[9]

Complaints requiring panel review in the study phase were typically complex and difficult differences-of-opinion situations that could not be resolved with the dealer, service agency, and manufacturer. In such cases, third-party volunteers were enlisted to make an on-site home visit. Volunteers did not need to be home economists as long as they were knowledgeable about the product or particular problem. Most volunteers were county agents of a statewide Cooperative Extension Service. Such local expertise reduced travel expenses and provided recognition of objectivity and impartiality.

Types of Complaints

Table 2 shows the type of products about which appliance consumers complained most frequently. Of the 17 appliances under MACAP's scope, refrigerator-freezers and kitchen ranges represented nearly two-thirds of all cases. Table 3 shows the type of problems most frequently experienced by complainants. Service and performance problems added to over two-thirds of all problem types. Fully 39 percent were resolved to the satisfaction of the consumer, and 44 percent were found to be unjustified or unsubstantiated.

Nolan reviewed the experience of ICAP by looking through the final report issued by the panel upon discontinuance of operations (Figure 2). He paid particular attention to the ICAP panel's review of their performance and procedures. ICAP had experienced difficulty in securing support of the insurance industry. The industry never really adopted the mediation concept. There also was not enough publicity, because of funding, to inform consumers that ICAP existed.

Nolan was also familiar with the failure of CRICAP. The problems with CRICAP lay primarily in the organizational structure of the panel, with all panelists being representatives of the industry. The procedures used by the panel also hindered performance. A major factor in failure was that the mediation process was cumbersome and overly lengthy. In addition, consumer acceptance of panel results was less than expected.

Nolan was sensitive to the question about which industries offered the most promise for the consumer action panel concept. He had a copy of a listing of the industries that received the most frequent complaints according to the United States Office of Consumer Affairs (Figure 3). He be-

---

[9]   This may occur if the complaint is a group complaint and not an individual claim, or if the issue has reached active litigation.

Table 2 MACAP COMPLAINTS RECEIVED BY TYPE OF PRODUCT

Type of Product	1977		1976		1975	
Refrigerator-freezer	1,188	34.3%	1,360	37.9%	1,558	39.4%
Range	1,040	30.0%	974	26.6%	1,045	26.4%
Washer	439	11.8%	417	11.4%	448	11.3%
Dishwasher	236	6.8%	246	6.7%	293	7.7%
Dryer	148	4.3%	204	5.5%	173	4.3%
Freezer	97	2.8%	164	4.4%	142	3.6%
Room air conditioner	155	4.5%	105	2.8%	153	3.8%
Washer/dryer	22	0.6%	36	0.9%	40	1.0%
Water heater	24	0.7%	15	0.5%	27	0.6%
Microwave oven	117	3.4%	88	2.4%	38	0.9%
Disposer	8	0.2%	21	0.5%	16	0.4%
Trash compactor	7	0.2%	18	0.4%	15	0.4%
Humidifier	1	—	2	—	3	0.1%
Dehumidifier	4	0.1%	3	—	4	0.1%
Incinerator	0	—	0	—	0	—
Other	12	0.3%	0	—	1	—
Total	3,468	100.0%	3,657	100.0%	3,956	100.0%

Source: MACAP 1977 Annual Audit, Chicago.

Table 3　MACAP COMPLAINTS BY TYPE
OF PROBLEM (TOTAL
COMPLAINTS RECEIVED
IN 1974)

Type of Problem	Percent of Total
Service	35.9
Delays for service and parts	13.1
Dissatisfaction with service	9.5
Alleged excessive repairs	6.7
Cost	6.6
Performance	32.5
Alleged defective appliance	13.0
General performance	12.0
Operating noise	2.8
Temperature maintenance	1.9
Running time	1.2
Other	1.6
Parts failure	10.4
Nonresponsiveness of manufacturers/dealers	3.6
Food loss	5.3
Warranties	3.5
Purchasing dissatisfaction	2.8
Damage in delivery	1.5
Misrepresentation	0.9
Inadequate buying information	0.4
Damaged finishes	3.3
Safety	2.0
Improper installation	0.1
Other	0.6
Total	100.0

lieved that several of the industries might benefit from use of consumer action panels.

The Speech

James Nolan looked at the pile of documents and information regarding consumer panels spread across his desk relating to consumer mediation panels. Nolan could well appreciate the work and intentions behind the panels. He admired the professionalism of those individuals on the unsuccessful panels who had taken the time and effort to diagnose their failure.

Now, thought Nolan, all he had to do was to organize his thoughts so that he could prepare the speech. He knew that SOCAP included in its membership most of the managers of consumer affairs departments for major companies. He was also aware, from the activities of the Chicago chapter of SOCAP, that the membership was quite knowledgeable about complaint handling, including mediation and arbitration procedures. Still, he felt that he could make a contribution to the annual SOCAP meeting. He began to draft his speech.

FIGURE 2   Insurance Consumer Action Panel*

Lessons Learned from the Pilot Period

Clearly, the pilot program did not achieve the expectations of its founders. While the organizational machinery worked well, there were too few cases (351) brought to ICAP for resolution to permit the drawing of valid conclusions about the usefulness of ICAP. Thus the experience was not an adequate test of the feasibility of an informal complaint-handling system in the insurance industry. Since the experience did not provide sufficient data to draw conclusions about generic or repeated problem areas, the panel was not in a position to render such advice to the insurance industry.

It is the panel's judgment that a number of factors contributed to the ineffectiveness of the pilot period. These factors are addressed below:

Assumptions of the Need. The United States Office of Consumer Affairs (OCA) received a large number of complaints against the insurance industry. Some insurance commissioners had agreed to forward unresolved complaints to the panel. Other insurance commissioners believed unresolved complaints were insignificant in number.

During the panel's existence, participating insurance commissioners forwarded only a few unresolved complaints. Why more complaints were not forwarded is not clear.

At the same time, conversations with selected executives in the insurance industry suggested that unresolved complaints are insignificant in number. They pointed out that the insurance industry, unlike other industries, already had a built-in mechanism for complaint resolution; namely, the state insurance commissioners. Thus the industry saw little need for an additional complaint-handling mechanism.

The issue of whether or not a need existed for a third-party,

* Abstracted from *End-of-Year Report of Insurance Consumer Action Panel Report* (Washington, D.C.: Professional Insurance Agents, 1978), pp. 8–17.

complaint-handling system in the insurance industry was considered of fundamental importance. Because of the opposing views of the OCA and the industry executives, the panel recommended research to prove or disprove the need.

PIA Sponsorship. The panel concluded the PIA's sole sponsorship of ICAP was inappropriate. For the panel to have worked effectively between the purchaser and the company, the panel needed the support of insurance companies. ICAP should have had a readily available point of contact in each company party to a dispute. Such was not the case with PIA sponsorship. PIA's membership consisted of independent insurance agents.

Insurance complaints involve companies, agents, and adjusting firms; thus the effective operation of ICAP required that it be sponsored by all members of the industry, with company support being paramount.

PIA Support. PIA's major contributions to ICAP were to organize the panel and hire the administrator. In addition, PIA presented papers about ICAP at industry conferences and conducted public relations about the test program. These efforts served as the primary means of informing the industry and consumers of the test program's existence and progress.

The ICAP panel report concluded these efforts were insufficient. Increased efforts should have been given to gaining the cooperation and support of the insurance companies or their trade associations. More attention should have been given to building the leadership function of ICAP. In particular, linking relationships between the panel and the affected companies were underdeveloped.

It appears that PIA acted as a facilitating agent, but additional attention should have been paid to defining the need of consumers and in particular the needs of companies and commissioners. There appeared to be a complete adoption of the notion that there were thousands of unresolved complaints.

Finally, the difficulties encountered in preparing and presenting cases to a panel located thousands of miles away from the affected consumer was not fully understood. The panel recommended regional ICAPs to facilitate communication with affected customers.

Undercapitalization of ICAP. By design, the pilot program was limited to complaints submitted by four participating state insurance commissioners. It was not intended that the general public would be encouraged or invited to submit complaints to ICAP during the test period. Consequently, ICAP communicated on a broad basis with consumers only to the extent that PIA's public relations efforts attracted the attention of the general media. Unsolicited consumer responses generated by this exposure were directly related to the intensity of the media coverage.

It is clear that consumer complaints will not find their way to ICAP unless the affected consumers are made aware of ICAP's existence. ICAP was in the unfortunate position of being unable to communicate with these consumers, given budgetary constraints. Further, such constraints limited ICAP's ability to win corporate participation. In short, the effective future operation of an ICAP required sufficient funding to promote the concept to the industry and affected consumers.

Commissioners Forwarding Complaints. The pilot program was based on the assumption that selected state insurance commissioners would forward their unresolved complaints. Initially it was believed that five State Insurance Commissioners had agreed to participate in this pilot program. Subsequently, one withdrew. Of the remaining four, only three forwarded cases, one of which forwarded only one.

Companies Not Convinced of Benefits. Insurance companies were not convinced of benefits they might derive from the existence of ICAP. Company executives not only did not support ICAP, they openly avoided involvement. Executives repeated claims that no significant number of unresolved complaints existed. Companies felt threatened by ICAP because they perceived it as a government-sponsored program. This notion was inadvertently reinforced by ICAP's introduction as a government-sponsored program. Further, the original ICAP letterhead had OCA shown as co-sponsor. Thus companies had ample reason to fear wider entanglement with still another government agency.

Finally, confusion existed over the meaning of unresolved complaints. Too often, unresolved complaints were understood to mean unsatisfactory resolution of claims. Company executives had difficulty understanding that complaints may not necessarily be related to specific claims.

In summary, the insurance industry for a variety of reasons was not favorably disposed to encouraging ICAP's continuance.

Conclusions

On the basis of the experience, the panel advanced two conclusions:

1. ICAP, in its present form, should be discontinued because it fails to have the support it needs to function effectively.
2. It is the judgment of the panel that the future of ICAP hinges on the determination of the real need for a third-party, complaint-handling system in the insurance area. The conflicting evidence on the need for an ICAP requires speedy resolution.

The dichotomy of views between government and industry needs to be investigated so that the facts of the matter can be documented. This matter should not be left to opinion.

Recommendations

Should the need for a third-party, complaint-handling system be validated and if ICAP were to be continued:

1. It should be designed to meet the needs of consumers *and* companies.
2. It must be sponsored by a trade association that represents the affected companies.
3. It should have a board of directors on which representatives of business, consumers and commissioners are represented.
4. It should encompass all areas of insurance, including health and life, since consumers have difficulty differentiating between one kind of insurance and another.
5. The panel should be expanded to nine including representatives from companies, state insurance departments, women, and minorities. Care should be taken to avoid people who, although fair and objective in their decision making, may be perceived as threatening to industry and/or consumer support.
6. Attention should be given to regionalizing the sphere of activity to make the ICAP panel more available to the affected consumers.
7. The design of an ICAP program must recognize the need to convey its existence to affected customers.
8. Finally, any subsequent activity should have financial support which is sufficient to achieve effective operations. Failure to provide an adequate level of funding amounts to strangling the program. It is the judgment of the panel that industry should either support the program adequately or deny support completely. A middle ground is an unsatisfactory solution.

FIGURE 3   Top Twenty Complaint Categories

The Office of Consumer Affairs (OCA) has compiled a list of the top 20 consumer complaints it received in 1977. The top 20 complaints have remained relatively constant with minor fluctuations over the past 4 years, with only one new complaint making the top 20 in 1977—the "Watches/Clock" category. Complaints in this area centered on the problems of service, especially when a timepiece has been sent to the manufacturer for repair. Also, many consumers seem to be having trouble with the LED watches.

"Automobile Tires" climbed from 12th place in 1976 to 10th place in 1977, possibly because many new car buyers did not receive a spare tire with their cars (as a result of a rubber strike in 1976). In addition, there has been an increase in the number of complaints about the quality of original equipment tires.

Here is the 1977 list by rank, category and percentage of total complaints received in each category*:

Rank	Category	% of Total
1	Automobiles	21.70
2	Mail order	9.65
3	Business practices	4.98
4	Credit	3.73
5	Appliances	3.38
6	Housing/real estate	2.54
7	Insurance	2.17
8	Food	2.04
9	Travel	2.01
10	Auto tires	1.69
11	Magazines	1.67
12	Advertising	1.64
13	Television/radio	1.61
14	Watches/clocks	1.31
15	Mobile homes/recreational vehicles	1.05
16	Utilities	1.01
17	Home repairs	0.09
18	Household	0.08
19	Movers	0.07
20	Medical/dental	0.07

* OCA stresses that it uses these categories in the broadest of terms. OCA is in the process of revising its product classification code to more accurately reflect complaint data received by the office.

Source: *Consumer News,* March 15, 1978, p. 3.

MAJOR APPLIANCE CONSUMER ACTION PANEL (B): MEDIATION OF A CONSUMER COMPLAINT*

Virginia L. Habeeb, chairperson and director of MACAP, was seated at the head of the conference table reviewing her agenda for the upcoming meeting. Habeeb was particularly pleased that James Nolan, executive administrator for MACAP, had gotten five of ten panel members to meet on

* This case is not intended to provide a precise account of the thinking of the parties involved.

such short notice, especially since MACAP members lived in locales scattered throughout the United States. Habeeb had elected to call this special meeting because the MACAP case load had been increasing steadily, even though the panel had met 20 times in the past 2 years. This meeting was intended to handle accumulated complaints on food loss due to refrigerator-freezer malfunctions.

The food-loss cases scheduled for consideration at the meeting had left the communication phase, where manufacturer and consumer attempted to settle their differences, and had entered the study or second phase. In the study phase, the panel acted as mediator and studied each case in depth. All necessary information was gathered from the manufacturer, retailer/service agency, and consumer by staff members. In some cases, an independent third party made an on-site investigation and filed a report. The panel then had a detailed summary of the events from both sides.

The panel's decisions could be closed as resolved or unresolved. Resolved cases occurred when the consumer accepted the panel's findings. Unresolved cases included those in which the panel, manufacturer, or consumer did not reach a mutual agreement. If the closing was based on manufacturer refusal, it was filed as "industry's responsibility," since the panel's recommendation had been vetoed. the same procedure applied to a consumer refusal. Depending upon the circumstances, the panel could decide the situation was out of jurisdiction. For example, a problem with a consumer appliance used for commercial purposes, would not be considered by MACAP.

Habeeb looked up and smiled a greeting as the MACAP panel members began entering the room. As they were getting settled and conversing with each other, Habeeb glanced around at them.

Seated to her immediate left was Mary Neil Alexander, an associate professor in home economics at Winthrop College, located in Rock Hill, South Carolina. Alexander had 20 years of experience in education, appliance industry, utility, and consumer fields. Seated next to her was Jason Annis. Annis was an engineering consultant from Manhattan, Kansas, and a researcher in mining, residential, and industrial air conditioning and ventilation and a former Kansas State University instructor in engineering. Talking with Annis was Elsie Fetterman, a professor of family economics, Cooperative Extension Service, University of Connecticut, Storrs, Connecticut. Fetterman was a family economics expert and an educator and administrator with over 27 years experience in consumer education. Seated to Habeeb's right was William F. White, a retired appliance service technician coordinator with Commonwealth Edison located in Chicago. White has over 30 years of experience as an appliance service technician and instructor in field service and service training. Talking with White was Edwin P.

Palumbo, executive director of the Rhode Island Consumers' Council and professor of economics at Providence College (see Figure 1).

The agenda, which had been prepared by Nolan, included 10 cases on food loss. Each panel member had received copies of the case files a week earlier, including a brief summary of the problem and MACAP staff findings. The panel was ready to consider the first case, a complaint of refrigerator-freezer malfunction filed by a couple from Woodstock, Georgia.

As outlined in Figures 2 to 8, the food-loss problem was complicated by the fact that the warranty on Mr. and Mrs. Logan's refrigerator-freezer had expired 2 months prior to the problem. The documentation provided by the Logans, together with the information supplied by Woodstock House Appliance Co., indicated that the problem was a recurrent one. The on-site inspection report filed by a MACAP volunteer verified the damage to carpet and ventilation ducting. The panel was now ready to discuss case 30794.

FIGURE 1   MACAP Panel Members*

Mary Neil Alexander —Associate Professor, School of Home Economics, Winthrop College, Rock Hill, South Carolina. A home economist with 20 years experience in the education, appliance industry, utility and consumer magazine fields.

> *"Having served consumers in a variety of professional capacities, with particular emphasis on household appliances—in education, with utilities and in industry, I view MACAP as a very special opportunity to serve American consumers and the industry which provides these important household goods.*
>
> *"MACAP has a unique role which is only possible through the cooperation of industry and consumers. This liaison function between a highly technical and often very specialized industry and a cross section of appliance users who have varied backgrounds cannot be fulfilled adequately in a simple, uniform procedure. As important as each consumer is, a fair resolution to each problem is helping to promote the interests of* all *consumers while strengthening the businesses designed to serve them."*

Dr. Jason C. Annis—Engineering Consultant, Manhattan, Kansas. Rescarcher in air quality in the fields of mining, residential and industrial air conditioning and kitchen ventilation, and educator in mechanical engineering, formerly with Kansas State University.

* *MACAP 5th Anniversary Report,* May 1975, pp. 7–8.

"I attempt to provide MACAP with an understanding of the compromises inherently involved in engineering design. The Panelists and staff understand 'defects in materials and workmanship' but I have tried to interject the concept of 'defects in engineering.' Coming from a small Midwest university town where many persons are competent to do their own repair, I am perhaps more sensitive to costs of repair and parts than the other Panelists.

"The Panel has a dual role—first, to act as ombudsman when the consumer has economically little recourse to other avenues; and secondly, to influence industry's complaint handling procedures to the point where a third party such as MACAP is no longer required.

"I have high hopes for the MACAP procedure and philosophy. Every consumer needs to understand his appliances better, manufacturers need to match the promises of their sales personnel to the real operation of their products and MACAP must act as a catalyst to see that it happens."

Dr. Elsie Fetterman—Professor of Family Economics, Cooperative Extension Service, University of Connecticut, Stoors. Family economics specialist, educator and administrator with over 27 years experience in a wide range of communications assignments in consumer education.

"When I was first invited to join MACAP, I was asked if I could give one day every six weeks to two months to work on Panel business. That was true in the beginning. If I had been asked to give fifty to sixty days a year to MACAP, I am sure I would have declined the invitation. However, the more involved I became with MACAP, the more excited I became and I found that I was volunteering more time because of the responsiveness of the manufacturers and consumers. When you see industry changing behavior, you feel that MACAP has made an important contribution to consumer needs."

Virginia Habeeb—Director, Editorial Services, New York. A writer, editor, and communications specialist with experience as a utility home economist and editor of a national magazine.

"I see MACAP not only as a complaint-handling mechanism but an effective consumer education source. A prime contribution I bring to the Panel is one of communications expertise. This enables me to help MACAP interpret consumer appliance problems into positive tools—such as pertinent press releases and publications. It is my hope that MACAP can help reduce the number of appliance complaints by promoting more effective communications between the consumer and dealer at point of purchase and informing the consumer on proper appliance use and care. Consumer education has been a successful activity with MACAP through the mutuality of trust that exists between its sponsors and the Panel, as well as the dedication of its staff."

Edwin P. Palumbo—Executive Director of the Rhode Island Consumers' Council, Providence and Professor of Economics, Providence College. An economist, lecturer, and author with special expertise in consumer affairs.

"I am pleased to be a MACAP panelist. I appreciate the opportunity to share in a personal way in its efforts to make a significant contribution to the development of an efficient, effective, and fair method for the resolution of consumer-business differences. For me there is much personal satisfaction in being a part of this effort; my associates on the Panel, along with staff, add an extra measure of satisfaction.

"I am particularly encouraged by the program's potential to contribute to a fuller understanding and enrichment of consumer-business relations generally. This potential is enhanced by awareness and sincere willingness to give attention to the numerous matters which need consideration in order to achieve the mutual trust in market transactions."

William F. White—Retired Appliance Service Technician Coordinator, Commonwealth Edison, Chicago. An appliance service technician and instructor with over 30 years experience in appliance field service and service training.

"Perhaps the most important contribution I bring to MACAP is that, while being on a limited, fixed pension income, I am more aware of the financial hardship of the retired consumer. I also bring a most important facet to MACAP in the form of practical experience with servicing major appliances; consumer's demands and needs at the time of service; and manufacturers' policies regarding warranty, parts and service availability, and service training.

"MACAP will and does work because of a complete cross section of available knowledge from the Panelists. My continuing efforts will be to convey to the other Panel members the practical side of in-house servicing of major appliances."

FIGURE 2   Arctic-Zephyr Refrigerator-Freezer

Warranty

Full One-Year Warranty on Mechanical or Electrical Parts and Mechanical Adjustments.

For one year from the date of purchase, when the refrigerator is installed and operated in accordance with the instructions in the Owners Manual and Installation Manual, _____ will repair or replace any mechanical or electrical parts in this refrigerator-freezer, if defective in material or workmanship, and perform any necessary adjustments at no charge.

The above warranty coverage applies to _____ refrigerators and refrigerator-freezers used for private family use only. If warranty service is needed, contact the nearest authorized service center located throughout the United States.

This warranty gives you specific legal rights, and you may also have other rights which vary from state to state.

FIGURE 3   Woodstock Home Appliance Co. Service Report

Call: M. B. Logan   Date: June 13, 1978
      212 Sabrina Court   Time: 4:30 PM
      Woodstock, GA   Service Agent: R. Rivers

  Item: Refrigerator, A. Zephyr
Model: ZA109C77492
Status: Warranty

Complaint: Cooling system stopped working.
Date Notified: June 13, 1977

  Work: Inspected unit—didn't find anything wrong. Everything hooked
         up OK. Owner said had stopped then started. Told her couldn't
         do anything if it was OK. Did find water in condensation channels
         so it looked like she was right. Turned thermostat on/off and it
         started-up alright. Looked at plug—it was OK. Door shut OK.
         Told owner to call if it stopped again.

Charge: Warranty work, 4:30–5:01, 31 minutes. Call exceeded 30 min-
         utes—1-hour charge/10.00.

subtotal $10.00   Certification of Work
tax   0.40
                _____
total $10.40
method of payment: Warranty

                              R. Rivers

FIGURE 4   Woodstock Home Appliance Co. Service Report

Call: M. B. Logan   Date: March 18, 1979
          212 Sabrina Court   Time: 11:39
          Woodstock, GA   Service Agent: Corbett, Mgr.

  Item: Refrigerator, A. Zephyr
Model: ZA109C77492
Status: Out of Warranty

Complaint: Stopped running and defrosted.
Date Notified: March 18, 1979.

  Work: Upon arrival, found unit had completely ceased to function. Con-
         ducted external inspection of wiring—found it intact and opera-
         tional. Inspected the interior electrical system at all points and
         upon removal of the interior thermostat cover saw a short circuit,
         indicated by a blackened area around a loose wire terminal that
         was in contact with metal side. Wire led to defrost timer—

mechanism damaged. Removed and replaced timer. Soldered terminal back into place, rewired. Tested circuit and cycled system several times—OK. Left refrigerator operating normally.

Charge: Timer assembly, Part ZA0T39277 - 28.00
Wire - .79
Labor 2-1/2 units @ 10.00/hr. - 25.00

subtotal	$53.79	Certification of Work Performed
tax	2.15	
total	$55.94	
method of payment:	Check	

M. A. Corbett

FIGURE 5   Letter to Mr. Logan from Service Outlet

Woodstock Home Appliance Co.
Canton Highway
Woodstock, GA 30188

March 21, 1979

Mr. Michael B. Logan
212 Sabrina Court
Woodstock, GA 30100

Dear Mr. Logan:

As you requested, this letter is to inform you that due to your warranty having lapsed I cannot authorize warranty coverage for repairs on your North Wind refrigerator-freezer. I cannot charge any work on your appliance to the company.

If you believed your refrigerator was not running properly you should have requested service before the warranty lapsed.

I am sure you will understand my position and the fact that I am acting under terms of the warranty.

Very truly yours,

M. A. Corbett
Manager

FIGURE 6 Letter from Chillbane Mfg. to Mr. Logan

1781 Loop West
Chicago, IL

April 17, 1979

Mr. Michael B. Logan
212 Sabrina Court
Woodstock, GA 30188

Dear Mr. Logan:

Mr. N. C. Meredith, Vice President of Production and Servicing, has requested that I investigate your complaint about your Arctic Zephyr refrigerator-freezer. I would like to be able to honor your request for warranty coverage concerning your food loss.

But, Mr. Logan, the problem in your case is that the warranty on your Arctic Zephyr refrigerator has expired. I have contacted the dealer you referred to in your letter and have discussed the matter with him. Mr. Corbett stated that he sent a trained service representative out to your home who carefully inspected your appliance. The service representative stated your appliance was fully operational.

I have carefully investigated the circumstances surrounding your complaint and I must reluctantly conclude that we cannot accept responsibility for your unit's failure since it was two months out of warranty. We sympathize with your feelings, but we feel we can only establish warranty standards for a reasonable amount of time. I trust you will understand our position. If I can be of any further service to you, please call me through our toll free telephone line at 800-123-4567.

Sincerely,

Patrick Flautt
Customer Service Manager
Chillbane Manufacturing

FIGURE 7   Letter to MACAP from Mr. Logan

Logan and Pollack
Attorneys at Law
771 Logan Street
Atlanta, Georgia 30308

April 27, 1979

Dear Sirs:

I am addressing your consumer mediation panel as a last resort prior to instituting litigation against the Chillbane Corporation, manufacturers of the Arctic Zephyr refrigerator, which I own.

I have been advised that your panel acts as mediator between consumers and appliance manufacturers if an impasse has been reached regarding warranty coverage and the like.

I have a complaint against the Chillbane Corporation in regard to the performance of their product and their subsequent failure to repair damages incurred as a result of their machine's failure.

My immediate complaint lies in the failure of the unit to execute the task it was designed for; i.e., refrigeration of its contents. A subsequent complaint concerns the damage incurred to my residence as a result of refrigerator failure. It would be simplest if I related the events chronologically. I have enclosed a diagram of my kitchen layout to assist you in understanding events.

I purchased my Arctic Zephyr deluxe model refrigerator from an authorized dealer for Chillbane Corporation on January 7, 1978. The retail outlet was company-owned and an authorized service center, located in Woodstock Georgia. My house had just been built when the refrigerator was delivered. The "authorized service representative" delivered and installed the refrigerator. He discussed the operation procedures with my wife and I, left the operating manual and dated warranty certificate, and departed.

The refrigerator operated normally until one morning in June. When I came into the kitchen and opened the refrigerator, I realized it had stopped operating. I had no idea how long it had been stopped. My wife called the service center as soon as they opened and requested a warranty service call. I was told by the repairman that as far as he could see, it was "OK." If it stopped again, we were to call the dealer.

After that visit the unit functioned normally, except for occasional periods where the temperature setting seemed to fluctuate or cycle up and down. If the thermostat device was "thumped" it cleared up immediately. This occasional problem did not appear to warrant a repair call.

However, on the morning of September 21, 1978 we found the unit had again stopped. I cycled the thermostat switch and waited to see if it would start. I was then distracted by a telephone call from my office. The call was rather lengthy and when I got back to the refrigerator it was running normally. I called the dealer and requested a repairman. Once again, the service call involved only a minor adjustment fully covered by the warranty. Unfortunately, neither I nor the repair shop can find the records of this second visit.

On March 18, 1979, my Arctic Zephyr malfunctioned again. My wife and I had gone to Savannah for St. Patricks Day. Upon our return, we found the Zephyr had failed completely while we were gone. The contents of the refrigerator and freezer, valued at $300 dollars, were completely spoiled.

In addition to this direct loss, there were also some other damages resulting from the system failure. The Arctic Zephyr freezer unit is an integral part of the main compartment. The freezer compartment sits over the main food compartment and has a lightweight panel door with a magnetic latch. To reach the freezer, the main door must be opened. I mentioned this feature so you will understand the following chain of events.

When the Zephyr's cooling system blew its last breath, the interior naturally began to defrost. The freezer compartment has an automatic ice maker. It seems the ice container leaks. When the ice melted, it pooled in the freezer compartment until the weight of the water forced that lightweight door open. The water then cascaded into the main compartment. The ice maker draws its supply, in part, from a condensation collector. Thus, you have the ice maker busily collecting condensation, cycling through its system, pumping into the compartment and hence to the bottom of the refrigerator. In addition, the frozen items defrosted and being soggy shifted and some fell out of the compartment. Some items apparently struck other items such as eggs; all of which gathered in the bottom of the compartment. Add to this other such items such as "Poppin Fresh Rolls" in tubes that required chilling. As they heated up, they exploded taking with them containers with contents such as orange juice.

I had a chance to appreciate this interaction of the Arctic Zephyr's contents because when I opened the refrigerator door the mess came pouring out over my then bare feet. My house is built in the "tri-level" style and the den is off the kitchen and the floor is 4-1/2 feet below it (see diagram). This mess proceeded to flow over the edge and onto the wall-to-wall carpet. As I stopped the flow with some dishcloths, I noticed the flow was also going down a floor vent of the central air and heat system.

I immediately requested a serviceman to come out to inspect the unit and repair it. The dealership manager came out and inspected the refrigerator, finding that a short circuit had caused the defrost timer to activate itself and then the defrost timer burned out, the refrigerator had turned itself off. The defrost timer was replaced and some rewiring also done. After inspecting the warranty, the manager announced that the unit was out of warranty and he would have to charge me for repairs. We discussed the matter, but the dealer, a Mr. Corbett, was adamant in his statements that he could not honor the warranty. He said he appreciated the nature of the situation, but "his hands were tied." Corbett gave me the name of a service manager at the nearest plant to contact. I also requested he give me a letter stating his stand on the issue.

The service area manager at the plant was a Mr. Garcia. It took five phone calls over five days to contact Mr. Garcia, even though his secretary took my name, number, and purpose of each call. Finally, when I threatened litigation, I was able to speak to Mr. Garcia. I stated my experiences and requested to know what I might be able to expect under the given circumstances. Mr. Garcia said he would have to review the case and would call me back. After several days I called him and had to go through a similar routine as the first time; repeated calls and then intimidation. Mr. Garcia said he was not authorized to consider my case at his level. He referred me to the Vice President for Customer Relations, a Mr. Meredith.

Mr. Meredith was not in to receive my repeated calls. I then sent a registered letter with a summation of events and a list of times I would contact him by telephone, for his convenience. In my next call, I was informed that Mr. Meredith was out of town inspecting plants and would be gone for one week.

This, then, is the situation as it stands. I have sought dialogue with the company at various levels to no avail. There has been no discussion, indeed I have been given the polite "brush-off." I contact your panel as a last resort. I am tired and disgusted with the entire affair. I can almost look forward to a meeting in court. It will be a much more expensive proposition for Chillbane. I believe, if they elect not to discuss the matter, that it will cost them far more in dollars and adverse publicity than a discussion and possible settlement would have. My intention here is simply to request a discussion with Chillbane. I simply wish to submit to them the idea of a "rule of reason"—are my actions those of a reasonable man given the circumstances? If Chillbane does not wish to consider it, I am sure the courts will.

Sincerely yours,

M. B. Logan

FIGURE 8   Volunteer On-Site Inspection Report

To: MACAP Panel

From: Mary Carol Trombley
             Home Economics Instructor, East Georgia College
             Case No: 30794

On-Site Inspection Report

Date: June 2, 1979

Report

I arrived at the Logan house and was met by both Mr. and Mrs. Logan. I was invited to inspect the area with or without their presence. I asked them to accompany me and to explain the problem.

After inspection of the refrigerator-freezer unit, I went down the stairs into the den and looked at the area immediately under the wall and below the refrigerator. The wall-to-wall carpet, a deep rust color, was bleached out to a yellowish color and the bristles were stiff and unyielding to the touch. The Logans said this condition persisted in spite of having been cleaned several times with rug cleaners. The stain is in the shape of a rough half circle, extending out from the wall in about a two-foot radius.

Comments

The time of the visit itself was not by precise appointment, I arrived unannounced and proceeded to the area immediately. The house is only a year and a half old and the kitchen is well designed and well kept. The refrigerator plug is the only electrical connection in the wall socket and the wiring is in sound condition. The design of the unit corresponds with Mr. Logan's description (as does the layout in his diagram). There has been damage to the carpet in the room below and there is a noticeable odor in the vicinity of the ventilation duct. The smell also pervades the house to a degree. The carpet stain appears to be deep and permanent, and in my experience will have to be replaced since it is of a wall-to-wall style.

I stopped at the service facilitiy and confirmed the first service call, but the second visit could not be confirmed. I was told that there had been two service technicians leave about that time, one of whom was released due to poor performance. Upon return to my office, I called the heating and air conditioning firm mentioned by Mr. Logan. I was told that the ducting in the kitchen area would have to be removed for cleaning and it would be cheaper to replace it.

Recommendation

I find Mr. Logan's report to be accurate and the nature of it to be sufficiently serious to be reviewed by the MACAP panel.

DAYS INNS OF AMERICA, INC.: USING CUSTOMER FEEDBACK AS AN INPUT INTO MARKETING DECISION MAKING

Roy B. Burnette, senior vice president of Marketing and Public Relations, Days Inns of America, Inc., settled in to his seat for the flight to San Francisco. He would preside the next day over the grand opening of his company's 310th motel, a 500-room facility near the San Francisco airport. He was particularly proud of this event, as it represented the first Days Inn to be opened on the West Coast. Consistent with the corporate expansion plan to reach 1,000 units by 1988, this would be the first of 200 Days Inns in California.

His mind flashed back to another flight 7 years earlier, when he had first met Cecil B. Day, Sr., founder of Days Inns of America, Inc. Burnette had just completed a tour of duty as a pilot in the Navy and was on his way to the University of Florida to begin studies in law. Day had engaged him in conversation on the flight and offered him an attractive position with a rapidly growing motel chain. Instead of going to law school, Burnette accepted the offer. After 5 years, he was named to his present position and, subsequently, to the board of directors of the privately held company.

His reverie interrupted by the flight attendant's request for beverage preference, Burnette opened his briefcase to remove materials he planned to review while in flight. The first item was a consultant's report written by a marketing professor from a southeastern business school. The mandate given to the consultant was to review the computerized customer feedback system used by Days Inns management to track customer satisfaction. The impetus for the study had come from the senior vice president for operations who had expressed concern over use of the system as an input in the determination of bonuses for motel managers. Apparently, several district managers had expressed concern over the accuracy of the reports. Since the system had been in place for over a year and had processed feedback from over 40,000 guests, the executive committee had agreed to fund the study, not only to determine whether it was a valid input into bonus computation, but also to determine the cost effectiveness of the feedback system.

The report was entitled "An Evaluation of Customer Feedback Measurement at Days Inns." The conclusions and recommendations from the report are shown in Figure 1. Burnette noted that the report contained a substantial number of recommendations. This was a bit surprising since the directive to the consultant had been simply to review the cost effectiveness of the system. Burnette had scheduled a meeting with the senior vice president of operations on the morning of his return to Atlanta, so he decided to review the report during the remainder of the flight.

FIGURE 1   Summary of Consultant's Conclusions and Recommendations

As stated earlier in this report, the review of the Customer Satisfaction Information System (CSIS) was conducted by interviews with key personnel, examination of 500 cards selected at random, and review of the past year's weekly summaries. The review shows that the system is used to identify and correct problems and, less frequently, to highlight and reward effective performance. The levels of reported satisfaction have risen consistently over the year to support the belief that the system is an effective means to provide accountability for guest satisfaction.

The review shows that there remains a substantial opportunity to expand the system into a positive marketing tool. Also, the system output can be enhanced to provide still better information to management at all levels of the company. The four principal conclusions of the study are offered, together with recommendations for each.

Conclusions and Recommendations

1. There is potential for system abuse by motel managers and front-desk personnel. No evidence was found to suggest that employees submit comment cards to the system. However, evidence was found which suggests that some properties are lax in keeping cards in all rooms at all times.

An exception report should be prepared for each property that has a response rate above 3 percent or below 0.5 percent. Since the company average response rate is 1.5 percent of room nights, the exception report would highlight properties that might not be following the system adequately. District managers would be responsible for followup with exceptional properties.

2. The system does not utilize fully the information provided by guests. The reports simply summarize responses from all guests. Further analysis of subgroups would provide additional insight on problem areas, as well as provide input for the market research function.

Exception reports should be developed to examine the satisfaction of first-time guests, business travelers, listed reasons for intentions to not return, and so forth. Such reports, run on a periodic basis, would suggest fruitful areas for management attention. For instance, any complaint that required corrective action could be highlighted on an exception report which would require followup action by the motel manager accountable to the district manager.

Presently, name and address data provided on about 65 percent of the cards is not captured in the computer system. Zip-code data could be used to develop profiles of guest origin under the assumption that all guests are equally likely to submit a card when an exceptional visit is experienced. Name and address data, when coupled with other data about the visit, could be used for ongoing market research efforts. For instance, 6 months or so after a visit, a questionnaire could be sent to determine additional experience with Days Inns. This leads directly to the third conclusion.

3. No follow-up is conducted with those guests who provide comments. A major opportunity exists for effective followup communications with several types of respondents.

All first-time guests should get a letter of welcome from the president of Days Inns. In addition, the letter should include a Days Inns directory and a coupon good for a 10 percent discount redeemable on a subsequent visit. Encouragement of repurchase should lead directly to the development of an expanded loyal customer base.

All guests who indicate that they will not choose Days Inns in the future should receive a follow-up questionnaire to determine the reasons for their dissatisfaction and to determine appropriate remedies. A trial of this recommendation to 150 dissatisfied guests produced a 50 percent response rate, of whom 73 percent indicated that they would try Days Inns again in the future.

All guests who take the time to write a letter to the company should receive a personally addressed letter promptly from customer relations. These letters should be added to the customer feedback computer reports. Copies of the letters should be forwarded to motel managers and district managers for further follow-up.

All other guests should receive a brief note expressing appreciation for their comments. The brief note should be appropriate to the nature of the comments provided.

4. Additional feedback information could be gained at little cost. In fact, the card could be redesigned to drop the questions that yield few useful data. Such questions could be replaced with others of more benefit to management.

Since motel satisfaction is often a function of friendly, prompt service, space for the name of an employee who provided exceptional service could be added to the card. This would provide management with an opportunity to highlight and reward superior service.

Since September Days Club is a major attraction for senior citizens, space could be provided on the card for those guests who desire more information about the club. Such guests could be sent an application form along with a copy of the *September Days* quarterly magazine.

It is recognized that adoption of the recommendations outlined in this report would increase substantially the cost of the customer feedback system. However, the increased information should provide benefits far in excess of the costs involved.

THE UNITED STATES LODGING INDUSTRY

The U.S. lodging industry was composed of both chain and independent hotels and motels. The services offered and the prices charged for these services ranged from bare-bones budget to luxurious and costly. Table 1 describes the size and occupancy of the 10 largest motel chains in the United States.

The chain segment of the U.S. lodging industry had expanded more than 50 percent in the past five years. In 1979, this segment accounted for an estimated 30 percent of the total U.S. lodging properties and 60 percent of the total U.S. rooms available.

Table 1 TOP TEN FULL-SERVICE LODGING CHAINS IN THE UNITED STATES

	Number of U.S. Properties	Rooms	Company-Owned	Franchise or Member	Management Contract	Average Single Rate	Average Occupancy (percent)
1. Holiday Inns	1,533	250,160	244	1,458	28	$27.81	74.3
2. Ramada Inns	607	85,500	113	494	3	25.00	72.0
3. Sheraton Hotels	315	67,706	19	279	17	32.04	71.8
4. Hilton Hotels	184	67,610	17	137	30	NA	73.0
5. Howard Johnsons	511	57,590	132	379	0	NA	NA
6. Days Inns of America, Inc.	304	42,900	65	240	0	17.88	75.0
7. Quality Inns International	310	35,700	26	283	2	NA	NA
8. Motel 6	272	28,000	272	0	0	12.60	81.0
9. Hyatt Hotels	52	26,000	3	35	14	41.91	75.0
10. Marriott Hotels	57	23,462	23	17	23	NA	80+

Note: Best Western International is excluded because all 1,713 properties are members but are not franchises or company-owned.

"Top 25 U.S. Lodging Chains," *Lodging Hospitality*, August 1979, p. 47.

In the lodging industry, the annual occupancy rate was the best indicator of successful performance. Days Inns consistently outperformed the industry average. In 1978, the Days Inns annual occupancy level was 74 percent, well above the industry average of 65 percent.

THE COMPANY

The Days Inns concept began with an idea Cecil B. Day, Sr., had while traveling with his family in New England in 1968. He realized the void in the lodging industry for meeting the needs of middle Americans—the family with two, three, or four children traveling on a limited budget. Day felt that families needed quality accommodations that cost considerably less than the existing motel alternatives.

Day was a successful realtor and president of Day Realty Associates, a company that specialized in building and operating apartments in the Atlanta area. Day was reminded of the concept when he traveled the next year to California. A good idea was becoming a potential business in his mind.

When he returned to Atlanta from California, Day designed a 60-unit motel module which combined budget and luxury features. His staff draftsman drew up the plans, but they were shelved until the spring of 1970. Day kept the idea in mind, however, for his experience in construction reaffirmed his belief that there was a way to offer budget-luxury accommodations on a sound business basis. Standardization of construction and operation throughout the chain would keep company costs down. Consequently, these savings could be passed on to the motel guest.

The Days Inns budget–luxury concept became a reality with the opening of the first Days Inns in Savannah Beach, Georgia, in April 1970. It became the first of the four-in-one budget–luxury stops which provided the traveler with lodging, self-service gasoline, a restaurant, and a gift shop. In addition, most properties provided guests with a swimming pool and children's playground. Operational economies centered on a central cash register for all operations. In addition, construction economies were created by a unique modular design which reduced greatly the assembly time at the lodging site.

The Days Inns concept caught on quickly. The chain was soon billed as the fastest growing chain in the world as it began to double in size every 6 months. By 1973, the American Hotel and Motel Association recognized Days Inns as one of the top 25 lodging chains in the United States. By 1977, Days Inns was the eighth largest lodging chain in the United States. By 1979, it had become sixth, with 305 properties and over 47,000 rooms in 27 states and Canada. Management planned to have 1,000 units by 1988, at which time it would be the second largest full-service lodging chain, behind Holiday Inns.

Even as a busy entrepreneur, Day found time to render service to civic, business, religious, and educational organizations. He was a member of the Young Presidents Organization and of The Conference Board. In addition, he was a trustee of Tift College and a trustee of Mercer University of Atlanta. He served as vice chairman and member of the board of directors for Haggai Institute of Singapore (formerly Evangelism International). He was on the board of managers of the American Bible Society. He had served as deacon in his church for several years.

Although Cecil Day had become nationally prominent in business, he did not forget his father's lessons in Christianity. In 1968, Day gave concrete expression to his dedication by organizing and funding a nonprofit organization known as Day Companies Foundation, which promoted research and conferences on Christianity in business.

The distribution of Bibles was another of Cecil Day's ideas. When a member of Gideons International complained to Day at a motel opening about guests stealing Bibles, Day responded, "Who needs a Bible more than a person who steals one?" As a result, a New Testament was placed in every Days Inns and Lodge room with the printed invitation on each copy, "take it with you." By 1978, Days Inns had distributed over 1 million Bibles since the program began in 1971.

The Days Inns commitment to Christian service extended to other areas as well. Not only was it one of the few corporate tithers in history, the company extended personal service to guests and employees through its Chaplain Services Department. The company also was committed firmly to a policy of no cocktail lounges in any of its properties. These commitments to Christian service made Days Inns quite popular with families and older couples. In fact, the September Days Club for persons over 55 developed by Days Inns in 1973 now had over 250,000 dues-paying members. Club members got discounts, a quarterly publication, and had several meetings each year which were well attended.

Organization of the Marketing Function

There were four distinct areas involved in Days Inns' marketing effort, all under Roy Burnette as the senior vice president of marketing and public relations. The sales department, headed by James Wright, was responsible for keeping Days Inns name before the travel industry. This department initiated and maintained contact with tour groups and travel agents.

The advertising department was responsible for spreading the Days

Inns name and reputation and was headed by Lew Strachan. One major thrust in advertising was the use of magazine supplements, and another was the use of billboards on interstate highways.

The public relations department had two branches. One branch, headed by Tom C. Lawler, was responsible for September Days Club and for gaining publicity on talk shows, in newspapers, and the lodging and business press. Barbara Baughman headed a branch responsible for grand opening and franchise relations. Franchisees participated in four seminars and three conferences during 1978.

Finally, a customer relations department was responsible for the handling of complaints and inquiries. The work in this area was of increasing importance, particularly with the implementation of the customer satisfaction information system.

Marketing Environment

Days Inns' marketing department forecasted an expansion of both the vacation/pleasure and business-related market segments, including those consumers specifically targeted by Days Inns (see Figure 2 for data on these segments). In particular, population growth trends indicated a shift toward an older population as well as an increase of the prime family oriented population segment because of the movement of the "baby-boom generation" into that stage. The results of these trends were expected to be more families, more vacations, and more use of Days Inns.

FIGURE 2   The Days Inns Customer

Days Inns recognized three distinct market segments:

- Lodging customers.
- Franchisees/investors.
- Investment banking community.

All three of these target markets were essential to the successful marketing of Days Inns; however, marketing focused on the lodging consumer market. A separate franchise development group was responsible for development of franchises and securing long-term financing.

The lodging consumer market had three major market segments. They were

- Vacation/pleasure (30 percent of total market).
- Business (50 percent of total market).
- Conventions (20 percent of total market).

However, because of the nature of the Days Inns product and their marketing objectives, Days Inns chose to market their product to the vacation/pleasure and business segments only.

The vacation/pleasure market segment consisted of consumers with a broad spectrum of backgrounds, characteristics, and needs. Within this spectrum, Days Inns chose to further segment the vacation/pleasure market segment into two target categories of consumers. They were:

Average Family (Days Inns description).   The following characteristics best described this target market.

- Median age of parents 25 to 49.
- One or more children.
- At least one vacation a year.
- Drive a car on vacation.
- Their origin is mainly the Midwest and Northeast.
- Their destination is mainly Florida.
- Desire value for money spent on lodging.

Senior Citizens (55 and older).   The target market was successfully and aggressively marketed to through Days Inns' September Days Club. September Days Club was the first and only club in the lodging industry for persons 55 years of age and over. September Days Club had a paid membership of more than a quarter of a million. Its membership encompassed all 50 states, Canada, and several foreign countries.

Members received plastic embossed membership cards for $5 per year, per individual or per couple. In addition to discounts on lodging, food, and gifts at participating Days Inns and Lodges, the club published a quarterly magazine, *September Days,* and offered reduced rates at rental car agencies and discounts at various theme parks and attractions. Some of these attractions offered as much as a 50 percent discount.

September Days Club was actively involved in planning national and regional conventions for its members. These meetings attracted thousands of members to various cities, including Atlanta, Orlando, Dallas, and Richmond–Williamsburg.

The general characteristics of the September Days Club membership were:

- Active individuals.
- Like people-oriented activities.
- Like clubs and club activities.
- Christian-oriented.
- Economy-minded.
- Desire value for their money spent on lodging.

> The business market segment also consisted of a broad spectrum of consumers. The sectors of this market targeted by Days Inns were the
>
> - Per diem businessperson.
> - Self-employed.
>
> Characteristically, these two target markets consisted of businesspeople who
>
> - Do extensive traveling in the areas served by Days Inns.
> - Have a need for economy lodging.
> - Find Days Inns convenient enough to their work to make it a viable purchase option.

Another important growth factor was the inflation rate. Company officials predicted that lodging consumers would become more economy-minded, placing more emphasis on saving money and in particular on receiving high perceived value for the money spent on lodging. Days Inns regarded this emphasis on value as a definite plus for the growth of their vacation/pleasure and business market segments.

A great potential for growth was indicated for the senior citizens' consumer market as well. This market segment represented an estimated 30 percent of the total vacation/pleasure market. The size of the September Days Club and its growth trend indicated that this market segment also perceived a need for economy and value.

Days Inns conducted research on lodging purchase decision making, and a ranking of consumer needs was developed. It showed that consumers looked for:

1. Value (perceived).
2. Convenience.
3. Amenities (color TV, telephone, double beds, etc.).
4. Clean room.
5. Low price.

Days Inns used its research as well as marketing information gathered through the "Customer Satisfaction Information System" to monitor changes in general consumer needs, and in particular, to monitor specific consumer compliments and complaints.

The computerized customer relations program was implemented in June 1978. Information from the "Customer Satisfaction Information System" allowed the identification of problem properties as well as those doing well. However, the greatest benefit was the ability to respond to specific customer complaints both by correcting problem situations and following up with the dissatisfied customer to resolve problems.

The Customer Satisfaction Information System

The customer feedback system came about because management wanted better information about guest comments. Prior to 1978, Days Inns, like most companies in the lodging industry, had a customer relations department and had customer comment cards. However, the management reports were prepared manually, which meant there were delays and there was difficulty in getting the kind of analysis that management needed.

Installed in June 1978, the system handled feedback from over 40,000 customers in its first year. In July 1979, all 64 company-owned properties were participating in the system. The franchise properties were scheduled to begin use of the system in fall 1979. At that time, the system was expected to process 5,000 customer comments per week from over 300 properties.

The system was designed to provide timely information to executives and general managers of individual properties. Specifically, the system was designed to:

- Identify overall level of guest satisfaction.
- Develop trend data on guest satisfaction.
- Identify most frequent complaints and compliments.
- Identify exceptional properties.
- Follow up on complaints and compliments.
- Evaluate and reward managers.

The system used a customer comment card, shown in Exhibit 4, for input. The customer comment card was postage paid, addressed to the Customer Relations Department. This ensured that all comments reached Days Inns Management. The variable cost to Days Inns, after printing 400,000 cards, was about 20 cents per comment received at headquarters.

Room-related problems which required immediate attention were directed to management by a tear-off part of the card. This ensured that a problem could be taken care of before a second guest was confronted by it. Many guests filled out this part of the card and handed it to the cashier at check out.

The card was designed so that information could be entered directly into the computer on the day the card arrived at Days Inns headquarters. The card, shown in Figure 3, included the data of most interest to management. The first nine questions were created from the most frequent compliments and complaints received by the Customer Relations Department.

FIGURE 3 Customer Comment Card

BUSINESS REPLY MAIL

NO POSTAGE STAMP NECESSARY IF MAILED IN THE UNITED STATES

FIRST CLASS
Permit No. 9017
Atlanta, Georgia

Postage will be paid by:

DAYS INNS OF AMERICA, INC.
2751 Buford Highway, N.E.
Atlanta, Georgia 30324

Attention: Customer Relations Department

CARTERSVILLE - 0070

DAYS INN

DATE(S) of STAY ____________

To help us serve you better, we would appreciate your opinions and comments. *Thank You!*

How satisfied were you with:	Very Satisfied	Satisfied	Dissatisfied
1. Cleanliness of room	1	2	3
2. Room supplies	1	2	3
3. Room maintenance	1	2	3
4. Employee attitude	1	2	3
5. Front desk service	1	2	3
6. Restaurant service	1	2	3
7. Restaurant food quality	1	2	3
8. Property maintenance	1	2	3
9. Reservations System	1	2	3

10. What is the purpose of your trip? Vacation 1 Business 2 Other 3

11. Have you ever stayed at Days Inn before? No 1 Once 2 2-5 times 3 Over 5 times 4

12. When you next travel, will you use Days Inn? Yes 1 Maybe 2 No 3

13. What did you like most about your stay?

____

____

____

14. What did you like least about your stay?

____

____

____

15. Your room number ____________
Name ______________________
Address ______________________
City ______________ State ☐☐ Zip ☐☐☐☐☐

Please drop this in the nearest mailbox. Postage has been paid by Days Inn. Thank You again!

Questions 10, 11, and 12 provided additional information for follow-up
and to allow analysis of complaints. Questions 13 and 14 let management
know what each guest thought was the most important positive and
negative part of the stay. The name and address allowed for follow-up.
About two-thirds of the respondents provided their name and address.

The computer was programmed to create an executive summary, containing all comments, which was reviewed at the weekly meeting of top executives. A second report, intended for general managers and district
managers, contained a summary of all comment cards received from each
property.

The executive summary, shown in Figure 4, provided an overview of
all customer feedback to the company. The report began with an overview
of current week comments compared to last week and year-to-date for each
of 12 questions. This allowed management to detect trends and to see if,
overall, their decisions were effective in promoting guest satisfaction. Page
three provided information on the one item customers like most about their
visit. The report also detailed responses to the open-ended question, "What
did you like least about your stay?" Last, a listing was provided of the exceptional properties, both good and bad, which deserved management attention. The worst properties were reviewed for the causes of guest
dissatisfaction. Analysis of the best properties gave insight into ways to improve all properties and thus the performance of the company.

The unit manager summary, a part of which is shown in Figure 5,
detailed the guest comments for an individual property, including comparison with previous periods and with company averages. The first four
pages of this report were similar in format to the executive summary, except that all data were for one property. The last page gave the local inn-
keeper feedback on room-related complaints and on relative performance
within the company.

Days Inns management used the system to improve the level of
customer acceptance. The company developed a baseline consisting of the
average satisfaction level achieved by the top 10 properties. That average
was the goal for all properties for fiscal year 1979–1980, beginning July 1,
1979. Each manager was judged compared to performance against the standard. The results were used in determination of salary adjustments and
bonus participation. Management also used the system as an input into
evaluation of customer contact employees. In addition, the system helped
management to allocate the capital improvement budget to those properties
which had the highest incidence of complaints related to physical condition
of the property.

The customer feedback about the system had been overwhelmingly
positive. Perhaps as a result of having the comment card in guest rooms,
the customer relations department received a threefold increase in un-

FIGURE 4 Guest Satisfaction Information System Executive Summary

GUEST SATISFACTION INFORMATION SYSTEM
EXECUTIVE SUMMARY
DAYS INNS OF AMERICA, INC.

GUEST RESPONSES TO COMMENT CARD QUESTIONS

	THIS PERIOD		LAST PERIOD		YEAR-TO-DATE	
	NBR	PERC	NBR	PERC	NBR	PERC
CLEANLINESS OF ROOM						
VERY SATISFIED	451	.50	391	.49	19461	.56
SATISFIED	247	.27	229	.28	8489	.24
DISSATISFIED	183	.20	167	.21	5872	.17
NO RESPONSE	21	.02	20	.03	1130	.03
ROOM SUPPLIES						
VERY SATISFIED	405	.45	361	.45	18642	.53
SATISFIED	299	.33	280	.35	10672	.31
DISSATISFIED	157	.17	133	.16	3619	.10
NO RESPONSE	41	.05	35	.04	2019	.06
ROOM MAINTENANCE						
VERY SATISFIED	390	.43	328	.41	16969	.49
SATISFIED	245	.27	240	.30	8709	.25
DISSATISFIED	209	.23	180	.22	6430	.18
NO RESPONSE	59	.07	59	.07	2843	.08
EMPLOYEE ATTITUDE						
VERY SATISFIED	426	.47	387	.48	18477	.53
SATISFIED	276	.31	253	.31	8998	.26
DISSATISFIED	93	.10	94	.12	3029	.09
NO RESPONSE	107	.12	76	.09	4447	.13
FRONT DESK SERVICE						
VERY SATISFIED	454	.50	409	.51	19554	.56
SATISFIED	269	.30	233	.29	8903	.26
DISSATISFIED	117	.13	111	.14	3766	.11
NO RESPONSE	62	.07	55	.07	2732	.08
RESTAURANT SERVICE						
VERY SATISFIED	268	.30	275	.34	12757	.37
SATISFIED	215	.24	207	.26	7583	.22
DISSATISFIED	122	.14	96	.12	4140	.12
NO RESPONSE	297	.33	230	.29	10479	.30
RESTAURANT FOOD QUALITY						
VERY SATISFIED	244	.27	271	.34	11098	.32
SATISFIED	261	.29	215	.27	9511	.27
DISSATISFIED	67	.07	80	.10	3288	.09
NO RESPONSE	330	.37	241	.30	11053	.32
PROPERTY MAINTENANCE						
VERY SATISFIED	339	.38	300	.37	14503	.42
SATISFIED	292	.32	261	.32	9760	.28
DISSATISFIED	134	.15	109	.14	3683	.11
NO RESPONSE	137	.15	137	.17	7005	.20
RESERVATION SYSTEM						
VERY SATISFIED	394	.44	358	.44	15935	.46
SATISFIED	175	.19	158	.20	5452	.16
DISSATISFIED	57	.06	64	.08	2056	.06
NO RESPONSE	276	.31	227	.28	11511	.33
PURPOSE OF TRIP						
VACATION	715	.79	674	.84	26383	.76
BUSINESS	87	.10	48	.06	3884	.11
OTHER	80	.09	74	.09	3600	.10
NO RESPONSE	20	.02	13	.02	1070	.03
EVER STAYED BEFORE						
NO	213	.24	208	.26	7507	.22
ONCE	121	.13	102	.13	3617	.10
2-5 TIMES	216	.24	187	.23	7490	.21
OVER 5 TIMES	340	.38	296	.37	15796	.45
NO RESPONSE	13	.01	14	.02	546	.02
WILL USE DAYS INN IN FUTURE						
YES	448	.50	394	.49	20545	.59
MAYBE	293	.33	281	.35	10131	.29
NO	138	.15	110	.14	3358	.10
NO RESPONSE	23	.03	22	.03	922	.03

GUEST COMMENTS

COMPLIMENTS	THIS PERIOD		LAST PERIOD		YEAR-TO-DATE	
	NBR	PERC	NBR	PERC	NBR	PERC
EFFICIENT DESK PERSONL	35	.04	32	.04	1650	.05
EFFICIENT WAITRESS	4	.00	1	.00	140	.00
CLEAN ROOM	90	.10	78	.10	3691	.11
GOOD FOOD	11	.01	10	.01	487	.01
QUICK RESTAURANT SERVC	14	.02	4	.01	261	.01
POOL	74	.08	63	.08	583	.02
RESERVATIONS	12	.01	12	.02	577	.02
PROPERTY APPEARANCE	4	.00	5	.01	137	.00

(continued)

FIGURE 4 *(continued)*

GUEST COMMENTS

COMPLAINTS	THIS PERIOD		LAST PERIOD		YEAR-TO-DATE	
	NBR	PERC	NBR	PERC	NBR	PERC
REASONABLE RATES	54	.06	67	.08	3015	.09
CONVENIENT LOCATION	72	.08	53	.07	2961	.09
COMFORTABLE ROOM	67	.07	53	.07	3406	.10
COMFORTABLE BEDS	46	.05	35	.04	2185	.06
QUIET	34	.04	25	.03	1492	.04
OTHER	105	.12	71	.09	3660	.11
NO RESPONSE	283	.31	298	.37	10715	.31
DIRTY ROOM	46	.05	54	.07	1992	.06
RUDE DESK PERSONNEL	23	.03	30	.04	1009	.03
INADEQUATE RM SUPPLIES	45	.05	32	.04	1246	.04
POOR ROOM MAINTENANCE	61	.07	51	.06	2868	.08
POOR FOOD QUALITY	18	.02	18	.02	1115	.03
SLOW RESTAURANT SERVICE	37	.04	37	.05	1697	.05
SLOW FRONT DESK SERVICE	3	.00	2	.00	128	.00
RESERVATNS NOT HONORED	8	.01	19	.02	660	.02
RATE TOO HIGH	16	.02	23	.03	485	.01
POOL	23	.03	19	.02	228	.01
INSECTS	38	.04	24	.03	1100	.03
PARKING	7	.01	14	.02	533	.02
DIRTY BATHROOM	21	.02	25	.03	1082	.03
AC/HEATING BROKEN	53	.06	33	.04	881	.03
NOT ENOUGH TOWELS	4	.00	19	.02	203	.01
TELEVISION	16	.02	7	.01	530	.02
ICE MACHINE	52	.06	36	.05	455	.01
BAD ODOR	11	.01	18	.02	468	.01
NOISE	9	.01	16	.02	1185	.03
OTHER	172	.19	107	.13	5255	.15
NO RESPONSE	240	.27	223	.28	11834	.34

BEST/WORST PROPERTIES

	BEST CURRENT PERIOD				BEST LAST PERIOD				BEST YEAR-TO-DATE	
RANK	PROPERTY		RATING	RANK	PROPERTY		RATING	RANK	PROPERTY		RATING
1	120	GEORGETOWN	+ 24.7	1	81	EMPORIA	+ 23.4	1	80	ROWLAND	+ 20.4
2	128	CARMEL CHURCH	+ 17.4	2	57	LUMBERTON	+ 17.2	2	126	WALTHALL	+ 20.3
3	126	WALTHALL	+ 17.3	3	126	WALTHALL	+ 15.3	3	128	CARMEL CHURCH	+ 15.0
4	38	MICANOPY	+ 16.9	4	55	KNOXVILLE	+ 15.0	4	39	ST AUGUSTINE	+ 13.7
5	62	ROCKY MOUNT	+ 13.5	5	121	RICHMOND KENTUCKY	+ 14.9	5	30	NORTH TIFTON (CHULA)	+ 13.5
6	91	OLD STONE MOUNTAIN L	+ 13.2	6	99	FAYETTEVILLE-WADE	+ 12.1	6	99	FAYETTEVILLE-WADE	+ 13.4
7	80	ROWLAND	+ 12.7	7	31	FORSYTH NORTH	+ 11.8	7	70	CARTERSVILLE	+ 13.3
8	82	MANNING	+ 12.7	8	83	JACKSONVILLE AIRPOR	+ 10.6	8	121	RICHMOND KENTUCKY	+ 12.6
9	55	KNOXVILLE	+ 11.0	9	30	NORTH TIFTON (CHULA)	+ 9.9	9	89	JELLICO	
10	121	RICHMOND KENTUCKY	+ 10.2	10	128	CARMEL CHURCH	+ 9.8	10	112	BENSON	+ 12.4

	WORST CURRENT PERIOD				WORST LAST PERIOD				WORST YEAR-TO-DATE	
RANK	PROPERTY		RATING	RANK	PROPERTY		RATING	RANK	PROPERTY		RATING
60	40	WILDWOOD	- 2.7	58	86	CHATTANOOGA	- 3.6	60	35	FLAGSHIP	+ 0.00
59	77	CLEVELAND AVE	- 2.4	57	44	LAKE PARK	- 2.1	59	52	SEA WORLD	+ 0.0
58	90	ASHLAND	- 2.3	56	66	NASHVILLE	- 1.9	58	71	DISNEY WORLD EAST	+ 0.5
57	111	RICHMOND-BYRD AIRPOR	- 1.9	55	77	CLEVELAND AVE	- 1.2	57	41	JACKSONVILLE - CAGLE	+ 0.7
56	41	JACKSONVILLE - CAGLE	- 1.8	54	90	ASHLAND	- 0.8	56	43	DAYTONA BEACH	+ 1.0
55	59	HENDERSON	- 1.2	53	52	SEA WORLD	- 0.5	55	111	RICHMOND-BYRD AIRPOR	+ 1.3
54	43	DAYTONA BEACH	- 1.2	52	35	FLAGSHIP	- 0.4	54	78	FORT WAYNE	+ 1.5
53	44	LAKE PARK	+ 0.0	51	88	SHALLOWFORD LODGE	- 0.2	53	77	CLEVELAND AVE	+ 1.7
52	86	CHATTANOOGA	+ 0.1	50	71	DISNEY WORLD EAST	+ 0.2	52	11	SAVANNAH BEACH	+ 1.8
51	85	BUFORD LODGE	+ 0.2	49	74	MACON	+ 0.2	51	74	MACON	+ 2.1

THIS PERIOD   RESPONSE RATES

THIS PERIOD	LAST PERIOD	YEAR-TO-DATE
0.016	0.016	0.022

NUMBER OF COMMENT CARDS THIS PERIOD =   902

FIGURE 5   Guest Satisfaction Imformation System
Unit Manager Summary

```
DATE  07/07/80                          GUEST SATISFACTION INFORMATION SYSTEM
                                              DAYS INNS OF AMERICA, INC.
REPORT-ID MWLP35                              2 WEEK UNIT MANAGER SUMMARY
  0011   SAVANNAH BEACH


                                        ROOM INFORMATION

                         NO DETAIL ROOM INFORMATION FOR THIS SITE

                                           RANKING

                       1)   THIS SITE RANKED  41  OUT OF  61
                            BASED ON AVG. RATING OF  + 3.4

                       2)   HIGHEST AVG. RATING = + 20.0

                       3)   LOWEST AVG. RATING = - 2.0

                       4)   AVERAGE RATING = + 6.4

                                        RESPONSE RATES

                              THIS PERIOD    YEAR-TO-DATE

                 THIS SITE        .006           .006

                 COMPANY          .022           .022
```

solicited letters and phone calls from customers, 70 percent of which was positive. In addition, the reports showed a steady increase in reported levels of satisfaction as problems were identified and resolved.

The only problem with the report was that occasionally there were properties which showed up on the best 10 list for several consecutive weeks with high response rates and overwhelmingly positive responses. Follow-up had shown that on occasion managers and/or front desk clerks had solicited responses from guests. Since the vast majority of all guests had satisfactory visits, such requests tended to distort the ratings and thus the overall rankings.

BURNETTE'S DILEMMA

The flight was nearly completed. The plane had begun its descent somewhere over Lake Tahoe. Burnette had read and reread the recommendations. He was pleased that the report supported the continuation of the system, but he was unsure about how to evaluate the several recommendations. In fact, he was concerned that the cost to implement all the suggestions could be prohibitive. More specifically, he was unsure about what to recommend about the continued use of the system as an input into bonuses for motel managers. However, he decided that the report should be discussed at the meeting with the senior vice president of operations. He also intended to add the report to the agenda for the next weekly meeting of the executive committee of Days Inns.

Commentaries

BUSINESS RESPONDS TO CONSUMERISM*

Spurred by Fear of Customer Revolts or Even More Laws, Industry Offers Simpler Products, New Warranties and Service

> First Banana: "Hey, did you hear about the man who crossed a parrot with a tiger?"
> Second Banana: "No! What did he get?"
> First Banana: "I don't know. But when it talks, you better listen!"

Whatever else consumerism is, it's beginning to look like a tigerish sort of parrot, and business, it seems, would do well to listen.

Some businesses are not only listening, they are doing something. Appliance makers are starting to print their warranties in clear English. Auto makers are trying to get new cars to customers with all the screws tightened and all the weatherstripping in place. Textile manufacturers are looking more closely at the clothes their products end up in, to make sure the fiber is really suited to the suit.

Every class of manufacturer whose product ends up sold at retail—from foods and finance service to toys and tires—is thinking, more or less intensively, about what to do when Ralph Nader, or Consumers Union's Walker Sandbach, or Senator Warren Magnuson (D-Wash.), or Representative Benjamin Rosenthal (D-N.Y.), or another of the growing corps of influential consumer protectors comes knocking at the door.

Impetus. Few businessmen make any secret of it: Fear is the spur. Banks and finance companies have had a taste of consumer credit regulation and worry that they may some day be held responsible for the reliability of products financed through notes they have bought. No one has to teach Detroit the power of safety crusades; performance, pricing, and warranty revision may come next. Overnight, the delicate credibility of the toy and baby-food industries could be destroyed all over the country. Cosmetic and drug manufacturers, regulated for years, are uncomfortably aware that what they have swallowed so far may be only the beginning.

Read, for example, a recent press release issued by the Democratic Study Group, an informal alliance of liberal congressmen. After warming up with an indictment of the Nixon Administration in the field of consumer protection, the group lists no fewer than 30 separate desired pieces of legislation to regulate business in its relations with the public: 10 laws dealing with product safety (including drugs, toys, tires, fish, eggs, and medical devices); five on consumer information (package labeling and pricing, product testing); six on deception and fraud; three on consumer credit; and six others that range from electric power reliability standards to the guarantee of reasonable access to liability insurance.

New weapons. A laundry list compiled by the Chamber of Commerce of the U.S. is even longer: 86 major bills before the Congress, and more dumped into the hopper every day.

The Nixon Administration itself, despite the Democrats' criticism, is readying a package of consumer-oriented legislation. In a recent speech, Mrs. Virginia Knauer, the President's consumer adviser (who has turned out to be just as tart-tongued as her Democratic predecessors), outlined the first bill in the program: an act that enables consumers economically injured by fraudulent or deceptive marketing practices to pool their small claims and bring "class actions" in the Federal courts. The proposed law is similar to several already introduced in Congress. Nader says such a bill is potentially the most powerful weapon that could be put in the hands of consumers.

If anyone, at this late date, thinks that all this is just so much political wind, he should glance at the major legislation of the past few years:

- The National Traffic & Motor Vehicle Safety Act, which took on the whole automobile industry.
- The Fair Packaging & Labeling Act, which was passed over the strenuous objection of the mammoth food industry.
- The Consumer Credit Protection Act, which vitally touches the banking and finance industries as well as every retail organization that grants credit.

If one thing can be said for the lawmakers, it is that they are not afraid to tackle the biggest. Consumerism is powerful politics. Senator

Magnuson used consumerism as a key issue in his sucessful drive for re-election last year. His theme: "Let's keep the big boys honest."

Senator Frank E. Moss (D-Utah), who recently won a signal victory over the cigarette makers, is considered by Republican strategists to be vulnerable next year in his bid for re-election. He recently scheduled a public hearing in connection with his campaign to tighten the Truth-in-Packaging Law. Where did he hold the hearing? Salt Lake City, of course.

Bandwagon.   Among politicians, consumer protection is becoming institutionalized, just as defense, taxation, space, oil, and banking. Staff assistants to senators are making careers of consumer protection; they spend much of their time keeping up their bosses' interest with a stream of clippings, reports, studies, gossip, draft bills, draft speeches.

Some legislators need no encouragement. For each session of Congress through the years, Representative Leonor K. Sullivan, a serene and comfortable lady who represents a Democratic district in St. Louis, has introduced an omnibus package of amendments to the Federal Food, Drug & Cosmetic Act (this year's version, all 120 pages of it, is designated H. R. 1235). She watches with equanimity as her bill dies in the Interstate & Foreign Commerce Committee. But every so often, bits and pieces of it turn up in other bills that do get passed, and she is perfectly prepared to continue submitting variations of her bill to the end of her Congressional career.

Furthermore, anyone in the business community who expects the Republicans to capture the Senate next year and overturn the consumerist establishment should reconsider. The consensus in Washington is that consumer protection is no longer the exclusive concern (if it ever was) of the liberal Democrats. Conservatives of the stripe of Senator John Tower (R-Tex.) are becoming interested. Votes, it seems, are votes, and everyone is a consumer.

Boiling point.   There's an explanation why consumer issues have become good politics. In the very broadest sense, consumerism can be defined as the bankruptcy of what the business schools have been calling the marketing concept.

For all the millions of words written on the subject in the last 20 years, the marketing concept is a fairly simple idea: The proper way to run a business, and especially a consumer-goods business, is to find out the customer's wants and needs, felt and unfelt. The next step is to work back through the chain from customer to manufacturer, and design and produce a product that fills those needs and wants better than anything else on the market. With proper attention to efficient production, good distribution, attractive packaging, and effective promotion, the manufacturer should have few troubles.

But the whole system, which has worked brilliantly since the mid-1950s, is precariously balanced on one assumption: that the consumer is capable of exercising intelligent choice, and inclined to exercise it. The consumer, it is said, "votes with her pocketbook."

More and more people are beginning to believe that the assumption is not at all self-evident. Dr. Peter F. Drucker, the management consultant, lectured the marketing conference of National Assn. of Manufacturers last April in these terms: "Consumerism means that the consumer looks upon the manufacturer as somebody who is interested, but who really doesn't know what the consumer's realities are. He regards the manufacturer as somebody who has not made the effort to find out, who does not understand the world in which the consumer lives, and who expects the consumer to be able to make distinctions which the consumer is neither able nor willing to make."

THE LONG REACH OF LIABILITY

If businessmen need any more incentive to take consumerism seriously, they can find it in the courts, where product liability law is rapidly expanding into a far-reaching doctrine of consumer protection. In just a few years, the legal position of manufacturers in product defect suits has been turned upside down. Once they were virtually immune; now they can be held liable for any injury their product causes—even injury caused by the sheer stupidity of the user.

The doctrine of "privity," the requirement of direct contact between the injured party and the party alleged to have been negligent, which protected manufacturers from legal action, has all but disappeared. In its place is the "strict liability" rule that requires only a showing that a specific error of manufacture or design led to an injury.

Proliferation. The switch has brought an explosion of thousands of product liability suits. Most still involve such things as exploding soft drink bottles and defective car brakes. But the courts are increasingly willing to interpret broadly what constitutes factory error.

Consider the case of the White Gearshift Knob:

Putting the finishing touches on 1949 models, Ford Motor Co. designers decided to make the plastic knob on the gear shift lever white rather than black. It was not a particularly momentous decision, causing no more comment than the switch back to black the following year. But the initial switch was fateful: It has involved Ford in a lengthy court battle over an $880,000 damage claim.

It seems that, colored white, tennite butyrate plastic reacts to sunlight, producing hairline cracks in the knob. In a 1962 accident, a passenger in a 1949 Ford was thrown up against the gearshift; the knob shattered and the lever went through her chest, paralyzing her. The jury found Ford at fault for using improper materials.

The verdict was appealed. And this year the South Carolina Supreme Court ordered a new trial on the basis of errors in the judge's charge to the jury. But, because of its strong language on car makers' responsibility for the "second collision," in which occupants are thrown against the interior of the car, the court's decision was cold comfort:

"An automobile manufacturer knows with certainty that many users of his product will be involved in collisions and that the incidence and extent of injury to them will frequently be determined by the placement, design, and construction of . . . shafts, levers, and knobs . . . A known risk of harm raises a duty of commensurate care."

New interpretations.   Many claims lawyers see the "doctrine of foreseeability" as a logical step.

Consumer protection spokesmen want products designed not only for use, but for anticipated misuse.

"A manufacturer is best able to evaluate the risks inherent in his product and figure out ways to avoid them," says Arnold B. Elkind, a noted negligence lawyer and head of the National Commission on Product Safety. Elkind thinks that the courts should protect not just the unwitting consumer from the consequences of a manufacturer's error, but also the "witless boobs" who misuse a product in ways that can be anticipated.

A year ago the Kentucky Court of Appeals saw it the same way. It held a manufacturer liable for damages that occurred when one of its vacuum cleaners was plugged into a 220-volt circuit and blew up. The label stated clearly that the product was to be used in 115-volt outlets, the court admitted, but failed to warn that the consequence of plugging it into anything hotter was disaster. "It may be doubted that a sign warning, 'Keep Off the Grass,' could be deemed sufficient to appraise a reasonable person that the grass was infested with deadly snakes," the court argued.

The threat of court action, Elkind thinks, will eventually push manufacturers in this direction.

In atomic physics, there is the concept of critical mass—a point at which enough fissionable material is present to support a violent reaction. The U.S. consumer economy is at the point of critical mass, and consumerism is the explosion. A great many things have come together at once:

Product complexity. "The product," complains John J. Nevin, the head of Ford Motor Co.'s central marketing staff, "is getting more complex as we are building it better. We've kept pace with complexity, but we haven't licked it.'' Few consumers can peer under the hood of an eight-cylinder, air-conditioned, power-assisted automobile and understand what is there.

The business boom. The country's productive capacity is beginning to gape at the seams under the pressure to get the goods out on the market at any cost. Last fall, the New York Times reported that 5% of certain classes of women's wear needed some repair by retailers before they could be placed on sale. Says one Detroit executive: ''Things have moved so fast —from 6 million cars to 9 million in less than a decade. How do you increase repair stalls fast enough?''

The marketing boomerang. In a sense, consumer marketing and advertising have been too successful. Convinced that quality and convenience are forever on the rise, that the technical genius of industry can work miracles, that the new is always better, that the computer can solve anything, the customer expects a lot that cannot be delivered. ''We are suffering'' says Herbert M. Cleaves, senior vice-president of General Foods, ''from a revolution of customers' rising expectations. The consumer never had it so good, but he wants to know 'what have you done for me lately?''' Marketing overkill is even harming products that do perform well. ''They've been screaming about how good their products are for so many years, people no longer believe them,'' says Morris Kaplan, technical director of Consumers Union.

Full employment. It's a truism that no one wants to be an auto mechanic or repairman anymore. There are better and easier jobs in the factories. And present repairmen are so beset by customers that they can't take the trouble they used to. Says John C. Bates, director of General Motors' service section: ''It's not that they don't do the work, but that they don't cater to the consumer anymore. If you get respect, you don't complain. Ten years ago, management in a dealer's repair shop had pretty good control over his people. As labor shortages developed, there's been an abrogation of control.''

Anomie, or the feeling of disorder and isolation; the sense, in short, that a bad situation has no bottom. The white, suburban, middle class, which constitutes the principal market for goods and services, believes that government is cold and unresponsive, that taxes are too high, that Negroes are too aggressive, that the Vietnam war will never end. The middle class is at its collective wit's end. And now the last refuge, the goods and services the suburbanite buys with his devalued dollars to support the good life, seems to have let him down.

Together, the discontents have produced the broadest consumer protection movement in U.S. history, a movement that is not only concerned with protecting consumers against physical harm and outright fraud, but that also attempts to guarantee performance, efficacy, and to regulate the total relationship between buyer and seller. In legal terms, emphasis has moved from torts to contracts.

"There is a lack of balance in the consumer's capacity to deal equally with the guy who's got an item to sell," says Senator Gaylord Nelson (D-Wis.) one of the most active consumerists in Congress. The aim is to redress that balance.

One appliance executive ticks off on his fingers the big issues that are coming up: safety, of course, and the problems of product recall; some machinery for the resolution of customer grievances; improvement and standardizations of product warranties; provision of a lot more information to the consumer on what he is buying and how well it will perform.

FACING UP TO REALITY

"The most encouraging thing," says General Electric Co.'s associate counsel, Winston H. Pickett, "is that businessmen are taking consumerism seriously and addressing themselves to it on a systematic and continuous basis." Adds a key man in a powerful Senate committee: "People are changing; or at least everyone is willing to play the game and make the right pronouncements."

Both men were addressing themselves to the No. 1 problem: How should business respond to the consumer challenge? The question—and its various answers—are likely to occupy a lot of high-priced time for a good many years to come. And that in itself is a problem. "We're not a huge company," says E. G. Higdon, president of Maytag Co., "and we don't have a lot of loose management with nothing to do. The consumerism boom is putting the time pressure on some of our top people. You don't go out and employ someone to go to Washington and sit down and listen. You have to send someone who knows this business, who is capable of representing us adequately, and who can come back with the proper information to let us form our own opinions."

Actually, the business response to government regulation has been fairly predictable over the years, and falls into several stages.

Deny everything. Nearly everyone goes through a phase of shock when hallowed business practices are questioned, and this is the automatic response.

Blame wrongdoing on the small, marginal companies. In any industry where fragmentation and ease of entry are the rule, the argument is popular that the major companies are blameless, but that the small outfits must cut corners to survive.

Discredit the critics. "Hell," says one Congressional staff man, "I've had publishers worried about circulation sales investigations down here peddling stuff on the Communist nature of consumerism based on 1942 documents."

Hire a public relations man. A big campaign to modify public opinion is alluring. But, as one PR man says, "there's no sense in a PR campaign if you have nothing to say."

Defang the legislation. Trade associations and Washington law firms are specialists in this, and it is often effective, at least for a while. It worked for the tobacco industry in 1965. It also worked in respect to the Truth-in-Packaging Law.

Launch a fact-finding committee to find out whether anything really needs to be improved in the way the company does business. The food industry is deeply involved in this now.

Actually do something, whether you think you are guilty or innocent. Carl Levin, a PR man who runs the Washington office of Burson-Marsteller, cites the case of his client, Reserve Mining Co., the big taconite processor in Minnesota. Reserve has been criticized for dumping ore tailings into Lake Superior. "Reserve thinks it's right," says Levin. "But if everyone's wearing a mini-skirt, you wear one too. Whether it's a real public interest or merely what the public thinks is its interest, it must be taken into account. They're trying to do something short of closing down the plant."

More and more businessmen are convinced that the rewards—or the avoidance of penalties—will come only in the later stages of this cycle. Says GE's Pickett: "You're going to do something voluntarily or involuntarily. These aren't fancied grievances. The dimensions are a matter of dispute, but not the existence of them."

How does industry answer these complaints? Consider the case of the food industry. Regulation is certainly nothing new, and the processors have been living with minimum standards of health and cleanliness for decades. But in the early 1960s, the proposals to regulate labeling on consumer packages cropped up. By the time the Fair Packaging & Labeling Act was passed in 1966, the grocery industry had earned a reputation for primitive intransigence that would have shamed a 19th Century railroad baron.

But packaging was only the beginning. Some of the labeling regulations are just being promulgated, and the industry is under attack on additives and plant inspection.

Introspection. In 1967, the Grocery Manufacturers Assn. commissioned a study by McKinsey Co. to try to get some new ideas. A number of alternatives were discarded, including a massive public relations campaign and an expensive continuing opinion survey to find out what is bugging the consumer. What finally came out of it all was the Consumer Research Institute, run by James Carman, a business administration professor from the University of California.

CRI is a foundation sponsored by major manufacturers that sell through supermarkets, by the National Assn. of Food Chains, the National Assn. of Wholesale Grocers of America, by several large ad agencies, and a group of magazines with a healthy interest in food advertising.

The studies themselves—planned or actual—vary in stature. Some of them merely put out brush fires, such as a study now in the works on cents-off deals in supermarkets.

A project in the planning stage is so-called "unit-pricing." Several bills now in Congress would require retails to stamp the price per ounce, or pound, or foot on packages. "We want to do some decent research," says Carman. "How much would it cost? Would it change the way goods are priced physically; that is, would the actual price-stamping have to change? Would it promote more or fewer pricing mistakes?"

Carman's biggest expenditure area is in consumer information studies. For example, one scholar is looking at the state of consumer testing and grading programs in Europe in an effort to determine whether a similar program would make sense in an American environment. Another project will study what product information consumers actually use.

Feedback. Carman's sponsors very much want to know what's bugging consumers. So far he has no answer.

The U.S. Chamber of Commerce thinks it has a method that might work. The chamber has designed a program that it is trying to sell to its local affiliates. The proposition: a series of local meetings between business and consumers designed to get some kind of feedback on dissatisfaction— and get some action on injustices.

There are other schemes. One of the original alternatives to Carman's institute was a national market research study proposed by A. Edward Miller, at the time (1967) president of Alfred Politz Research, and now president of World Publishing Co. Miller's scheme involved a $100,000 study, jointly paid for by government and industry to isolate the areas of consumer discontent.

Miller also proposed a continuing study, called the Consumer Index of Buying Satisfaction, to provide both the regulators and the regulated with something better than letters of complaint as a clue to consumer dissatisfaction.

CRI is the packaged-goods producers' principal effort at the moment. Individual companies, of course, are doing more. General Foods, for example, early this year set up the Center for Applied Nutrition, which is charged with research into the problems of nutrition and hunger. It is no secret that one of the issues of increasing interest to the consumerists is whether convenience foods are more or less nourishing than food the housewife prepares herself, and whether consumers think they are getting more sustenance than they really are.

LIKELY NEW TARGETS

The major dialogue in the business community is taking place not in the food industry but among the durable goods makers, which are less accustomed to severe regulation. They are, to put it bluntly, in a sweat. The areas that are bugging them are warranties, repair, reliability, consumer grievance mechanisms, and product safety. And the principal argument is how fast to move to head off unwelcome regulation.

The battleground is over industry-wide product standards and product certification. Are they desirable? Are they prudent? Are they anticompetitive? The National Commission on Product Safety, appointed by the President, distrusts self-regulation and is pushing for federal standards and surveillance. The commission has gone so far as to enlist the Antitrust Div. of the Justice Dept. In May, Arnold B. Elkind, chairman of the commission, asked Assistant Attorney General Richard W. McLaren for an advisory letter on the antitrust implications of self-regulation. In June, McLaren replied, and his very cautious response has provided ammunition for the warring points of view.

In July, for example, the commission announced that Justice does not think voluntary safety standards necessarily violate the laws, but that setting such standards "would appear to be a task more appropriately entrusted to a governmental body than private groups of manufacturers."

True, McLaren said that, but the statement was taken out of a context that bore on quite a different point. Donald L. Peyton, managing director of the United States of American Standards Institute (USASI), a private organization supported by trade associations to promulgate voluntary standards, has photocopies of McLaren's letter and the safety commission's press release. He implies that Elkind distorted McLaren's views to frighten industry away from self-regulation.

But a careful reading of McLaren's statement reveals that Elkind need distort nothing: The general tenor of McLaren's opinion is that self-regulation could be extremely dangerous.

Dilemma. There's nothing surprising in that. The anti-competitive aspects of voluntary codes have been recognized for years. A product standard rigged to favor one or two producers, or a certification program too costly for small manufacturers, is very likely in violation of the antitrust statutes.

APPLIANCE MAKER COMES CLEAN

"Who in business is really doing something to make the consumerists happy?"

A few weeks ago, when a Business Week report asked congressmen, regulators, committee staffers, public relations men, and association representatives that question, the response more often than not was: "Why don't you go see the Whirlpool people; they come to mind first."

In the present atmosphere of Washington, this adds up to an accolade that should entitle Elisha Gray II, Whirlpool Corp.'s chairman, to a medal the size of a dinner plate.

But from the vantage point of Benton Harbor, Mich., where Whirlpool maintains its headquarters, it certainly doesn't appear as if the company's washing machines are inlaid with rare gems—and it certainly doesn't give the machines away.

But Whirlpool's modest programs designed to get the floundering consumer up on dry ground appear both practical and commonsensical. They include:

- A 24-hour "cool line," free-of-charge, enabling customers to telephone from anywhere in the country to gripe, ask about service, get product and usage information, or request such things as spare owner manuals. The two-year-old service has fielded some 11,000 calls so far this year, and averages 125 per day.

- A letter in housewife's language in place of warranty certificates, telling customers what they can expect.

- "Reputation" ads, for which Whirlpool has been spending about 20% of its advertising budget. A notable one ran last October in Life and Look. "If you have a gripe," it ran, "let the manufacturer know." The ad offered a preaddressed letter which the reader simply could scribble on and mail. "Dear Mr. Upton," it began—and the rest was blank. "We got about 2,700 responses to that," says Stephen Upton, Whirlpool's consumer services vice-president, "and they're still coming in."

- A buy-guide that is attached to appliances, showing major product characteristics and features: motor size, operating time, water temperature and pressure, water consumption, weight. The head of a consumer testing organization points out that the guide tells the housewife everything but how well the washing machine will wash clothes.

Whirlpool was also the first company in the industry to pay for all in-warranty service calls. "Back in the early 1960s," says Upton, "the discount store was taking a larger and larger percentage of sales. But because they were working on a smaller profit margin, many did not lay aside an amount for the in-warranty labor for which they were responsible."

So Whirlpool took the warranty service out of the dealers' hands. "The service agent just writes out a regular bill to us, sends it in at his regular out-of-warranty rates so that he makes a profit, and we pay it," Upton explains. "It also gives us a complete record of all in-warranty claims anywhere in the country so we can see immediately what components are failing."

Payoff. The expenses are borne by adding a little extra to the distributor cost of each appliance as it is sold. The extra goes into a pot to pay for warranty repairs. Some of the extra charge is passed on to the consumer, but the increment is small enough to keep Whirlpool competitive. Reason: The dealer, who once had to put aside a portion of his gross markup for in-warranty sevice expense, is now able to shave his margin a little.

Says Upton: "In the last three years, our rate of increase in sales of the Whirlpool line has tripled that of the industry. Our interest in the consumer has to be one of the main reasons."

Juel Ranum, board chairman of the Assn. of Home Appliance Manufacturers, an organization that is doing more than most in the area of performance standards and consumer grievance, puts the fears of industry very explicitly indeed: "The one thing I haven't heard in Washington is what a politician would do if a company in his particular area were threatened by standards that it was unwilling or unable to meet. This is a real dilemma, because if the standards are to mean anything, they will have to raise the level, not lower it. At the present time, if we as an industry attempted to write a standard that every single manufacturer could not meet now, it would be absolutely construed as a violation of antitrust laws, as an attempt to drive some companies out of business."

The danger is no illusion. USASI's Peyton admits: "I can get GE and Westinghouse to reduce current leakage. But the standard would put 50 manufacturers out of business."

Nevertheless, USASI (the name will soon be changed to American National Standards Institute because the Federal Trade Commission thinks the present name sounds deceptively like an arm of the U.S. government) believes that voluntary certification is both safe and feasible, despite the opposition or lethargy of some of its members. Says one of Peyton's associates: "We have a consumer council loaded with consumer-oriented manufacturers, some of whom are sitting on it to make sure that no standards are written on his industry."

Yardsticks. USASI recently launched a national certification program that will offer something of a breakthrough in self-certification for performance.

Peyton would like to see graded standards, which would get an industry off the antitrust hook by finding room for manufacturers of every degree of efficiency and size. "There's nothing illegal, immoral, or fattening about component performance levels for a whole industry," he says. "Why not have performance points as well as price points and market the product accordingly?"

One reason, says a testing engineer, is that it is harder to do than most people in or out of Washington think. "Take tires. Quality grade labeling is an almost impossible situation. Everyone's been working on it, but the chore is beyond man's knowledge and they're a year past the deadline for Commerce Dept. regulations."

There are other reasons why people in industry doubt USASI's success. Companies joining the certification program must satisfy USASI that product liability insurance covered USASI. Testing costs are also higher under the program because the testing laboratory that actually administered the certification standard would have to post a bond with USASI for the life of the program plus 10 years. To be legal, the certification must be open to any company. Says one observer: "Suppose a company that's not an association member came along and asked for the USASI seal. He hasn't contributed a nickel to the association's certification program, which includes expensive advertising to acquaint the public with its value. The first time a Hong Kong air-conditioner importer comes along, USASI is down the drain."

Debate. USASI is not the only institution pushing reluctant manufacturers to adopt some form of self-certification. Hoffman Beagle, president of Electrical Testing Laboratories, one of the oldest independent testing labs in the business, thinks that self-certification sponsored by an industry association can work.

He has made it work in a few cases. For example, the aluminum window manufacturers administered their own program for years, but found that the inspection system left something to be desired. In 1963, Beagle's laboratory took over policing of the standards, including random sampling of production. "We have in all our programs sole authority without recourse to determine the facts of compliance. If we gig someone, it costs them money."

Beagle is puzzled by the consumerist issue. "You'd think the woods would be full of new clients these days," he says. "But it is not so." He doesn't think cost is the reason. "I have yet to find an industry where a viable certification program could not be instituted at a cost per unit that leaves the pricing structure unaffected," Beagle says.

Others disagree. Baron Whitaker, president of Underwriters' Laboratories, which certifies electrical safety, puts his finger on a fundamental paradox in trying to graft consumer protection measures onto a sophisticated market economy. "If you put in extra safety features or extend product life, the cost has to come out of somewhere. There's no Santa Claus."

Delicate balance. To understand exactly what all this means in terms of competing in a cutthroat market, maintaining dealer margins, and maintaining pricing points in the volume segments of a business, listen to John W. Craig, senior vice-president of the appliance division of Admiral Corp.: "Does attention to the consumer cost money? Certainly it does. You get nothing free any more. The only solution is cost-improvement programs. Our engineering, purchasing, and manufacturing departments have annual requirements set up calling for taking a certain amount off manufacturing costs without interfering with performance, features, or reliability."

In the face of that kind of optimism, a lot of marketing men can only grin wryly. In most hardgoods industries—including the automobile business, where it has been raised to a high art—cost control and engineering adjustments are matters of a fraction of a cent. The whole point: to bring in the product somehow at a competitive price level in the face of rising costs. The trick is to do it without losing much of the quality or durability. A major program of improvement in response to consumerist demands plays havoc with such a delicately balanced system. It is the lucky company that can raise its prices enough to cover the costs and still meet competition.

Herd instinct. These competitive pressures are precisely why whole industries try to act together on new standards, as Senator Magnuson points out in his book, The Dark Side of the Marketplace: "When asked why they had not incorporated the $2 instinctive release on their wringer washing machine, one company admitted that even such a small expenditure that would require some alterations in production would require a higher price, giving competitors an edge in a low-income market, where every dollar-off counts. . . . Recently, an automotive engineer told me that many in the auto industry were secretly glad that a law was passed, mandating the use of the safety features by all companies, for competition had long prevented their adoption by one company alone.''

The problem of how to satisfy everyone in the system at once pops up everywhere you look.

The problem of repair, for example, is both knotty and expensive. GE has erected a huge edifice to solve it: factory service branches which now account for 80% of its major appliance service calls.

Detroit revs up.   The auto industry naturally is in the biggest bind. Ford is gearing up its HEVAC (heating, ventilation, air conditioning) laboratory, which will experiment with modular design for car climate control systems, among other things. The reason: air-conditioning is the company's biggest warranty headache, and it shows up early enough to be covered by even the shortest warranty period.

For the first time, too, Ford is asking its engineers to consider ease and accessibility of repair when they design a car, especially at the lower-priced end. The luxury models, whose owners presumably don't care one way or the other, will still emphasize style over fast—and cheap—repair. "Lee Iacocca [executive vice-president of Ford] can't stand exposed screw heads," says one man, "so there are none in the Continental." When you want to fix a car, it's nice to be able quickly to find the screws that hold it together.

The experiment with Maverick, which is billed as a repair-it-yourself car, is another indication of Ford's direction. The owner's manual is not all that easy to follow, but the company claims the last Ford with such a manual was the 1931 Model A Ford car.

GM is experimenting with a program, still in the pilot stage, in which an inspector selects a new car at random from a dealer's lot and drives it. GM calls it the "Would-I-buy-this-car test."

Sharper focus.   The auto companies are paying a lot of attention to the "short-term" quality problems, the ones that show up in the first 10 days of a car's life: vent leaks, faulty door handles, and the like. Building quality through basic engineering and design is more difficult and more time-consuming. But Ford's Nevin points out that even the little repairable items may represent basic design failure. "Take a vacuum or electrical system where there is routinely a 5% defect rate. Maybe the plant simply can't build the part to that design."

Finally, there is the problem of customer relations. GM's Bates believes that the attitude of people dealing with consumers has a lot to do with customer satisfaction. So early this year the company began a series of meetings for dealer employees on owner relations that eventually clocked 37,000 employees. GM is also setting up incentive programs for mechanics.

It makes contributions to a fund for mechanics with the best repair records, based on how often or seldom a customer who has just had his car fixed has to return for another go-around.

TIRE MAKERS' BUMPY RECALL CAMPAIGN

What happens when an unprepared industry runs into the consumer buzz-saw is clearly illustrated by the recent woes of the tire manufacturers.

The question of tire safety has been around a long time. But the 1966 National Traffic & Motor Vehicle Safety Act for the first time required auto manufacturers to recall cars and parts—including the original equipment tires—when safety-related defects are discovered.

Through a Congressional oversight, replacement tires were not mentioned in the law.

Late in 1968, the National Highway Safety Bureau found that one of every 11 tires it tested failed to meet Federal safety standards. Ralph Nader got hold of the report and spread it all over the newspapers. The Safety Bureau began pressuring Akron to institute voluntary recall programs, and the industry was in trouble.

Recalls. Finally, in January, 1969, Mohawk Rubber Co. announced that it was recalling 10,000 of its 7.35 x 14 Airflo tires—about half the company's 1968 production of that model—and would replace them with its costlier Bonanza tires. Since then, there have been at least eight more recalls, and Akron has found that rubber doesn't always bounce back:

- Mohawk retrieved 3,356 of the 10,000 tires, but 2,776 of these were from inventory. Only 580 came from customers.
- General Tire & Rubber Co. went searching for 42,000 General Jet tires, but can account for only 8,259.
- Goodyear Tire & Rubber Co. got a great deal of publicity when an upside down "6" in a tire mold caused a figure in the load rating to look like a "9." But only eight of the 2,000 tires involved have been found.

Obviously, hunting down tires is a lot harder than recalling autos. While there are 29,000 car dealerships in the country, there are at least 250,000 places to buy tires. Besides, car dealers know who buys their cars; tire dealers know only in the case of credit purchases.

Compliance. To launch a recall campaign, a rubber company sends a registered letter to the dealers involved and covers media with news releases. The company will call in all tires of a particular serial number and destroy them, even though only a handful might prove defective.

Because of the dismal performance of the recall campaigns, Senator Gaylord Nelson (D-Wis.) introduced an Administration-backed bill last April that would require tire makers to notify owners by letter of any suspected defects in their tires, and to replace the tires with new ones. To comply, manufacturers would have to keep track of who owned all tires.

To everyone's surprise the Rubber Manufacturers Assn. backed the bill, although the industry had resisted two earlier versions. But by this time, the handwriting was on the wall, and RMA admitted that the companies had been designing a voluntary recall system for more than a year.

By the time the Nelson bill gets through Congress—perhaps as early as January—all manufacturers will have onstream an alphanumeric code that tells the week the tire was made, who made it and in which plant, and the size and style.

Snags.   The code, which replaces the individual manufacturer's serial numbers with more detailed and standardized information, is merely an identification system. More important—and more difficult—is to get customers to fill out registration cards with their names and addresses and the code numbers of the tires they buy—and then return the cards.

Mohawk found in its experiments earlier this year that the return of its postage-paid registration cards was high when the dealers cooperated fully. Firestone Tire & Rubber Co. found, in its own series of tests, that purchasers seldom returned the registration cards when left to their own devices. Returns from company-owned stores were best, but still poor.

Goodyear already has prepared a registration card in anticipation of the law. The customer has to pay the postage, but Goodyear hopes the strong wording will induce him to spend the 6¢: "Important! Your tire identification number must be registered now for your protection under Federal motor vehicle law."

Criticism.   Tire men complain that the law puts no pressure on dealers to see that the registration cards are returned. Nor are tire executives enthralled at the prospect of keeping records on the 200-million tires they make every year. "The logistics are staggering," moans one. Manufacturers swallow hard when they think of the cost. Independent studies put the cost at between $2 and $2.50 per tire (about half what Nader claims auto makers pay for original equipment). Uniroyal, Inc., has estimated it will cost 75¢ just to register a tire, while Cooper Tire & Rubber Co. figures the program will add 2% a year to its manufacturing cost, even if not a single tire is recalled.

Saddest of all, claim tire men privately, the whole recall program is unnecessary. "The defects we're talking about simply don't cause accidents," says one. "As far as we can tell, tires are involved in less than 1% of all car accidents, and in those cases it's almost always because the tire was bald, not because it was defective. If anybody thinks he's going to save any lives with all this, he's kidding himself."

Satisfying the consumerists isn't all headache by any means. Celanese figured out a set of end-use licensing standards for its Fortrel and Arnel fibers that is widely known in consumerist circles. Celanese got into the program because it was a late starter in an industry dominated by DuPont's brand names, and it felt it had to invest real money in building confidence in its merchandise. The lure: the ad budget Celanese spends to support the products of everyone from the mill to the cutter that makes the clothing. To get Celanese's money, everyone has to conform to the standards the company has established.

A HAZY OUTLOOK

In the struggle over the new consumerism, businessmen are often angry, and even more often bewildered. But by and large, they don't appear to be cynical.

If they were, the record shows that probably the safest course would be to let Congress pass any sort of regulatory bill it pleased, then sit back and watch the regulators fail to enforce it.

Consider, for example, the Fair Packaging & Labeling Act—"Truth-in-Packaging"—enacted in 1966. It will come as a surprise to many people who remember the publicity generated by the bill's passage that, despite the redesign of a host of supermarket packages to conform with the act's provisions, some parts of the law are still not officially in effect. The effective date for drug and cosmetics packages is now Dec. 31. Food packaging regulation went into effect only two months ago.

In some instances, even the official dates may prove unrealistic. One section of the act, for example, charges FDA with promulating regulations governing "cents-off" deal labels on packages. FDA has yet to issue such regulations. Exactly why is in some dispute. A Senate Commerce Committee staffer believes that FDA, with all its other problems, simply assigned a low priority to the intricacies of promotional labeling. But other observers maintain that the agency simply found the task beyond its capabilities, that it just doesn't know enough about high-powered packaged goods marketing to draw up meaningful rules.

Trials and errors. To do it justice, FDA has made a number of efforts to stretch its limited resources.

Two years ago, the agency launched an experiment in self-inspection with General Foods to see whether food manufacturers could manage the surveilance of food processing on their own. The experiment was conducted in GF's modern plant in Dover, Del., and covered two products—a gelatin dessert (a "low risk" product) and a custard ("high risk").

The program has undergone a series of modifications, and will be terminated this month. The result: "It worked not as well as we both had hoped," according to GF's Herbert Cleaves. The problem was the endless paperwork involved in reporting to Washington—a chore to produce, and certainly a chore to read. Cleaves thinks that "with refinements" self-certification can be made feasible in the food industry. If the biggest and most modern food processors could take some of the strain off FDA, it would have more resources to police smaller operators.

Despite imaginative ideas like these, however, an internal study group set up by FDA recently declared that the agency "had been unable to develop the kind of concerted and coordinated efforts needed to deal adequately and simultaneously with problems of pesticide residues, food sanitation, chemical additives, microbiological contamination, drug and device safety and efficacy, hazardous household products, medicated animal feeds, and myriad other problems." In short, said the study group, "we are currently not equipped to cope with the challenge."

Frustrations.   The Federal Trade Commission is not in much better shape. It is an agency, as Louis M. Kohlmeier, Jr., points out in his new book, The Regulators, that was designed by Congress to be the national expert on monopoly and economic concentration and has ended up as the national authority on phoney chinchilla-farming schemes. As a matter of fact, to any business reporter who regularly sees FTC's fat packets of new releases cross his desk, it sometimes seems that the commission's major activity is enjoining infractions of the fur-labeling act in Bent Spoon, North Dakota.

What has happened, of course, is that FTC has over the years been saddled with responsibility for a variety of consumer protection measures —mainly involving deception and fraud—which it is not really equipped to handle.

The load on FTC is so great, and the administrative machinery so cumbersome, that it is the despair of the commissioners. Mary Gardiner Jones, a liberal Republican commissioner, asserts that the commissioners, no matter how well intentioned, have no time to get out into the business world to see what's going on, and certainly no time to think about a rational and imaginative regulatory policy regarding the marketing of consumer goods.

The result is a very real frustration, even for businesses facing the threat of regulation. Both the home appliance manufacturers and the auto people have been waiting a year for the final draft of FTC's promised report on warranty practices.

What makes them impatient, of course, is the pending warranty legislation in Congress. Early drafts of both the House and Senate bills are tough, and, in the opinion of many in industry, almost impossible to live with. They include not only the requirement for a full parts-and-labor express warranty if any guarantee of product performance is offered at all, but a section requiring compulsory arbitration of warranty grievances. The specter of compulsory arbitration over the repair of a $10 toaster makes the appliance men's hair curl. So they are counting on the FTC report to put matters in somewhat better perspective.

Similarly, the synthetic fiber and textile industry is discouraged over the delay in reporting on the amendment to the Flammable Fabrics Act. The amendment, ramrodded by Senator Magnuson, was passed 18 months ago. The Secretary of Commerce was supposed to define the extent and nature of the textile fire hazard by end-use of the fabric and report recommendations to the industry. Only two small sections of the report have been issued, and the industry is still waiting for the rest. "They just haven't done their homework," says an executive of one big fiber producer.

Uncertainties.   More than one businessman has said in exasperation—though never on the record—that thoroughgoing enforcement of existing laws would in some ways be preferable to the arbitrary system of random prosecution. Business sits around waiting for lightning to strike. "It's an awful way to try to build an intelligent policy of response to legislation," one man complains.

Then, too, Kohlmeier argues in his book that the regulatory agencies are more concerned with protecting the interest of the regulated industries than with the needs of the consuming public. His argument is persuasive, particularly in regard to the Interstate Commerce Commission, which has consistently maintained a floor under freight rates, and the Federal Communications Commission, which is generally regarded to have botched the allocation of television frequencies.

Businessmen faced with specific new regulation, however, don't always believe they have a friend at the regulatory agency. They may not be afraid of the regulators now but they are genuinely scared about the potential for regulation in the age of consumerism. Ralph Nader predicted recently that within the next decade some businessmen will end up in jail if their products injure a consumer.

THE CHALLENGE OF PRODUCT SAFETY: A POSITIVE APPROACH PROGRAM FOR PRODUCT SAFETY*

By John J. Williams

Safety awareness at all levels, and well-planned
and executed special programs have decreased product
recalls and liability litigations for Rockwell-Standard.

Rockwell-Standard, manufacturers of mechanical components for heavy-duty trucks and commercial vehicles, have always been safety conscious, but increased public concern over safety has led us to intensify our efforts in this area and to establish new and more formal programs to further assure the safety of our products and reduce the number of recalls.

The first, and by far the most important step toward a successful product safety program, is to get the whole team thinking. The concern and desire to produce safe products must permeate throughout the entire organization. Management already has considerable motivation to produce safe products from a business viewpoint. The ever present objective of maintaining a good company reputation and public image are strong motivators. However, in today's environment with the growing concern for product safety, as evidenced by the many product recall campaigns, consumer organizations, the National Traffic & Motor Vehicle Safety Act of 1966, the Occupational Health & Safety Act of 1970, the Consumer Product Safety Act of 1972, and resulting Federal Safety Standards, plus the increasing incidence of product liability lawsuits, it is safe to say that management is safety conscious. Thus, the real challenge towards achieving our desired safety awareness was not with upper management, but entailed disseminating management's concern to those not directly involved with managing the business.

SAFETY AWARENESS

The actions we took at Rockwell-Standard to achieve the desired product safety awareness involved: 1) establishing a top management level safety committee; 2) establishing a permanent product safety organizational entity: 3) documenting policy and responsibilities; and 4) implementing

* John Williams is manager of product safety, Rockwell Standard Group, Rockwell International. This paper was presented at the Industrial Research Institute Fall Meeting, November, 1977.

safety awareness motivational activities. These four actions became the foundation for our present successful product safety program. Because of their importance in not only starting but maintaining any product safety program I would like to share with you the approaches we took.

First we established a 9-man safety committee composed of Rockwell-Standard vice president level personnel plus our corporate legal counsel. This group meets monthly for at least 1½ hours. Establishment of policy, leadership, and coordination of product safety activities, are their primary functions. The committee acts as a decision-making body, and during the monthly meetings is briefed on status, corrective actions underway, and recommended actions associated with product safety and product liability, and responds by approval or redirection. In addition, they also provide the management push for priority accomplishment of assigned actions. All material presented to the safety committee is screened and organized by our safety office, in advance of the meeting which facilitates covering the normal lengthy agenda in the short time allowed.

Next we established a safety office with a permanent two-man staff (now up to four men) devoted solely to product safety activities. Although closely allied to engineering, this office is outside of the engineering organization and reports to the vice president of technical operations. This office developed all of the documentation, procedures, and briefings used to implement our product safety program, and is the heart of the continuing activity.

The third element of our awareness program was the issuance of a Rockwell-Standard product safety manual signed by our group president. This document stated the company policy regarding product safety in very specific terms and also how the policy was to be administered including applicable responsibilities for all functional organizations. Wide distribution was achieved and this manual is compulsory reading for new personnel in many job classifications. Revisions and additions are periodically made to the manual to document additional policy statements and requirements associated with our expanding product safety program.

The fourth step in our safety awareness activity was to take our message to the personnel in our manufacturing plants, those men on the firing line who are in the best spot to stop defects from getting out of our plants. We assembled a 10-minute hard hitting briefing that was presented around the clock to groups at shift changes until every man at all of our plants had attended. The presentation emphasized the individual's involvement with product safety, how he could contribute and why he personally, as well as our company, should be concerned. The motivational impact obtained was overwhelming. Follow on plant briefings are scheduled yearly, with a poster program plus articles in the plant papers periodically reminding personnel of our concern for product safety.

ROUTINE SAFETY ACTIVITIES

Now I will review some of our key efforts aimed at avoiding safety problems. I will first briefly mention the relatively routine activities, which though probably conventional elsewhere, are important to achieving a successful product safety program. The first of these is our time-phased design reviews—as many as six during the development of a new product. The importance of good design reviews at the right time cannot be overemphasized. This is where we require the design team to prove that product safety received the proper emphasis in relation to other considerations of performance, conformance to all requirements, maintainability, producibility, reliability and cost. The use of a checklist at design reviews assures that all the important considerations are adequately covered. During design reviews we put heavy emphasis on the usage of time-proven designs. We also strive to achieve a design life on safety related parts that exceeds vehicle life, but where this is not possible, then the issuance of appropriate inspection/maintenance instructions becomes critical. Sometimes specific safety precautions are even added directly on the product.

We have specific criteria that dictates the timing of our various design reviews. Our final design review on a new product may be unique in that it is scheduled one year after initial production hardware was put in service. This either serves as a confirmation of design adequacy based upon actual field usage, or provides early indication of required changes.

Regardless of all of the sophisticated analysis processes available, nothing substitutes for a good test program prior to production. Besides extensive laboratory testing, and testing on our own instrumented test vehicles, it is our normal practice to obtain limited field experience in a selected truck fleet prior to full scale production. I appreciate that this field testing under actual environmental conditions is a luxury not feasible on many products, but since we have the opportunity we take full advantage of it.

Good technical publications for use by customers and field service personnel are also important. In our publications, which are many and varied, we not only define the correct maintenance and repair, but provide clear warnings regarding the hazards created by improper repair procedures.

Another important area is quality control. There will always be controversy regarding too much vs too little Q.C. when evaluated against cost effectiveness. However, when considering safety related parts and the consequences of a defective part finding its way into highway usage, it is generally agreed that there are areas where Q.C. cannot be compromised. We subject all safety related parts to stringent purchasing and inspection requirements. In our organization we have a group staff Q.C. function and manufacturing plant level Q.C. The group staff Q.C. establish policy, issue procedures, audit procedure implementation, and also audit actual production quality. Plant level Q.C. reports directly to the plant engineering manager and is thus removed somewhat from the pressures of plant manufacturing.

SPECIAL SAFETY PROGRAMS

There are three processes we have implemented at Rockwell-Standard that undoubtedly have been large contributors to our successful product safety program. The first of these is our SRC (Safety Related Component) program. This entailed identifying all of the safety related parts in our product lines and actually stamping all applicable drawings with an SRC stamp. Further, on each of these drawings all safety critical characteristics (such as material, process, dimension, torque, etc.) were coded with the special symbol. Considerable engineering effort was expended in this drawing markup activity, but it was certainly effective in getting our safety message throughout all of engineering.

With all of our safety parts and critical characteristics coded we were then able to implement our special quality control procedures, which as mentioned earlier involved more stringent purchasing and inspection requirements. The net result was that with realigned, but not increased, inspection activity we have achieved an improvement in the quality of safety parts leaving our plants. We have also introduced traceability requirements on all safety parts.

Another very significant part of our SRC program was implementing a procedure that requires that any manufacturing deviation to a safety related component must be approved by the product safety manager. This provides an independent evaluation outside of the influence of manufacturing pressure of the performance effects of the proposed deviation. In today's environment of material shortages this deviation procedure is being taxed but serves as an effective check and balance.

The next of the big three in our safety program is our application analysis process. The courts have indicated that we as manufacturers are expected to know how our products are being used, and further not to sell if the usage would be unsafe. With these requirements in mind we require potential customers to fill out an application approval request form with pertinent vehicle and usage characteristics. This data is then fed into our computerized application analysis programs and the correct axle, brake, etc. for the application is selected. This analysis process has also been recently expanded to consider compliance to applicable Federal Safety Standards. Upon selection of the appropriate size products for the application, this data is entered on the lower portion of the same sheet submitted by the customer and returned to him as Rockwell's approval for the specific usage defined.

In order to enforce use of this system all Rockwell-Standard sales data carries the notation that warranty is contingent upon usage as approved by our engineering department. As a cross check of the system all purchase orders received are checked against a printout of application approvals. If no approval is on record a follow-up system is triggered to obtain the customer's approval request data. We have established a target of 100% approvals on all products sold and so far have made good progress toward achieving that goal. In the not too distant future we intend to enforce achievement of the goal by refusing to honor any purchase order that does not reference an approved application.

Lastly, but by no means last in importance, is our potential safety problem (PSP) investigation system. Any reported field problem on a safety related component is immediately brought to the attention of our safety office. Copies of these safety related field reports are all printed on redborder paper to obtain special attention by all recipients. The key element, however, of the PSP system is that each such report initiates an investigative file that cannot be closed until resolved. Resolution might involve extensive field inspections, testing, special field instructions, or in some cases even a product recall campaign. Whatever the eventual outcome, each PSP item receives priority attention by all involved personnel and must be resolved to the satisfaction of the group safety committee before the file is closed. This system is in a way similar to the requirement on manned spacecraft hardware wherein any failure during test must be resolved as to cause, prior to completion of the failure report. It worked for our spacecraft hardware and the same philosophy is now finding application to truck components.

In conclusion, our product safety program is working because of the following salient facts: a) policy and procedures were documented; b) top management support was provided; c) all personnel were made aware of policy and what was expected of them individually; d) safety related components were identified and subjected to special handling throughout design and manufacturing; e) product potential usage is throughly analyzed; and f) any known field safety problems receive priority attention until resolved.

We are proud of our product safety program at Rockwell-Standard, and are gratified to see our recall campaigns and product liability litigations decreasing in opposition to the national trend. Our Positive Approach is paying dividends.

HOW TO DEAL WITH PROFESSIONAL
CONSUMER ACTIVISTS*
By Arthur R. Schulze

Marketing today involves more than locating and fulfilling consumer needs. It also entails counteracting professional consumer activists who make a living by attacking your products, according to Arthur R. Schulze, group vice president, General Mills Inc., Minneapolis.

Speaking at a recent Food and Drug Law Institute symposium in Charleston, S.C., Schulze said unfavorable publicity by consumer activists has "awakened us to the realities of a new marketing environment."

Schulze said marketers must learn to deal with professional consumer activists, but he used the marketing of breakfast cereal to illustrate his point.

"The cereal industry's experience with presweetened cereals is a good example," he said at the symposium, entitled *Getting the Message Across.*

"Almost 30 years ago, the cereal industry realized that most breakfast cereals, cooked or ready-to-eat, were consumed with sugar added. Thus, the idea of presweetened cereals was born.

"The extra convenience to consumers of adding sugar in the factory, plus the resulting differences in product texture and eating quality, proved successful. Presweetened cereals came on to represent about 30% of the total breakfast cereal volume, a market share which continues to the present day.

"From a nutritional standpoint, the cereal industry has known all along that sugar does not replace cereal grain. Presweetened cereal usually provides no more sugar than that which is added by consumers to regular cereals, which is very little.

"Since we knew all of this, we assumed that consumers would also know, and that there should be no reason to 'speak out' in ways other than our normal advertising.

"We found it hard to acknowledge that getting the message across should require anything beyond advertising, despite a growing awareness that consumers were beginning to receive, from other sources, product information which was inaccurate.

"But, the times have changed. Not only has the past decade seen the emergence of consumer activism, it has seen the emergence of consumer activism as a *profession.*

* Arthur R. Schulze, "How to Deal with Professional Consumer Activists," August 10, 1979, pp. 1, 2. Reprinted from *Marketing News,* published by the American Marketing Association.

"Today all of us are faced with critics who make a living by attacking our products or services. Quite literally, their income depends largely on their abilities to convincingly assail our products."

Schulze pointed out that consumer groups are well-organized and directed by intelligent, well-meaning people. "They are able to spend 100% of their time crusading for a cause," he said. "They are often highly successful."

As an example, he mentioned the Action for Children's Television (ACT) organization, which has succeeded in altering the nature of broadcasting to children.

"These groups are well-financed," he said. "With the passage of the Magnuson-Moss Act by Congress, many consumer groups have found the (federal) government a significant source of funds."

Consumers Union, he said, has 2 million members and annual gross revenues of $25 million from its publications. Still, it received $325,000 in Magnuson-Moss funds last year.

"Robert Choate's Council on Children, Media, and Merchandising also received nearly $200,000," Schulze said.

Consumer groups, he feels can exert influence far out of proportion to their size because of America's current interest in self-improvement and fulfillment, including health and nutrition.

"How can you possibly oppose a group with such a well-chosen and official-sounding name as the Safe Food Institute?" he asked.

"Perhaps it is these names, which connote such respectability, that enable activists to make such statements as, 'the food industry is literally killing us producing foods that cause cancer and heart disease.' Or, 'it's about time for the FTC to stop Kelloggs from lying to our children.'

"Heard often enough, and without positive refutation by the food industry, this kind of nonsense achieves credibility and acceptance among the American people."

Schulze said the first consumer activist to assail the cereal industry was Choate. In 1970 he published a list which ranked cereals by nutritional value.

"Those of us who manufactured breakfast cereals ranked high on Choate's list saw sales of those brands increase sharply," he said. "Other brands placed down on the list, saw sales slump. This immediate consumer reaction to unfavorable publicity awakened us to the realities of a new marketing environment."

Schulze said two General Mills brands, Mr. Wonderful's Surprise and Total, also "felt the activists' sting." Published reports by consumer activists about sugar content and allegations of over-pricing "had an adverse impact on sales," he admitted.

"The professional activist has changed our marketing environment," he said. "But there's been another change, too: the emergence of the activists' sympathetic counterpart in Washington."

The placement of consumer activists into positions of authority in regulatory agencies (like the FTC) and government advisory groups has affected the industry, he added, citing proposed FTC rules that would ban children's advertising.

"I am worried that many of us in the food industry think this is an isolated problem of concern only to those companies which market breakfast cereals or confections to children," he said.

"Lest you be surrounded by a false sense of security, I want to impress upon you that the children's advertising issue now before the FTC may well be the leading edge of a very long sword aimed at drastically changing *all* advertising.

"Once a precedent has been established with foods containing sugar, it will be possible to attack other food advertising.

"If barriers to the advertising of sugared foods can be erected, how long will it be before foods containing salt come under attack? Or foods that are high in fat?

"I think that most of us agree, whatever your feelings about the value of advertising, that the 'leading edge' could produce drastic changes in our way of doing business with consumers."

Schulze said companies, and marketing executives in particular, could use the following strategy to counteract negative, or inaccurate publicity by consumer activists:

1. Organize a top-level management team to identify the issues, define corporate objectives/strategies, and assign duties.

2. Initiate a comprehensive fact-finding mission so you're as knowledgeable about the issues as the activists. Consult outside experts, initiate special research, conduct interviews with consumers, and analyze available survey data.

3. Identify key target audiences, just as you would do in developing a marketing media plan for one of your new products. Employ direct contacts with government officials, media, academia, and others who exert influence on public policy.

4. Discuss the issues with your employees and stockholders. They want facts and you must do your best to provide them.

5. Launch an aggressive communications campaign, utilizing key executives. Have them speak out on TV, radio, and in the newspapers. Provide reporters with sufficient background information so that they are knowledgeable enough to deal with both industry and activist spokesmen. Bring the key issues to the attention of editorial writers and commentators, espeially those believed to be thought-leaders, who exert an influence on readers or viewers.

6. Create positive industry momentum, mostly by demonstrating in the public media that many arguments on the issues are emotional in nature and not supported by facts.

Schulze said General Mills followed this strategy.

"You must have commitment and support at the highest levels of company management," he said. "Line management must also be involved.

"To get the message across you must be willing to commit resources, not just money but also time and people. It requires a long-term effort.

"Establishing your position and credibility on an issue doesn't happen overnight. Effective advertising campaigns require continuing frequency as well as reach. So does the task of changing people's attitudes."

WHY DOES MANAGEMENT ALLOW INCOMPETENTS TO HANDLE COMPLAINTS?*

A Feature Report

In travels around the country I always read the Action Line columns. Typical of what I find is the following from *The Dallas Morning News* on Friday, March 9, 1979:

> *Last April a purchase made by another customer, whose account number differed from mine by two digits, appeared on my Neiman-Marcus bill. Although I have called numerous times I have not been able to get the erroneous charge taken off my account. Last month a man in Neiman's credit department promised to take care of it, but my next bill not only still had the unauthorized charge but also failed to credit my account with a payment I made two months ago for merchandise I did buy.*

RT knows that Nieman-Marcus doesn't want to give this kind of service. N–M grew and prospered by showing concern about customers—by inundating them with good service.

When the Action column called (and it obviously got attention) the result was that they removed the erroneous charge twice and credited the missing payment twice! It took another call from the newspaper to get the account corrected—and then the customer was afraid to charge for three months to be sure that new mistakes didn't show up.

RT thought: There was a day when larger stores had a "Complaint Department." The window was clearly marked and the customer could come to it. If the customer called in (and in those ancient days many

---

* "Why Does Management Allow Incompetents to Handle Complaints?" *Retailing Today,* April 1979, Lafayette, California, used with permission.

customers who had good accounts did not have telephones), they were connected with the Complaint Department.

Who manned (or womaned) the complaint department? The best and most experienced clerk in the office. This was a job that people were promoted to—and got extra pay for filling. Today the person on the complaint desk would be called a "customer's advocate" or even an "ombudsman." They prided themselves on clearly understanding the customer's problem applying their knowledge of the store system to that problem, resolving the problem, advising the customer of the action taken—AND KEEPING THE PERSON AS A CUSTOMER.

What happens today? Anyone answers the telephone—often the least experienced person in the store. There is no such thing as a complaint office or complaint desk. There are no special instructions about who shall handle complaints. The senior people don't want to be interrupted by customers. The person who answers the phone may be new, untrained, a short-hour person, or even a Kelly Girl.

The story of this disdain for the customer travels to many places.

People tell their friends about their problem with your store. People write to Action Line columns in newspapers or consumer reporters at radio or TV stations. These consumer advocates properly disclose the name of the offending retailer so that other customers can be alerted about the way your store handles your customers.

Your policy should be a simple one. The best person in the department handles complaints. If someone else happens to receive the complaint they are to record it and bring it to the attention of the responsible person in the shortest possible time. The responsible person is to resolve the problem, report back to the customer, record the action taken, and follow up with the customer after an appropriate interval.

The cheapest thing for a retailer to do is to keep an existing customer; the most expensive thing is to try to attract a new customer. It is appropriate to reprint an item that United Parcel Service ran in *Pickup* years ago. UPS found it in a publication called *Be a Friendly Floridian.*

Remember Me?

I'm the fellow who goes into a restaurant and patiently waits while the waitresses finish their visiting before taking my order.

I'm the fellow who goes into a department store and stands quietly while the sales clerks finish their little chit-chat.

I'm the fellow who drives into a service station and never blows his horn but lets the attendant take his sweet time.

You might say I'm the good guy—But do you know who else I am? I'm the fellow who never comes back.

It amuses me to see business spending so much money each year to get me back when I was there in the first place! All they really needed to do was give me some service and extend a little courtesy and I would have still been their customer.

CHELSEA, THE ADULT SOFT DRINK: A CASE STUDY OF CORPORATE SOCIAL RESPONSIBILITY*

A corporation can regulate itself on social matters if it establishes a meaningful two-way dialogue with consumers.

By Keith M. Jones
Anheuser-Busch, Inc.

Following World War II, the pent-up needs of American consumers were unleashed in the domestic marketplace. An unending stream of new consumer products resulted, and the marketing concept was born. Simply put, the marketing concept argued that products existed solely to fill consumer needs. Products were not purchased for their intrinsic value, but rather to satisfy a consumer need. The simple logic of the marketing concept was irresistible, so manufacturers began marketing their products instead of simply producing them.

LIMITS OF THE MARKETING CONCEPT

As the marketing concept flowered and consumer need research rivaled the aerospace program in detail, competition among manufacturers extended far beyond the characteristics of the product itself. Products were enlarged to become the "augmented product" of Theodore Levitt. The "augmented product" was articulated by Professor Levitt in his mid-60's best seller, "The Marketing Mode" as:

> . . . a new kind of competition that is in galloping ascendance in the world today. This is the competition of product augmentation: not competition be-

---

* Keith M. Jones, "Chelsea. The Adult Soft Drink: A Case Study of Corporate Social Responsibility," *Journal of Contemporary Business,* 7. no. 4., used with permission.

tween what companies produce in their factories, but between what they add to their factory output in the form of packaging, services, advertising, customer advice, financing, delivery arrangements, warehousing, and other things that people value.

As the augmented product achieved full dimensions, consumer needs to be fulfilled became increasingly complex: ego needs, status needs, and needs for conspicuous display of affluence. Ordering just a "scotch" whiskey for example was insufficient. Brand name scotch was required, and certain brands such as Johnnie Walker Black Label filled social needs that Johnnie Walker himself could never have imagined.

Product augmentation stretched the marketing concept to its furthest limits, and conflicts began to appear. Conflicts occurred between augmented products satisfying social needs and the larger role of the corporation in society. The need for convenient aerosol cosmetics conflicted with preservation of the environment. The stress and tension release provided by tobacco products conflicted with human longevity. The need for social lubricants conflicted with the social costs of alochol abuse.

MARKETING CONCEPT VERSUS SOCIAL RESPONSIBILITY

What happened to corporations whose pursuit of the marketing concept conflicted with their larger role as a responsible social citizen? Historically there were three consequences:

- The product in question was publicly screened for social negatives.
- The federal government was the screening agent.
- The press had a field day at company expense.

There can be no doubt that the marketplace demands and deserves products free of social negatives. However, there is an alternative to coercive and often punitive governmental intervention. A corporation can self-screen its products by directly involving consumer opinion leaders. A case in point is the social screening of Chelsea, a controversial soft drink test-marketed by Anheuser-Busch. Rather than wait for governmental direction, Anheuser-Busch employed a unique approach to resolve a conflict situation—consumer participation.

The following discussion of the Chelsea experience consists of two segments. First, the Chelsea product and the controversy is briefly reviewed. Second, a step-by-step description of the social screening process is detailed.

CHELSEA, THE CONTROVERSIAL PRODUCT

Chelsea was the culmination of more than two years of consumer needs research which indicated that adults wanted a soft beverage with three characteristics:

- Less sweet, drier taste
- All natural ingredients
- Social acceptability as an alternative to alcoholic beverages

The resulting product was a light blend of all natural apple, lemon, lime, and ginger flavors. Since Chelsea was pasteurized, no artificial preservatives were needed and it had no caffeine or saccharin either. Because Chelsea contained one-third less sugar than regular soft drinks, there were one-third fewer calories. To compensate for the body of sugar, a malt product was added which contained about one-half of one percent of alcohol fermented naturally. Like apple cider, ginger ale, and beer, Chelsea was a golden color with a frothy head.

An Adult Soft Drink

The product was reviewed by the Federal Bureau of Alcohol, Tobacco and Firearms (BATF) and the alcohol control boards of five test market states and was found to fit the FDA and state definitions of a soft drink. In summary, Chelsea was a natural, less sweet, adult soft drink.

Chelsea, the Augmented Product

To fulfill the adult need for a socially acceptable alcohol substitute, augmentation was required. First, a sophisticated package was selected with the sleek, thin shape and distinctive foil labeling an adult would expect. Next, Chelsea was priced higher than regular soft drinks to reinforce the "Cadillac" image of a natural, adult product. Finally, an advertising campaign was developed to communicate Chelsea as an extraordinary soft drink for extraordinary people aged 25 or older. Because Chelsea was "Not-So" sweet, "Not-So" heavy, "Not-So" artificial and "Not-So" ordinary as other soft drinks, the advertising slogan was the "Not-So" Soft Drink. Thus natural, less sweet Chelsea, with its packaging, pricing, and advertising augmentation entered into market test.

CHELSEA, THE CONTROVERSY

In Virginia test markets, Chelsea conflicted with the social concerns of several individuals and organizations. The Virginia Nurses' Association voted to boycott Chelsea. Seventh-Day Adventists condemned Chelsea as a contributor to the problem of alcohol abuse. Local educators, church groups and PTA councils even pressured store managers to remove Chelsea from their shelves. Press coverage of the Virginia controversy led to network television exposure and Chelsea became a national issue. Finally, respected national figures such as Senator Orrin Hatch (Chairman, Senate Sub-Committee on Alcoholism and Alcohol Abuse) and H.E.W. Secretary Joseph Califano publicly denounced the product and its manufacturer.

How Could a Natural Soft Drink Be So Controversial?

How could the first natural soft drink with less sugar and no chemicals or preservatives become so controversial? The problem was that although Chelsea was targeted for adults, it was by definition a soft drink, and therefore purchasable by children. Chelsea critics argued that children did not need a socially acceptable alcohol substitute because they could not consume alcohol in the first place. Reasonable people suggested that however unintended, the augmented product Chelsea was in conflict with the social responsibility of a major corporation.

THE MANAGEMENT DECISION TO ACT

Corporations interpreting social responsibility as simple profit maximization may have done nothing at this point. It would have been easy to argue "tough-it-out" or "let the marketplace decide." Anheuser-Busch management, however, realized that action was required, and the process of social screening was initiated. Because the screening process had to be conducted objectively, without the pressure of time, and would intimately involve Chelsea critics, the first step was to defuse the controversy. Therefore all Chelsea manufacture, advertising and promotion was suspended on October 21, five weeks after test market start-up. The suspension was a signal to Chelsea critics that the company valued its social responsibility more than Chelsea profits.

DYNAMICS OF THE SOCIAL SCREENING PROCESS

The screening process is much easier to describe than to conduct. In essence the purpose of the process was to eliminate the conflict between corporate activity and larger social goals. At Anheuser-Busch the social screening process consisted of four steps:

Step I: Visible corporate commitment to social responsibility
Step II: Identification of the social issue
Step III: Active participation of consumer opinion leaders
Step IV: Public communication of screening results.

While the following discussion explores each step in detail, it should be pointed out that all four steps are intertwined in a continuous process and should not be considered as independent actions.

VISIBLE CORPORATE COMMITMENT

Effective social screening is impossible without commitment to social responsiveness at the highest levels of the corporation. Such commitment is not easy to demonstrate. It's not a matter of public relations, or of truth in advertising. It's not a matter of subsidizing the local symphony or of generosity during United Fund drives. It is a matter of ordering priorities. Corporate economic ends must clearly become subordinate to larger social objectives. Importantly, this ranking of priorities must be performed by top management. In the case of Chelsea, August A. Busch, III, chief executive officer and board chairman, made it perfectly clear that corporate responsiveness was a higher than profit and loss contribution.

Not only was this commitment made clear *inside* the corporation, but visible commitment was also communicated *outside* the corporation. For Anheuser-Busch, the October 21 public suspension of Chelsea manufacture, advertising and promotion conveyed this commitment.

Identification of the Social Issue

The best intentions are in vain if the corporate social screening process misidentifies or fails to identify the source of the conflict in question. With Chelsea, the basic social issue was not easy to pinpoint, and there were a few red herrings. The issue, for example, was not that children could purchase Chelsea. Restricting sales to minors would not have solved the problem. Nor was intoxication the issue (about 17 ten ounce bottles consumed in an hour would have been required for intoxication—more than a child's stomach capacity). The social issue in the Chelsea case was much more complex. The issue was one of social conditioning. Critics claimed that Chelsea could act to predispose children toward alcohol consumption because Chelsea product packaging and advertising suggested beer in some respects.

No quantitative data existed to refute or substantiate the predisposition claim, so its validity became a matter of opinion. Therefore, Anheuser-Busch consulted outside experts. Medical experts, religious leaders, authorities on alcoholism, and educators were involved. When their expert opinion confirmed that the "Stepping Stone" theory of Chelsea critics could be true, the required action was obvious. Those elements of the augmented product, Chelsea, which would act to precondition children had to be eliminated.

Active Participation of Consumer Opinion Leaders

At this point, the executive might ask, "Who is running the company anyway?" Isn't the manager who invites outsiders into the decision making process abdicating his managerial responsibilities? Of course not. The consumer participants are only a sounding board, a mini-board of directors individually selected for expertise on the specific social issue identified in Step II. The corporate manager selects the outsiders, presents action plans to them, and is responsible for channeling their input in a manner which benefits the corporation. What about confidentiality? If the consumer participants exposed confidential information to the press or to competitors, wouldn't the whole screening process backfire? There was always such a risk. However, Anheuser-Busch felt the risk was outweighed by the benefit of articulate social input, and therefore selected consumer participants of demonstrated personal integrity who would respect confidentiality requests. The consumer participants included: the Director of Adolescent Medicine at a leading Virginia university, the Director of the Center for Research on Media and Children at the Wharton School of Business, members of the Virginia Nurses' Association, members of the Potomac Council of Seventh-Day Adventists and, of course, the staff of U.S. Senator Orrin Hatch. All of these individuals strictly adhered to our confidentiality requests and made significant contributions to the screening process. More specifically, each opinion leader was included in two tasks:

- Articulating social issues to be dealt with
- Previewing Anheuser-Busch's proposed action plan

In retrospect, the participation of outside opinion leaders was the key to successful social screening because through this process, the severest Chelsea critics became proponents of the revised product.

THE CHELSEA ACTION PLAN

Based on constructive consumer input, verified by independent market research, Anheuser-Busch revised Chelsea by eliminating those elements which could act to "predispose" children while preserving the original concept of a natural, less sweet soft drink for adults. Accordingly, the alcohol was virtually removed, the foaminess was dramatically reduced, the "Not-So" Soft Drink advertising was dropped, and the bottle was changed from clear to emerald green glass. Furthermore, the Anheuser-Busch name was reduced in size on the label and positioned behind "Soft Drink Division" in order to more clearly communicate soft drink identity.

The outside participants previewed the revised product and its augmentation support and offered their public approval. Now the stage was set to complete the social screening process and inform the public of the results.

PUBLIC COMMUNICATION OF SCREENING RESULTS

When Step I (visible corporate social commitment) is sincerely taken, the responsible manager understands that the screening process is an integral part of augmented product marketing and not a public relations tool. Therefore, rather than use advertising or a major public relations program, Anheuser-Busch management chose to conduct a national press conference to communicate the screening results. On December 12, less than two months after the screening process was initiated, a socially screened Chelsea was announced at the National Press Club in Washington, D.C. More importantly, several key outside participants in the screening process (including Senator Hatch's staff, the Virginia Nurses' Association, and the Potomac Council of Seventh-Day Adventists) attended the press conference and issued public statements commending the new product and its manufacturer.

Defusing a Potentially Damaging Situation

As a result, a potentially damaging situation was turned into one of those rare instances where all parties won. Chelsea critics won because they were able to change the marketing thrust of a major corporation. Anheuser-Busch won because new Chelsea more clearly fit consumer needs than the original product. The biggest winner, however, was the consumer who benefited from the exercise of democracy in the marketplace without footing the bill for governmental intervention.

THE CHELSEA EXPERIENCE: A SUMMARY

One of the most difficult challenges facing contemporary managers is the task of identifying those situations when the corporation's larger role as a social unit transcends short term profit motives. When such a situation does arise, responsible corporations require a process for resolving conflict. The Chelsea experience is offered as a case study of one corporation's process in action—the process of consumer participatory social screening.

Of course, the social screening process is not risk-free, nor is it appropriate in every conflict situation. Once initiated, the corporation is obligated to follow the process through. Once outside consumer opinion leader input is solicited, the corporation may forfeit the option of "doing nothing." Pursued to the extreme, the screening process could snowball management into socially positive actions that made poor business sense. In the Chelsea case, there was the possibility that the product and marketing revisions consisted of "throwing out the baby with the bath water." While it is still too early to tell if the Chelsea screening was economically successful, one point is already clear: a corporation can regulate itself on social matters if it establishes a meaningful two-way dialogue with the consumer.

HOW YOUNG MARKETER CAN HELP
INSTILL SOCIAL AWARENESS*
By Larry J. Rosenberg

The scene is a breakfast cereal division of a large manufacturing firm. Full of idealism and energy, the recent marketing-major graduate tackles her first product manager assignment—a dry breakfast cereal brand that has been on the market more than 40 years.

* Larry J. Rosenburg is an Associate Professor of Marketing at New York University's Graduate School of Business Administration. Reprinted from *Marketing News,* February 11, 1977, p. 4. Published by the American Marketing Association.

The company's staff nutritionists have assured our junior executive that the product is healthful, thanks to vitamin fortification. She has no reason to doubt their word. It seems logical for her to recommend a repositioning of the brand through advertising that emphasizes the nutritional value of the cereal set in more nostalgic times.

But then along come nutritionists outside the company who scoff at such a cereal and such a message. Some state, "There is a crisis in the American breakfast." Others say, "Health is how you live, not just what you eat."

Assuming that our product manager grasps the meaning of corporate social responsibility, the dilemma is one that she or other marketing specialists may sooner or later have to face: a management concerned primarily with marketing the product profitably versus outside pressures to deal with various other aspects of the relationships between the product, consumers, and society.

This is an increasingly familiar situation in many industries besides packaged foods—drugs, toys, automobiles, banking, airlines, just to name a few.

What do you tell junior-level marketing people or marketing students about coping with social responsibility in marketing? There are plenty of books and articles that explain why marketing *must* recognize new social realities and what actions companies (meaning upper management) can take. However, not many of these offer guidance to new marketing specialists who are getting on-the-job training in the need to achieve solid sales and profit results in order to advance their careers.

Focusing on the product manager, here are some things he or she can do when faced with apparent (or real) conflict between conventional marketing and social responsibility.

First, the product manager must question the relative merits of accusations or suggestions made by critics. In most instances the clarity of the issue is related directly to the completeness of the data and to the degree of objectivity of the product manager. The truly objective product manager must be fully informed on both sides of the question in order to be better able to decide what is socially responsible. He or she will, for example, learn what the critics (in our example, certain nutritionists) have to say, will check the records of those making the accusations or suggestions to determine what the base of their argument is—be it scientific, moralistic, social, or political, will get various outside opinions from reliable sources, and will systematically weigh the results as they affect marketing decisions.

Having decided that a problem related to social responsibility does exist and that something should be done about it, the product manager's next move is to transmit this information to a higher level of marketing management. Besides the disclosure of a problem, recommendations may be spelled out. Where management shows itself receptive to this kind of information, our new product manager will have little more to do than to hand in the results of his or her labor, and management will take it from there.

Too often, however, executives greet such unsolicited material as unwelcome. Their attitude is to ask why marketing (with the prime objective of profit) should get itself involved in anything as new, amorphous, and risky as social responsibility?

Another problem is that the management itself may be in conflict. One issue that often involves management conflict is the timing of marketing strategy related to social responsibility. Obviously when a crisis is boiling and the necessity of reacting is immediate, the only alternative is action. When the pressures appear to be future ones, opinions will range. On the one hand people are saying, "Wait until the crisis actually hits and in the meantime enjoy the flexibility of conventional marketing strategy." On the other hand are those suggesting that if social pressures on marketing activities are inevitable, then there is no time like the present to begin to anticipate the situation by planning a marketing strategy that deals with the approaching storm.

Where management is in conflict within itself or is concerned mainly with short-term profit or sales, these attitudes usually are quickly made clear to the junior marketing ranks. In such instances, assuming that the product manager has some social conscience and really believes he or she has a case, how can he or she help management to recognize and/or accept an increased measure of social responsibility?

Informing and gaining the cooperation of an uninformed and/or a reluctant management usually requires a carefully planned strategy. Before presenting a report on the specific problem, musts in strategy might be:

1. To ascertain who the sponsors of the *current* marketing strategy are, and, as diplomatically as possible, begin to test their response to the controversial data. For example, our breakfast cereal product manager operates under many divisional and corporate constraints on product marketing. Therefore, she will have to sound out her case at a higher level of the firm and identify the positions where she encounters resistance to change. What she discovers will certainly affect the manner in which she should present her case.

2. To understand how the organization makes major marketing decisions—in the division and in the company at large. Then to find those executives who appear to have sympathetic learnings towards the social issues (either because they are oriented toward social responsibility or because they are realists who recognize an idea whose time has come). Also to find other allies in the corporation—persons who will be likely to sympathize with your ideas. Discuss the situation openly and frankly with as many of these sympathetic persons as possible. Ask their advice on how best to pre-

sent the material and, where possible, ascertain to what degree you can expect their backing.

3. To write reports and memos which in subtle ways focus on the new realities in the environment and therefore the new assumptions you feel are needed regarding marketing strategy. Hopefully you can get some of your allies to do the same thing in their interoffice communications.

4. Find out what the top executives of your corporation have said about the subject and quote them wherever possible. Also, recognize the phenomenon that what top management says doesn't always filter down to the operational people. The operational people have profit and/or sales performance goals, but the reward system rarely accommodates amorphous social variables. The pro-social quotes of top executives should be featured as reinforcements in the junior marketing specialist's communications.

5. Keep a special eye on what the competition is doing in implementing social responsibility in marketing. You may run into your competitor's people at trade associations, professional meetings, chapter meetings, or over cocktails. Also read what the trade press reports and tune in to what your salespeople pick up. This information is particularly forceful when used to point what the competition is doing (or failing to do) with regard to the specific issue at hand.

Having all the pertinent data at hand, the next step is to decide on the format for presentation of the information to make it as meaningful as possible. With a management which likes to hear about profit or return on investment, the issue might best be presented in terms of these opportunities for the firm. Thus the company might be asked to weigh the costs of adopting the desired socially responsible strategy against the costs in the event that government and/or consumers listen to the critics.

Since many executives wonder at the erosion of the marketplace which often occurs in the face of public pressure and government regulation, it could be pointed out that where social responsibility is incorporated into the profit outlook, government may not feel it needs to intervene any further. Here, too, cost could be considered in terms of the flexibility of taking marketing action when one wishes to, rather than when the government orders it. With every layer of government regulation, the flexibility of the corporation is reduced, and this, in turn, may reduce marketing innovation (new products, packages, pricing approaches, promotion campaigns, and so on). And innovation is the key to the health of our organizations and, according to Peter Drucker, the primary mission or life-force of a corporation.

This "self-interest" strategy also may show that when the company alters its current policy to accommodate consumer welfare, it "buys" good will. Still another strategy may be to point out that those firms ignoring their responsibility to the consumer and/or the public often find that the problem comes back to haunt them later. Besides government regulation, there may be complaints by activist consumers, negative public opinion, and adverse media exposure—all with possible resulting loss of sales. This latter argument can be very effective if backed up by concrete examples full of figures or worst-outcome scenarios.

Finally, sooner or later, the product manager comes face to face not only with the questions of loyalty to the corporation but also loyalty to the industry (which helps build professional pride) and loyalty to society (which can build personal pride). People who come out of marketing education programs should treat themselves as professionals who are trying to be conscious of standards (corporate, social, and personal) and to encourage the application of such standards.

Not all companies, however, are going to respond, no matter how well the case is presented.

But for those early in their careers as marketing people, who feel strongly enough about their convictions and believe that social responsibility is a rational marketing approach for the late 1970s, there are a growing number of companies whose attitudes *have* changed and whose management would not have it any other way.

Bibliography

BOOKS

AAKER, DAVID A. and GEORGE S. DAY. *Consumerism: Search for the Consumer Interest.* 2nd edition. New York: The Free Press, 1974.

ALLVINE, FRED C. *Highway Robbery: An Analysis of the Gasoline Crisis.* Bloomington, Ind.: Indiana University Press, 1974.

———, and JAMES M. PATTERSON. *Competition, Ltd.: The Marketing of Gasoline.* Bloomington, Ind.: Indiana University Press, 1972.

ANDREASEN, ALAN R., ed. *Improving Inner-City Marketing.* Chicago: American Marketing Association, 1972.

———. *The Disadvantaged Consumer.* New York: The Free Press, 1975.

BACKMAN, JULES. *Advertising and Competition.* New York: New York University Press, 1967.

BAUER, RAYMOND A. and STEPHEN A. GREYSER. *Advertising in America: The Consumer View.* Cambridge, Mass · Harvard University Press, 1968.

BERRY, LEONARD L. and JAMES S. HENSEL. *Marketing and the Social Environment: A Readings Text.* New York: Petrocelli Books, 1973.

BISHOP, F. P. *Ethics of Advertising.* London: Robert Hale Ltd., 1949.

BISHOP, JAMES, JR. and HENRY W. HUBBARD. *Let the Seller Beware.* Washington, D.C.: The National Press, 1969.

BJORK, GORDON C. *Private Enterprise and Public Interest.* Englewood Cliffs, N.J.: Prentice-Hall, Inc., 1969.

BORDEN, NEIL H. *The Economic Effects of Advertising.* Chicago: Richard D. Irwin, Inc., 1942.

CADY, JOHN F. *Drugs on the Market.* Lexington, Mass.: Lexington Books, 1975.

CAPLOVITZ, DAVID. *The Poor Pay More.* New York: The Free Press, 1967.

CHAMBER OF COMMERCE OF THE UNITED STATES. *Business and the Consumer—A Program for the Seventies.* Washington, D.C.: Chamber of Commerce, 1970.

COMANOR, WILLIAM S. and THOMAS A. WILSON. *Advertising and Market Power.* Cambridge, Mass.: Harvard University Press, 1974.

CROSS, JENNIFER. *The Supermarket Trap.* Bloomington, Ind.: Indiana University Press, 1970.

DIVITA, SAL and FRANK MCLAUGHLIN, eds. *Consumer Complaints: Public Policy Alternatives.* Washington, D.C.: Acropolis Books, 1974.

FIRESTONE, O. J. *The Economic Implications of Advertising.* London: Eyre Methuen Company, 1967.

FISK, GEORGE. *Marketing and the Ecological Crisis.* New York: Harper & Row, Publishers, Inc., 1974.

FURUHASHI, HUGH J. and E. JEROME MCCARTHY. *Social Issues of Marketing in American Economy.* Columbus, Ohio: Grid, Inc., 1971.

GAEDEKE, RALPH M. *Marketing in Private and Public Nonprofit Organizations: Perspectives and Illustrations.* Santa Monica, Calif.: Goodyear Publishing Co., Inc., 1977.

GALBRAITH, JOHN KENNETH. *Economics and the Public Purpose.* Boston: Houghton Mifflin Company, 1973.

GIST, RONALD R. *Marketing and Society: Text and Cases.* 2nd edition. Hinsdale, Ill.: The Dryden Press, 1974.

GRAY, IRWIN, with ALBERT L. BASES, CHARLES H. MARTIN, and ALEXANDER STERNBERG. *Product Liability: A Management Response.* New York: AMACOM, 1975.

GREEN, MARK J., ed. *The Monopoly Makers: Ralph Nader's Study Group Report on Regulation and Competition.* New York: Grossman Publishers, 1973.

HEILBRONER, ROBERT L. *In the Name of Profit: Profiles in Corporate Irresponsibility.* Garden City, N.Y.: Doubleday & Company, Inc., 1972.

HENION, KARL E., II. *Ecological Marketing.* Columbus, Ohio: Grid, Inc., 1976.

HOWARD, JOHN A. and JAMES HULBERT. *Advertising and the Public Interest: A Staff Report to the Federal Trade Commission.* Chicago: Crain Communications, Inc., 1973.

HOWARD, MARSHALL C. *Legal Aspects of Marketing.* New York: McGraw-Hill Book Company, 1964.

JONES, MARY GARDINER and DAVID M. GARDNER, eds. *Consumerism: A New Force in Society.* Lexington, Mass.: Lexington Books, 1976.

KANGUN, NORMAN. *Society and Marketing: An Unconventional View.* New York: Harper & Row, Publishers, Inc., 1972.

KAPP, K. WILLIAM. *The Social Costs of Private Enterprise.* New York: Schocken Books, 1971.

KELLEY, WILLIAM T., ed. *The New Consumerism: Selected Readings.* Columbus, Ohio: Grid, Inc., 1973.

KINTNER, EARL W. *A Primer on the Law of Deceptive Practices.* New York: Macmillan Publishing Co., Inc., 1971.

KOHLMEIER, LOUIS M., JR. *The Regulators.* New York: Harper & Row, Publishers, Inc., 1970.

KOTLER, PHILIP. *Marketing for Nonprofit Organizations.* Englewood Cliffs, N.J.: Prentice-Hall, Inc., 1975.

LAVIDGE, ROBERT J. and ROBERT J. HOLLOWAY, eds. *Marketing and Society: The Challenge.* Homewood, Ill.: Richard D. Irwin, Inc., 1969.

LAZER, WILLIAM and EUGENE J. KELLEY. *Social Marketing: Perspectives and Viewpoints.* Homewood, Ill.: Richard D. Irwin, Inc., 1973.

LEVY, SIDNEY J. and GERALD ZALTMAN. *Marketing, Society, and Conflict.* Englewood Cliffs, N.J.: Prentice-Hall, Inc., 1975.

LOVELOCK, CHRISTOPHER H. and CHARLES P. WEINBERG. *Cases in Public and Nonprofit Marketing.* Palo Alto, Calif.: The Scientific Press, 1977.

MAGNUSON, WARREN G. and JEAN CARPER. *The Dark Side of the Marketplace.* Englewood Cliffs, N.J.: Prentice-Hall, Inc., 1968.

MORRIS, RUBY TURNER. *Consumers Union—Method, Implications, Weaknesses and Strengths.* New London, Conn.: Litfield Publications, 1971.

MOSS, FRANK E. *Initiatives in Corporate Responsibility.* Washington, D.C.: U.S. Government Printing Office, 1972.

MOYER, REED and MICHAEL D. HUTT. *Macro Marketing: A Social Perspective.* 2nd edition. New York: John Wiley & Sons, Inc., 1978.

MURRAY, BARBARA B., ed. *Consumerism: The Eternal Triangle.* Pacific Palisades, Calif.: Goodyear Publishing Co., Inc., 1973.

NADEL, MARK V. *The Politics of Consumer Protection.* New York: The Bobbs-Merrill Co., Inc., 1971.

NADER, RALPH. *Unsafe At Any Speed.* Revised edition. New York: Grossman Publishers, 1970.

———, ed. *The Consumer and Corporate Accountability.* New York: Harcourt Brace Jovanovich, 1973.

PALAMOUNTAIN, JOSEPH CORNWALL, JR. *The Politics of Distribution.* Cambridge, Mass.: Harvard University Press, 1955.

PERRY, DONALD L. *Social Marketing Strategies: Conservation Issues and Analysis.* Pacific Palisades, Calif.: Goodyear Publishing Co., Inc., 1976.

PETERSON, MARY BENNETT. *The Regulated Consumer.* Los Angeles: Nash Publishing, 1971.

PETERSON, ROBIN T., ed. *Marketing and Society: Selected Readings.* New York: MSS Educational Publishing Co., Inc., 1970.

POTTER, DAVID M. *People of Plenty: Economic Abundance and the American Character.* Chicago: University of Chicago Press, 1954.

PRESTON, LEE E., ed. *Social Issues in Marketing.* Glenview, Ill.: Scott, Foresman and Co., 1968.

————, and JAMES E. POST. *Private Management and Public Policy.* Englewood Cliffs, N.J.: Prentice-Hall, Inc., 1975.

RIDGEWAY, JAMES. *The Politics of Ecology.* New York: E. P. Dutton & Co., Inc., 1970.

ROTHSCHILD, MICHAEL L., ed. *Incomplete Bibliography of Works Relating to Marketing for Public Sector and Nonprofit Organizations.* Revised edition. Boston: Intercollegiate Case Clearing House, 1977.

SANFORD, DAVID, ed. *Hot War on the Consumer.* New York: Pitman Publishing Corp., 1969.

————. *Who Put the Con in Consumer?* New York: Liveright, 1972.

SCOTT, RICHARD A. and NORTON E. MARKS, eds. *Marketing and Its Environment.* Belmont, Calif.: Wadsworth Publishing Co., Inc., 1969.

SENTRY INSURANCE. *Consumerism at the Crossroads: A National Opinion Research Survey of Public, Activist, Business and Regulator Attitudes toward the Consumer Movement.* Hartford, Conn: 1978.

SETHI, S. PRAKASH. *Promises of the Good Life: Social Consequences of Private Marketing Decisions.* Homewood, Ill.: Richard D. Irwin, Inc., 1979.

SEXTON, DONALD E., JR. *Groceries in the Ghetto.* Lexington, Mass.: Lexington Books, 1973.

SHETH, JAGDISH N. and PETER L. WRIGHT, eds. *Marketing Analysis for Societal Problems.* Urbana, Ill.: University of Illinois Press, 1974.

SIMON, JULIAN L. *Issues in the Economics of Advertising.* Urbana, Ill.: University of Illinois Press, 1970.

STERN, LOUIS W. and JOHN R. GRABNER, eds. *Competition in the Marketplace.* Glenview, Ill.: Scott, Foresman and Co., 1970.

STIGLER, GEORGE J. *The Intellectual and the Marketplace.* Vol. 3. Chicago: University of Chicago Press, 1967.

STURDIVANT, FREDERICK D., ed. *The Ghetto Marketplace.* New York: The Free Press, 1969.

TROELSTRUP, ARCH W. *The Consumer in American Society.* New York: McGraw-Hill Book Company, 1970.

TUCKER, W. T. *The Social Context of Economic Behavior.* New York: Holt, Rinehart and Winston, 1964.

WARE, CAROLINE F. *The Consumer Goes to War.* New York: Funk & Wagnalls, Inc., 1942.

WASSON, CHESTER; FREDERICK D. STURDIVANT; and DAVID H. McCONAUGHY. *Competition and Human Behavior.* New York: Appleton-Century-Crofts, 1968.

WEBSTER, FREDERICK E., JR. *Social Aspects of Marketing.* Englewood Cliffs, N.J.: Prentice-Hall, Inc., 1974.

WINTER, RALPH, JR. *The Consumer Advocate versus the Consumer.* Washington, D.C.: American Enterprise Institute, 1972.

WISH, JOHN R. and STEPHEN H. GAMBLE. *Marketing and Social Issues: An Action Reader.* New York: John Wiley & Sons, Inc., 1971.

ARTICLES

AAKER, DAVID A. and GEORGE S. DAY. "Corporate Responses to Consumerism Pressures," *Harvard Business Review,* November–December 1972, pp. 114–124.

ACKERMAN, ROBERT W. "How Companies Respond to Social Demands." *Harvard Business Review,* July–August 1973, pp. 88–98.

"Ads Are Finally Getting Bleeped at the FTC." *Business and Society Review,* Summer 1978, pp. 38–46.

"Ads Start to Take Hold in the Professions." *Business Week,* July 24, 1978, pp. 122, 124.

"The Aerosol Debate." *Newsweek,* June 23, 1975, pp. 63–64.

ALPERT, H. "Consumer Concerns: Questions and Answers." *50 Plus,* August 1979, p. 43.

ANDERSON, ROBERT L. and R. EUGENE KLIPPEL. "An Empirical Test of a Public Policy Decision Model: The Evaluation of Prescription Drug Price Advertising." *American Marketing Association Educators Conference Proceedings,* 1977, pp. 280–285.

ANDERSON, THOMAS W., JR. and WILLIAM H. CUNNINGHAM. "The Socially Conscious Consumer." *Journal of Marketing.* July 1972, pp. 23–31.

———, KARL E. HENION, and ELI P. COX III. "Socially vs. Ecologically Responsible Consumers." *American Marketing Association Combined Conference Proceedings,* 1974, pp. 304–311.

ANDREASEN, ALAN R. "Ghetto Marketing Life Cycle." *Journal of Marketing Research,* February 1978, pp. 20–28.

"Are the Television Networks Selling Too Many Ads?" *Business Week,* September 18, 1978, pp. 26–27.

ARMSTRONG, GARY M. and FREDERICK A. RUSS. "Detecting Deception in Advertising." *MSU Business Topics,* Spring 1975, pp. 21–31.

ARMSTRONG, J. SCOTT and WALTER A. MAJOROS. "Marketing Decisions and Social Responsibility." Paper delivered at the Institute of Management Sciences Meetings, Houston, Tex., April 1972.

AUSTIN, J. PAUL. "World Marketing as a New Force for Peace." *Journal of Marketing,* January 1966, pp. 1–3.

AUSTIN, ROBERT W. "Responsibility for Social Change." *Harvard Business Review,* July–August 1965, pp. 45–52.

BACKMAN, JULES. "Is Advertising Wasteful?" *Journal of Marketing,* January 1968, pp. 2–8.

BANKS, SEYMOUR. "Public Policy on Ads to Children." *Journal of Advertising Research,* August 1975, pp. 7–12.

BARKSDALE, HIRAM C. and BILL DARDEN. "Marketers' Attitudes toward the Marketing Concept." *Journal of Marketing,* October 1971, pp. 29–36.

———, and WILLIAM D. PERREAULT, JR. "Changes in Consumer Attitudes toward Marketing, Consumerism, and Government Regulation." *Journal of Consumer Affairs,* Winter 1976, pp. 121–135.

BARTELS, ROBERT. "A Model for Ethics in Marketing." *Journal of Marketing,* January 1967, pp. 20–26.

"Battle Looms as FTC Seeks Product Standards Control." *Industrial Marketing,* January 1979, p. 64.

BAUER, RAYMOND A. and STEPHEN A. GREYSER. The Dialogue That Never Happens." *Harvard Business Review.* November–December 1967, pp. 2–4, 6, 8, 10, 12, 186, 188, 190.

BECKER, BORIS, W. "The Image of Advertising Truth: Is Being Truthful Enough?" *Journal of Marketing,* July 1970, pp. 67–68.

BELL, MARTIN L. and C. WILLIAM EMORY. "The Faltering Marketing Concept." *Journal of Marketing,* October 1971, pp. 37–42.

BENNIGSON, ARNOLD I. "Product Liability—Procedures and Manufacturers Beware." *Research Management,* March 1975, pp. 16–19.

BERNACCHI, M. D. and KEN KONO. "Information in the Market Place: Behavioral View on *Caveat Venditor* versus *Caveat Emptor." American Marketing Association Educators Conference Proceedings,* 1977, pp. 355–357.

BERRY, LEONARD L. "A New Age for Marketing and Business." *Industrial Banker,* December 1970, pp. 5–8, 24.

———. "The Challenges of Marketing: A Field in Transition." *Southern Journal of Business,* January 1971, pp. 75–84.

———. "Consumerism, Marketing and the Small Businessman." *The Journal of Small Business Management,* Summer 1972, pp. 14–19.

———. "Marketing Challenges in the Age of the People." *MSU Business Topics,* Winter 1972, pp. 7–13.

———. "Social and Economic Discontinuity and Marketing." *American Marketing Association Educators Conference Proceedings,* Series No. 41, 1977, p. 543.

———, and PAUL J. SOLOMON. "Generalizing about Low-Income Food Shoppers: A Word of Caution." *Journal of Retailing,* Summer 1971, pp. 41–51.

BLANKENSHIP, A. B. "Point of View: Consumerism and Consumer Research." *Journal of Advertising Research,* August 1971, pp. 44–47.

BLOOM, PAUL N. "Advertising in the Professions: The Critical Issues." *Journal of Marketing,* July 1977, pp. 103–110.

BLUM, MILTON L., JOHN B. STEWART, and EDWARD W. WHEATLEY. "Consumer Affairs: Viability of the Corporate Response." *Journal of Marketing,* April 1974, pp. 13–19.

BOGART, LEO. "Is All This Advertising Really Necessary?" *Association for Consumer Research Conference Proceedings,* 1975, pp. 12–16.

BOWERMAN, FRANK R. "Managing Solid Waste Disposal." *California Management Review,* Spring 1972, pp. 104–106.

BRANDT, MICHAEL T. and IVAN L. PRESTON. "The Federal Trade Commission's Use of Evidence to Determine Deception." *Journal of Marketing,* January 1977, pp. 54–62.

BRIEN, RICHARD H., BETSY D. GELB, and WILLIAM D. TRAMMELL. "The Challenge to Marketing Dominance." *Business Horizons,* February 1972, pp. 23–30.

BROWNE, M. NEIL and PAUL F. HAAS. "Social Responsibilty and Market Performance." *MSU Business Topics,* Autumn 1971, pp. 7–10.

BUELL, J. "Sovereign Consumer." *Progressive,* February 1979, p. 32.

BUSCH, PAUL. "A Review and Critical Evaluation of the Consumer Product Safety Commission: Marketing Management Implications." *Journal of Marketing,* October 1976, pp. 41–49.

BUSKIRK, RICHARD H. and JAMES T. ROTHE. "Consumerism—An Interpretation." *Journal of Marketing,* October 1970, pp. 61–65.

"Can Janine Understand an Ad?" *Media Decisions,* June 1978, pp. 59–63.

CAPITMAN, WILLIAM G. "Morality in Advertising—A Public Imperative." *MSU Business Topics,* Spring 1971, pp. 21–26.

CARNAHAN, W. and S. MILMO. "Comparative Advertising Attracts Divergent Views." *Advertising Age,* November 21, 1977, p. 84.

CARR, ALBERT Z. "Can an Executive Afford a Conscience?" *Harvard Business Review,* July–August 1970, pp. 58–64.

CHAKRABARTI, ALOK K. and WILLIAM E. SOUDER. "Government Policies· Barriers or Stimuli to New Product Innovation." *American Marketing Association Educators Conference Proceedings,* 1977, pp. 196–198.

CHARRON, PEGGY. "Children's TV: Sugar and Vice and Nothing Nice." *Business and Society Review,* Summer 1977, pp. 65–70.

"Children's Advertising: Behind the Candy-Coated Message." *Technology Review,* June–July 1979, pp. 74–77.

CLASON, EARL A. "Marketing Ethics and the Consumer." *Harvard Business Review,* January–February 1967, pp. 79–86.

COHEN, DOROTHY. "Surrogate Indicators and Deception in Advertising." *Journal of Marketing,* July 1972, pp. 10–15.

———. "The Federal Trade Commission and the Regulation of Advertising in the Consumer Interest." *Journal of Marketing,* January 1969, pp. 40–44.

COHN, JULES. "Is Business Meeting the Challenge of Urban Affairs?" *Harvard Business Review*, March–April 1970, pp. 68–72.

COMMONER, BARRY. "A Businessman's Primer on Ecology." *Business and Society Review*, Spring 1972, pp. 45–53.

"Consumer Protection: What's at Issue." *Nation's Business*, August 1977, pp. 18–22.

CORNFELD, RICHARD S. "A New Approach to an Old Remedy: Corrective Advertising and the Federal Trade Commission." *Iowa Law Review*, February 1976, pp. 693–721.

CORSON, JOHN J. "A Corporate Social Audit?" *The Center Magazine*, January–February 1972, pp. 62–65.

CORWIN, E. "Why FDA Bans Harmful Substances." *FDA Consumer*, December 1978, pp. 6–9.

"Cows with a Kick." *Time*, April 19, 1976, p. 76.

CRACCO, ETIENNE and JACQUES ROSTENNE. "The Socio-ecological Product." *MSU Business Topics*, Summer 1971, pp. 27–34.

CRAIG, SAMUEL C. and JOHN M. McCANN. "Communicating Energy Conservation Information to Consumers: A Field Experiment." *American Marketing Association Educators Conference Proceedings*, 1977, pp. 432–436.

CRAVENS, DAVID W. and GERALD E. HILLS. "Consumerism: A Perspective for Business." *Business Horizons*, August 1970, pp. 21–28.

CULLEY, JAMES D. "Perceptions of Children's Television Advertising: An Empirical Investigation of the Beliefs and Attitudes of Consumer, Industry, and Government Respondents." *Association for Consumer Research Conference Proceedings*, 1974, pp. 879–890.

CUNNINGHAM, ISABELLA C. M. and WILLIAM H. CUNNINGHAM. "Standards for Advertising Regulation." *Journal of Marketing*, October 1977, pp. 92–97.

CUNNINGHAM, ROSS M. "Brand Loyalty—What, Where, How Much?" *Harvard Business Review*, January–February 1956, pp. 116–128.

CURLEY, JAMES, WILLIAM LAZER, and C. ATKIN. "The Experts Look at Children's Television." *Journal of Broadcasting*, Winter 1976, pp. 3–22.

DARDIS, RACHEL and DIANE HYMAN. "Cost Benefit Analysis of Consumer Protection Programs." *Association for Consumer Research Conference Proceedings*, 1976, pp. 121–125.

DAWSON, LESLIE M. "Marketing Science in the Age of Aquarius." *Journal of Marketing*, July 1971, pp. 66–72.

DAY, GEORGE S. "Assessing the Effects of Information Disclosure Requirements." *Journal of Marketing*, April 1976, pp. 42–52.

———, and DAVID A. AAKER. "A Guide to Consumerism." *Journal of Marketing*, July 1970, pp. 12–19.

DENNEY, M. "Public Demands on Business: A Research Frontier." *Asso-*

ciation for Consumer Research Conference Proceedings, 1975, pp. 269–275.

DILLON, TOM. "What is Deceptive Advertising?" *Journal of Advertising Research,* October 1973, pp. 9–12.

"Distribution Knot Strangling Consumers?" *Business Week,* September 18, 1978, p. 44.

DONOHUE, T. "The Effects of Commercials on Children." *Journal of Advertising Research,* December 1975, pp. 41–47.

DRUCKER, PETER F. "Marketing and Economic Development." *Journal of Marketing,* January 1958, pp. 252–259.

———. "The Shame of Marketing." *Marketing/Communications,* August 1969, pp. 60–64.

DUNN, DONALD. "If the Product Is the Problem, Do You Censor the Ads?" *Business Week,* April 3, 1978, p. 90.

DYER, ROBERT F. "The 'Corrective Advertising' Remedy of the FTC: An Experimental Approach." *Journal of Marketing,* January 1974, pp. 48–54.

———, and PHILLIP G. KUEHL. "Longitudinal Study of Corrective Advertising." *Journal of Marketing Research,* February 1978, pp. 39–48.

———, and TERENCE A. SHIMP. "Enhancing the Role of Marketing Research in Public Policy Decision-Making." *Journal of Marketing,* January 1977, pp. 63–67.

"Effects of Comparative Ads Studied." *Editor and Publisher,* January 21, 1978, p. 22.

EL ANSARY, ADEL and OSCAR L. KRAMER, JR. "Social Marketing: The Family Planning Experience." *Journal of Marketing,* July 1973, pp. 1–7.

FABER, RONALD, and SCOTT WARD. "Children's Understanding of Using Products Safely." *Journal of Marketing,* October 1977, pp. 39–44.

"Fading Ralph Nader Rewrites His Strategy." *Business Week,* April 9, 1979, p. 72.

FARLEY, JOHN U. and HAROLD J. LEAVITT. "Marketing and Population Problems." *Journal of Marketing,* July 1971, pp. 28–33.

FARMER, RICHARD N. "Would You Really Want Your Daughter to Marry a Marketing Man?" *Journal of Marketing,* January 1967, pp. 1–3.

———. "Would You Want Your Son to Marry a Marketing Lady?" *Journal of Marketing,* January 1977, pp. 15–18.

FELDMAN, LAURENCE P. "New Legislation and the Prospects of Real Warranty Reforms." *Journal of Marketing,* July 1976, pp. 41–47.

———. "Societal Adaptation: A New Challenge for Marketing." *Journal of Marketing,* July 1971, pp. 54–60.

FISK, GEORGE. "Guidelines for Warranty Service after Sale." *Journal of Marketing,* January 1970, pp. 63–67.

"Food Poisoning: It Doesn't Have to Be a Threat." *Food Service Marketing,* December 1976, pp. 41–42.

FORD, GARY T. "Adoption of Consumer Policies of States." *Journal of Marketing Research,* February 1978, pp. 49–57.

FRENCH, WARREN A. and HIRAM C. BARKSDALE. "Food Labeling Regulations: Efforts toward Full Disclosure." *Journal of Marketing,* July 1974, pp. 14–19.

"FTC Challenge to the Legal Profession." *Business Week,* January 9, 1978, p. 23.

"FTC's Authority Would Be Cut by Senate Panel." *The Wall Street Journal,* November 21, 1979, p. 2.

"FTC's Tougher Tactics for Regulating Business." *Business Week,* May 19, 1975, p. 66.

GARDNER, DAVID M. "Deception in Advertising: A Conceptual Approach." *Journal of Marketing,* January 1975, pp. 40–46.

GARDNER, MERYL, ANDREW MITCHELL, and RICHARD STAELIN. "The Effects of Attacks and Inoculations in a Public Policy Context: A Cognitive Structure Approach." *American Marketing Association Educators Conference Proceedings,* Series No. 41, 1977, pp. 292–297.

GELB, BETSY D. and RICHARD BRIEN. "Survival and Social Responsibility: Themes for Marketing Education and Management." *Journal of Marketing,* April 1967, pp. 3–9.

GOLDEN, LINDA L. "Consumer Reactions to Comparative Advertising." *Association for Consumer Research Conference Proceedings,* 1975, pp. 63–67.

GOLDMAN, ARIEH. "Confined Shopping Behavior among Low Income Consumers: An Empirical Test." *Journal of Marketing Research,* February 1978, pp. 11–19.

GOODMAN, CHARLES S. "Do the Poor Pay More?" *Journal of Marketing,* January 1968, pp. 19–24.

GRANZIN, KENT L. and GARY M. GRIKSCHEIT. "What Is Consumerism?" *Association for Consumer Research Conference Proceedings,* 1975, pp. 68–72.

GRAVEREAU, VICTOR P., LEONARD J. KONOPA, AND JIM L. GRIMM. "Attitudes of Industrial Buyers toward Selected Social Issues." *Industrial Marketing Management,* June 1978, pp. 199–207.

GRAY, ELISHA. "Changing Values in the Business Society." *Business Horizons,* August 1968, pp. 21–26.

GRETHER, E. T. "Business Responsibility toward the Market." *California Management Review,* Fall 1969, pp. 33–42.

GREYSER, STEPHEN A. "Advertising: Attacks and Counters." *Harvard Business Review,* March–April 1972, pp. 22–36.

GRIFFITH, THOMAS. "Payoff Is Not 'Accepted Practice.'" *Fortune,* August 1975, pp. 122-25, 200, 202, 205.

GROSS, EDWIN J. "Needed: Consumer Ombudsmen." *Business and Society,* Autumn 1968, pp. 22-27.

"Growing Worry over the Chemicals in Food." *Changing Times,* January 1977, pp. 37-40.

GUILTINAN, JOSEPH. "Planned and Evolutionary Changes in Distribution Channels." *Journal of Retailing,* Summer 1974, pp. 79-91, 103.

——, and NONYELU NWOKOYE. "Reverse Channels for Recycling: An Analysis of Alternatives and Public Policy Implications." *American Marketing Association Combined Conference Proceedings,* Spring and Fall 1974, pp. 341-346.

HANNON, BRUCE. "Energy Conservation and the Consumer." *Science,* July 11, 1975, pp. 95-102.

HARRIS, KING. "The Candy Breakfast Case." *The Nation,* March 3, 1979, p. 242.

HAYNES, ROBERT. "The Environmental Scene: Just How Bad Is the View?" *Business and Society Review/Innovation,* Winter 1972-73, pp. 73-80.

HEMPEL, DONALD J. and LARRY J. ROSENBERG. "Consumer Satisfaction: A Neglected Link?" *Association for Consumer Research Conference Proceedings,* 1975, pp. 261-268.

HENDERSON, HAZEL. "Ecologists versus Economists." *Harvard Business Review,* July-August 1973, pp. 153-56.

HENION, KARL E. "The Effect of Ecologically Relevant Information on Detergent Sales." *Journal of Marketing Research,* February 1972, pp. 10-14.

HERRMANN, ROBERT O. "Consumerism. Its Goals, Organizations, and Future." *Journal of Marketing,* October 1970, pp. 55-60.

HODSON, JOHN. "The Social and Economic Context of Advertising." *Journal of the Royal Society of Arts,* July 1964, pp. 1-10.

HOLDEN, C. "Battle Heats Up over Sugared Cereals." *Science,* December 2, 1977, pp. 902-903.

HOPKINSON, THOMAS G. "New Battleground: Consumer Interest." *Harvard Business Review,* September-October 1964, pp. 97-104.

HOWARD, A. "Battle over Comparative Ads." *Dun's Review,* November 1977, pp. 60-62.

HOWARD, JOHN A. and JAMES HULBERT. "Advertising and the Public Interest." *Journal of Advertising Research,* December 1974, pp. 33-39.

"How Consumer Organizations Rate Corporations." *Business and Society Review/Innovation,* Autumn 1972, pp. 87-93.

"How to Get the FDA's Attention." *FDA Consumer,* May 1979, pp. 10-12.

HUNT, H. KEITH. "Decision Points in FTC Deceptive Advertising Matters." *Journal of Advertising,* Spring 1977, p. 28.

HUNT, SHELBY D. "The Nature and Scope of Marketing." *Journal of Marketing,* July 1976, pp. 17–28.

HUSTAD, THOMAS P. and EDGAR A. PESSEMIER. "Will the Real Consumer Activist Please Stand Up: An Examination of Consumers Opinions about Marketing Practices." *Journal of Marketing Research,* August 1973, pp. 319–324.

"The Industry Gets a Controversial Watchdog." *Business Week,* May 12, 1973, pp. 130–133.

ISAKSON, HANS R. and ALEX R. MAURIZL. "The Consumer Economics of Unit Pricing." *Journal of Marketing Research,* August 1973, pp. 277–285.

JACOBY, JACOB and CONSTANCE SMALL. "The FDA Approach to Defining Misleading Advertising." *Journal of Marketing,* October 1972, pp. 65–73.

JENSEN, WALTER, JR., EDWARD M. MAZZE, and DUKE NORDLINGER STERN. "The Consumer Product Safety Act: A Special Case in Consumerism." *Journal of Marketing,* October 1973, pp. 68–71.

JOHNSON, JEAN. "Death to the Boob Tube." *Business and Society Review,* Summer 1978, p. 79.

KARPATKIN, RHODA H. "Should the FTC Limit TV Advertising to Children?" *Consumer Reports,* August 1978, p. 432.

KASSARJIAN, HAROLD H. "Incorporating Ecology into Marketing Strategy: The Case of Air Pollution." *Journal of Marketing,* July 1971, pp. 61–65.

KATZ, ROBERT N. and S. PRAKASH SETHI. "Extension of Criminal Liability to Corporate Executives for Subordinate's Actions: Some Implications of the Acme Markets Case." *American Marketing Association Educators Conference Proceedings,* 1977, pp. 482–485.

KERIN, ROGER A. and ROBERT A. PETERSON. "Selected Insights into the Dynamics of Ecologically Responsible Behavior." *American Institute for Decision Sciences Proceedings,* 1974, p. 33.

KEY, HERBERT. "Children's Responses to Advertising: Who's Really to Blame?" *Journal of Advertising,* Winter 1974, pp. 26–30.

KIECHEL, WALTER. "Food Giants Struggle to Stay in Step with Consumers." *Fortune,* September 11, 1978, pp. 50–56.

KINNEAR, THOMAS C. and SADRUDIN A. AHMED. "Ecologically Concerned Consumers: Who Are They?" *Journal of Marketing,* April 1974, pp. 20–24.

————, and JAMES R. TAYLOR. "The Effect of Ecological Concern on Brand Perceptions." *Journal of Marketing Research,* May 1973, pp. 191–197.

KLINE, F. GERALD, PETER V. MILLER, and ANDREW J. MORRISON. "Communication Issues in Different Public Health Areas." *Association for Consumer Research Conference Proceedings,* 1975, pp. 290–294.

KOTLER, PHILIP. "A Generic Concept of Marketing." *Journal of Marketing,* April 1972, pp. 46–54.

———. "Overview of Political Candidate Marketing." *Association for Consumer Research Conference Proceedings,* 1974, pp. 761–770.

———. "What Consumerism Means for Marketing." *Harvard Business Review,* May–June 1972, pp. 48–57.

———, and R. A. CONNER. "Marketing Professional Services." *Journal of Marketing,* January 1977, pp. 71–76.

———, and SIDNEY J. LEVY. "Demarketing, Yes Demarketing." *Harvard Business Review,* November–December 1971, pp. 74–80.

———, and GERALD ZALTMAN. "Social Marketing: An Approach to Planned Social Change." *Journal of Marketing,* July 1971, pp. 3–12.

KRUGMAN, HERBERT E. "The Impact of Television Advertising: Learning without Involvement." *Public Opinion Quarterly,* Fall 1965, pp. 349–356.

KUEIIL, PHILIP G. and GARY T. FORD. "The Promotion of Medical and Legal Services." *American Marketing Association Educators Conference Proceedings,* 1977, pp. 39–44.

KUSHNER, LAWRENCE. "Consumer Product Safety Commission: What It Is and What It's Doing." *Research Management,* March 1975, pp. 12–15.

LA BARBERA, PRISCILLA ANN. "Consumer Participation in the Regulatory System." *American Marketing Association Educators Conference Proceedings,* 1977, p. 533.

LACZNIAK, R. GENE, ROBERT L. LUSCH, and PATRICK M. MURPHY. "Social Marketing: Its Ethical Dimensions." *Journal of Marketing,* Spring 1979, pp. 26–36.

LAVIDGE, ROBERT J. "The Growing Responsibilities of Marketing." *Journal of Marketing,* January 1970, pp. 25–28.

LAZER, WILLIAM. "Marketing's Changing Social Relationships." *Journal of Marketing,* January 1969, pp. 3–9.

LEVITT, THEODORE. "Branding on Trial." *Harvard Business Review,* March–April 1966, pp. 113–115.

———. "The Morality (?) of Advertising." *Harvard Business Review,* July 1970, pp. 84–92.

LOUDENBACK, LYNN J. and JOHN W. GOEBEL. "Marketing in the Age of Strict Liability." *Journal of Marketing,* January 1974, pp. 62–66.

LUCK, DAVID J. "Broadening the Concept of Marketing—Too Far." *Journal of Marketing,* January 1969, pp. 10–15.

LUNDSTROM, WILLIAM J. and DONALD SCIGLIMPAGLIA. "Sex Role Portrayals in Advertising." *Journal of Marketing,* July 1977, pp. 72–79.

LYLES, JEAN CAFFEY. "Sugar and the School Kids." *The Christian Century,* March 7, 1979, p. 237.

"Madison Avenue's Response to Its Critics." *Business Week,* June 10, 1972, pp. 44–54.

MAIN, JEREMY. "Industry Still Has Something to Learn about Congress." *Fortune,* February 1967, pp. 128–129, 191–192, 194.

MARKIN, ROM J. and CHEM L. NARAYANA. "Behavior Control: Are Consumers beyond Freedom and Dignity?" *Association for Consumer Research Conference Proceedings,* 1975, pp. 222–228.

MASON, KENNETH. "Responsibility for What's on the Tube." *Business Week,* August 13, 1979, p. 14.

MCCLINTOCK, CHARLES C. "Issues in Establishing and Enforcing Professional Research Ethics and Standards." *Association for Consumer Research Conference Proceedings,* 1976, pp. 258–260.

MCDOUGALL, GORDON H. G. "Comparative Advertising: Consumer Issues and Attitudes." *American Marketing Association Educators Conference Proceedings,* 1977, pp. 286–291.

MCGANN, ANTHONY F. and NILS-ERIK AABY. "The Relationships among Advertising, Economic Development and Consumer Welfare: An Examination of Recent World-Wide Evidence." *Association for Consumer Research Conference Proceedings,* 1974, pp. 643–654.

MCGUIRE, E. PATRICK. "New Opportunities in Consumerism." *Conference Board Record,* December 1979, pp. 41–43.

MCNEAL, JAMES U. "Advertising in the 'Age of Me'." *Business Horizons,* August 1979, pp. 34–38.

MILSTEIN, JEFFERY S. "Attitudes, Knowledge, and Behavior of American Consumers Regarding Energy Conservation with Some Implications for Governmental Action." *Association for Consumer Research Conference Proceedings,* 1976, pp. 315–321.

MINDAK, WILLIAM A. and H. MALCOLM BYBEE. "Marketing's Application to Fund Raising." *Journal of Marketing,* July 1971, pp. 13–18.

"More Give-Take between FTC and Cereal Makers." *Broadcasting,* November 28, 1977, pp. 26–27.

MORIN, BERNARD A. "Consumerism Revisited." *MSU Business Topics,* Summer 1970, pp. 47–51.

———, and THOMAS L. WHEELEN. "Status Report on Consumer Protection of the State Level." *American Marketing Association Educators Conference Proceedings,* 1977, p. 534.

MURDOCK, GENE W. "Liability of Advertising Agencies for Deceptive Advertising." *American Marketing Association Educators Conference Proceedings,* 1977, pp. 203–207.

NARVER, JOHN C. "Some Observations on the Impact of Antitrust Merger Policy in Marketing." *Journal of Marketing,* January 1969, pp. 24–31.

NASON, ROBERT W. and J. SCOTT ARMSTRONG. "Role Conflict: Society's Dilemma with Excellence in Marketing." *Wharton Quarterly,* Fall 1972, pp. 13–16.

NAYAC, P. and L. J. ROSENBERG. "Does Open Dating of Food Benefit the Consumer?" *Journal of Retailing,* Summer 1975, pp. 10–20.

NELSON, PHILIP. "The Economic Consequences of Advertising." *Journal of Business,* April 1975, pp. 213–241.

NICKELS, WILLIAM G. and EARNESTINE HARGROVE. "A New Societal Marketing Concept." *American Marketing Association Educators Conference Proceedings,* 1977, p. 541.

OLIVAREZ, GRACIELA. "The 'Poor' Are an 'Easy Target' at Budget-Cutting Time." *U.S. News and World Report,* January 22, 1979, pp. 24–27.

OLSON, JERRY C. and PHILIP A. DOVER. "Cognitive Effects of Deceptive Advertising." *Journal of Marketing Research,* February 1978, pp. 29–38.

"Packagers Told Consider Customer Rights." *Marketing News,* January 17, 1975, p. 4.

PATTERSON, JAMES M. "What Are the Social and Ethical Responsibilities of Marketing Executives?" *Journal of Marketing,* July 1966, pp. 12–15.

PETERSON, ESTHER. "Consumerism as a Retailer's Asset." *Harvard Business Review,* May–June 1974, pp. 91–101.

PETERSON, ROBERT A. and ROGER A. KERIN. "The Female Role in Advertisements: Some Experimental Evidence." *Journal of Marketing,* October 1977, pp. 59–63.

"Product Liability: The Search for Solutions." *Nation's Business,* August 1977, pp. 24–31.

"Product Protection on TV? Forget It." *Media,* January 1978, pp. 64–65.

"Professional Societies and Advertising Bans." *The CPA Journal,* July 1976, p. 5.

"Professions: Ethical Monopoly." *Economist,* December 9, 1978, p. 56.

"Putting the Lid on Kid Vid." *Sales Management,* July 1971, p. 40.

RADOS, DAVID L. "Product Liability: Tougher Ground Rules." *Harvard Business Review,* July–August 1969, pp. 144–152.

RATCHFORD, BRIAN T. "Banning Unsafe Products: A Framework for Policy Analysis." *American Marketing Association Educators Conference Proceedings,* 1977, pp. 362–365.

RAY, MICHAEL L. and SCOTT WARD. "Experimentation for Pretesting Public Health Programs: The Case of the Anti-drug Abuse Campaigns." *Association for Consumer Research Conference Proceedings,* 1975, pp. 278–286.

———, and WILLIAM L. WILKE. "Fear: The Potential of an Appeal Neglected by Marketing." *Journal of Marketing,* January 1970, pp. 55–56.

RESNICK, ALAN J., PETER B. B. TURNEY, and J. BARRY MASON. "Marketers Turn to 'Counter-segmentation'." *Harvard Business Review,* September–October 1979, pp. 100–106.

ROBERTSON, LEON S. "Consumer Response to Seat Belt Use Campaigns and Inducements: Implications for Public Health Strategies." *Association for Consumer Research Conference Proceedings,* 1975, pp. 287–289.

ROBERTSON, THOMAS S. "The Impact of Television Advertising on Children." *Wharton Quarterly,* Fall 1972, pp. 38–41.

ROSENBERG, LARRY J. and LOUIS W. STERN. "Toward the Analysis of Conflict in Distribution Channels: A Descriptive Model." *Journal of Marketing,* October 1970, pp. 40–47.

ROTHSCHILD, MICHAEL L. "Political Advertising: A Neglected Policy Issue in Marketing." *Journal of Marketing Research,* February 1978, pp. 58–71.

RUSSO, J. EDWARD. "When Do Advertisements Mislead the Consumer? An Answer from Experimental Psychology." *Association for Consumer Research Conference Proceedings,* 1975, pp. 273–275.

SCAMMON, DEBRA. "Comparative Advertising: A Reexamination of the Issues." *Journal of Consumer Affairs,* Winter 1978, pp. 381–392.

SCHLINGER, MARY JANE. "The Role of Mass Communications in Promoting Public Health." *Association for Consumer Research Conference Proceedings,* 1975, pp. 302–305.

SCHNAPPER, ERIC. "Consumer Legislation and the Poor." *Yale Law Journal,* 1967, pp. 745–792.

SCHWARTZ, GEORGE. "The Successful Fight against a Federal Consumer Protection Agency." *MSU Business Topics,* Summer 1979.

SHAPIRO, BENSON P. "Marketing for Nonprofit Organizations." *Harvard Business Review,* September–October 1973, pp. 123–132.

"Should an Ad Identify Brand X?" *Business Week,* September 24, 1979, p. 156.

SMITH, BETTY F. and RACHEL DARDIS. "Cost Benefit Analysis of Consumer Product Safety Standards." *The Journal of Consumer Affairs,* Summer 1977, pp. 34–46.

SRIVASTAVA, RAJENDRA K. and ROHIT DESHPANDE. "The Management of Marketing-Conflict: Implications for Public Policy." *American Marketing Association Educators Conference Proceedings,* 1977, p. 542.

STEINER, ROBERT L. "Does Advertising Lower Consumer Prices?" *Journal of Marketing,* October 1973, pp. 19–26.

STERN, LOUIS L. "Consumer Protection via Self-regulation." *Journal of Marketing,* July 1971, pp. 46–58.

———. "Perspective on Public Policy: Comments on the 'Great Debate'." *Journal of Marketing,* January 1969, pp. 32–39.

STOCK, F. "Professional Advertising." *American Journal of Public Health,* December 1978, pp. 1207–1209.

"Study Cites Value of Comparative Ads but Warns Effect Hinges on Honesty." *Broadcasting,* August 29 1977, p. 52.

STURDIVANT, FREDERICK D. "Better Deal for Ghetto Shoppers." *Harvard Business Review,* March–April 1968, pp. 130–139.

———. "The Limits of Black Capitalism." *Harvard Business Review,* January–February 1969, pp. 122–128.

———. "Social Issues and Policy: Some Observations about Marketing Scholarship." *Journal of Marketing Research,* February 1978, pp. 1–2.

———, and A. BENTON COCANOUGHER. "What Are Ethical Marketing Practices?" *Harvard Business Review,* November–December 1973, pp. 10, 12, 176.

———, and WALTER T. WILHELM. "Poverty, Minorities, and Consumer Exploitation." *Social Science Quarterly,* December 1968, pp. 643–650.

TAKAS, ANDREW. "Societal Marketing: A Businessman's Perspective." *Journal of Marketing,* October 1974, pp. 2–7.

TOOTELIAN, DENNIS H. "Attitudinal and Cognitive Readiness: Key Dimensions for Consumer Legislation." *Journal of Marketing,* July 1975, pp. 61–64.

TROMBETTA, WILLIAM L. and TIMOTHY L. WILSON. "Foreseeability of Misuse and Abnormal Use of Products by the Consumer." *Journal of Marketing,* July 1975, pp. 48–55.

UDELL, GERALD G. and PHILIP J. FISCHER. "The FTC Improvement Act." *Journal of Marketing,* April 1977, pp. 81–86.

UDELL, JON G. "How Important Is Pricing in Competitive Strategy?" *Journal of Marketing,* January 1964, pp. 44–48.

VANKATESH, ALLADI. "Changing Roles of Women—Some Empirical Findings with Marketing Implications." *American Marketing Association Educators Conference Proceedings,* 1977, pp. 417–422.

VARBLE, DALE L. "Social and Environmental Considerations in New Product Development." *Journal of Marketing,* October 1972, pp. 11–15.

WALKER, ORVILLE C. and NEIL M. FORD. "Can 'Cooling-Off Laws' Really Protect the Consumer?" *Journal of Marketing,* April 1970, pp. 53–58.

WARD, SCOTT. "Compromise in Commercials for Children." *Harvard Business Review,* November 1978, pp. 128–136.

———. "Kid's TV—Marketing on the Hot Seat." *Harvard Business Review,* July–August 1972, pp. 16–28, 150–151.

WARLAND, REX H., ROBERT O. HERRMAN, and JANE WILLITS. "Dissatisfied Consumers: Who Gets Upset and Who Takes Action." *Journal of Consumer Affairs,* Winter 1975, pp. 148–163.

WATERS, HARRY F. "Sugar in the Morning . . ." *Newsweek,* April 23, 1979, p. 137.

WAX, SAUL BARRY. "Social Science Inputs to Public Policy Formulation: Massachusetts and the Unit Pricing Regulations." *Association for Consumer Research Conference Proceedings,* 1974, pp. 915–924.

WEAVER, K. MARK and O. C. FERRELL. "The Impact of Corporate Policy on Reported Ethical Beliefs and Behavior of Marketing Practitioners." *American Marketing Association Educators Conference Proceedings,* 1977, pp. 477–481.

WEBSTER, FREDERICK E., JR. "Does Business Misunderstand Consumerism?" *Harvard Business Review,* September–October 1973, pp. 89–97.

WEISS, E. B. "Marketers Fiddle While Consumers Burn." *Harvard Business Review,* July–August 1968, pp. 45–53.

WERNER, RAY O. "Marketing and the U.S. Supreme Court, 1968–1974." *Journal of Marketing,* January 1977, pp. 32–43.

"What Do Consumers Want to See on Food Labels?" *Consumer Reports,* October 1979, p. 591.

"What's Good about Ads to Kids? Three Ad Groups Tell Their Side." *Advertising Age,* November 27, 1978, p. 2.

"When Does Food Become a Drug?" *Product Marketing,* January 1977, p. 7.

WILKIE, WILLIAM L. and PAUL W. FARRIS. "Comparison Advertising: Problems and Potential." *Journal of Marketing,* October 1975, pp. 7–15.

———, and DAVID M. GARDNER. "The Role of Marketing Research in Public Decision Making." *Journal of Marketing,* January 1974, pp. 38–47.

WILLENBORG, JOHN F. and ROBERT E. PITTS. "Gasoline Prices: Their Effect on Consumer Behavior and Attitudes." *Journal of Marketing,* January 1977, pp. 24–31.

WILSON, AUBREY. "Professions and the Marketplace." *Accountant,* January 6, 1977, pp. 9–11.

WOODSIDE, ARCH G. "Advertisers' Willingness to Substantiate Their Claims." *Journal of Consumer Affairs,* Summer 1977, pp. 135–144.

ZALTMAN, GERALD and ILAN VERTINSKY. "Health Service Marketing: A Suggested Model." *Journal of Marketing,* July 1971, pp. 19–27.

ZIKMUND, WILLIAM G. and WILLIAM J. STANTON. "Recycling Solid Wastes: A Channels-of-Distribution Problem." *Journal of Marketing,* July 1971, pp. 34–39.

Name Index

Louis, Arthur M., 45, 52, 53
Luken, Rep. Thomas (D-OH), 106, 108
Lurie, William L., 273, 275
Lynch, Mitchell C., 38
McAfee, Jerry, 10
McCuen, Joy, 150
McDonald, Maurice E., 145, 395
McDonald, Richard, 145
MacDougall, A. Kent, 95, 109
McGovern, Sen. George (D SD), 309
McGuire, E. Patrick, 125, 370
McIntyre, Larry, 313–28
McLaren, Richard W., 443
McLaughlin, Frank, 395
McNamara, Robert S., 345
MacNeil, Robert, 36
Magnuson, Sen. Warren (D-WA), 436, 447
Main, Jeremy, 205, 371
Manos, John, 46–48
Marcial, Gene, 144
Marks, Clifford, 289
Martin, Richard, 185
Matt, Morris, 307
Matulis, Delores, 257
Mayer, Jean, 308
Melton, R. B., 327
Merriam, Robert, 327–51
Metz, Tim, 148
Miller, A. Edward, 440
Miller, Sanford, 103
Millstein, Ira, 276
Mitford, Jessica, 237, 244
Modrall, Andrew, 236
Molina, Mario, 130
Moore, Sidney L., 211
Moran, John J., 30, 39
Morton, Cameron, 236
Moss, Rep. John E., 45, 46, 48, 52, 54
Moss, Sen. Frank (D-UT), 224, 235, 304, 436
Mrak, Emil M., 191
Nader, Ralph, 45, 49, 54, 185, 284, 304, 370, 449
Nalen, Craig, 209
Naunton, Ena, 287
Nelson, Gaylord, 440
Nesheim, Robert O., 306
Nessitt, Alfred, 88, 90–93
Nevin, John J., 438
Nevins, Barbara, 94
Nigut, William, 98
Niles, John, 285
Nixon, Richard M., 335, 341–51
Nolan, James F., 393–406
Norton, W. W., 187
O'Connor, John J., 36
Office, Gerald S., Jr., 148
Oxenfeldt, Alfred R., 220
Pace, Nicholas, 37, 38
Packard, Vance, 215
Paine, Thomas, 334
Pallen, Harvey, 287–89
Palumbo, Edwin P., 408, 410
Paolucci, Felix, 286
Papas, Susan, 37–38

Paul, Mitch, 200
Payton, Donald L., 445
Pearce, Alan, 197
Peltzman, Sam, 126
Pertschuk, Michael, 14, 195, 200, 269
Peterson, Esther, 224, 234, 374
Petkas, Peter J., 185
Pettis, Charles, 186
Pickett, Neil, 105
Pickett, Winston H., 440
Pines, Wayne, 283
Pitofsky, Robert, 270
Pollard, Joseph, 282
Porter, Sylvia, 36, 73
Post, Hyde, 313
Pressler, Sen. Larry (R-ND), 354
Pyle, Christopher, 186
Quinn, Taylor, 102
Raether, Howard D., 242
Ranum, Juel, 445
Reddish, Jeanette M., 144
Reetz, John, 151
Reich, Robert, 270
Renner, Janet F., 391
Revson, Charles, 25
Rhodes, Seth, 288
Richardson, Stanley, 287–89
Rickinbach, Betty, 392
Riley, Richard, 52, 55, 57
Ring, Markus, 367
Rishel, George Fox, 105
Roberts, John, 376 92
Robertson, Thomas, 311
Robicheaux, Robert, 294
Robinson, Larry M., 371
Roche, James, 370
Rodino, Peter, 355
Roll, L. C., 307
Roosevelt, Kermit, 349
Rosen, Gary, 288
Rosenbert, Larry J., 481
Rosenthal, Benjamin, 386
Ross, Sam M., 358
Rossiter, John, 311
Rostenne, Jacques, 25
Rowland, Sherwood F., 130, 132
Rule, Elton H., 198
Russo, J. Edward, 4
Rynearson, Edward H., 190
Sachs, Reynold M., 127–28
Sammons, Steve, 151
Samuelson, Robert J., 279
Saunders, Ernest, 364
Savy, William A., 335
Schellhardt, Timothy D., 272
Schottland, Stanley, 273
Schulze, Arthur R., 459
Schwartz, Daniel, 106
Schylen, Peter J., 149
Sebrell, W. H., 306
Selby, Ted, 208
Shaprio, Irving S., 278
Shenefield, John H., 277
Sherry, Louis, 202

Subject Index